Walt Disney

UNCLE $CROOGE
and
Donald Duck

The

DoN RosA

Library

Volume Two

Walt Disney

UNCLE $CROOGE
and
Donald Duck

Return to Plain Awful

FANTAGRAPHICS BOOKS

The Don Rosa Library

Editor: David Gerstein
Supervising Editor: Gary Groth
Color Restoration: Kneon Transitt and Digikore Studios
Series Designer: Tony Ong
Designers: David Gerstein and Keeli McCarthy
Production: Paul Baresh
Associate Publisher: Eric Reynolds
Publisher: Gary Groth

Fantagraphics Books
7563 Lake City Way NE
Seattle, Washington 98115

For a free full-color catalogue of comics and cartooning, call 1-800-657-1100. Our books may be viewed–and purchased–on our website at www.fantagraphics.com.

The Editor would like to thank: Scott Burnley, John Clark, Susan Daigle-Leach, Thomas Jensen, Dan Shane, David Terzopoulos, Solveig Thime, and Joe Torcivia.

First Fantagraphics Books edition: November 2014

ISBN 978-1-60699-780-2

Printed in China

Table of Contents

All stories and text features written and drawn by Don Rosa except where noted.
All stories lettered by John Clark except where noted.

Preface

By Don Rosa

This volume covers the most diverse group of projects of my entire so-called "career," even though that "career" was still in its earliest stages. As you'll see from the autobiographical feature in the back of the book, there was a lot happening to me in this two-year period—working for four different Disney publishers, a stint working for Walt Disney TV Animation, and even a frightening time of unemployment. During this early stage in my Duck work, there were also many "firsts." Here's a sort of "teaser" for the widely varied contents of this volume. It contains—

FREE POSTER INSIDE OF
Return TO
PLAIN AWFUL

This ornately-lettered banner was created by Gladstone editor John Clark for the cover of *Donald Duck Adventures* 12 (1989), the first edition of Rosa's "Return to Plain Awful." The "free poster" referred to was a reproduction of Carl Barks' new "Plain Awful" painting (see page 175).

The ***first and only*** Duck story I ever wrote that was completely *rejected* by my editor with no interest in a rewrite, but which I later completed for a *different* publisher!

The ***first and only*** Duck story I ever wrote that was not ultimately drawn in finished form, by me or anyone else.

The ***first and only*** Duck script I ever wrote that was intended to be drawn by another artist (and was!).

The ***first and only*** time that I wrote and drew (at least in storyboard script form) a story that actually featured Mickey Mouse.

My ***first and only*** "collaboration" (after a fashion) on a story with my lifelong inspiration, Carl Barks himself!

The ***first and only*** story I ever did directly for Disney Comics, Inc., Disney's short-lived 1990s in-house comics publishing firm.

The ***first and only*** stories I ever did for the Dutch Disney comics publisher, then known as Oberon.

The ***first and only*** *DuckTales* story I ever wrote.

The ***first*** full-blown sequel to a beloved old Carl Barks classic that I was ever asked to create.

The ***first*** new nemesis I ever created for Uncle Scrooge.

The ***first*** of several Duck stories I wrote based on a plot idea loosely inspired by a favorite old movie (which, being a huge movie buff, I am actually proud to admit).

Along with all these firsts, there are also a few stories in here that fans have regarded as their favorites of my career, and also many covers that Gladstone Publishing asked me to draw based on their reprinting of Barks stories that had no original cover art. Drawing such covers was naturally a great thrill for me!

All in all... by golly, now that I've written this preface, I've made it all seem so interesting that I'm anxious to read this book myself! •

MEANWHILE...
HA! THESE EIGHT-CORNERED FRYERS ARE REGULAR HOMING CHICKENS! THEY'RE LEADING ME STRAIGHT TO THE LOST CITY!
C'MON! WE'RE FOLLOWING THESE CRITTERS NOW!
CHICKENS!? SQUARE CHICKENS?!!
DON'T TELL ME YOU ARE SEARCHING FOR SQUARE EGGS, SEÑOR?
HOW DID YOU--?

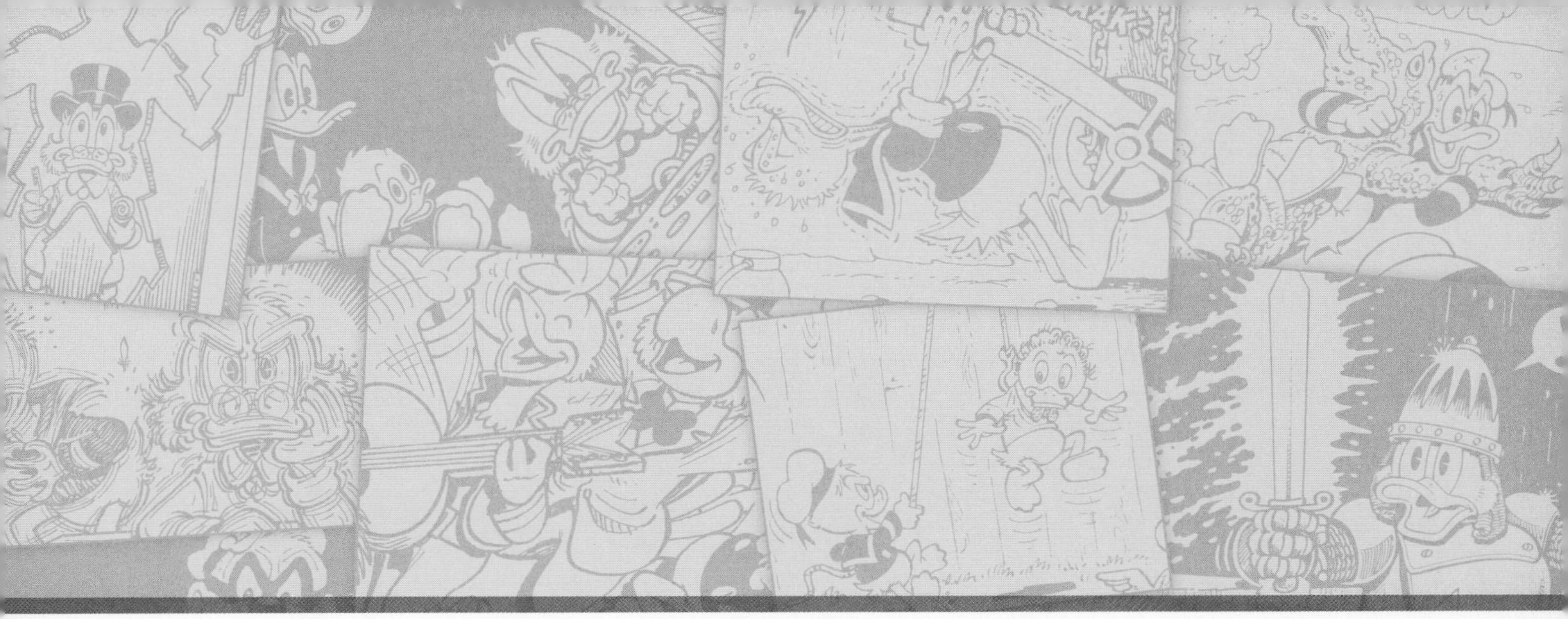

The Stories

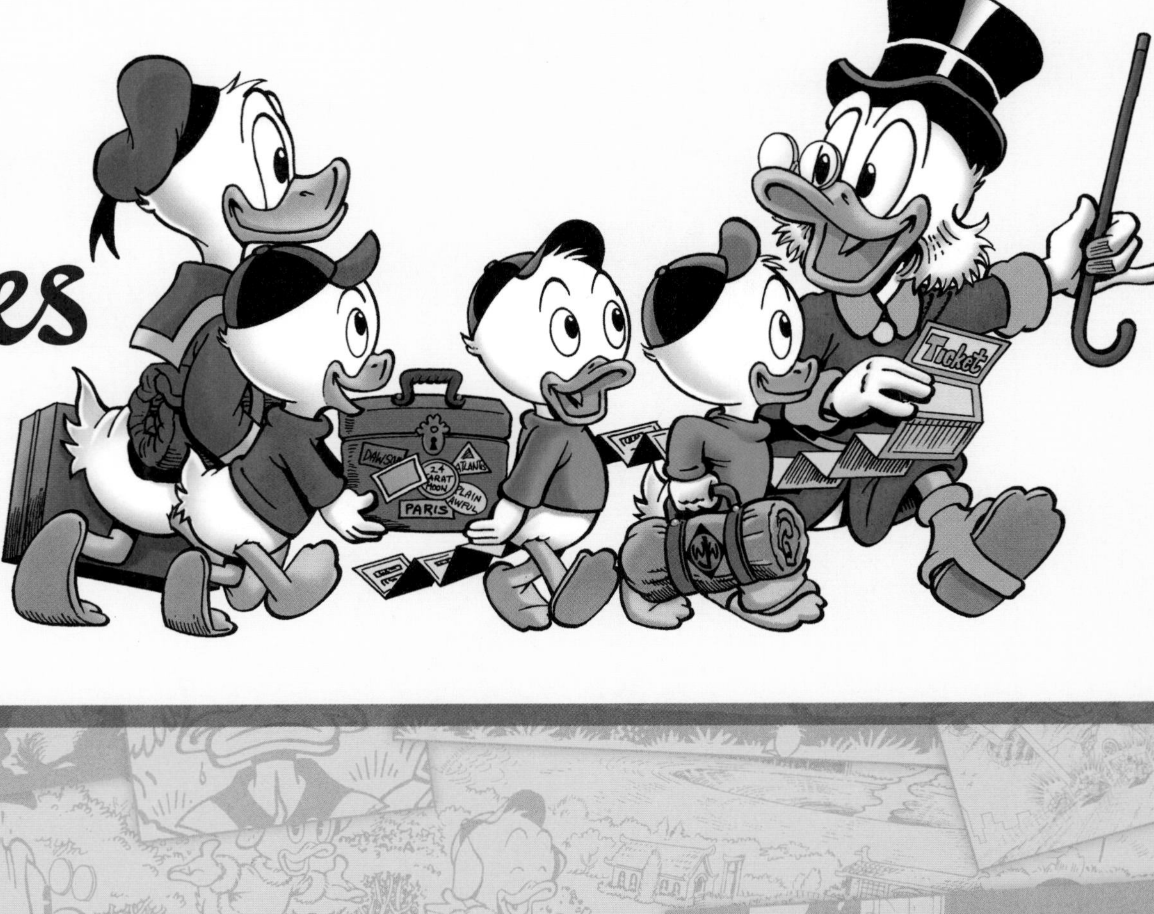
Ticket
PARIS

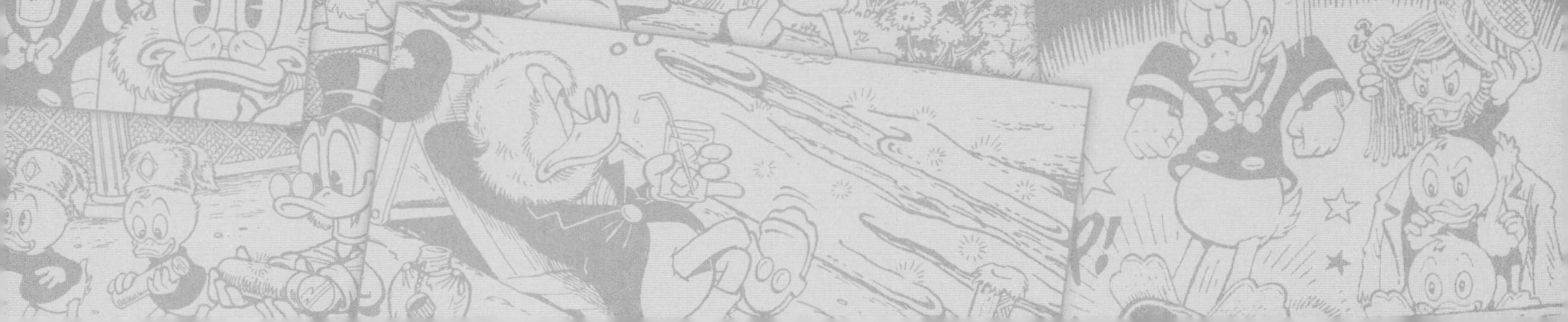

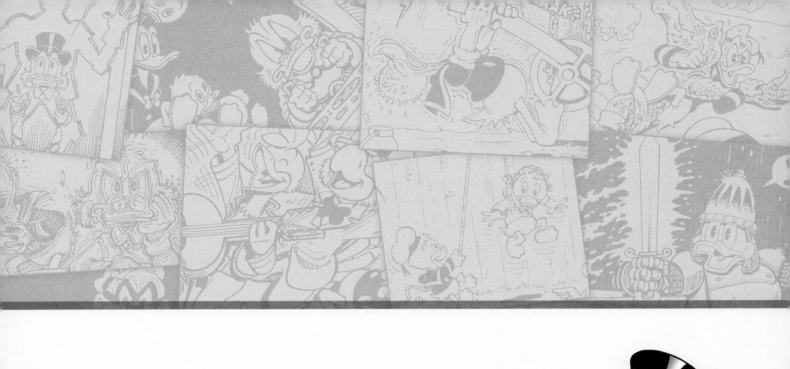

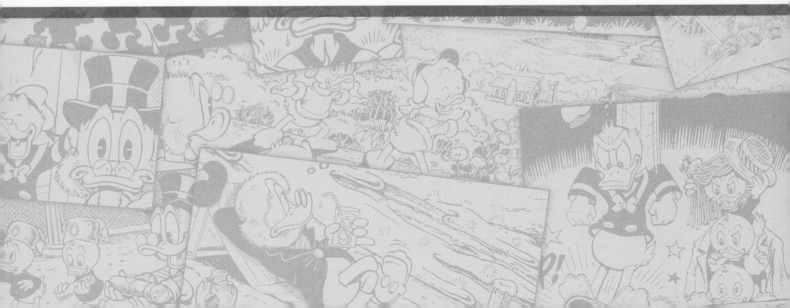

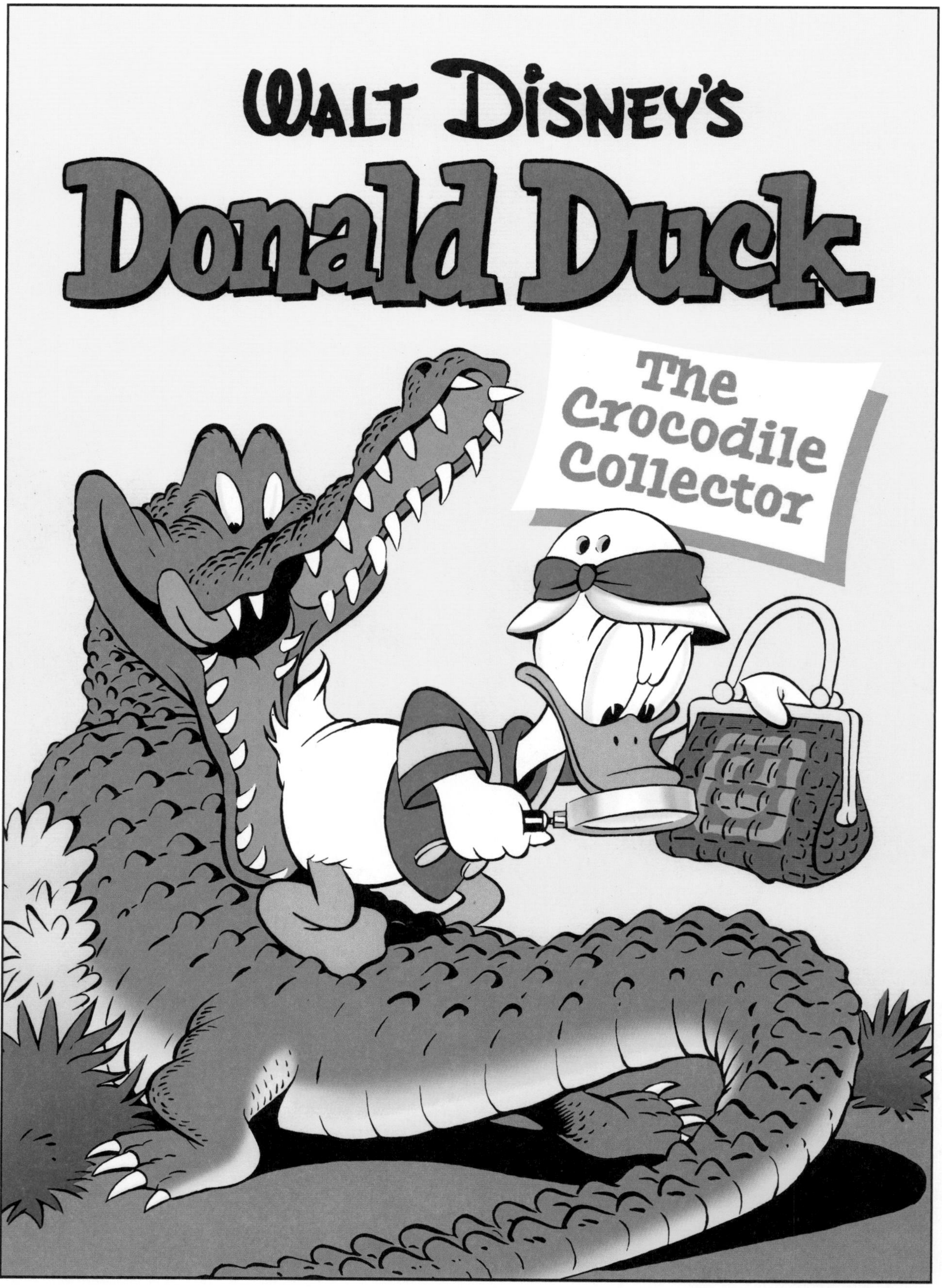
WALT DISNEY'S
Donald Duck
The Crocodile Collector

THE CROCODILE COLLECTOR
Cover by Carl Barks from Donald Duck *Four Color* 348, September 1951;
new color by Digikore Studios

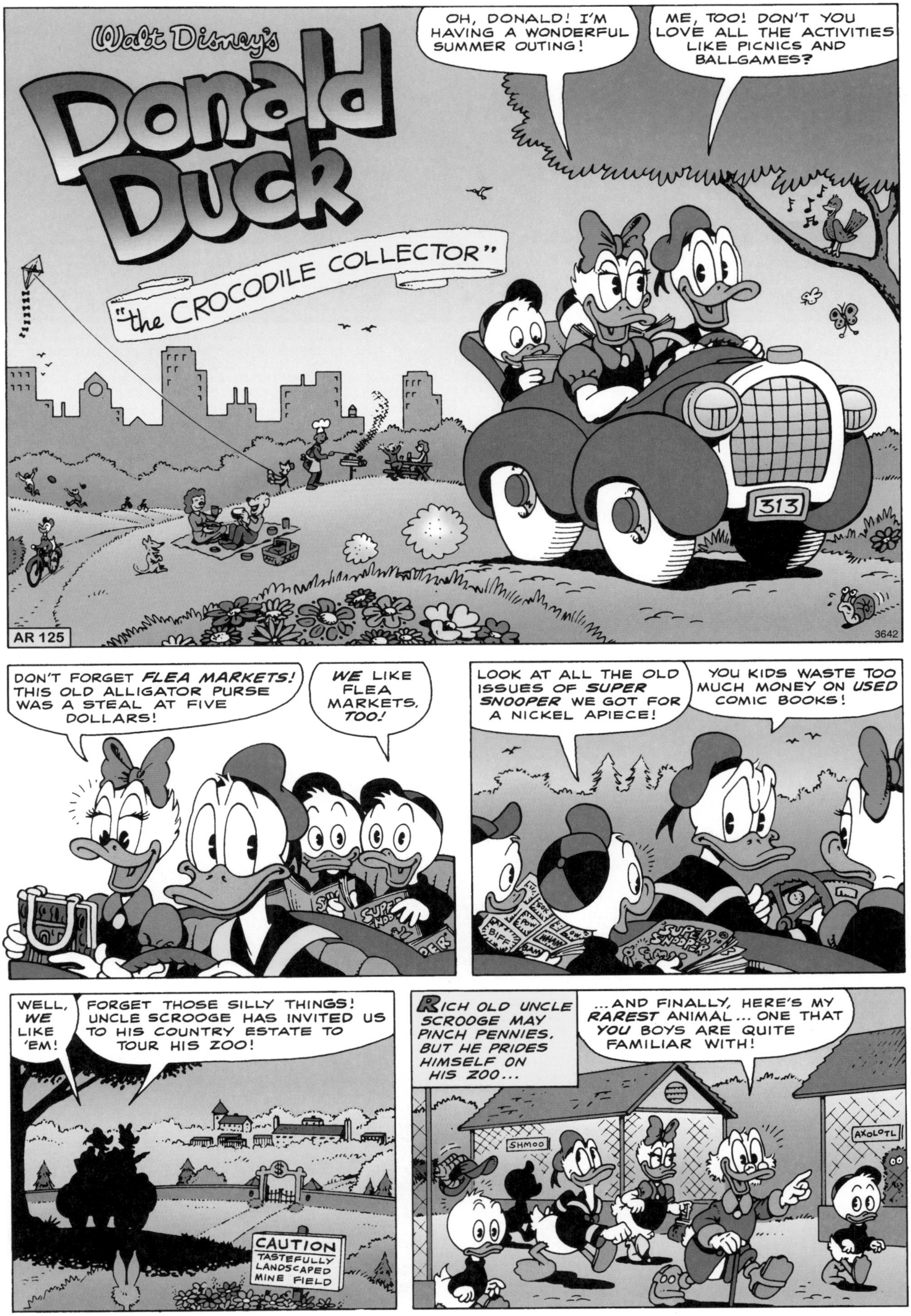
Walt Disney's
Donald Duck
"the CROCODILE COLLECTOR"
OH, DONALD! I'M HAVING A WONDERFUL SUMMER OUTING!
ME, TOO! DON'T YOU LOVE ALL THE ACTIVITIES LIKE PICNICS AND BALLGAMES?
313
AR 125
3642
DON'T FORGET FLEA MARKETS! THIS OLD ALLIGATOR PURSE WAS A STEAL AT FIVE DOLLARS!
WE LIKE FLEA MARKETS, TOO!
LOOK AT ALL THE OLD ISSUES OF SUPER SNOOPER WE GOT FOR A NICKEL APIECE!
YOU KIDS WASTE TOO MUCH MONEY ON USED COMIC BOOKS!
SUPER SNOOPER COMIC
WELL, WE LIKE 'EM!
FORGET THOSE SILLY THINGS! UNCLE SCROOGE HAS INVITED US TO HIS COUNTRY ESTATE TO TOUR HIS ZOO!
CAUTION
TASTEFULLY LANDSCAPED MINE FIELD
RICH OLD UNCLE SCROOGE MAY PINCH PENNIES, BUT HE PRIDES HIMSELF ON HIS ZOO...
...AND FINALLY, HERE'S MY RAREST ANIMAL... ONE THAT YOU BOYS ARE QUITE FAMILIAR WITH!
SHMOO
AXOLOTL

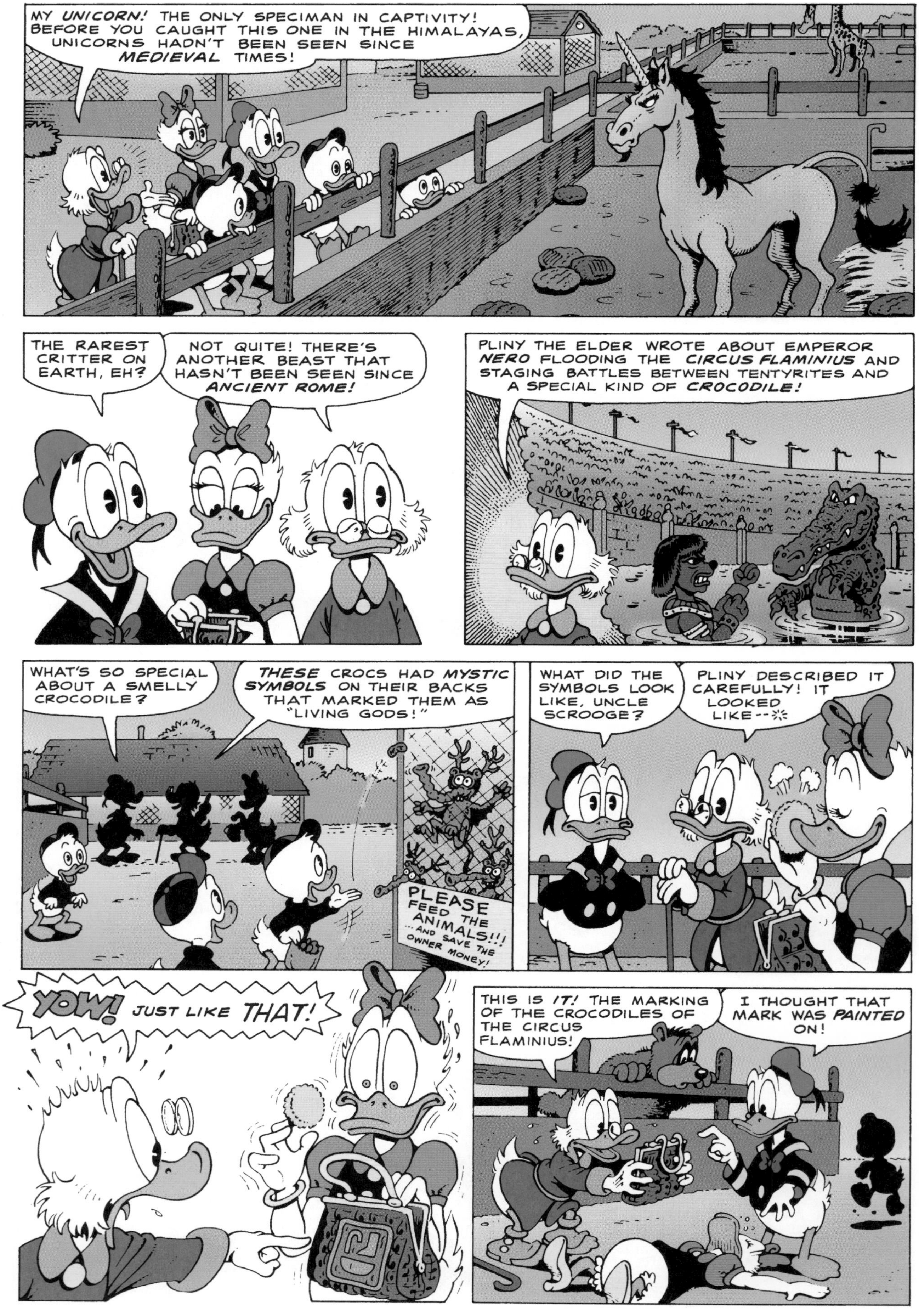
MY UNICORN! THE ONLY SPECIMAN IN CAPTIVITY! BEFORE YOU CAUGHT THIS ONE IN THE HIMALAYAS, UNICORNS HADN'T BEEN SEEN SINCE MEDIEVAL TIMES!
THE RAREST CRITTER ON EARTH, EH?
NOT QUITE! THERE'S ANOTHER BEAST THAT HASN'T BEEN SEEN SINCE ANCIENT ROME!
PLINY THE ELDER WROTE ABOUT EMPEROR NERO FLOODING THE CIRCUS FLAMINIUS AND STAGING BATTLES BETWEEN TENTYRITES AND A SPECIAL KIND OF CROCODILE!
WHAT'S SO SPECIAL ABOUT A SMELLY CROCODILE?
THESE CROCS HAD MYSTIC SYMBOLS ON THEIR BACKS THAT MARKED THEM AS "LIVING GODS!"
PLEASE FEED THE ANIMALS!!! ...AND SAVE THE OWNER MONEY!
WHAT DID THE SYMBOLS LOOK LIKE, UNCLE SCROOGE?
PLINY DESCRIBED IT CAREFULLY! IT LOOKED LIKE--
YOW! JUST LIKE THAT!
THIS IS IT! THE MARKING OF THE CROCODILES OF THE CIRCUS FLAMINIUS!
I THOUGHT THAT MARK WAS PAINTED ON!

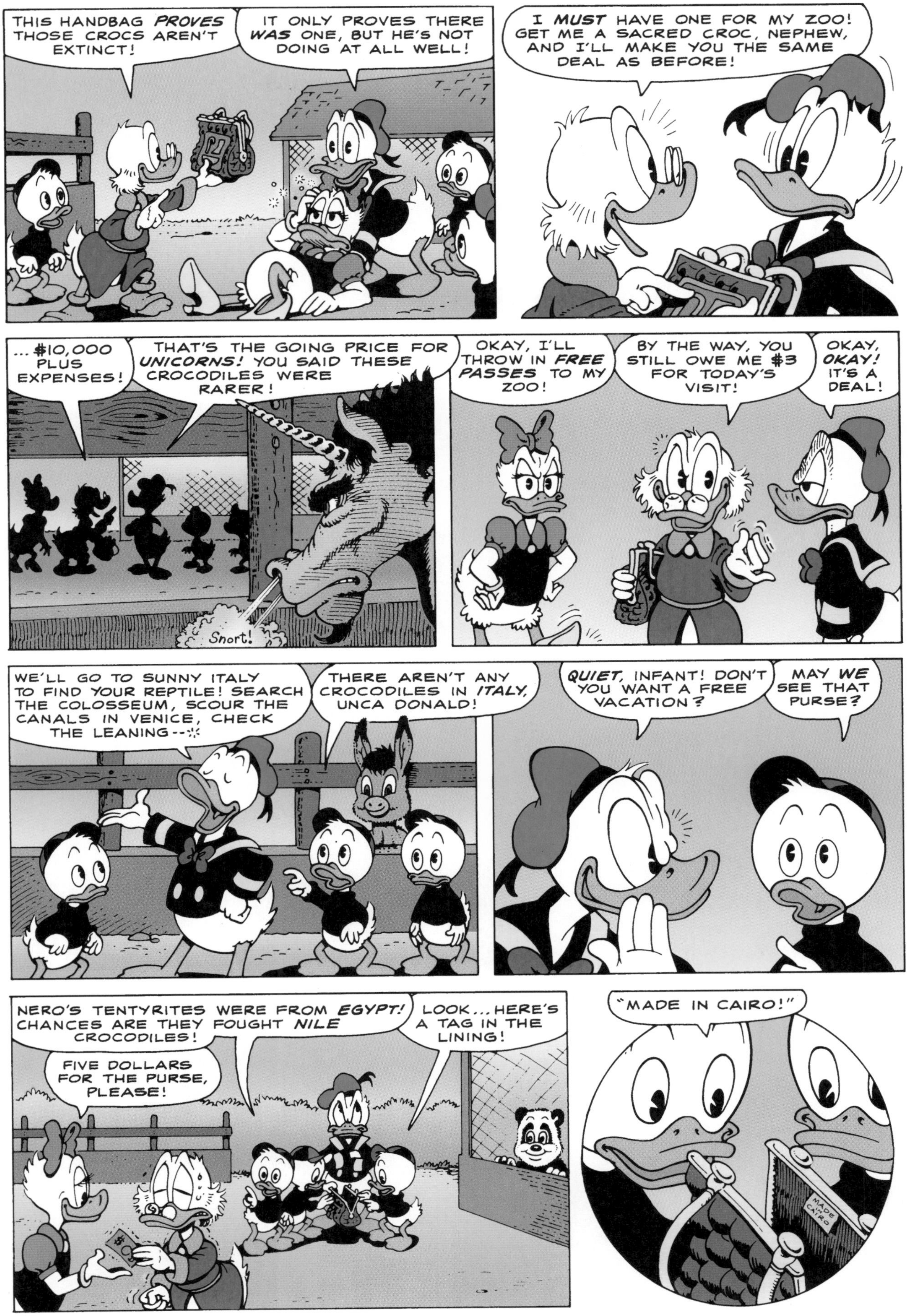
THIS HANDBAG PROVES THOSE CROCS AREN'T EXTINCT!
IT ONLY PROVES THERE WAS ONE, BUT HE'S NOT DOING AT ALL WELL!
I MUST HAVE ONE FOR MY ZOO! GET ME A SACRED CROC, NEPHEW, AND I'LL MAKE YOU THE SAME DEAL AS BEFORE!
...$10,000 PLUS EXPENSES!
THAT'S THE GOING PRICE FOR UNICORNS! YOU SAID THESE CROCODILES WERE RARER!
Snort!
OKAY, I'LL THROW IN FREE PASSES TO MY ZOO!
BY THE WAY, YOU STILL OWE ME $3 FOR TODAY'S VISIT!
OKAY, OKAY! IT'S A DEAL!
WE'LL GO TO SUNNY ITALY TO FIND YOUR REPTILE! SEARCH THE COLOSSEUM, SCOUR THE CANALS IN VENICE, CHECK THE LEANING--
THERE AREN'T ANY CROCODILES IN ITALY, UNCA DONALD!
QUIET, INFANT! DON'T YOU WANT A FREE VACATION?
MAY WE SEE THAT PURSE?
NERO'S TENTYRITES WERE FROM EGYPT! CHANCES ARE THEY FOUGHT NILE CROCODILES!
FIVE DOLLARS FOR THE PURSE, PLEASE!
LOOK... HERE'S A TAG IN THE LINING!
"MADE IN CAIRO!"
MADE IN CAIRO

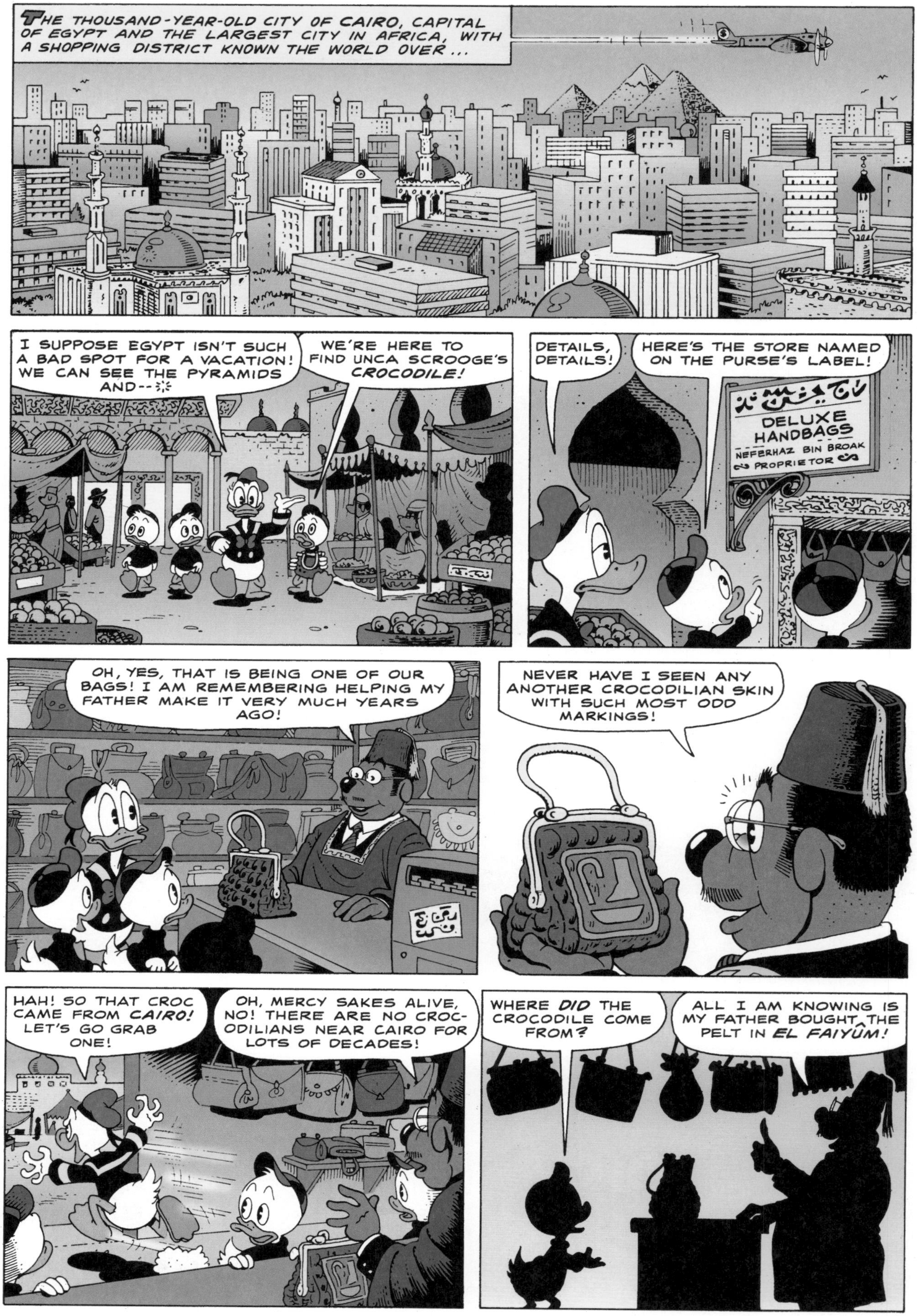
THE THOUSAND-YEAR-OLD CITY OF CAIRO, CAPITAL OF EGYPT AND THE LARGEST CITY IN AFRICA, WITH A SHOPPING DISTRICT KNOWN THE WORLD OVER...
I SUPPOSE EGYPT ISN'T SUCH A BAD SPOT FOR A VACATION! WE CAN SEE THE PYRAMIDS AND--
WE'RE HERE TO FIND UNCA SCROOGE'S CROCODILE!
DETAILS, DETAILS!
HERE'S THE STORE NAMED ON THE PURSE'S LABEL!
DELUXE HANDBAGS
NEFERHAZ BIN BROAK
PROPRIETOR
OH, YES, THAT IS BEING ONE OF OUR BAGS! I AM REMEMBERING HELPING MY FATHER MAKE IT VERY MUCH YEARS AGO!
NEVER HAVE I SEEN ANY ANOTHER CROCODILIAN SKIN WITH SUCH MOST ODD MARKINGS!
HAH! SO THAT CROC CAME FROM CAIRO! LET'S GO GRAB ONE!
OH, MERCY SAKES ALIVE, NO! THERE ARE NO CROCODILIANS NEAR CAIRO FOR LOTS OF DECADES!
WHERE DID THE CROCODILE COME FROM?
ALL I AM KNOWING IS MY FATHER BOUGHT THE PELT IN EL FAIYÛM!

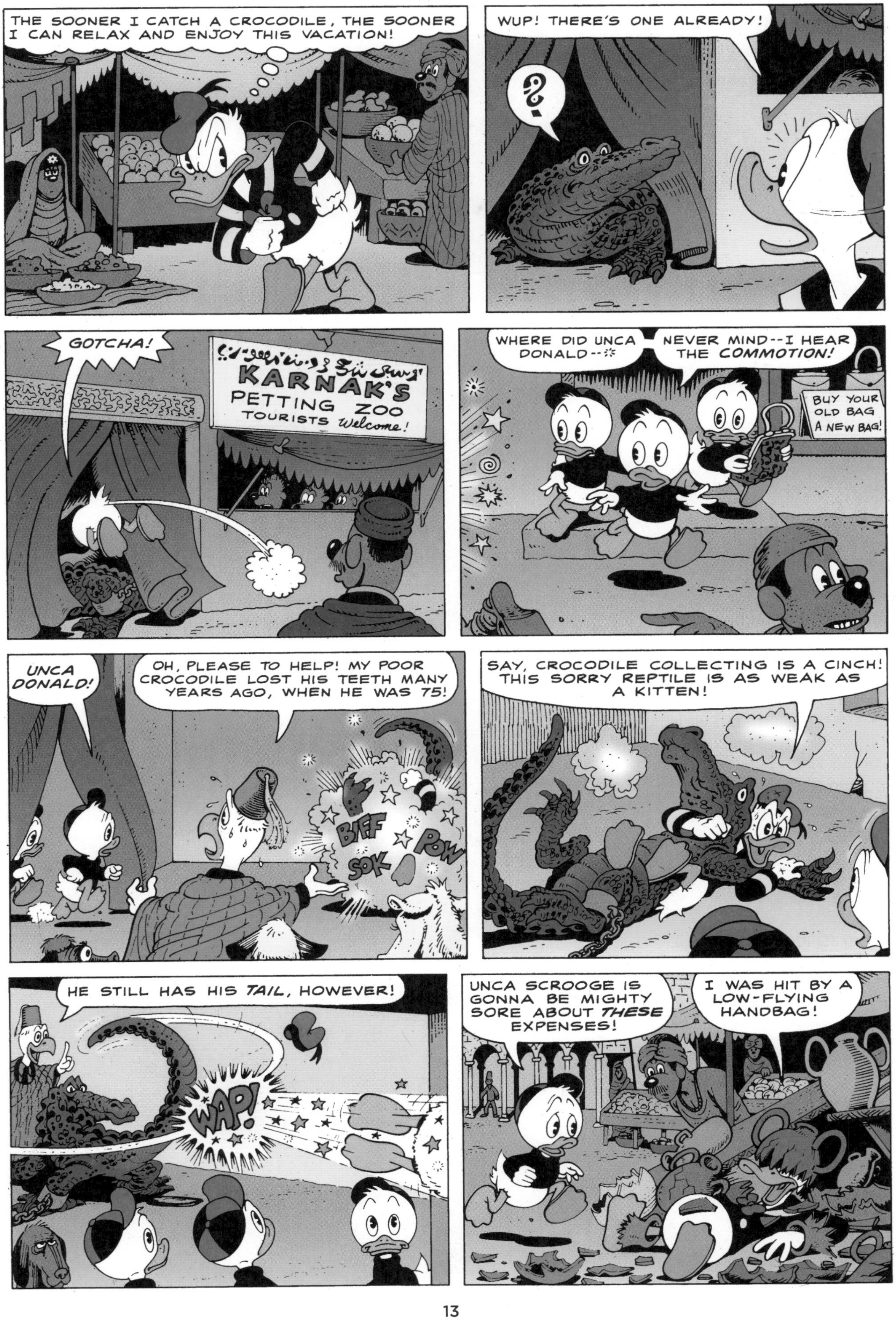
THE SOONER I CATCH A CROCODILE, THE SOONER I CAN RELAX AND ENJOY THIS VACATION!
WUP! THERE'S ONE ALREADY!
?
GOTCHA!
KARNAK'S PETTING ZOO
TOURISTS Welcome!
WHERE DID UNCA DONALD--
NEVER MIND--I HEAR THE COMMOTION!
BUY YOUR OLD BAG A NEW BAG!
UNCA DONALD!
OH, PLEASE TO HELP! MY POOR CROCODILE LOST HIS TEETH MANY YEARS AGO, WHEN HE WAS 75!
BIFF
SOK
POW
SAY, CROCODILE COLLECTING IS A CINCH! THIS SORRY REPTILE IS AS WEAK AS A KITTEN!
HE STILL HAS HIS TAIL, HOWEVER!
WAP!
UNCA SCROOGE IS GONNA BE MIGHTY SORE ABOUT THESE EXPENSES!
I WAS HIT BY A LOW-FLYING HANDBAG!

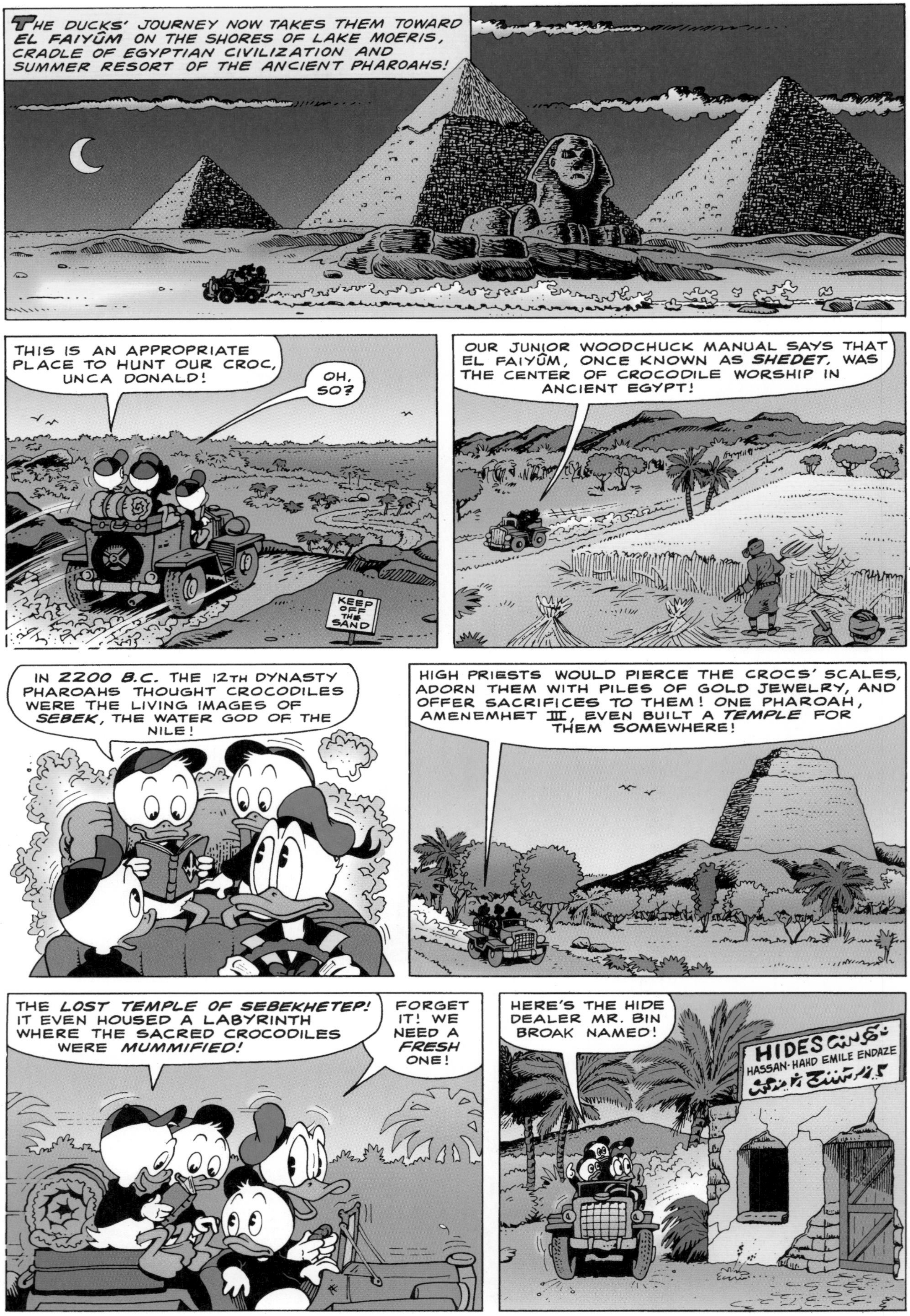
THE DUCKS' JOURNEY NOW TAKES THEM TOWARD EL FAIYÛM ON THE SHORES OF LAKE MOERIS, CRADLE OF EGYPTIAN CIVILIZATION AND SUMMER RESORT OF THE ANCIENT PHAROAHS!
THIS IS AN APPROPRIATE PLACE TO HUNT OUR CROC, UNCA DONALD!
OH, SO?
KEEP OFF THE SAND
OUR JUNIOR WOODCHUCK MANUAL SAYS THAT EL FAIYÛM, ONCE KNOWN AS SHEDET, WAS THE CENTER OF CROCODILE WORSHIP IN ANCIENT EGYPT!
IN 2200 B.C. THE 12TH DYNASTY PHAROAHS THOUGHT CROCODILES WERE THE LIVING IMAGES OF SEBEK, THE WATER GOD OF THE NILE!
HIGH PRIESTS WOULD PIERCE THE CROCS' SCALES, ADORN THEM WITH PILES OF GOLD JEWELRY, AND OFFER SACRIFICES TO THEM! ONE PHAROAH, AMENEMHET III, EVEN BUILT A TEMPLE FOR THEM SOMEWHERE!
THE LOST TEMPLE OF SEBEKHETEP! IT EVEN HOUSED A LABYRINTH WHERE THE SACRED CROCODILES WERE MUMMIFIED!
FORGET IT! WE NEED A FRESH ONE!
HERE'S THE HIDE DEALER MR. BIN BROAK NAMED!
HIDES
HASSAN-HAHD EMILE ENDAZE

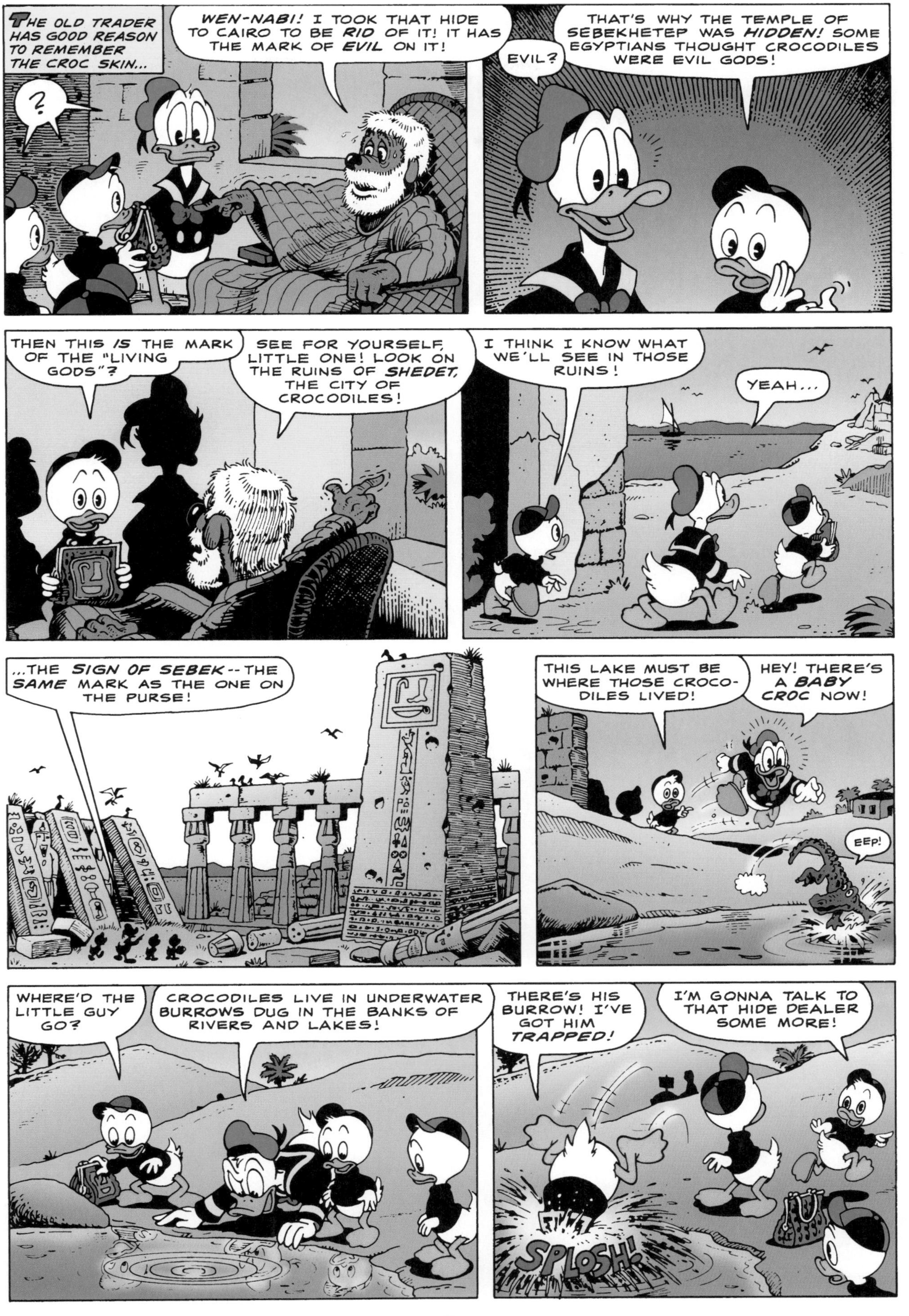
THE OLD TRADER HAS GOOD REASON TO REMEMBER THE CROC SKIN...
?
WEN-NABI! I TOOK THAT HIDE TO CAIRO TO BE RID OF IT! IT HAS THE MARK OF EVIL ON IT!
EVIL?
THAT'S WHY THE TEMPLE OF SEBEKHETEP WAS HIDDEN! SOME EGYPTIANS THOUGHT CROCODILES WERE EVIL GODS!
THEN THIS IS THE MARK OF THE "LIVING GODS"?
SEE FOR YOURSELF, LITTLE ONE! LOOK ON THE RUINS OF SHEDET, THE CITY OF CROCODILES!
I THINK I KNOW WHAT WE'LL SEE IN THOSE RUINS!
YEAH...
...THE SIGN OF SEBEK -- THE SAME MARK AS THE ONE ON THE PURSE!
THIS LAKE MUST BE WHERE THOSE CROCODILES LIVED!
HEY! THERE'S A BABY CROC NOW!
EEP!
WHERE'D THE LITTLE GUY GO?
CROCODILES LIVE IN UNDERWATER BURROWS DUG IN THE BANKS OF RIVERS AND LAKES!
THERE'S HIS BURROW! I'VE GOT HIM TRAPPED!
I'M GONNA TALK TO THAT HIDE DEALER SOME MORE!
SPLOSH!

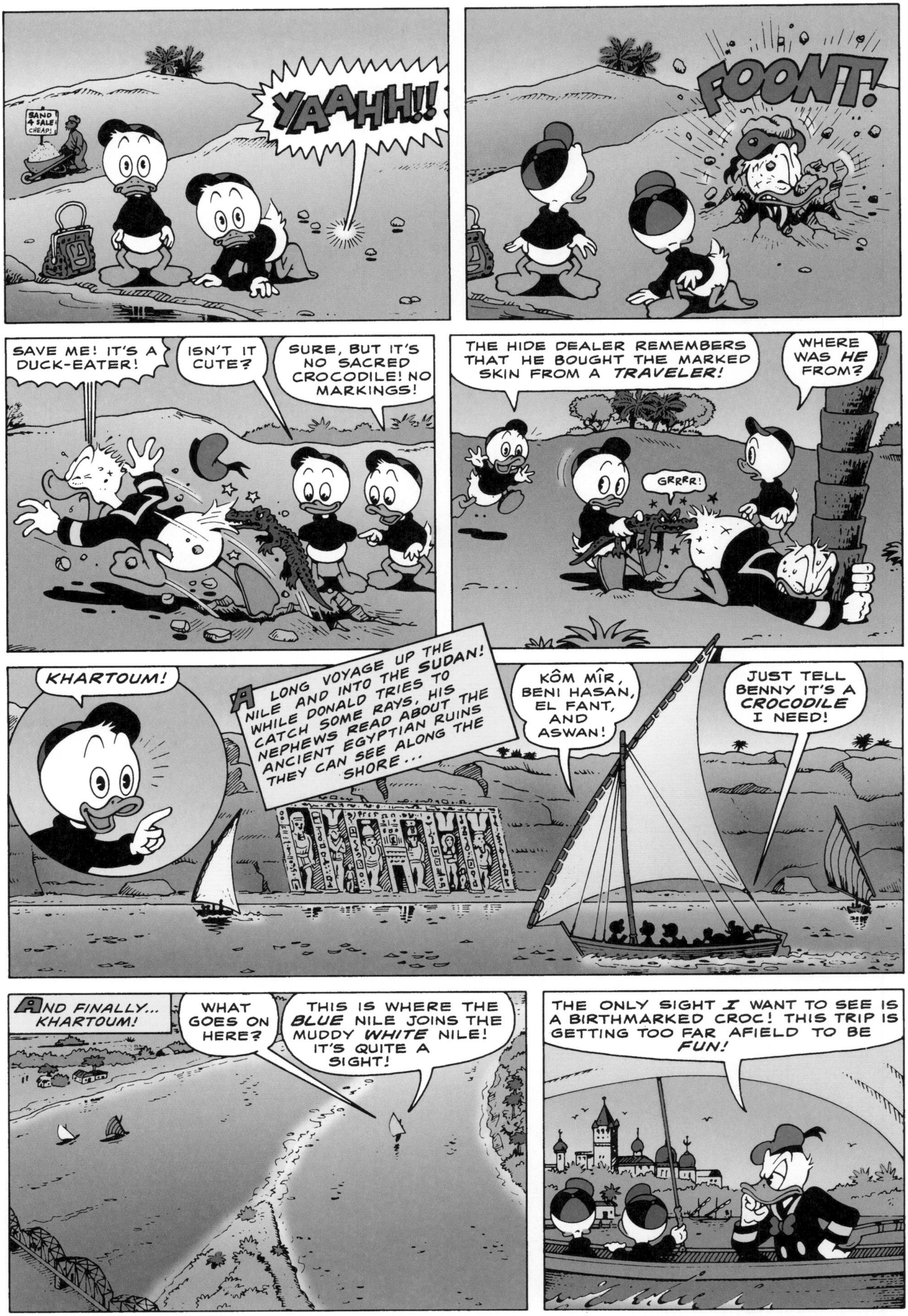
SAND 4 SALE CHEAP!
YAAHH!!
FOONT!
SAVE ME! IT'S A DUCK-EATER!
ISN'T IT CUTE?
SURE, BUT IT'S NO SACRED CROCODILE! NO MARKINGS!
THE HIDE DEALER REMEMBERS THAT HE BOUGHT THE MARKED SKIN FROM A TRAVELER!
WHERE WAS HE FROM?
GRRRR!
KHARTOUM!
A LONG VOYAGE UP THE NILE AND INTO THE SUDAN! WHILE DONALD TRIES TO CATCH SOME RAYS, HIS NEPHEWS READ ABOUT THE ANCIENT EGYPTIAN RUINS THEY CAN SEE ALONG THE SHORE...
KÔM MÎR, BENI HASAN, EL FANT, AND ASWAN!
JUST TELL BENNY IT'S A CROCODILE I NEED!
AND FINALLY... KHARTOUM!
WHAT GOES ON HERE?
THIS IS WHERE THE BLUE NILE JOINS THE MUDDY WHITE NILE! IT'S QUITE A SIGHT!
THE ONLY SIGHT I WANT TO SEE IS A BIRTHMARKED CROC! THIS TRIP IS GETTING TOO FAR AFIELD TO BE FUN!

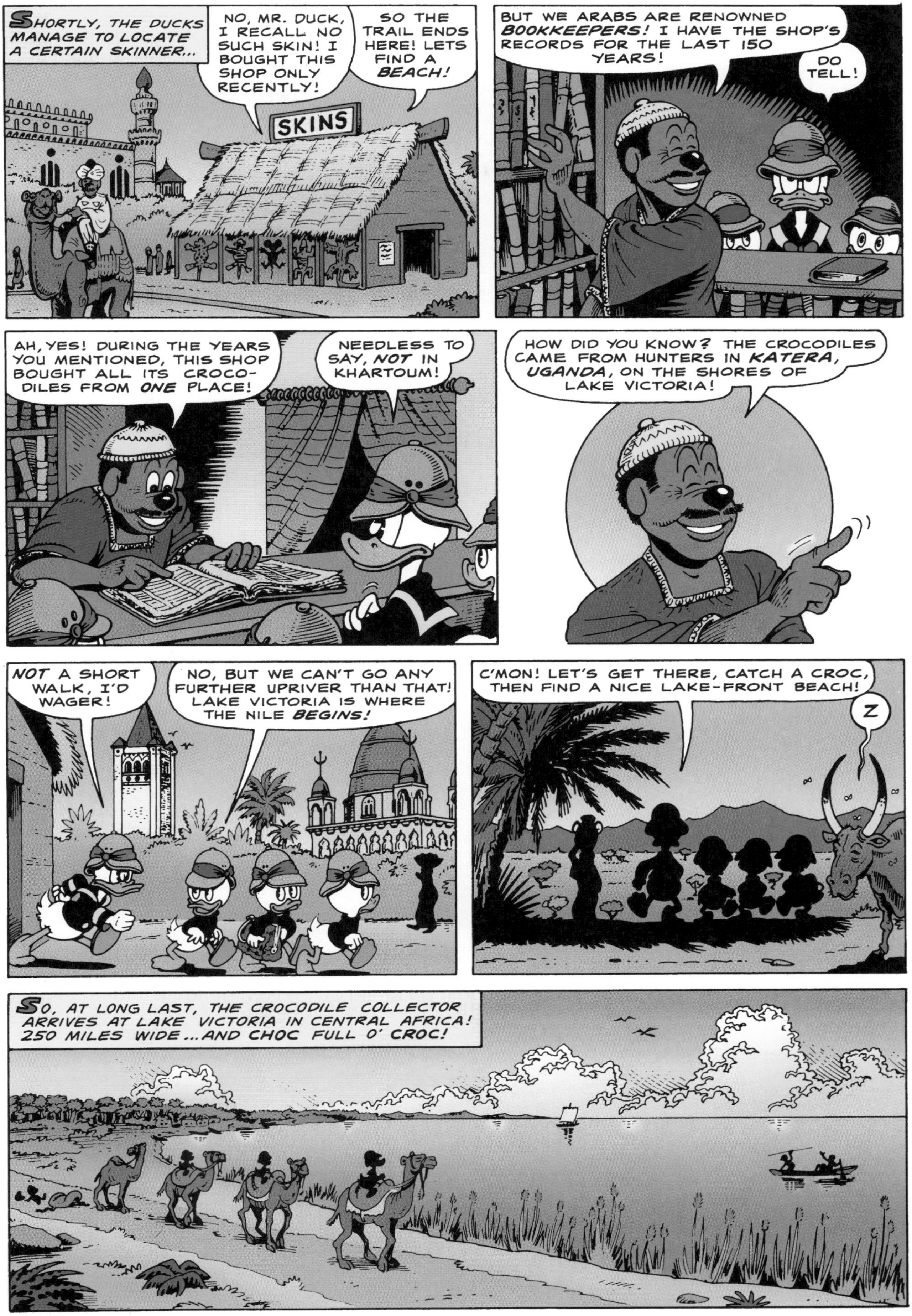
SHORTLY, THE DUCKS MANAGE TO LOCATE A CERTAIN SKINNER...
NO, MR. DUCK, I RECALL NO SUCH SKIN! I BOUGHT THIS SHOP ONLY RECENTLY!
SO THE TRAIL ENDS HERE! LETS FIND A BEACH!
SKINS
BUT WE ARABS ARE RENOWNED BOOKKEEPERS! I HAVE THE SHOP'S RECORDS FOR THE LAST 150 YEARS!
DO TELL!
AH, YES! DURING THE YEARS YOU MENTIONED, THIS SHOP BOUGHT ALL ITS CROCODILES FROM ONE PLACE!
NEEDLESS TO SAY, NOT IN KHARTOUM!
HOW DID YOU KNOW? THE CROCODILES CAME FROM HUNTERS IN KATERA, UGANDA, ON THE SHORES OF LAKE VICTORIA!
NOT A SHORT WALK, I'D WAGER!
NO, BUT WE CAN'T GO ANY FURTHER UPRIVER THAN THAT! LAKE VICTORIA IS WHERE THE NILE BEGINS!
C'MON! LET'S GET THERE, CATCH A CROC, THEN FIND A NICE LAKE-FRONT BEACH!
Z
SO, AT LONG LAST, THE CROCODILE COLLECTOR ARRIVES AT LAKE VICTORIA IN CENTRAL AFRICA! 250 MILES WIDE...AND CHOC FULL O' CROC!

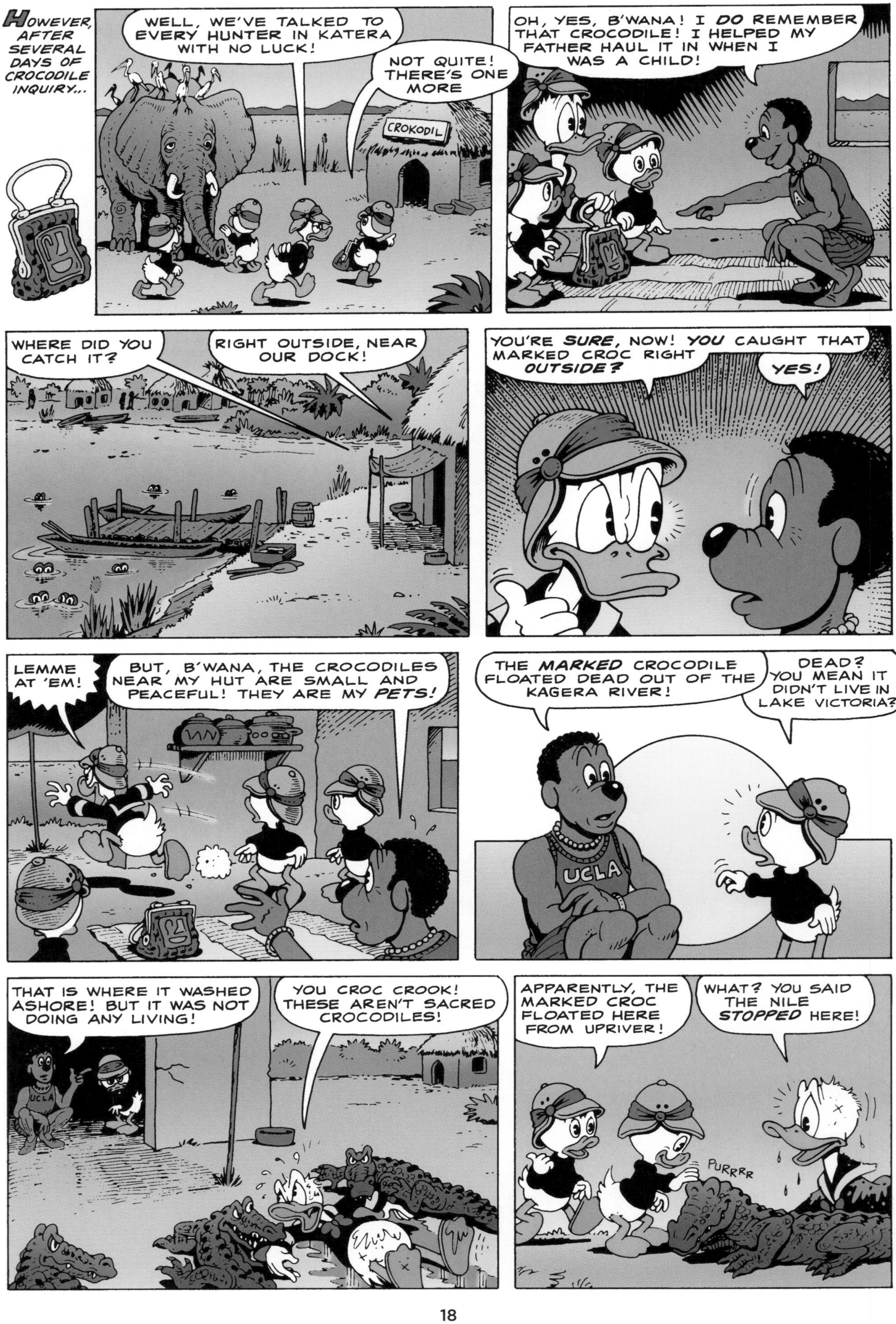
HOWEVER, AFTER SEVERAL DAYS OF CROCODILE INQUIRY...
WELL, WE'VE TALKED TO EVERY HUNTER IN KATERA WITH NO LUCK!
NOT QUITE! THERE'S ONE MORE
CROKODIL
OH, YES, B'WANA! I DO REMEMBER THAT CROCODILE! I HELPED MY FATHER HAUL IT IN WHEN I WAS A CHILD!
WHERE DID YOU CATCH IT?
RIGHT OUTSIDE, NEAR OUR DOCK!
YOU'RE SURE, NOW! YOU CAUGHT THAT MARKED CROC RIGHT OUTSIDE?
YES!
LEMME AT 'EM!
BUT, B'WANA, THE CROCODILES NEAR MY HUT ARE SMALL AND PEACEFUL! THEY ARE MY PETS!
THE MARKED CROCODILE FLOATED DEAD OUT OF THE KAGERA RIVER!
DEAD? YOU MEAN IT DIDN'T LIVE IN LAKE VICTORIA?
UCLA
THAT IS WHERE IT WASHED ASHORE! BUT IT WAS NOT DOING ANY LIVING!
YOU CROC CROOK! THESE AREN'T SACRED CROCODILES!
APPARENTLY, THE MARKED CROC FLOATED HERE FROM UPRIVER!
WHAT? YOU SAID THE NILE STOPPED HERE!
PURRRR

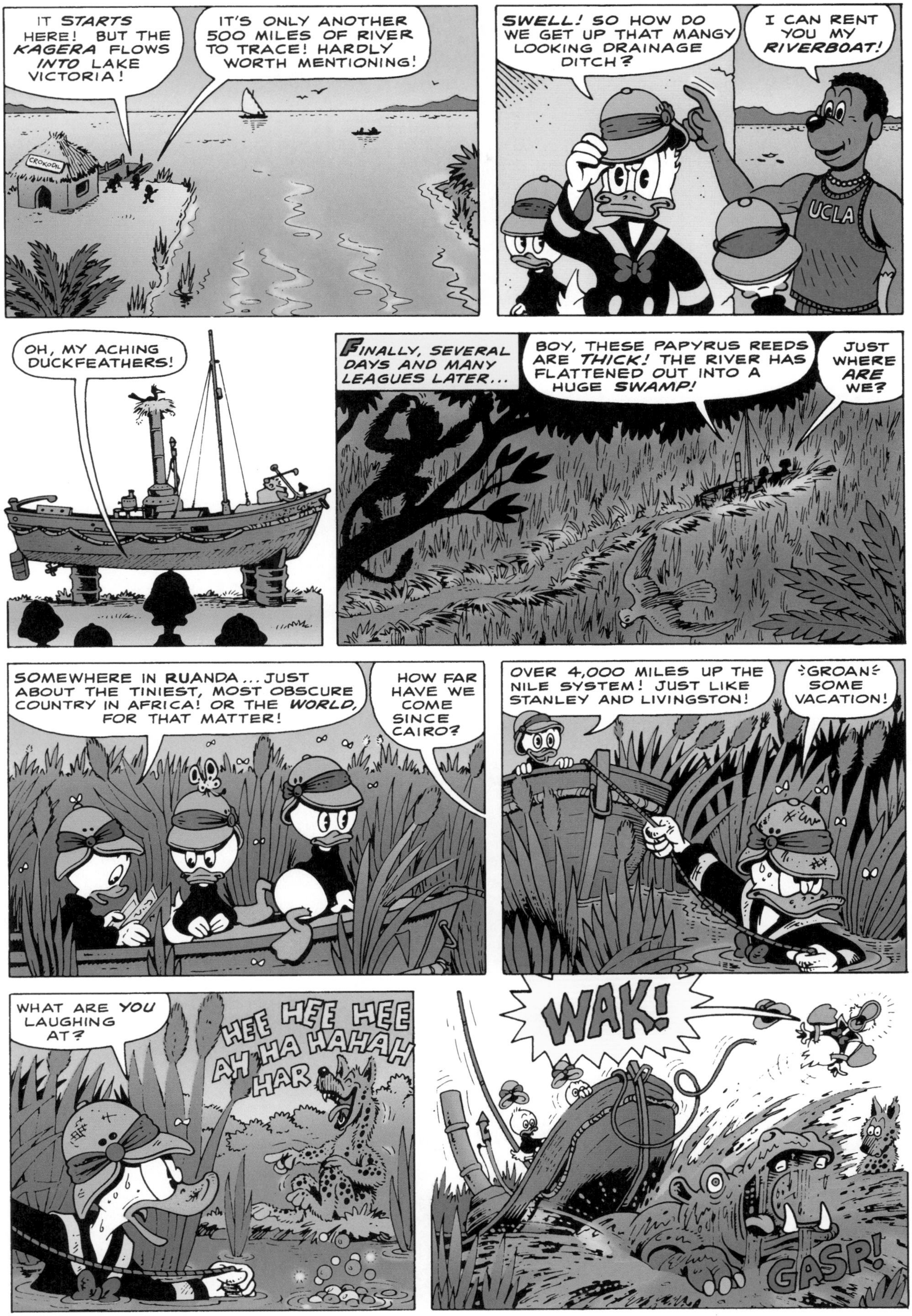
IT STARTS HERE! BUT THE KAGERA FLOWS INTO LAKE VICTORIA!
IT'S ONLY ANOTHER 500 MILES OF RIVER TO TRACE! HARDLY WORTH MENTIONING!
CROKODIL
SWELL! SO HOW DO WE GET UP THAT MANGY LOOKING DRAINAGE DITCH?
I CAN RENT YOU MY RIVERBOAT!
UCLA
OH, MY ACHING DUCKFEATHERS!
FINALLY, SEVERAL DAYS AND MANY LEAGUES LATER...
BOY, THESE PAPYRUS REEDS ARE THICK! THE RIVER HAS FLATTENED OUT INTO A HUGE SWAMP!
JUST WHERE ARE WE?
SOMEWHERE IN RUANDA... JUST ABOUT THE TINIEST, MOST OBSCURE COUNTRY IN AFRICA! OR THE WORLD, FOR THAT MATTER!
HOW FAR HAVE WE COME SINCE CAIRO?
OVER 4,000 MILES UP THE NILE SYSTEM! JUST LIKE STANLEY AND LIVINGSTON!
GROAN SOME VACATION!
WHAT ARE YOU LAUGHING AT?
HEE HEE HEE AH HA HAHAH HAR
WAK!
GASP!

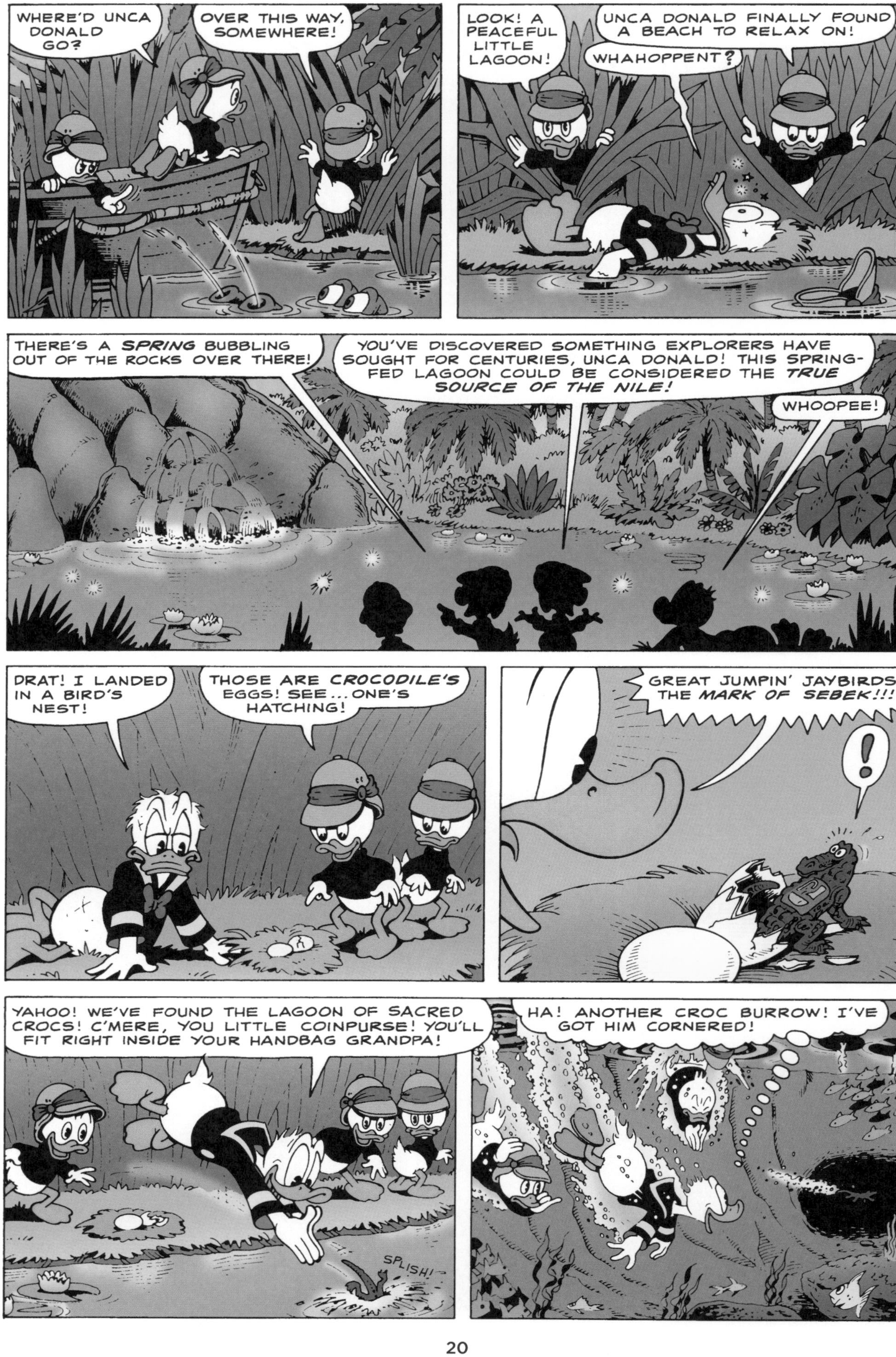
WHERE'D UNCA DONALD GO?
OVER THIS WAY, SOMEWHERE!
LOOK! A PEACEFUL LITTLE LAGOON!
UNCA DONALD FINALLY FOUND A BEACH TO RELAX ON!
WHAHOPPENT?
THERE'S A SPRING BUBBLING OUT OF THE ROCKS OVER THERE!
YOU'VE DISCOVERED SOMETHING EXPLORERS HAVE SOUGHT FOR CENTURIES, UNCA DONALD! THIS SPRING-FED LAGOON COULD BE CONSIDERED THE TRUE SOURCE OF THE NILE!
WHOOPEE!
DRAT! I LANDED IN A BIRD'S NEST!
THOSE ARE CROCODILE'S EGGS! SEE... ONE'S HATCHING!
GREAT JUMPIN' JAYBIRDS! THE MARK OF SEBEK!!!
!
YAHOO! WE'VE FOUND THE LAGOON OF SACRED CROCS! C'MERE, YOU LITTLE COINPURSE! YOU'LL FIT RIGHT INSIDE YOUR HANDBAG GRANDPA!
SPLISH!
HA! ANOTHER CROC BURROW! I'VE GOT HIM CORNERED!

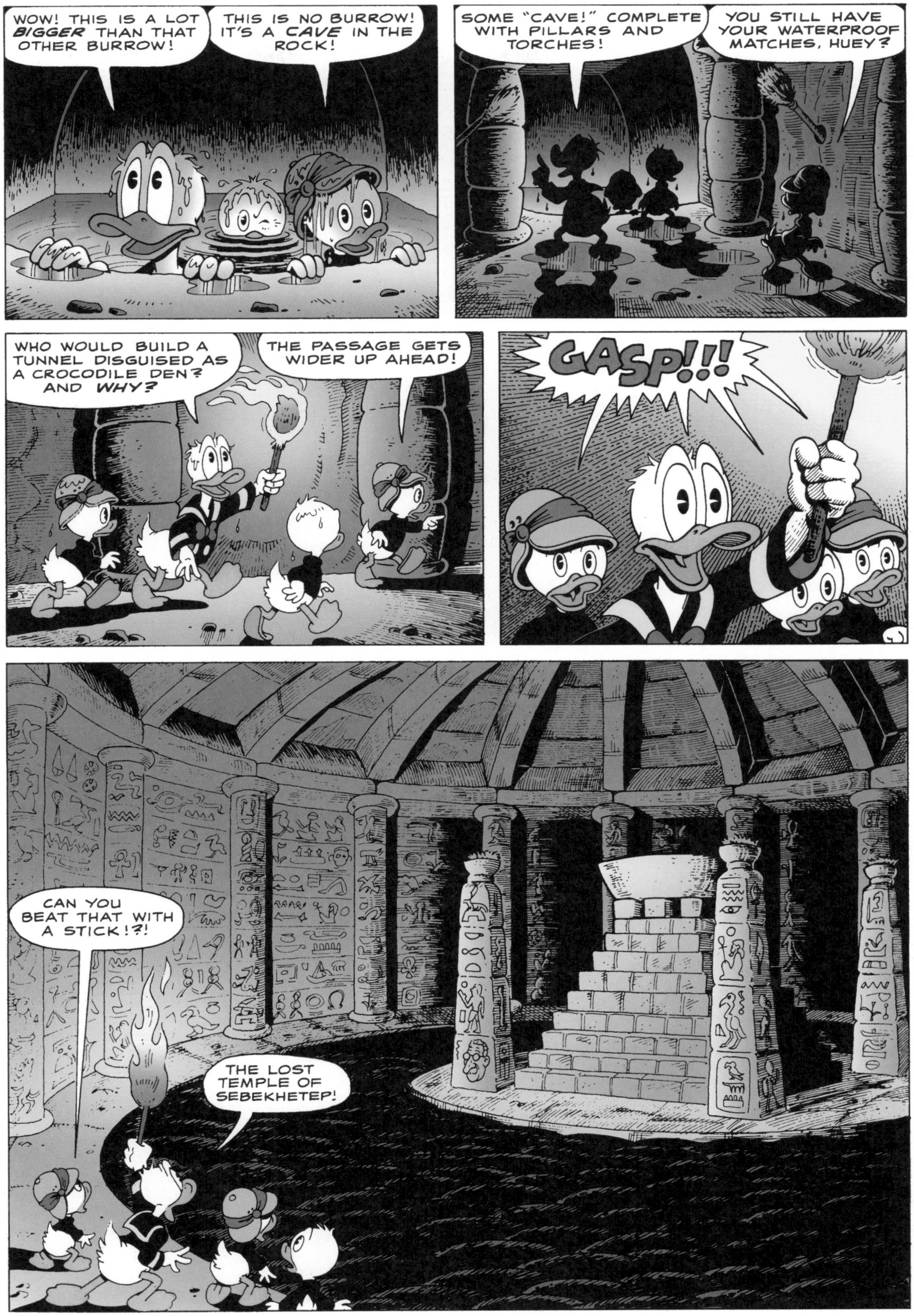

WOW! THIS IS A LOT BIGGER THAN THAT OTHER BURROW!
THIS IS NO BURROW! IT'S A CAVE IN THE ROCK!
SOME "CAVE!" COMPLETE WITH PILLARS AND TORCHES!
YOU STILL HAVE YOUR WATERPROOF MATCHES, HUEY?
WHO WOULD BUILD A TUNNEL DISGUISED AS A CROCODILE DEN? AND WHY?
THE PASSAGE GETS WIDER UP AHEAD!
GASP!!!
CAN YOU BEAT THAT WITH A STICK!?!
THE LOST TEMPLE OF SEBEKHETEP!

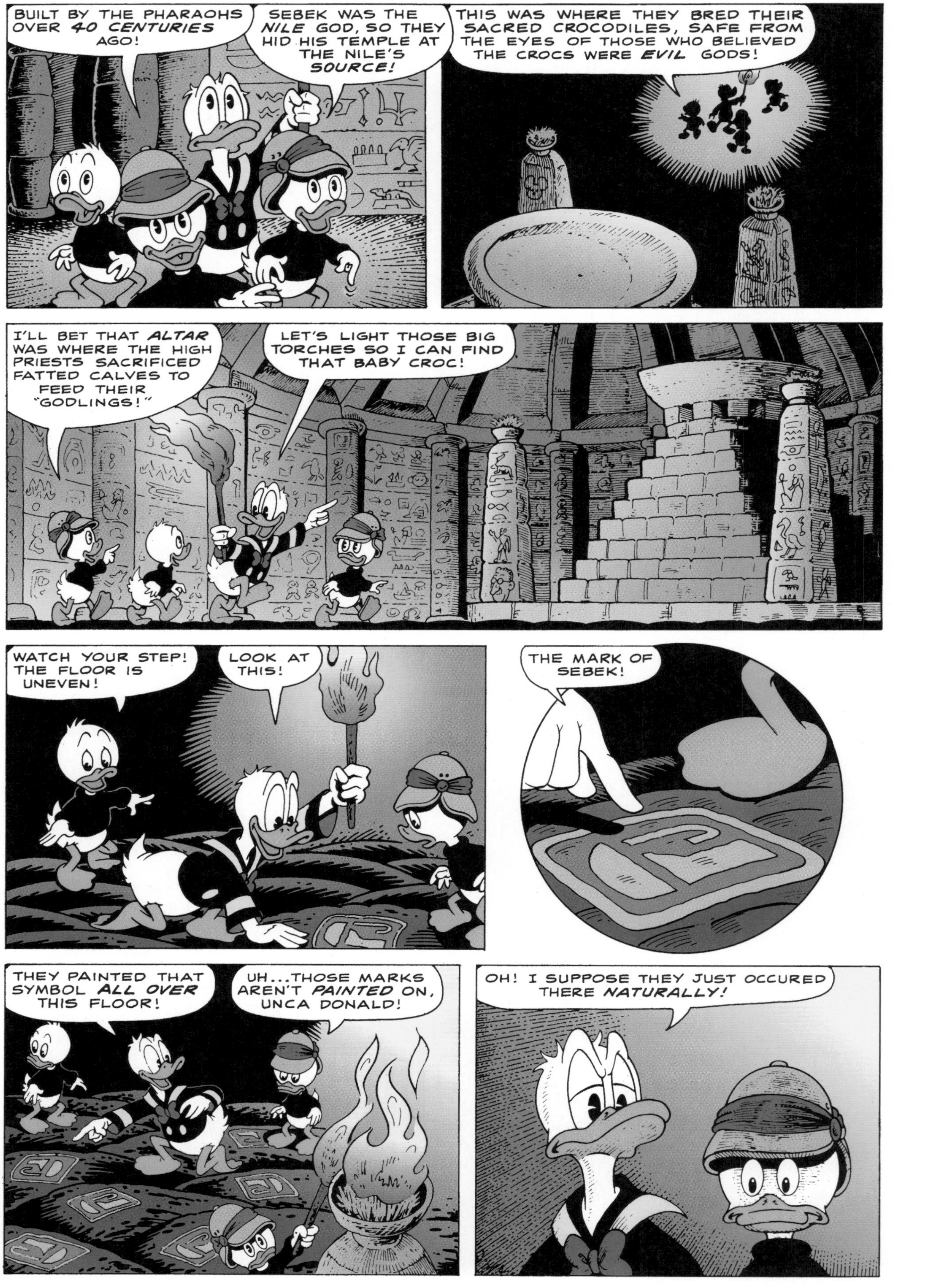
BUILT BY THE PHARAOHS OVER 40 CENTURIES AGO!
SEBEK WAS THE NILE GOD, SO THEY HID HIS TEMPLE AT THE NILE'S SOURCE!
THIS WAS WHERE THEY BRED THEIR SACRED CROCODILES, SAFE FROM THE EYES OF THOSE WHO BELIEVED THE CROCS WERE EVIL GODS!
I'LL BET THAT ALTAR WAS WHERE THE HIGH PRIESTS SACRIFICED FATTED CALVES TO FEED THEIR "GODLINGS!"
LET'S LIGHT THOSE BIG TORCHES SO I CAN FIND THAT BABY CROC!
WATCH YOUR STEP! THE FLOOR IS UNEVEN!
LOOK AT THIS!
THE MARK OF SEBEK!
THEY PAINTED THAT SYMBOL ALL OVER THIS FLOOR!
UH...THOSE MARKS AREN'T PAINTED ON, UNCA DONALD!
OH! I SUPPOSE THEY JUST OCCURED THERE NATURALLY!

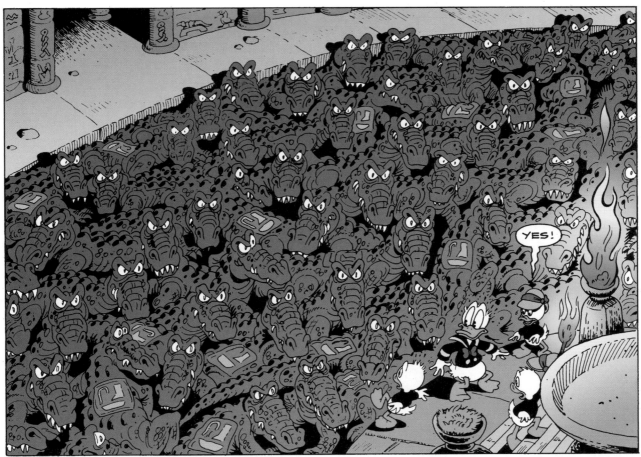

YES!

OH, MY SOCKS AND SHOES!

THIS IS *STILL* THEIR DEN! THEY MUST BE IN HERE TAKING A DAYTIME SNOOZE!

AND *WE* WOKE 'EM UP!

LOOKS LIKE WE'RE *TRAPPED* ON THE ALTAR ISLAND!

GREAT! IT'S TIME FOR *BREAKFAST* AND WE'RE SITTING ON THEIR PLATE LIKE FOUR *SAUSAGE LINKS!*

SAY... DO YOU FEEL A DRAFT?

YOU'RE WORRIED ABOUT *CATCHING A COLD* AT A TIME LIKE THIS?

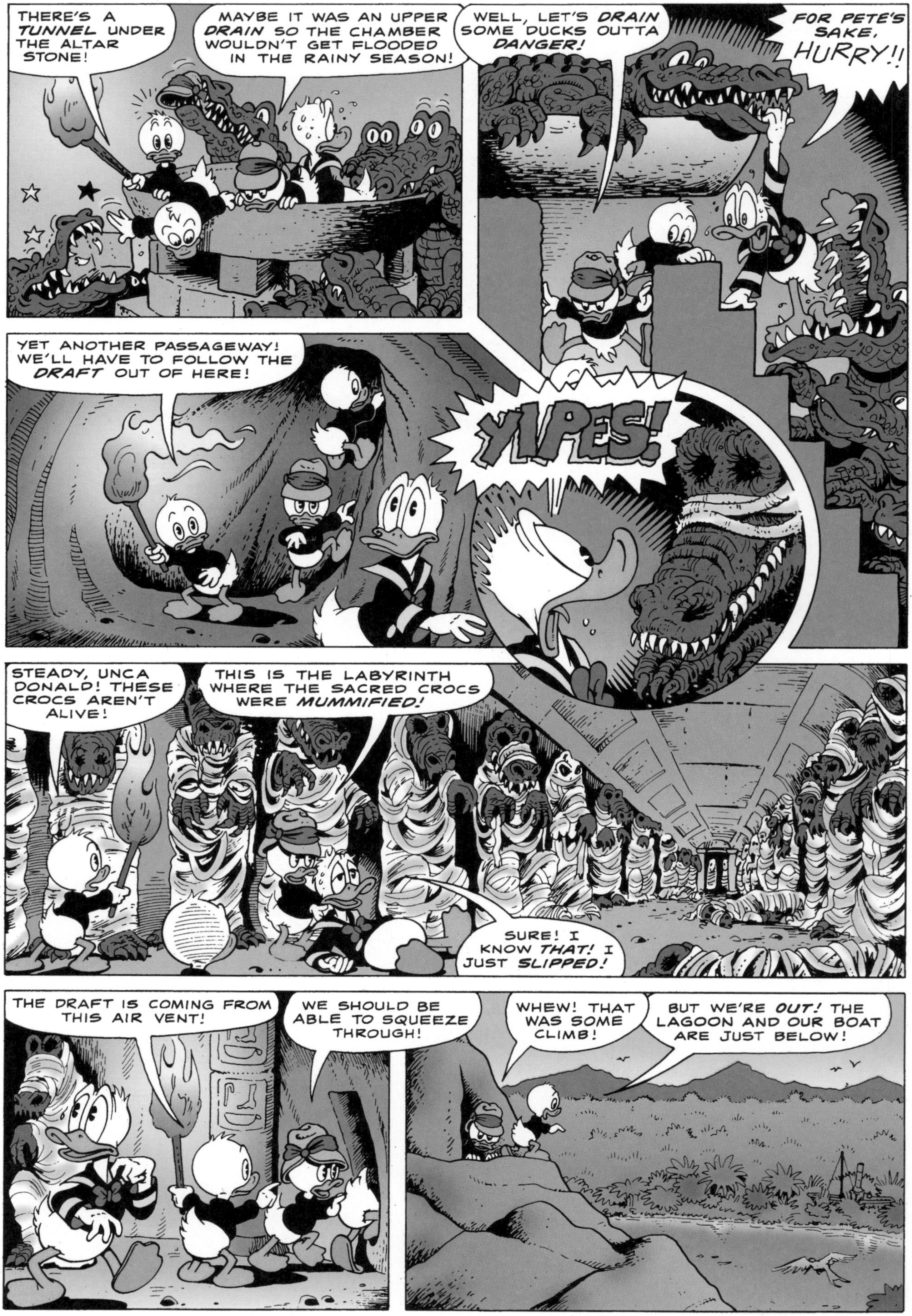
THERE'S A TUNNEL UNDER THE ALTAR STONE!
MAYBE IT WAS AN UPPER DRAIN SO THE CHAMBER WOULDN'T GET FLOODED IN THE RAINY SEASON!
WELL, LET'S DRAIN SOME DUCKS OUTTA DANGER!
FOR PETE'S SAKE, HURRY!!
YET ANOTHER PASSAGEWAY! WE'LL HAVE TO FOLLOW THE DRAFT OUT OF HERE!
YIPES!
STEADY, UNCA DONALD! THESE CROCS AREN'T ALIVE!
THIS IS THE LABYRINTH WHERE THE SACRED CROCS WERE MUMMIFIED!
SURE! I KNOW THAT! I JUST SLIPPED!
THE DRAFT IS COMING FROM THIS AIR VENT!
WE SHOULD BE ABLE TO SQUEEZE THROUGH!
WHEW! THAT WAS SOME CLIMB!
BUT WE'RE OUT! THE LAGOON AND OUR BOAT ARE JUST BELOW!

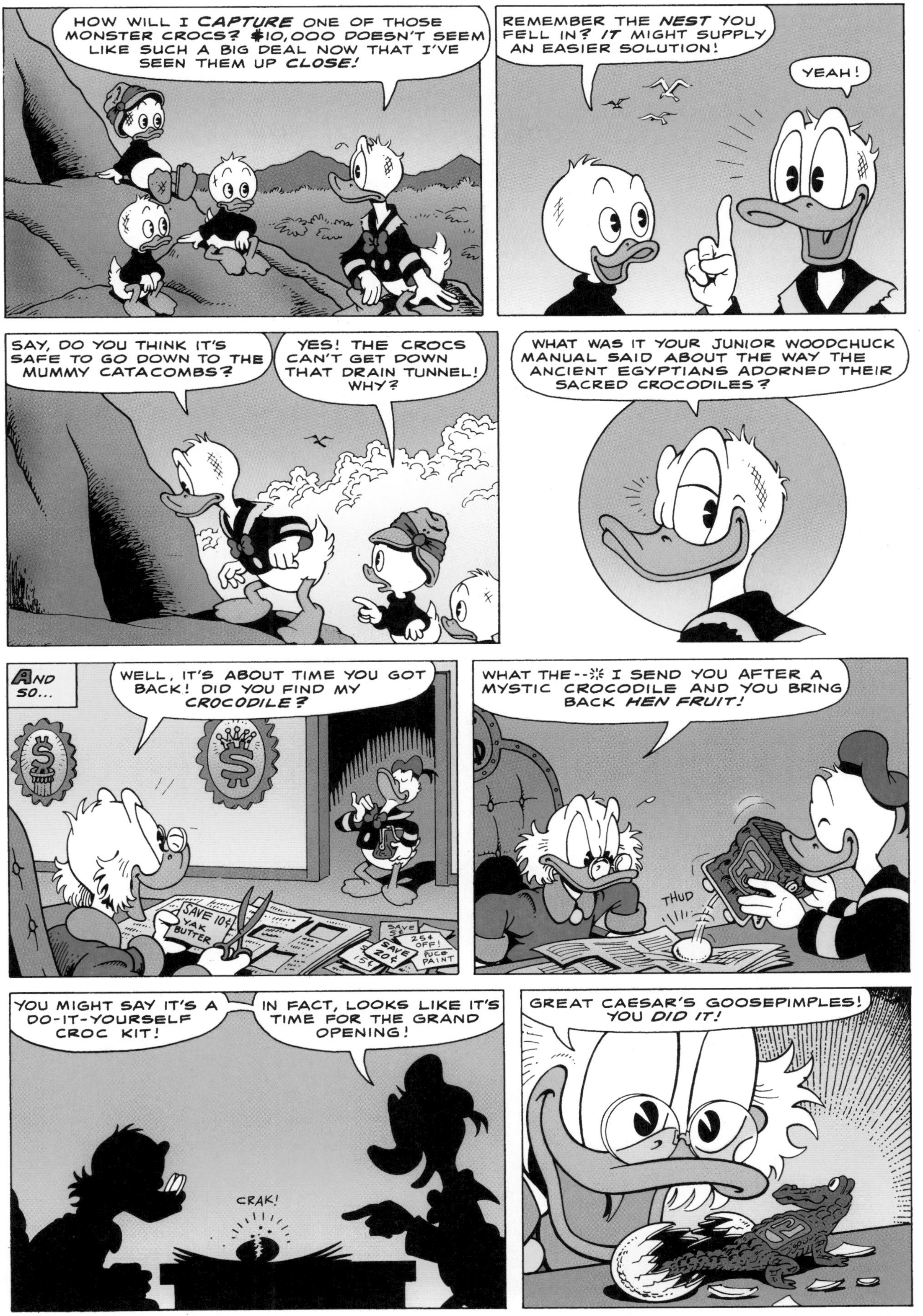
HOW WILL I CAPTURE ONE OF THOSE MONSTER CROCS? $10,000 DOESN'T SEEM LIKE SUCH A BIG DEAL NOW THAT I'VE SEEN THEM UP CLOSE!
REMEMBER THE NEST YOU FELL IN? IT MIGHT SUPPLY AN EASIER SOLUTION!
YEAH!
SAY, DO YOU THINK IT'S SAFE TO GO DOWN TO THE MUMMY CATACOMBS?
YES! THE CROCS CAN'T GET DOWN THAT DRAIN TUNNEL! WHY?
WHAT WAS IT YOUR JUNIOR WOODCHUCK MANUAL SAID ABOUT THE WAY THE ANCIENT EGYPTIANS ADORNED THEIR SACRED CROCODILES?
AND SO...
WELL, IT'S ABOUT TIME YOU GOT BACK! DID YOU FIND MY CROCODILE?
SAVE 10¢ YAK BUTTER
SAVE 5¢
25¢ OFF!
SAVE 20¢
15¢
PUCE PAINT
WHAT THE--※ I SEND YOU AFTER A MYSTIC CROCODILE AND YOU BRING BACK HEN FRUIT!
THUD
YOU MIGHT SAY IT'S A DO-IT-YOURSELF CROC KIT!
IN FACT, LOOKS LIKE IT'S TIME FOR THE GRAND OPENING!
CRAK!
GREAT CAESAR'S GOOSEPIMPLES! YOU DID IT!

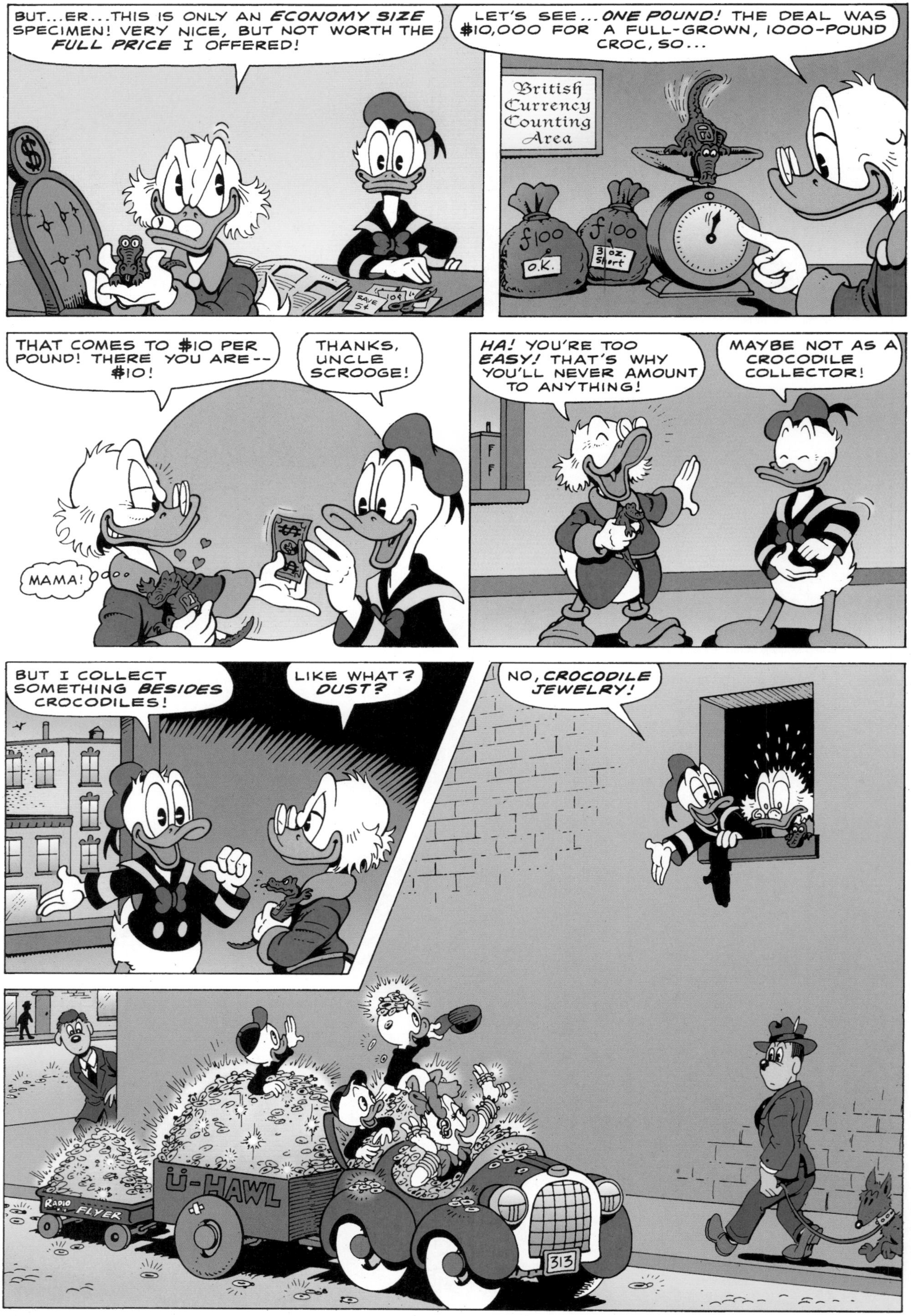
BUT...ER...THIS IS ONLY AN ECONOMY SIZE SPECIMEN! VERY NICE, BUT NOT WORTH THE FULL PRICE I OFFERED!
LET'S SEE...ONE POUND! THE DEAL WAS $10,000 FOR A FULL-GROWN, 1000-POUND CROC, SO...
British Currency Counting Area
£100
O.K.
£100
3 oz. Short
THAT COMES TO $10 PER POUND! THERE YOU ARE-- $10!
THANKS, UNCLE SCROOGE!
MAMA!
HA! YOU'RE TOO EASY! THAT'S WHY YOU'LL NEVER AMOUNT TO ANYTHING!
MAYBE NOT AS A CROCODILE COLLECTOR!
BUT I COLLECT SOMETHING BESIDES CROCODILES!
LIKE WHAT? DUST?
NO, CROCODILE JEWELRY!
U-HAWL
RADIO FLYER
313

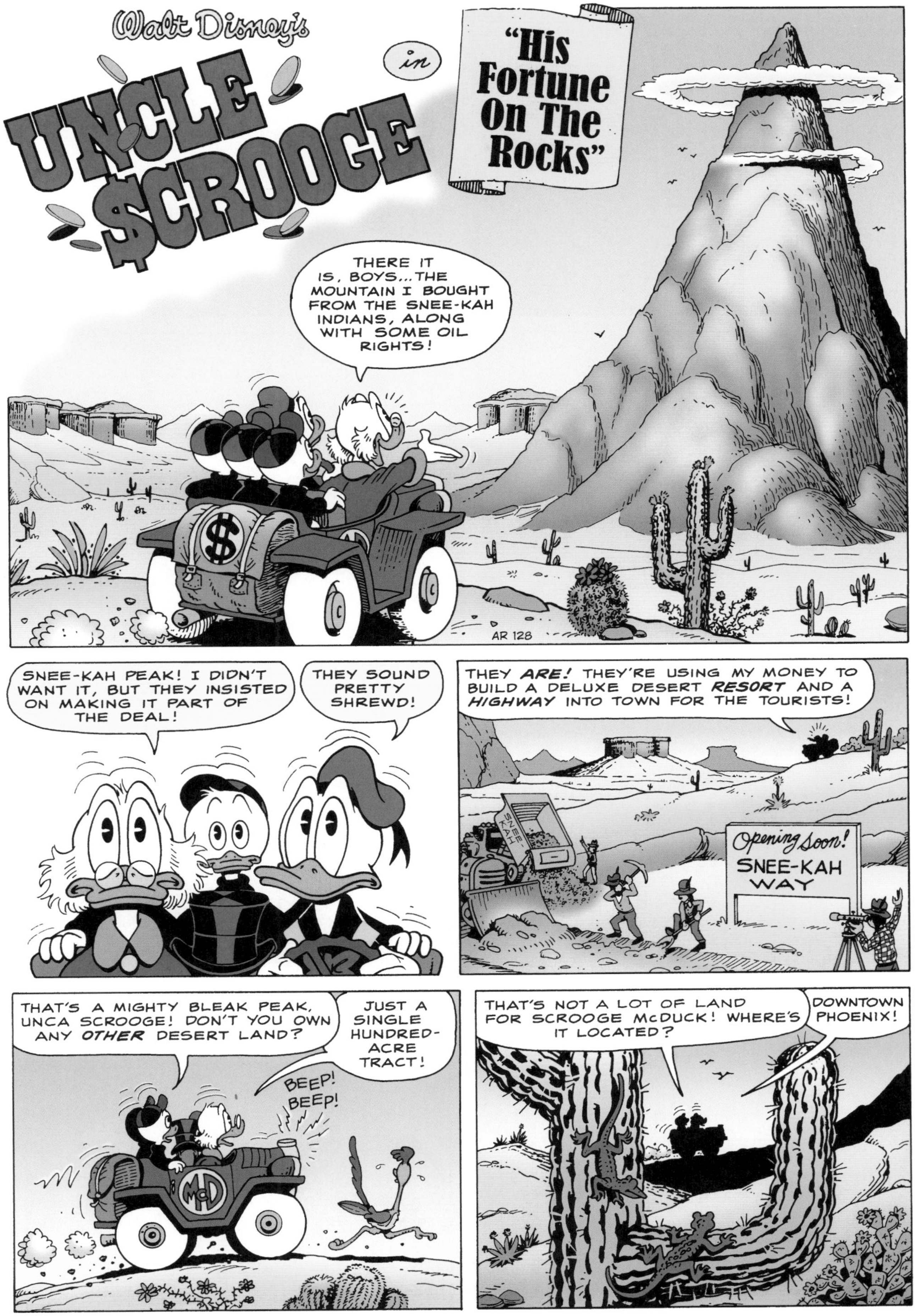

Walt Disney's
UNCLE $CROOGE
in
"His Fortune On The Rocks"
THERE IT IS, BOYS... THE MOUNTAIN I BOUGHT FROM THE SNEE-KAH INDIANS, ALONG WITH SOME OIL RIGHTS!
AR 128
SNEE-KAH PEAK! I DIDN'T WANT IT, BUT THEY INSISTED ON MAKING IT PART OF THE DEAL!
THEY SOUND PRETTY SHREWD!
THEY *ARE!* THEY'RE USING MY MONEY TO BUILD A DELUXE DESERT *RESORT* AND A *HIGHWAY* INTO TOWN FOR THE TOURISTS!
Opening Soon! SNEE-KAH WAY
THAT'S A MIGHTY BLEAK PEAK, UNCA SCROOGE! DON'T YOU OWN ANY *OTHER* DESERT LAND?
JUST A SINGLE HUNDRED-ACRE TRACT!
BEEP! BEEP!
THAT'S NOT A LOT OF LAND FOR SCROOGE McDUCK! WHERE'S IT LOCATED?
DOWNTOWN PHOENIX!

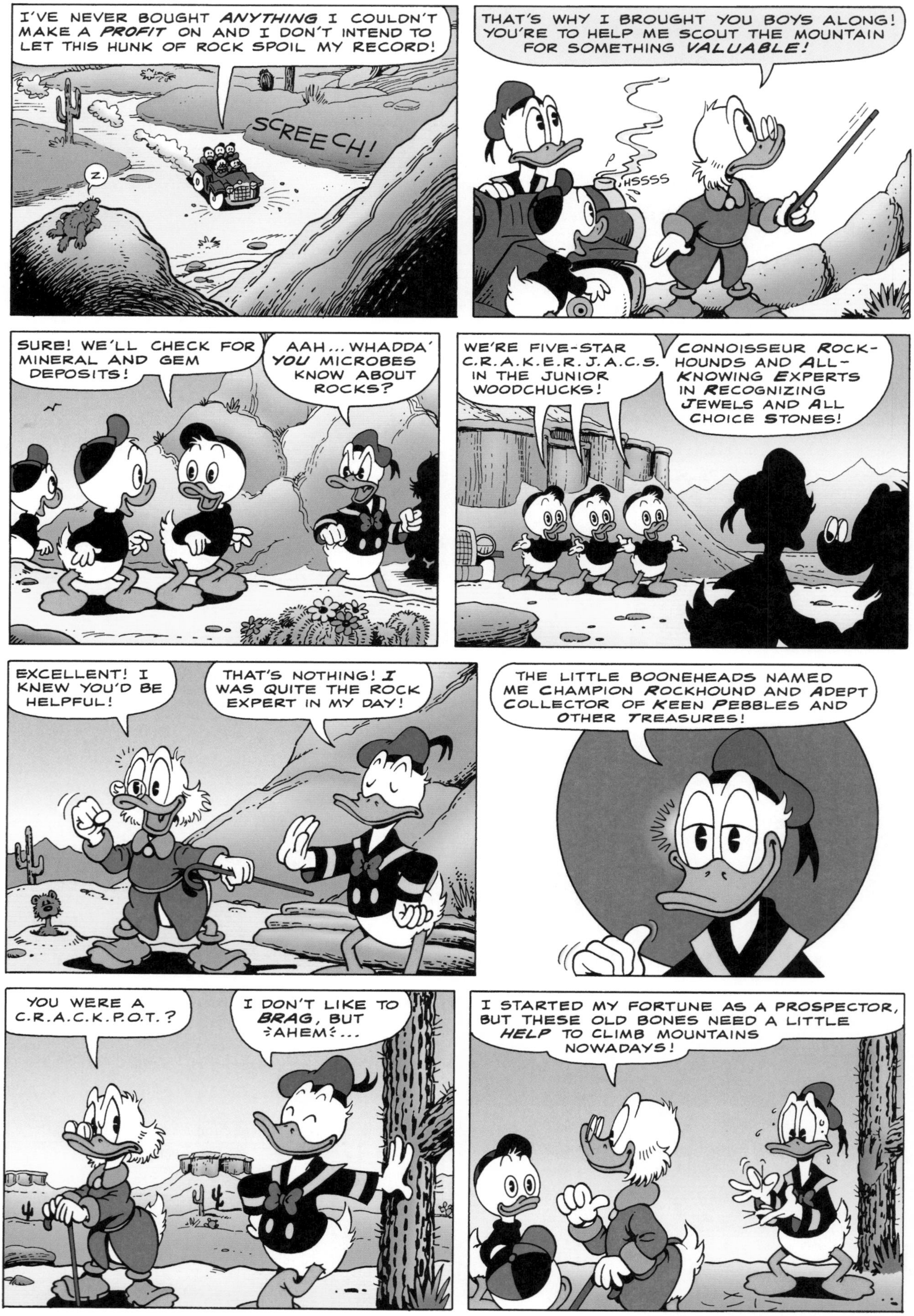
I'VE NEVER BOUGHT ANYTHING I COULDN'T MAKE A PROFIT ON AND I DON'T INTEND TO LET THIS HUNK OF ROCK SPOIL MY RECORD!
SCREECH!
Z.
THAT'S WHY I BROUGHT YOU BOYS ALONG! YOU'RE TO HELP ME SCOUT THE MOUNTAIN FOR SOMETHING VALUABLE!
HSSSS
SURE! WE'LL CHECK FOR MINERAL AND GEM DEPOSITS!
AAH... WHADDA' YOU MICROBES KNOW ABOUT ROCKS?
WE'RE FIVE-STAR C.R.A.K.E.R.J.A.C.S. IN THE JUNIOR WOODCHUCKS!
CONNOISSEUR ROCK-HOUNDS AND ALL-KNOWING EXPERTS IN RECOGNIZING JEWELS AND ALL CHOICE STONES!
EXCELLENT! I KNEW YOU'D BE HELPFUL!
THAT'S NOTHING! I WAS QUITE THE ROCK EXPERT IN MY DAY!
THE LITTLE BOONEHEADS NAMED ME CHAMPION ROCKHOUND AND ADEPT COLLECTOR OF KEEN PEBBLES AND OTHER TREASURES!
YOU WERE A C.R.A.C.K.P.O.T.?
I DON'T LIKE TO BRAG, BUT ⁓AHEM⁓...
I STARTED MY FORTUNE AS A PROSPECTOR, BUT THESE OLD BONES NEED A LITTLE HELP TO CLIMB MOUNTAINS NOWADAYS!

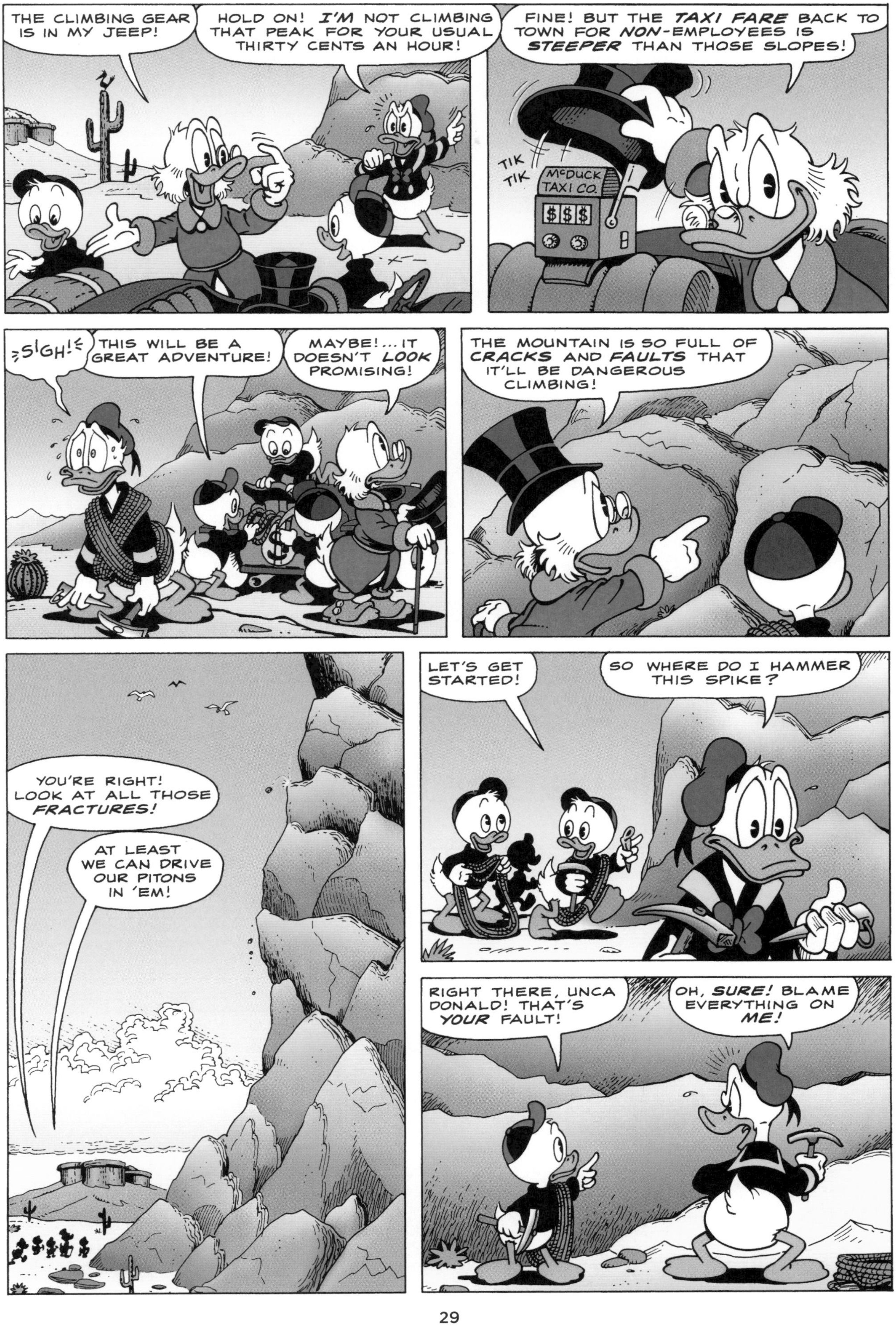
THE CLIMBING GEAR IS IN MY JEEP!
HOLD ON! I'M NOT CLIMBING THAT PEAK FOR YOUR USUAL THIRTY CENTS AN HOUR!
FINE! BUT THE TAXI FARE BACK TO TOWN FOR NON-EMPLOYEES IS STEEPER THAN THOSE SLOPES!
TIK TIK
McDUCK TAXI CO.
$$$
SIGH!
THIS WILL BE A GREAT ADVENTURE!
MAYBE!...IT DOESN'T LOOK PROMISING!
THE MOUNTAIN IS SO FULL OF CRACKS AND FAULTS THAT IT'LL BE DANGEROUS CLIMBING!
YOU'RE RIGHT! LOOK AT ALL THOSE FRACTURES!
AT LEAST WE CAN DRIVE OUR PITONS IN 'EM!
LET'S GET STARTED!
SO WHERE DO I HAMMER THIS SPIKE?
RIGHT THERE, UNCA DONALD! THAT'S YOUR FAULT!
OH, SURE! BLAME EVERYTHING ON ME!

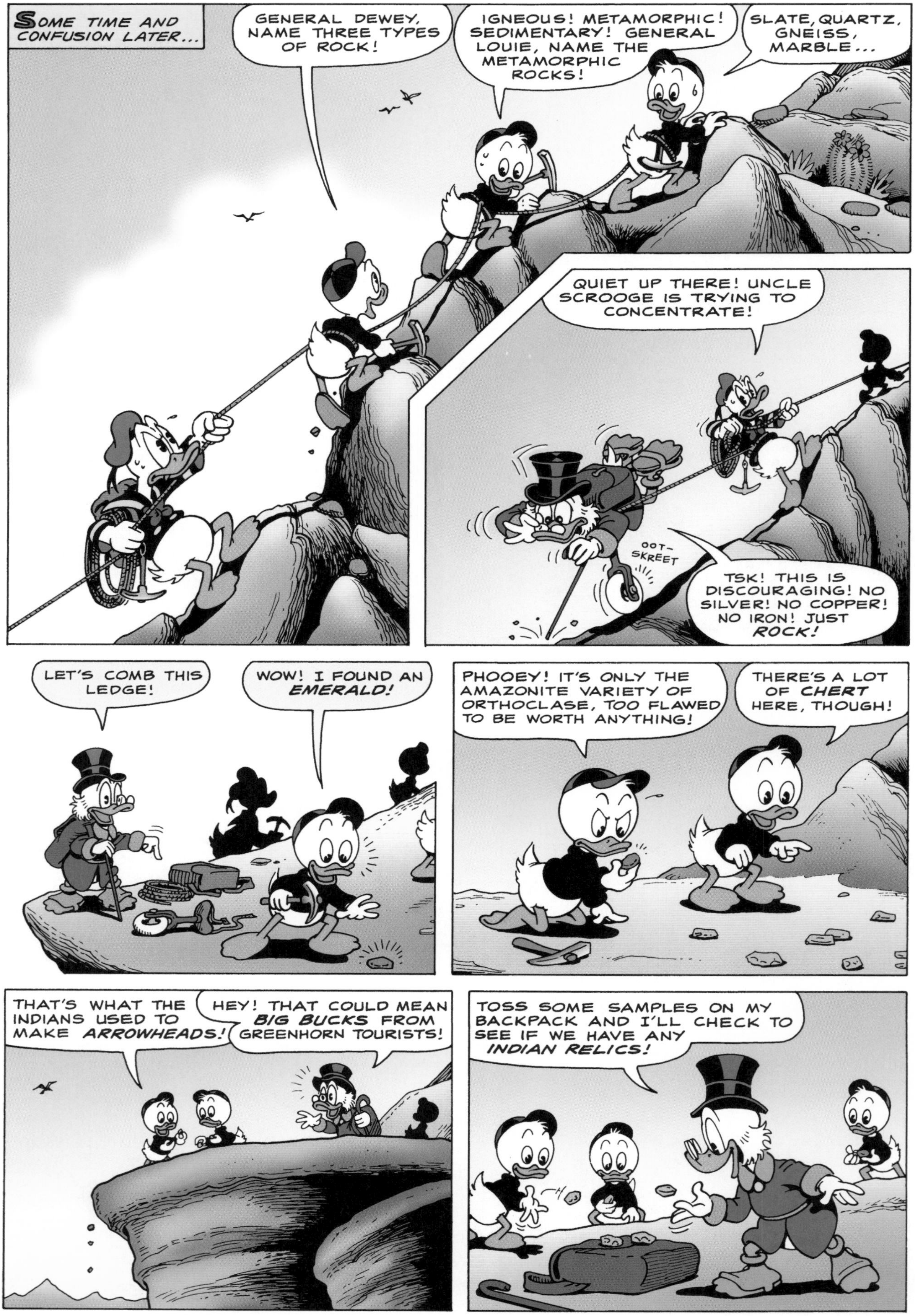
SOME TIME AND CONFUSION LATER...
GENERAL DEWEY, NAME THREE TYPES OF ROCK!
IGNEOUS! METAMORPHIC! SEDIMENTARY! GENERAL LOUIE, NAME THE METAMORPHIC ROCKS!
SLATE, QUARTZ, GNEISS, MARBLE...
QUIET UP THERE! UNCLE SCROOGE IS TRYING TO CONCENTRATE!
OOT-SKREET
TSK! THIS IS DISCOURAGING! NO SILVER! NO COPPER! NO IRON! JUST ROCK!
LET'S COMB THIS LEDGE!
WOW! I FOUND AN EMERALD!
PHOOEY! IT'S ONLY THE AMAZONITE VARIETY OF ORTHOCLASE, TOO FLAWED TO BE WORTH ANYTHING!
THERE'S A LOT OF CHERT HERE, THOUGH!
THAT'S WHAT THE INDIANS USED TO MAKE ARROWHEADS!
HEY! THAT COULD MEAN BIG BUCKS FROM GREENHORN TOURISTS!
TOSS SOME SAMPLES ON MY BACKPACK AND I'LL CHECK TO SEE IF WE HAVE ANY INDIAN RELICS!

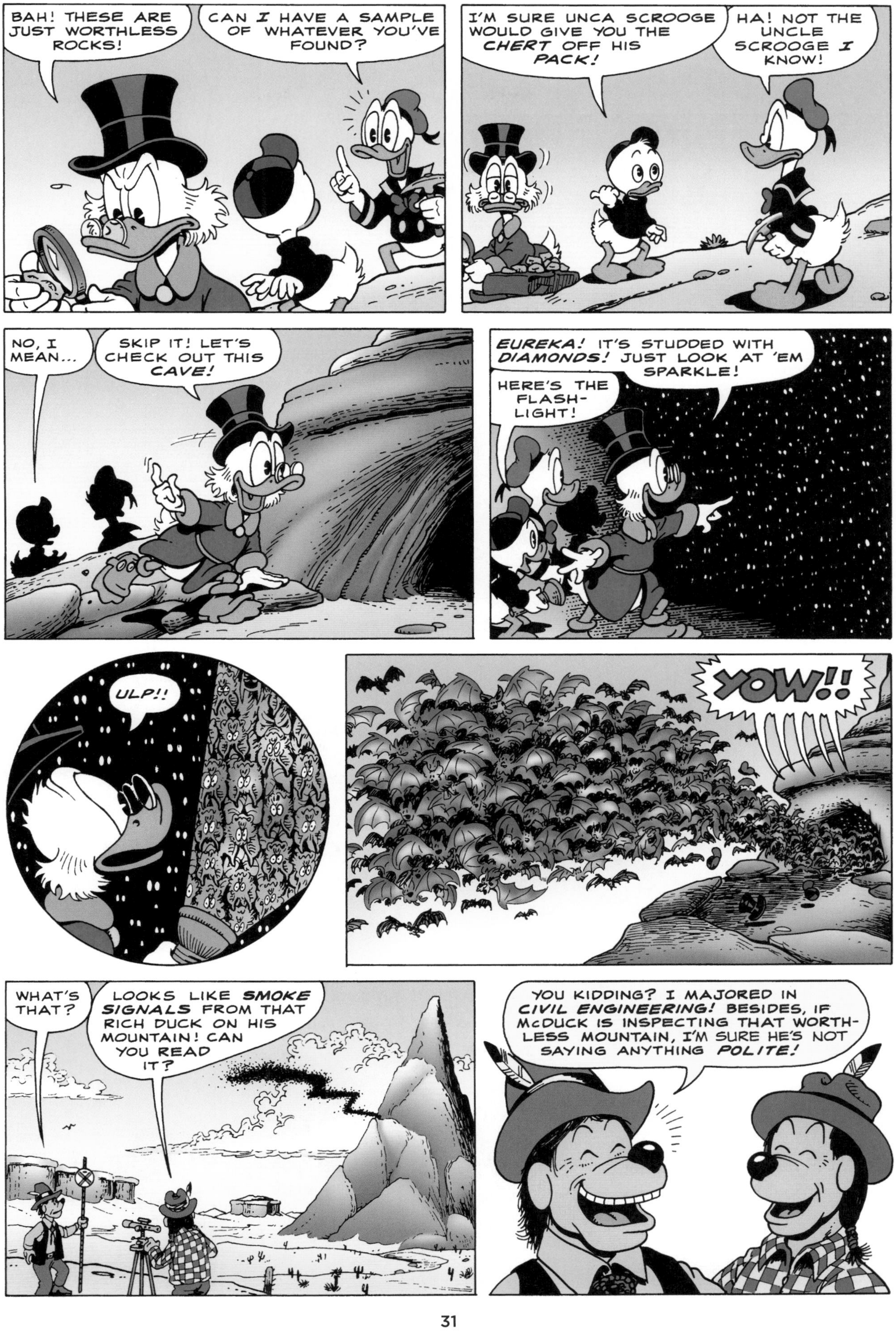

BAH! THESE ARE JUST WORTHLESS ROCKS!
CAN *I* HAVE A SAMPLE OF WHATEVER YOU'VE FOUND?
I'M SURE UNCA SCROOGE WOULD GIVE YOU THE *CHERT* OFF HIS *PACK!*
HA! NOT THE UNCLE SCROOGE *I* KNOW!
NO, I MEAN...
SKIP IT! LET'S CHECK OUT THIS *CAVE!*
EUREKA! IT'S STUDDED WITH *DIAMONDS!* JUST LOOK AT 'EM SPARKLE!
HERE'S THE FLASH-LIGHT!
ULP!!
YOW!!
WHAT'S THAT?
LOOKS LIKE *SMOKE SIGNALS* FROM THAT RICH DUCK ON HIS MOUNTAIN! CAN YOU READ IT?
YOU KIDDING? I MAJORED IN *CIVIL ENGINEERING!* BESIDES, IF McDUCK IS INSPECTING THAT WORTH-LESS MOUNTAIN, I'M SURE HE'S NOT SAYING ANYTHING *POLITE!*

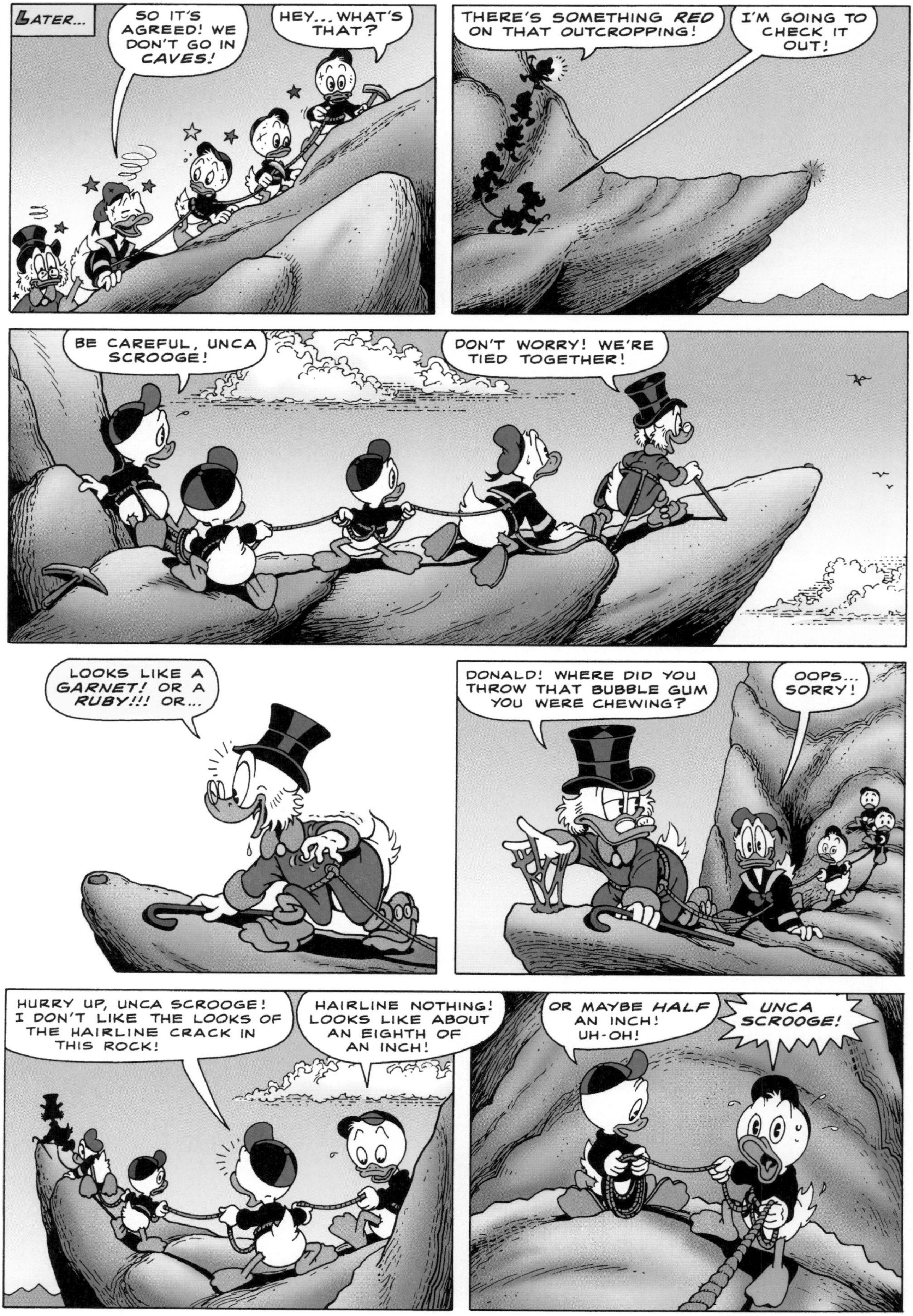
LATER...
SO IT'S AGREED! WE DON'T GO IN CAVES!
HEY... WHAT'S THAT?
THERE'S SOMETHING RED ON THAT OUTCROPPING!
I'M GOING TO CHECK IT OUT!
BE CAREFUL, UNCA SCROOGE!
DON'T WORRY! WE'RE TIED TOGETHER!
LOOKS LIKE A GARNET! OR A RUBY!!! OR...
DONALD! WHERE DID YOU THROW THAT BUBBLE GUM YOU WERE CHEWING?
OOPS... SORRY!
HURRY UP, UNCA SCROOGE! I DON'T LIKE THE LOOKS OF THE HAIRLINE CRACK IN THIS ROCK!
HAIRLINE NOTHING! LOOKS LIKE ABOUT AN EIGHTH OF AN INCH!
OR MAYBE HALF AN INCH! UH-OH!
UNCA SCROOGE!

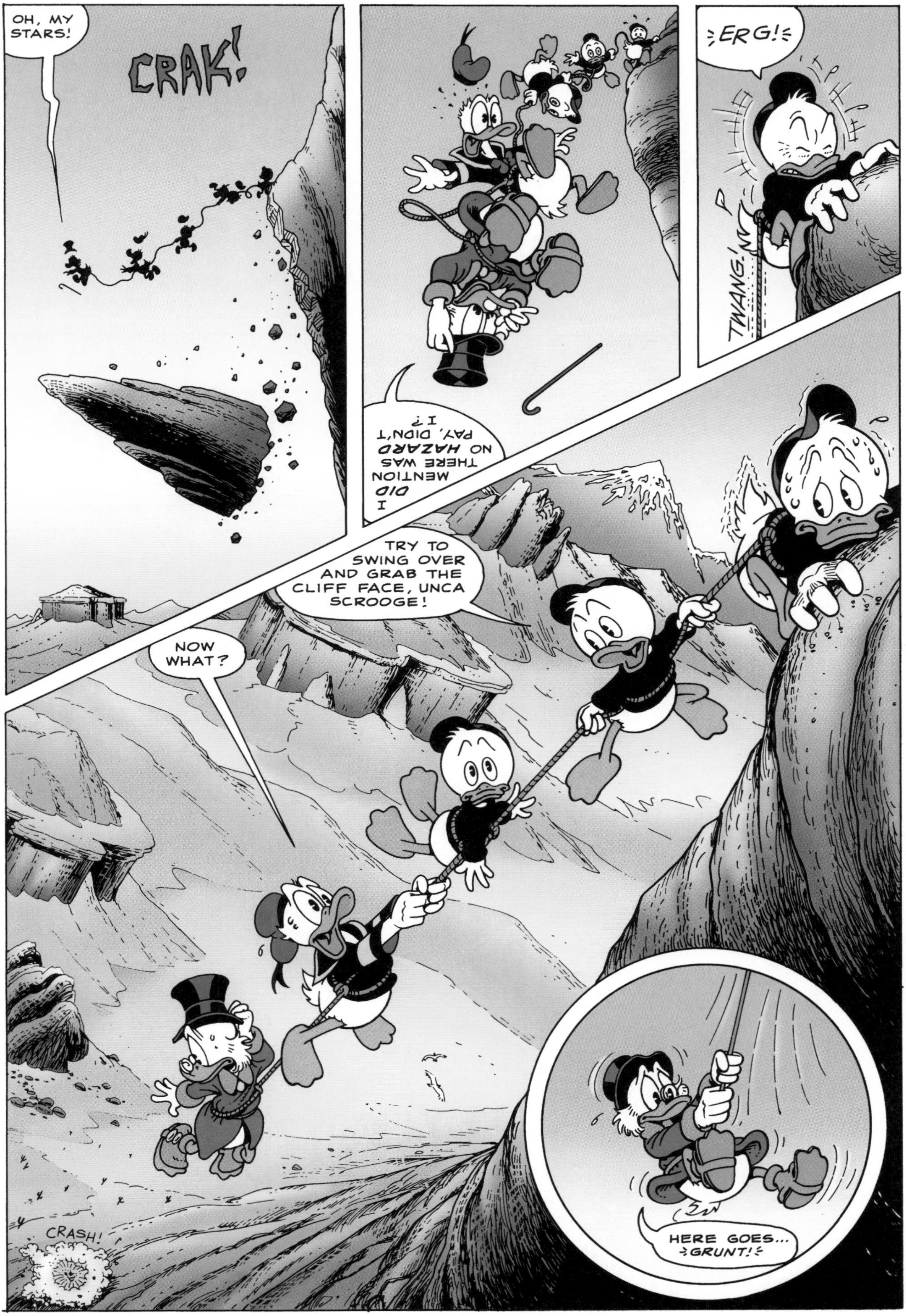
OH, MY STARS!
CRAK!
I DID MENTION THERE WAS NO HAZARD PAY, DIDN'T I?
ERG!
TWANG!
TRY TO SWING OVER AND GRAB THE CLIFF FACE, UNCA SCROOGE!
NOW WHAT?
CRASH!
HERE GOES... GRUNT!

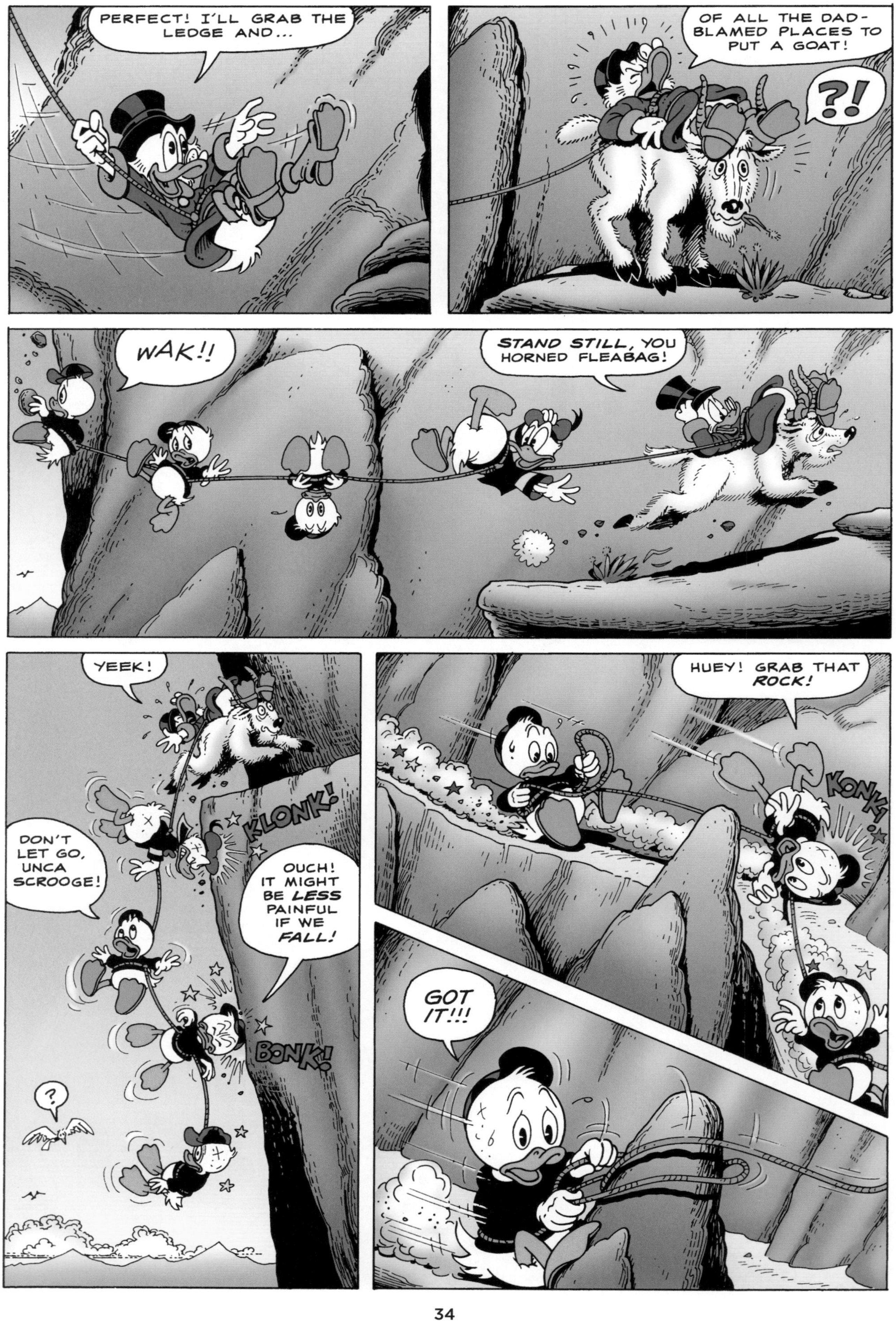
PERFECT! I'LL GRAB THE LEDGE AND...
OF ALL THE DAD-BLAMED PLACES TO PUT A GOAT!
?!
WAK!!
STAND STILL, YOU HORNED FLEABAG!
YEEK!
KLONK!
DON'T LET GO, UNCA SCROOGE!
OUCH! IT MIGHT BE LESS PAINFUL IF WE FALL!
BONK!
?
HUEY! GRAB THAT ROCK!
KONK!
GOT IT!!!

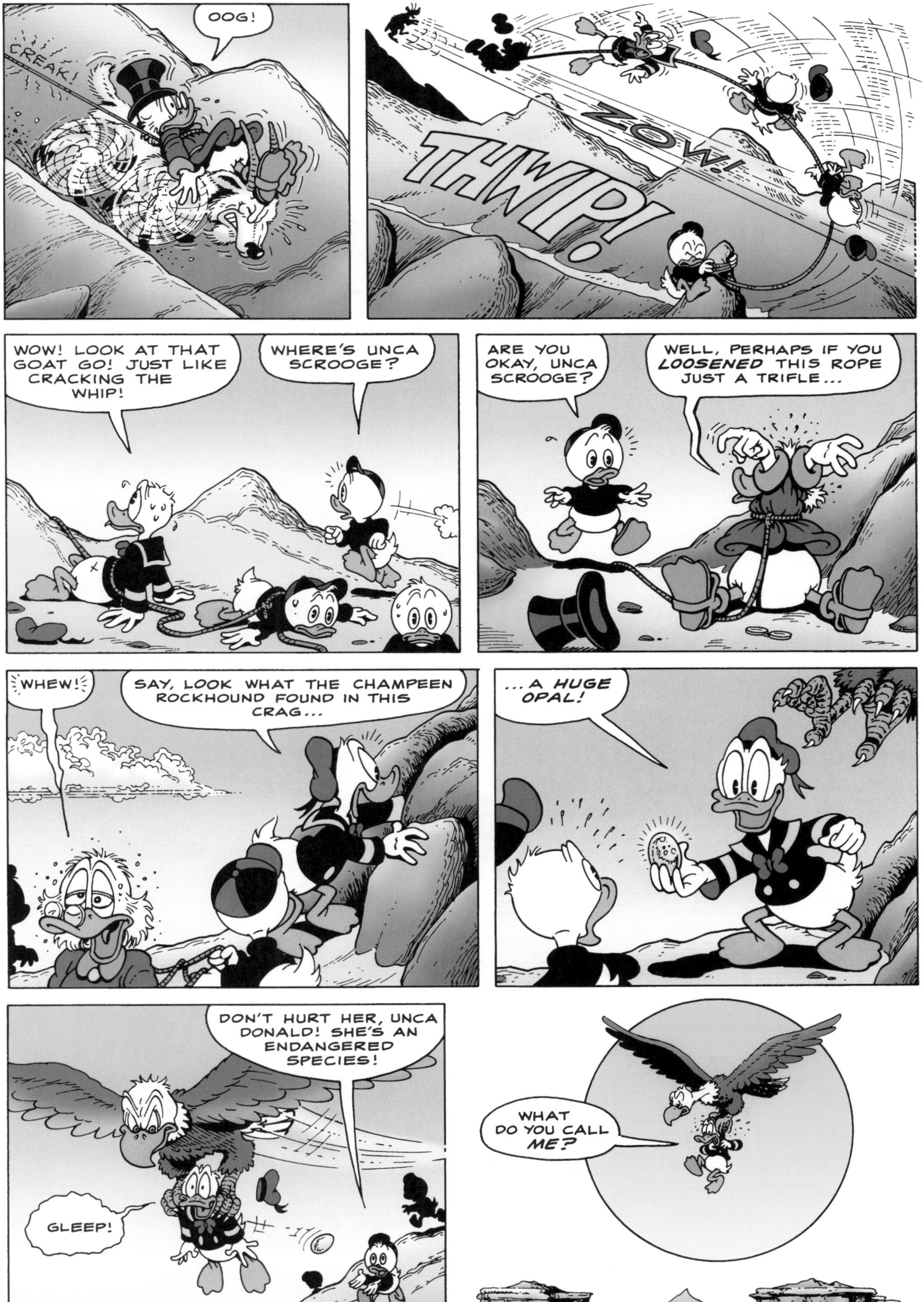
OOG!
CREAK!
ZOW!
THWIP!
WOW! LOOK AT THAT GOAT GO! JUST LIKE CRACKING THE WHIP!
WHERE'S UNCA SCROOGE?
ARE YOU OKAY, UNCA SCROOGE?
WELL, PERHAPS IF YOU LOOSENED THIS ROPE JUST A TRIFLE...
WHEW!
SAY, LOOK WHAT THE CHAMPEEN ROCKHOUND FOUND IN THIS CRAG...
...A HUGE OPAL!
DON'T HURT HER, UNCA DONALD! SHE'S AN ENDANGERED SPECIES!
GLEEP!
WHAT DO YOU CALL ME?

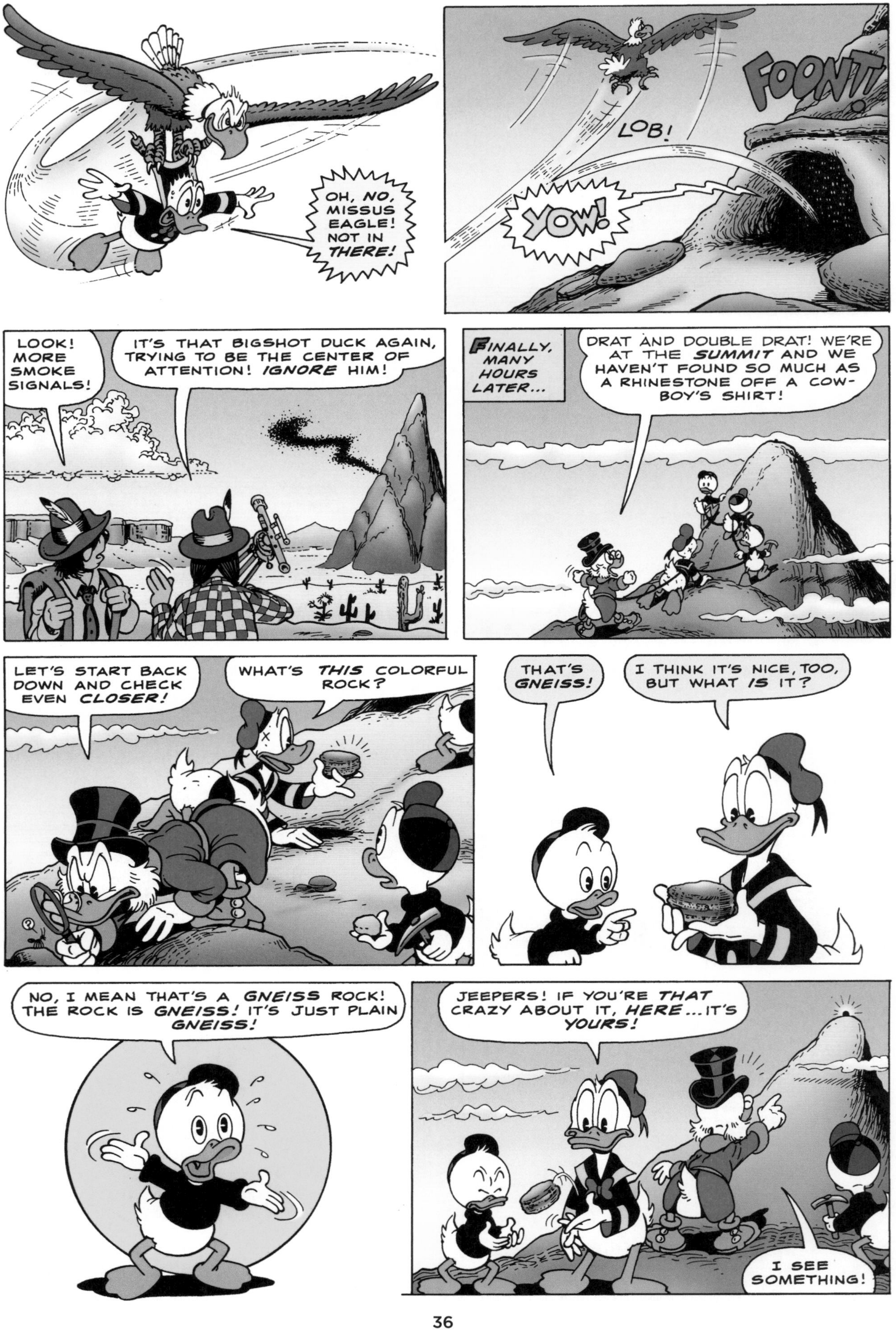
OH, NO, MISSUS EAGLE! NOT IN THERE!
FOONT!
LOB!
YOW!
LOOK! MORE SMOKE SIGNALS!
IT'S THAT BIGSHOT DUCK AGAIN, TRYING TO BE THE CENTER OF ATTENTION! IGNORE HIM!
FINALLY, MANY HOURS LATER...
DRAT AND DOUBLE DRAT! WE'RE AT THE SUMMIT AND WE HAVEN'T FOUND SO MUCH AS A RHINESTONE OFF A COW-BOY'S SHIRT!
LET'S START BACK DOWN AND CHECK EVEN CLOSER!
WHAT'S THIS COLORFUL ROCK?
THAT'S GNEISS!
I THINK IT'S NICE, TOO, BUT WHAT IS IT?
NO, I MEAN THAT'S A GNEISS ROCK! THE ROCK IS GNEISS! IT'S JUST PLAIN GNEISS!
JEEPERS! IF YOU'RE THAT CRAZY ABOUT IT, HERE... IT'S YOURS!
I SEE SOMETHING!

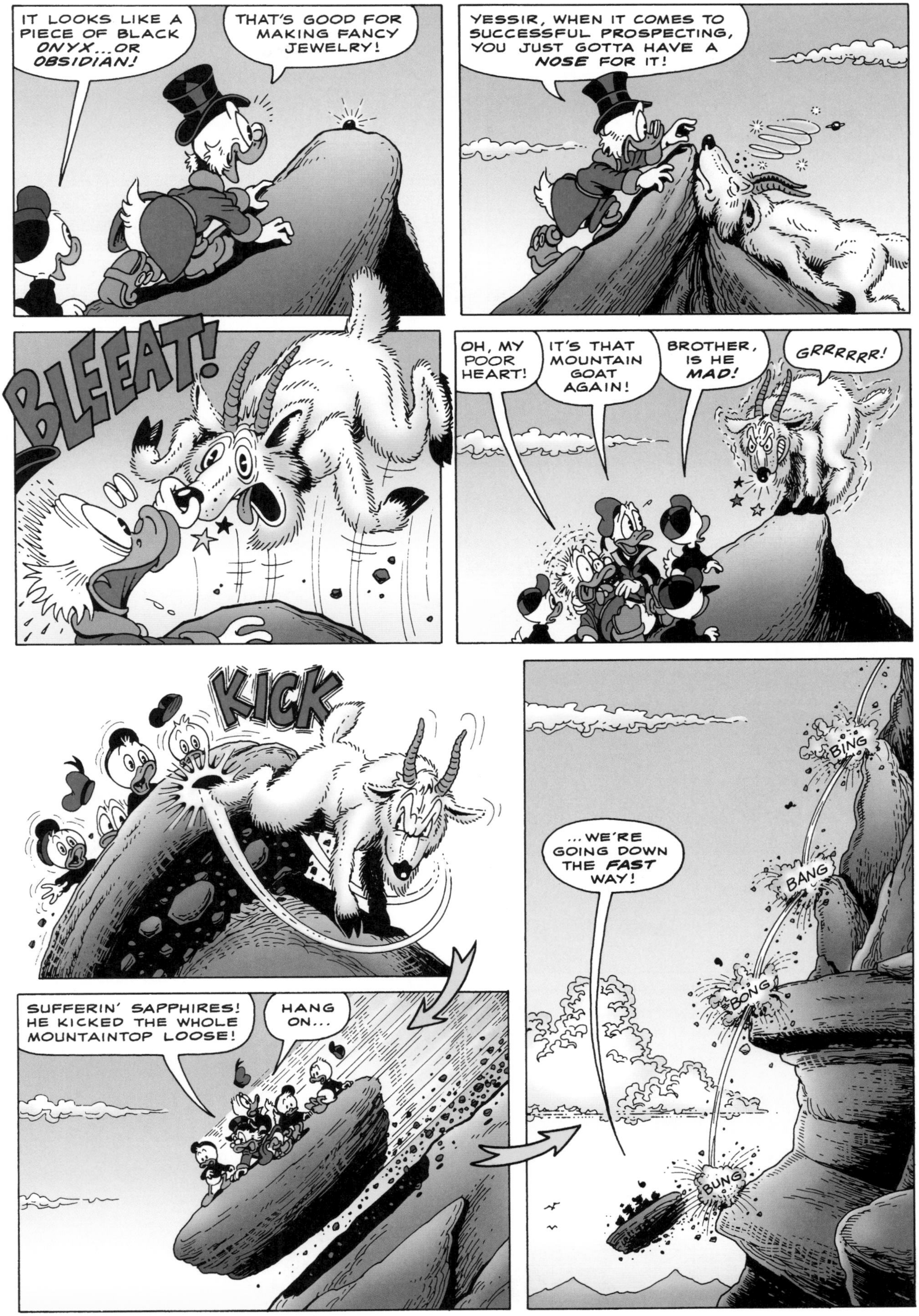
IT LOOKS LIKE A PIECE OF BLACK ONYX...OR OBSIDIAN!
THAT'S GOOD FOR MAKING FANCY JEWELRY!
YESSIR, WHEN IT COMES TO SUCCESSFUL PROSPECTING, YOU JUST GOTTA HAVE A NOSE FOR IT!
BLEEAT!
OH, MY POOR HEART!
IT'S THAT MOUNTAIN GOAT AGAIN!
BROTHER, IS HE MAD!
GRRRRRR!
KICK
SUFFERIN' SAPPHIRES! HE KICKED THE WHOLE MOUNTAINTOP LOOSE!
HANG ON...
...WE'RE GOING DOWN THE FAST WAY!
BING
BANG
BONG
BUNG

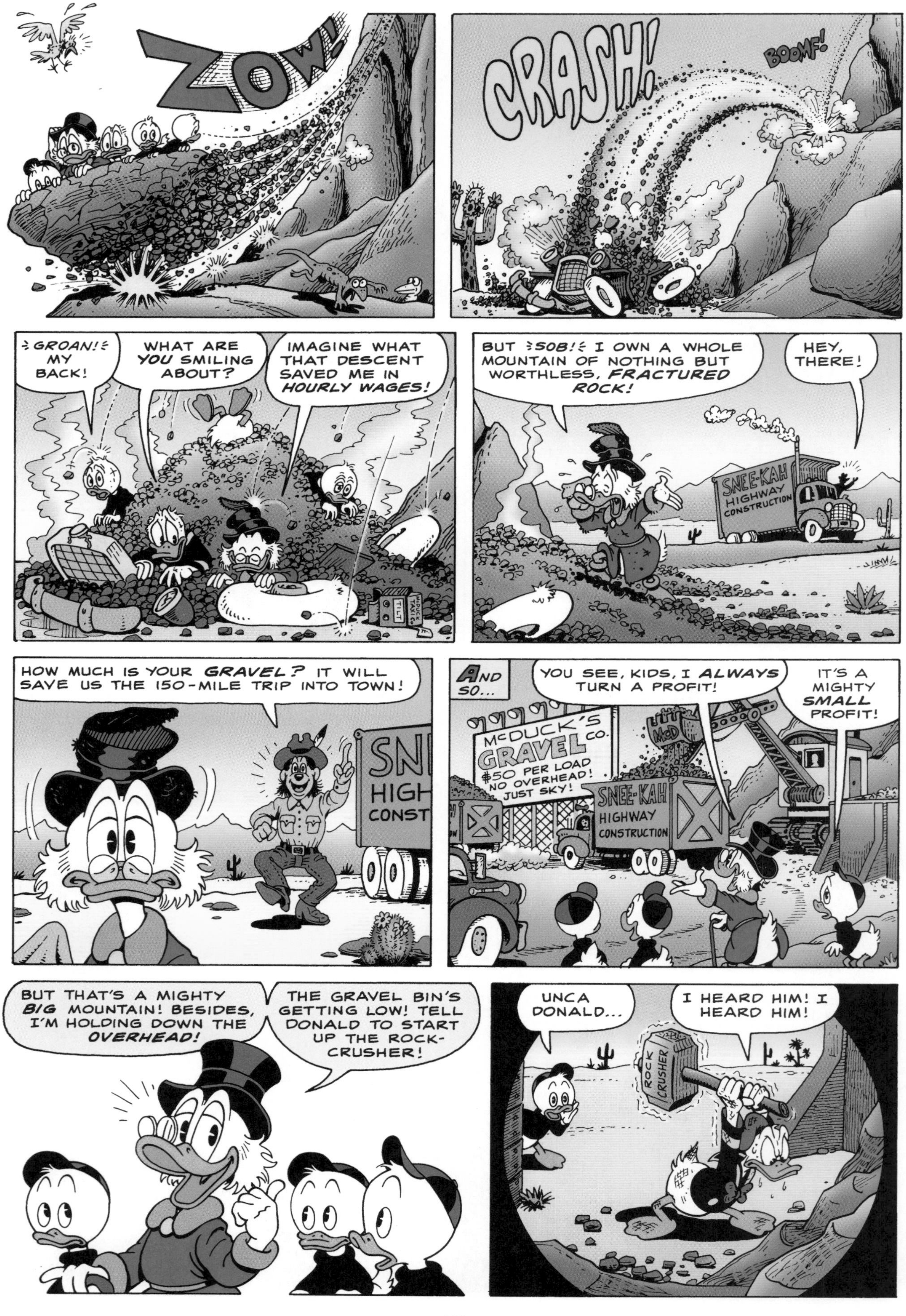
ZOW!
CRASH!
BOOMF!
GROAN! MY BACK!
WHAT ARE YOU SMILING ABOUT?
IMAGINE WHAT THAT DESCENT SAVED ME IN HOURLY WAGES!
TILT
BUT SOB! I OWN A WHOLE MOUNTAIN OF NOTHING BUT WORTHLESS, FRACTURED ROCK!
HEY, THERE!
SNEE-KAH HIGHWAY CONSTRUCTION
HOW MUCH IS YOUR GRAVEL? IT WILL SAVE US THE 150-MILE TRIP INTO TOWN!
AND SO...
YOU SEE, KIDS, I ALWAYS TURN A PROFIT!
IT'S A MIGHTY SMALL PROFIT!
McDUCK'S GRAVEL CO. $50 PER LOAD NO OVERHEAD! JUST SKY!
SNEE-KAH HIGHWAY CONSTRUCTION
BUT THAT'S A MIGHTY BIG MOUNTAIN! BESIDES, I'M HOLDING DOWN THE OVERHEAD!
THE GRAVEL BIN'S GETTING LOW! TELL DONALD TO START UP THE ROCK-CRUSHER!
UNCA DONALD...
I HEARD HIM! I HEARD HIM!
ROCK CRUSHER

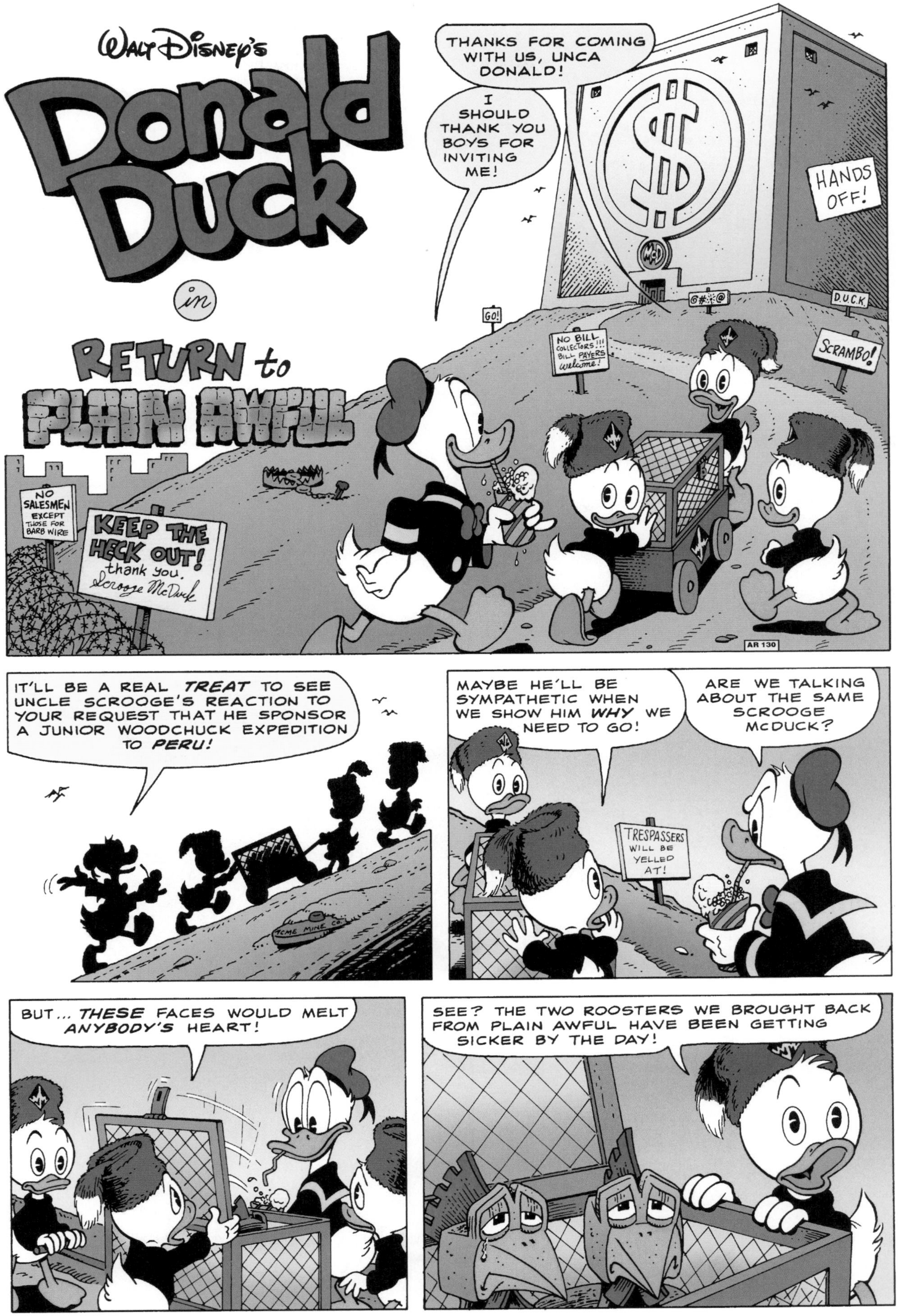

Walt Disney's
Donald Duck
in
RETURN to PLAIN AWFUL
THANKS FOR COMING WITH US, UNCA DONALD!
I SHOULD THANK YOU BOYS FOR INVITING ME!
HANDS OFF!
GO!
NO BILL COLLECTORS!!! BILL PAYERS welcome!
D.U.C.K.
SCRAMBO!
NO SALESMEN EXCEPT THOSE FOR BARB WIRE
KEEP THE HECK OUT! thank you. Scrooge McDuck
AR 130
IT'LL BE A REAL TREAT TO SEE UNCLE SCROOGE'S REACTION TO YOUR REQUEST THAT HE SPONSOR A JUNIOR WOODCHUCK EXPEDITION TO PERU!
ACME MINE CO.
MAYBE HE'LL BE SYMPATHETIC WHEN WE SHOW HIM WHY WE NEED TO GO!
ARE WE TALKING ABOUT THE SAME SCROOGE McDUCK?
TRESPASSERS WILL BE YELLED AT!
BUT... THESE FACES WOULD MELT ANYBODY'S HEART!
SEE? THE TWO ROOSTERS WE BROUGHT BACK FROM PLAIN AWFUL HAVE BEEN GETTING SICKER BY THE DAY!

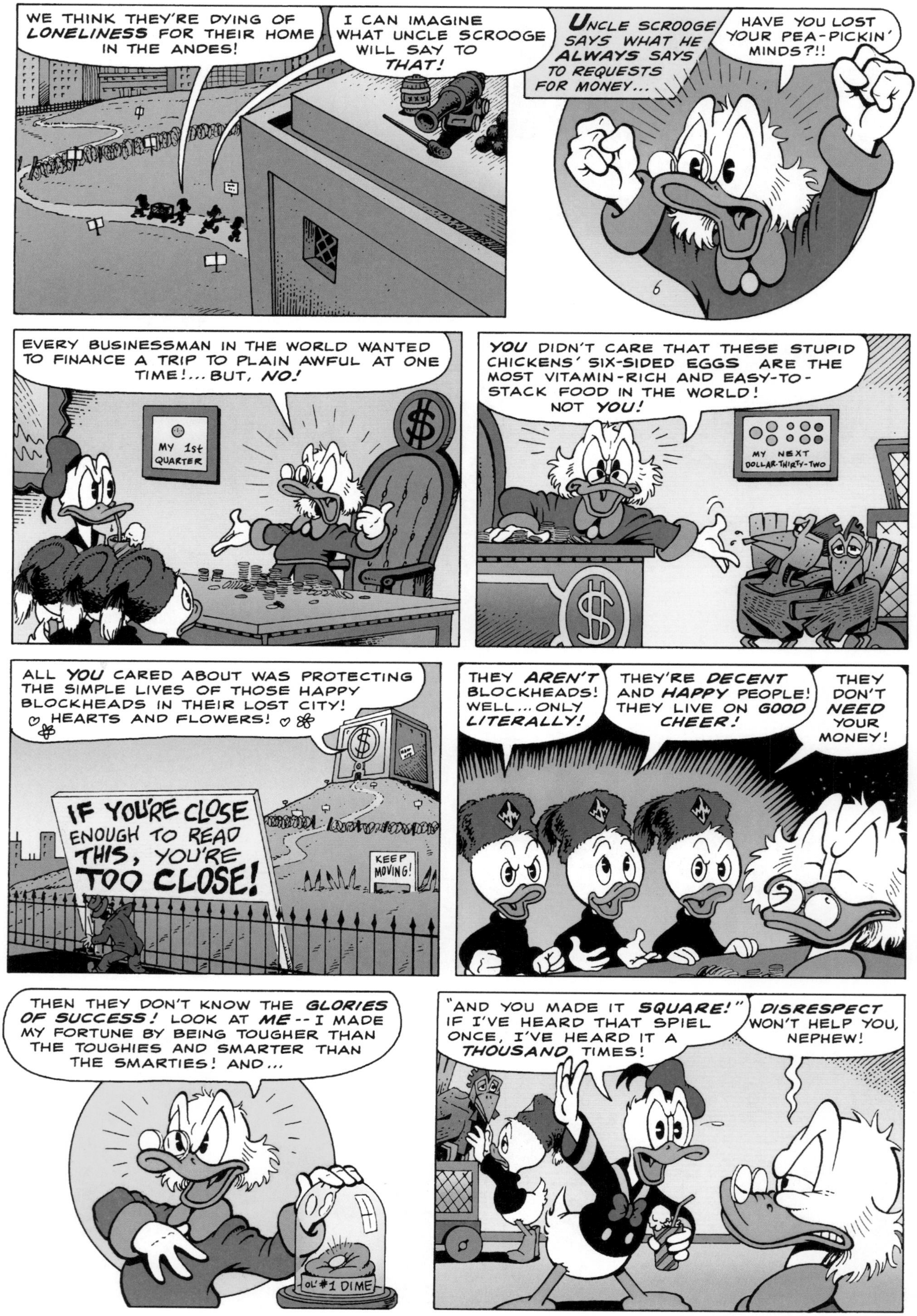

WE THINK THEY'RE DYING OF LONELINESS FOR THEIR HOME IN THE ANDES!
I CAN IMAGINE WHAT UNCLE SCROOGE WILL SAY TO THAT!
UNCLE SCROOGE SAYS WHAT HE ALWAYS SAYS TO REQUESTS FOR MONEY...
HAVE YOU LOST YOUR PEA-PICKIN' MINDS?!!
EVERY BUSINESSMAN IN THE WORLD WANTED TO FINANCE A TRIP TO PLAIN AWFUL AT ONE TIME!... BUT, NO!
MY 1st QUARTER
YOU DIDN'T CARE THAT THESE STUPID CHICKENS' SIX-SIDED EGGS ARE THE MOST VITAMIN-RICH AND EASY-TO-STACK FOOD IN THE WORLD! NOT YOU!
MY NEXT DOLLAR-THIRTY-TWO
ALL YOU CARED ABOUT WAS PROTECTING THE SIMPLE LIVES OF THOSE HAPPY BLOCKHEADS IN THEIR LOST CITY! HEARTS AND FLOWERS!
IF YOU'RE CLOSE ENOUGH TO READ THIS, YOU'RE TOO CLOSE!
KEEP MOVING!
THEY AREN'T BLOCKHEADS! WELL... ONLY LITERALLY!
THEY'RE DECENT AND HAPPY PEOPLE! THEY LIVE ON GOOD CHEER!
THEY DON'T NEED YOUR MONEY!
THEN THEY DON'T KNOW THE GLORIES OF SUCCESS! LOOK AT ME -- I MADE MY FORTUNE BY BEING TOUGHER THAN THE TOUGHIES AND SMARTER THAN THE SMARTIES! AND...
OL' #1 DIME
"AND YOU MADE IT SQUARE!" IF I'VE HEARD THAT SPIEL ONCE, I'VE HEARD IT A THOUSAND TIMES!
DISRESPECT WON'T HELP YOU, NEPHEW!

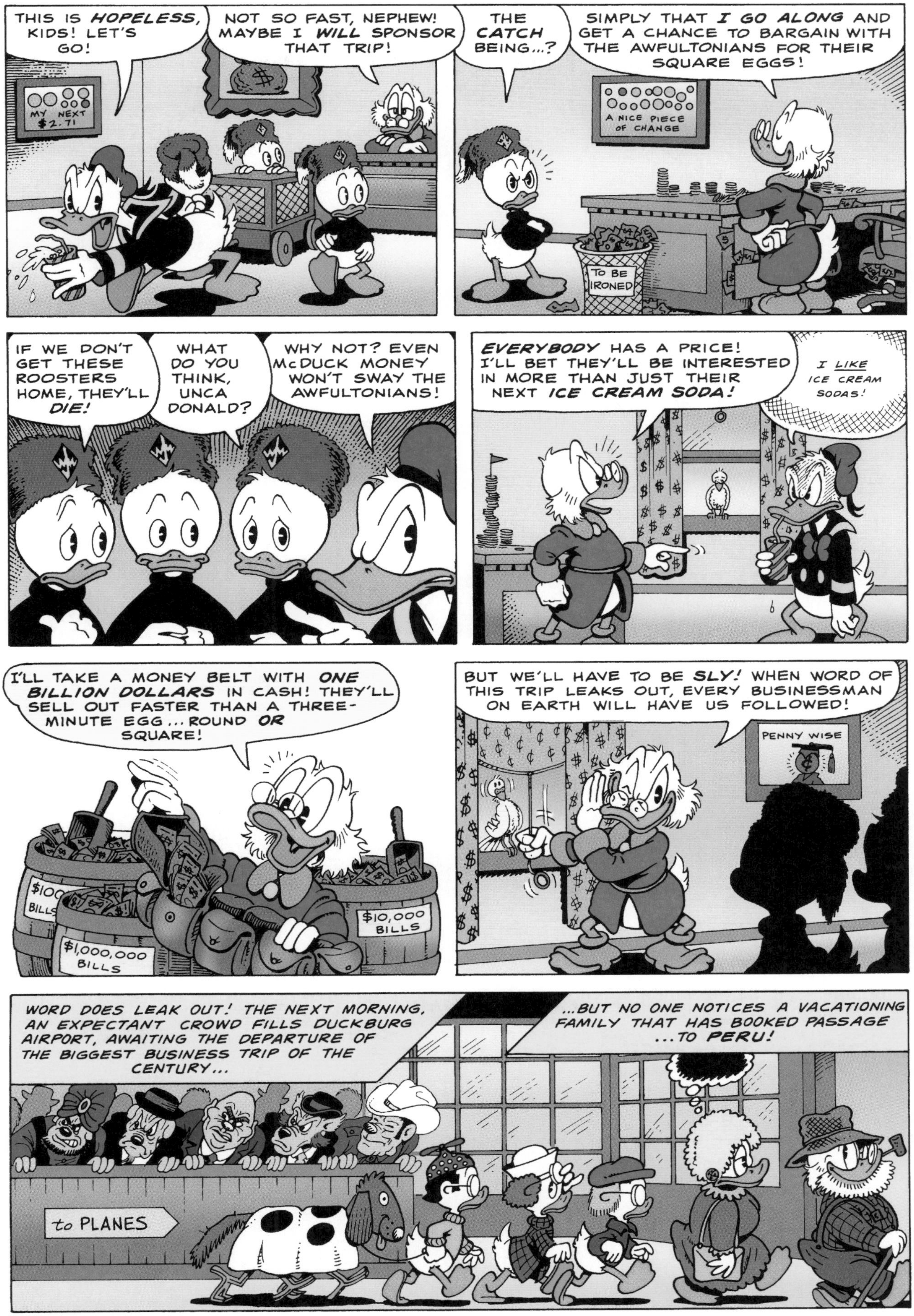
THIS IS HOPELESS, KIDS! LET'S GO!
NOT SO FAST, NEPHEW! MAYBE I WILL SPONSOR THAT TRIP!
MY NEXT $2.71
THE CATCH BEING...?
SIMPLY THAT I GO ALONG AND GET A CHANCE TO BARGAIN WITH THE AWFULTONIANS FOR THEIR SQUARE EGGS!
A NICE PIECE OF CHANGE
TO BE IRONED
IF WE DON'T GET THESE ROOSTERS HOME, THEY'LL DIE!
WHAT DO YOU THINK, UNCA DONALD?
WHY NOT? EVEN McDUCK MONEY WON'T SWAY THE AWFULTONIANS!
EVERYBODY HAS A PRICE! I'LL BET THEY'LL BE INTERESTED IN MORE THAN JUST THEIR NEXT ICE CREAM SODA!
I LIKE ICE CREAM SODAS!
I'LL TAKE A MONEY BELT WITH ONE BILLION DOLLARS IN CASH! THEY'LL SELL OUT FASTER THAN A THREE-MINUTE EGG...ROUND OR SQUARE!
$10,000 BILLS
$1,000,000 BILLS
BUT WE'LL HAVE TO BE SLY! WHEN WORD OF THIS TRIP LEAKS OUT, EVERY BUSINESSMAN ON EARTH WILL HAVE US FOLLOWED!
PENNY WISE
WORD DOES LEAK OUT! THE NEXT MORNING, AN EXPECTANT CROWD FILLS DUCKBURG AIRPORT, AWAITING THE DEPARTURE OF THE BIGGEST BUSINESS TRIP OF THE CENTURY...
...BUT NO ONE NOTICES A VACATIONING FAMILY THAT HAS BOOKED PASSAGE ...TO PERU!
to PLANES

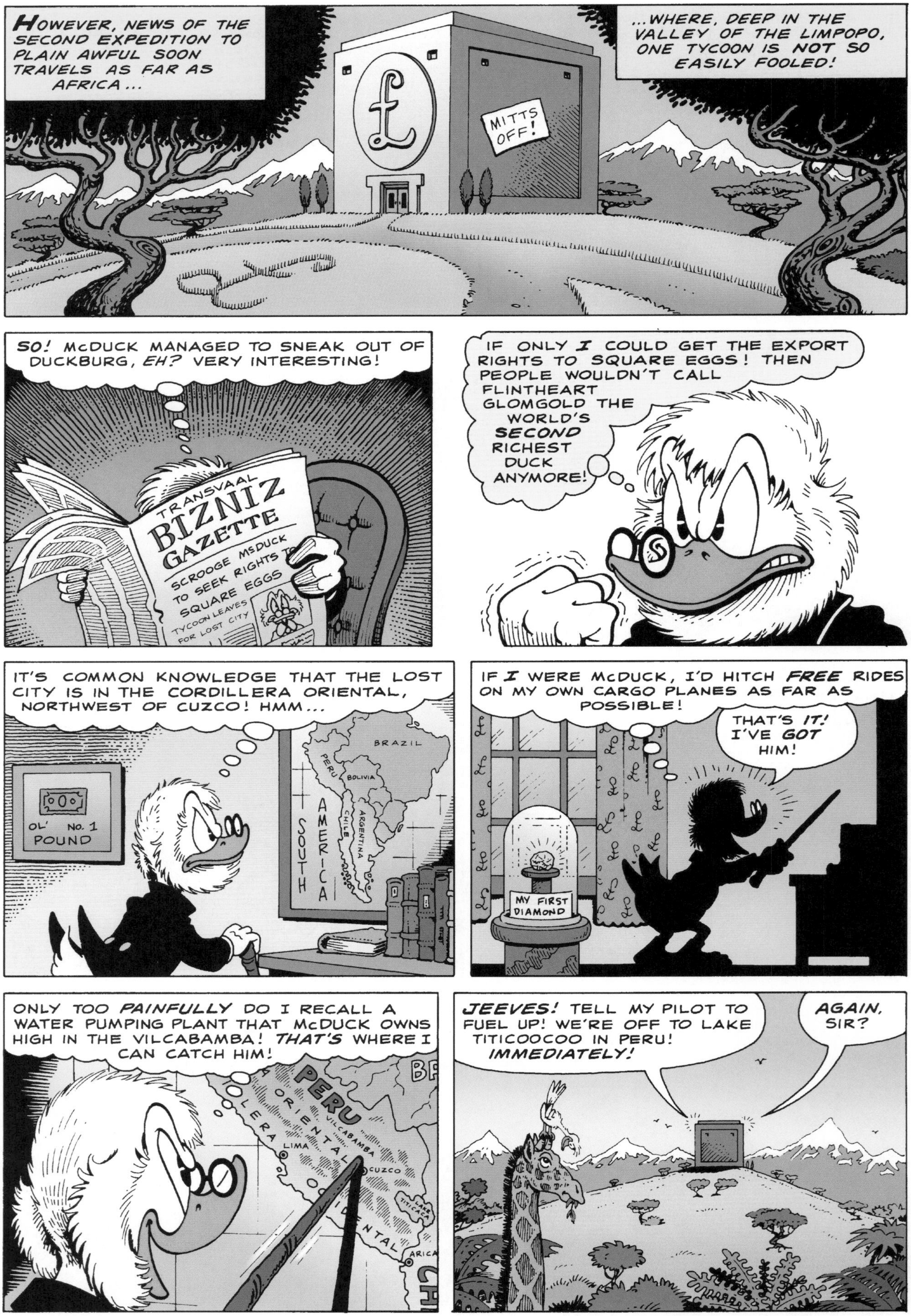
HOWEVER, NEWS OF THE SECOND EXPEDITION TO PLAIN AWFUL SOON TRAVELS AS FAR AS AFRICA...
...WHERE, DEEP IN THE VALLEY OF THE LIMPOPO, ONE TYCOON IS NOT SO EASILY FOOLED!
MITTS OFF!
SO! McDUCK MANAGED TO SNEAK OUT OF DUCKBURG, EH? VERY INTERESTING!
TRANSVAAL BIZNIZ GAZETTE
SCROOGE McDUCK TO SEEK RIGHTS TO SQUARE EGGS
TYCOON LEAVES FOR LOST CITY
IF ONLY I COULD GET THE EXPORT RIGHTS TO SQUARE EGGS! THEN PEOPLE WOULDN'T CALL FLINTHEART GLOMGOLD THE WORLD'S SECOND RICHEST DUCK ANYMORE!
IT'S COMMON KNOWLEDGE THAT THE LOST CITY IS IN THE CORDILLERA ORIENTAL, NORTHWEST OF CUZCO! HMM...
OL' No. 1 POUND
BRAZIL
PERU
BOLIVIA
SOUTH AMERICA
CHILE
ARGENTINA
IF I WERE McDUCK, I'D HITCH FREE RIDES ON MY OWN CARGO PLANES AS FAR AS POSSIBLE!
THAT'S IT! I'VE GOT HIM!
MY FIRST DIAMOND
ONLY TOO PAINFULLY DO I RECALL A WATER PUMPING PLANT THAT McDUCK OWNS HIGH IN THE VILCABAMBA! THAT'S WHERE I CAN CATCH HIM!
PERU
VILCABAMBA
LIMA
CUZCO
LAKE TITICACA
ARICA
JEEVES! TELL MY PILOT TO FUEL UP! WE'RE OFF TO LAKE TITICOOCOO IN PERU! IMMEDIATELY!
AGAIN, SIR?

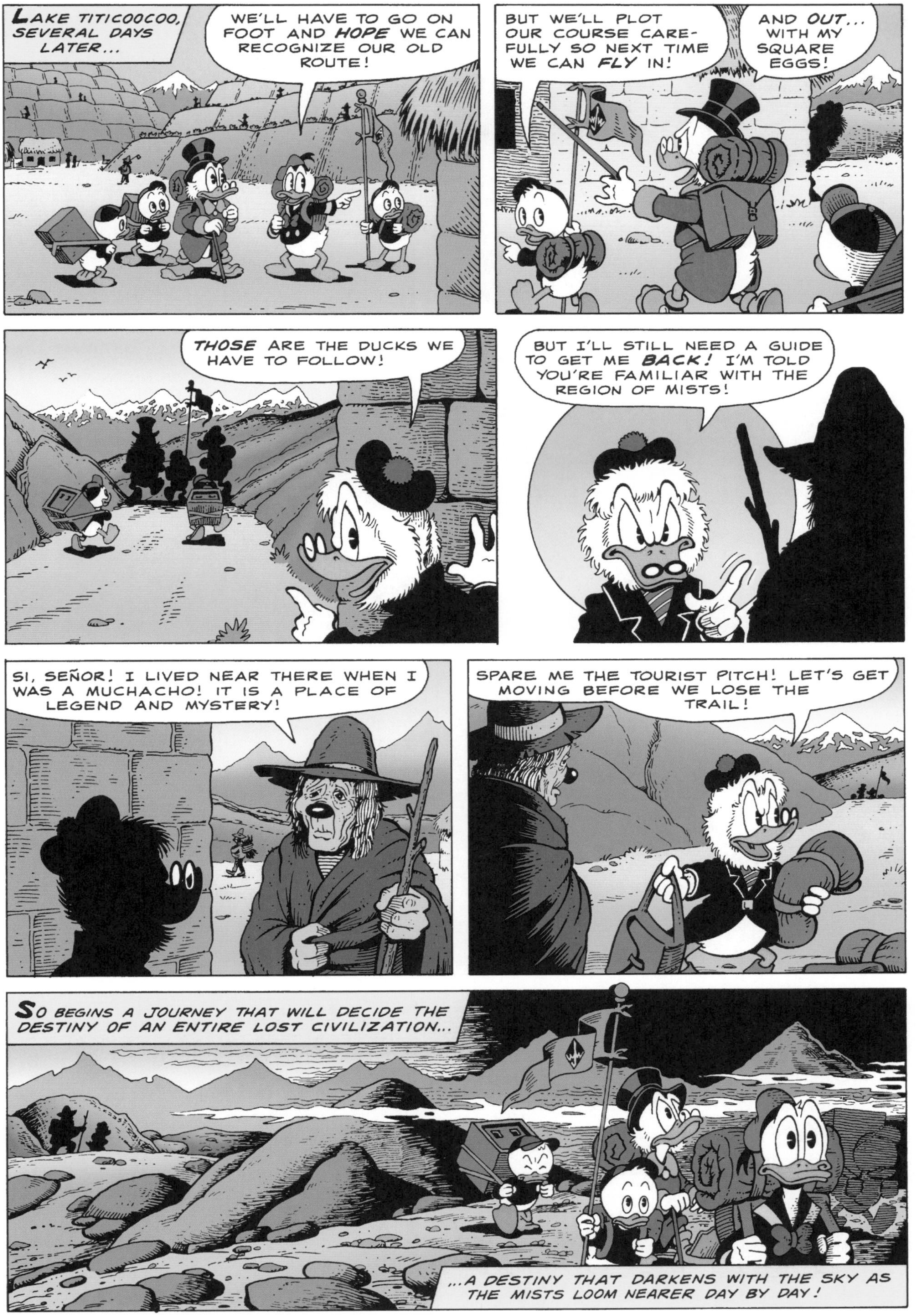
LAKE TITICOOCOO, SEVERAL DAYS LATER...
WE'LL HAVE TO GO ON FOOT AND HOPE WE CAN RECOGNIZE OUR OLD ROUTE!
BUT WE'LL PLOT OUR COURSE CAREFULLY SO NEXT TIME WE CAN FLY IN!
AND OUT... WITH MY SQUARE EGGS!
THOSE ARE THE DUCKS WE HAVE TO FOLLOW!
BUT I'LL STILL NEED A GUIDE TO GET ME BACK! I'M TOLD YOU'RE FAMILIAR WITH THE REGION OF MISTS!
SI, SEÑOR! I LIVED NEAR THERE WHEN I WAS A MUCHACHO! IT IS A PLACE OF LEGEND AND MYSTERY!
SPARE ME THE TOURIST PITCH! LET'S GET MOVING BEFORE WE LOSE THE TRAIL!
SO BEGINS A JOURNEY THAT WILL DECIDE THE DESTINY OF AN ENTIRE LOST CIVILIZATION...
...A DESTINY THAT DARKENS WITH THE SKY AS THE MISTS LOOM NEARER DAY BY DAY!

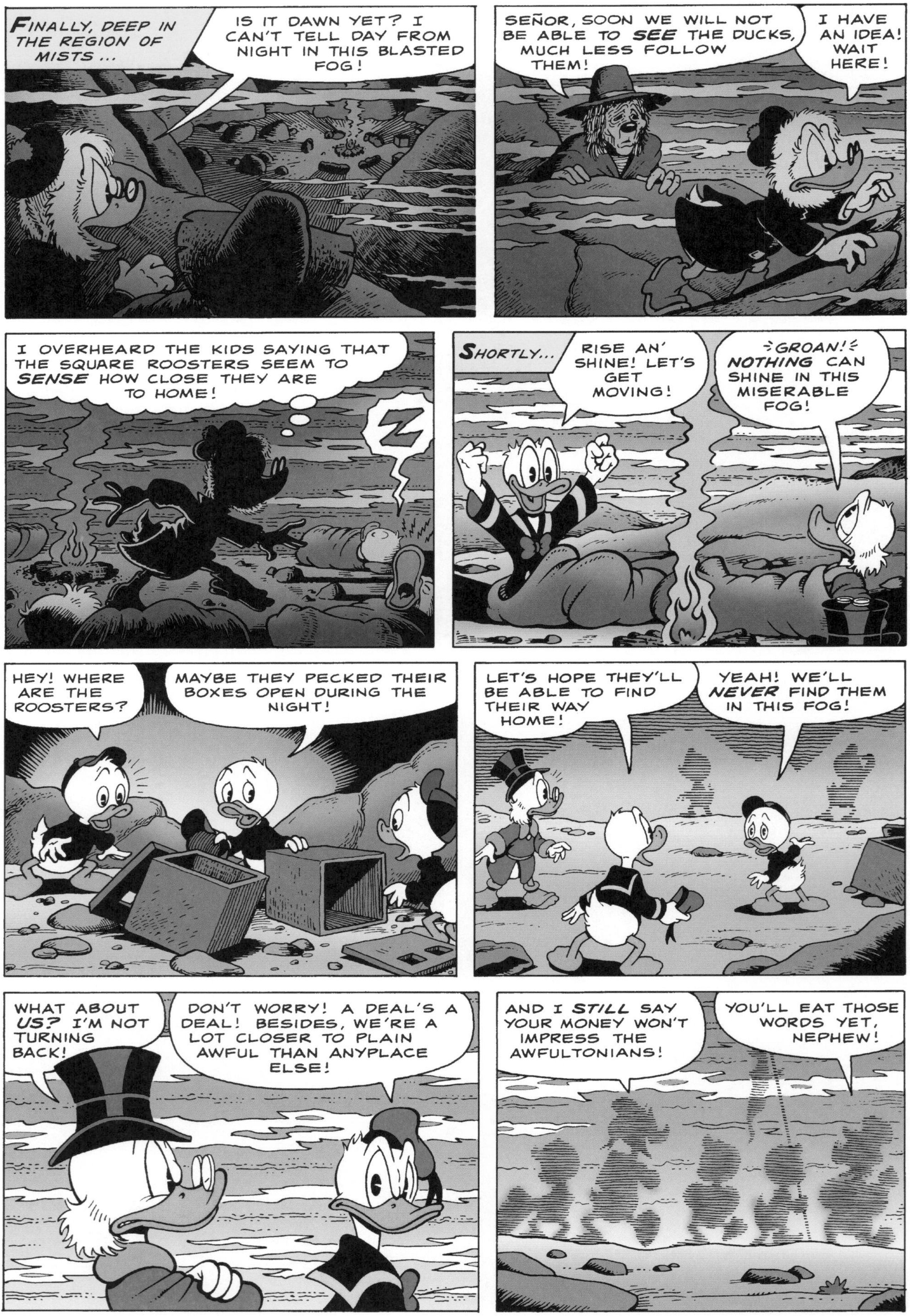
FINALLY, DEEP IN THE REGION OF MISTS ...
IS IT DAWN YET? I CAN'T TELL DAY FROM NIGHT IN THIS BLASTED FOG!
SEÑOR, SOON WE WILL NOT BE ABLE TO SEE THE DUCKS, MUCH LESS FOLLOW THEM!
I HAVE AN IDEA! WAIT HERE!
I OVERHEARD THE KIDS SAYING THAT THE SQUARE ROOSTERS SEEM TO SENSE HOW CLOSE THEY ARE TO HOME!
Z
SHORTLY...
RISE AN' SHINE! LET'S GET MOVING!
GROAN!
NOTHING CAN SHINE IN THIS MISERABLE FOG!
HEY! WHERE ARE THE ROOSTERS?
MAYBE THEY PECKED THEIR BOXES OPEN DURING THE NIGHT!
LET'S HOPE THEY'LL BE ABLE TO FIND THEIR WAY HOME!
YEAH! WE'LL NEVER FIND THEM IN THIS FOG!
WHAT ABOUT US? I'M NOT TURNING BACK!
DON'T WORRY! A DEAL'S A DEAL! BESIDES, WE'RE A LOT CLOSER TO PLAIN AWFUL THAN ANYPLACE ELSE!
AND I STILL SAY YOUR MONEY WON'T IMPRESS THE AWFULTONIANS!
YOU'LL EAT THOSE WORDS YET, NEPHEW!

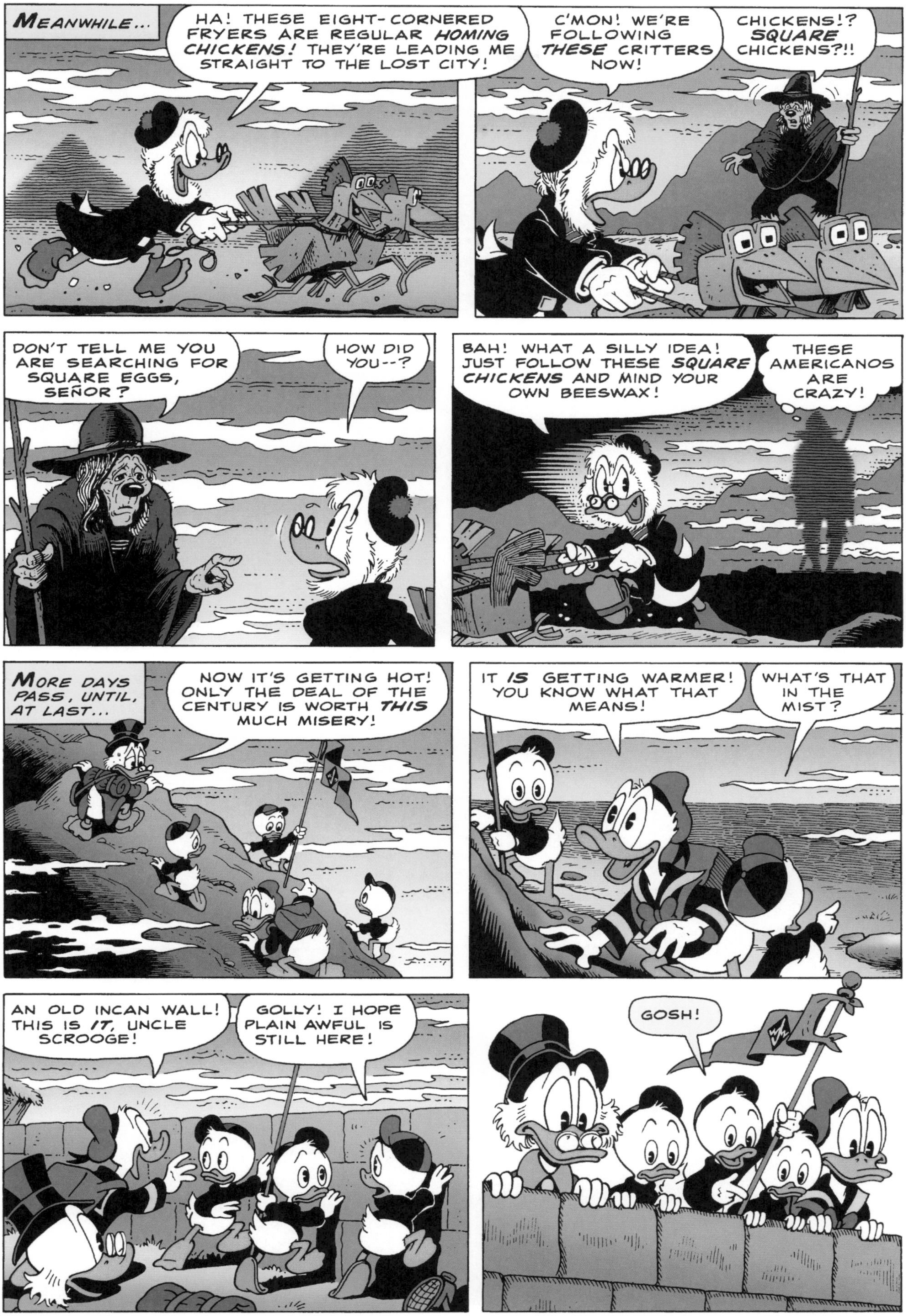
MEANWHILE...
HA! THESE EIGHT-CORNERED FRYERS ARE REGULAR HOMING CHICKENS! THEY'RE LEADING ME STRAIGHT TO THE LOST CITY!
C'MON! WE'RE FOLLOWING THESE CRITTERS NOW!
CHICKENS!? SQUARE CHICKENS?!!
DON'T TELL ME YOU ARE SEARCHING FOR SQUARE EGGS, SEÑOR?
HOW DID YOU--?
BAH! WHAT A SILLY IDEA! JUST FOLLOW THESE SQUARE CHICKENS AND MIND YOUR OWN BEESWAX!
THESE AMERICANOS ARE CRAZY!
MORE DAYS PASS, UNTIL, AT LAST...
NOW IT'S GETTING HOT! ONLY THE DEAL OF THE CENTURY IS WORTH THIS MUCH MISERY!
IT IS GETTING WARMER! YOU KNOW WHAT THAT MEANS!
WHAT'S THAT IN THE MIST?
AN OLD INCAN WALL! THIS IS IT, UNCLE SCROOGE!
GOLLY! I HOPE PLAIN AWFUL IS STILL HERE!
GOSH!

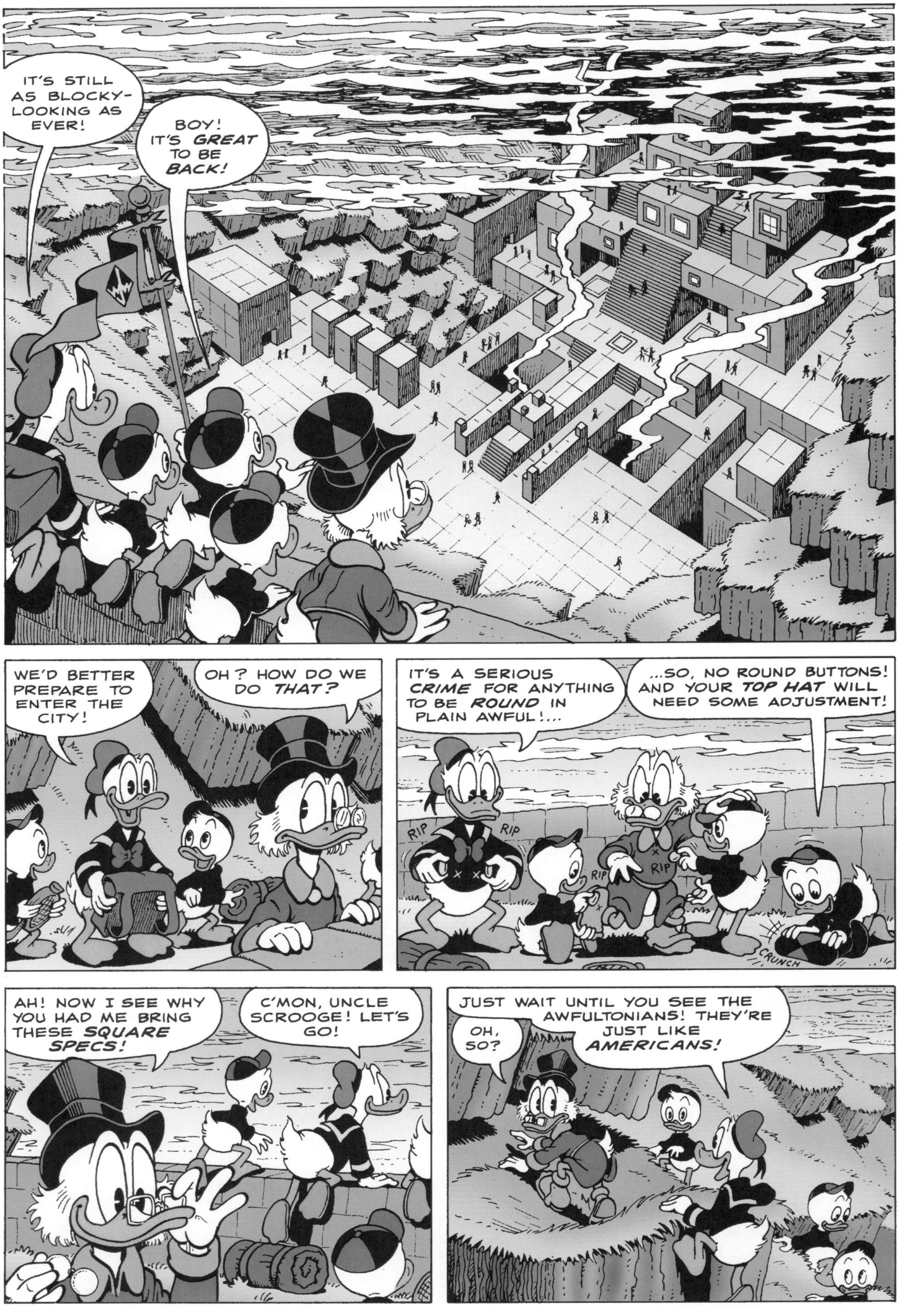
IT'S STILL AS BLOCKY-LOOKING AS EVER!
BOY! IT'S GREAT TO BE BACK!
WE'D BETTER PREPARE TO ENTER THE CITY!
OH? HOW DO WE DO THAT?
IT'S A SERIOUS CRIME FOR ANYTHING TO BE ROUND IN PLAIN AWFUL!...
...SO, NO ROUND BUTTONS! AND YOUR TOP HAT WILL NEED SOME ADJUSTMENT!
RIP
RIP
RIP
RIP
CRUNCH
AH! NOW I SEE WHY YOU HAD ME BRING THESE SQUARE SPECS!
C'MON, UNCLE SCROOGE! LET'S GO!
JUST WAIT UNTIL YOU SEE THE AWFULTONIANS! THEY'RE JUST LIKE AMERICANS!
OH, SO?

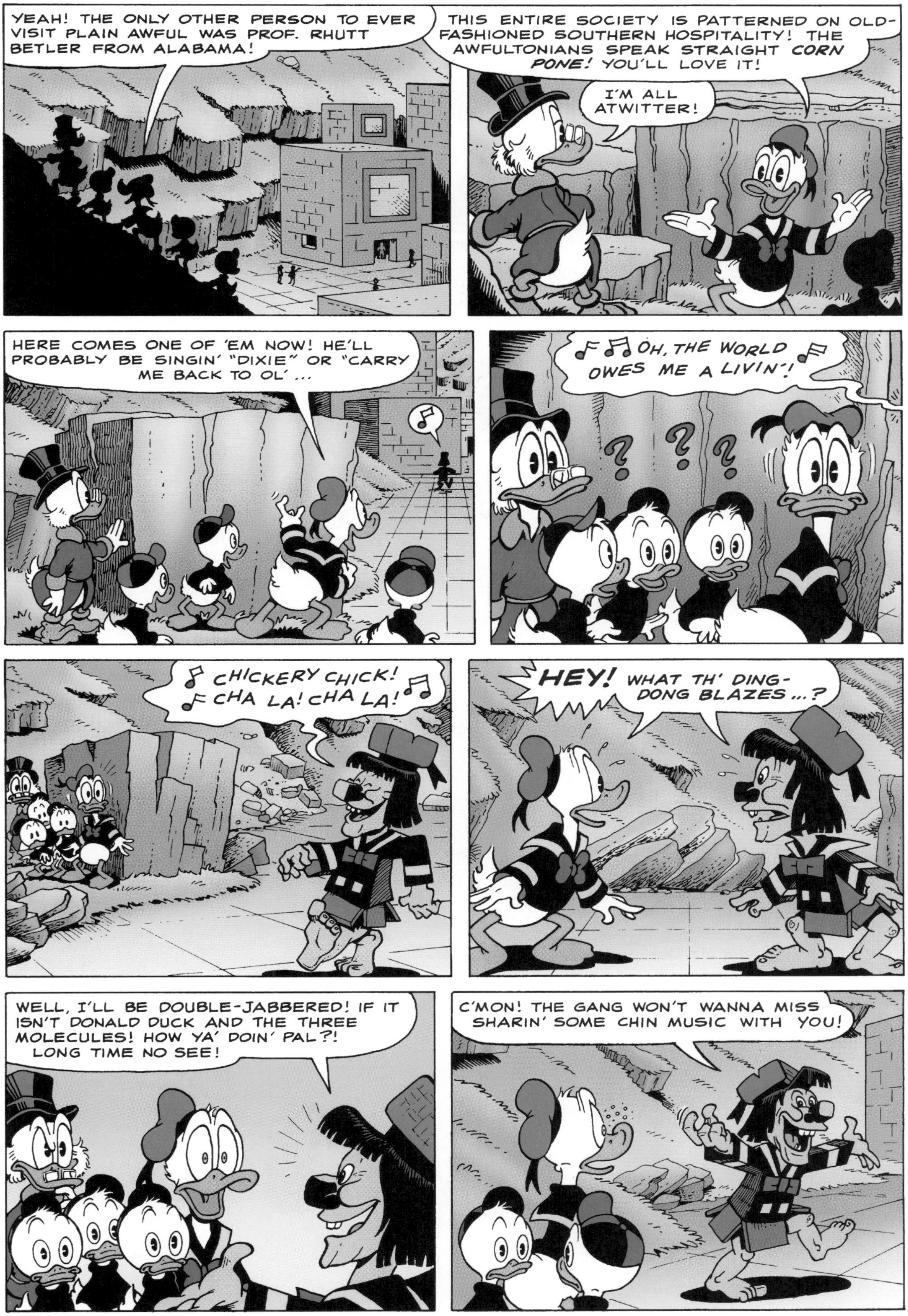
YEAH! THE ONLY OTHER PERSON TO EVER VISIT PLAIN AWFUL WAS PROF. RHUTT BETLER FROM ALABAMA!
THIS ENTIRE SOCIETY IS PATTERNED ON OLD-FASHIONED SOUTHERN HOSPITALITY! THE AWFULTONIANS SPEAK STRAIGHT CORN PONE! YOU'LL LOVE IT!
I'M ALL ATWITTER!
HERE COMES ONE OF 'EM NOW! HE'LL PROBABLY BE SINGIN' "DIXIE" OR "CARRY ME BACK TO OL' ...
OH, THE WORLD OWES ME A LIVIN'!
CHICKERY CHICK! CHA LA! CHA LA!
HEY! WHAT TH' DING-DONG BLAZES ...?
WELL, I'LL BE DOUBLE-JABBERED! IF IT ISN'T DONALD DUCK AND THE THREE MOLECULES! HOW YA' DOIN' PAL?! LONG TIME NO SEE!
C'MON! THE GANG WON'T WANNA MISS SHARIN' SOME CHIN MUSIC WITH YOU!

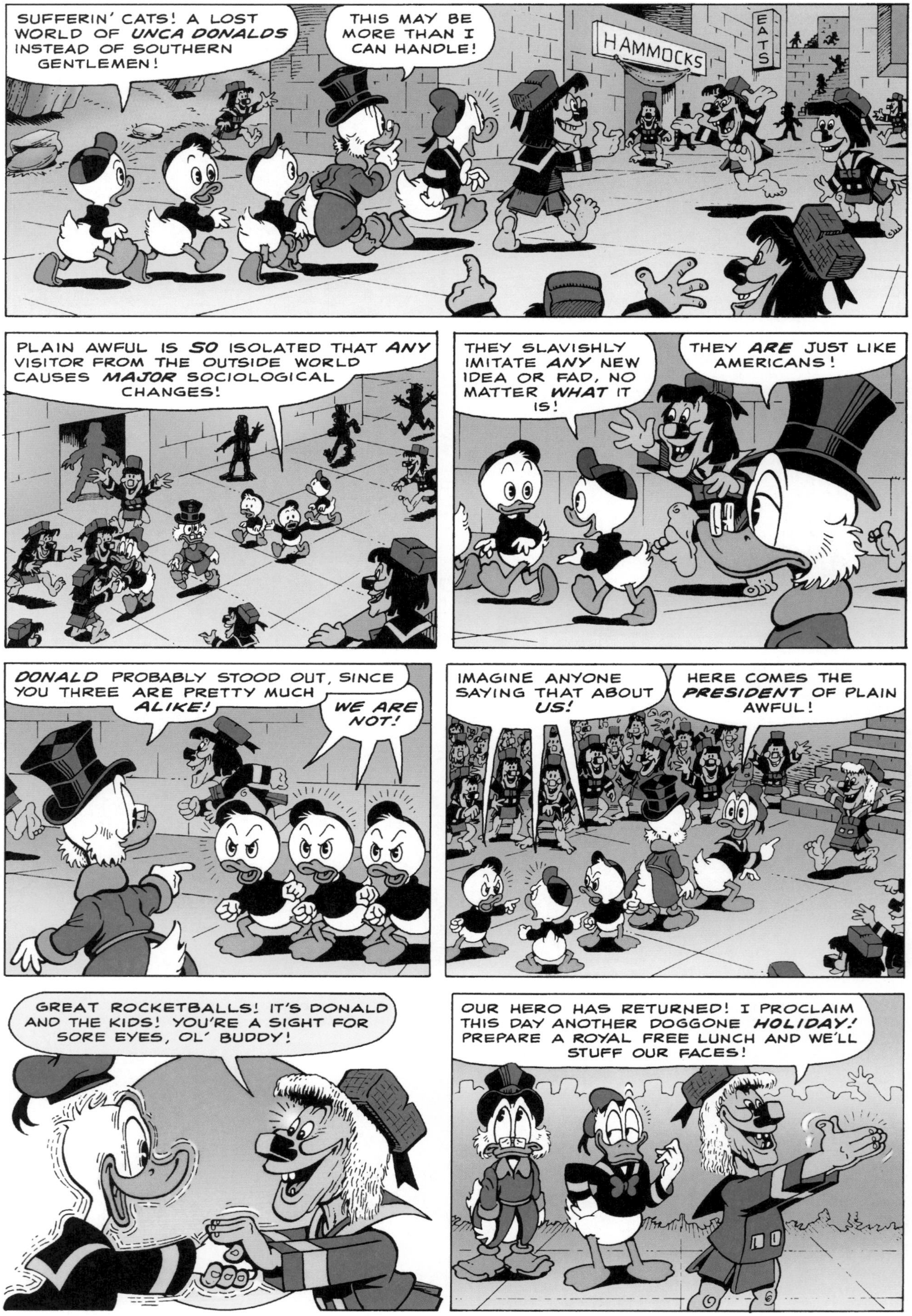

SUFFERIN' CATS! A LOST WORLD OF UNCA DONALDS INSTEAD OF SOUTHERN GENTLEMEN!
THIS MAY BE MORE THAN I CAN HANDLE!
HAMMOCKS
EATS
PLAIN AWFUL IS SO ISOLATED THAT ANY VISITOR FROM THE OUTSIDE WORLD CAUSES MAJOR SOCIOLOGICAL CHANGES!
THEY SLAVISHLY IMITATE ANY NEW IDEA OR FAD, NO MATTER WHAT IT IS!
THEY ARE JUST LIKE AMERICANS!
DONALD PROBABLY STOOD OUT, SINCE YOU THREE ARE PRETTY MUCH ALIKE!
WE ARE NOT!
IMAGINE ANYONE SAYING THAT ABOUT US!
HERE COMES THE PRESIDENT OF PLAIN AWFUL!
GREAT ROCKETBALLS! IT'S DONALD AND THE KIDS! YOU'RE A SIGHT FOR SORE EYES, OL' BUDDY!
OUR HERO HAS RETURNED! I PROCLAIM THIS DAY ANOTHER DOGGONE HOLIDAY! PREPARE A ROYAL FREE LUNCH AND WE'LL STUFF OUR FACES!

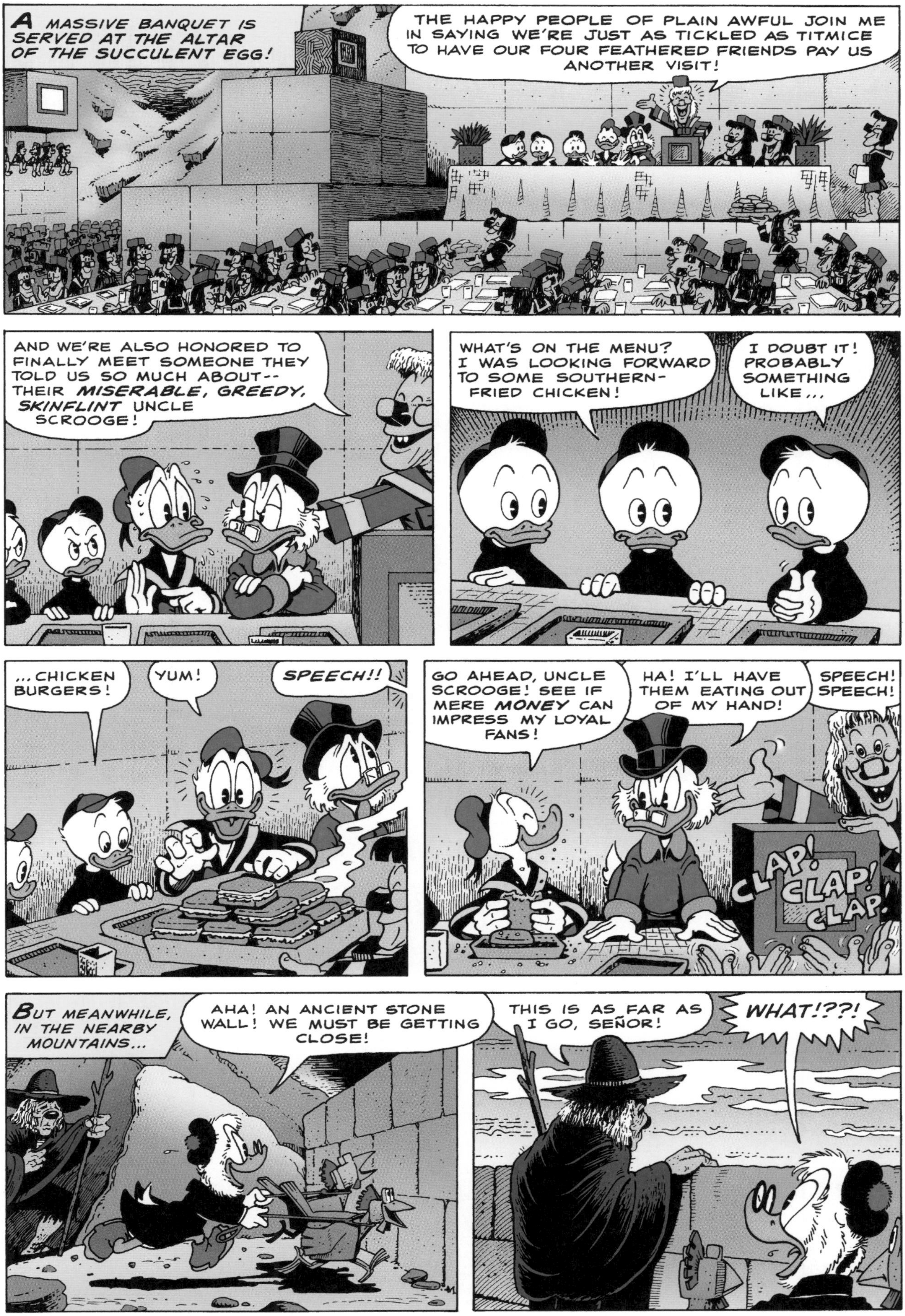
A MASSIVE BANQUET IS SERVED AT THE ALTAR OF THE SUCCULENT EGG!
THE HAPPY PEOPLE OF PLAIN AWFUL JOIN ME IN SAYING WE'RE JUST AS TICKLED AS TITMICE TO HAVE OUR FOUR FEATHERED FRIENDS PAY US ANOTHER VISIT!
AND WE'RE ALSO HONORED TO FINALLY MEET SOMEONE THEY TOLD US SO MUCH ABOUT-- THEIR MISERABLE, GREEDY, SKINFLINT UNCLE SCROOGE!
WHAT'S ON THE MENU? I WAS LOOKING FORWARD TO SOME SOUTHERN-FRIED CHICKEN!
I DOUBT IT! PROBABLY SOMETHING LIKE...
...CHICKEN BURGERS!
YUM!
SPEECH!!
GO AHEAD, UNCLE SCROOGE! SEE IF MERE MONEY CAN IMPRESS MY LOYAL FANS!
HA! I'LL HAVE THEM EATING OUT OF MY HAND!
SPEECH! SPEECH!
CLAP! CLAP! CLAP!
BUT MEANWHILE, IN THE NEARBY MOUNTAINS...
AHA! AN ANCIENT STONE WALL! WE MUST BE GETTING CLOSE!
THIS IS AS FAR AS I GO, SEÑOR!
WHAT!??!

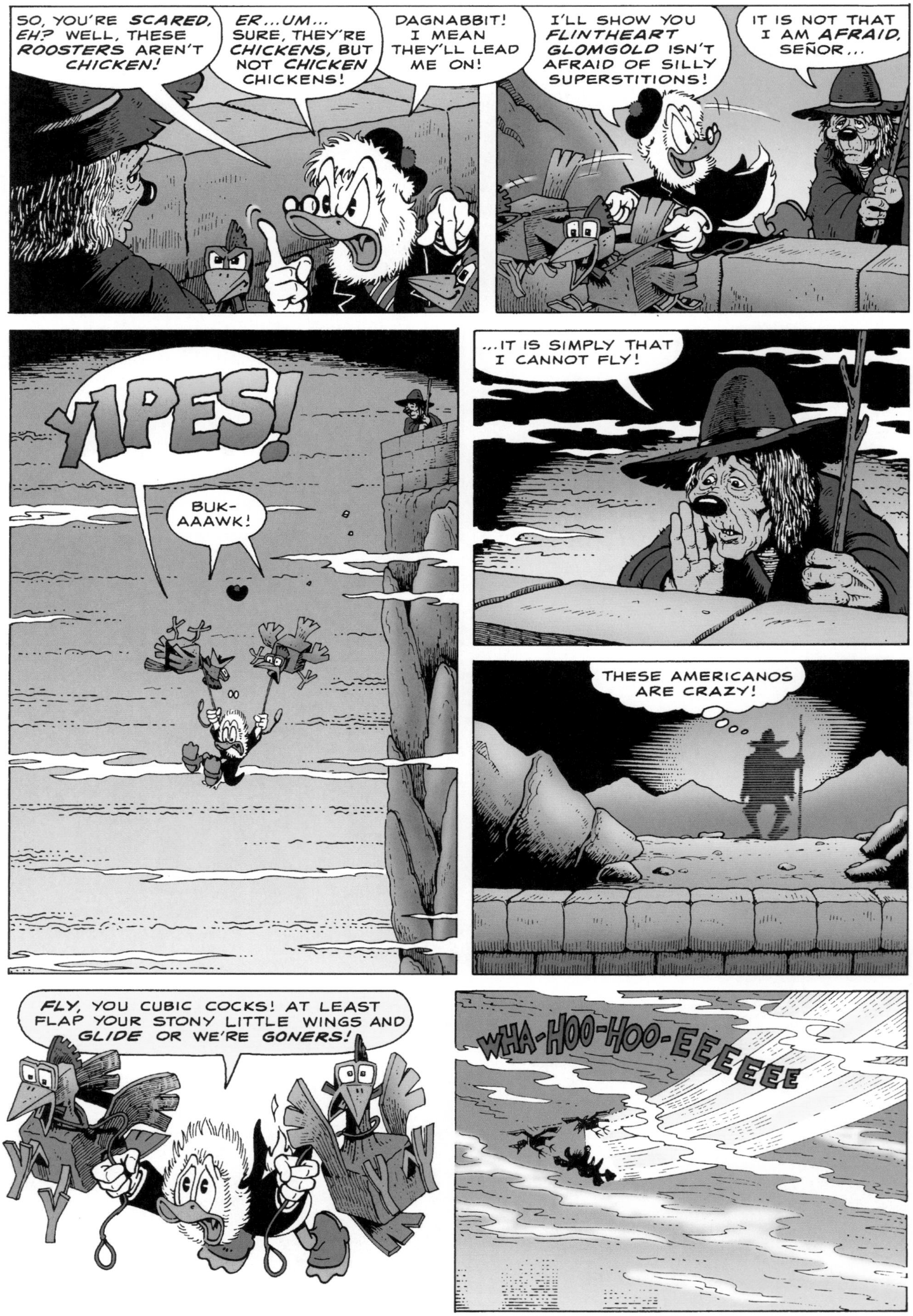
SO, YOU'RE SCARED, EH? WELL, THESE ROOSTERS AREN'T CHICKEN!
ER...UM... SURE, THEY'RE CHICKENS, BUT NOT CHICKEN CHICKENS!
DAGNABBIT! I MEAN THEY'LL LEAD ME ON!
I'LL SHOW YOU FLINTHEART GLOMGOLD ISN'T AFRAID OF SILLY SUPERSTITIONS!
IT IS NOT THAT I AM AFRAID, SEÑOR...
YIPES!
BUK-AAAWK!
...IT IS SIMPLY THAT I CANNOT FLY!
THESE AMERICANOS ARE CRAZY!
FLY, YOU CUBIC COCKS! AT LEAST FLAP YOUR STONY LITTLE WINGS AND GLIDE OR WE'RE GONERS!
WHA-HOO-HOO-EEEEEE

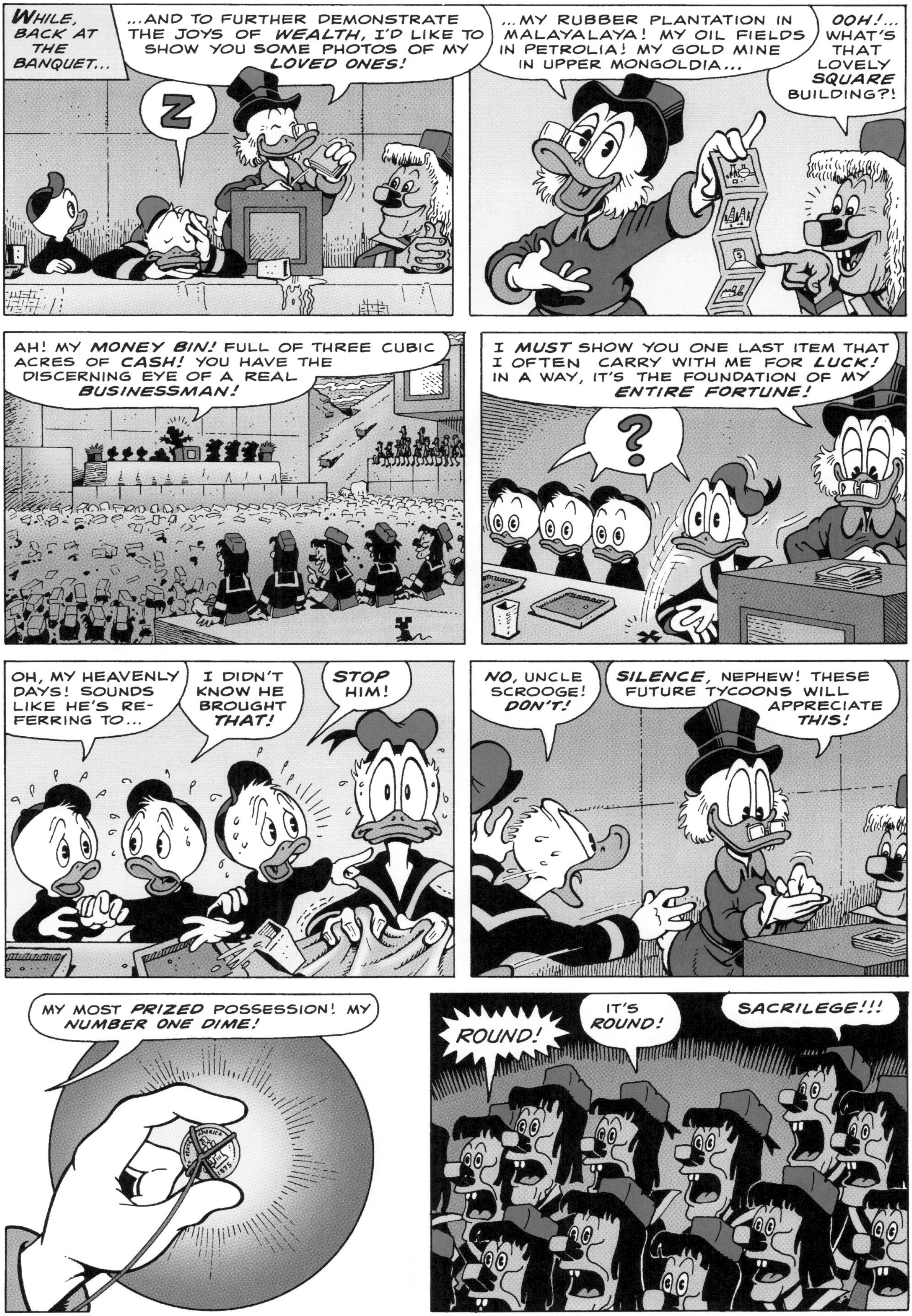
WHILE, BACK AT THE BANQUET...
...AND TO FURTHER DEMONSTRATE THE JOYS OF WEALTH, I'D LIKE TO SHOW YOU SOME PHOTOS OF MY LOVED ONES!
Z
...MY RUBBER PLANTATION IN MALAYALAYA! MY OIL FIELDS IN PETROLIA! MY GOLD MINE IN UPPER MONGOLDIA...
OOH!... WHAT'S THAT LOVELY SQUARE BUILDING?!
AH! MY MONEY BIN! FULL OF THREE CUBIC ACRES OF CASH! YOU HAVE THE DISCERNING EYE OF A REAL BUSINESSMAN!
I MUST SHOW YOU ONE LAST ITEM THAT I OFTEN CARRY WITH ME FOR LUCK! IN A WAY, IT'S THE FOUNDATION OF MY ENTIRE FORTUNE!
?
OH, MY HEAVENLY DAYS! SOUNDS LIKE HE'S RE- FERRING TO...
I DIDN'T KNOW HE BROUGHT THAT!
STOP HIM!
NO, UNCLE SCROOGE! DON'T!
SILENCE, NEPHEW! THESE FUTURE TYCOONS WILL APPRECIATE THIS!
MY MOST PRIZED POSSESSION! MY NUMBER ONE DIME!
ROUND!
IT'S ROUND!
SACRILEGE!!!

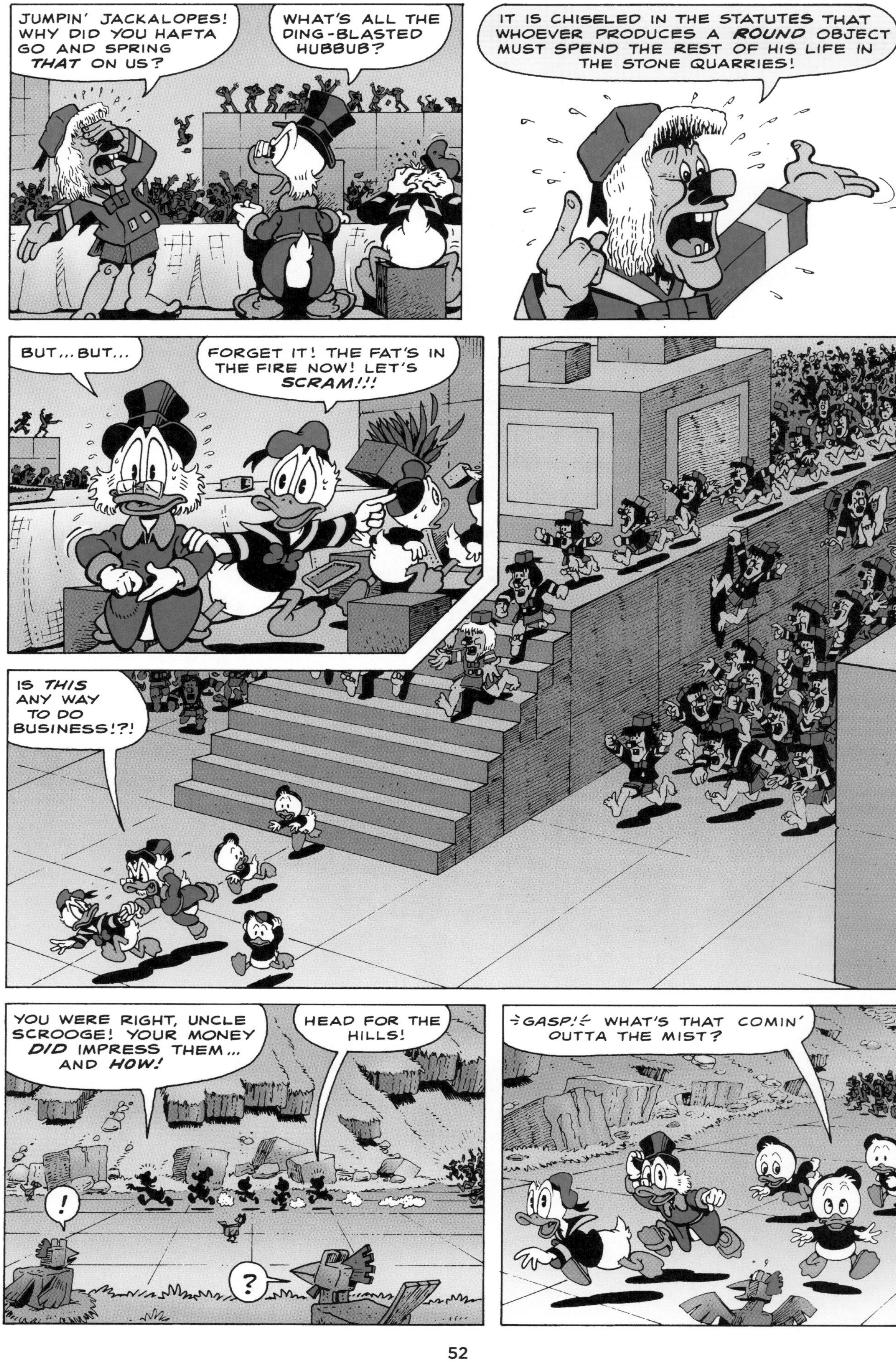
JUMPIN' JACKALOPES! WHY DID YOU HAFTA GO AND SPRING *THAT* ON US?
WHAT'S ALL THE DING-BLASTED HUBBUB?
IT IS CHISELED IN THE STATUTES THAT WHOEVER PRODUCES A *ROUND* OBJECT MUST SPEND THE REST OF HIS LIFE IN THE STONE QUARRIES!
BUT... BUT...
FORGET IT! THE FAT'S IN THE FIRE NOW! LET'S *SCRAM!!!*
IS *THIS* ANY WAY TO DO BUSINESS!?!
YOU WERE RIGHT, UNCLE SCROOGE! YOUR MONEY *DID* IMPRESS THEM... AND *HOW!*
HEAD FOR THE HILLS!
!
?
GASP! WHAT'S THAT COMIN' OUTTA THE MIST?

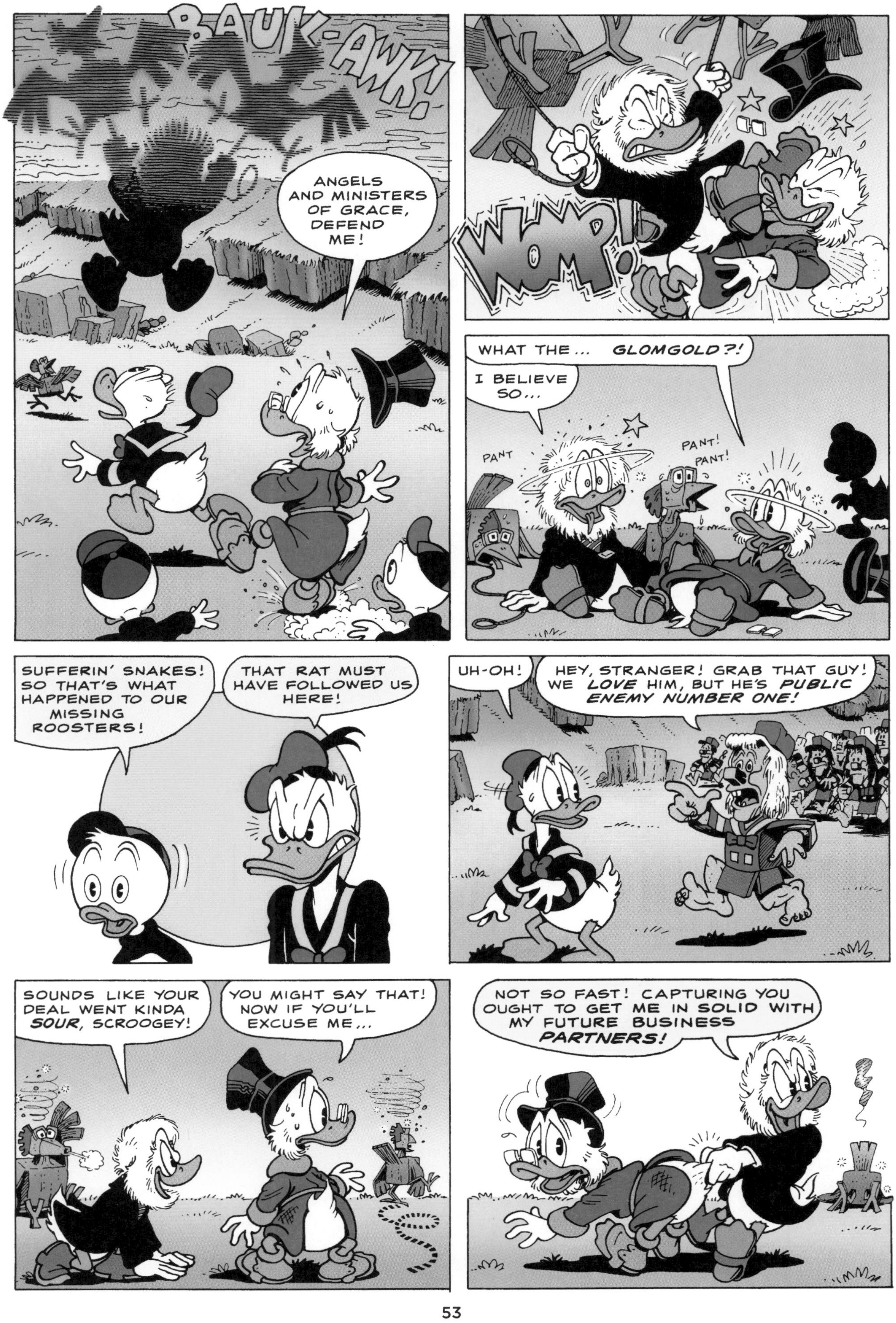
BAUK-AWK!
ANGELS AND MINISTERS OF GRACE, DEFEND ME!
WOMP!
WHAT THE... GLOMGOLD?!
I BELIEVE SO...
PANT
PANT! PANT!
SUFFERIN' SNAKES! SO THAT'S WHAT HAPPENED TO OUR MISSING ROOSTERS!
THAT RAT MUST HAVE FOLLOWED US HERE!
UH-OH!
HEY, STRANGER! GRAB THAT GUY! WE LOVE HIM, BUT HE'S PUBLIC ENEMY NUMBER ONE!
SOUNDS LIKE YOUR DEAL WENT KINDA SOUR, SCROOGEY!
YOU MIGHT SAY THAT! NOW IF YOU'LL EXCUSE ME...
NOT SO FAST! CAPTURING YOU OUGHT TO GET ME IN SOLID WITH MY FUTURE BUSINESS PARTNERS!

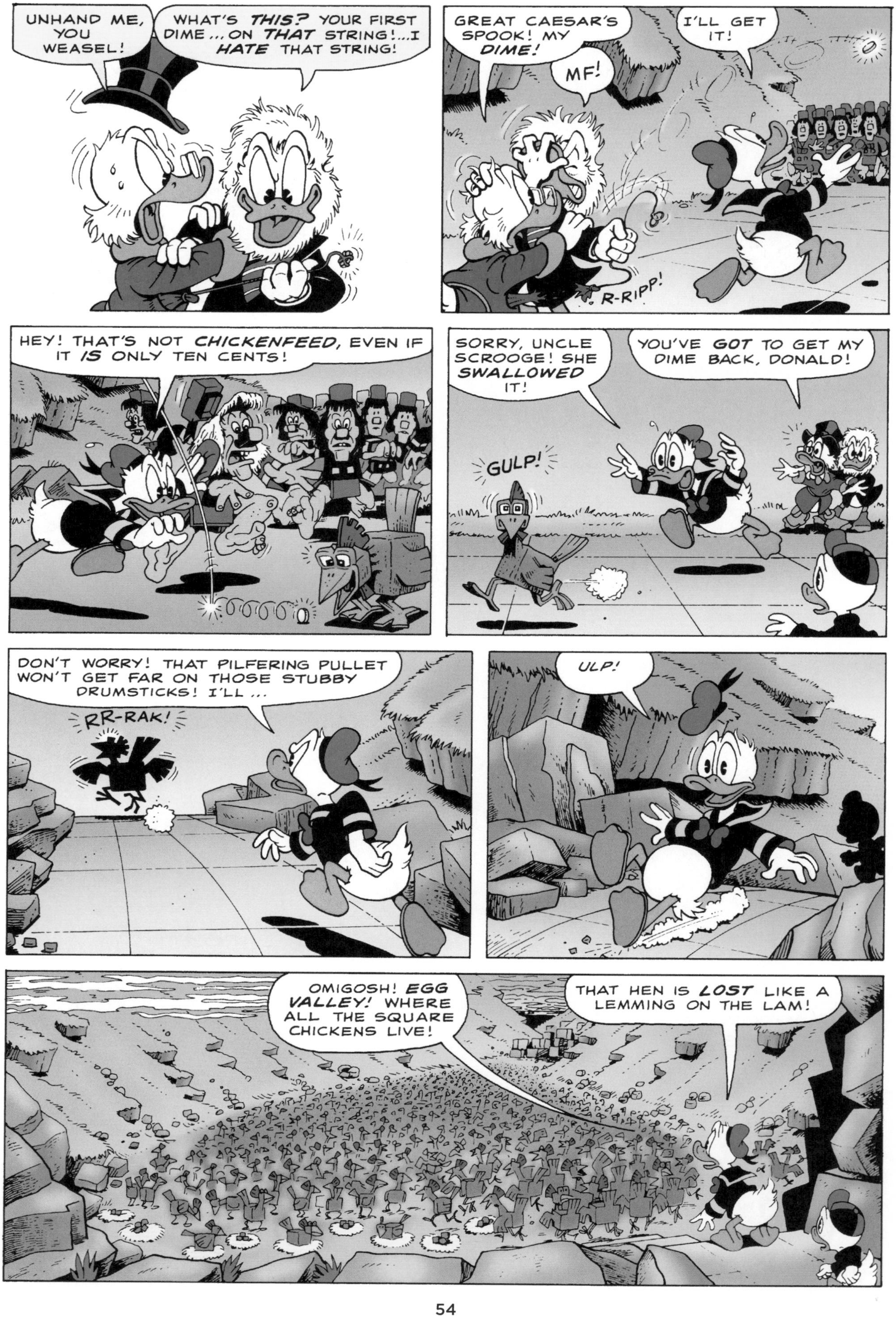
UNHAND ME, YOU WEASEL!
WHAT'S THIS? YOUR FIRST DIME ... ON THAT STRING! ... I HATE THAT STRING!
GREAT CAESAR'S SPOOK! MY DIME!
MF!
I'LL GET IT!
R-RIPP!
HEY! THAT'S NOT CHICKENFEED, EVEN IF IT IS ONLY TEN CENTS!
SORRY, UNCLE SCROOGE! SHE SWALLOWED IT!
YOU'VE GOT TO GET MY DIME BACK, DONALD!
GULP!
DON'T WORRY! THAT PILFERING PULLET WON'T GET FAR ON THOSE STUBBY DRUMSTICKS! I'LL ...
RR-RAK!
ULP!
OMIGOSH! EGG VALLEY! WHERE ALL THE SQUARE CHICKENS LIVE!
THAT HEN IS LOST LIKE A LEMMING ON THE LAM!

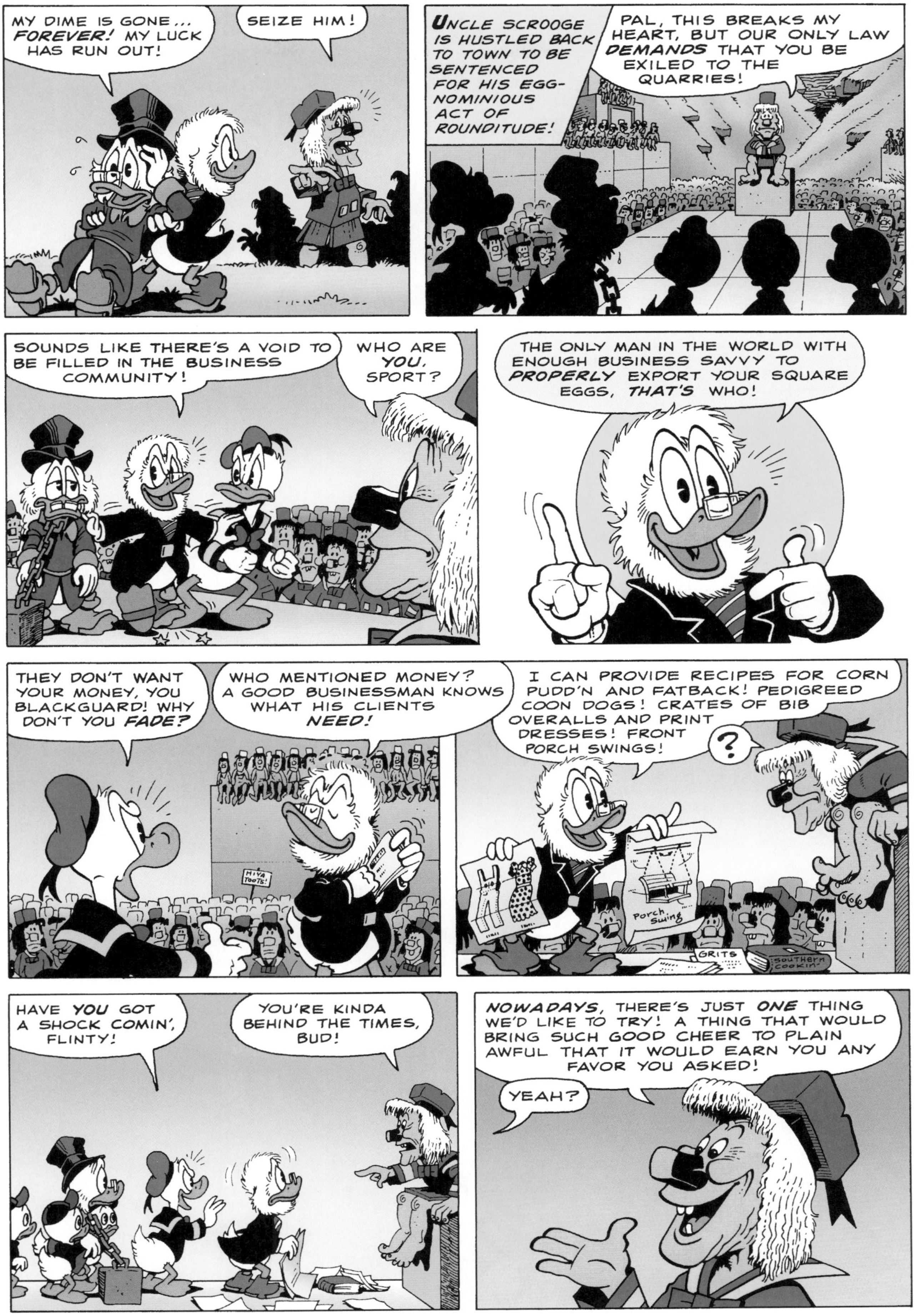
MY DIME IS GONE... FOREVER! MY LUCK HAS RUN OUT!
SEIZE HIM!
UNCLE SCROOGE IS HUSTLED BACK TO TOWN TO BE SENTENCED FOR HIS EGG-NOMINIOUS ACT OF ROUNDITUDE!
PAL, THIS BREAKS MY HEART, BUT OUR ONLY LAW DEMANDS THAT YOU BE EXILED TO THE QUARRIES!
SOUNDS LIKE THERE'S A VOID TO BE FILLED IN THE BUSINESS COMMUNITY!
WHO ARE YOU, SPORT?
THE ONLY MAN IN THE WORLD WITH ENOUGH BUSINESS SAVVY TO PROPERLY EXPORT YOUR SQUARE EGGS, THAT'S WHO!
THEY DON'T WANT YOUR MONEY, YOU BLACKGUARD! WHY DON'T YOU FADE?
WHO MENTIONED MONEY? A GOOD BUSINESSMAN KNOWS WHAT HIS CLIENTS NEED!
HIYA TOOTS!
I CAN PROVIDE RECIPES FOR CORN PUDD'N AND FATBACK! PEDIGREED COON DOGS! CRATES OF BIB OVERALLS AND PRINT DRESSES! FRONT PORCH SWINGS!
?
Porch Swing
GRITS
Southern Cookin'
HAVE YOU GOT A SHOCK COMIN', FLINTY!
YOU'RE KINDA BEHIND THE TIMES, BUD!
NOWADAYS, THERE'S JUST ONE THING WE'D LIKE TO TRY! A THING THAT WOULD BRING SUCH GOOD CHEER TO PLAIN AWFUL THAT IT WOULD EARN YOU ANY FAVOR YOU ASKED!
YEAH?

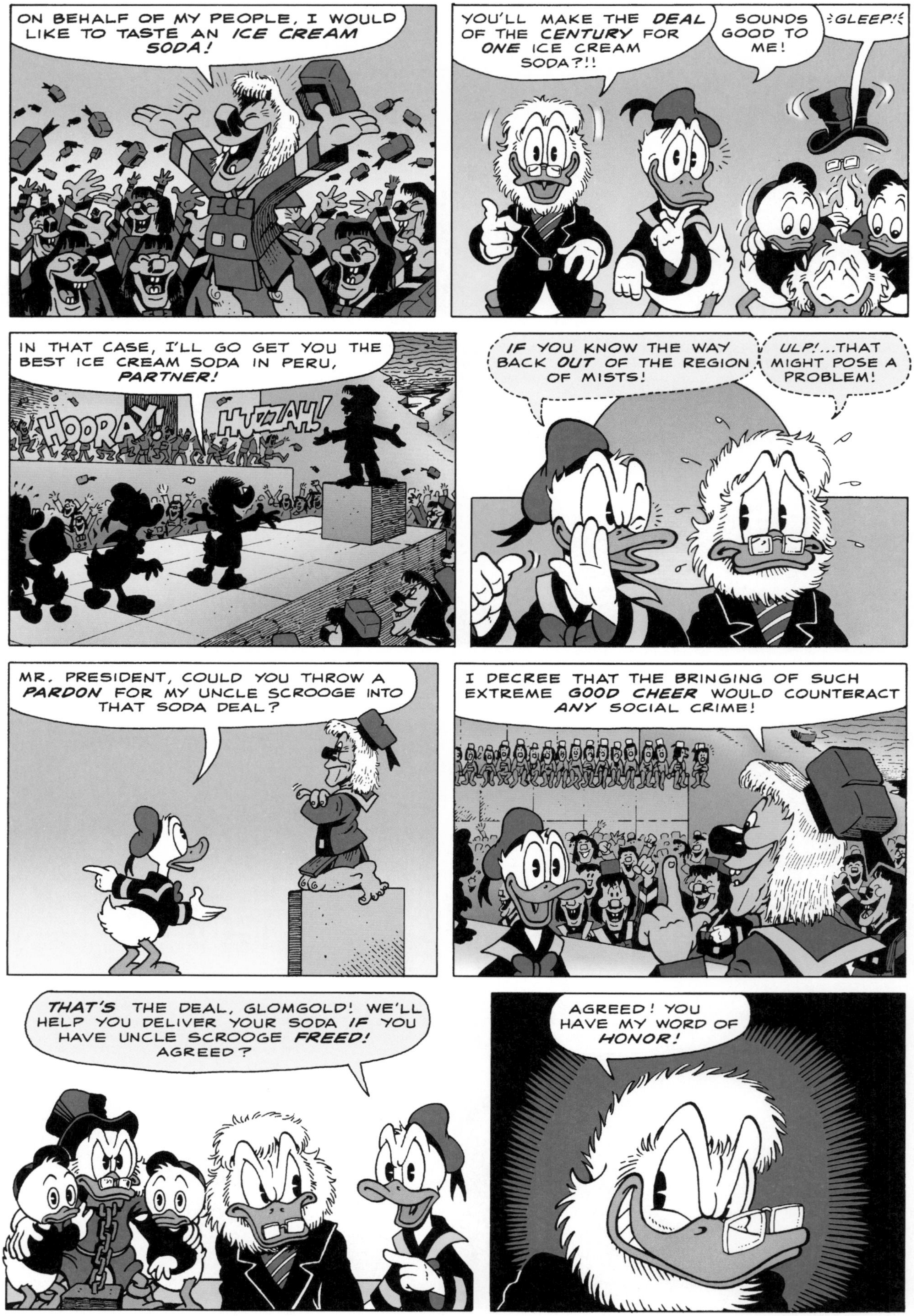

ON BEHALF OF MY PEOPLE, I WOULD LIKE TO TASTE AN *ICE CREAM SODA!*
YOU'LL MAKE THE *DEAL* OF THE *CENTURY* FOR *ONE* ICE CREAM SODA?!!
SOUNDS GOOD TO ME!
GLEEP!
IN THAT CASE, I'LL GO GET YOU THE BEST ICE CREAM SODA IN PERU, *PARTNER!*
HOORAY!
HUZZAH!
IF YOU KNOW THE WAY BACK *OUT* OF THE REGION OF MISTS!
ULP!...THAT MIGHT POSE A PROBLEM!
MR. PRESIDENT, COULD YOU THROW A *PARDON* FOR MY UNCLE SCROOGE INTO THAT SODA DEAL?
I DECREE THAT THE BRINGING OF SUCH EXTREME *GOOD CHEER* WOULD COUNTERACT *ANY* SOCIAL CRIME!
THAT'S THE DEAL, GLOMGOLD! WE'LL HELP YOU DELIVER YOUR SODA *IF* YOU HAVE UNCLE SCROOGE *FREED!* AGREED?
AGREED! YOU HAVE MY WORD OF *HONOR!*

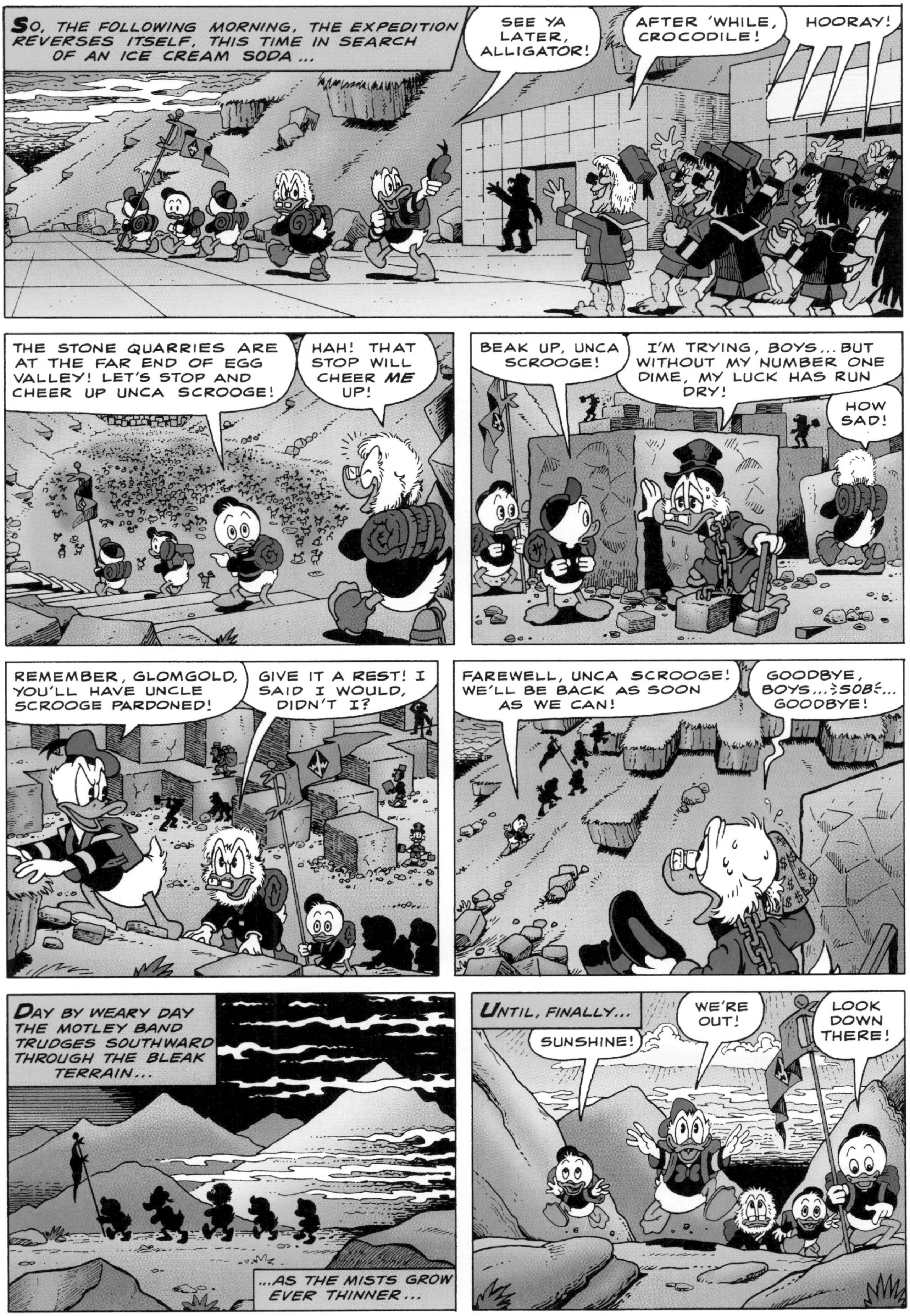
So, the following morning, the expedition reverses itself, this time in search of an ice cream soda...
SEE YA LATER, ALLIGATOR!
AFTER 'WHILE, CROCODILE!
HOORAY!
THE STONE QUARRIES ARE AT THE FAR END OF EGG VALLEY! LET'S STOP AND CHEER UP UNCA SCROOGE!
HAH! THAT STOP WILL CHEER ME UP!
BEAK UP, UNCA SCROOGE!
I'M TRYING, BOYS... BUT WITHOUT MY NUMBER ONE DIME, MY LUCK HAS RUN DRY!
HOW SAD!
REMEMBER, GLOMGOLD, YOU'LL HAVE UNCLE SCROOGE PARDONED!
GIVE IT A REST! I SAID I WOULD, DIDN'T I?
FAREWELL, UNCA SCROOGE! WE'LL BE BACK AS SOON AS WE CAN!
GOODBYE, BOYS... SOB... GOODBYE!
Day by weary day the motley band trudges southward through the bleak terrain...
...as the mists grow ever thinner...
Until, finally...
SUNSHINE!
WE'RE OUT!
LOOK DOWN THERE!

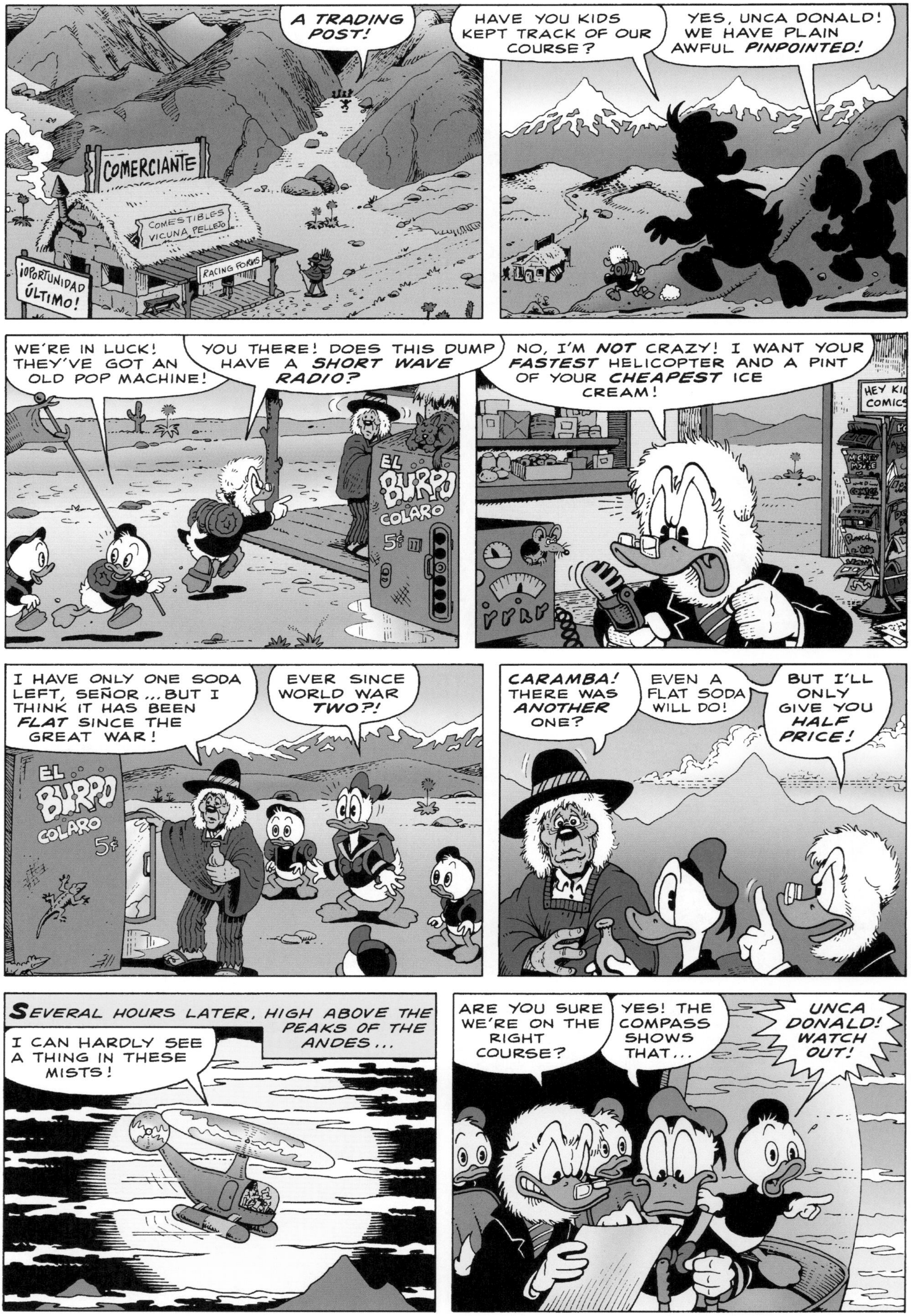
A TRADING POST!
COMERCIANTE
COMESTIBLES VICUNA PELLEJO
RACING FORMS
¡OPORTUNIDAD ÚLTIMO!
HAVE YOU KIDS KEPT TRACK OF OUR COURSE?
YES, UNCA DONALD! WE HAVE PLAIN AWFUL PINPOINTED!
WE'RE IN LUCK! THEY'VE GOT AN OLD POP MACHINE!
YOU THERE! DOES THIS DUMP HAVE A SHORT WAVE RADIO?
EL BURPO COLARO 5¢
NO, I'M NOT CRAZY! I WANT YOUR FASTEST HELICOPTER AND A PINT OF YOUR CHEAPEST ICE CREAM!
HEY KIDS COMICS
I HAVE ONLY ONE SODA LEFT, SEÑOR ... BUT I THINK IT HAS BEEN FLAT SINCE THE GREAT WAR!
EVER SINCE WORLD WAR TWO?!
EL BURPO COLARO 5¢
CARAMBA! THERE WAS ANOTHER ONE?
EVEN A FLAT SODA WILL DO!
BUT I'LL ONLY GIVE YOU HALF PRICE!
SEVERAL HOURS LATER, HIGH ABOVE THE PEAKS OF THE ANDES...
I CAN HARDLY SEE A THING IN THESE MISTS!
ARE YOU SURE WE'RE ON THE RIGHT COURSE?
YES! THE COMPASS SHOWS THAT...
UNCA DONALD! WATCH OUT!

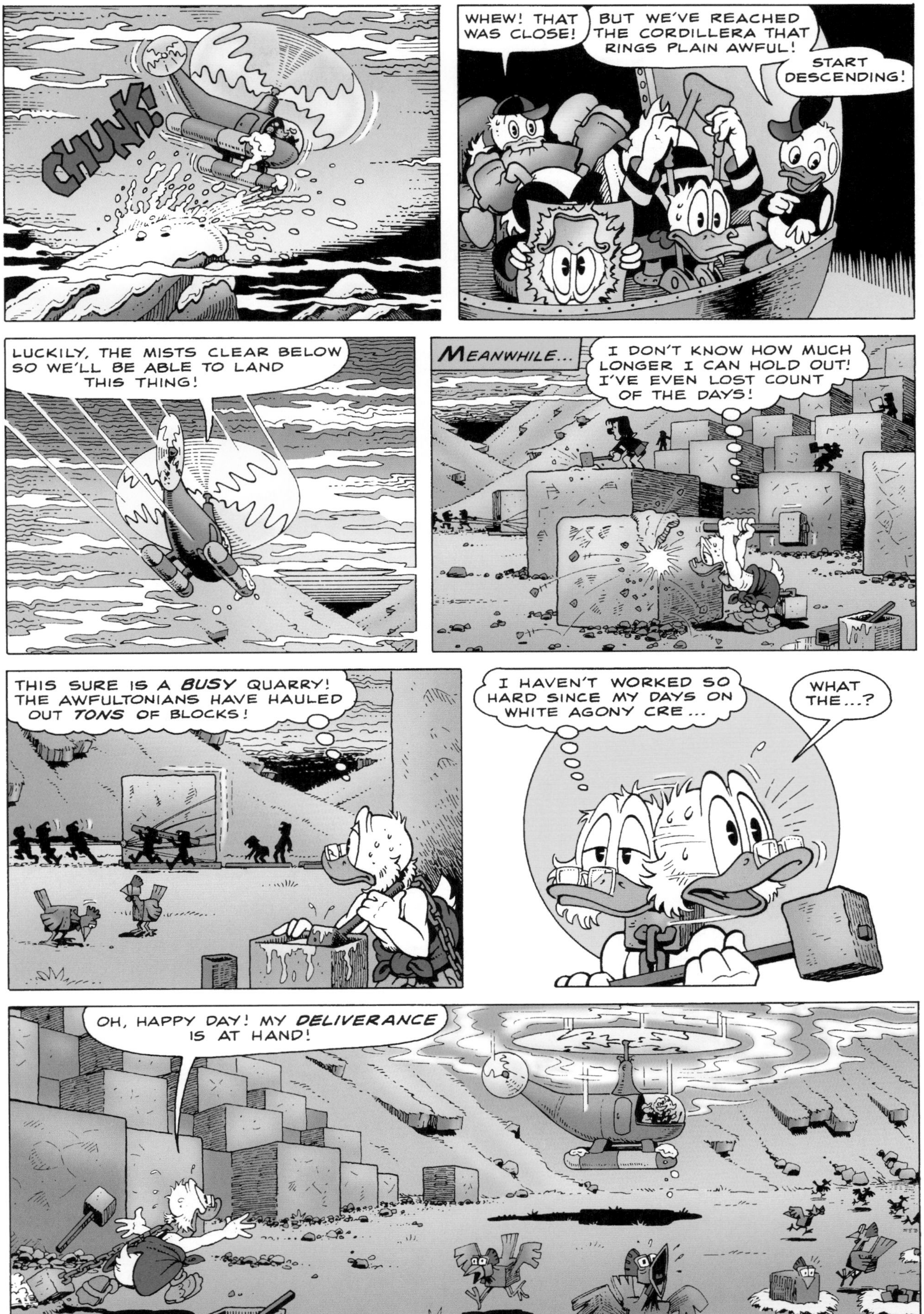
CHUNK!
WHEW! THAT WAS CLOSE!
BUT WE'VE REACHED THE CORDILLERA THAT RINGS PLAIN AWFUL!
START DESCENDING!
LUCKILY, THE MISTS CLEAR BELOW SO WE'LL BE ABLE TO LAND THIS THING!
MEANWHILE...
I DON'T KNOW HOW MUCH LONGER I CAN HOLD OUT! I'VE EVEN LOST COUNT OF THE DAYS!
THIS SURE IS A BUSY QUARRY! THE AWFULTONIANS HAVE HAULED OUT TONS OF BLOCKS!
I HAVEN'T WORKED SO HARD SINCE MY DAYS ON WHITE AGONY CRE...
WHAT THE...?
OH, HAPPY DAY! MY DELIVERANCE IS AT HAND!

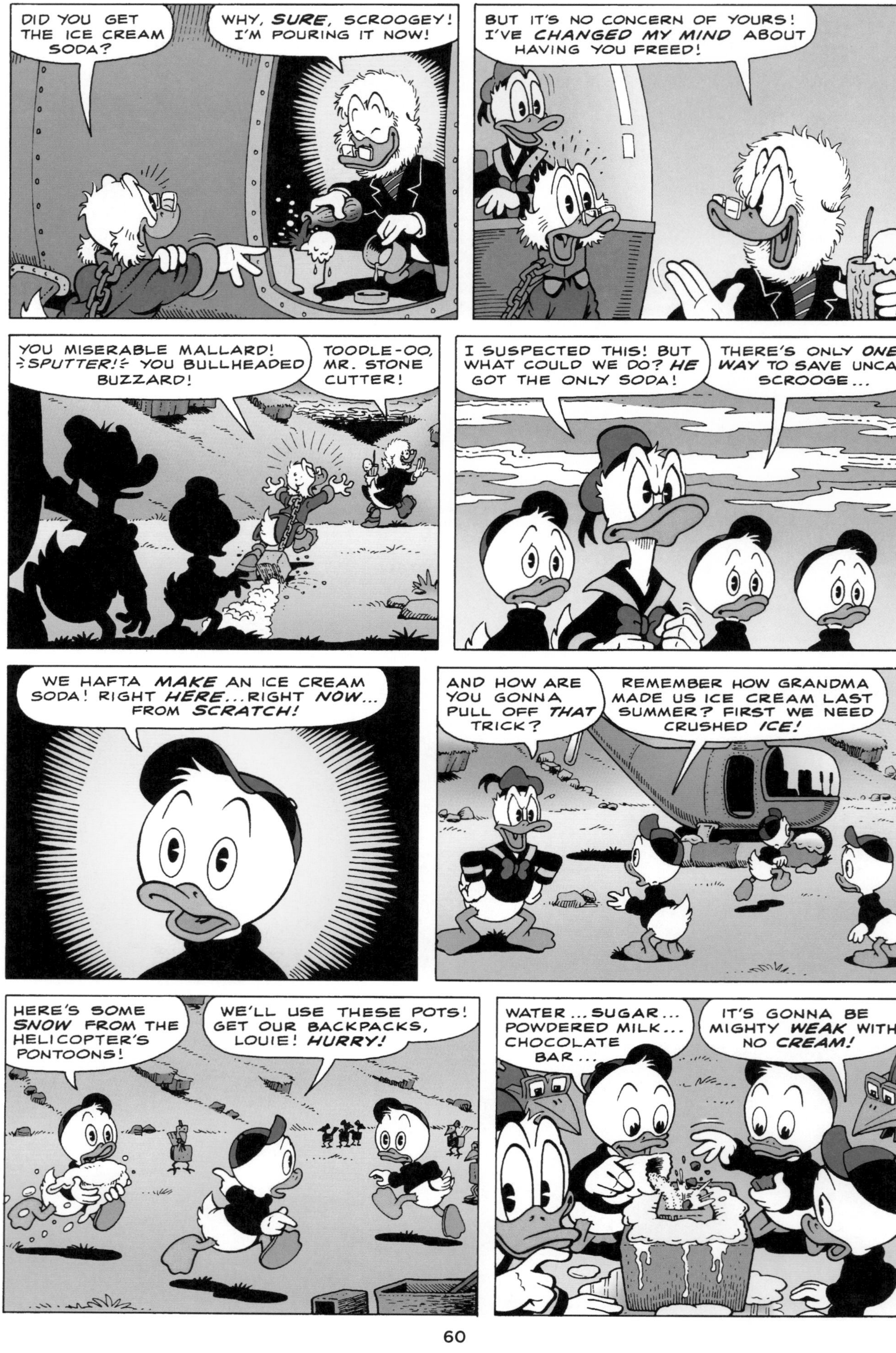
DID YOU GET THE ICE CREAM SODA?
WHY, SURE, SCROOGEY! I'M POURING IT NOW!
BUT IT'S NO CONCERN OF YOURS! I'VE CHANGED MY MIND ABOUT HAVING YOU FREED!
YOU MISERABLE MALLARD! SPUTTER! YOU BULLHEADED BUZZARD!
TOODLE-OO, MR. STONE CUTTER!
I SUSPECTED THIS! BUT WHAT COULD WE DO? HE GOT THE ONLY SODA!
THERE'S ONLY ONE WAY TO SAVE UNCA SCROOGE...
WE HAFTA MAKE AN ICE CREAM SODA! RIGHT HERE... RIGHT NOW... FROM SCRATCH!
AND HOW ARE YOU GONNA PULL OFF THAT TRICK?
REMEMBER HOW GRANDMA MADE US ICE CREAM LAST SUMMER? FIRST WE NEED CRUSHED ICE!
HERE'S SOME SNOW FROM THE HELICOPTER'S PONTOONS!
WE'LL USE THESE POTS! GET OUR BACKPACKS, LOUIE! HURRY!
WATER... SUGAR... POWDERED MILK... CHOCOLATE BAR...
IT'S GONNA BE MIGHTY WEAK WITH NO CREAM!

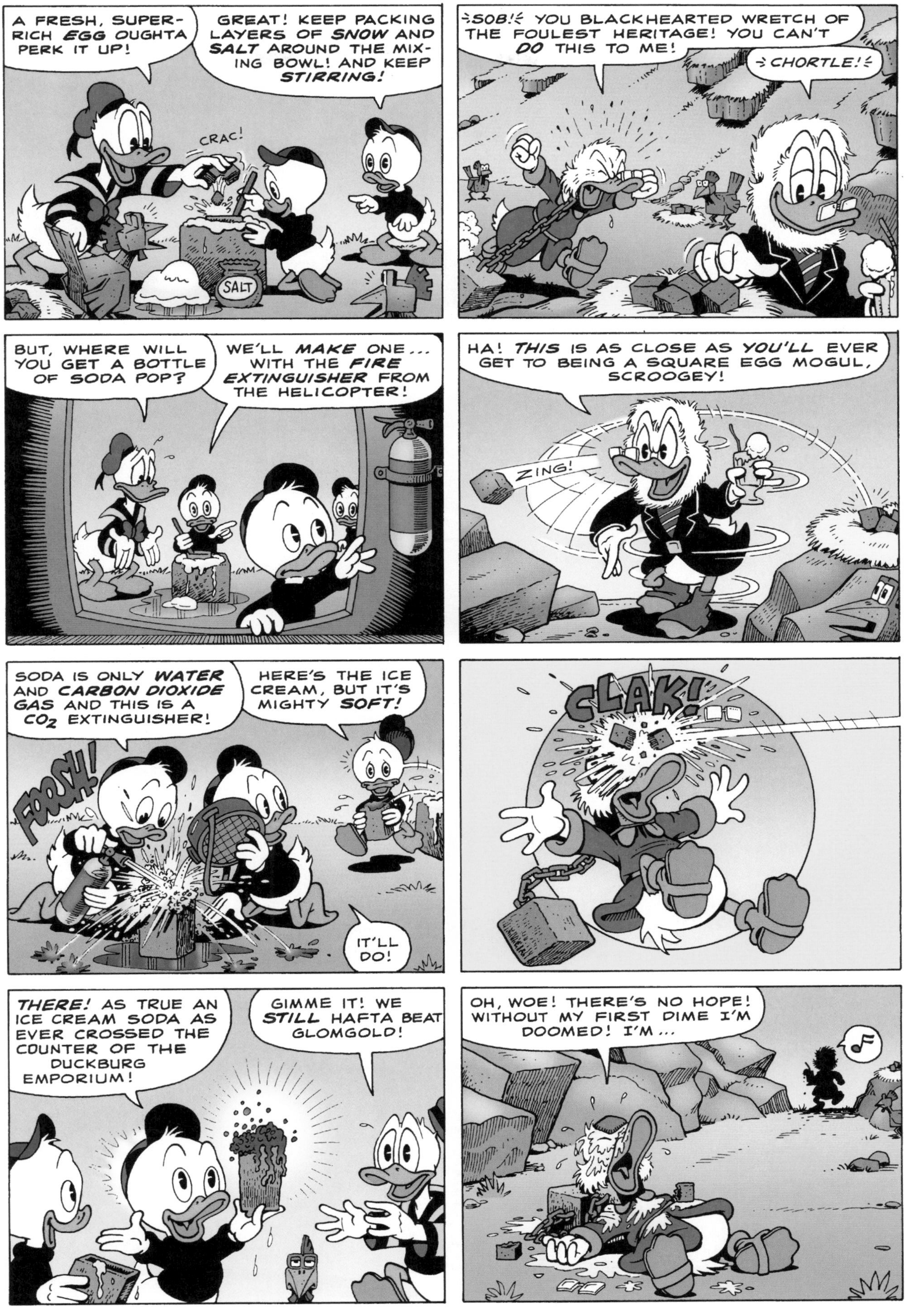
A FRESH, SUPER-RICH EGG OUGHTA PERK IT UP!
GREAT! KEEP PACKING LAYERS OF SNOW AND SALT AROUND THE MIXING BOWL! AND KEEP STIRRING!
CRAC!
SALT
SOB! YOU BLACKHEARTED WRETCH OF THE FOULEST HERITAGE! YOU CAN'T DO THIS TO ME!
CHORTLE!
BUT, WHERE WILL YOU GET A BOTTLE OF SODA POP?
WE'LL MAKE ONE... WITH THE FIRE EXTINGUISHER FROM THE HELICOPTER!
HA! THIS IS AS CLOSE AS YOU'LL EVER GET TO BEING A SQUARE EGG MOGUL, SCROOGEY!
ZING!
SODA IS ONLY WATER AND CARBON DIOXIDE GAS AND THIS IS A CO_2 EXTINGUISHER!
HERE'S THE ICE CREAM, BUT IT'S MIGHTY SOFT!
FOOSH!
IT'LL DO!
CLAK!
THERE! AS TRUE AN ICE CREAM SODA AS EVER CROSSED THE COUNTER OF THE DUCKBURG EMPORIUM!
GIMME IT! WE STILL HAFTA BEAT GLOMGOLD!
OH, WOE! THERE'S NO HOPE! WITHOUT MY FIRST DIME I'M DOOMED! I'M...

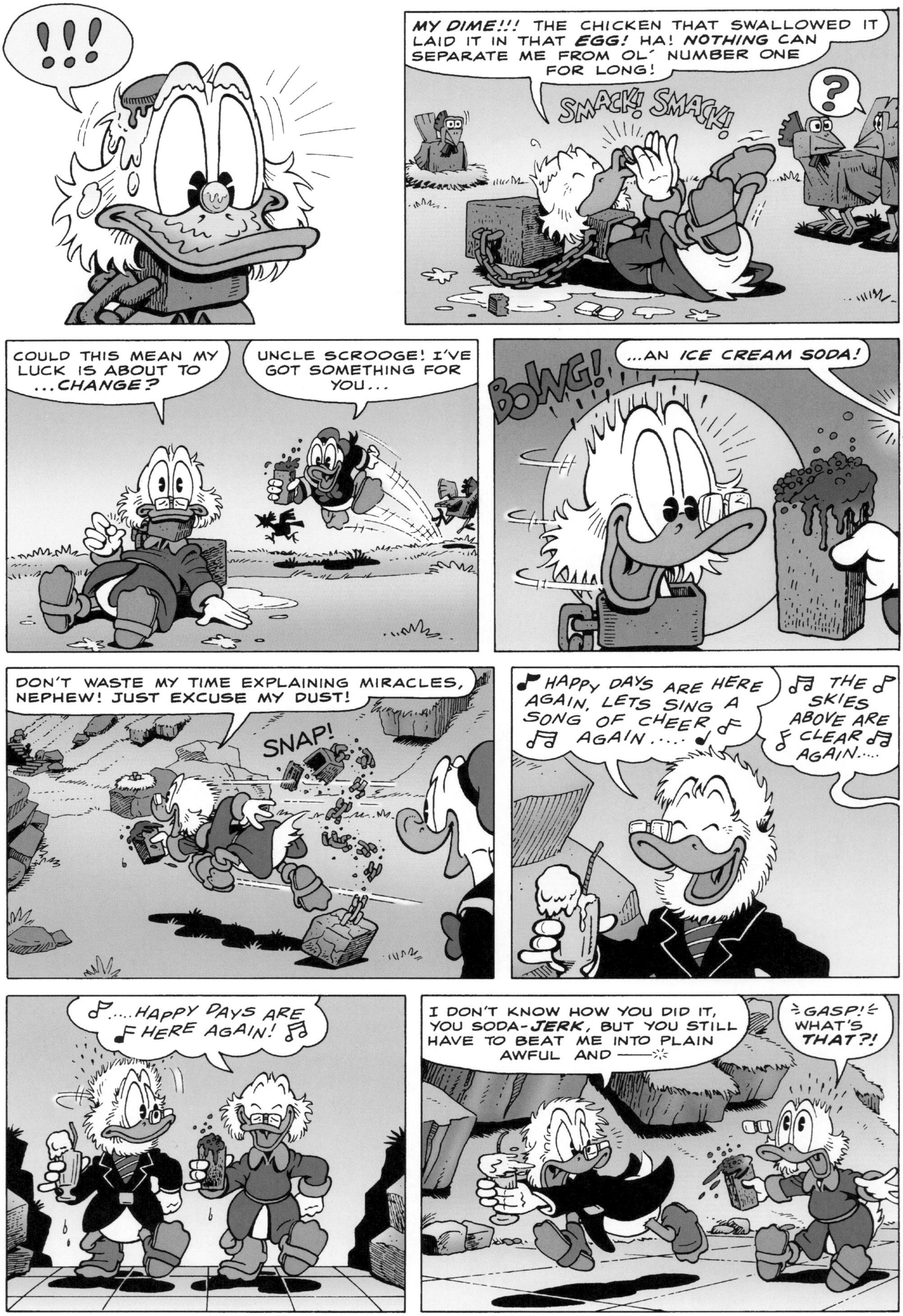
!!!
MY DIME!!! THE CHICKEN THAT SWALLOWED IT LAID IT IN THAT EGG! HA! NOTHING CAN SEPARATE ME FROM OL' NUMBER ONE FOR LONG!
SMACK! SMACK!
?
COULD THIS MEAN MY LUCK IS ABOUT TO ...CHANGE?
UNCLE SCROOGE! I'VE GOT SOMETHING FOR YOU...
BOING!
...AN ICE CREAM SODA!
DON'T WASTE MY TIME EXPLAINING MIRACLES, NEPHEW! JUST EXCUSE MY DUST!
SNAP!
HAPPY DAYS ARE HERE AGAIN, LETS SING A SONG OF CHEER AGAIN.....
THE SKIES ABOVE ARE CLEAR AGAIN....
.....HAPPY DAYS ARE HERE AGAIN!
I DON'T KNOW HOW YOU DID IT, YOU SODA-JERK, BUT YOU STILL HAVE TO BEAT ME INTO PLAIN AWFUL AND——
GASP! WHAT'S THAT?!

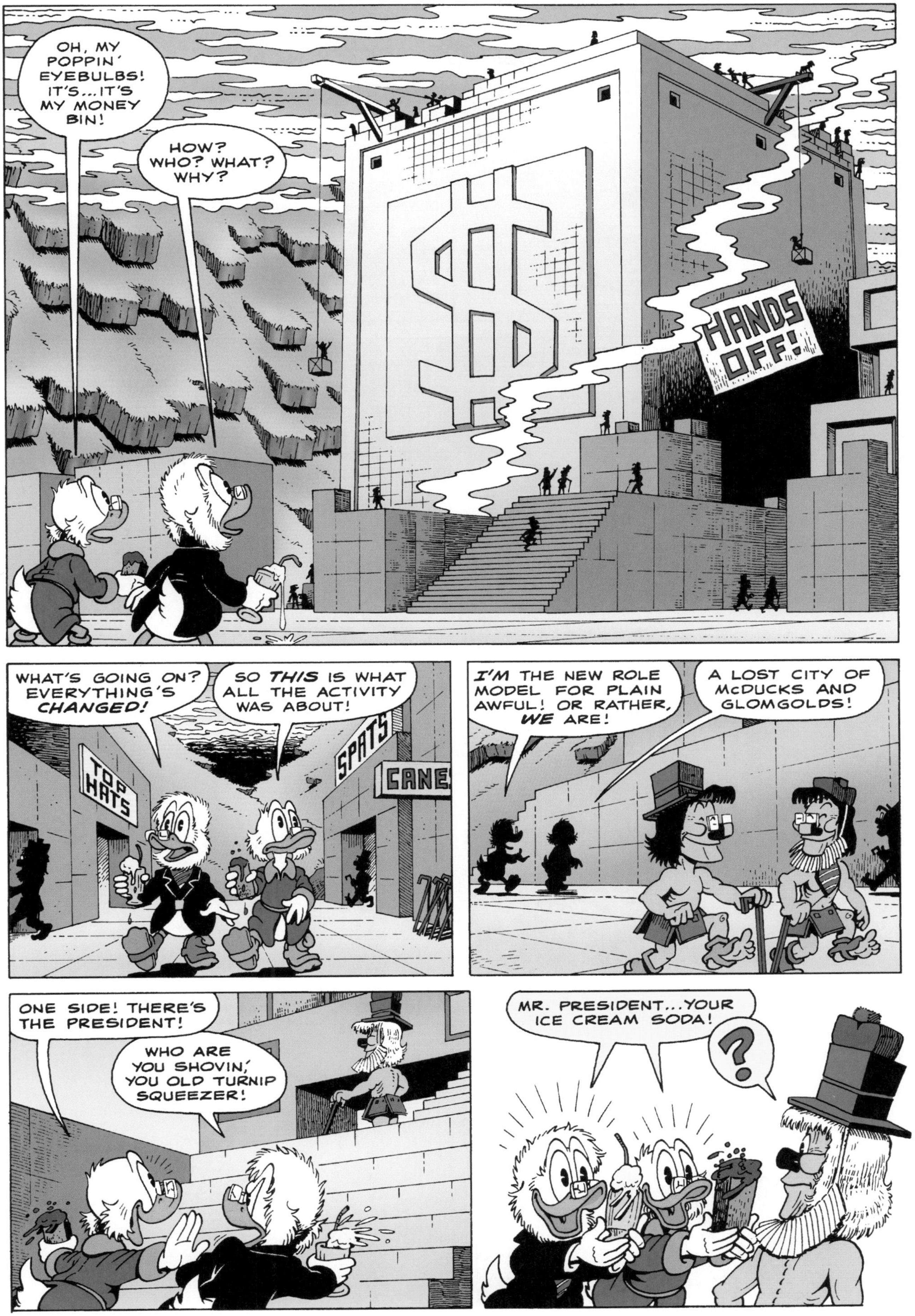
OH, MY POPPIN' EYEBULBS! IT'S...IT'S MY MONEY BIN!
HOW? WHO? WHAT? WHY?
HANDS OFF!
WHAT'S GOING ON? EVERYTHING'S CHANGED!
SO THIS IS WHAT ALL THE ACTIVITY WAS ABOUT!
TOP HATS
SPATS
CANES
I'M THE NEW ROLE MODEL FOR PLAIN AWFUL! OR RATHER, WE ARE!
A LOST CITY OF McDUCKS AND GLOMGOLDS!
ONE SIDE! THERE'S THE PRESIDENT!
WHO ARE YOU SHOVIN', YOU OLD TURNIP SQUEEZER!
MR. PRESIDENT...YOUR ICE CREAM SODA!
?

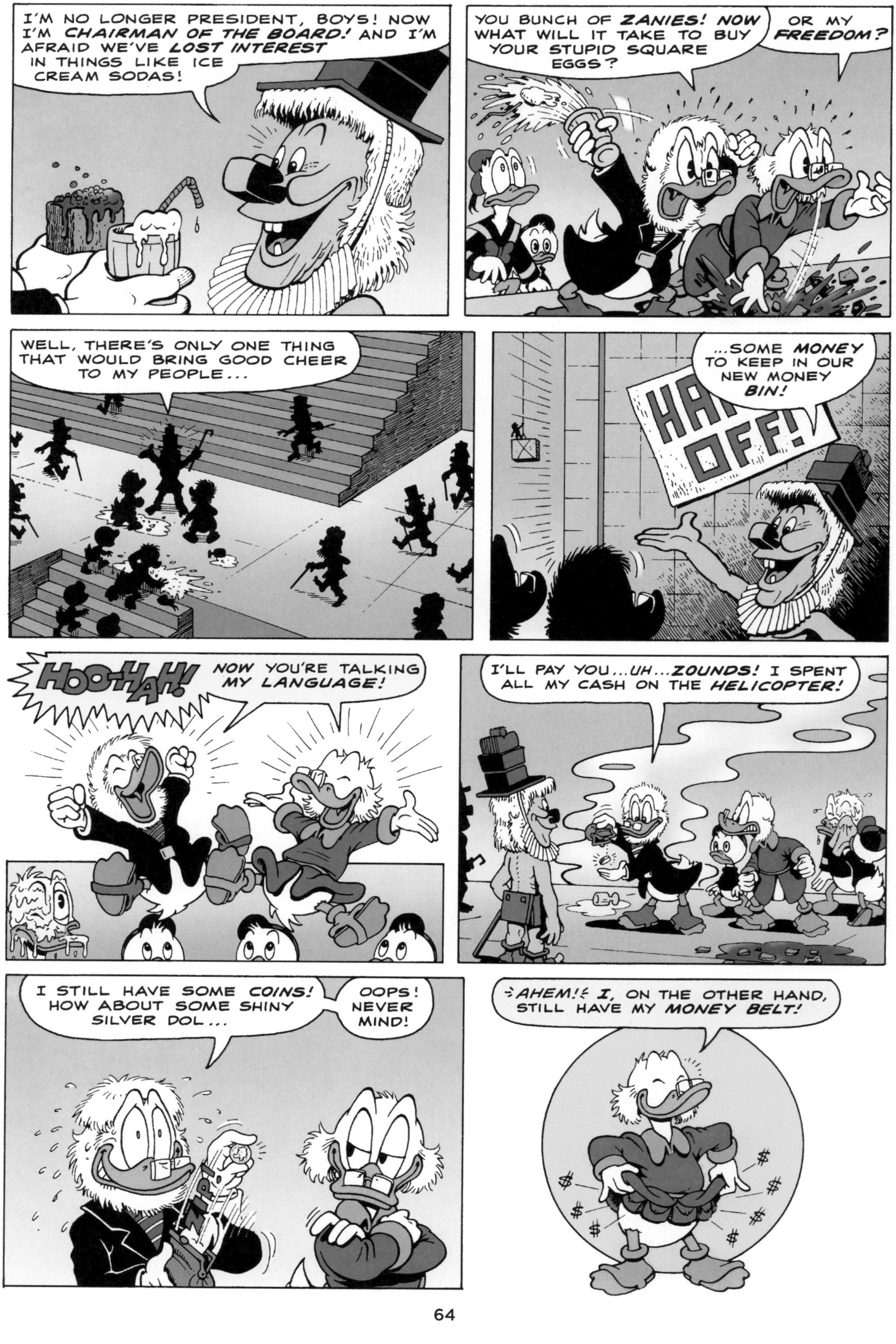

I'M NO LONGER PRESIDENT, BOYS! NOW I'M *CHAIRMAN OF THE BOARD!* AND I'M AFRAID WE'VE *LOST INTEREST* IN THINGS LIKE ICE CREAM SODAS!
YOU BUNCH OF *ZANIES! NOW* WHAT WILL IT TAKE TO BUY YOUR STUPID SQUARE EGGS?
OR MY *FREEDOM?*
WELL, THERE'S ONLY ONE THING THAT WOULD BRING GOOD CHEER TO MY PEOPLE...
...SOME *MONEY* TO KEEP IN OUR NEW MONEY *BIN!*
HOO-HAH!
NOW YOU'RE TALKING *MY LANGUAGE!*
I'LL PAY YOU...UH...*ZOUNDS!* I SPENT ALL MY CASH ON THE *HELICOPTER!*
I STILL HAVE SOME *COINS!* HOW ABOUT SOME SHINY SILVER DOL...
OOPS! NEVER MIND!
AHEM! I, ON THE OTHER HAND, STILL HAVE MY *MONEY BELT!*

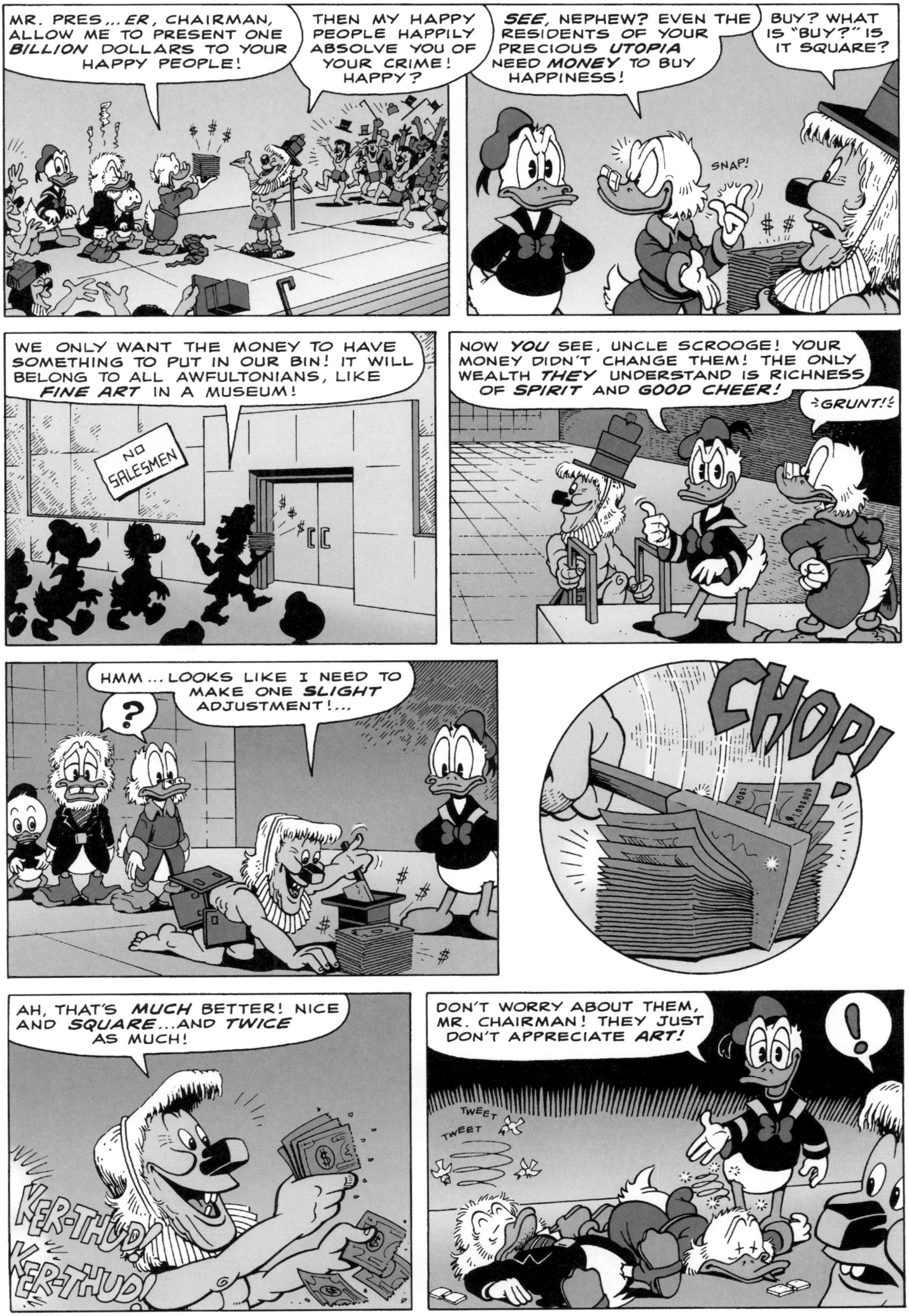

MR. PRES... ER, CHAIRMAN, ALLOW ME TO PRESENT ONE BILLION DOLLARS TO YOUR HAPPY PEOPLE!
THEN MY HAPPY PEOPLE HAPPILY ABSOLVE YOU OF YOUR CRIME! HAPPY?
SEE, NEPHEW? EVEN THE RESIDENTS OF YOUR PRECIOUS UTOPIA NEED MONEY TO BUY HAPPINESS!
BUY? WHAT IS "BUY?" IS IT SQUARE?
SNAP!
WE ONLY WANT THE MONEY TO HAVE SOMETHING TO PUT IN OUR BIN! IT WILL BELONG TO ALL AWFULTONIANS, LIKE FINE ART IN A MUSEUM!
NO SALESMEN
NOW YOU SEE, UNCLE SCROOGE! YOUR MONEY DIDN'T CHANGE THEM! THE ONLY WEALTH THEY UNDERSTAND IS RICHNESS OF SPIRIT AND GOOD CHEER!
GRUNT!
?
HMM... LOOKS LIKE I NEED TO MAKE ONE SLIGHT ADJUSTMENT!...
CHOP!
AH, THAT'S MUCH BETTER! NICE AND SQUARE... AND TWICE AS MUCH!
KER-THUD!
KER-THUD!
DON'T WORRY ABOUT THEM, MR. CHAIRMAN! THEY JUST DON'T APPRECIATE ART!
!
TWEET
TWEET

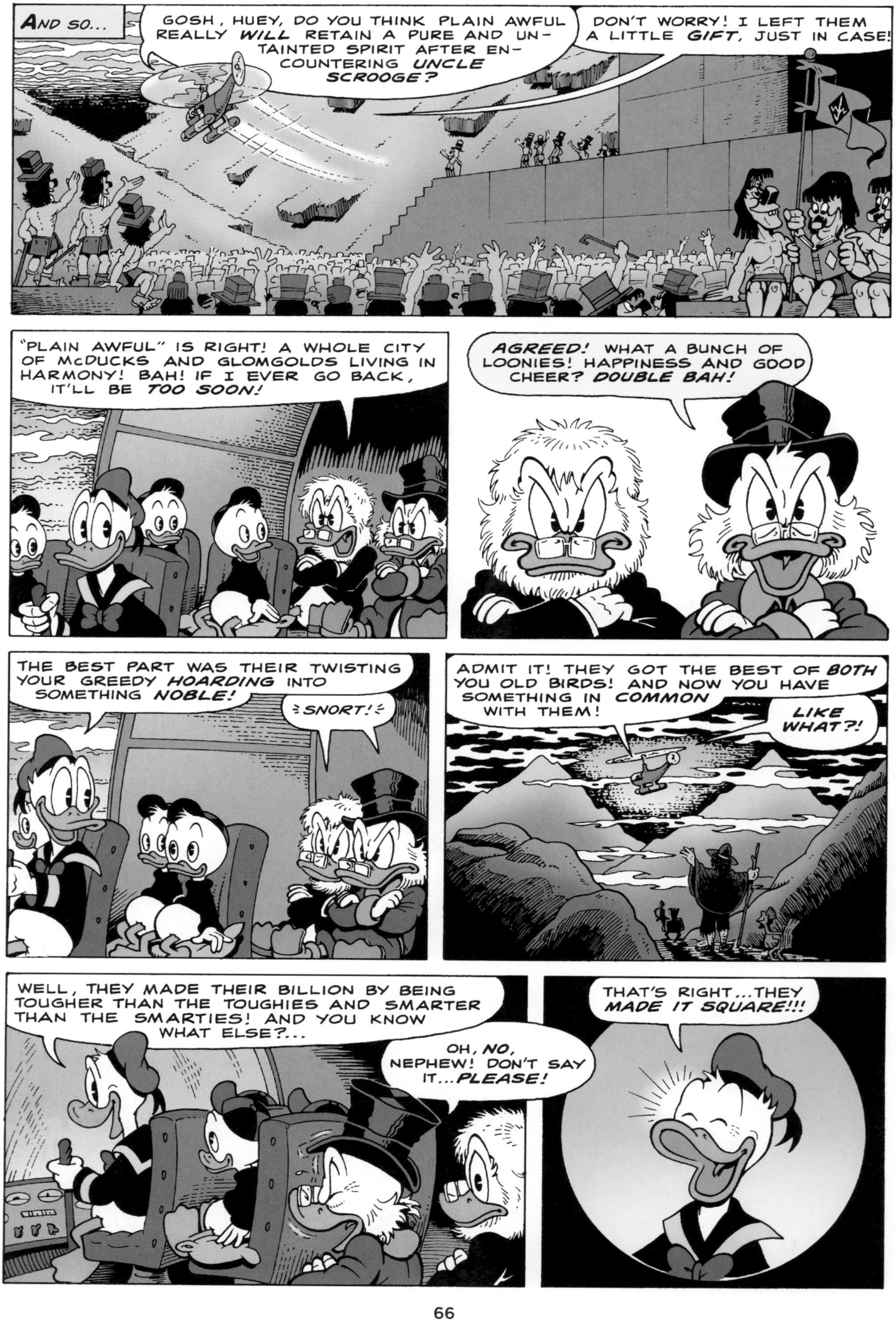
AND SO...
GOSH, HUEY, DO YOU THINK PLAIN AWFUL REALLY WILL RETAIN A PURE AND UNTAINTED SPIRIT AFTER ENCOUNTERING UNCLE SCROOGE?
DON'T WORRY! I LEFT THEM A LITTLE GIFT, JUST IN CASE!
"PLAIN AWFUL" IS RIGHT! A WHOLE CITY OF McDUCKS AND GLOMGOLDS LIVING IN HARMONY! BAH! IF I EVER GO BACK, IT'LL BE TOO SOON!
AGREED! WHAT A BUNCH OF LOONIES! HAPPINESS AND GOOD CHEER? DOUBLE BAH!
THE BEST PART WAS THEIR TWISTING YOUR GREEDY HOARDING INTO SOMETHING NOBLE!
SNORT!
ADMIT IT! THEY GOT THE BEST OF BOTH YOU OLD BIRDS! AND NOW YOU HAVE SOMETHING IN COMMON WITH THEM!
LIKE WHAT?!
WELL, THEY MADE THEIR BILLION BY BEING TOUGHER THAN THE TOUGHIES AND SMARTER THAN THE SMARTIES! AND YOU KNOW WHAT ELSE?...
OH, NO, NEPHEW! DON'T SAY IT... PLEASE!
THAT'S RIGHT... THEY MADE IT SQUARE!!!

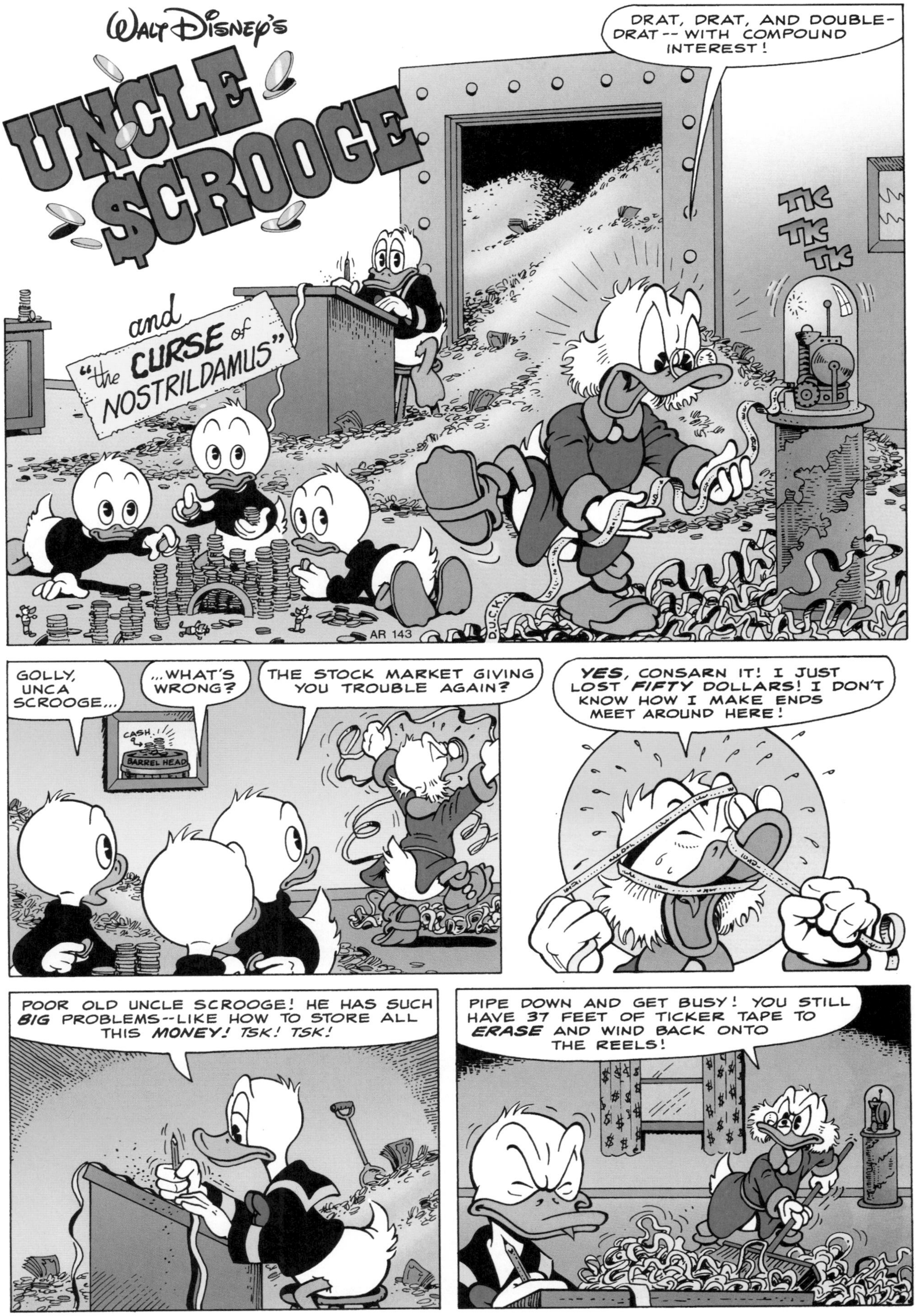
WALT DISNEY'S
UNCLE $CROOGE
and "the CURSE of NOSTRILDAMUS"
DRAT, DRAT, AND DOUBLE-DRAT--WITH COMPOUND INTEREST!
TIC TIC TIC
AR 143
GOLLY, UNCA SCROOGE...
...WHAT'S WRONG?
THE STOCK MARKET GIVING YOU TROUBLE AGAIN?
CASH BARREL HEAD
YES, CONSARN IT! I JUST LOST FIFTY DOLLARS! I DON'T KNOW HOW I MAKE ENDS MEET AROUND HERE!
POOR OLD UNCLE SCROOGE! HE HAS SUCH BIG PROBLEMS--LIKE HOW TO STORE ALL THIS MONEY! TSK! TSK!
PIPE DOWN AND GET BUSY! YOU STILL HAVE 37 FEET OF TICKER TAPE TO ERASE AND WIND BACK ONTO THE REELS!

AND DO A BETTER JOB THIS TIME! I CAN STILL SEE SOME OLD QUOTES ABOUT A DROP IN WHITE STAR OCEANLINES STOCK!

I NEVER *COULD* GET OUT ALL THAT STUFF ABOUT THE TITANIC SINKING! I THINK IT'S ABOUT TIME YOU BOUGHT SOME *FRESH* TAPE!

ERASE!

BAH! I WOULD'VE *SOLD* THAT STOCK IF I'D KNOWN ABOUT THAT STUPID ICEBERG! IF ONLY I COULD FORESEE THE *FUTURE!*

ALMIGHTY DOLLAR

WELL, ONLY *NOSTRILDAMUS* COULD DO *THAT!*

YEAH! HA HA!

NOSTRIL-WHOZIS?

NOSTRILDAMUS! THE 16TH CENTURY *ASTROLOGER!* HE COULD *SEE THE FUTURE!*

HMPH! 16TH CENTURY ASTROLOGERS ARE NEVER AROUND WHEN YOU *NEED* 'EM!

ALMIGHTY DOLLAR

ACCORDING TO THE *LEGEND,* YOU ONLY NEED HIS *MEDALLION!*

OH, SO? WHAT LEGEND IS THAT?

SHOO!

THE JUNIOR WOODCHUCKS GUIDEBOOK QUOTES NOSTRILDAMUS AS SAYING THAT WHOEVER WEARS HIS *MYSTIC* MEDALLION WILL GAIN HIS *POWERS!*

$

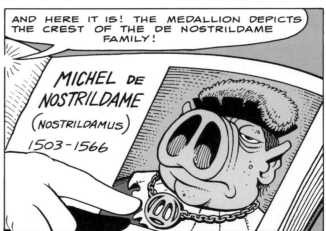

AND HERE IT IS! THE MEDALLION DEPICTS THE CREST OF THE DE NOSTRILDAME FAMILY!

MICHEL DE NOSTRILDAME
(NOSTRILDAMUS)
1503-1566

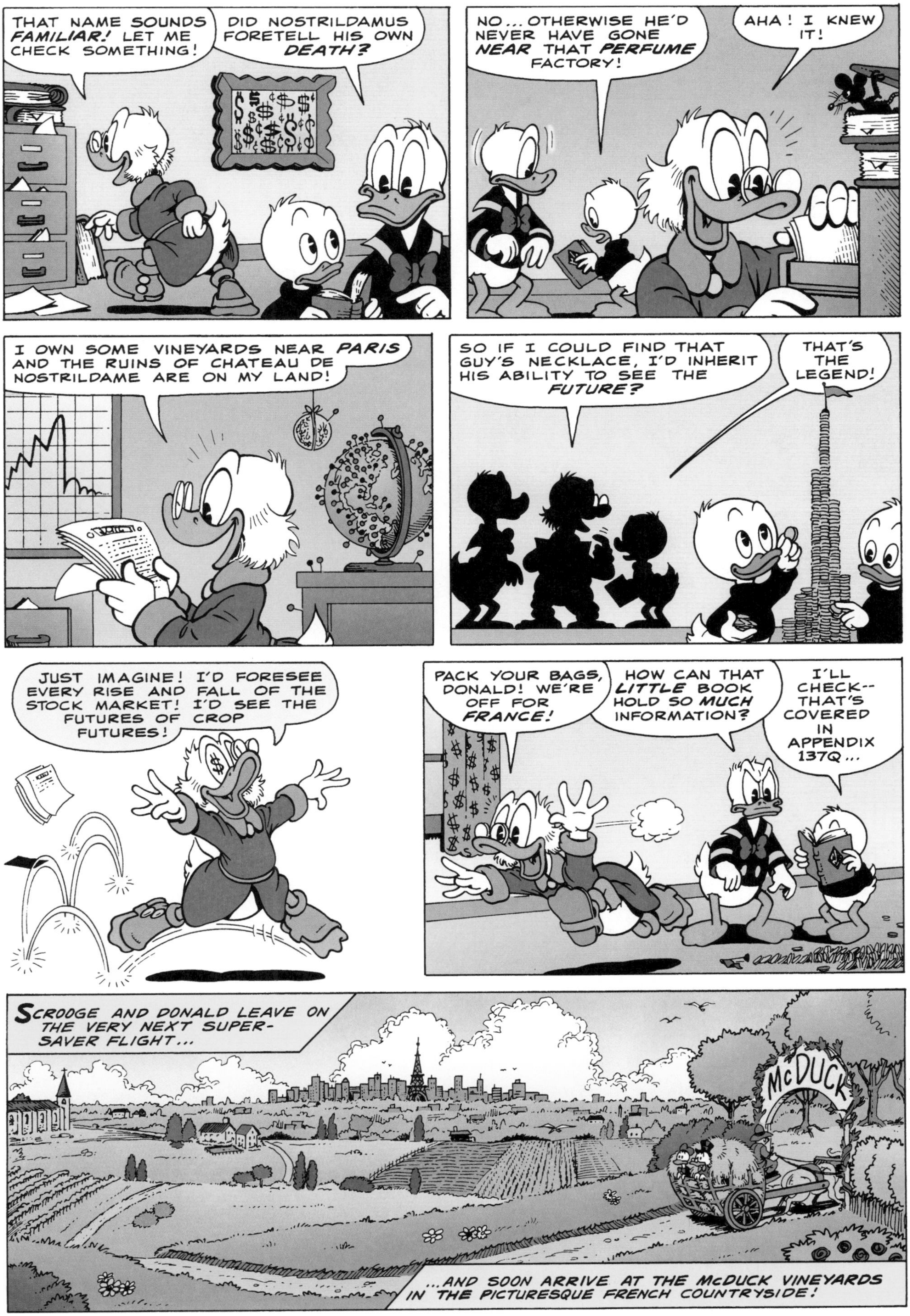
THAT NAME SOUNDS FAMILIAR! LET ME CHECK SOMETHING!
DID NOSTRILDAMUS FORETELL HIS OWN DEATH?
NO... OTHERWISE HE'D NEVER HAVE GONE NEAR THAT PERFUME FACTORY!
AHA! I KNEW IT!
I OWN SOME VINEYARDS NEAR PARIS AND THE RUINS OF CHATEAU DE NOSTRILDAME ARE ON MY LAND!
SO IF I COULD FIND THAT GUY'S NECKLACE, I'D INHERIT HIS ABILITY TO SEE THE FUTURE?
THAT'S THE LEGEND!
JUST IMAGINE! I'D FORESEE EVERY RISE AND FALL OF THE STOCK MARKET! I'D SEE THE FUTURES OF CROP FUTURES!
PACK YOUR BAGS, DONALD! WE'RE OFF FOR FRANCE!
HOW CAN THAT LITTLE BOOK HOLD SO MUCH INFORMATION?
I'LL CHECK-- THAT'S COVERED IN APPENDIX 137Q...
SCROOGE AND DONALD LEAVE ON THE VERY NEXT SUPER-SAVER FLIGHT...
McDUCK
...AND SOON ARRIVE AT THE McDUCK VINEYARDS IN THE PICTURESQUE FRENCH COUNTRYSIDE!

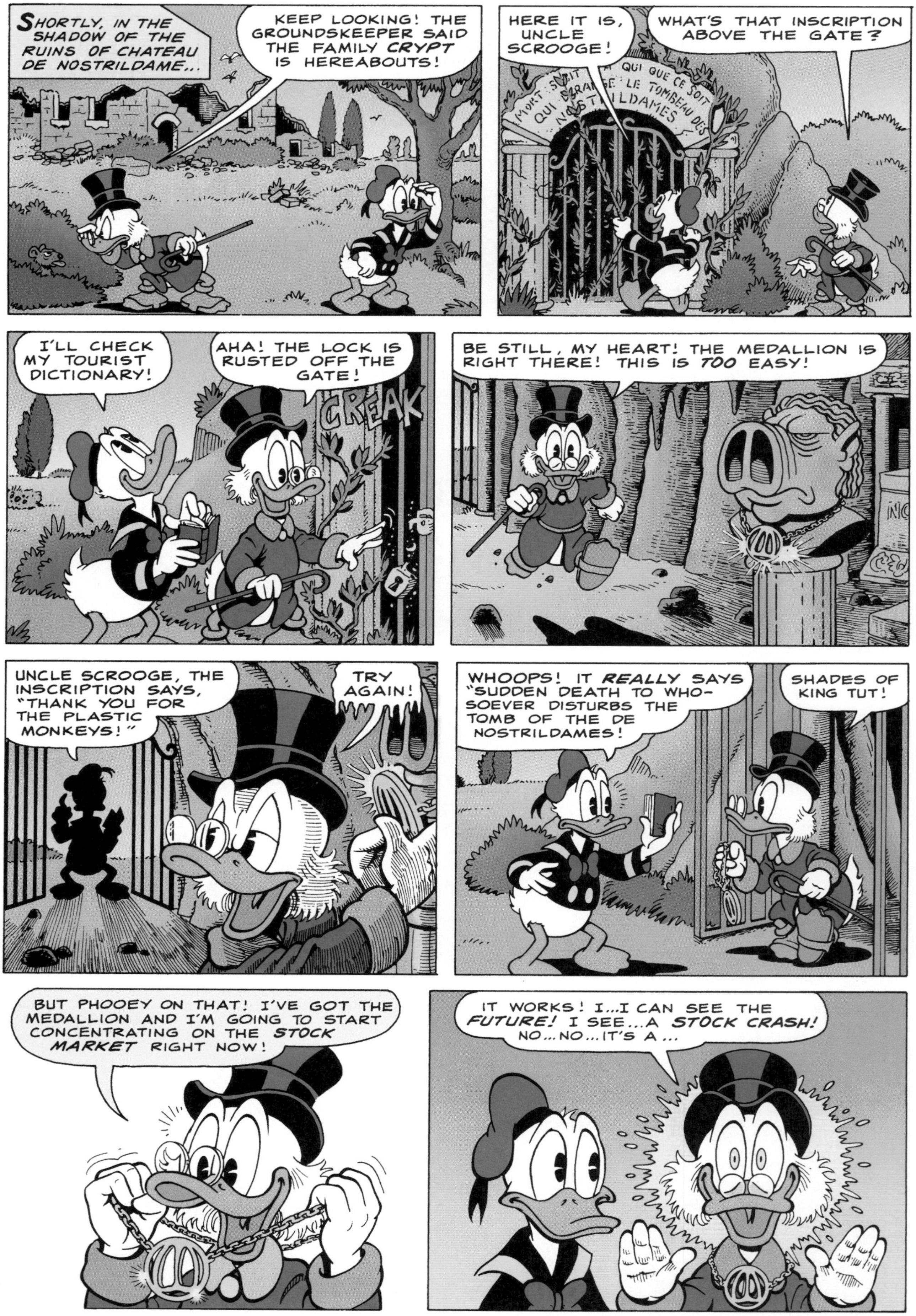
SHORTLY, IN THE SHADOW OF THE RUINS OF CHATEAU DE NOSTRILDAME...
KEEP LOOKING! THE GROUNDSKEEPER SAID THE FAMILY CRYPT IS HEREABOUTS!
HERE IT IS, UNCLE SCROOGE!
WHAT'S THAT INSCRIPTION ABOVE THE GATE?
I'LL CHECK MY TOURIST DICTIONARY!
AHA! THE LOCK IS RUSTED OFF THE GATE!
CREAK
BE STILL, MY HEART! THE MEDALLION IS RIGHT THERE! THIS IS TOO EASY!
UNCLE SCROOGE, THE INSCRIPTION SAYS, "THANK YOU FOR THE PLASTIC MONKEYS!"
TRY AGAIN!
WHOOPS! IT REALLY SAYS "SUDDEN DEATH TO WHO-SOEVER DISTURBS THE TOMB OF THE DE NOSTRILDAMES!
SHADES OF KING TUT!
BUT PHOOEY ON THAT! I'VE GOT THE MEDALLION AND I'M GOING TO START CONCENTRATING ON THE STOCK MARKET RIGHT NOW!
IT WORKS! I...I CAN SEE THE FUTURE! I SEE...A STOCK CRASH! NO...NO...IT'S A...

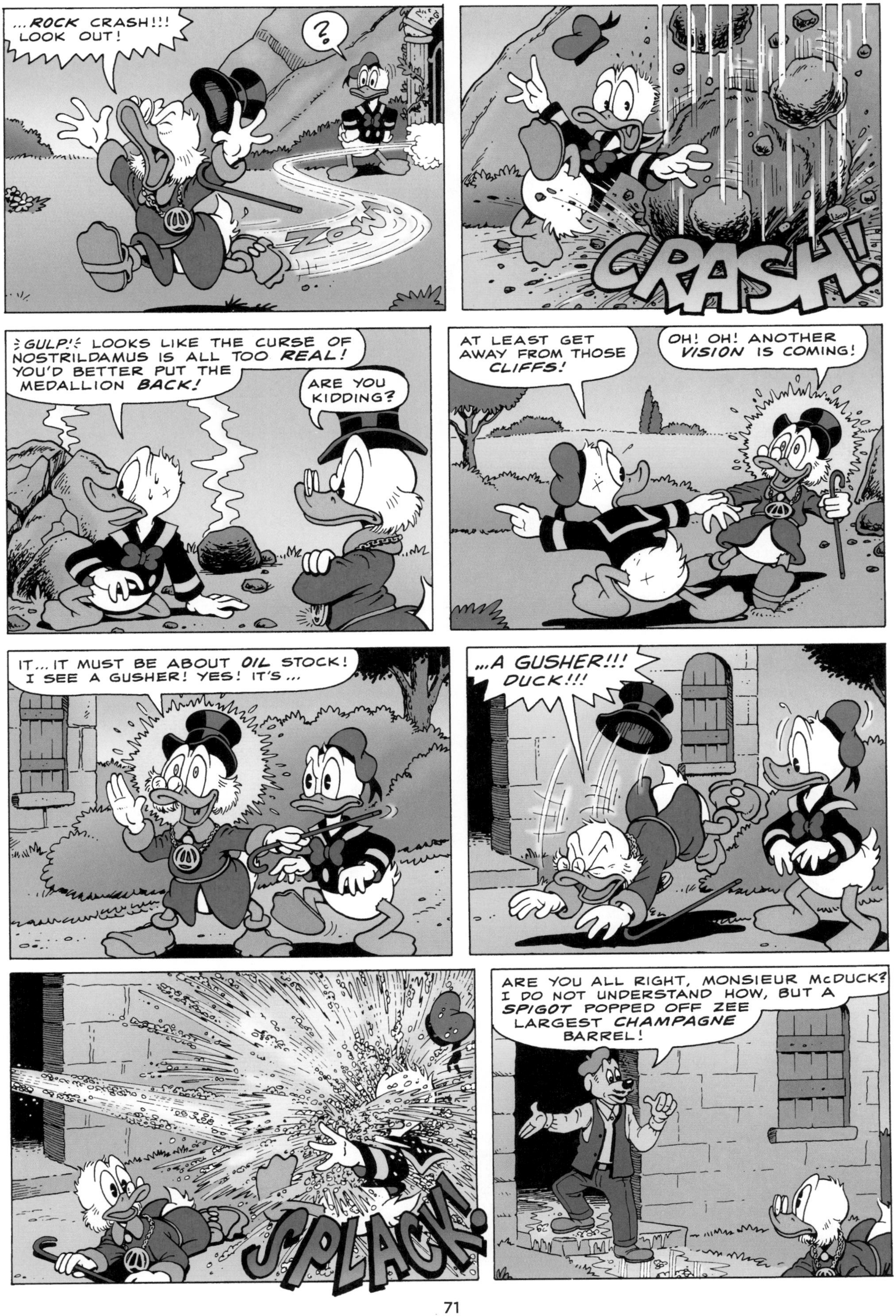
...ROCK CRASH!!! LOOK OUT!
?
ZOW!
CRASH!
GULP! LOOKS LIKE THE CURSE OF NOSTRILDAMUS IS ALL TOO REAL! YOU'D BETTER PUT THE MEDALLION BACK!
ARE YOU KIDDING?
AT LEAST GET AWAY FROM THOSE CLIFFS!
OH! OH! ANOTHER VISION IS COMING!
IT... IT MUST BE ABOUT OIL STOCK! I SEE A GUSHER! YES! IT'S...
...A GUSHER!!! DUCK!!!
SPLACK!
ARE YOU ALL RIGHT, MONSIEUR McDUCK? I DO NOT UNDERSTAND HOW, BUT A SPIGOT POPPED OFF ZEE LARGEST CHAMPAGNE BARREL!

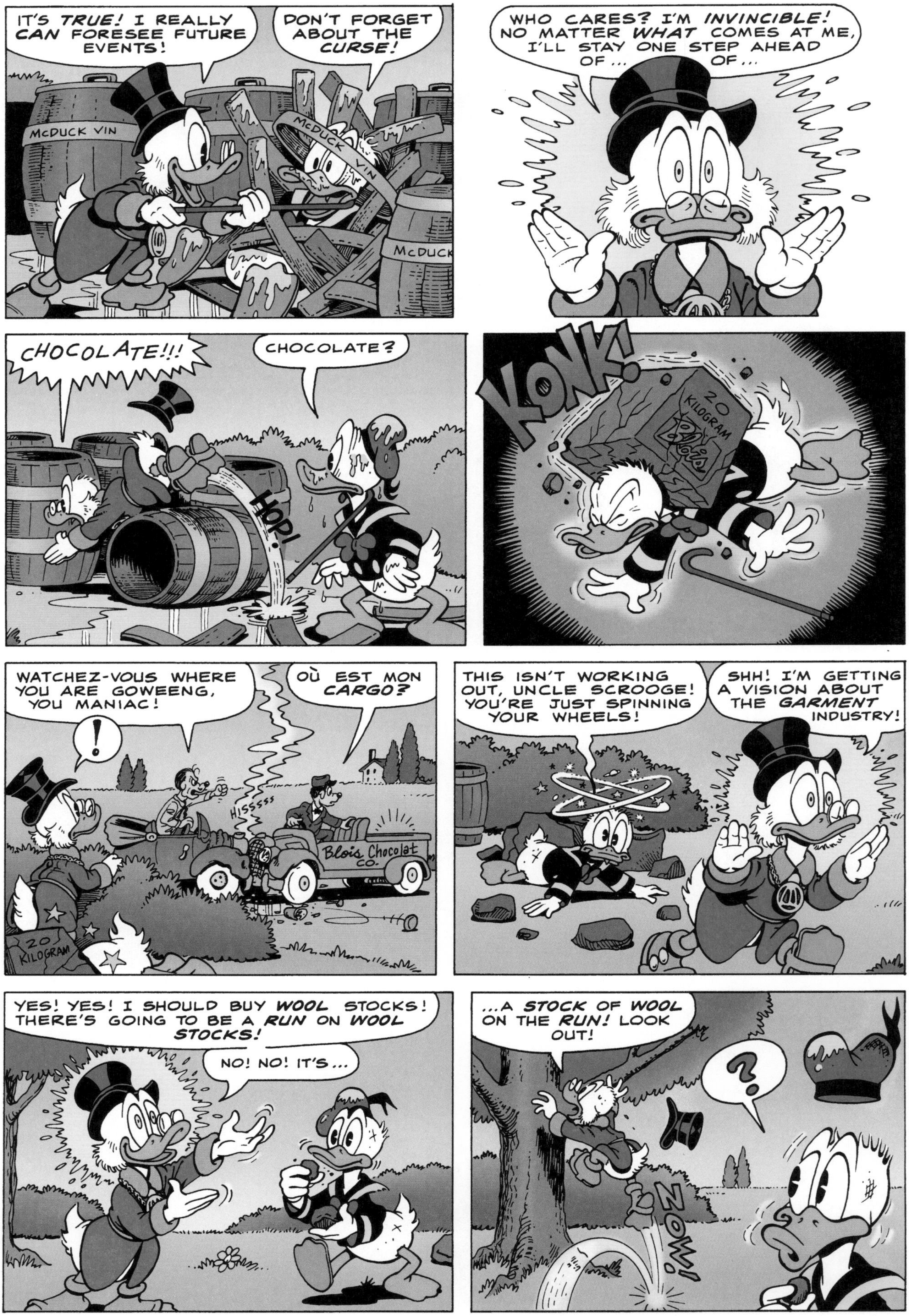
IT'S TRUE! I REALLY CAN FORESEE FUTURE EVENTS!
DON'T FORGET ABOUT THE CURSE!
McDUCK VIN
McDUCK VIN
McDUCK
WHO CARES? I'M INVINCIBLE! NO MATTER WHAT COMES AT ME, I'LL STAY ONE STEP AHEAD OF... OF...
CHOCOLATE!!!
CHOCOLATE?
HOP!
KONK!
20 KILOGRAM
Blois
WATCHEZ-VOUS WHERE YOU ARE GOWEENG, YOU MANIAC!
OÙ EST MON CARGO?
!
HISSSSS
Blois Chocolat Co.
20 KILOGRAM
THIS ISN'T WORKING OUT, UNCLE SCROOGE! YOU'RE JUST SPINNING YOUR WHEELS!
SHH! I'M GETTING A VISION ABOUT THE GARMENT INDUSTRY!
YES! YES! I SHOULD BUY WOOL STOCKS! THERE'S GOING TO BE A RUN ON WOOL STOCKS!
NO! NO! IT'S...
...A STOCK OF WOOL ON THE RUN! LOOK OUT!
?
ZOW!

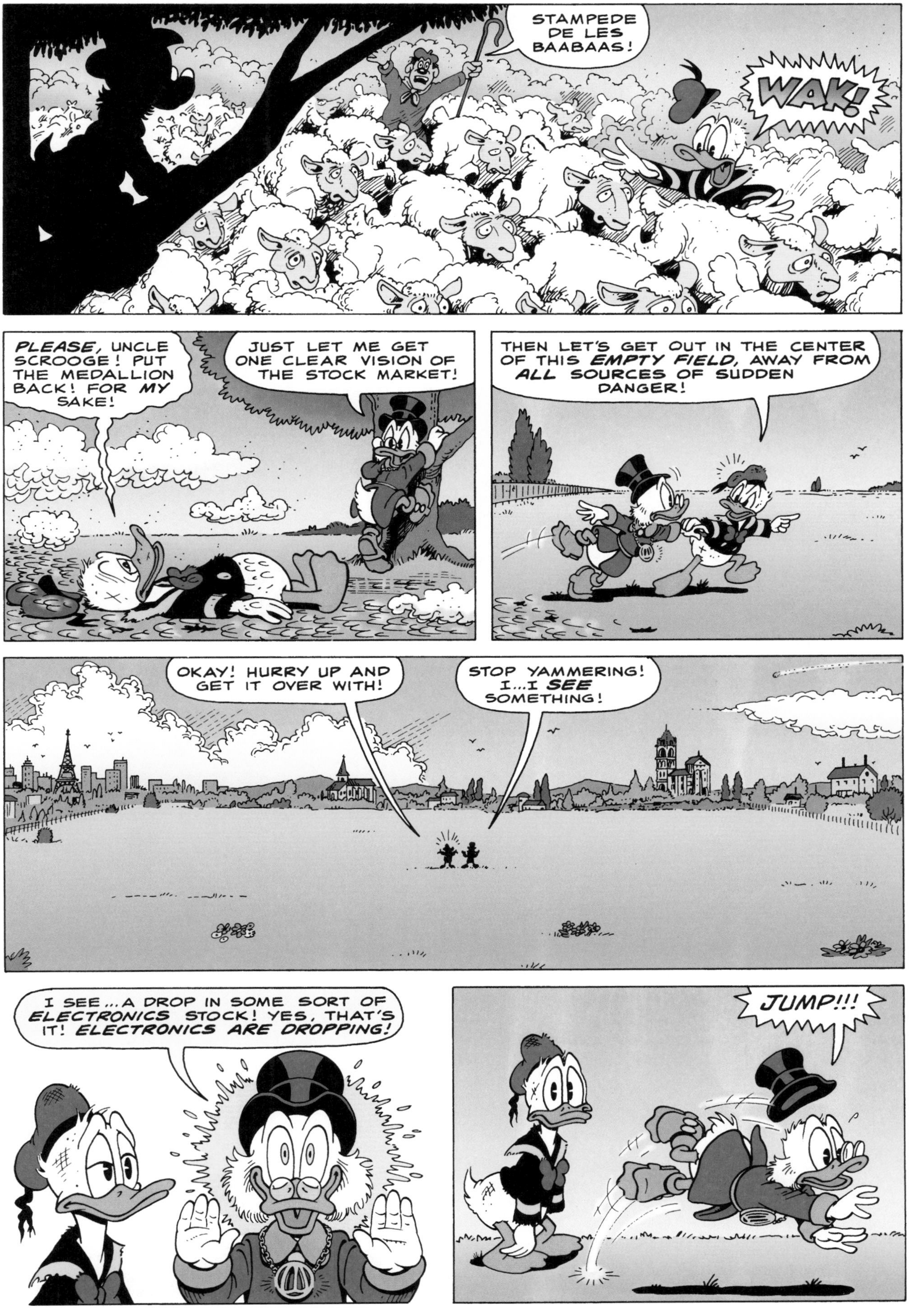
STAMPEDE DE LES BAABAAS!
WAK!
PLEASE, UNCLE SCROOGE! PUT THE MEDALLION BACK! FOR MY SAKE!
JUST LET ME GET ONE CLEAR VISION OF THE STOCK MARKET!
THEN LET'S GET OUT IN THE CENTER OF THIS EMPTY FIELD, AWAY FROM ALL SOURCES OF SUDDEN DANGER!
OKAY! HURRY UP AND GET IT OVER WITH!
STOP YAMMERING! I...I SEE SOMETHING!
I SEE... A DROP IN SOME SORT OF ELECTRONICS STOCK! YES, THAT'S IT! ELECTRONICS ARE DROPPING!
JUMP!!!

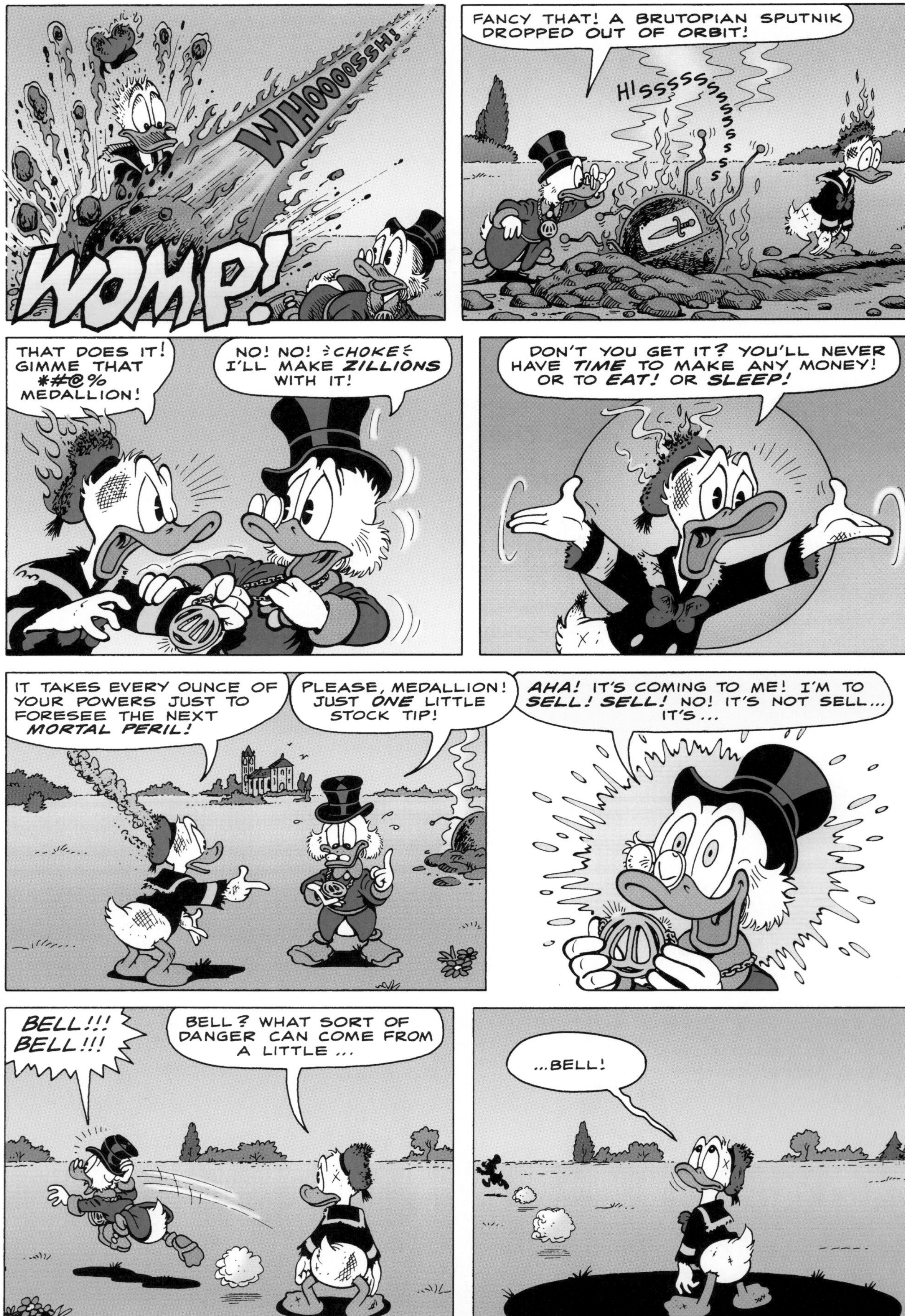
WHOOOOSSSH!
WOMP!
FANCY THAT! A BRUTOPIAN SPUTNIK DROPPED OUT OF ORBIT!
HISSSSSSSSSSSS
THAT DOES IT! GIMME THAT *#@% MEDALLION!
NO! NO! CHOKE I'LL MAKE ZILLIONS WITH IT!
DON'T YOU GET IT? YOU'LL NEVER HAVE TIME TO MAKE ANY MONEY! OR TO EAT! OR SLEEP!
IT TAKES EVERY OUNCE OF YOUR POWERS JUST TO FORESEE THE NEXT MORTAL PERIL!
PLEASE, MEDALLION! JUST ONE LITTLE STOCK TIP!
AHA! IT'S COMING TO ME! I'M TO SELL! SELL! NO! IT'S NOT SELL... IT'S...
BELL!!! BELL!!!
BELL? WHAT SORT OF DANGER CAN COME FROM A LITTLE ...
...BELL!

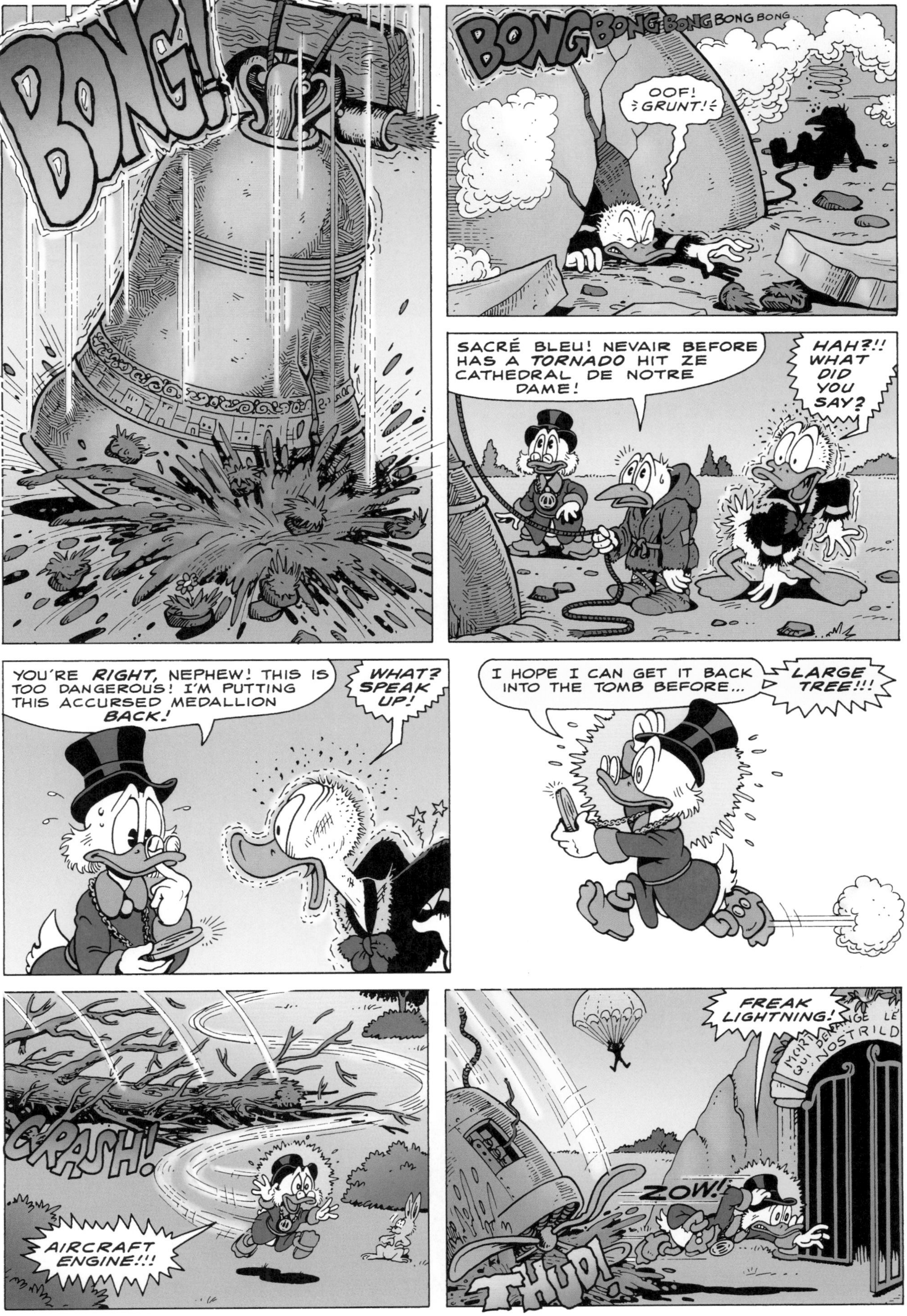
BONG!
BONG BONG BONG BONG BONG...
OOF! GRUNT!
SACRÉ BLEU! NEVAIR BEFORE HAS A TORNADO HIT ZE CATHEDRAL DE NOTRE DAME!
HAH?!! WHAT DID YOU SAY?
YOU'RE RIGHT, NEPHEW! THIS IS TOO DANGEROUS! I'M PUTTING THIS ACCURSED MEDALLION BACK!
WHAT? SPEAK UP!
I HOPE I CAN GET IT BACK INTO THE TOMB BEFORE...
LARGE TREE!!!
CRASH!
AIRCRAFT ENGINE!!!
FREAK LIGHTNING!
MORT
QUI
LE
NOSTRILD
ZOW!
THUD!

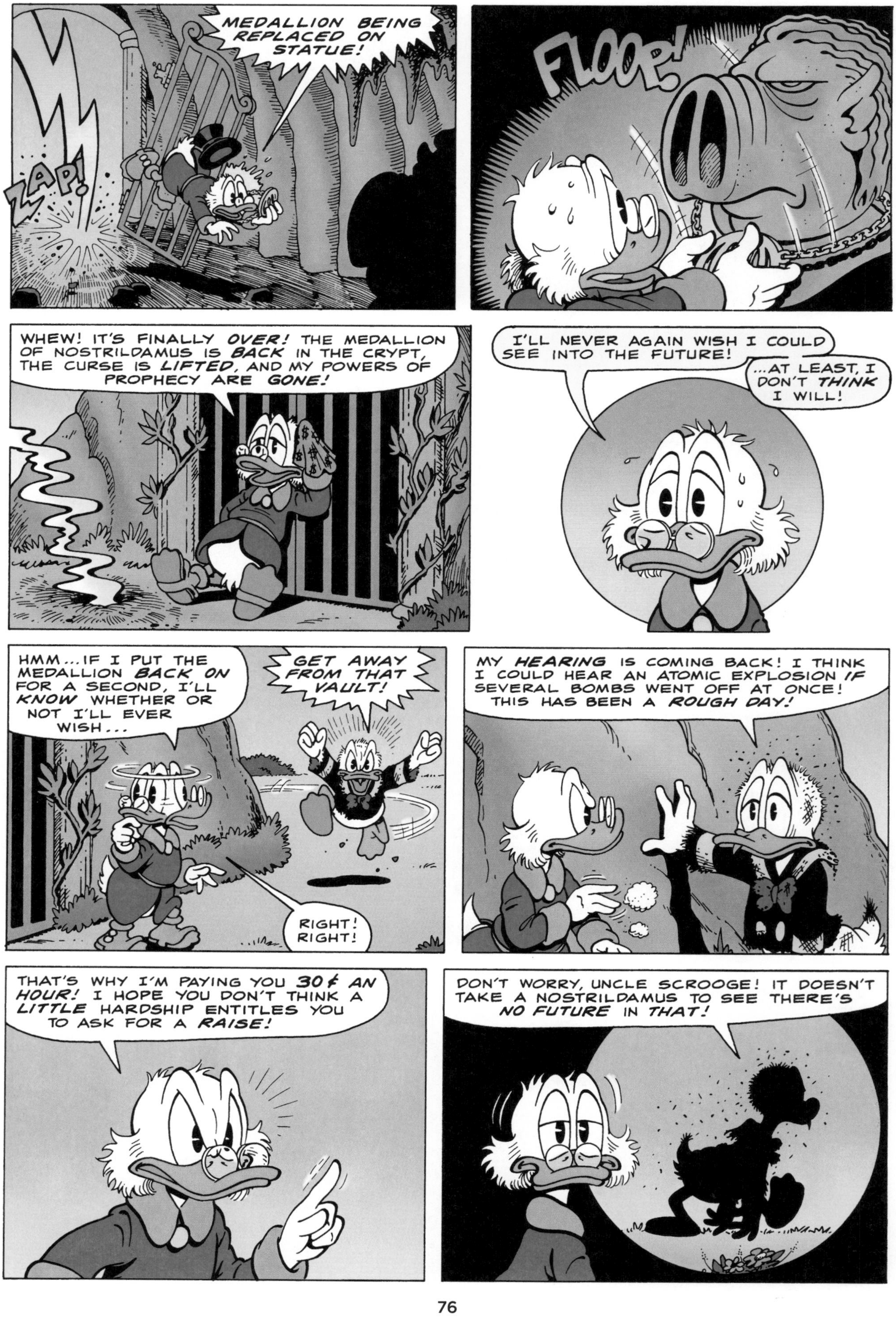
MEDALLION BEING REPLACED ON STATUE!
ZAP!
FLOOP!
WHEW! IT'S FINALLY OVER! THE MEDALLION OF NOSTRILDAMUS IS BACK IN THE CRYPT, THE CURSE IS LIFTED, AND MY POWERS OF PROPHECY ARE GONE!
I'LL NEVER AGAIN WISH I COULD SEE INTO THE FUTURE!
...AT LEAST, I DON'T THINK I WILL!
HMM... IF I PUT THE MEDALLION BACK ON FOR A SECOND, I'LL KNOW WHETHER OR NOT I'LL EVER WISH...
GET AWAY FROM THAT VAULT!
RIGHT! RIGHT!
MY HEARING IS COMING BACK! I THINK I COULD HEAR AN ATOMIC EXPLOSION IF SEVERAL BOMBS WENT OFF AT ONCE! THIS HAS BEEN A ROUGH DAY!
THAT'S WHY I'M PAYING YOU 30¢ AN HOUR! I HOPE YOU DON'T THINK A LITTLE HARDSHIP ENTITLES YOU TO ASK FOR A RAISE!
DON'T WORRY, UNCLE SCROOGE! IT DOESN'T TAKE A NOSTRILDAMUS TO SEE THERE'S NO FUTURE IN THAT!

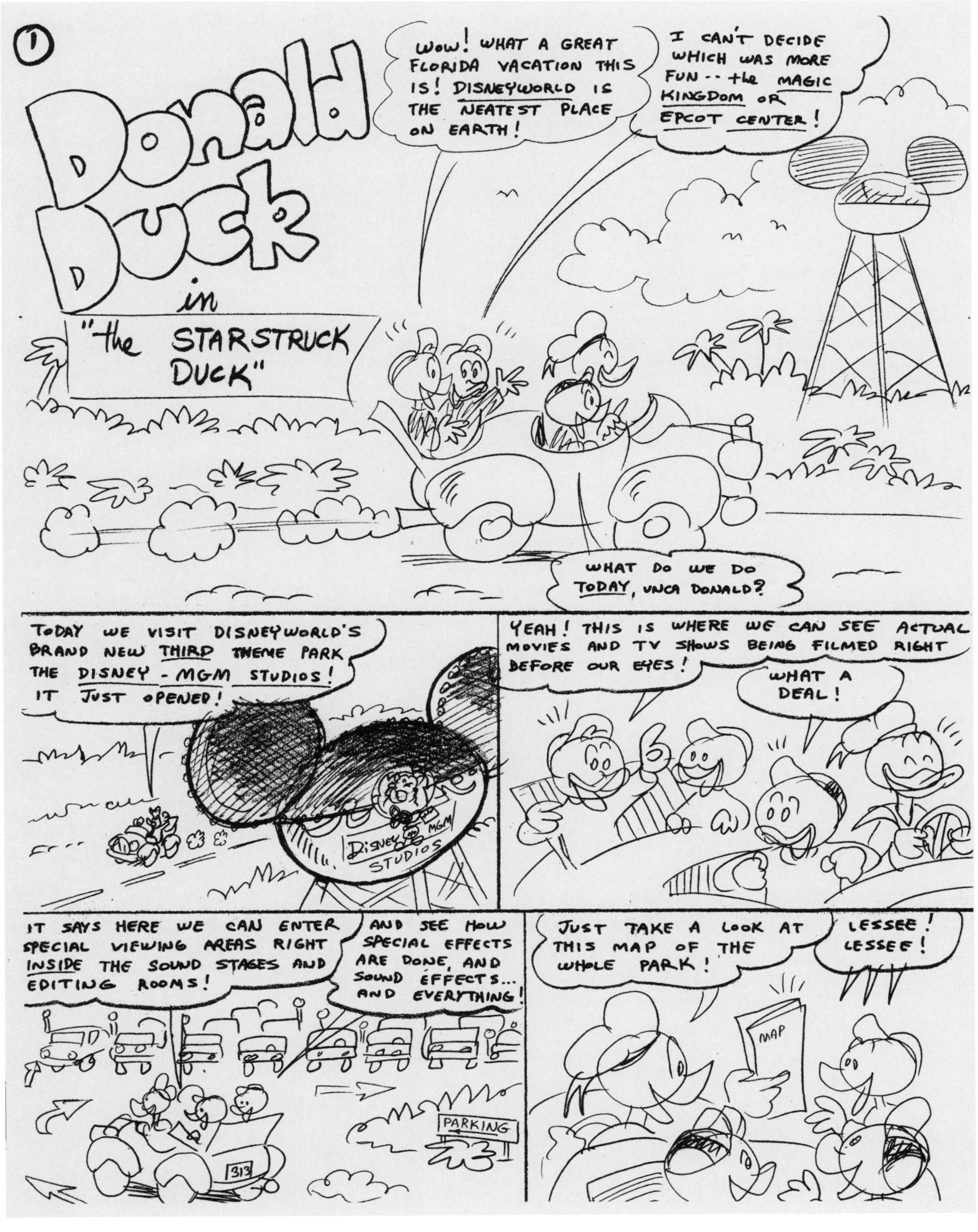
1
Donald Duck
in
"the STARSTRUCK DUCK"
WOW! WHAT A GREAT FLORIDA VACATION THIS IS! DISNEYWORLD IS THE NEATEST PLACE ON EARTH!
I CAN'T DECIDE WHICH WAS MORE FUN -- the MAGIC KINGDOM OR EPCOT CENTER!
WHAT DO WE DO TODAY, UNCA DONALD?
TODAY WE VISIT DISNEYWORLD'S BRAND NEW THIRD THEME PARK THE DISNEY-MGM STUDIOS! IT JUST OPENED!
DISNEY MGM STUDIOS
YEAH! THIS IS WHERE WE CAN SEE ACTUAL MOVIES AND TV SHOWS BEING FILMED RIGHT BEFORE OUR EYES!
WHAT A DEAL!
IT SAYS HERE WE CAN ENTER SPECIAL VIEWING AREAS RIGHT INSIDE THE SOUND STAGES AND EDITING ROOMS!
AND SEE HOW SPECIAL EFFECTS ARE DONE, AND SOUND EFFECTS... AND EVERYTHING!
PARKING
313
JUST TAKE A LOOK AT THIS MAP OF THE WHOLE PARK!
LESSEE! LESSEE!
MAP

("The Starstruck Duck" appears in rough, black and white form because a finished version was never created. See page 178 for the story behind the story.)

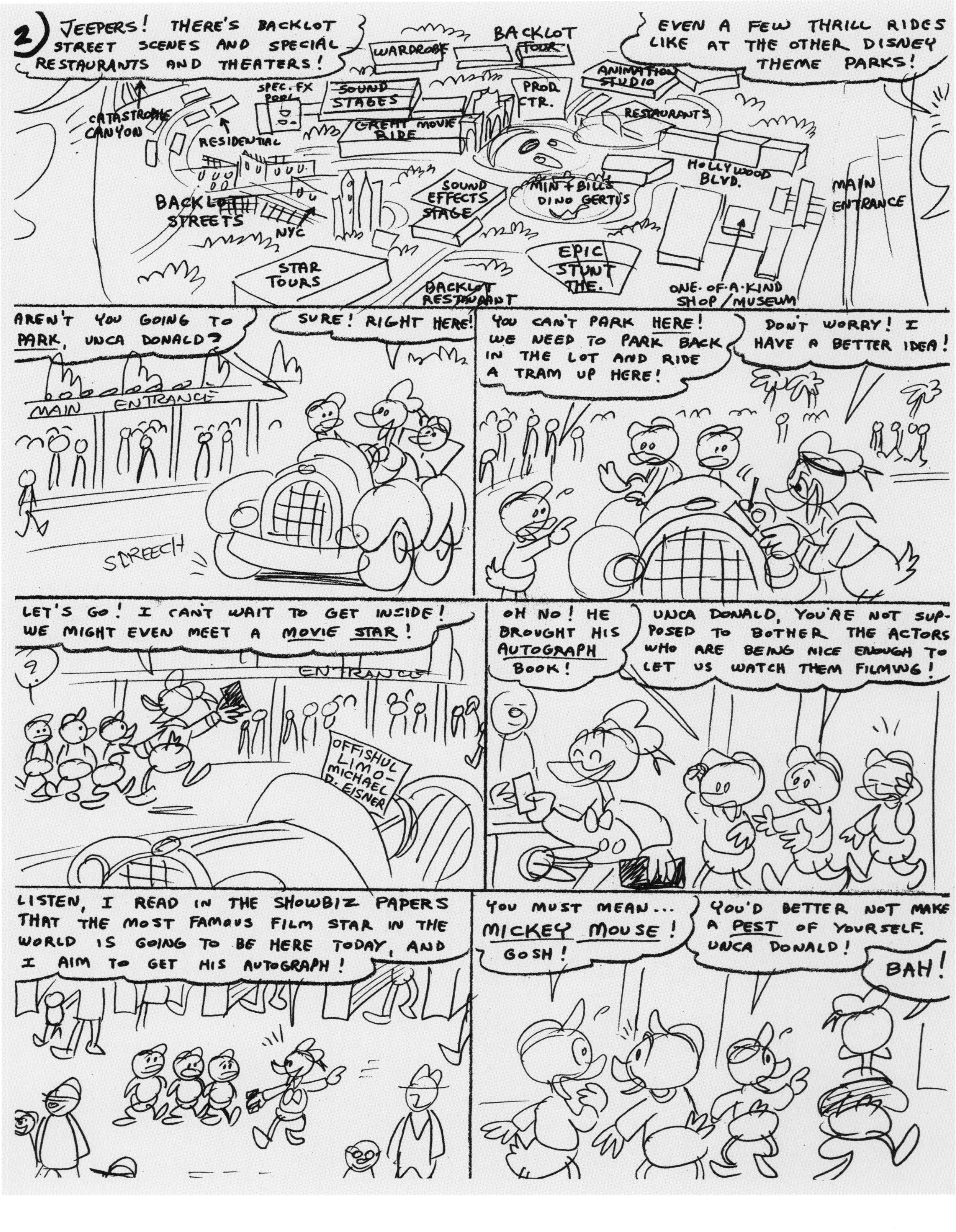
2) JEEPERS! THERE'S BACKLOT STREET SCENES AND SPECIAL RESTAURANTS AND THEATERS!
EVEN A FEW THRILL RIDES LIKE AT THE OTHER DISNEY THEME PARKS!
BACKLOT TOUR
WARDROBE
ANIMATION STUDIO
SPEC. FX POOL
SOUND STAGES
PROD. CTR.
CATASTROPHE CANYON
RESIDENTIAL
GREAT MOVIE RIDE
RESTAURANTS
HOLLYWOOD BLVD.
MAIN ENTRANCE
BACKLOT STREETS
NYC
SOUND EFFECTS STAGE
MIN + BILL'S DINO GERTIE'S
STAR TOURS
BACKLOT RESTAURANT
EPIC STUNT THE.
ONE-OF-A-KIND SHOP/MUSEUM
AREN'T YOU GOING TO PARK, UNCA DONALD?
SURE! RIGHT HERE!
MAIN ENTRANCE
SCREECH
YOU CAN'T PARK HERE! WE NEED TO PARK BACK IN THE LOT AND RIDE A TRAM UP HERE!
DON'T WORRY! I HAVE A BETTER IDEA!
LET'S GO! I CAN'T WAIT TO GET INSIDE! WE MIGHT EVEN MEET A MOVIE STAR!
?
ENTRANCE
OFFISHUL LIMO - MICHAEL D. EISNER
OH NO! HE BROUGHT HIS AUTOGRAPH BOOK!
UNCA DONALD, YOU'RE NOT SUPPOSED TO BOTHER THE ACTORS WHO ARE BEING NICE ENOUGH TO LET US WATCH THEM FILMING!
LISTEN, I READ IN THE SHOWBIZ PAPERS THAT THE MOST FAMOUS FILM STAR IN THE WORLD IS GOING TO BE HERE TODAY, AND I AIM TO GET HIS AUTOGRAPH!
YOU MUST MEAN... MICKEY MOUSE! GOSH!
YOU'D BETTER NOT MAKE A PEST OF YOURSELF, UNCA DONALD!
BAH!

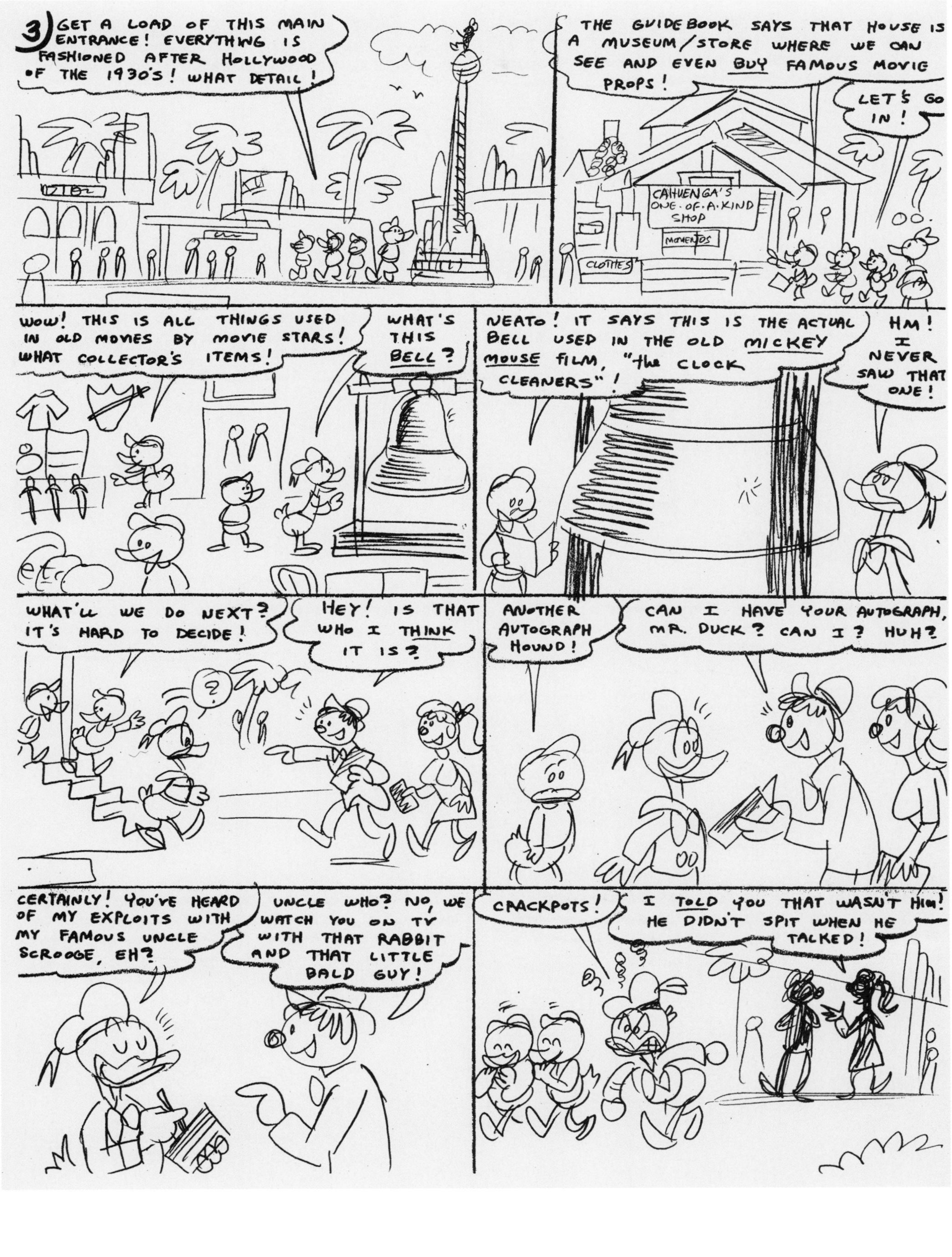
3
GET A LOAD OF THIS MAIN ENTRANCE! EVERYTHING IS FASHIONED AFTER HOLLYWOOD OF THE 1930'S! WHAT DETAIL!
THE GUIDEBOOK SAYS THAT HOUSE IS A MUSEUM/STORE WHERE WE CAN SEE AND EVEN BUY FAMOUS MOVIE PROPS!
LET'S GO IN!
CAHUENGA'S ONE·OF·A·KIND SHOP
MOMENTOS
CLOTHES
WOW! THIS IS ALL THINGS USED IN OLD MOVIES BY MOVIE STARS! WHAT COLLECTOR'S ITEMS!
WHAT'S THIS BELL?
NEATO! IT SAYS THIS IS THE ACTUAL BELL USED IN THE OLD MICKEY MOUSE FILM, "the CLOCK CLEANERS"!
HM! I NEVER SAW THAT ONE!
WHAT'LL WE DO NEXT? IT'S HARD TO DECIDE!
HEY! IS THAT WHO I THINK IT IS?
ANOTHER AUTOGRAPH HOUND!
CAN I HAVE YOUR AUTOGRAPH, MR. DUCK? CAN I? HUH?
CERTAINLY! YOU'VE HEARD OF MY EXPLOITS WITH MY FAMOUS UNCLE SCROOGE, EH?
UNCLE WHO? NO, WE WATCH YOU ON TV WITH THAT RABBIT AND THAT LITTLE BALD GUY!
CRACKPOTS!
I TOLD YOU THAT WASN'T HIM! HE DIDN'T SPIT WHEN HE TALKED!

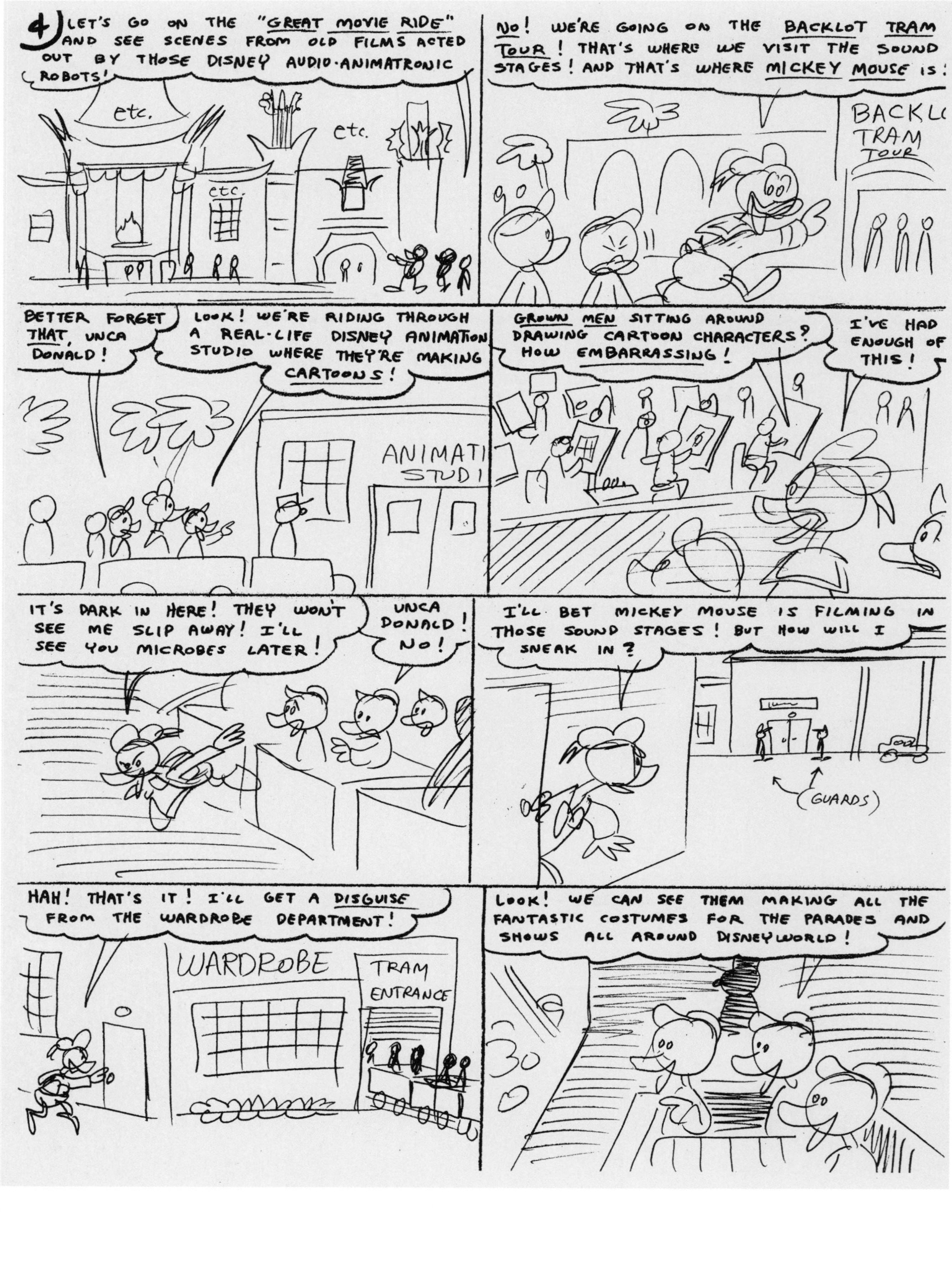
4
LET'S GO ON THE "GREAT MOVIE RIDE" AND SEE SCENES FROM OLD FILMS ACTED OUT BY THOSE DISNEY AUDIO-ANIMATRONIC ROBOTS!
etc.
etc.
etc.
NO! WE'RE GOING ON THE BACKLOT TRAM TOUR! THAT'S WHERE WE VISIT THE SOUND STAGES! AND THAT'S WHERE MICKEY MOUSE IS!
BACKLO
TRAM
TOUR
BETTER FORGET THAT, UNCA DONALD!
LOOK! WE'RE RIDING THROUGH A REAL-LIFE DISNEY ANIMATION STUDIO WHERE THEY'RE MAKING CARTOONS!
ANIMATI
STUDI
GROWN MEN SITTING AROUND DRAWING CARTOON CHARACTERS? HOW EMBARRASSING!
I'VE HAD ENOUGH OF THIS!
IT'S DARK IN HERE! THEY WON'T SEE ME SLIP AWAY! I'LL SEE YOU MICROBES LATER!
UNCA DONALD! NO!
I'LL BET MICKEY MOUSE IS FILMING IN THOSE SOUND STAGES! BUT HOW WILL I SNEAK IN?
(GUARDS)
HAH! THAT'S IT! I'LL GET A DISGUISE FROM THE WARDROBE DEPARTMENT!
WARDROBE
TRAM ENTRANCE
LOOK! WE CAN SEE THEM MAKING ALL THE FANTASTIC COSTUMES FOR THE PARADES AND SHOWS ALL AROUND DISNEYWORLD!

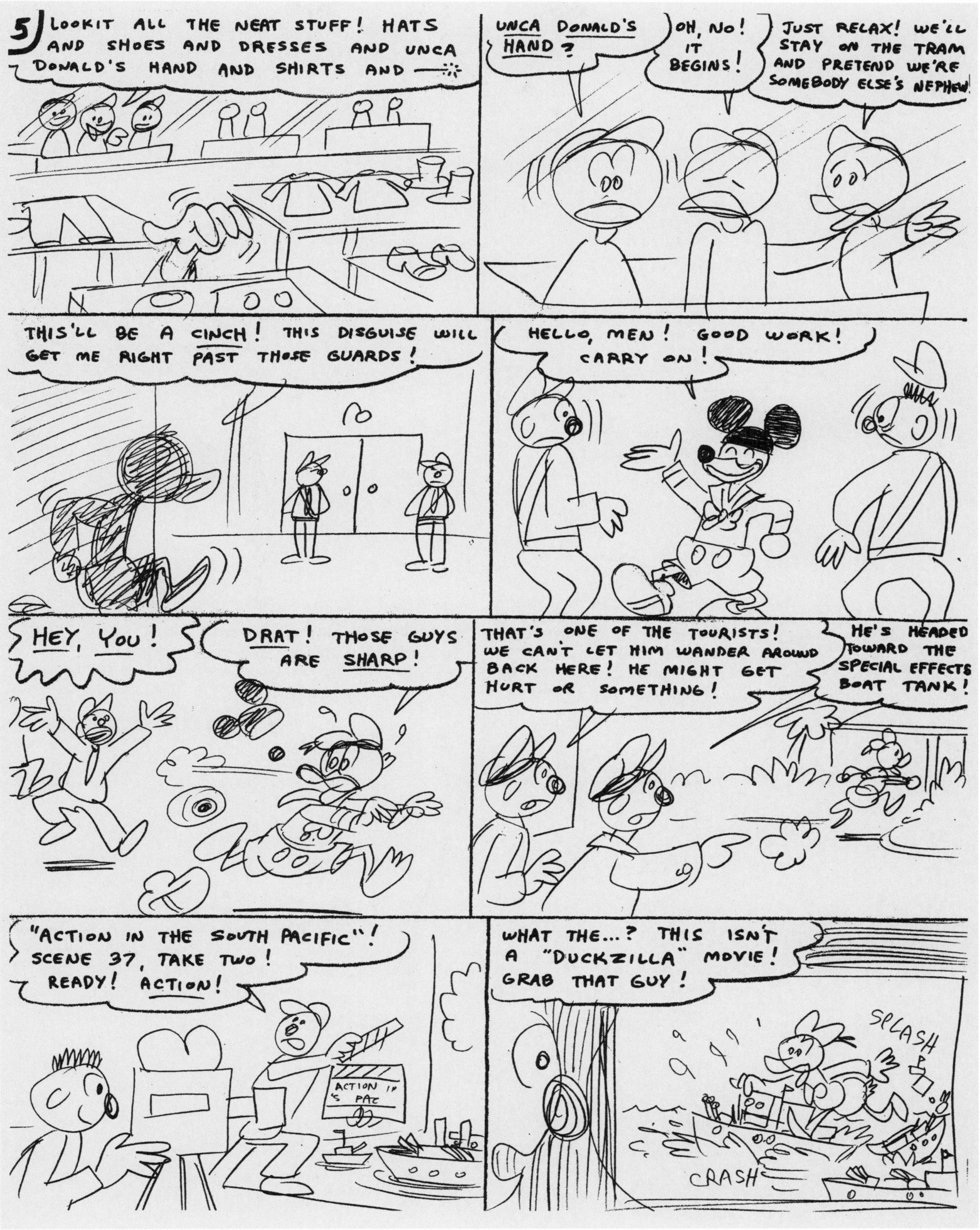
5
LOOKIT ALL THE NEAT STUFF! HATS AND SHOES AND DRESSES AND UNCA DONALD'S HAND AND SHIRTS AND —
UNCA DONALD'S HAND?
OH, NO! IT BEGINS!
JUST RELAX! WE'LL STAY ON THE TRAM AND PRETEND WE'RE SOMEBODY ELSE'S NEPHEW!
THIS'LL BE A CINCH! THIS DISGUISE WILL GET ME RIGHT PAST THOSE GUARDS!
HELLO, MEN! GOOD WORK! CARRY ON!
HEY, YOU!
DRAT! THOSE GUYS ARE SHARP!
THAT'S ONE OF THE TOURISTS! WE CAN'T LET HIM WANDER AROUND BACK HERE! HE MIGHT GET HURT OR SOMETHING!
HE'S HEADED TOWARD THE SPECIAL EFFECTS BOAT TANK!
"ACTION IN THE SOUTH PACIFIC"! SCENE 37, TAKE TWO! READY! ACTION!
ACTION IN S PAC
WHAT THE...? THIS ISN'T A "DUCKZILLA" MOVIE! GRAB THAT GUY!
SPLASH
CRASH

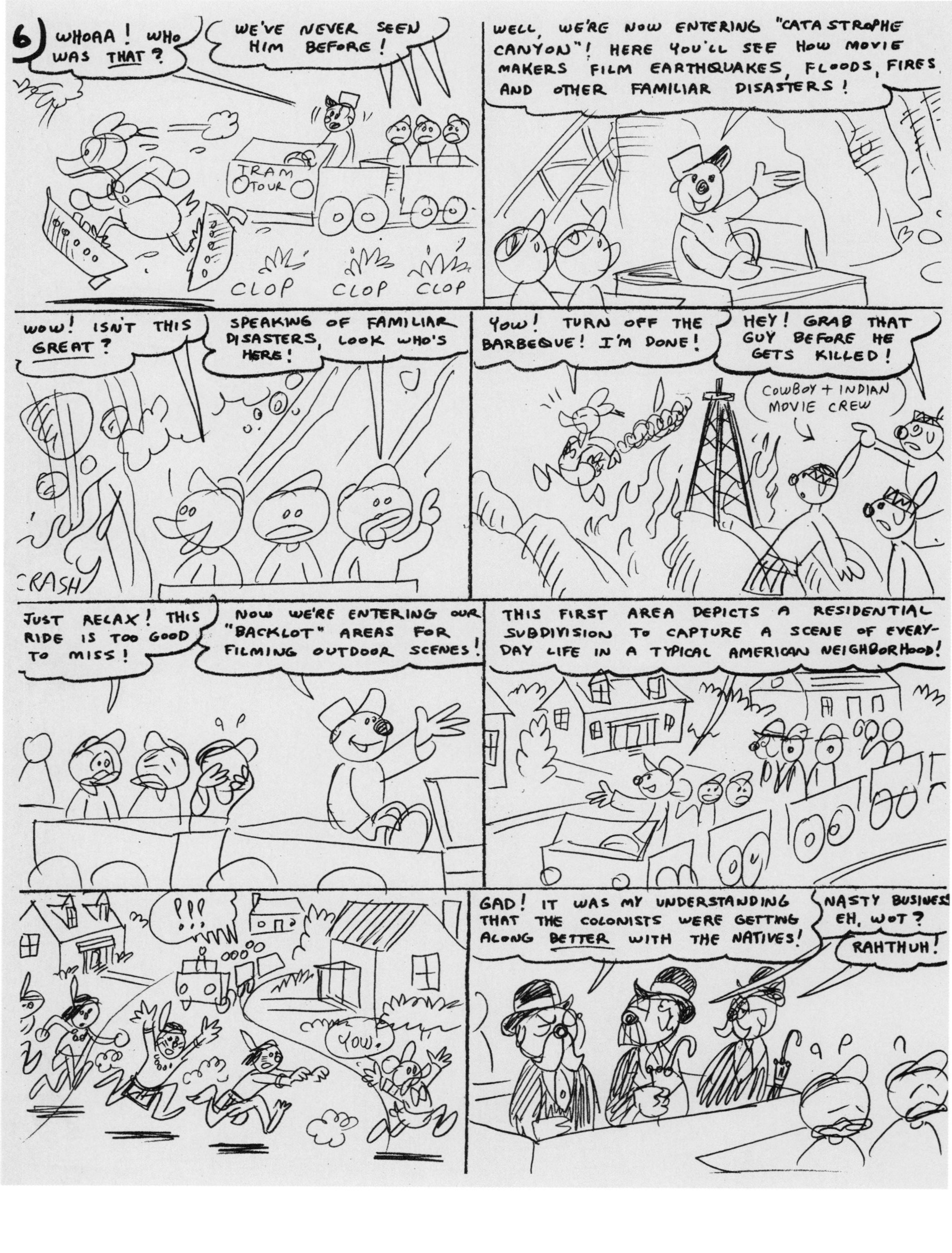
6)
WHOAA! WHO WAS THAT?
WE'VE NEVER SEEN HIM BEFORE!
TRAM TOUR
CLOP CLOP CLOP
WELL, WE'RE NOW ENTERING "CATASTROPHE CANYON"! HERE YOU'LL SEE HOW MOVIE MAKERS FILM EARTHQUAKES, FLOODS, FIRES AND OTHER FAMILIAR DISASTERS!
WOW! ISN'T THIS GREAT?
SPEAKING OF FAMILIAR DISASTERS, LOOK WHO'S HERE!
CRASH
YOW! TURN OFF THE BARBEQUE! I'M DONE!
HEY! GRAB THAT GUY BEFORE HE GETS KILLED!
COWBOY + INDIAN MOVIE CREW
JUST RELAX! THIS RIDE IS TOO GOOD TO MISS!
NOW WE'RE ENTERING OUR "BACKLOT" AREAS FOR FILMING OUTDOOR SCENES!
THIS FIRST AREA DEPICTS A RESIDENTIAL SUBDIVISION TO CAPTURE A SCENE OF EVERY-DAY LIFE IN A TYPICAL AMERICAN NEIGHBORHOOD!
!??
YOW!
GAD! IT WAS MY UNDERSTANDING THAT THE COLONISTS WERE GETTING ALONG BETTER WITH THE NATIVES!
NASTY BUSINESS EH, WOT?
RAHTHUH!

7)
THERE HE GOES! HE'S IN THE "NEW YORK" BACKLOT SET!
HA! I'LL LOSE THESE GUARDS IN THIS ALLEY!
ZOW!
CRASH
RIP
KLUNK!
CREEAK!
CLUNK!
THAT WAS A GREAT BACKSTAGE TOUR! WHAT'S NEXT?
LET'S GO TO THE "EPIC STUNT THEATER" AND SEE HOW MOVIE STUNTMEN WORK!
CRASH
WHEW! I NEED TO LAY LOW AND REST A MOMENT! KNOCKING OVER THE CHRYSLER BUILDING CAN WEAR A BODY OUT!
HA HA! THIS IS COOL! THAT COWBOY THREW THE OTHER ONE OVER THE BAR!
THE PROGRAM SAYS THIS IS WHEN THEY SWITCH HIM FOR A DUMMY!
CRASH
POW
WATCH IT, TEX! YOU ALMOST LANDED ON ME! I OUGHTTA—
WHIT!

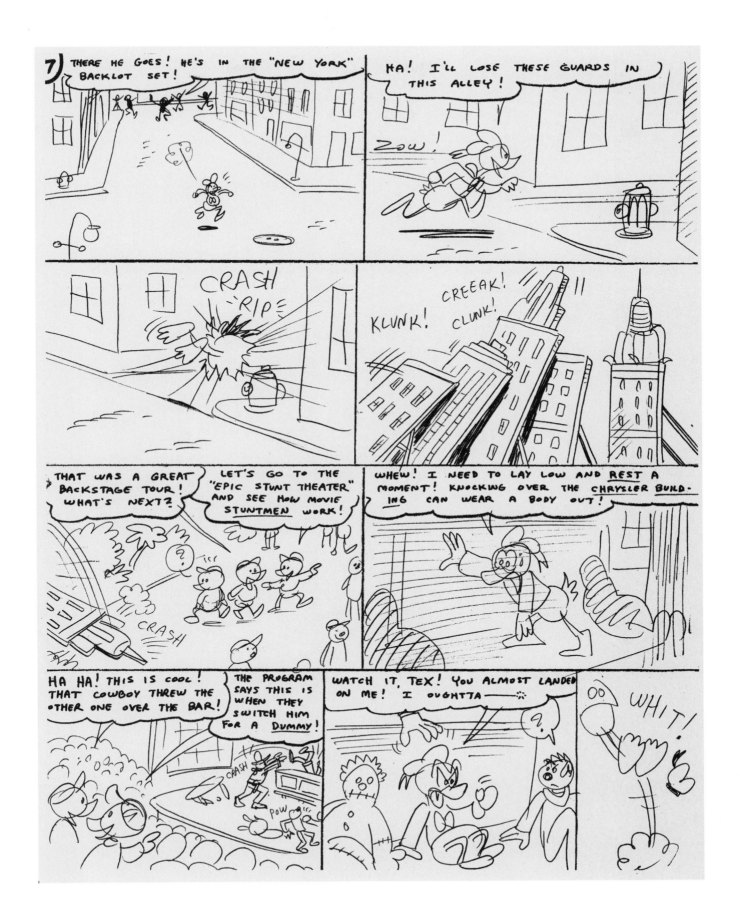

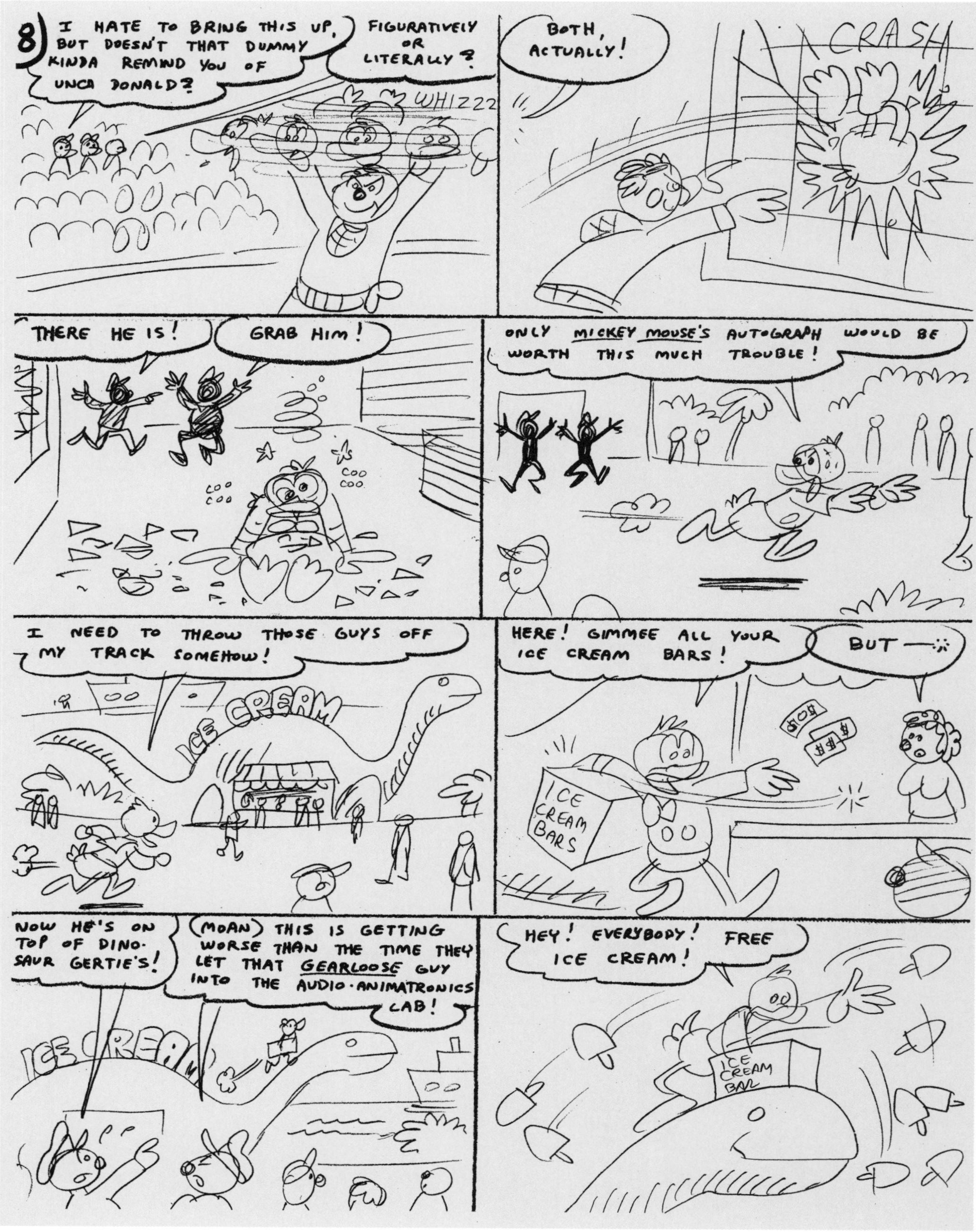
8)
I HATE TO BRING THIS UP, BUT DOESN'T THAT DUMMY KINDA REMIND YOU OF UNCA DONALD?
FIGURATIVELY OR LITERALLY?
WHIZZZ
BOTH, ACTUALLY!
CRASH
THERE HE IS!
GRAB HIM!
COO COO
COO COO
ONLY MICKEY MOUSE'S AUTOGRAPH WOULD BE WORTH THIS MUCH TROUBLE!
I NEED TO THROW THOSE GUYS OFF MY TRACK SOMEHOW!
ICE CREAM
HERE! GIMMEE ALL YOUR ICE CREAM BARS!
BUT —
ICE CREAM BARS
NOW HE'S ON TOP OF DINO-SAUR GERTIE'S!
(MOAN) THIS IS GETTING WORSE THAN THE TIME THEY LET THAT GEARLOOSE GUY INTO THE AUDIO-ANIMATRONICS LAB!
ICE CREAM
HEY! EVERYBODY! FREE ICE CREAM!
ICE CREAM BAR

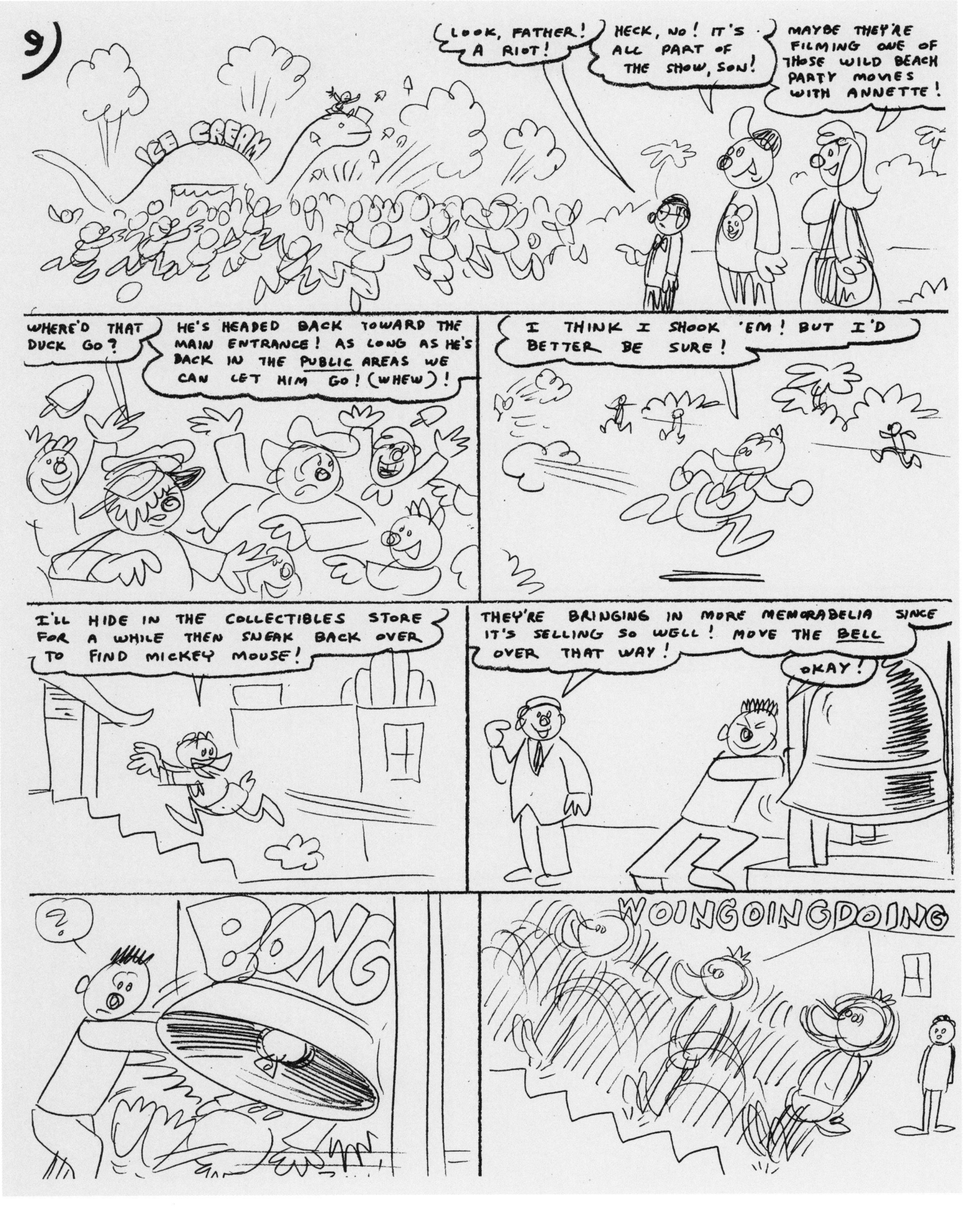
9)
LOOK, FATHER! A RIOT!
HECK, NO! IT'S ALL PART OF THE SHOW, SON!
MAYBE THEY'RE FILMING ONE OF THOSE WILD BEACH PARTY MOVIES WITH ANNETTE!
ICE CREAM
WHERE'D THAT DUCK GO?
HE'S HEADED BACK TOWARD THE MAIN ENTRANCE! AS LONG AS HE'S BACK IN THE PUBLIC AREAS WE CAN LET HIM GO! (WHEW)!
I THINK I SHOOK 'EM! BUT I'D BETTER BE SURE!
I'LL HIDE IN THE COLLECTIBLES STORE FOR A WHILE THEN SNEAK BACK OVER TO FIND MICKEY MOUSE!
THEY'RE BRINGING IN MORE MEMORABELIA SINCE IT'S SELLING SO WELL! MOVE THE BELL OVER THAT WAY!
OKAY!
?
BONG
WOINGOINGDOING

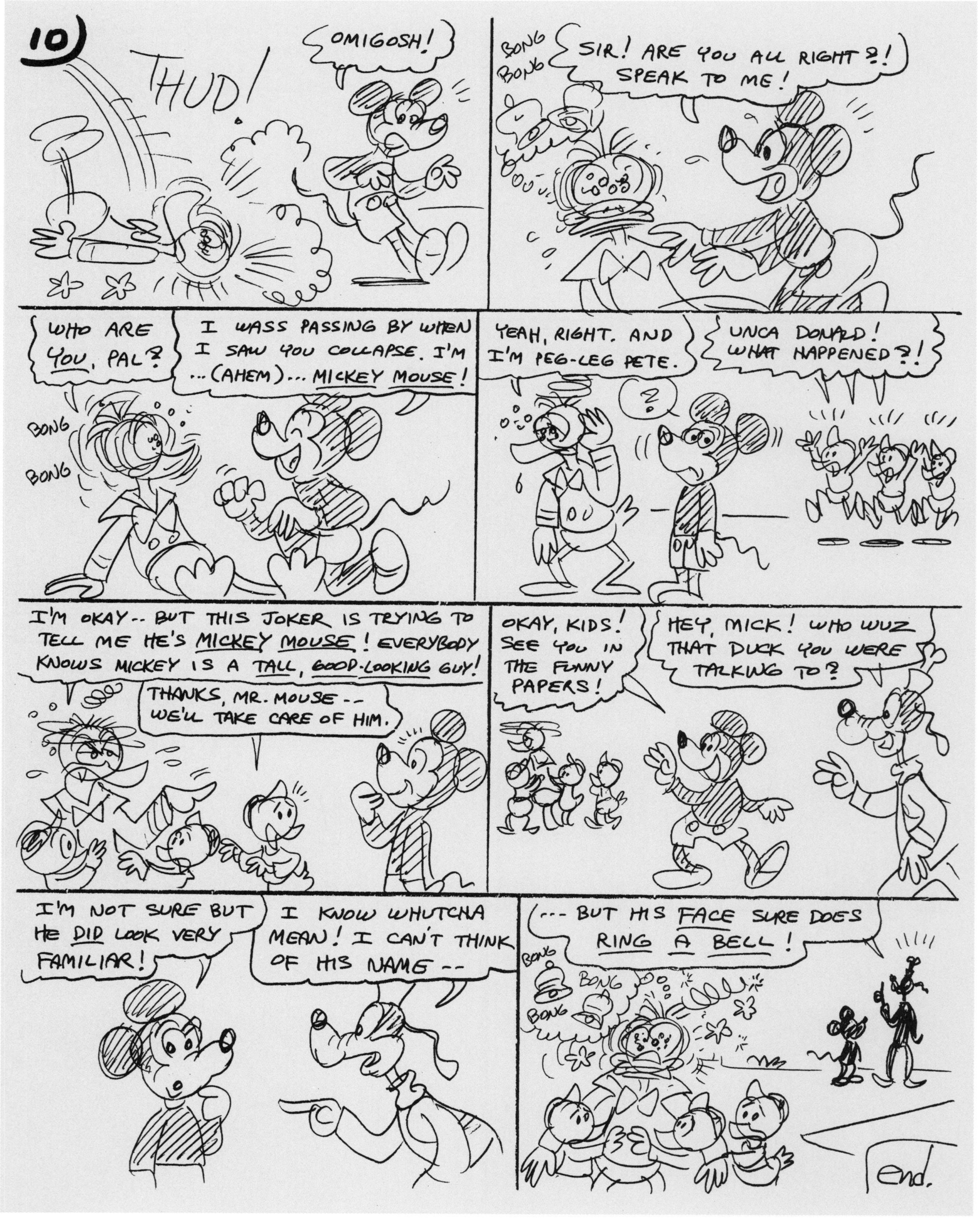
10)
THUD!
OMIGOSH!
BONG BONG
SIR! ARE YOU ALL RIGHT?! SPEAK TO ME!
WHO ARE YOU, PAL?
I WASS PASSING BY WHEN I SAW YOU COLLAPSE. I'M ...(AHEM)... MICKEY MOUSE!
BONG
BONG
YEAH, RIGHT. AND I'M PEG-LEG PETE.
UNCA DONALD! WHAT HAPPENED?!
I'M OKAY-- BUT THIS JOKER IS TRYING TO TELL ME HE'S MICKEY MOUSE! EVERYBODY KNOWS MICKEY IS A TALL, GOOD-LOOKING GUY!
THANKS, MR. MOUSE -- WE'LL TAKE CARE OF HIM.
OKAY, KIDS! SEE YOU IN THE FUNNY PAPERS!
HEY, MICK! WHO WUZ THAT DUCK YOU WERE TALKING TO?
I'M NOT SURE BUT HE DID LOOK VERY FAMILIAR!
I KNOW WHUTCHA MEAN! I CAN'T THINK OF HIS NAME --
--- BUT HIS FACE SURE DOES RING A BELL!
BONG
BONG
BONG
End.

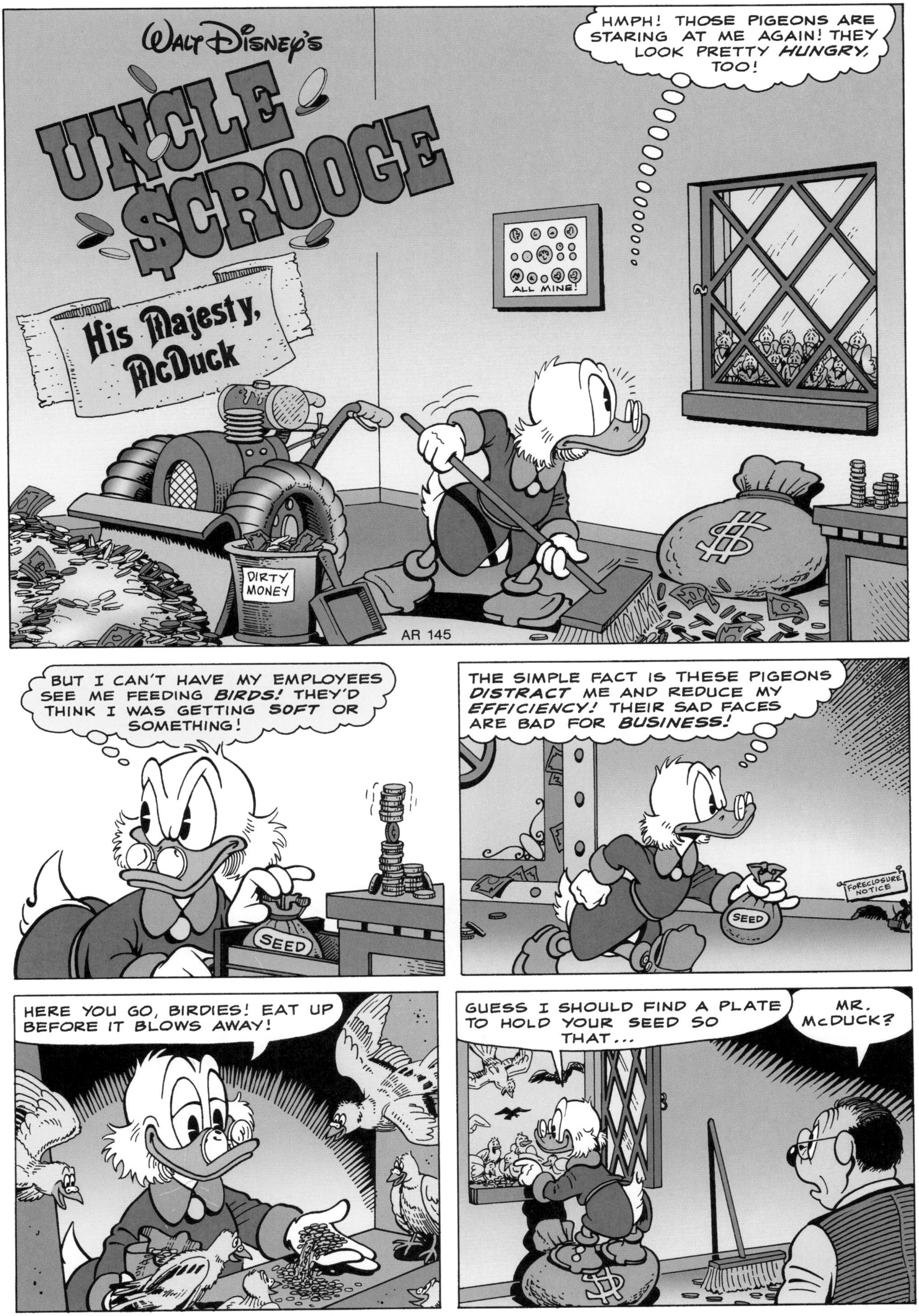
WALT DISNEY'S
UNCLE $CROOGE
His Majesty, McDuck
HMPH! THOSE PIGEONS ARE STARING AT ME AGAIN! THEY LOOK PRETTY HUNGRY, TOO!
ALL MINE!
DIRTY MONEY
AR 145
BUT I CAN'T HAVE MY EMPLOYEES SEE ME FEEDING BIRDS! THEY'D THINK I WAS GETTING SOFT OR SOMETHING!
SEED
THE SIMPLE FACT IS THESE PIGEONS DISTRACT ME AND REDUCE MY EFFICIENCY! THEIR SAD FACES ARE BAD FOR BUSINESS!
FORECLOSURE NOTICE
SEED
HERE YOU GO, BIRDIES! EAT UP BEFORE IT BLOWS AWAY!
GUESS I SHOULD FIND A PLATE TO HOLD YOUR SEED SO THAT...
MR. McDUCK?

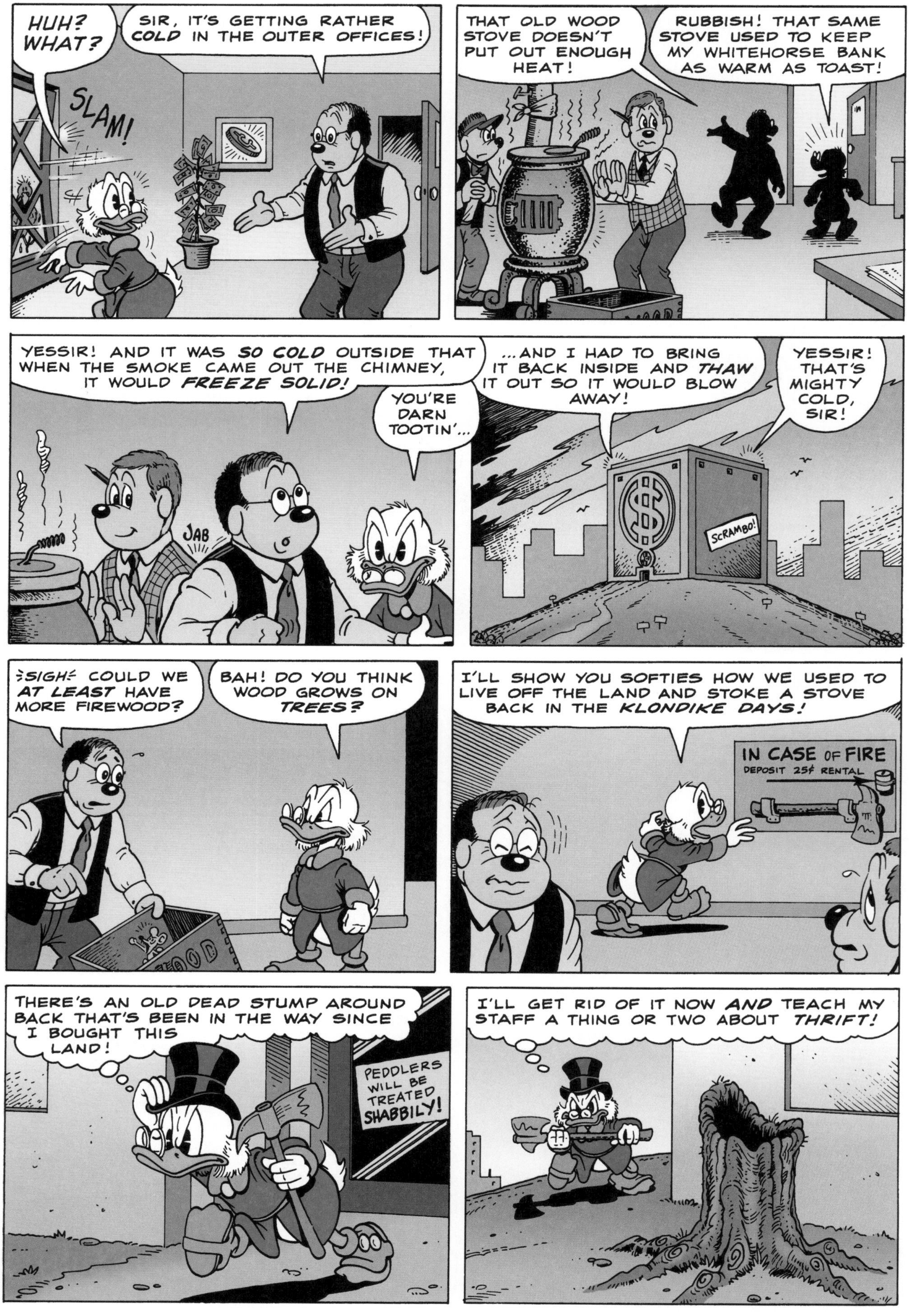
HUH? WHAT?
SIR, IT'S GETTING RATHER COLD IN THE OUTER OFFICES!
SLAM!
THAT OLD WOOD STOVE DOESN'T PUT OUT ENOUGH HEAT!
RUBBISH! THAT SAME STOVE USED TO KEEP MY WHITEHORSE BANK AS WARM AS TOAST!
YESSIR! AND IT WAS SO COLD OUTSIDE THAT WHEN THE SMOKE CAME OUT THE CHIMNEY, IT WOULD FREEZE SOLID!
YOU'RE DARN TOOTIN'...
JAB
...AND I HAD TO BRING IT BACK INSIDE AND THAW IT OUT SO IT WOULD BLOW AWAY!
YESSIR! THAT'S MIGHTY COLD, SIR!
SCRAMBO!
≶SIGH≶ COULD WE AT LEAST HAVE MORE FIREWOOD?
BAH! DO YOU THINK WOOD GROWS ON TREES?
I'LL SHOW YOU SOFTIES HOW WE USED TO LIVE OFF THE LAND AND STOKE A STOVE BACK IN THE KLONDIKE DAYS!
IN CASE OF FIRE
DEPOSIT 25¢ RENTAL
THERE'S AN OLD DEAD STUMP AROUND BACK THAT'S BEEN IN THE WAY SINCE I BOUGHT THIS LAND!
PEDDLERS WILL BE TREATED SHABBILY!
I'LL GET RID OF IT NOW AND TEACH MY STAFF A THING OR TWO ABOUT THRIFT!

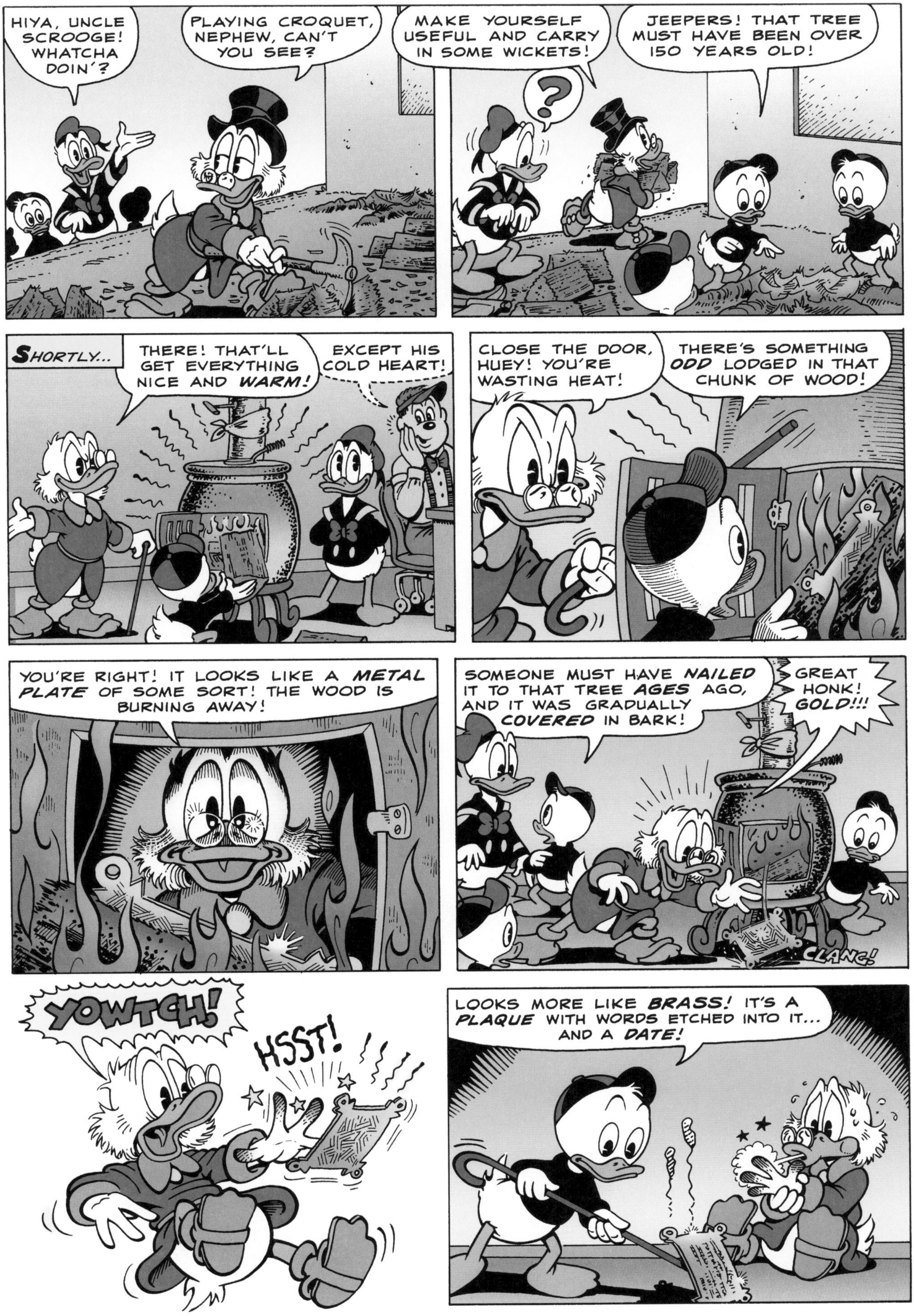
HIYA, UNCLE SCROOGE! WHATCHA DOIN'?
PLAYING CROQUET, NEPHEW, CAN'T YOU SEE?
MAKE YOURSELF USEFUL AND CARRY IN SOME WICKETS!
?
JEEPERS! THAT TREE MUST HAVE BEEN OVER 150 YEARS OLD!
SHORTLY...
THERE! THAT'LL GET EVERYTHING NICE AND WARM!
EXCEPT HIS COLD HEART!
CLOSE THE DOOR, HUEY! YOU'RE WASTING HEAT!
THERE'S SOMETHING ODD LODGED IN THAT CHUNK OF WOOD!
YOU'RE RIGHT! IT LOOKS LIKE A METAL PLATE OF SOME SORT! THE WOOD IS BURNING AWAY!
SOMEONE MUST HAVE NAILED IT TO THAT TREE AGES AGO, AND IT WAS GRADUALLY COVERED IN BARK!
GREAT HONK! GOLD!!!
CLANG!
YOWTCH!
HSST!
LOOKS MORE LIKE BRASS! IT'S A PLAQUE WITH WORDS ETCHED INTO IT... AND A DATE!

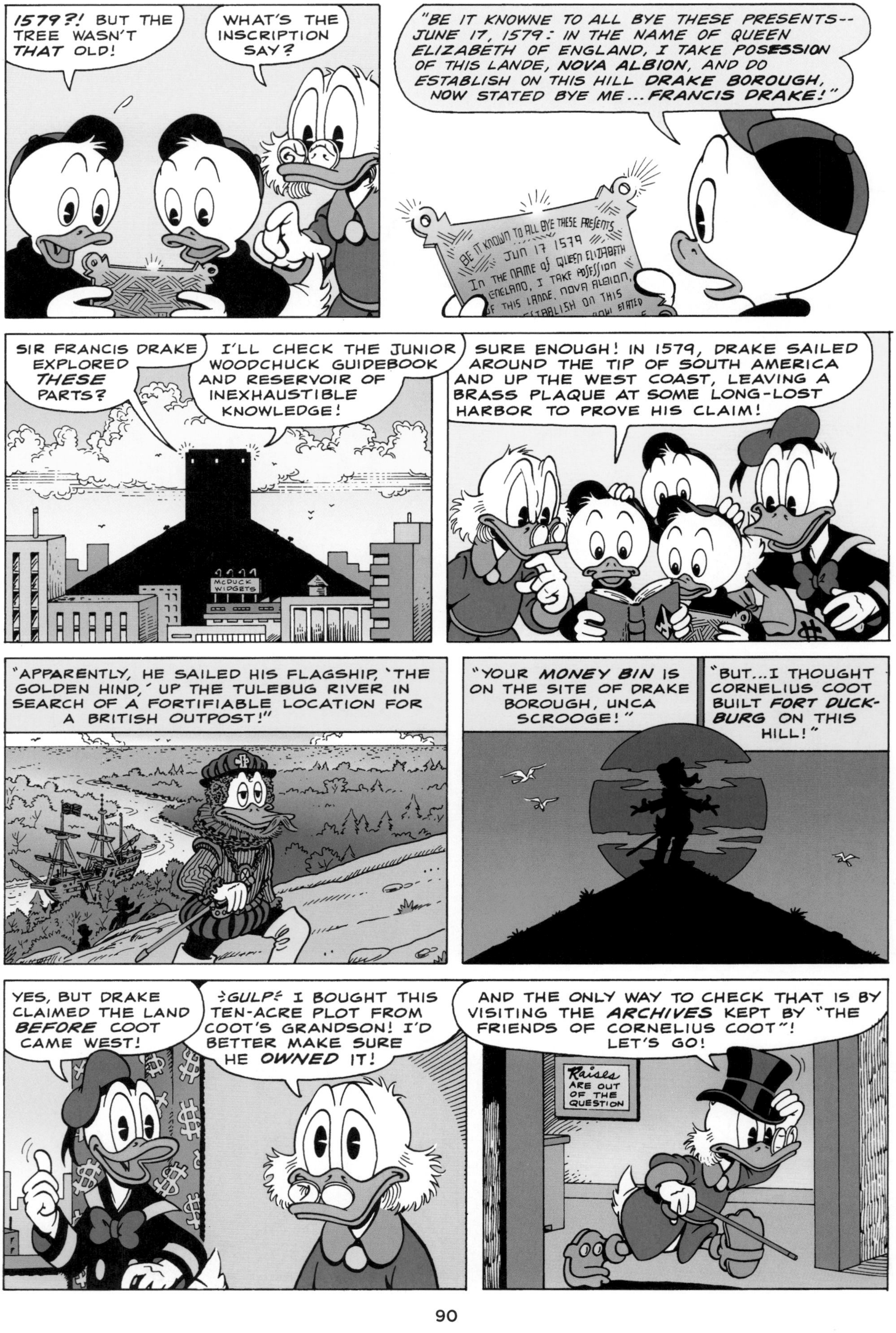
1579?! BUT THE TREE WASN'T THAT OLD!
WHAT'S THE INSCRIPTION SAY?
"BE IT KNOWNE TO ALL BYE THESE PRESENTS-- JUNE 17, 1579: IN THE NAME OF QUEEN ELIZABETH OF ENGLAND, I TAKE POSESSION OF THIS LANDE, NOVA ALBION, AND DO ESTABLISH ON THIS HILL DRAKE BOROUGH, NOW STATED BYE ME... FRANCIS DRAKE!"
BE IT KNOWN TO ALL BYE THESE PRESENTS
JUN 17 1579
IN THE NAME OF QUEEN ELIZABETH
ENGLAND, I TAKE POSESSION
OF THIS LANDE, NOVA ALBION,
ESTABLISH ON THIS
SIR FRANCIS DRAKE EXPLORED THESE PARTS?
I'LL CHECK THE JUNIOR WOODCHUCK GUIDEBOOK AND RESERVOIR OF INEXHAUSTIBLE KNOWLEDGE!
McDUCK WIDGETS
SURE ENOUGH! IN 1579, DRAKE SAILED AROUND THE TIP OF SOUTH AMERICA AND UP THE WEST COAST, LEAVING A BRASS PLAQUE AT SOME LONG-LOST HARBOR TO PROVE HIS CLAIM!
"APPARENTLY, HE SAILED HIS FLAGSHIP, 'THE GOLDEN HIND,' UP THE TULEBUG RIVER IN SEARCH OF A FORTIFIABLE LOCATION FOR A BRITISH OUTPOST!"
"YOUR MONEY BIN IS ON THE SITE OF DRAKE BOROUGH, UNCA SCROOGE!"
"BUT... I THOUGHT CORNELIUS COOT BUILT FORT DUCKBURG ON THIS HILL!"
YES, BUT DRAKE CLAIMED THE LAND BEFORE COOT CAME WEST!
GULP I BOUGHT THIS TEN-ACRE PLOT FROM COOT'S GRANDSON! I'D BETTER MAKE SURE HE OWNED IT!
AND THE ONLY WAY TO CHECK THAT IS BY VISITING THE ARCHIVES KEPT BY "THE FRIENDS OF CORNELIUS COOT"! LET'S GO!
Raises ARE OUT OF THE QUESTION

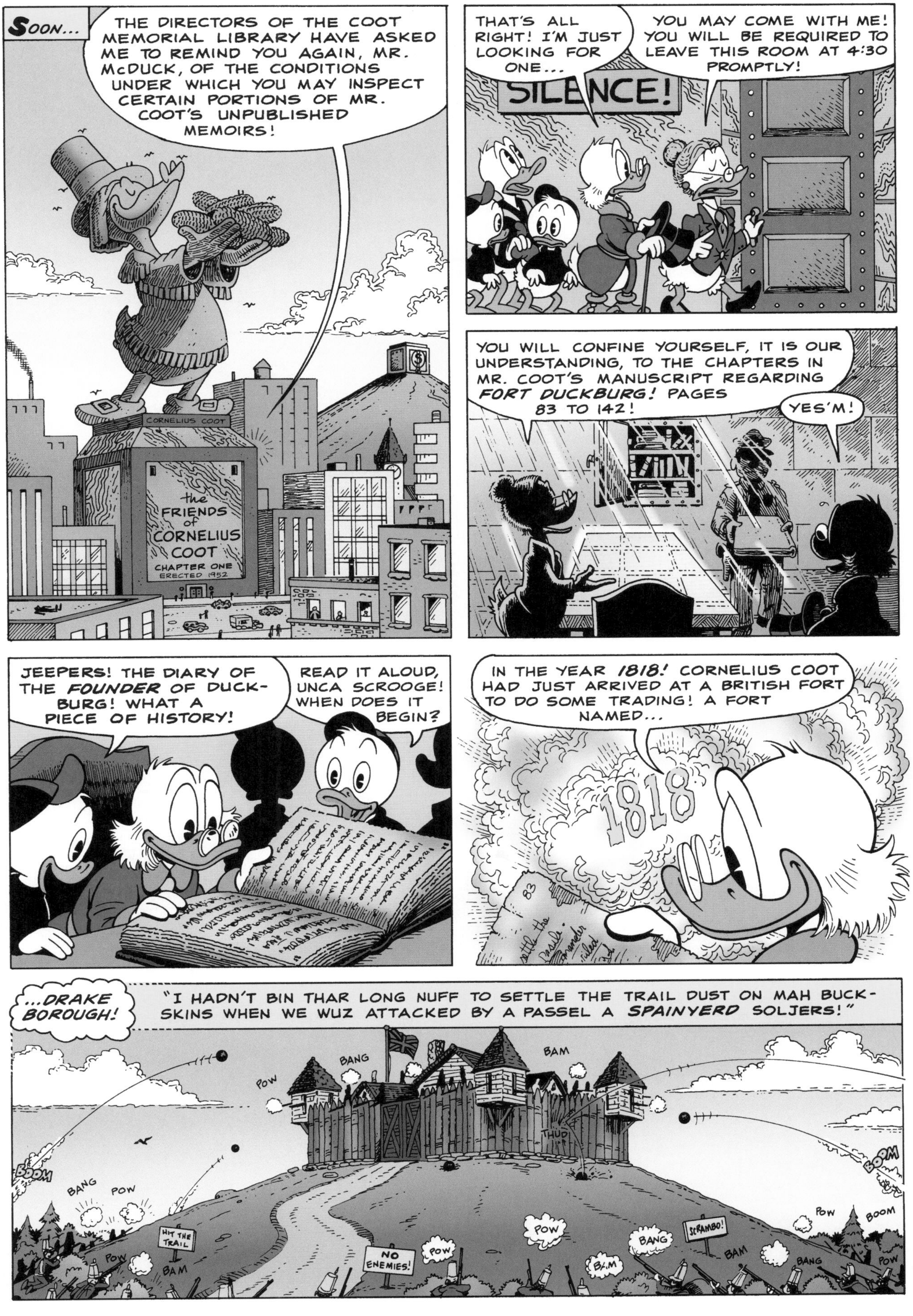
SOON...
THE DIRECTORS OF THE COOT MEMORIAL LIBRARY HAVE ASKED ME TO REMIND YOU AGAIN, MR. McDUCK, OF THE CONDITIONS UNDER WHICH YOU MAY INSPECT CERTAIN PORTIONS OF MR. COOT'S UNPUBLISHED MEMOIRS!
CORNELIUS COOT
the FRIENDS of CORNELIUS COOT CHAPTER ONE ERECTED 1952
THAT'S ALL RIGHT! I'M JUST LOOKING FOR ONE...
YOU MAY COME WITH ME! YOU WILL BE REQUIRED TO LEAVE THIS ROOM AT 4:30 PROMPTLY!
SILENCE!
YOU WILL CONFINE YOURSELF, IT IS OUR UNDERSTANDING, TO THE CHAPTERS IN MR. COOT'S MANUSCRIPT REGARDING FORT DUCKBURG! PAGES 83 TO 142!
YES'M!
JEEPERS! THE DIARY OF THE FOUNDER OF DUCKBURG! WHAT A PIECE OF HISTORY!
READ IT ALOUD, UNCA SCROOGE! WHEN DOES IT BEGIN?
IN THE YEAR 1818! CORNELIUS COOT HAD JUST ARRIVED AT A BRITISH FORT TO DO SOME TRADING! A FORT NAMED...
1818
...DRAKE BOROUGH!
"I HADN'T BIN THAR LONG NUFF TO SETTLE THE TRAIL DUST ON MAH BUCKSKINS WHEN WE WUZ ATTACKED BY A PASSEL A SPAINYERD SOLJERS!"
BANG
POW
BAM
THUD
BOOM
HIT THE TRAIL
NO ENEMIES!
SCRAMBO!
BLAM

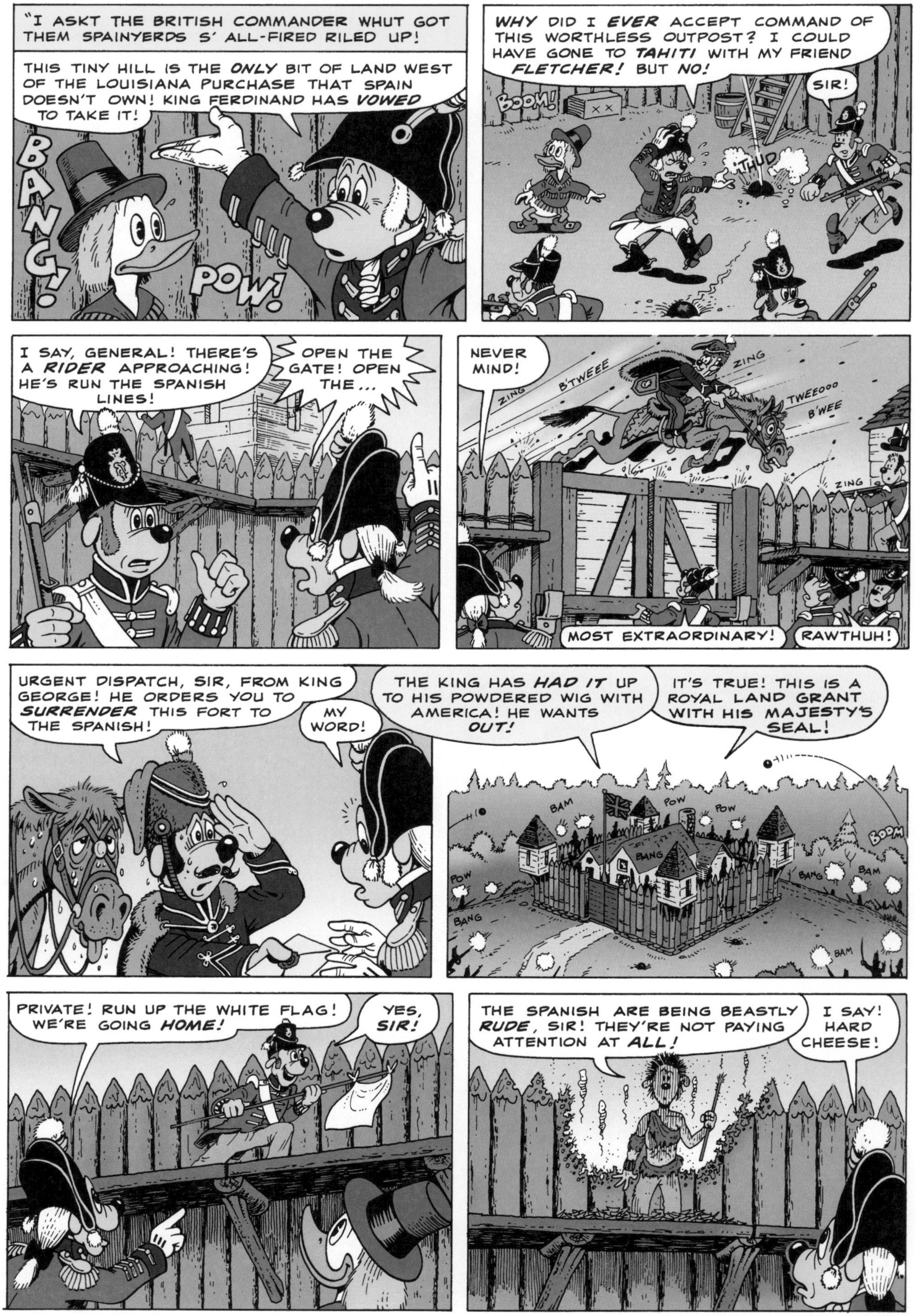
"I ASKT THE BRITISH COMMANDER WHUT GOT THEM SPAINYERDS S' ALL-FIRED RILED UP!
THIS TINY HILL IS THE ONLY BIT OF LAND WEST OF THE LOUISIANA PURCHASE THAT SPAIN DOESN'T OWN! KING FERDINAND HAS VOWED TO TAKE IT!
BANG!
POW!
WHY DID I EVER ACCEPT COMMAND OF THIS WORTHLESS OUTPOST? I COULD HAVE GONE TO TAHITI WITH MY FRIEND FLETCHER! BUT NO!
SIR!
BOOM!
THUD
I SAY, GENERAL! THERE'S A RIDER APPROACHING! HE'S RUN THE SPANISH LINES!
OPEN THE GATE! OPEN THE...
NEVER MIND!
ZING
B'TWEEE
ZING
TWEEooo
B'WEE
ZING
MOST EXTRAORDINARY!
RAWTHUH!
URGENT DISPATCH, SIR, FROM KING GEORGE! HE ORDERS YOU TO SURRENDER THIS FORT TO THE SPANISH!
MY WORD!
THE KING HAS HAD IT UP TO HIS POWDERED WIG WITH AMERICA! HE WANTS OUT!
IT'S TRUE! THIS IS A ROYAL LAND GRANT WITH HIS MAJESTY'S SEAL!
BAM
POW
POW
BOOM
BANG
POW
BANG
BAM
BANG
BAM
PRIVATE! RUN UP THE WHITE FLAG! WE'RE GOING HOME!
YES, SIR!
THE SPANISH ARE BEING BEASTLY RUDE, SIR! THEY'RE NOT PAYING ATTENTION AT ALL!
I SAY! HARD CHEESE!

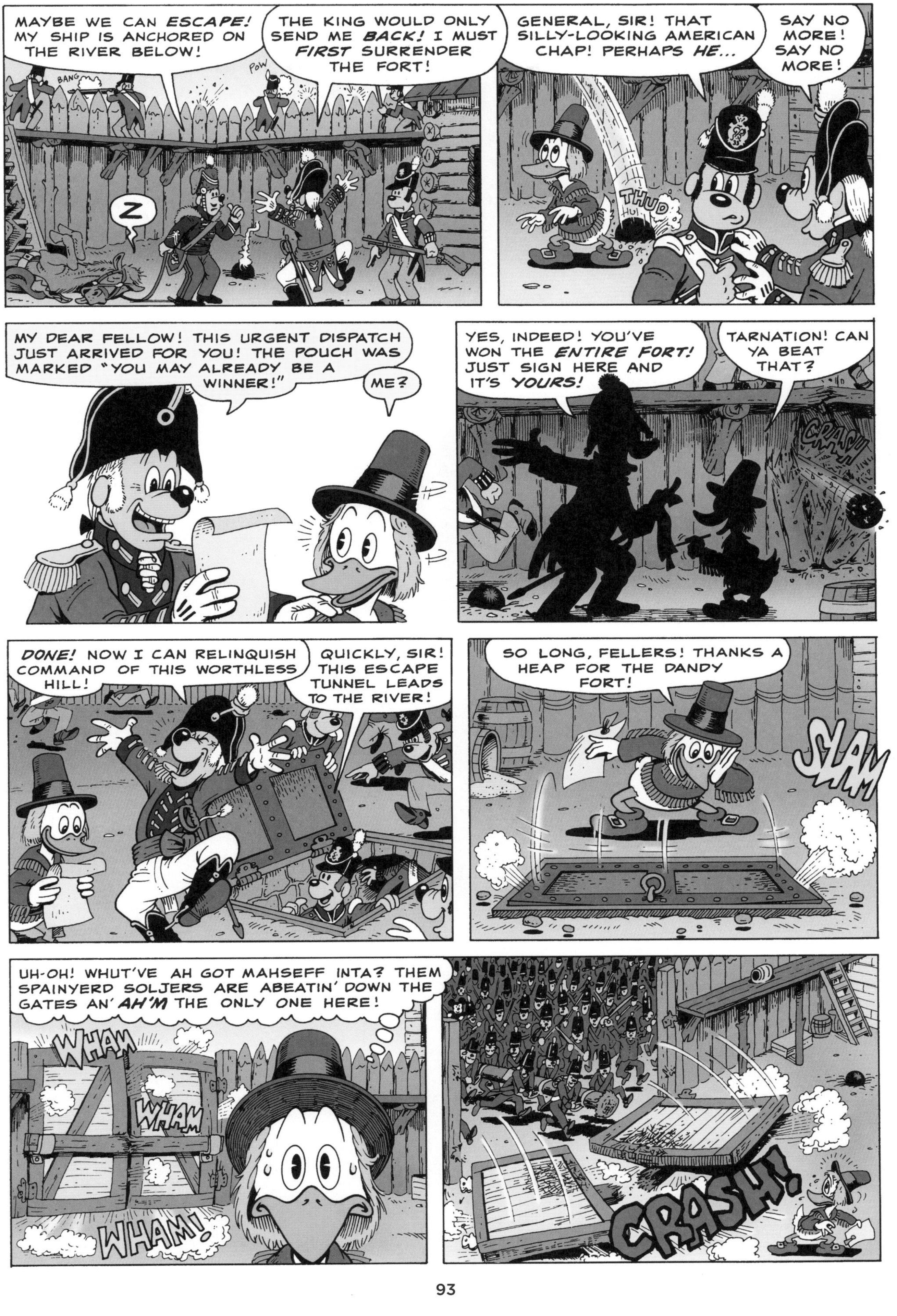
MAYBE WE CAN ESCAPE! MY SHIP IS ANCHORED ON THE RIVER BELOW!
THE KING WOULD ONLY SEND ME BACK! I MUST FIRST SURRENDER THE FORT!
BANG
POW
Z
GENERAL, SIR! THAT SILLY-LOOKING AMERICAN CHAP! PERHAPS HE...
SAY NO MORE! SAY NO MORE!
THUD
MY DEAR FELLOW! THIS URGENT DISPATCH JUST ARRIVED FOR YOU! THE POUCH WAS MARKED "YOU MAY ALREADY BE A WINNER!"
ME?
YES, INDEED! YOU'VE WON THE ENTIRE FORT! JUST SIGN HERE AND IT'S YOURS!
TARNATION! CAN YA BEAT THAT?
CRASH
DONE! NOW I CAN RELINQUISH COMMAND OF THIS WORTHLESS HILL!
QUICKLY, SIR! THIS ESCAPE TUNNEL LEADS TO THE RIVER!
SO LONG, FELLERS! THANKS A HEAP FOR THE DANDY FORT!
SLAM
UH-OH! WHUT'VE AH GOT MAHSEFF INTA? THEM SPAINYERD SOLJERS ARE ABEATIN' DOWN THE GATES AN' AH'M THE ONLY ONE HERE!
WHAM
WHAM
WHAM!
CRASH!

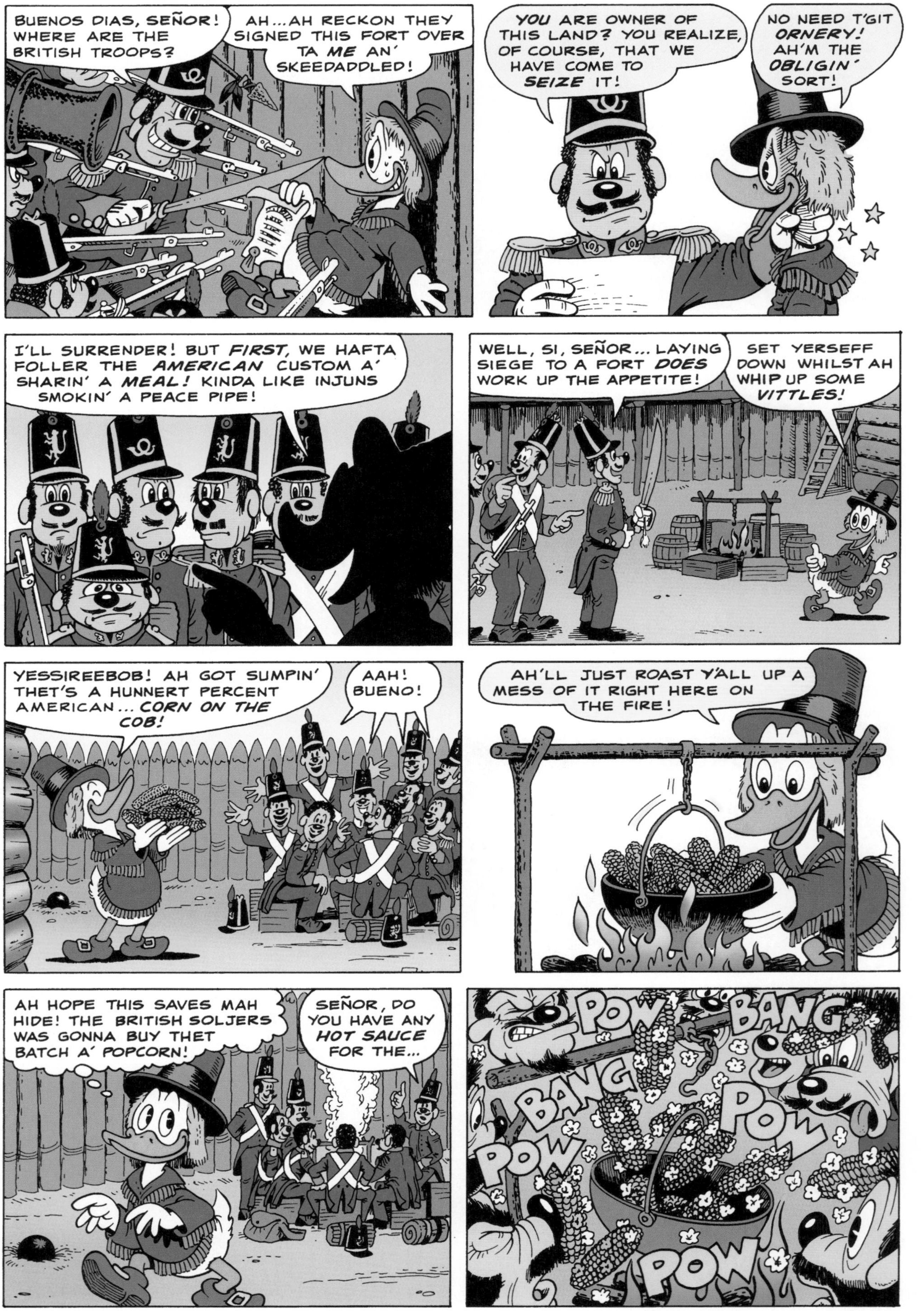
BUENOS DIAS, SEÑOR! WHERE ARE THE BRITISH TROOPS?
AH... AH RECKON THEY SIGNED THIS FORT OVER TA *ME* AN' SKEEDADDLED!
YOU ARE OWNER OF THIS LAND? YOU REALIZE, OF COURSE, THAT WE HAVE COME TO *SEIZE* IT!
NO NEED T'GIT *ORNERY!* AH'M THE *OBLIGIN'* SORT!
I'LL SURRENDER! BUT *FIRST,* WE HAFTA FOLLER THE *AMERICAN* CUSTOM A' SHARIN' A *MEAL!* KINDA LIKE INJUNS SMOKIN' A PEACE PIPE!
WELL, SI, SEÑOR... LAYING SIEGE TO A FORT *DOES* WORK UP THE APPETITE!
SET YERSEFF DOWN WHILST AH WHIP UP SOME *VITTLES!*
YESSIREEBOB! AH GOT SUMPIN' THET'S A HUNNERT PERCENT AMERICAN... *CORN ON THE COB!*
AAH! BUENO!
AH'LL JUST ROAST Y'ALL UP A MESS OF IT RIGHT HERE ON THE FIRE!
AH HOPE THIS SAVES MAH HIDE! THE BRITISH SOLJERS WAS GONNA BUY THET BATCH A' POPCORN!
SEÑOR, DO YOU HAVE ANY *HOT SAUCE* FOR THE...
POW
BANG
BANG
POW
POW
POW

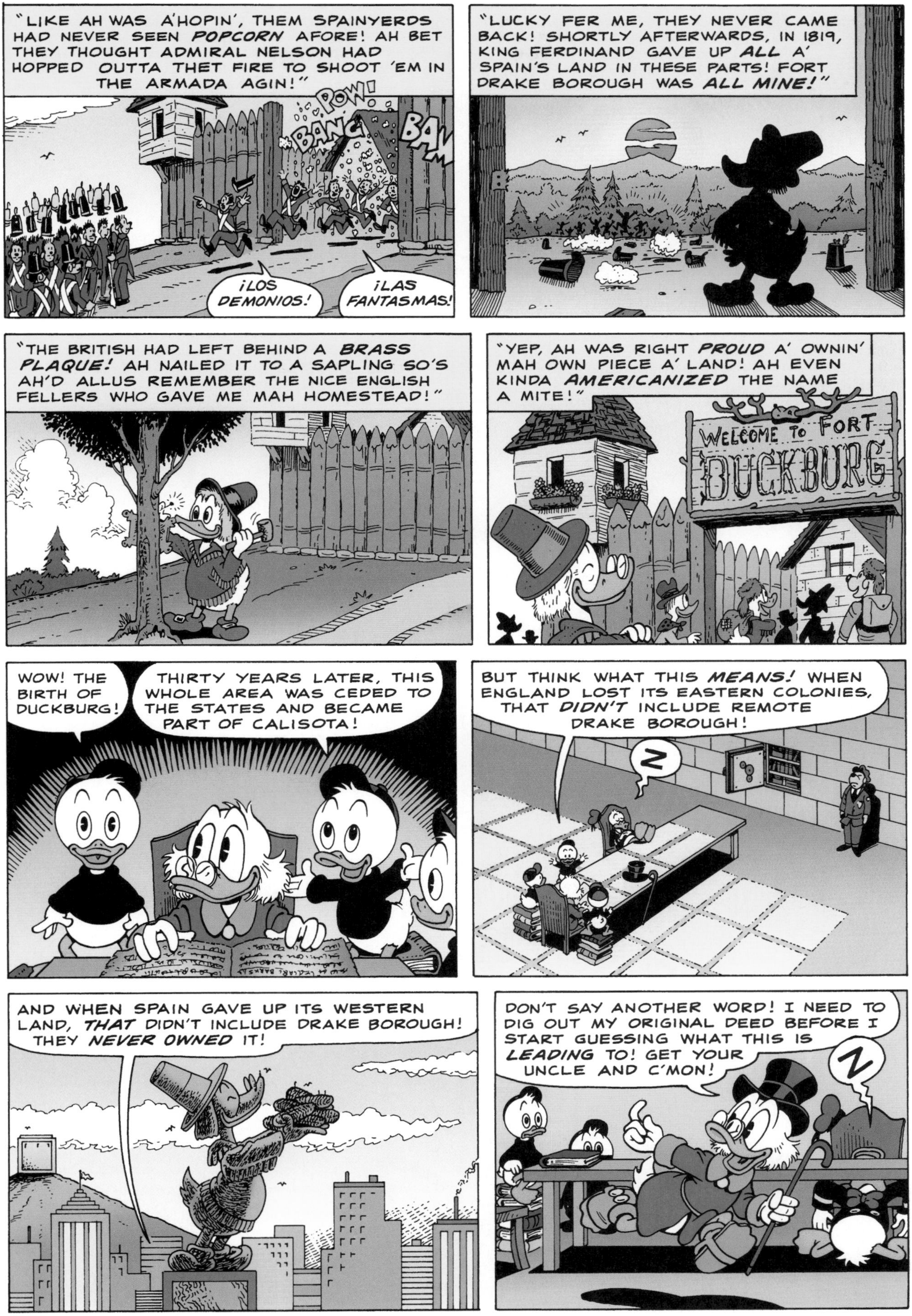
"LIKE AH WAS A'HOPIN', THEM SPAINYERDS HAD NEVER SEEN POPCORN AFORE! AH BET THEY THOUGHT ADMIRAL NELSON HAD HOPPED OUTTA THET FIRE TO SHOOT 'EM IN THE ARMADA AGIN!"
POW!
BANG
BAM
¡LOS DEMONIOS!
¡LAS FANTASMAS!
"LUCKY FER ME, THEY NEVER CAME BACK! SHORTLY AFTERWARDS, IN 1819, KING FERDINAND GAVE UP ALL A' SPAIN'S LAND IN THESE PARTS! FORT DRAKE BOROUGH WAS ALL MINE!"
"THE BRITISH HAD LEFT BEHIND A BRASS PLAQUE! AH NAILED IT TO A SAPLING SO'S AH'D ALLUS REMEMBER THE NICE ENGLISH FELLERS WHO GAVE ME MAH HOMESTEAD!"
"YEP, AH WAS RIGHT PROUD A' OWNIN' MAH OWN PIECE A' LAND! AH EVEN KINDA AMERICANIZED THE NAME A MITE!"
WELCOME TO FORT DUCKBURG
WOW! THE BIRTH OF DUCKBURG!
THIRTY YEARS LATER, THIS WHOLE AREA WAS CEDED TO THE STATES AND BECAME PART OF CALISOTA!
BUT THINK WHAT THIS MEANS! WHEN ENGLAND LOST ITS EASTERN COLONIES, THAT DIDN'T INCLUDE REMOTE DRAKE BOROUGH!
Z
AND WHEN SPAIN GAVE UP ITS WESTERN LAND, THAT DIDN'T INCLUDE DRAKE BOROUGH! THEY NEVER OWNED IT!
DON'T SAY ANOTHER WORD! I NEED TO DIG OUT MY ORIGINAL DEED BEFORE I START GUESSING WHAT THIS IS LEADING TO! GET YOUR UNCLE AND C'MON!
Z

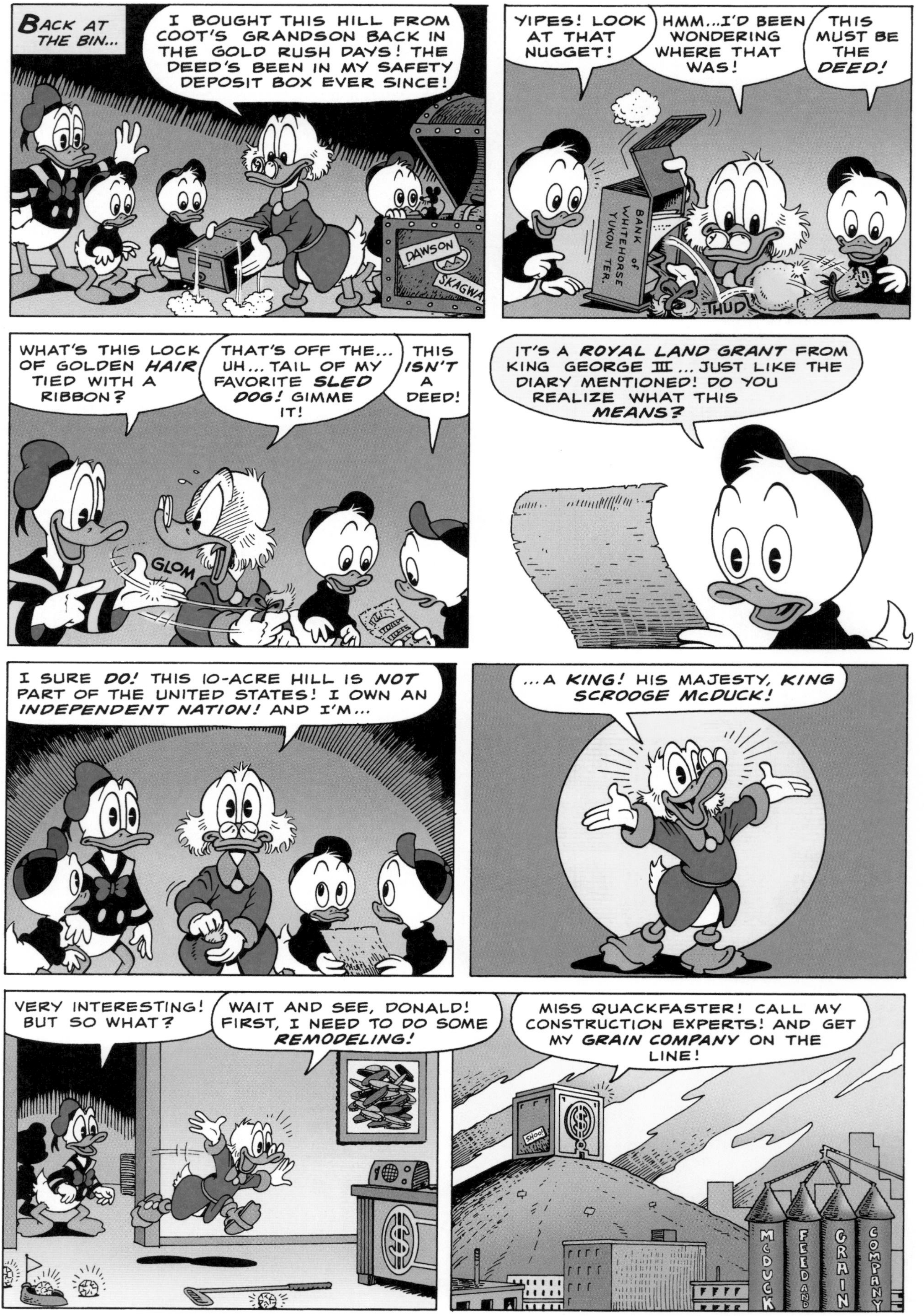
BACK AT THE BIN...
I BOUGHT THIS HILL FROM COOT'S GRANDSON BACK IN THE GOLD RUSH DAYS! THE DEED'S BEEN IN MY SAFETY DEPOSIT BOX EVER SINCE!
DAWSON
SKAGWA
YIPES! LOOK AT THAT NUGGET!
HMM...I'D BEEN WONDERING WHERE THAT WAS!
THIS MUST BE THE DEED!
BANK of WHITEHORSE YUKON TER.
THUD
WHAT'S THIS LOCK OF GOLDEN HAIR TIED WITH A RIBBON?
THAT'S OFF THE... UH... TAIL OF MY FAVORITE SLED DOG! GIMME IT!
THIS ISN'T A DEED!
GLOM
IT'S A ROYAL LAND GRANT FROM KING GEORGE III... JUST LIKE THE DIARY MENTIONED! DO YOU REALIZE WHAT THIS MEANS?
I SURE DO! THIS 10-ACRE HILL IS NOT PART OF THE UNITED STATES! I OWN AN INDEPENDENT NATION! AND I'M...
...A KING! HIS MAJESTY, KING SCROOGE McDUCK!
VERY INTERESTING! BUT SO WHAT?
WAIT AND SEE, DONALD! FIRST, I NEED TO DO SOME REMODELING!
MISS QUACKFASTER! CALL MY CONSTRUCTION EXPERTS! AND GET MY GRAIN COMPANY ON THE LINE!
SHOO!
McDUCK FEED AND GRAIN COMPANY

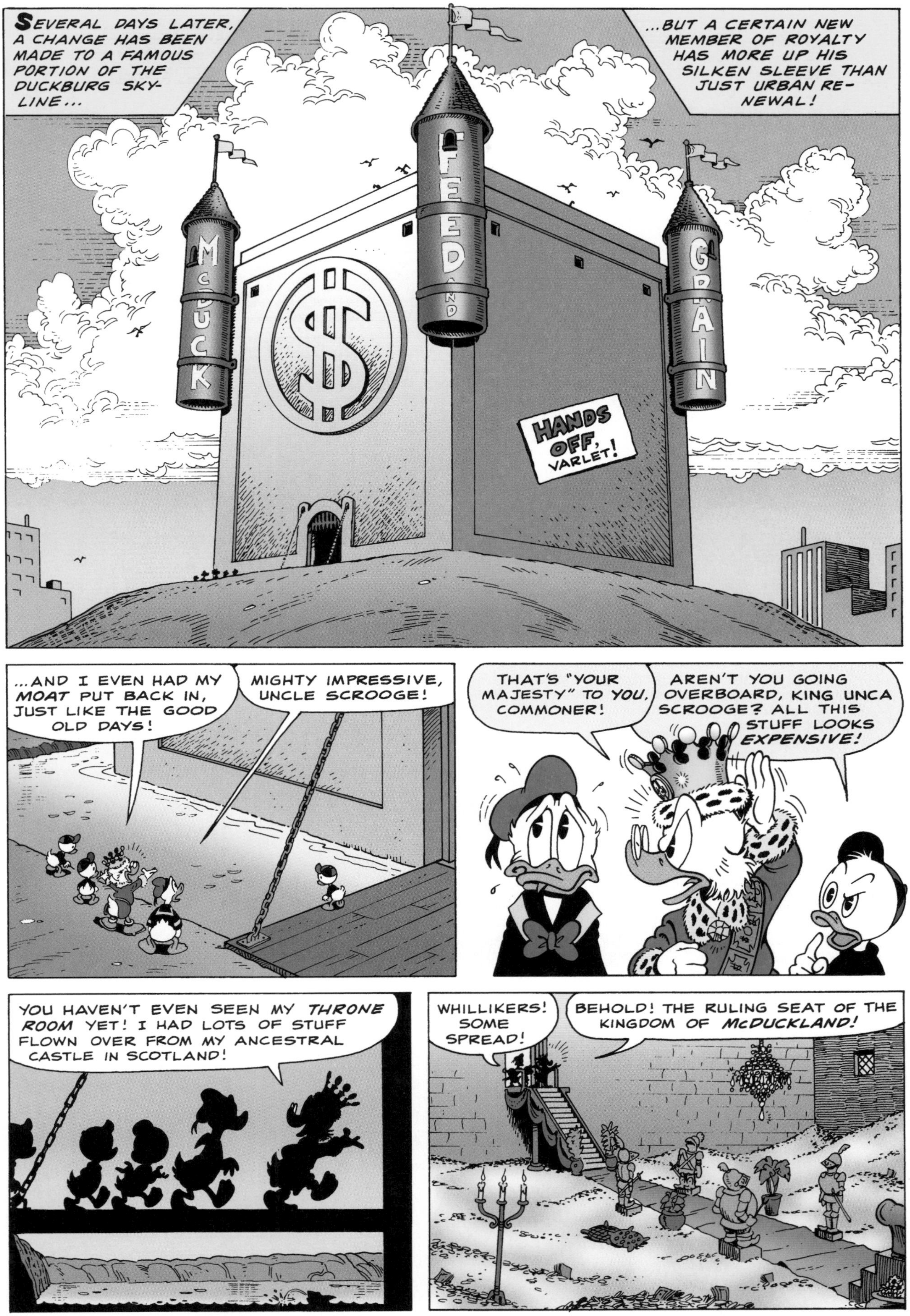
SEVERAL DAYS LATER, A CHANGE HAS BEEN MADE TO A FAMOUS PORTION OF THE DUCKBURG SKY-LINE...
...BUT A CERTAIN NEW MEMBER OF ROYALTY HAS MORE UP HIS SILKEN SLEEVE THAN JUST URBAN RE-NEWAL!
McDUCK
FEED AND
GRAIN
HANDS OFF, VARLET!
...AND I EVEN HAD MY MOAT PUT BACK IN, JUST LIKE THE GOOD OLD DAYS!
MIGHTY IMPRESSIVE, UNCLE SCROOGE!
THAT'S "YOUR MAJESTY" TO YOU, COMMONER!
AREN'T YOU GOING OVERBOARD, KING UNCA SCROOGE? ALL THIS STUFF LOOKS EXPENSIVE!
YOU HAVEN'T EVEN SEEN MY THRONE ROOM YET! I HAD LOTS OF STUFF FLOWN OVER FROM MY ANCESTRAL CASTLE IN SCOTLAND!
WHILLIKERS! SOME SPREAD!
BEHOLD! THE RULING SEAT OF THE KINGDOM OF McDUCKLAND!

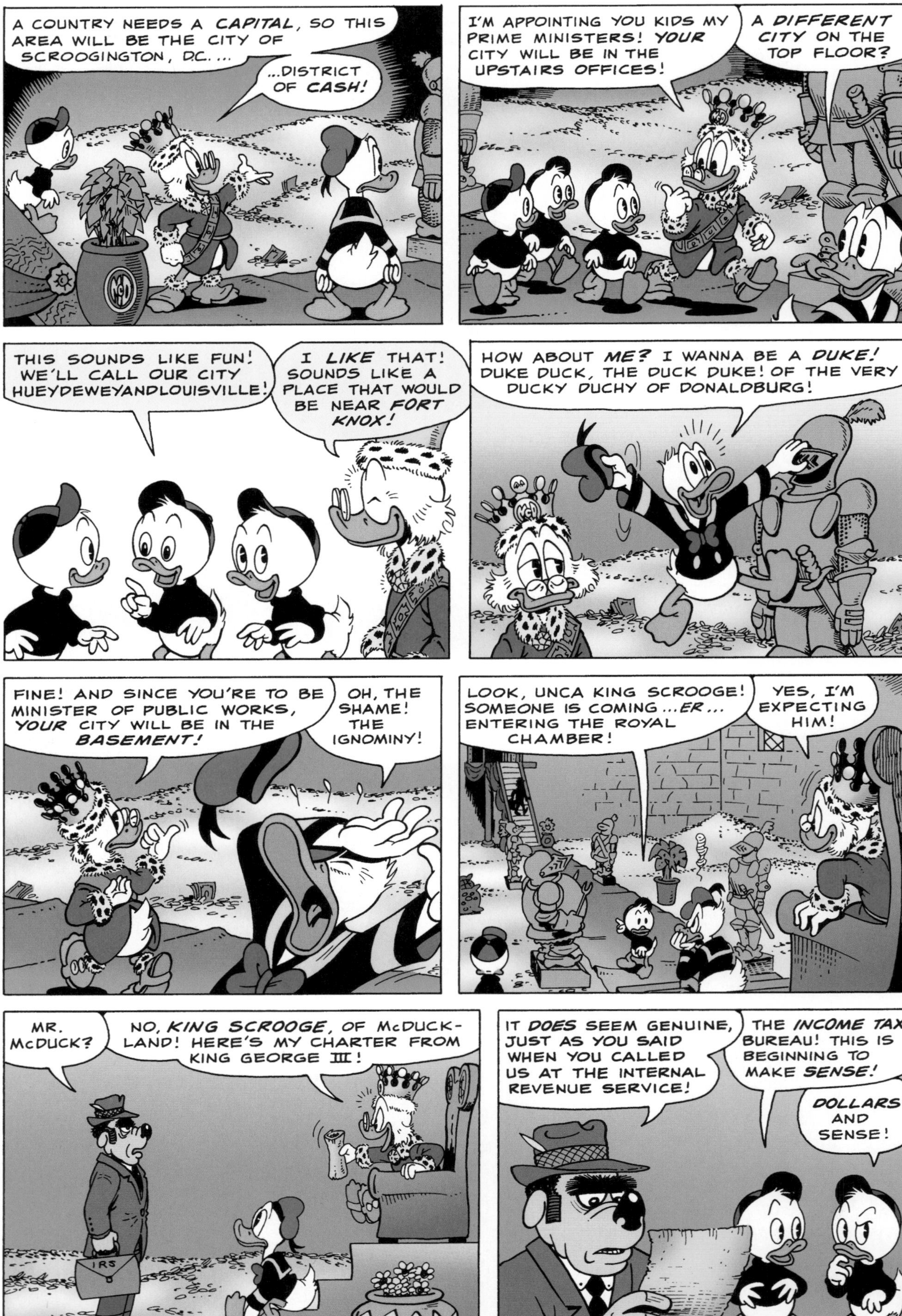
A COUNTRY NEEDS A CAPITAL, SO THIS AREA WILL BE THE CITY OF SCROOGINGTON, D.C. ...
...DISTRICT OF CASH!
I'M APPOINTING YOU KIDS MY PRIME MINISTERS! YOUR CITY WILL BE IN THE UPSTAIRS OFFICES!
A DIFFERENT CITY ON THE TOP FLOOR?
THIS SOUNDS LIKE FUN! WE'LL CALL OUR CITY HUEYDEWEYANDLOUISVILLE!
I LIKE THAT! SOUNDS LIKE A PLACE THAT WOULD BE NEAR FORT KNOX!
HOW ABOUT ME? I WANNA BE A DUKE! DUKE DUCK, THE DUCK DUKE! OF THE VERY DUCKY DUCHY OF DONALDBURG!
FINE! AND SINCE YOU'RE TO BE MINISTER OF PUBLIC WORKS, YOUR CITY WILL BE IN THE BASEMENT!
OH, THE SHAME! THE IGNOMINY!
LOOK, UNCA KING SCROOGE! SOMEONE IS COMING ...ER... ENTERING THE ROYAL CHAMBER!
YES, I'M EXPECTING HIM!
MR. McDUCK?
NO, KING SCROOGE, OF McDUCK-LAND! HERE'S MY CHARTER FROM KING GEORGE III!
IRS
IT DOES SEEM GENUINE, JUST AS YOU SAID WHEN YOU CALLED US AT THE INTERNAL REVENUE SERVICE!
THE INCOME TAX BUREAU! THIS IS BEGINNING TO MAKE SENSE!
DOLLARS AND SENSE!

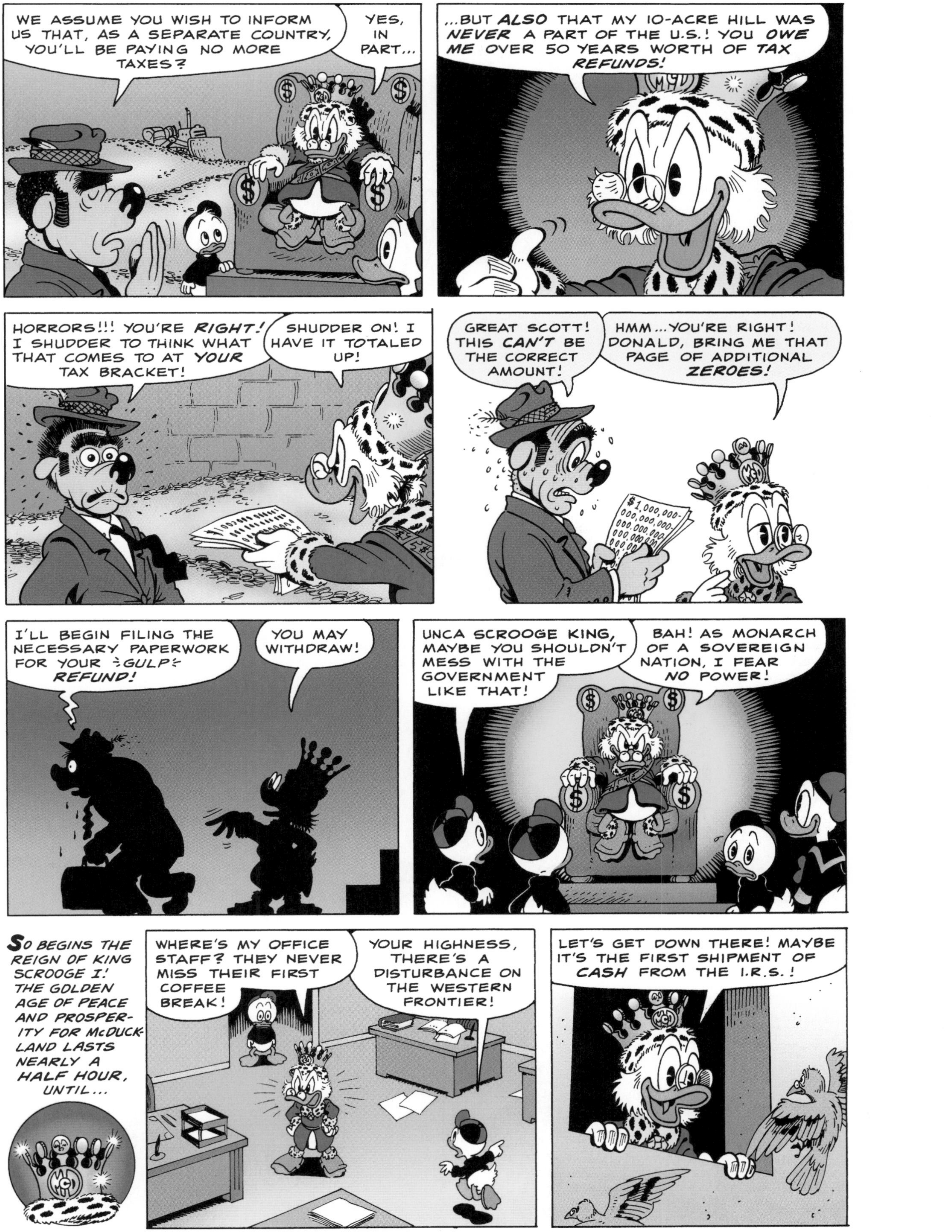

WE ASSUME YOU WISH TO INFORM US THAT, AS A SEPARATE COUNTRY, YOU'LL BE PAYING NO MORE TAXES?
YES, IN PART...
...BUT ALSO THAT MY 10-ACRE HILL WAS NEVER A PART OF THE U.S.! YOU OWE ME OVER 50 YEARS WORTH OF TAX REFUNDS!
HORRORS!!! YOU'RE RIGHT! I SHUDDER TO THINK WHAT THAT COMES TO AT YOUR TAX BRACKET!
SHUDDER ON! I HAVE IT TOTALED UP!
GREAT SCOTT! THIS CAN'T BE THE CORRECT AMOUNT!
HMM... YOU'RE RIGHT! DONALD, BRING ME THAT PAGE OF ADDITIONAL ZEROES!
$1,000,000,000,000,000,000,000,000,000,000,000
I'LL BEGIN FILING THE NECESSARY PAPERWORK FOR YOUR ÷GULP÷ REFUND!
YOU MAY WITHDRAW!
UNCA SCROOGE KING, MAYBE YOU SHOULDN'T MESS WITH THE GOVERNMENT LIKE THAT!
BAH! AS MONARCH OF A SOVEREIGN NATION, I FEAR NO POWER!
SO BEGINS THE REIGN OF KING SCROOGE I! THE GOLDEN AGE OF PEACE AND PROSPERITY FOR McDUCKLAND LASTS NEARLY A HALF HOUR, UNTIL...
WHERE'S MY OFFICE STAFF? THEY NEVER MISS THEIR FIRST COFFEE BREAK!
YOUR HIGHNESS, THERE'S A DISTURBANCE ON THE WESTERN FRONTIER!
LET'S GET DOWN THERE! MAYBE IT'S THE FIRST SHIPMENT OF CASH FROM THE I.R.S.!

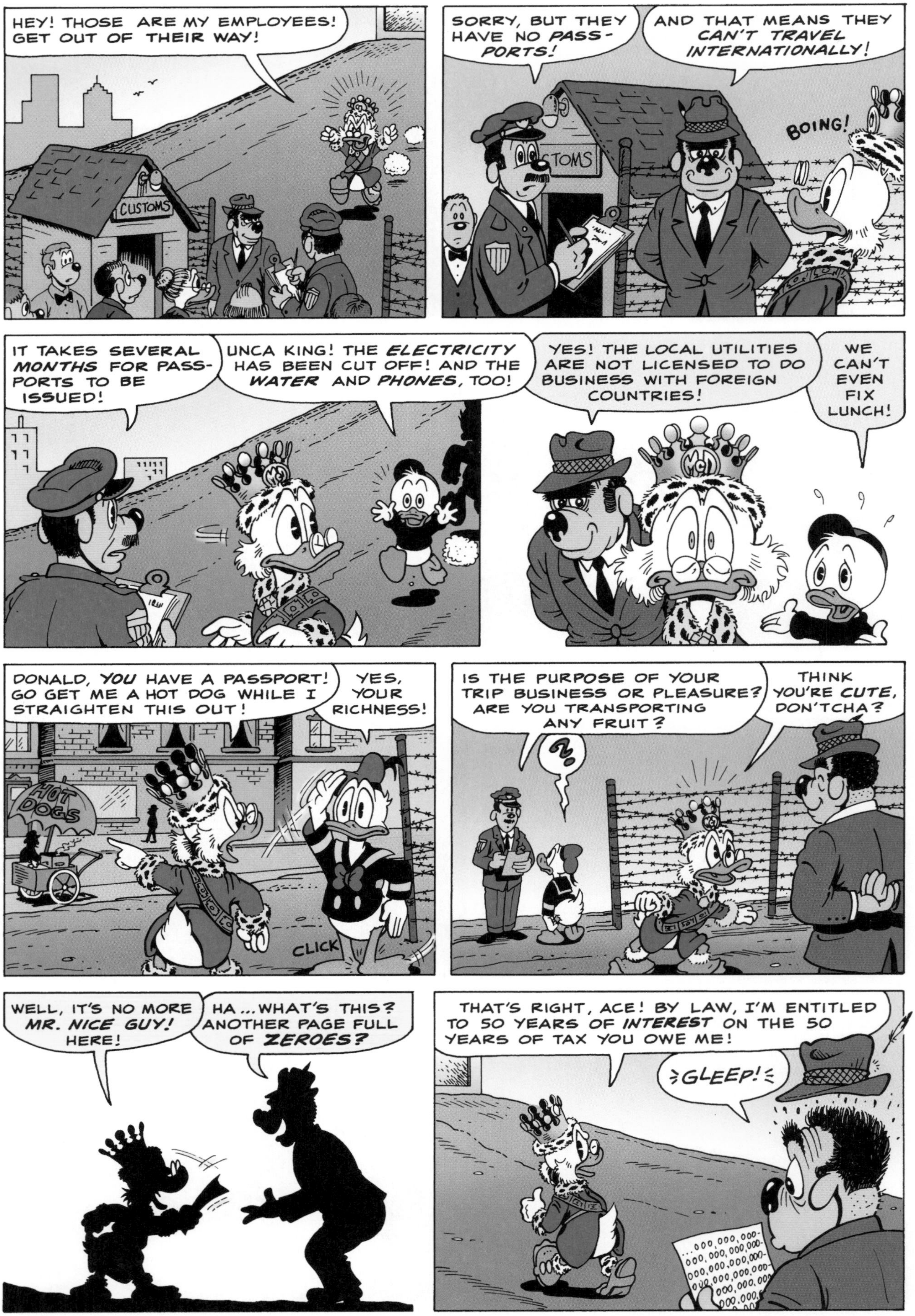
HEY! THOSE ARE MY EMPLOYEES! GET OUT OF THEIR WAY!
CUSTOMS
SORRY, BUT THEY HAVE NO PASS-PORTS!
AND THAT MEANS THEY CAN'T TRAVEL INTERNATIONALLY!
BOING!
IT TAKES SEVERAL MONTHS FOR PASS-PORTS TO BE ISSUED!
UNCA KING! THE ELECTRICITY HAS BEEN CUT OFF! AND THE WATER AND PHONES, TOO!
YES! THE LOCAL UTILITIES ARE NOT LICENSED TO DO BUSINESS WITH FOREIGN COUNTRIES!
WE CAN'T EVEN FIX LUNCH!
DONALD, YOU HAVE A PASSPORT! GO GET ME A HOT DOG WHILE I STRAIGHTEN THIS OUT!
YES, YOUR RICHNESS!
HOT DOGS
CLICK
IS THE PURPOSE OF YOUR TRIP BUSINESS OR PLEASURE? ARE YOU TRANSPORTING ANY FRUIT?
THINK YOU'RE CUTE, DON'TCHA?
WELL, IT'S NO MORE MR. NICE GUY! HERE!
HA ... WHAT'S THIS? ANOTHER PAGE FULL OF ZEROES?
THAT'S RIGHT, ACE! BY LAW, I'M ENTITLED TO 50 YEARS OF INTEREST ON THE 50 YEARS OF TAX YOU OWE ME!
GLEEP!

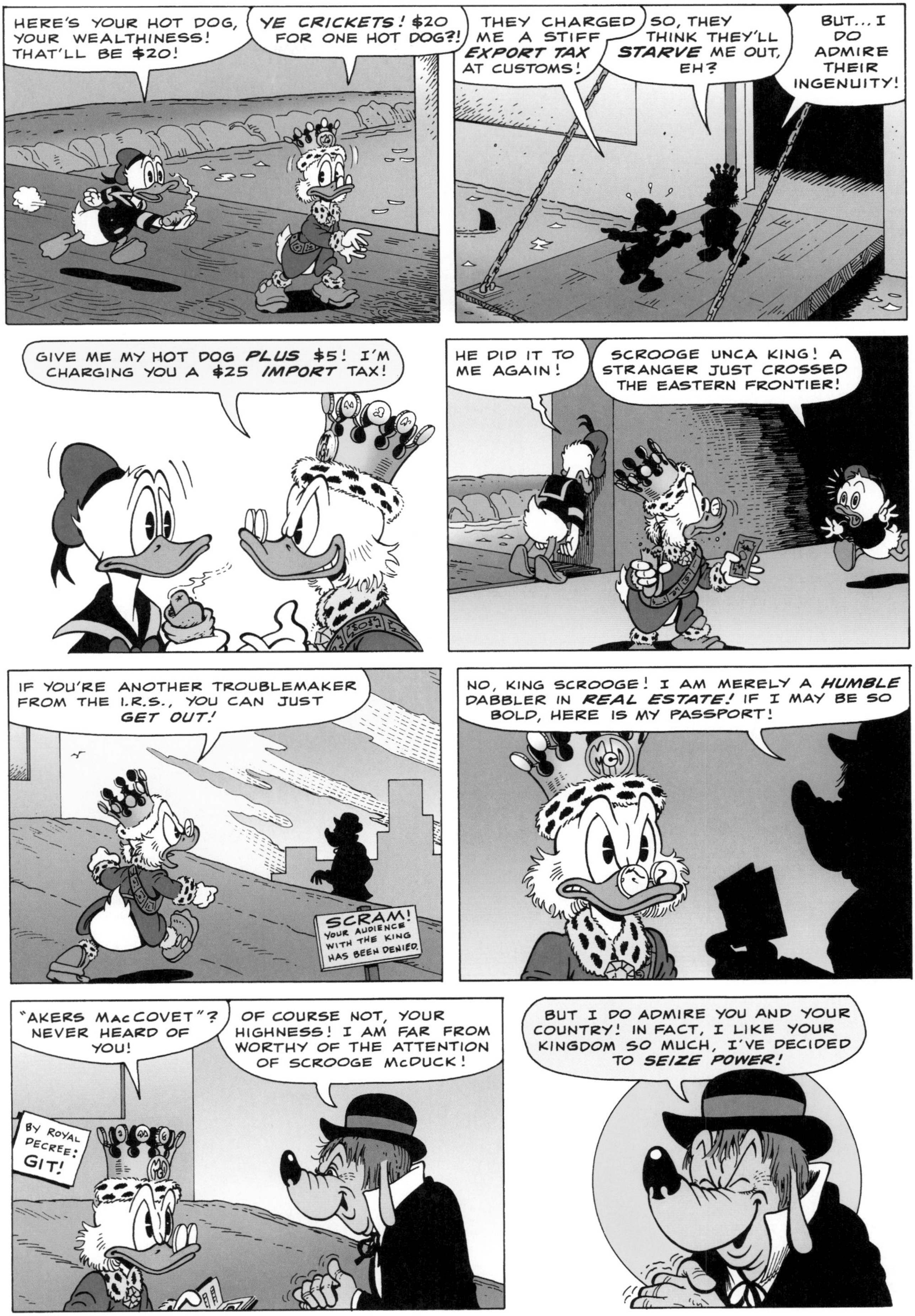

HERE'S YOUR HOT DOG, YOUR WEALTHINESS! THAT'LL BE $20!
YE CRICKETS! $20 FOR ONE HOT DOG?!
THEY CHARGED ME A STIFF EXPORT TAX AT CUSTOMS!
SO, THEY THINK THEY'LL STARVE ME OUT, EH?
BUT... I DO ADMIRE THEIR INGENUITY!
GIVE ME MY HOT DOG PLUS $5! I'M CHARGING YOU A $25 IMPORT TAX!
HE DID IT TO ME AGAIN!
SCROOGE UNCA KING! A STRANGER JUST CROSSED THE EASTERN FRONTIER!
IF YOU'RE ANOTHER TROUBLEMAKER FROM THE I.R.S., YOU CAN JUST GET OUT!
SCRAM! YOUR AUDIENCE WITH THE KING HAS BEEN DENIED.
NO, KING SCROOGE! I AM MERELY A HUMBLE DABBLER IN REAL ESTATE! IF I MAY BE SO BOLD, HERE IS MY PASSPORT!
BY ROYAL DECREE: GIT!
"AKERS MacCOVET"? NEVER HEARD OF YOU!
OF COURSE NOT, YOUR HIGHNESS! I AM FAR FROM WORTHY OF THE ATTENTION OF SCROOGE McDUCK!
BUT I DO ADMIRE YOU AND YOUR COUNTRY! IN FACT, I LIKE YOUR KINGDOM SO MUCH, I'VE DECIDED TO SEIZE POWER!

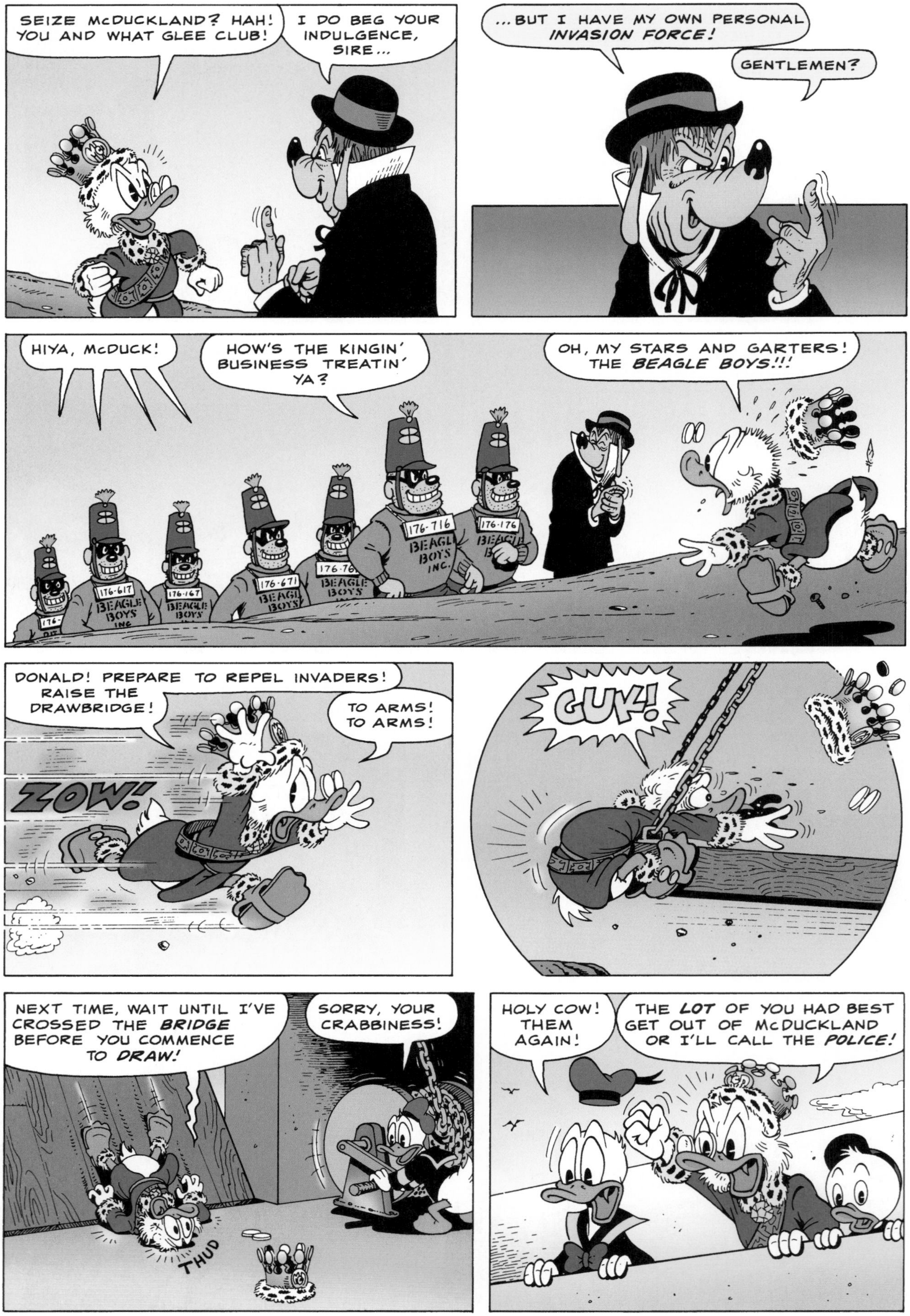
SEIZE McDUCKLAND? HAH! YOU AND WHAT GLEE CLUB!
I DO BEG YOUR INDULGENCE, SIRE...
...BUT I HAVE MY OWN PERSONAL INVASION FORCE!
GENTLEMEN?
HIYA, McDUCK!
HOW'S THE KINGIN' BUSINESS TREATIN' YA?
OH, MY STARS AND GARTERS! THE BEAGLE BOYS!!!
176-716
BEAGLE BOYS INC.
176-176
176-671
176-617
176-167
DONALD! PREPARE TO REPEL INVADERS! RAISE THE DRAWBRIDGE!
TO ARMS! TO ARMS!
ZOW!
GUK!
NEXT TIME, WAIT UNTIL I'VE CROSSED THE BRIDGE BEFORE YOU COMMENCE TO DRAW!
SORRY, YOUR CRABBINESS!
THUD
HOLY COW! THEM AGAIN!
THE LOT OF YOU HAD BEST GET OUT OF McDUCKLAND OR I'LL CALL THE POLICE!

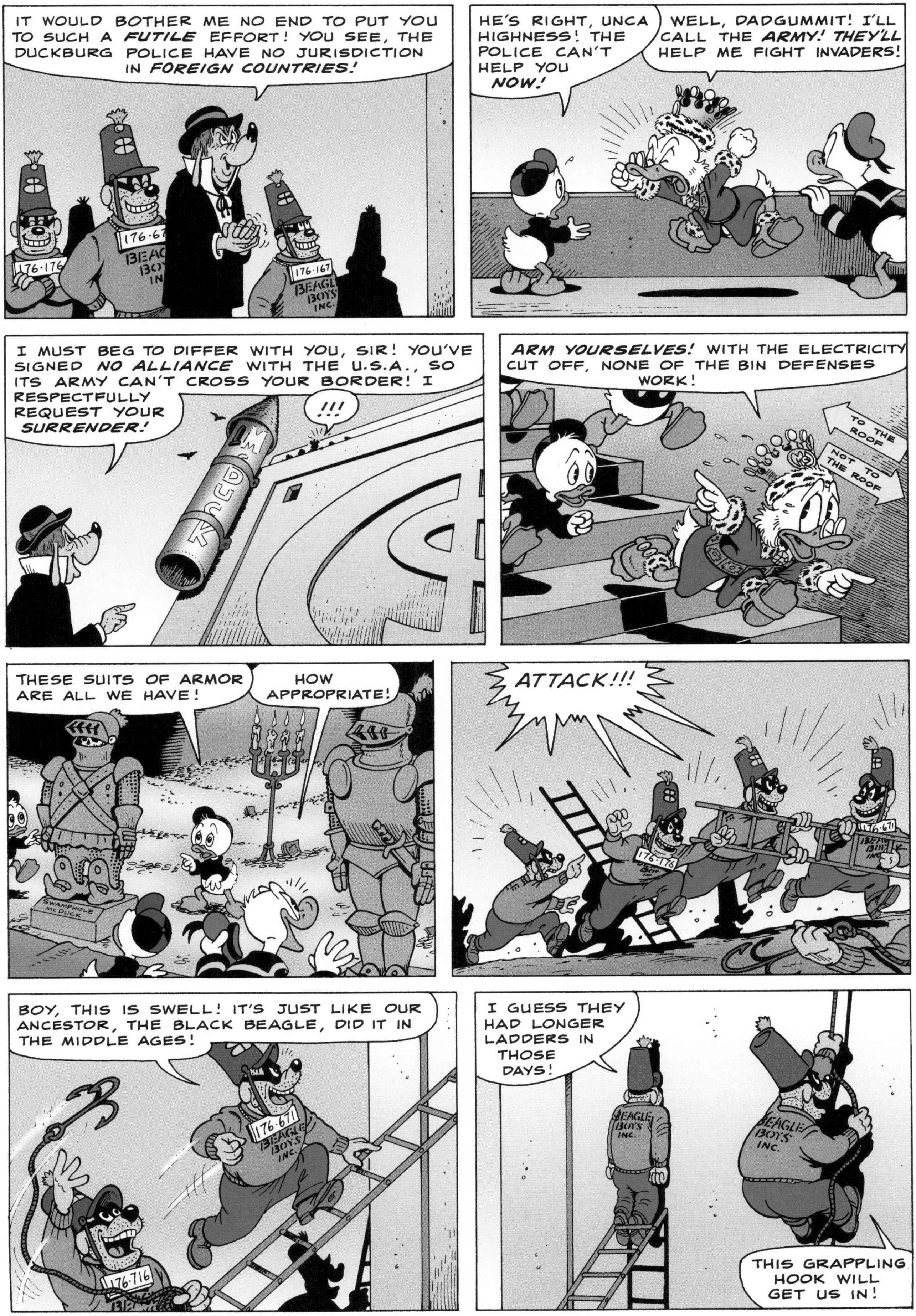
IT WOULD BOTHER ME NO END TO PUT YOU TO SUCH A FUTILE EFFORT! YOU SEE, THE DUCKBURG POLICE HAVE NO JURISDICTION IN FOREIGN COUNTRIES!
176-176
176-67
BEAG BOYS IN
176-167
BEAGLE BOYS INC.
HE'S RIGHT, UNCA HIGHNESS! THE POLICE CAN'T HELP YOU NOW!
WELL, DADGUMMIT! I'LL CALL THE ARMY! THEY'LL HELP ME FIGHT INVADERS!
I MUST BEG TO DIFFER WITH YOU, SIR! YOU'VE SIGNED NO ALLIANCE WITH THE U.S.A., SO ITS ARMY CAN'T CROSS YOUR BORDER! I RESPECTFULLY REQUEST YOUR SURRENDER!
!!!
McDUCK
ARM YOURSELVES! WITH THE ELECTRICITY CUT OFF, NONE OF THE BIN DEFENSES WORK!
TO THE ROOF
NOT TO THE ROOF
THESE SUITS OF ARMOR ARE ALL WE HAVE!
HOW APPROPRIATE!
SWAMPHOLE McDUCK
ATTACK!!!
176-176
176-671
BOY, THIS IS SWELL! IT'S JUST LIKE OUR ANCESTOR, THE BLACK BEAGLE, DID IT IN THE MIDDLE AGES!
176-671
BEAGLE BOYS INC.
176-716
I GUESS THEY HAD LONGER LADDERS IN THOSE DAYS!
BEAGLE BOYS INC.
BEAGLE BOYS INC.
THIS GRAPPLING HOOK WILL GET US IN!

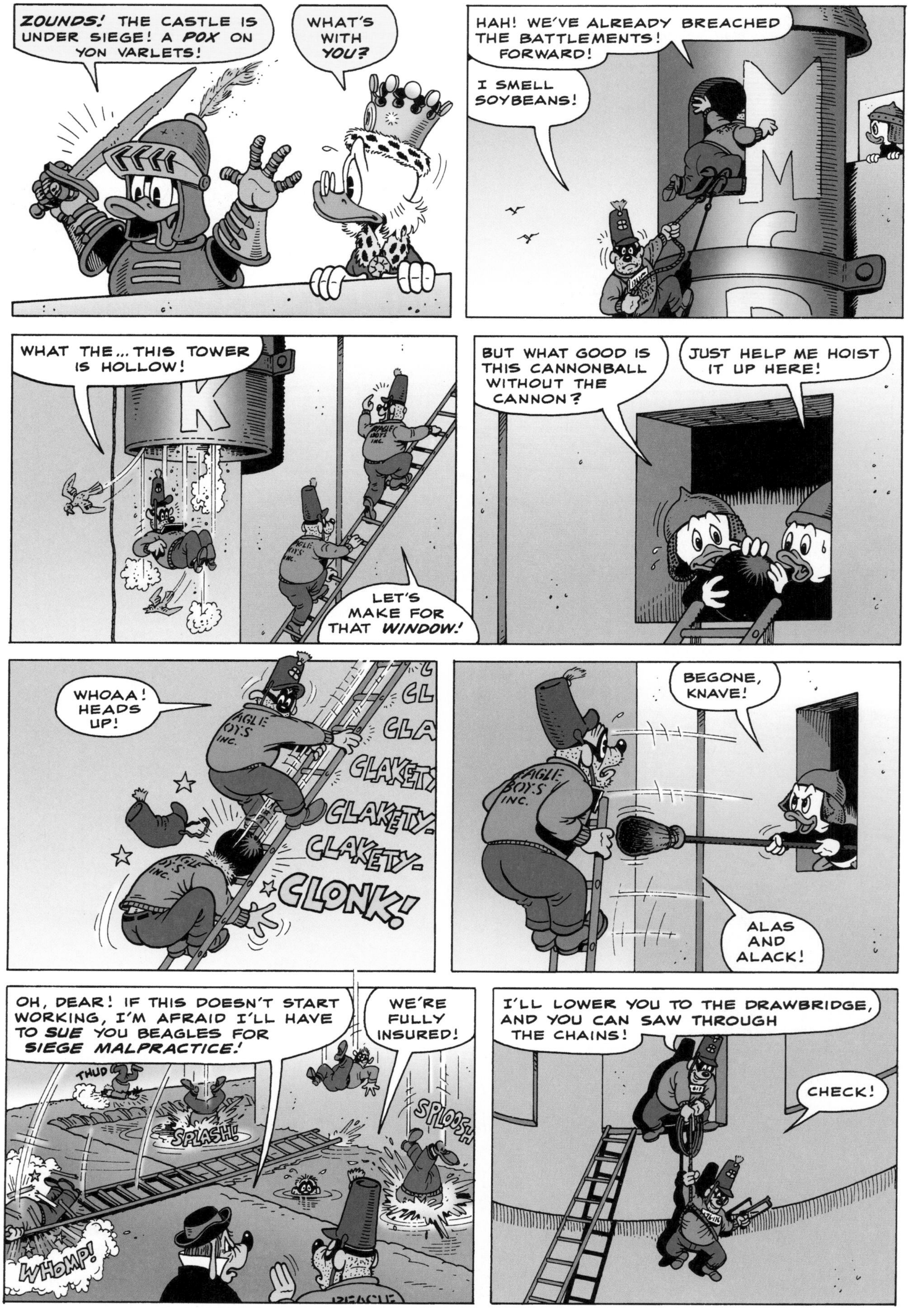
ZOUNDS! THE CASTLE IS UNDER SIEGE! A POX ON YON VARLETS!
WHAT'S WITH YOU?
HAH! WE'VE ALREADY BREACHED THE BATTLEMENTS! FORWARD!
I SMELL SOYBEANS!
WHAT THE... THIS TOWER IS HOLLOW!
LET'S MAKE FOR THAT WINDOW!
BUT WHAT GOOD IS THIS CANNONBALL WITHOUT THE CANNON?
JUST HELP ME HOIST IT UP HERE!
WHOAA! HEADS UP!
CLAKETY-
CLAKETY-
CLAKETY-
CLONK!
BEGONE, KNAVE!
ALAS AND ALACK!
OH, DEAR! IF THIS DOESN'T START WORKING, I'M AFRAID I'LL HAVE TO SUE YOU BEAGLES FOR SIEGE MALPRACTICE!
WE'RE FULLY INSURED!
THUD
SPLASH!
SPLOOSH
WHOMP!
I'LL LOWER YOU TO THE DRAWBRIDGE, AND YOU CAN SAW THROUGH THE CHAINS!
CHECK!

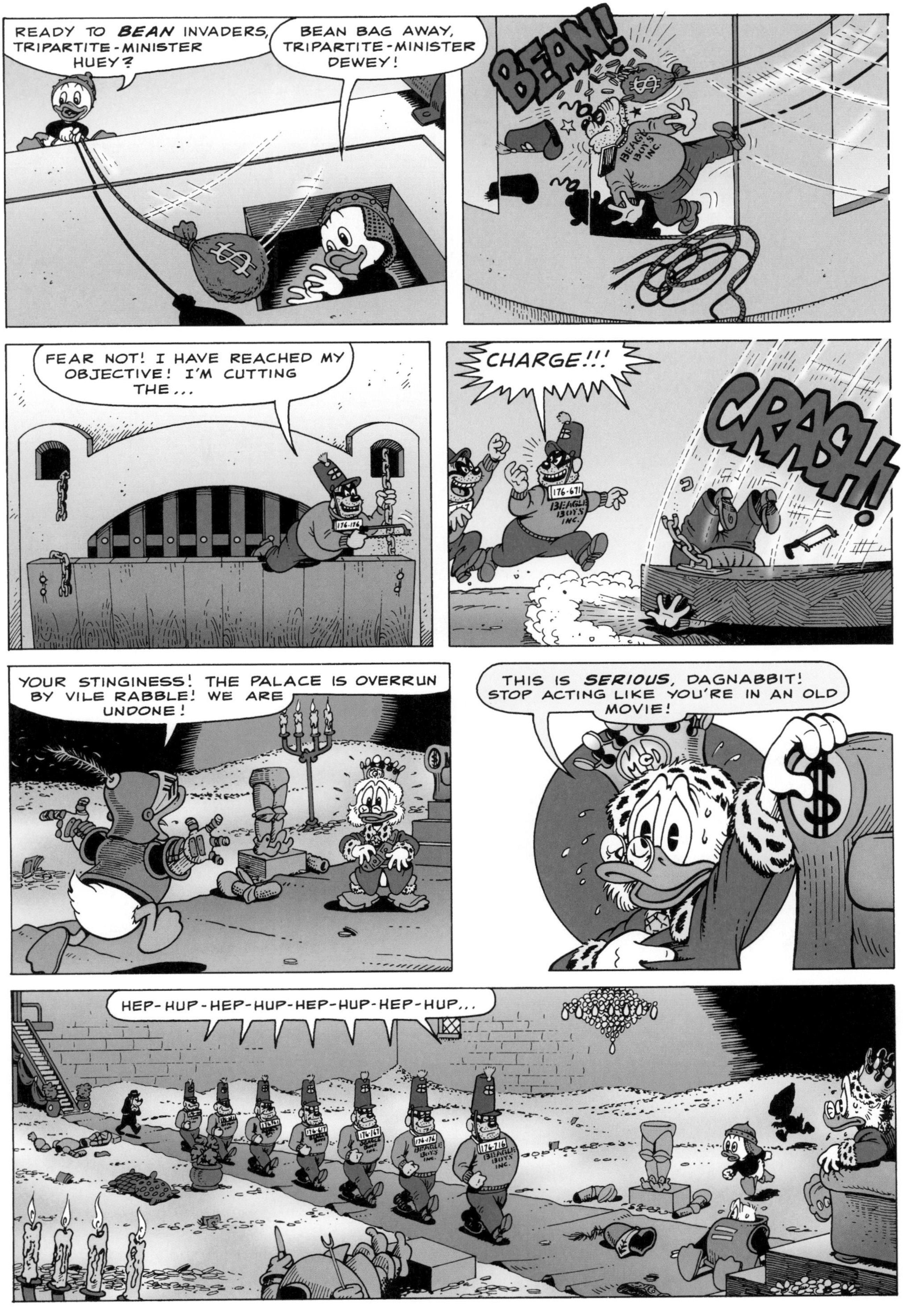
READY TO BEAN INVADERS, TRIPARTITE-MINISTER HUEY?
BEAN BAG AWAY, TRIPARTITE-MINISTER DEWEY!
BEAN!
BEAGLE BOYS INC.
FEAR NOT! I HAVE REACHED MY OBJECTIVE! I'M CUTTING THE...
176-176
CHARGE!!!
176-671
BEAGLE BOYS INC.
CRASH!
YOUR STINGINESS! THE PALACE IS OVERRUN BY VILE RABBLE! WE ARE UNDONE!
THIS IS SERIOUS, DAGNABBIT! STOP ACTING LIKE YOU'RE IN AN OLD MOVIE!
McD
HEP-HUP-HEP-HUP-HEP-HUP-HEP-HUP...
176-617
176-176
176-716
BEAGLE BOYS INC.

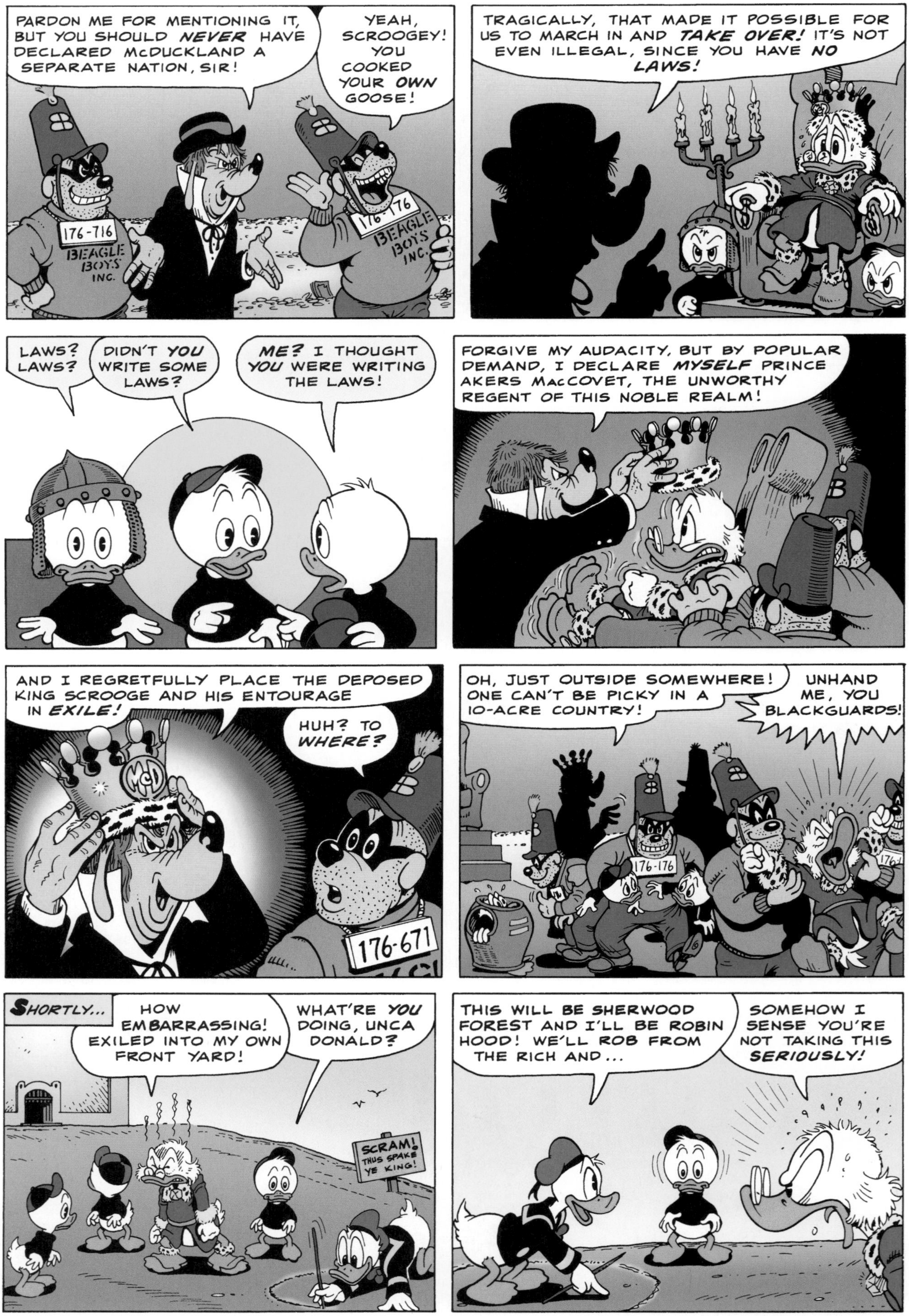
PARDON ME FOR MENTIONING IT, BUT YOU SHOULD NEVER HAVE DECLARED McDUCKLAND A SEPARATE NATION, SIR!
YEAH, SCROOGEY! YOU COOKED YOUR OWN GOOSE!
176-716
BEAGLE BOYS INC.
176-176
BEAGLE BOYS INC.
TRAGICALLY, THAT MADE IT POSSIBLE FOR US TO MARCH IN AND TAKE OVER! IT'S NOT EVEN ILLEGAL, SINCE YOU HAVE NO LAWS!
LAWS? LAWS?
DIDN'T YOU WRITE SOME LAWS?
ME? I THOUGHT YOU WERE WRITING THE LAWS!
FORGIVE MY AUDACITY, BUT BY POPULAR DEMAND, I DECLARE MYSELF PRINCE AKERS MacCOVET, THE UNWORTHY REGENT OF THIS NOBLE REALM!
AND I REGRETFULLY PLACE THE DEPOSED KING SCROOGE AND HIS ENTOURAGE IN EXILE!
HUH? TO WHERE?
176-671
OH, JUST OUTSIDE SOMEWHERE! ONE CAN'T BE PICKY IN A 10-ACRE COUNTRY!
UNHAND ME, YOU BLACKGUARDS!
176-176
SHORTLY...
HOW EMBARRASSING! EXILED INTO MY OWN FRONT YARD!
WHAT'RE YOU DOING, UNCA DONALD?
SCRAM! THUS SPAKE YE KING!
THIS WILL BE SHERWOOD FOREST AND I'LL BE ROBIN HOOD! WE'LL ROB FROM THE RICH AND...
SOMEHOW I SENSE YOU'RE NOT TAKING THIS SERIOUSLY!

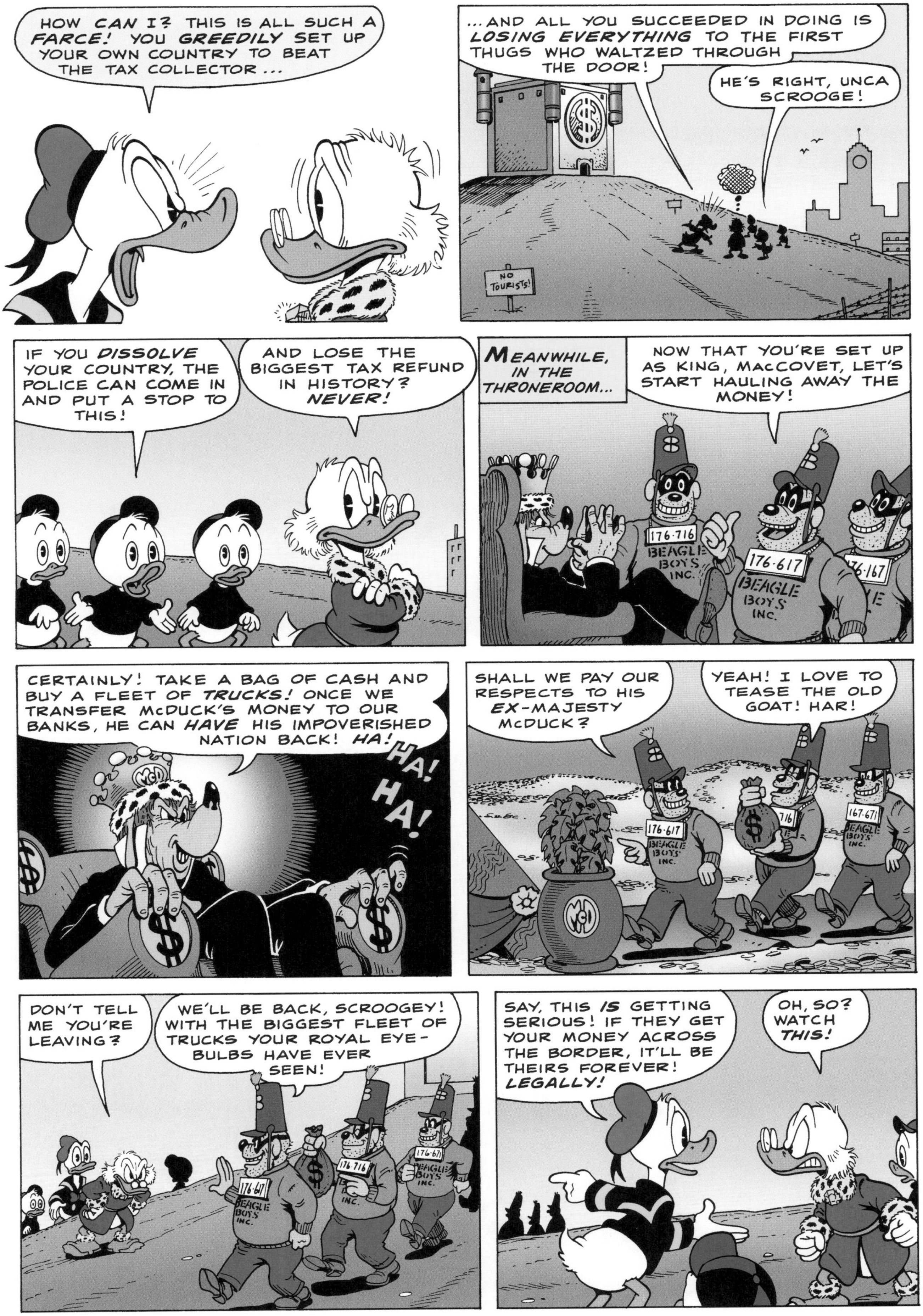
HOW CAN I? THIS IS ALL SUCH A FARCE! YOU GREEDILY SET UP YOUR OWN COUNTRY TO BEAT THE TAX COLLECTOR...
...AND ALL YOU SUCCEEDED IN DOING IS LOSING EVERYTHING TO THE FIRST THUGS WHO WALTZED THROUGH THE DOOR!
HE'S RIGHT, UNCA SCROOGE!
NO TOURISTS!
IF YOU DISSOLVE YOUR COUNTRY, THE POLICE CAN COME IN AND PUT A STOP TO THIS!
AND LOSE THE BIGGEST TAX REFUND IN HISTORY? NEVER!
MEANWHILE, IN THE THRONEROOM...
NOW THAT YOU'RE SET UP AS KING, MACCOVET, LET'S START HAULING AWAY THE MONEY!
176-716
BEAGLE BOYS INC.
176-617
BEAGLE BOYS INC.
CERTAINLY! TAKE A BAG OF CASH AND BUY A FLEET OF TRUCKS! ONCE WE TRANSFER McDUCK'S MONEY TO OUR BANKS, HE CAN HAVE HIS IMPOVERISHED NATION BACK! HA!
HA! HA! HA!
SHALL WE PAY OUR RESPECTS TO HIS EX-MAJESTY McDUCK?
YEAH! I LOVE TO TEASE THE OLD GOAT! HAR!
176-617
BEAGLE BOYS INC.
167-671
BEAGLE BOYS INC.
DON'T TELL ME YOU'RE LEAVING?
WE'LL BE BACK, SCROOGEY! WITH THE BIGGEST FLEET OF TRUCKS YOUR ROYAL EYE-BULBS HAVE EVER SEEN!
176-617
BEAGLE BOYS INC.
176-716
176-671
BEAGLE BOYS INC.
SAY, THIS IS GETTING SERIOUS! IF THEY GET YOUR MONEY ACROSS THE BORDER, IT'LL BE THEIRS FOREVER! LEGALLY!
OH, SO? WATCH THIS!

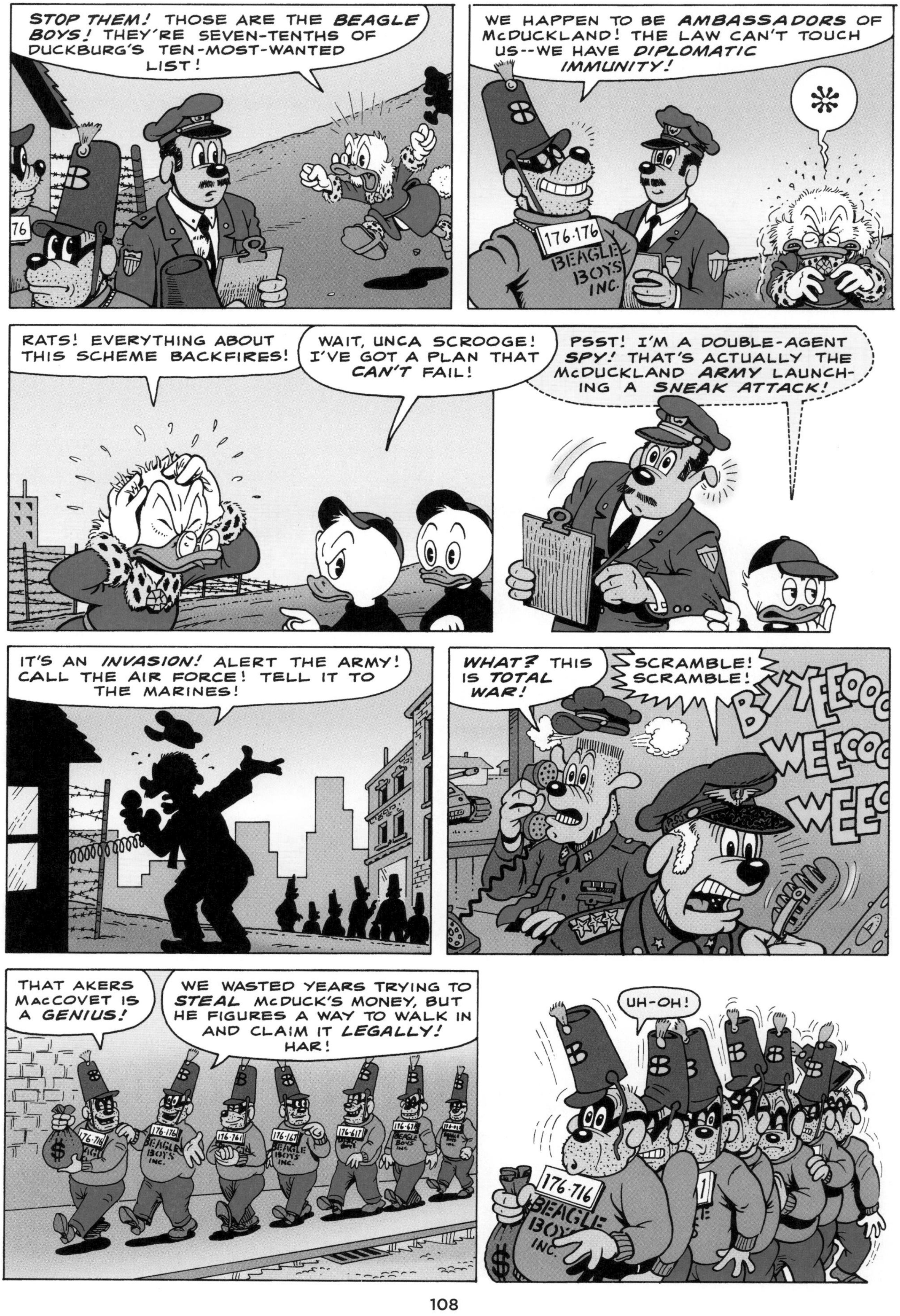
STOP THEM! THOSE ARE THE BEAGLE BOYS! THEY'RE SEVEN-TENTHS OF DUCKBURG'S TEN-MOST-WANTED LIST!
176-176
BEAGLE BOYS INC.
WE HAPPEN TO BE AMBASSADORS OF McDUCKLAND! THE LAW CAN'T TOUCH US--WE HAVE DIPLOMATIC IMMUNITY!
RATS! EVERYTHING ABOUT THIS SCHEME BACKFIRES!
WAIT, UNCA SCROOGE! I'VE GOT A PLAN THAT CAN'T FAIL!
PSST! I'M A DOUBLE-AGENT SPY! THAT'S ACTUALLY THE McDUCKLAND ARMY LAUNCHING A SNEAK ATTACK!
IT'S AN INVASION! ALERT THE ARMY! CALL THE AIR FORCE! TELL IT TO THE MARINES!
WHAT? THIS IS TOTAL WAR!
SCRAMBLE! SCRAMBLE!
BYYEEOOO
WEECOO
WEE
THAT AKERS MacCOVET IS A GENIUS!
WE WASTED YEARS TRYING TO STEAL McDUCK'S MONEY, BUT HE FIGURES A WAY TO WALK IN AND CLAIM IT LEGALLY! HAR!
UH-OH!
176-716
BEAGLE BOYS INC.

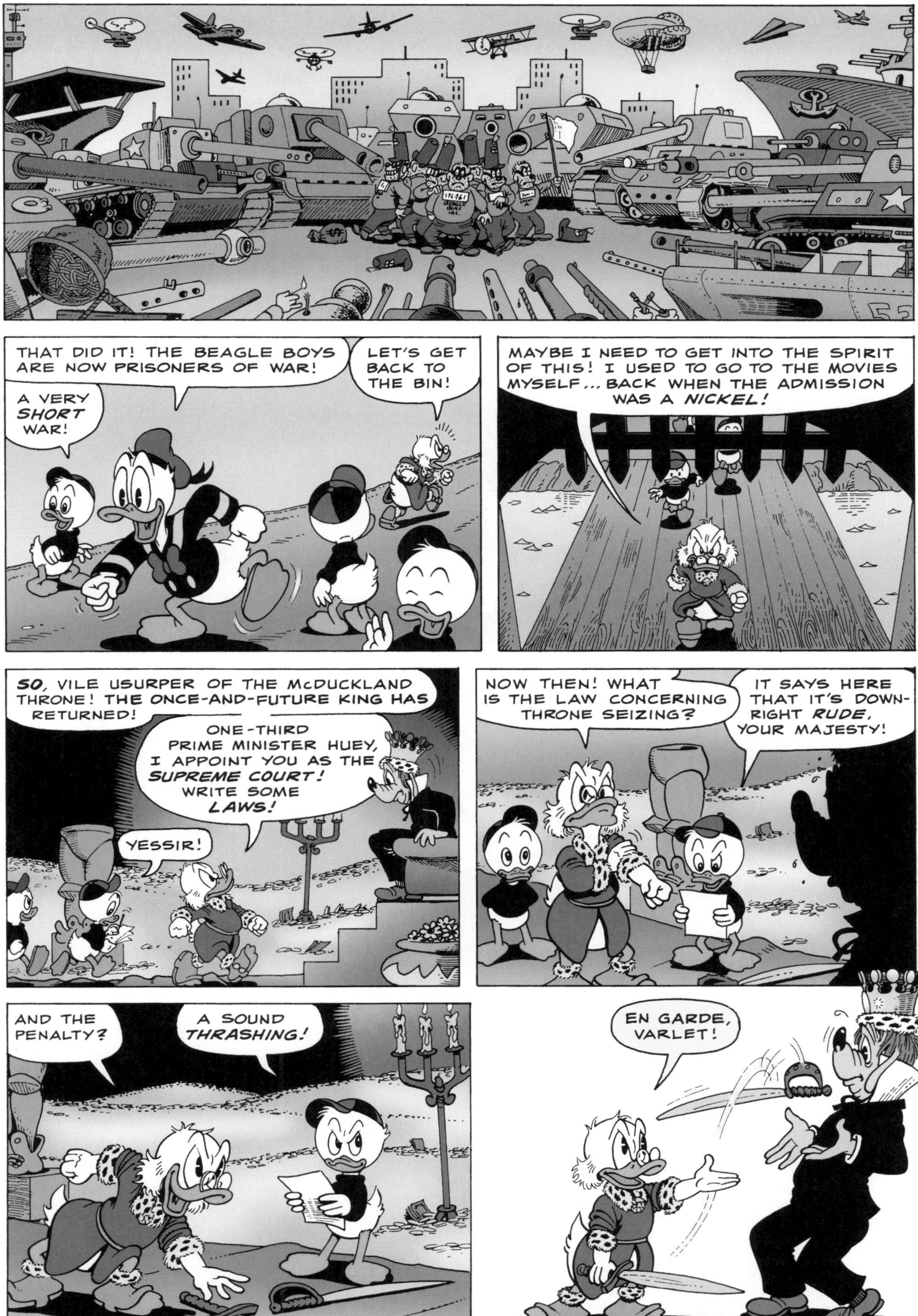
THAT DID IT! THE BEAGLE BOYS ARE NOW PRISONERS OF WAR!
A VERY SHORT WAR!
LET'S GET BACK TO THE BIN!
MAYBE I NEED TO GET INTO THE SPIRIT OF THIS! I USED TO GO TO THE MOVIES MYSELF... BACK WHEN THE ADMISSION WAS A NICKEL!
SO, VILE USURPER OF THE McDUCKLAND THRONE! THE ONCE-AND-FUTURE KING HAS RETURNED!
ONE-THIRD PRIME MINISTER HUEY, I APPOINT YOU AS THE SUPREME COURT! WRITE SOME LAWS!
YESSIR!
NOW THEN! WHAT IS THE LAW CONCERNING THRONE SEIZING?
IT SAYS HERE THAT IT'S DOWNRIGHT RUDE, YOUR MAJESTY!
AND THE PENALTY?
A SOUND THRASHING!
EN GARDE, VARLET!

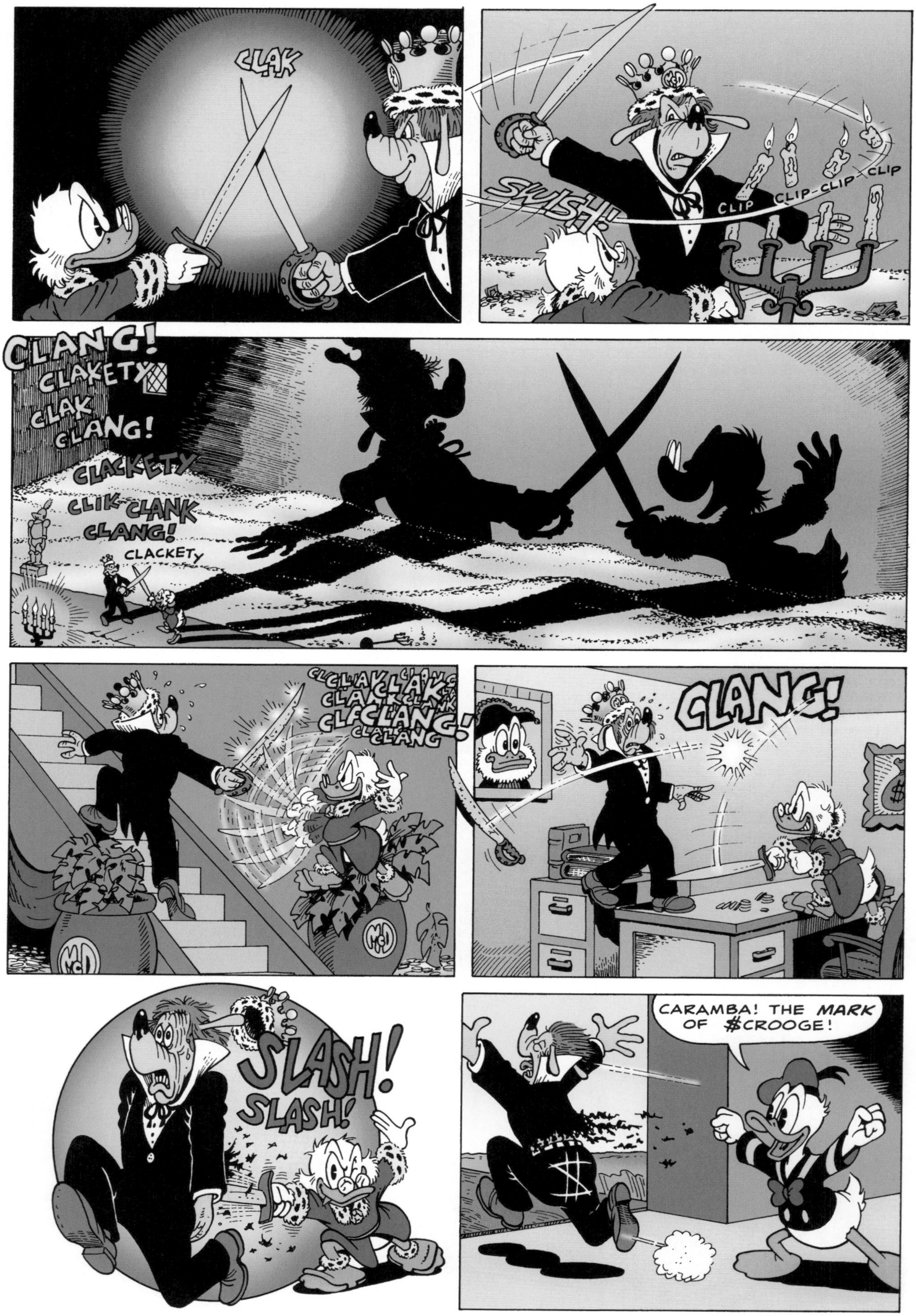
CLAK
SWISH!
CLIP CLIP-CLIP-CLIP
CLANG!
CLAKETY
CLAK
CLANG!
CLACKETY
CLIK CLANK
CLANG!
CLACKETY
CLANG!
SLASH!
SLASH!
CARAMBA! THE MARK OF $CROOGE!

THE RIGHTFUL KING HAS BEEN RESTORED TO HIS THRONE! PRETTY BUSY FIRST DAY IN THIS MONARCHY!

≳GULP!≲ IT'S NOT OVER YET! TURN AROUND!

MONEY MONEY MONEY

OH, DELIVER ME! THE BEAGLE BOYS!

WE THOUGHT YOU WERE ALL PRISONERS OF WAR!

176·617 BEAGLE BOYS INC.

176·176 BEAGLE BOYS INC.

S.McDUCK

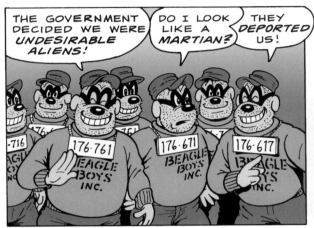

THE GOVERNMENT DECIDED WE WERE UNDESIRABLE ALIENS!

DO I LOOK LIKE A MARTIAN?

THEY DEPORTED US!

·716

176·761 BEAGLE BOYS INC.

176·671 BEAGLE BOYS INC.

176·617 BEAGLE BOYS INC.

WE CAN'T LEAVE McDUCKLAND, SO WE DON'T WANT YOUR MONEY!

BESIDES, WE'RE NOW ON McDUCKLAND WELFARE! YOU HAFTA FEED AND HOUSE US!

UK-WUK!

176·671 BEAGLE BOYS INC.

176·617 BEAGLE BOYS INC.

THERE'S NO END TO THE TROUBLE YOU'RE CAUSING YOURSELF!

IT'S WORTH IT! THAT TAX REFUND WILL PAY FOR THE HUMILIATION OF BEING THE BEAGLES' FOSTER FATHER!

UNCA SCROOGE, THE MAYOR OF DUCKBURG TO SEE YOU!

QUIET! WE'RE TRYIN' TA SLEEP!

WHEN'S LUNCH AROUND HERE?

WHAT DO YOU WANT?

I CAME ABOUT THE TAX REFUND THAT DUCKBURG OWES YOU, MR....ER... KING SCROOGE!

SAY, THAT'S RIGHT! I'VE PAID CITY TAXES, TOO! WOW!

I'M AFRAID THAT DUCKBURG SIMPLY CAN'T AFFORD TO REPAY YOU!

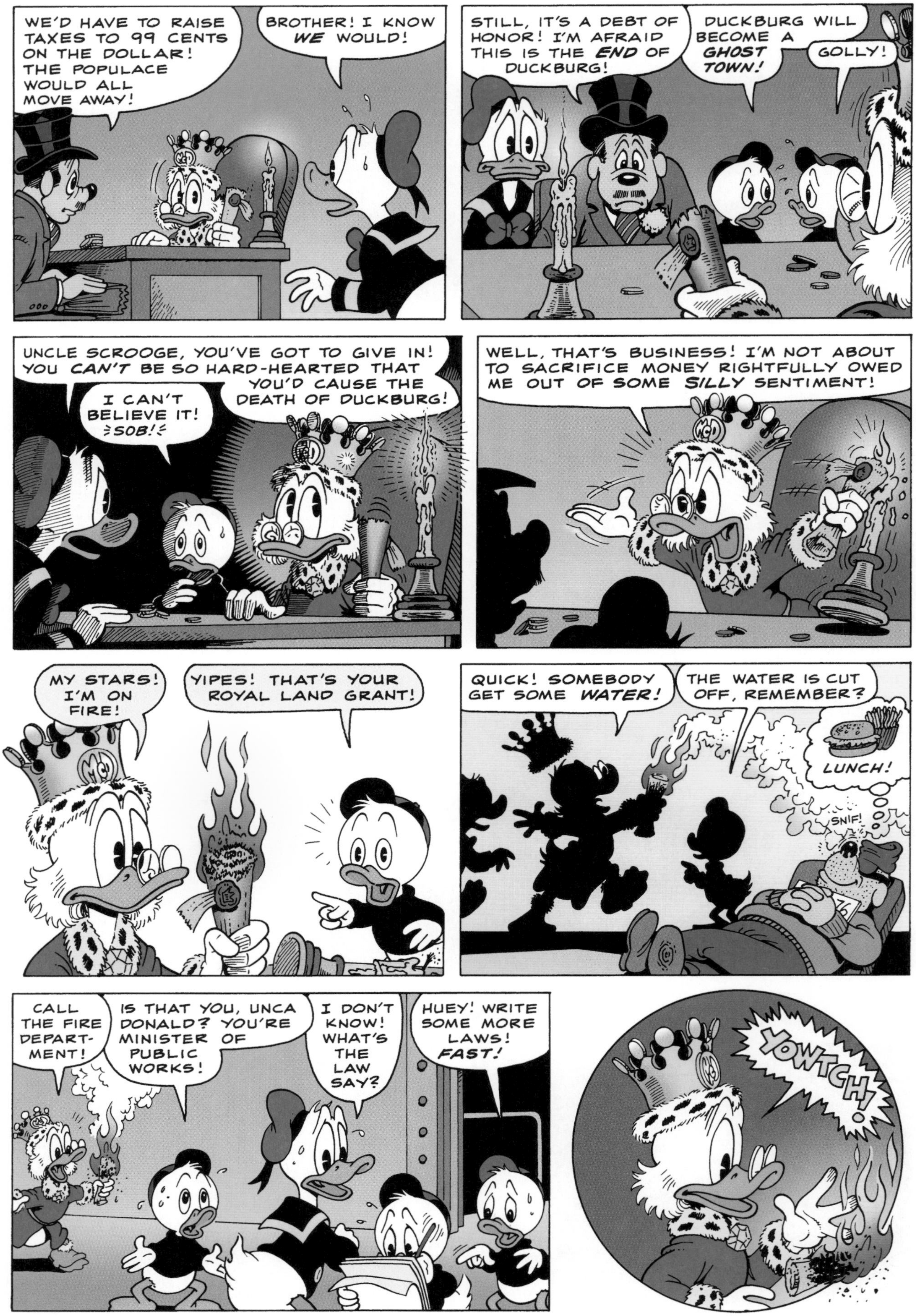
WE'D HAVE TO RAISE TAXES TO 99 CENTS ON THE DOLLAR! THE POPULACE WOULD ALL MOVE AWAY!
BROTHER! I KNOW WE WOULD!
STILL, IT'S A DEBT OF HONOR! I'M AFRAID THIS IS THE END OF DUCKBURG!
DUCKBURG WILL BECOME A GHOST TOWN!
GOLLY!
UNCLE SCROOGE, YOU'VE GOT TO GIVE IN! YOU CAN'T BE SO HARD-HEARTED THAT YOU'D CAUSE THE DEATH OF DUCKBURG!
I CAN'T BELIEVE IT! SOB!
WELL, THAT'S BUSINESS! I'M NOT ABOUT TO SACRIFICE MONEY RIGHTFULLY OWED ME OUT OF SOME SILLY SENTIMENT!
MY STARS! I'M ON FIRE!
YIPES! THAT'S YOUR ROYAL LAND GRANT!
QUICK! SOMEBODY GET SOME WATER!
THE WATER IS CUT OFF, REMEMBER?
LUNCH!
SNIF!
CALL THE FIRE DEPART-MENT!
IS THAT YOU, UNCA DONALD? YOU'RE MINISTER OF PUBLIC WORKS!
I DON'T KNOW! WHAT'S THE LAW SAY?
HUEY! WRITE SOME MORE LAWS! FAST!
YOWTCH!

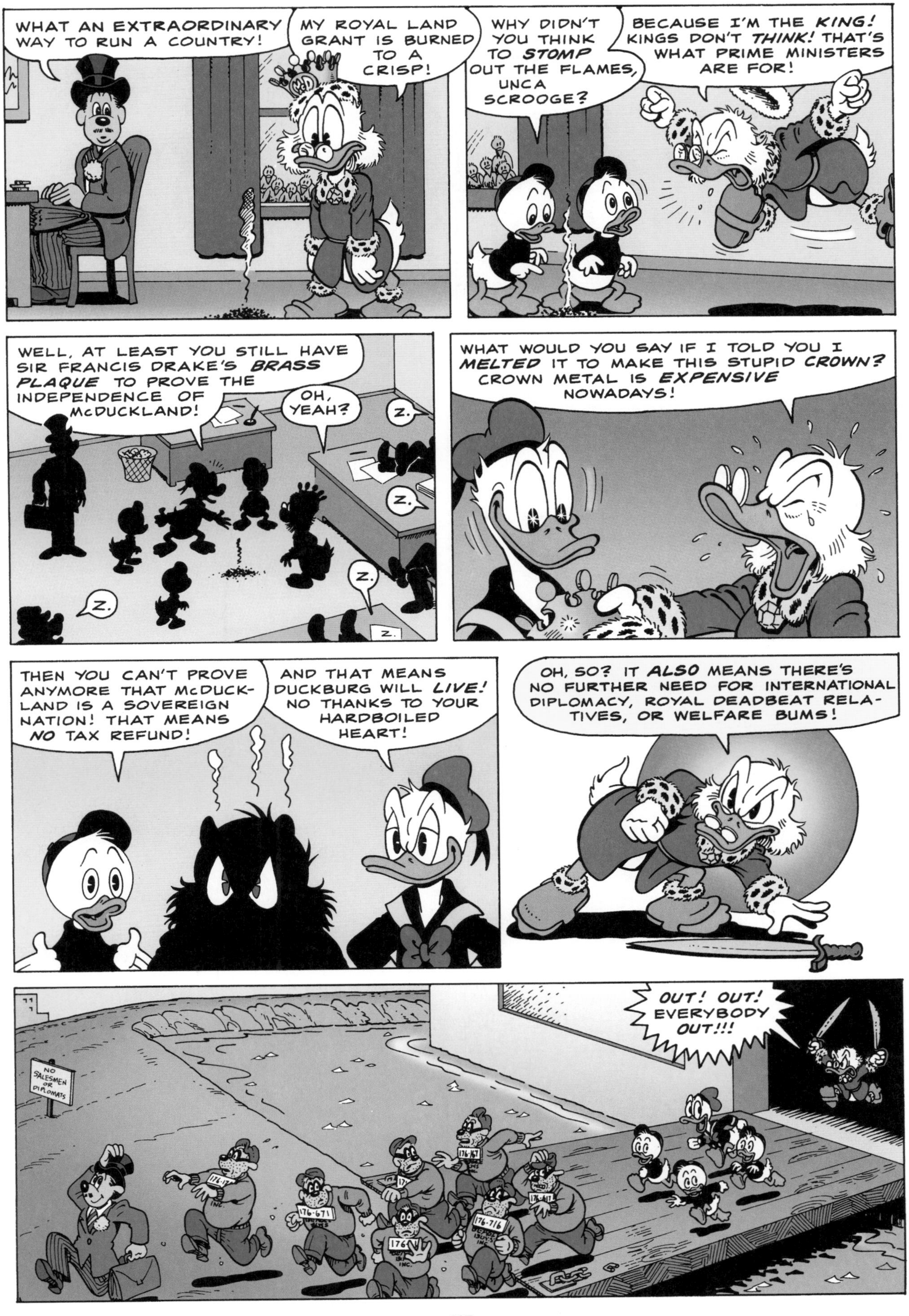
WHAT AN EXTRAORDINARY WAY TO RUN A COUNTRY!
MY ROYAL LAND GRANT IS BURNED TO A CRISP!
WHY DIDN'T YOU THINK TO STOMP OUT THE FLAMES, UNCA SCROOGE?
BECAUSE I'M THE KING! KINGS DON'T THINK! THAT'S WHAT PRIME MINISTERS ARE FOR!
WELL, AT LEAST YOU STILL HAVE SIR FRANCIS DRAKE'S BRASS PLAQUE TO PROVE THE INDEPENDENCE OF McDUCKLAND!
OH, YEAH?
Z.
Z.
Z.
Z.
Z.
WHAT WOULD YOU SAY IF I TOLD YOU I MELTED IT TO MAKE THIS STUPID CROWN? CROWN METAL IS EXPENSIVE NOWADAYS!
THEN YOU CAN'T PROVE ANYMORE THAT McDUCKLAND IS A SOVEREIGN NATION! THAT MEANS NO TAX REFUND!
AND THAT MEANS DUCKBURG WILL LIVE! NO THANKS TO YOUR HARDBOILED HEART!
OH, SO? IT ALSO MEANS THERE'S NO FURTHER NEED FOR INTERNATIONAL DIPLOMACY, ROYAL DEADBEAT RELATIVES, OR WELFARE BUMS!
OUT! OUT! EVERYBODY OUT!!!
NO SALESMEN OR DIPLOMATS

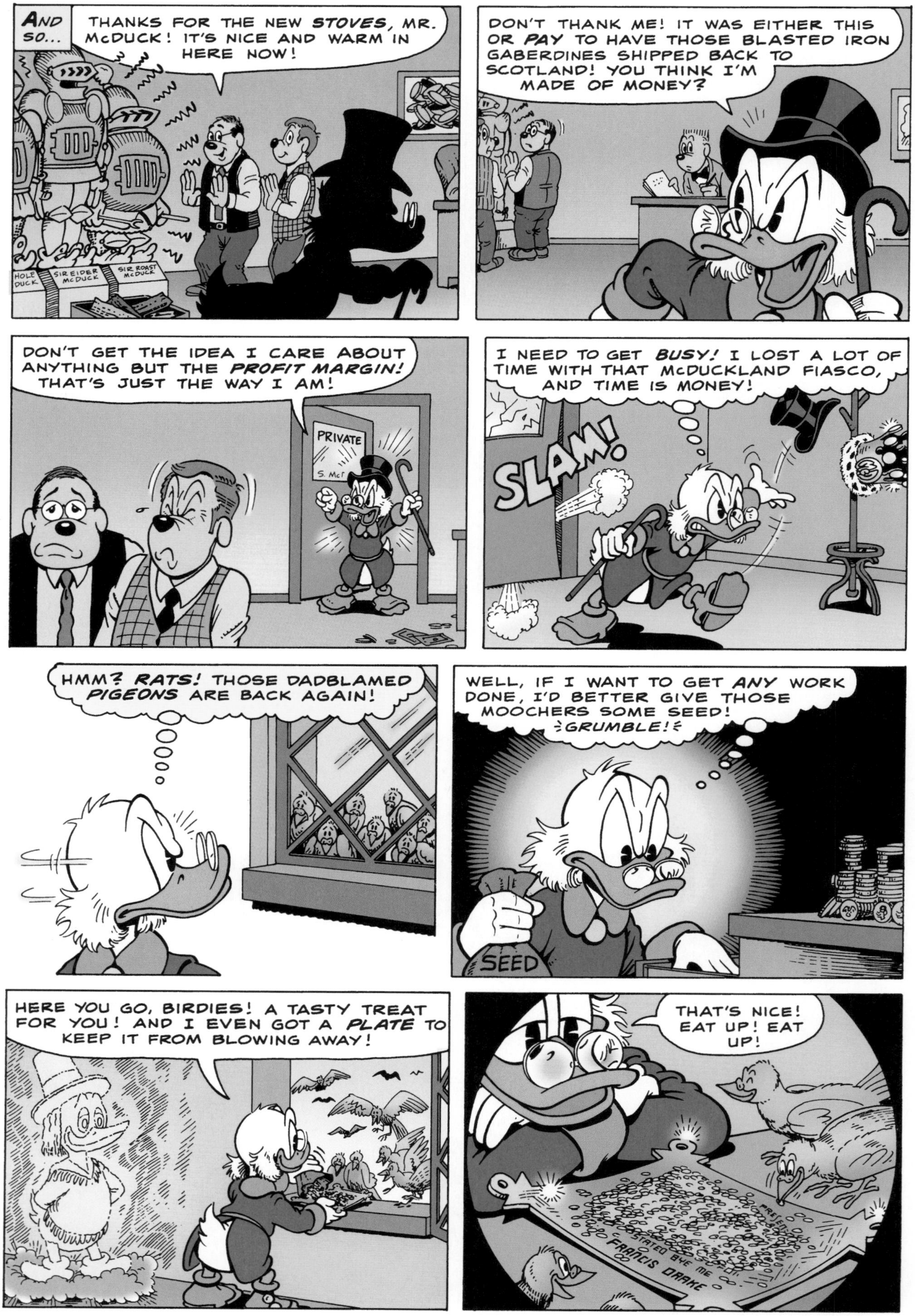
AND SO...
THANKS FOR THE NEW STOVES, MR. McDUCK! IT'S NICE AND WARM IN HERE NOW!
HOLE DUCK
SIR EIDER McDUCK
SIR ROAST McDUCK
DON'T THANK ME! IT WAS EITHER THIS OR PAY TO HAVE THOSE BLASTED IRON GABERDINES SHIPPED BACK TO SCOTLAND! YOU THINK I'M MADE OF MONEY?
DON'T GET THE IDEA I CARE ABOUT ANYTHING BUT THE PROFIT MARGIN! THAT'S JUST THE WAY I AM!
PRIVATE
I NEED TO GET BUSY! I LOST A LOT OF TIME WITH THAT McDUCKLAND FIASCO, AND TIME IS MONEY!
SLAM!
HMM? RATS! THOSE DADBLAMED PIGEONS ARE BACK AGAIN!
WELL, IF I WANT TO GET ANY WORK DONE, I'D BETTER GIVE THOSE MOOCHERS SOME SEED! GRUMBLE!
SEED
HERE YOU GO, BIRDIES! A TASTY TREAT FOR YOU! AND I EVEN GOT A PLATE TO KEEP IT FROM BLOWING AWAY!
THAT'S NICE! EAT UP! EAT UP!
STATED BYE ME
FRANCIS DRAKE

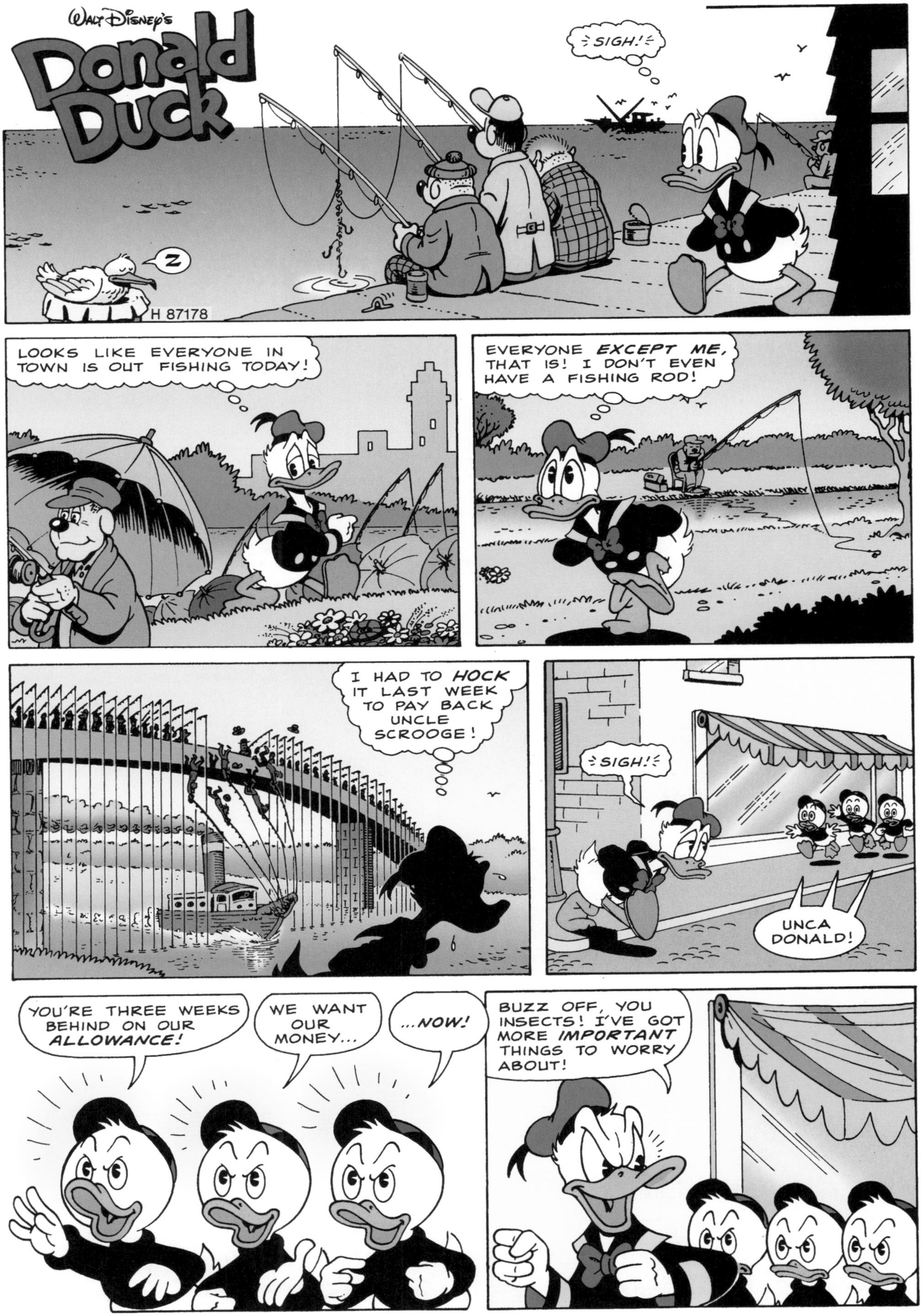
Walt Disney's
Donald Duck
SIGH!
Z
H 87178
LOOKS LIKE EVERYONE IN TOWN IS OUT FISHING TODAY!
EVERYONE EXCEPT ME, THAT IS! I DON'T EVEN HAVE A FISHING ROD!
I HAD TO HOCK IT LAST WEEK TO PAY BACK UNCLE SCROOGE!
SIGH!
UNCA DONALD!
YOU'RE THREE WEEKS BEHIND ON OUR ALLOWANCE!
WE WANT OUR MONEY...
...NOW!
BUZZ OFF, YOU INSECTS! I'VE GOT MORE IMPORTANT THINGS TO WORRY ABOUT!

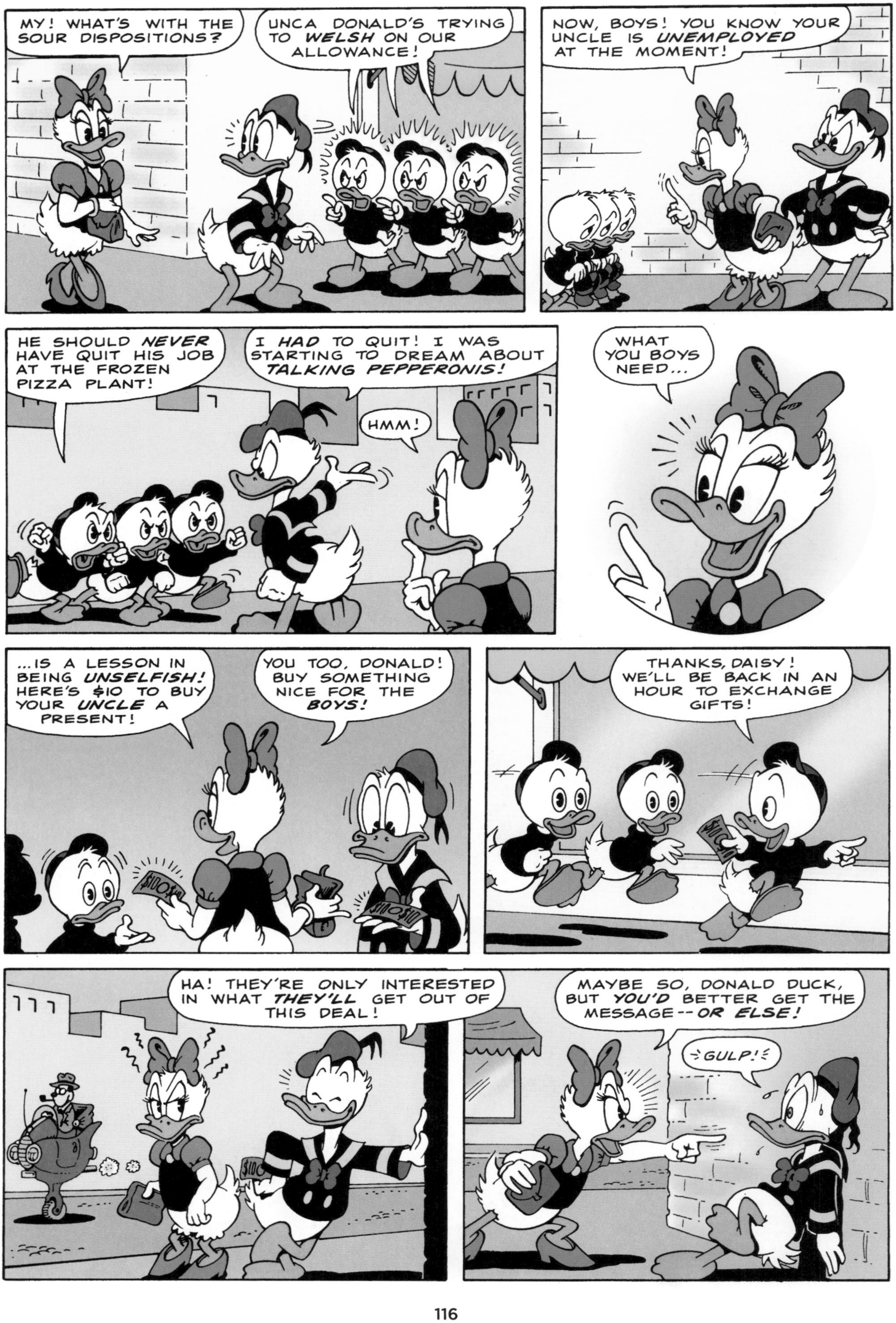
MY! WHAT'S WITH THE SOUR DISPOSITIONS?
UNCA DONALD'S TRYING TO WELSH ON OUR ALLOWANCE!
NOW, BOYS! YOU KNOW YOUR UNCLE IS UNEMPLOYED AT THE MOMENT!
HE SHOULD NEVER HAVE QUIT HIS JOB AT THE FROZEN PIZZA PLANT!
I HAD TO QUIT! I WAS STARTING TO DREAM ABOUT TALKING PEPPERONIS!
HMM!
WHAT YOU BOYS NEED...
...IS A LESSON IN BEING UNSELFISH! HERE'S $10 TO BUY YOUR UNCLE A PRESENT!
YOU TOO, DONALD! BUY SOMETHING NICE FOR THE BOYS!
THANKS, DAISY! WE'LL BE BACK IN AN HOUR TO EXCHANGE GIFTS!
HA! THEY'RE ONLY INTERESTED IN WHAT THEY'LL GET OUT OF THIS DEAL!
MAYBE SO, DONALD DUCK, BUT YOU'D BETTER GET THE MESSAGE--OR ELSE!
GULP!

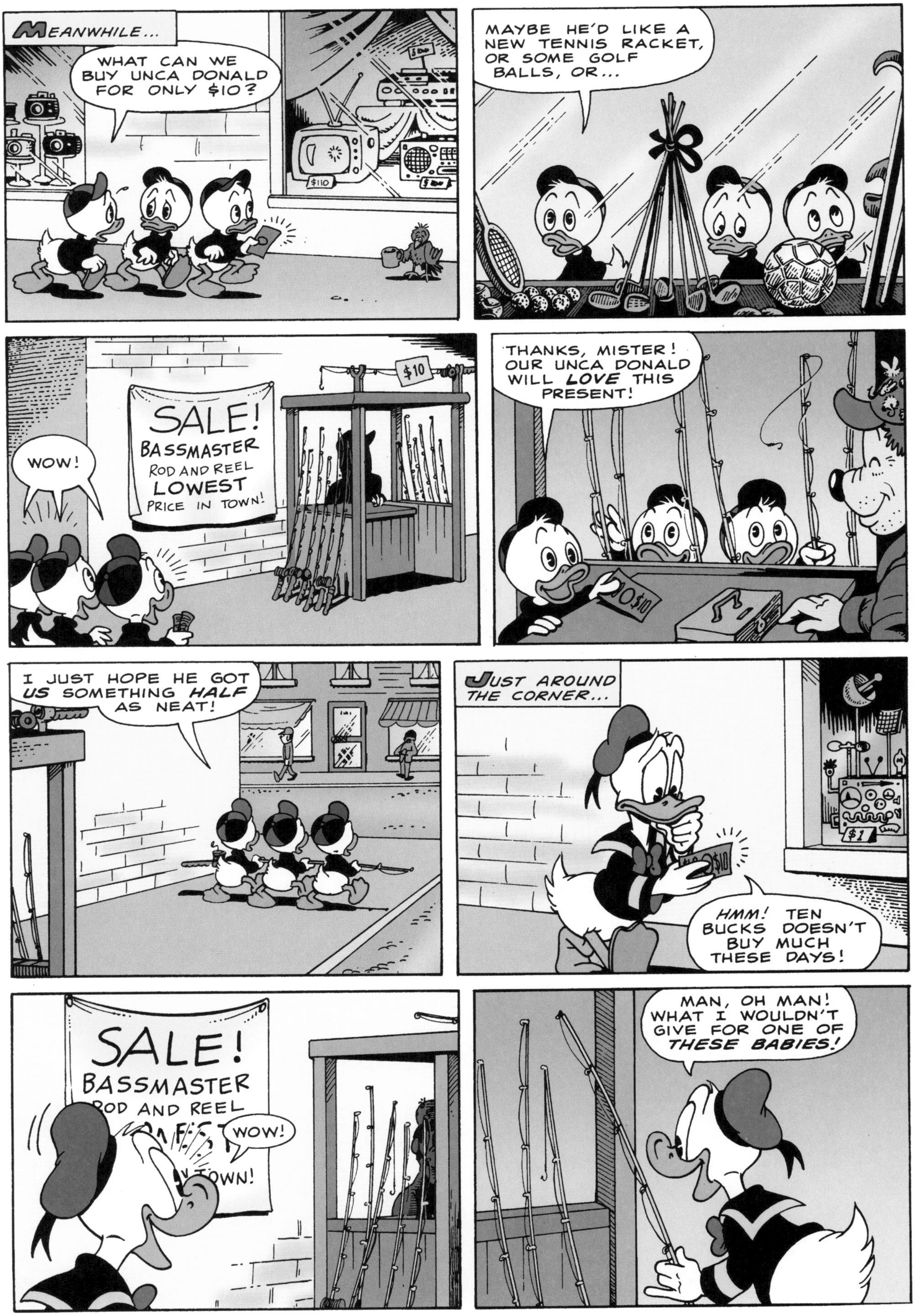
MEANWHILE...
WHAT CAN WE BUY UNCA DONALD FOR ONLY $10?
$110
MAYBE HE'D LIKE A NEW TENNIS RACKET, OR SOME GOLF BALLS, OR...
$10
SALE! BASSMASTER ROD AND REEL LOWEST PRICE IN TOWN!
WOW!
THANKS, MISTER! OUR UNCA DONALD WILL LOVE THIS PRESENT!
I JUST HOPE HE GOT US SOMETHING HALF AS NEAT!
JUST AROUND THE CORNER...
$1
HMM! TEN BUCKS DOESN'T BUY MUCH THESE DAYS!
SALE! BASSMASTER ROD AND REEL
WOW!
MAN, OH MAN! WHAT I WOULDN'T GIVE FOR ONE OF THESE BABIES!

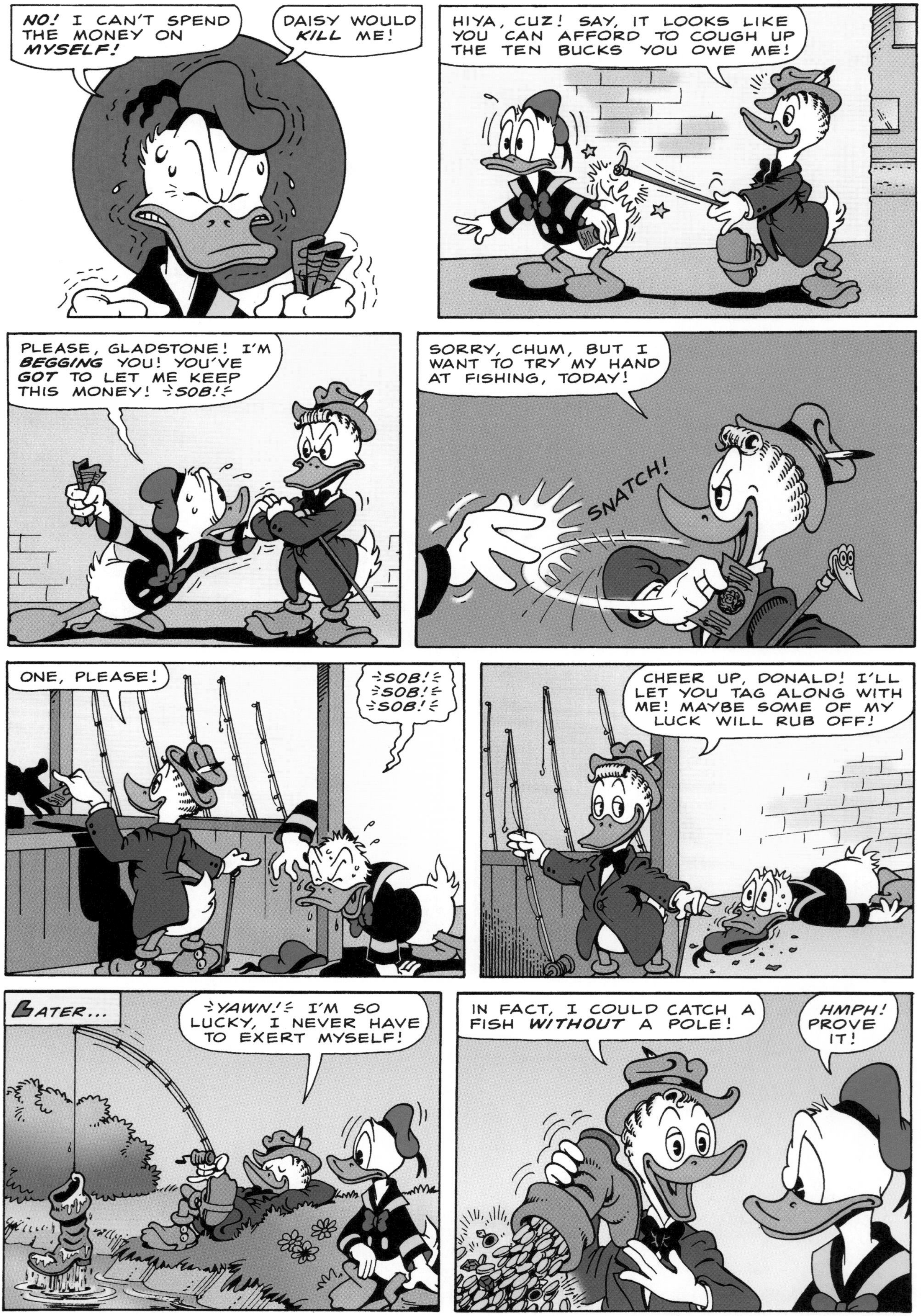
NO! I CAN'T SPEND THE MONEY ON MYSELF!
DAISY WOULD KILL ME!
HIYA, CUZ! SAY, IT LOOKS LIKE YOU CAN AFFORD TO COUGH UP THE TEN BUCKS YOU OWE ME!
PLEASE, GLADSTONE! I'M BEGGING YOU! YOU'VE GOT TO LET ME KEEP THIS MONEY! -SOB!-
SORRY, CHUM, BUT I WANT TO TRY MY HAND AT FISHING, TODAY!
SNATCH!
ONE, PLEASE!
-SOB!- -SOB!- -SOB!-
CHEER UP, DONALD! I'LL LET YOU TAG ALONG WITH ME! MAYBE SOME OF MY LUCK WILL RUB OFF!
LATER...
-YAWN!- I'M SO LUCKY, I NEVER HAVE TO EXERT MYSELF!
IN FACT, I COULD CATCH A FISH WITHOUT A POLE!
HMPH! PROVE IT!

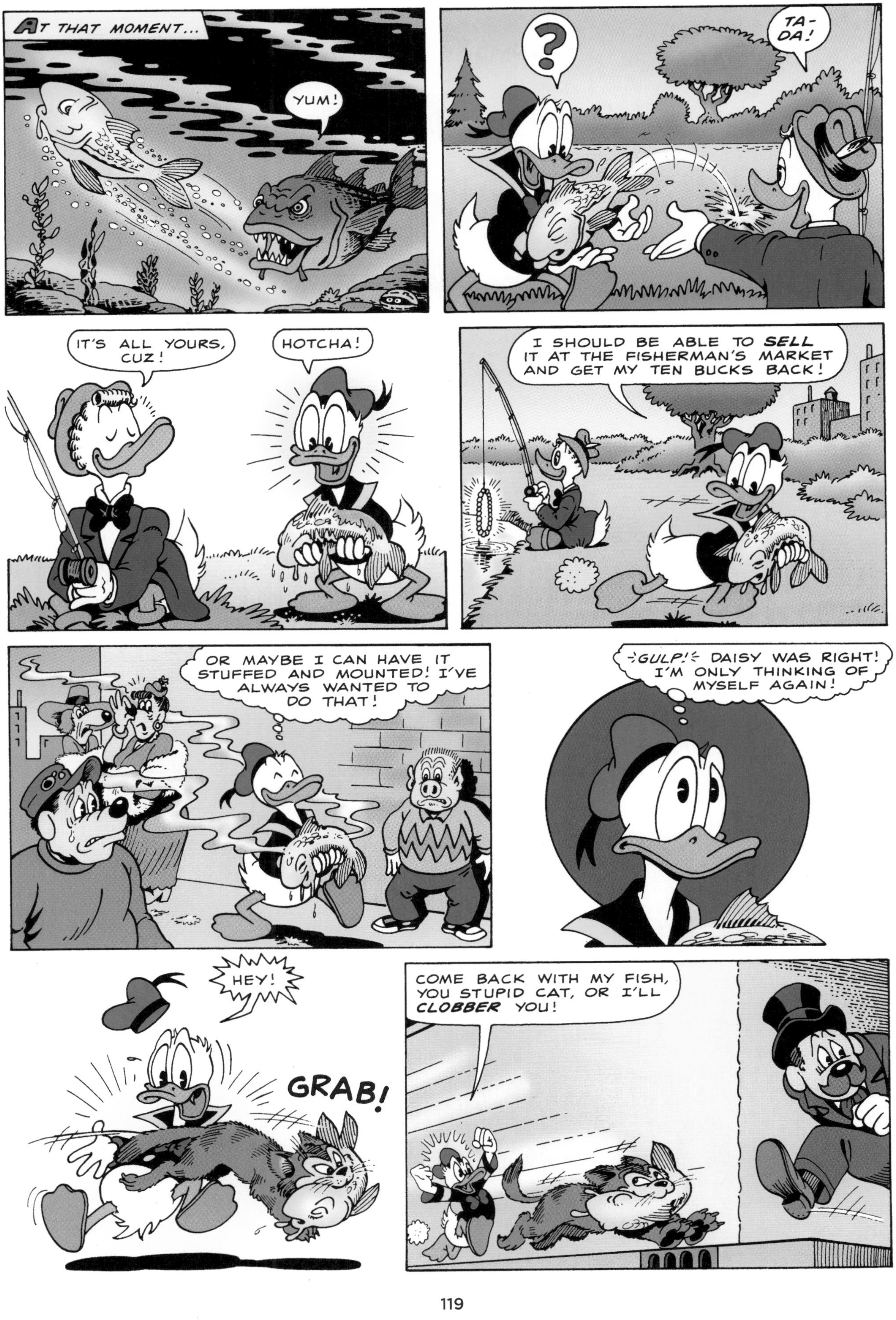
AT THAT MOMENT...
YUM!
?
TA-DA!
IT'S ALL YOURS, CUZ!
HOTCHA!
I SHOULD BE ABLE TO SELL IT AT THE FISHERMAN'S MARKET AND GET MY TEN BUCKS BACK!
OR MAYBE I CAN HAVE IT STUFFED AND MOUNTED! I'VE ALWAYS WANTED TO DO THAT!
GULP! DAISY WAS RIGHT! I'M ONLY THINKING OF MYSELF AGAIN!
HEY!
GRAB!
COME BACK WITH MY FISH, YOU STUPID CAT, OR I'LL CLOBBER YOU!

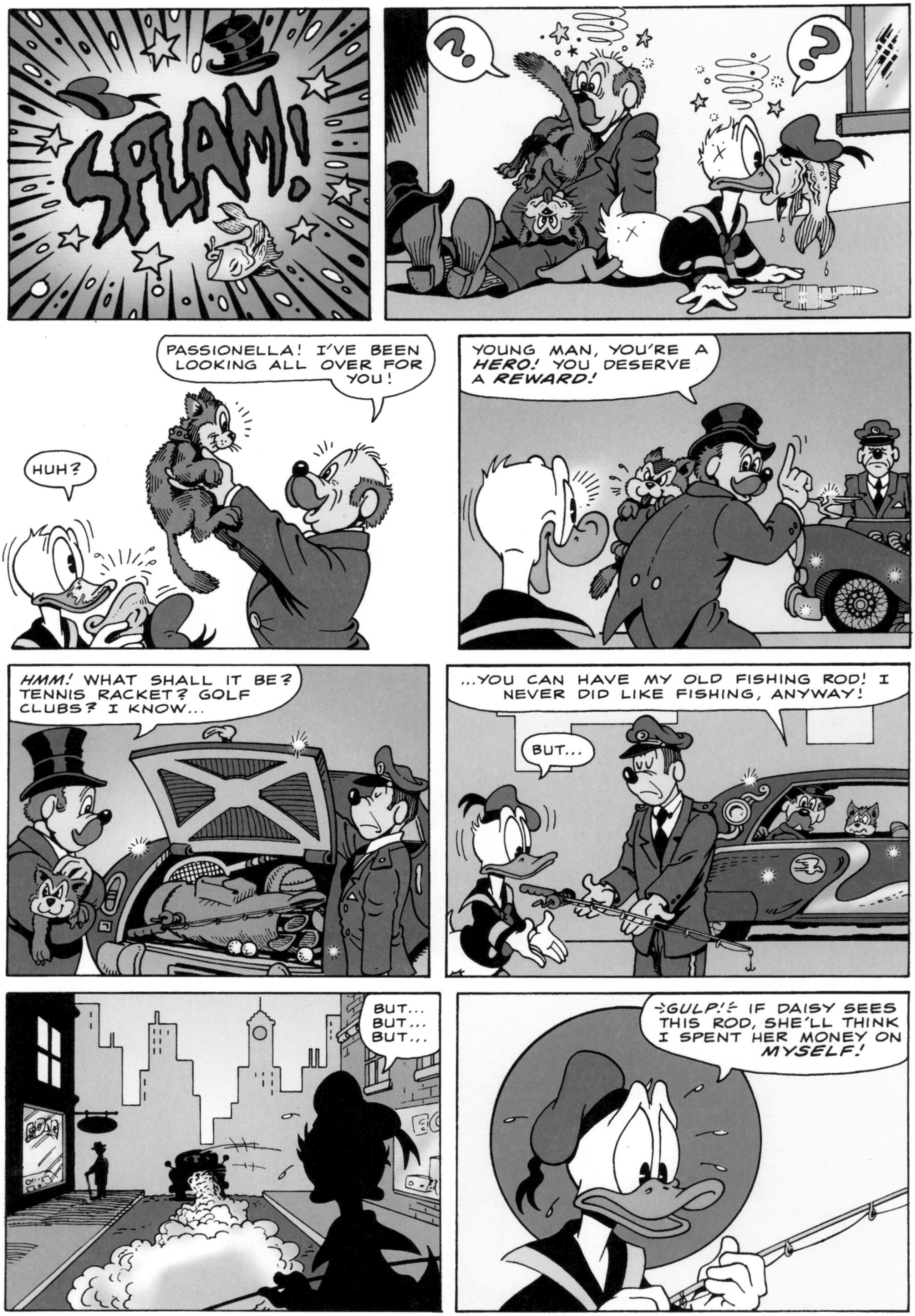
SPLAM!
?
?
PASSIONELLA! I'VE BEEN LOOKING ALL OVER FOR YOU!
HUH?
YOUNG MAN, YOU'RE A *HERO!* YOU DESERVE A *REWARD!*
HMM! WHAT SHALL IT BE? TENNIS RACKET? GOLF CLUBS? I KNOW...
...YOU CAN HAVE MY OLD FISHING ROD! I NEVER DID LIKE FISHING, ANYWAY!
BUT...
BUT... BUT... BUT...
GULP! IF DAISY SEES THIS ROD, SHE'LL THINK I SPENT HER MONEY ON *MYSELF!*

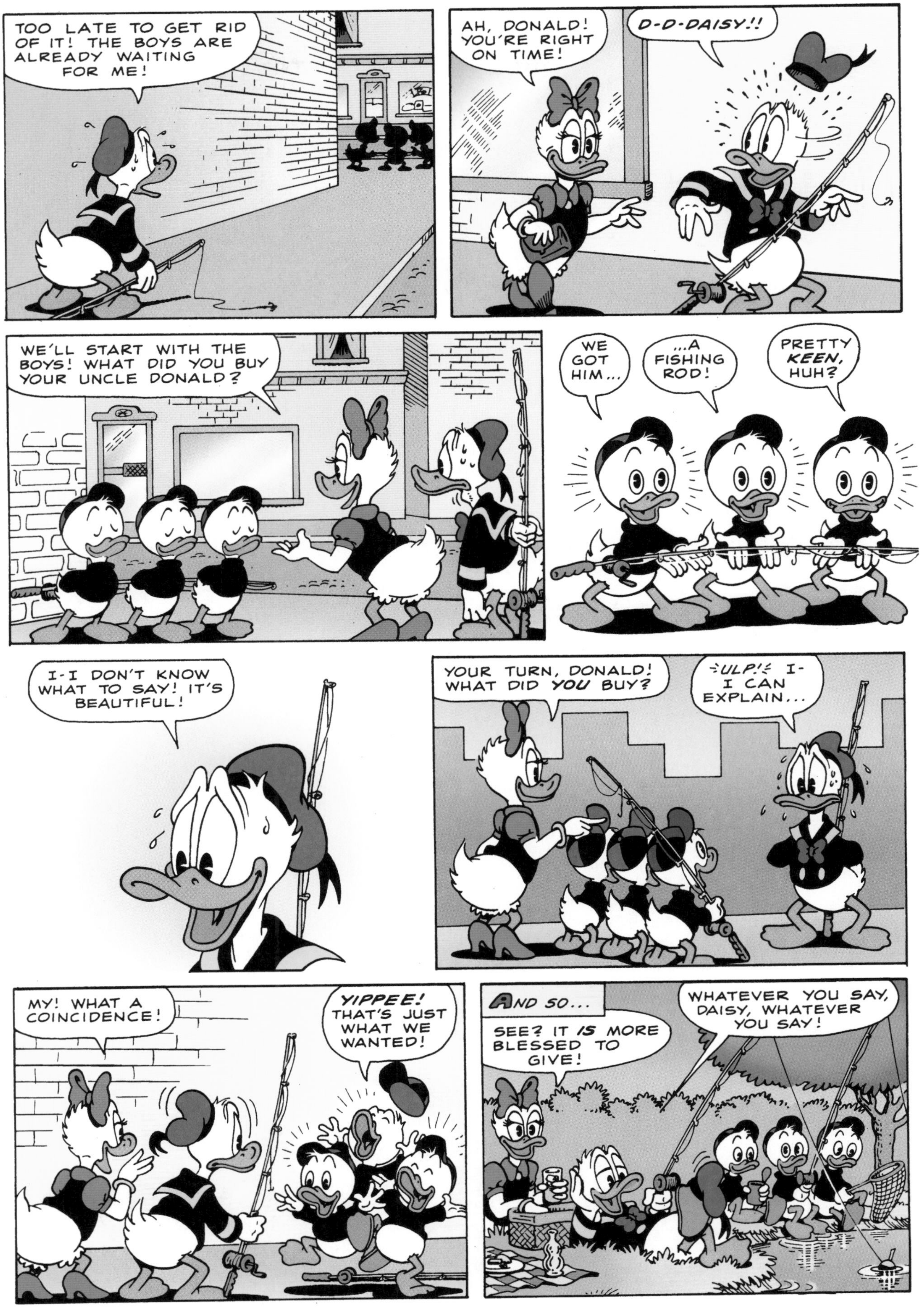
TOO LATE TO GET RID OF IT! THE BOYS ARE ALREADY WAITING FOR ME!
AH, DONALD! YOU'RE RIGHT ON TIME!
D-D-DAISY!!
WE'LL START WITH THE BOYS! WHAT DID YOU BUY YOUR UNCLE DONALD?
WE GOT HIM...
...A FISHING ROD!
PRETTY KEEN, HUH?
I-I DON'T KNOW WHAT TO SAY! IT'S BEAUTIFUL!
YOUR TURN, DONALD! WHAT DID YOU BUY?
ULP! I- I CAN EXPLAIN...
MY! WHAT A COINCIDENCE!
YIPPEE! THAT'S JUST WHAT WE WANTED!
AND SO...
SEE? IT IS MORE BLESSED TO GIVE!
WHATEVER YOU SAY, DAISY, WHATEVER YOU SAY!

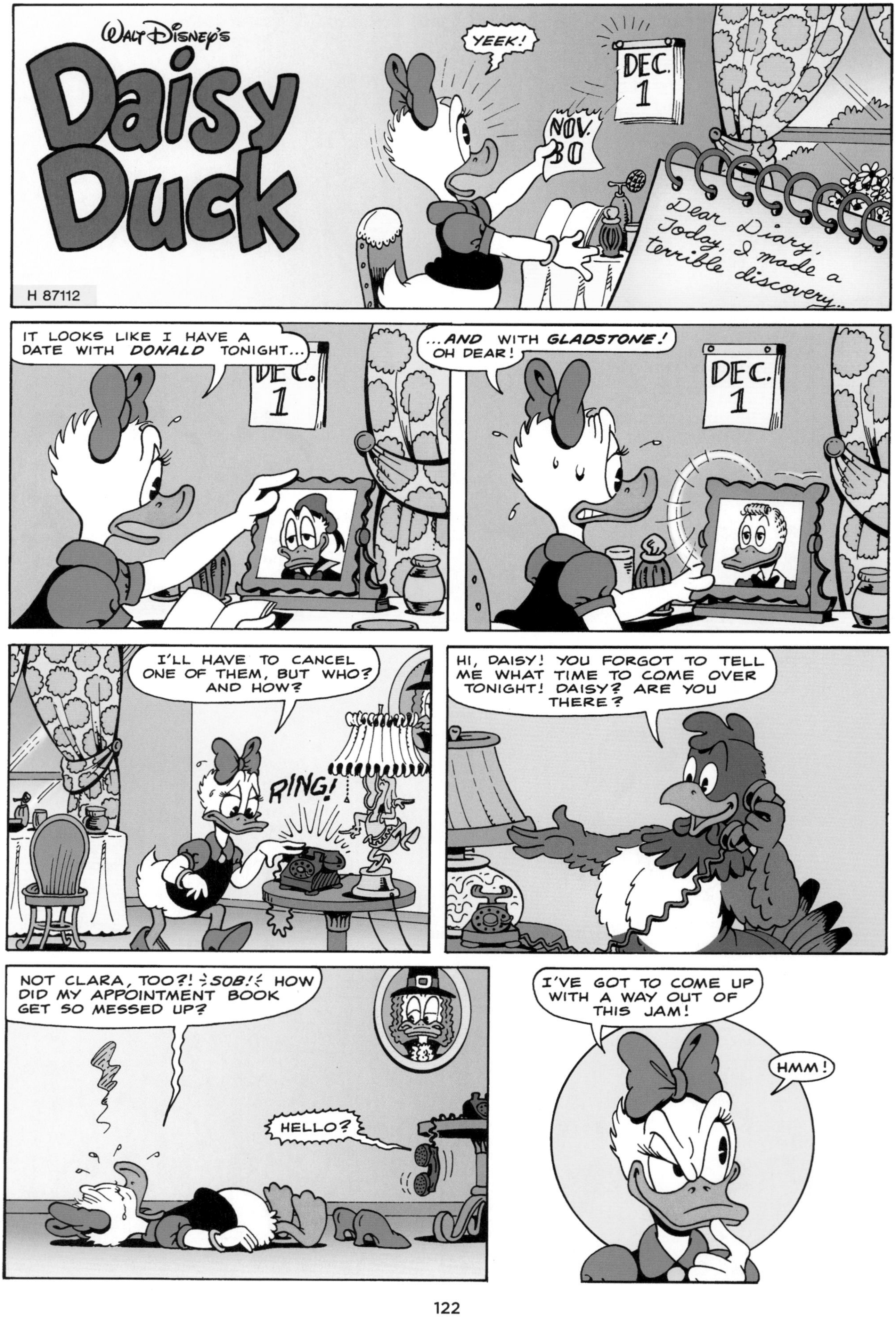

WALT DISNEY'S
Daisy Duck
YEEK!
DEC. 1
NOV. 30
Dear Diary, Today, I made a terrible discovery...
H 87112
IT LOOKS LIKE I HAVE A DATE WITH DONALD TONIGHT...
DEC. 1
...AND WITH GLADSTONE! OH DEAR!
DEC. 1
I'LL HAVE TO CANCEL ONE OF THEM, BUT WHO? AND HOW?
RING!
HI, DAISY! YOU FORGOT TO TELL ME WHAT TIME TO COME OVER TONIGHT! DAISY? ARE YOU THERE?
NOT CLARA, TOO?! SOB! HOW DID MY APPOINTMENT BOOK GET SO MESSED UP?
HELLO?
I'VE GOT TO COME UP WITH A WAY OUT OF THIS JAM!
HMM!

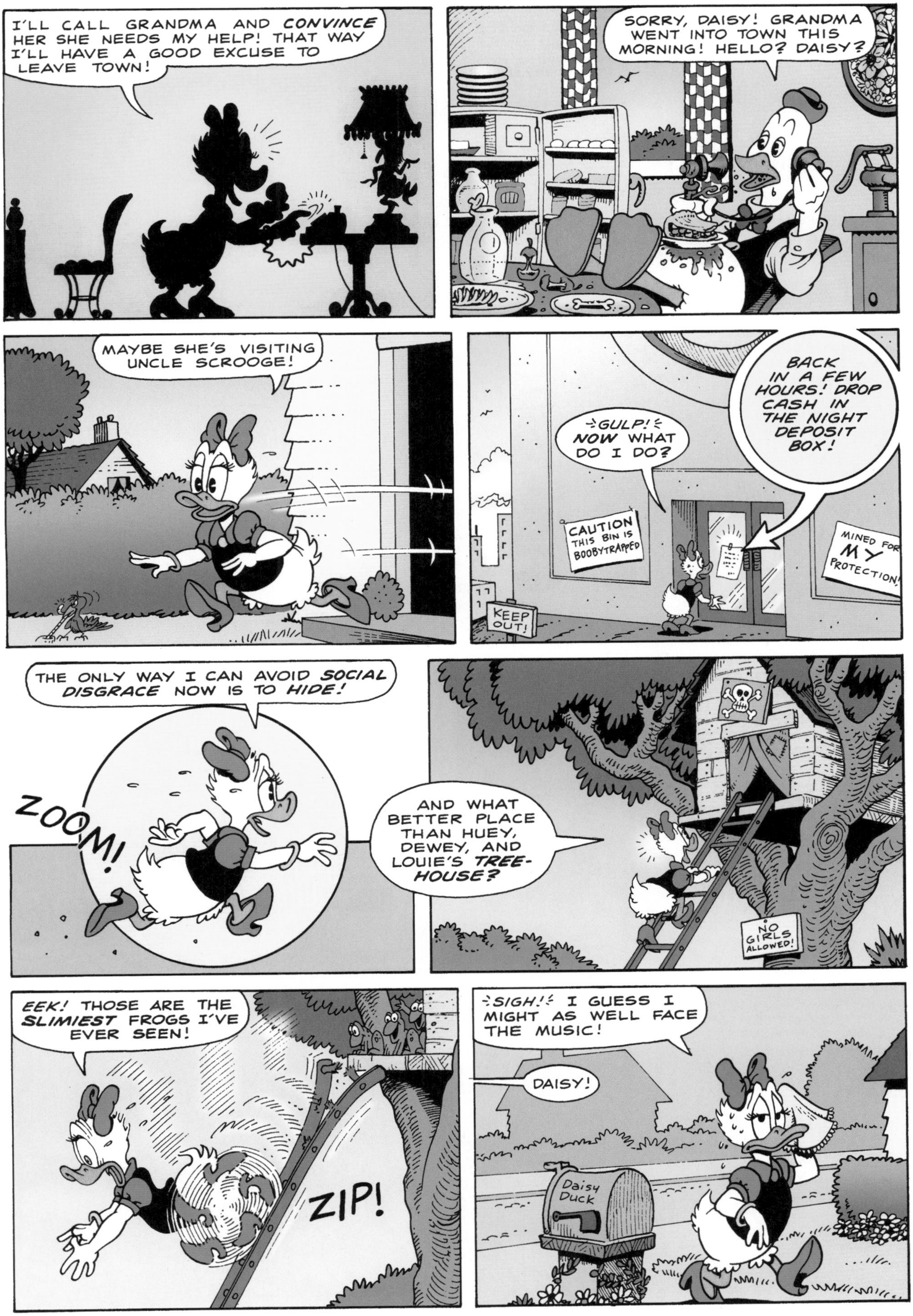
I'LL CALL GRANDMA AND CONVINCE HER SHE NEEDS MY HELP! THAT WAY I'LL HAVE A GOOD EXCUSE TO LEAVE TOWN!
SORRY, DAISY! GRANDMA WENT INTO TOWN THIS MORNING! HELLO? DAISY?
MAYBE SHE'S VISITING UNCLE SCROOGE!
GULP! NOW WHAT DO I DO?
BACK IN A FEW HOURS! DROP CASH IN THE NIGHT DEPOSIT BOX!
CAUTION THIS BIN IS BOOBYTRAPPED
MINED FOR MY PROTECTION!
KEEP OUT!
THE ONLY WAY I CAN AVOID SOCIAL DISGRACE NOW IS TO HIDE!
ZOOM!
AND WHAT BETTER PLACE THAN HUEY, DEWEY, AND LOUIE'S TREE-HOUSE?
NO GIRLS ALLOWED!
EEK! THOSE ARE THE SLIMIEST FROGS I'VE EVER SEEN!
ZIP!
SIGH! I GUESS I MIGHT AS WELL FACE THE MUSIC!
DAISY!
Daisy Duck

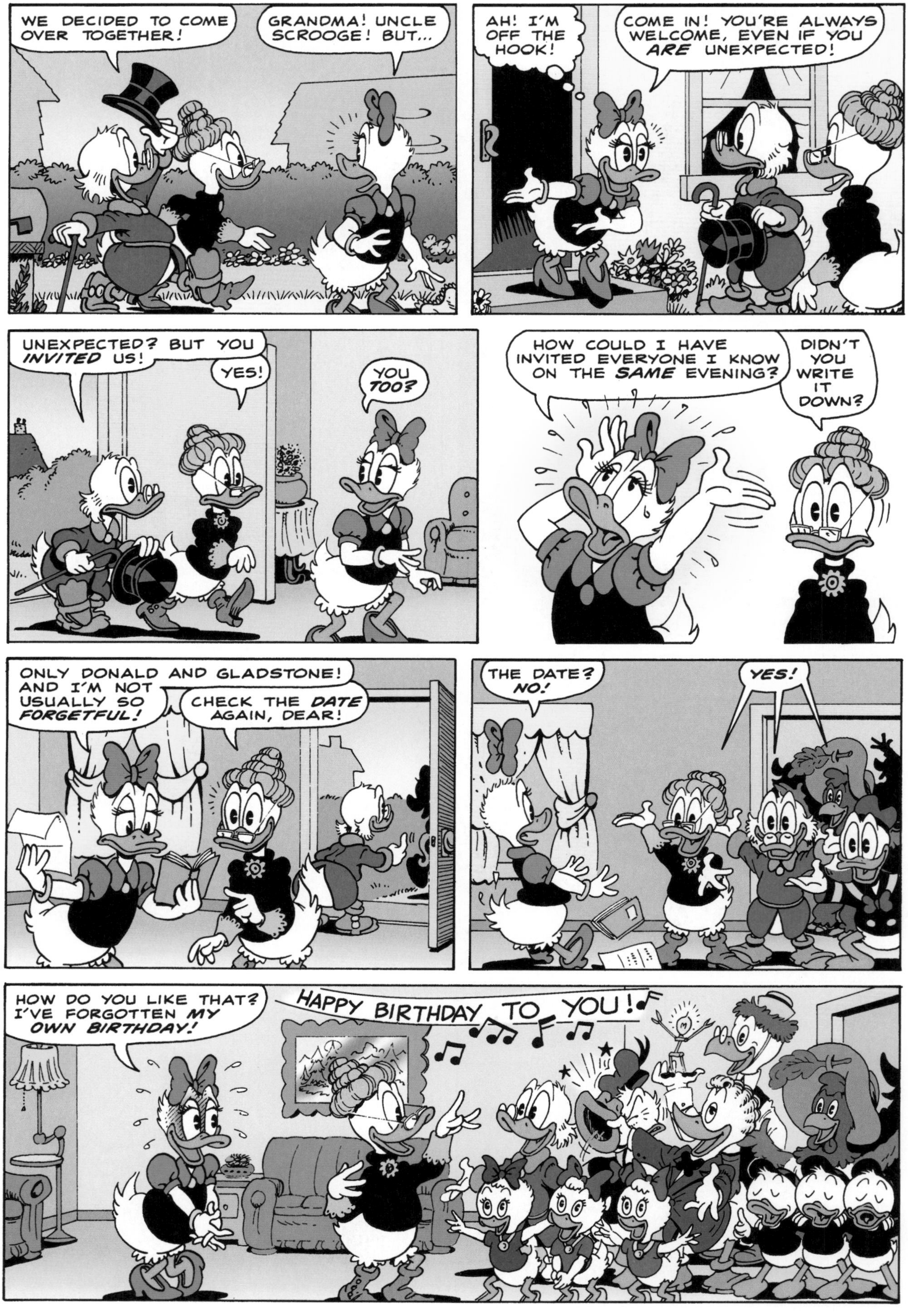

WE DECIDED TO COME OVER TOGETHER!
GRANDMA! UNCLE SCROOGE! BUT...
AH! I'M OFF THE HOOK!
COME IN! YOU'RE ALWAYS WELCOME, EVEN IF YOU *ARE* UNEXPECTED!
UNEXPECTED? BUT YOU *INVITED* US!
YES!
YOU *TOO?*
HOW COULD I HAVE INVITED EVERYONE I KNOW ON THE *SAME* EVENING?
DIDN'T YOU WRITE IT DOWN?
ONLY DONALD AND GLADSTONE! AND I'M NOT USUALLY SO *FORGETFUL!*
CHECK THE *DATE* AGAIN, DEAR!
THE DATE? *NO!*
YES!
HOW DO YOU LIKE THAT? I'VE FORGOTTEN *MY OWN BIRTHDAY!*
HAPPY BIRTHDAY TO YOU!

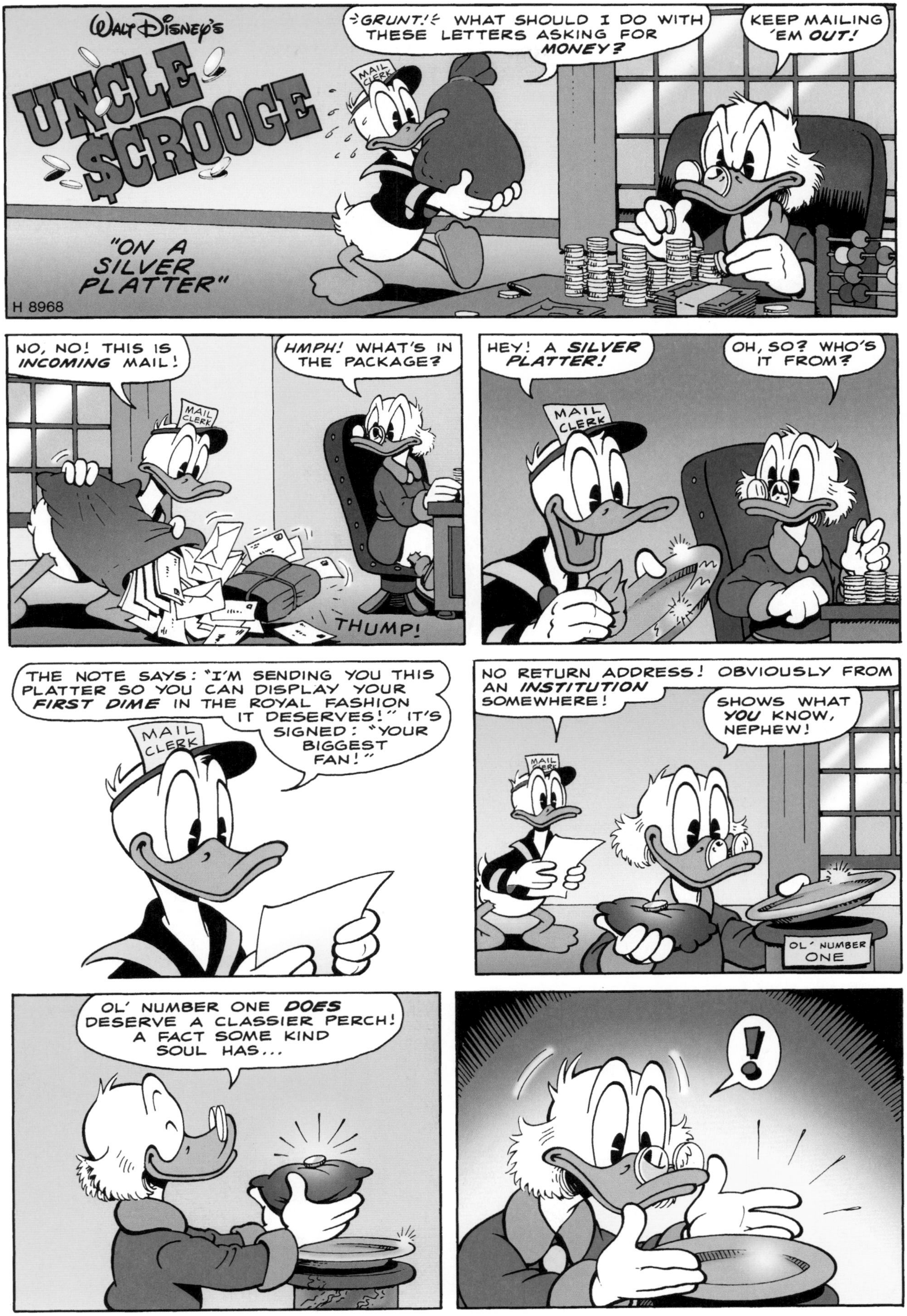
WALT DISNEY'S
UNCLE $CROOGE
"ON A SILVER PLATTER"
H 8968
-GRUNT!- WHAT SHOULD I DO WITH THESE LETTERS ASKING FOR MONEY?
KEEP MAILING 'EM OUT!
MAIL CLERK
NO, NO! THIS IS INCOMING MAIL!
HMPH! WHAT'S IN THE PACKAGE?
THUMP!
HEY! A SILVER PLATTER!
OH, SO? WHO'S IT FROM?
THE NOTE SAYS: "I'M SENDING YOU THIS PLATTER SO YOU CAN DISPLAY YOUR FIRST DIME IN THE ROYAL FASHION IT DESERVES!" IT'S SIGNED: "YOUR BIGGEST FAN!"
NO RETURN ADDRESS! OBVIOUSLY FROM AN INSTITUTION SOMEWHERE!
SHOWS WHAT YOU KNOW, NEPHEW!
OL' NUMBER ONE
OL' NUMBER ONE DOES DESERVE A CLASSIER PERCH! A FACT SOME KIND SOUL HAS...
!

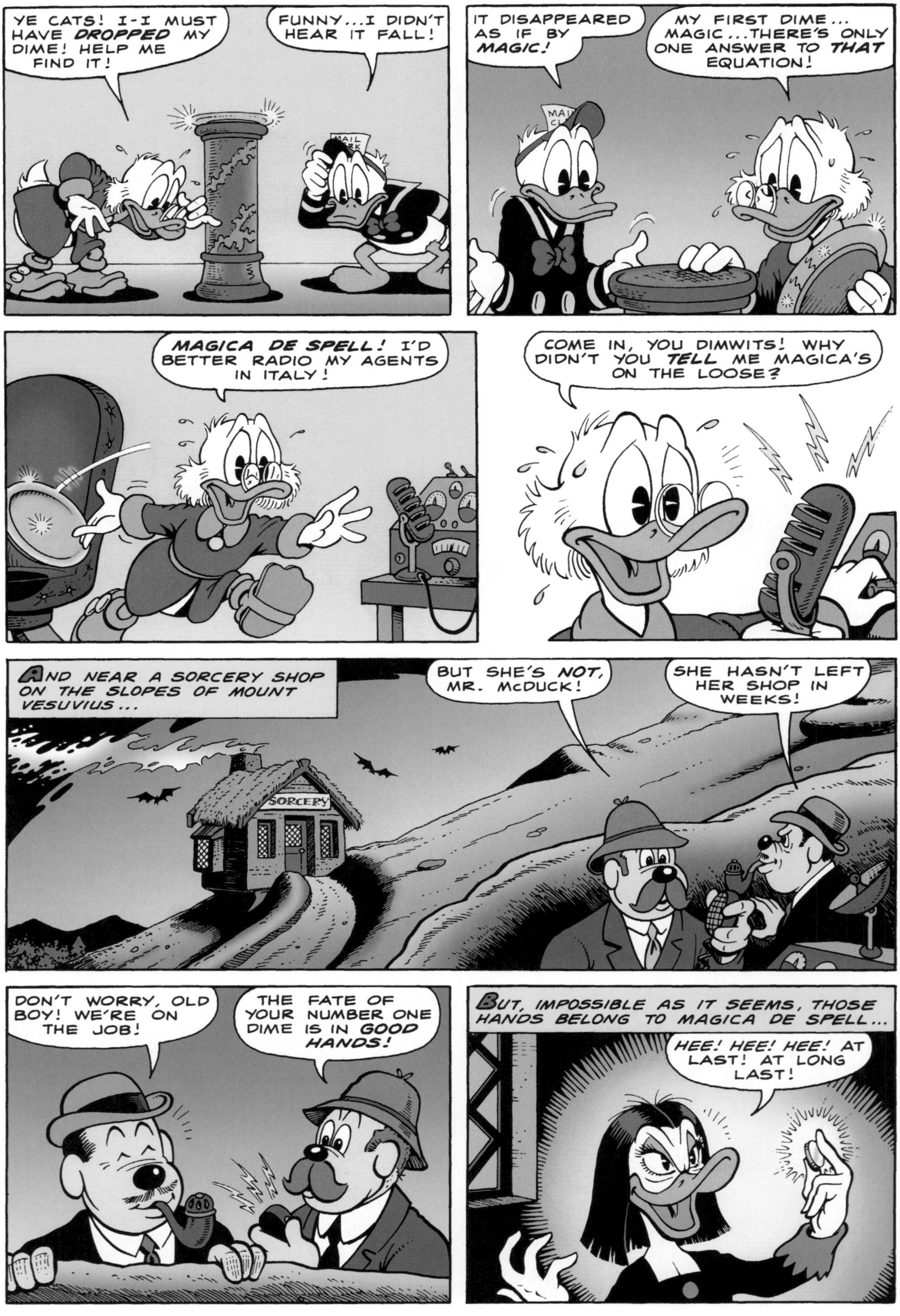

YE CATS! I-I MUST HAVE DROPPED MY DIME! HELP ME FIND IT!
FUNNY...I DIDN'T HEAR IT FALL!
IT DISAPPEARED AS IF BY MAGIC!
MY FIRST DIME... MAGIC...THERE'S ONLY ONE ANSWER TO THAT EQUATION!
MAGICA DE SPELL! I'D BETTER RADIO MY AGENTS IN ITALY!
COME IN, YOU DIMWITS! WHY DIDN'T YOU TELL ME MAGICA'S ON THE LOOSE?
AND NEAR A SORCERY SHOP ON THE SLOPES OF MOUNT VESUVIUS...
SORCERY
BUT SHE'S NOT, MR. McDUCK!
SHE HASN'T LEFT HER SHOP IN WEEKS!
DON'T WORRY, OLD BOY! WE'RE ON THE JOB!
THE FATE OF YOUR NUMBER ONE DIME IS IN GOOD HANDS!
BUT, IMPOSSIBLE AS IT SEEMS, THOSE HANDS BELONG TO MAGICA DE SPELL...
HEE! HEE! HEE! AT LAST! AT LONG LAST!

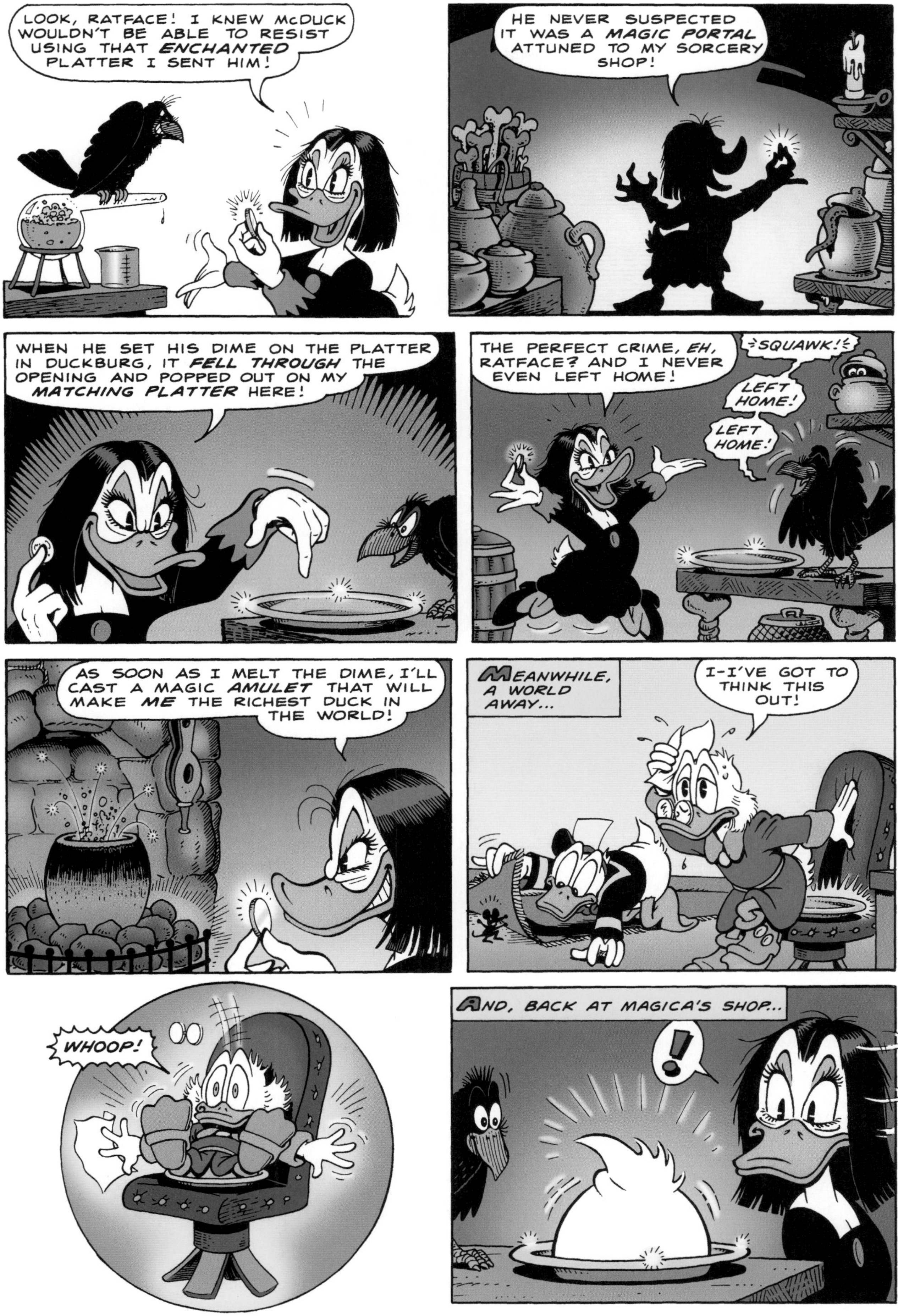
LOOK, RATFACE! I KNEW McDUCK WOULDN'T BE ABLE TO RESIST USING THAT ENCHANTED PLATTER I SENT HIM!
HE NEVER SUSPECTED IT WAS A MAGIC PORTAL ATTUNED TO MY SORCERY SHOP!
WHEN HE SET HIS DIME ON THE PLATTER IN DUCKBURG, IT FELL THROUGH THE OPENING AND POPPED OUT ON MY MATCHING PLATTER HERE!
THE PERFECT CRIME, EH, RATFACE? AND I NEVER EVEN LEFT HOME!
SQUAWK!
LEFT HOME!
LEFT HOME!
AS SOON AS I MELT THE DIME, I'LL CAST A MAGIC AMULET THAT WILL MAKE ME THE RICHEST DUCK IN THE WORLD!
MEANWHILE, A WORLD AWAY...
I-I'VE GOT TO THINK THIS OUT!
WHOOP!
AND, BACK AT MAGICA'S SHOP...
!

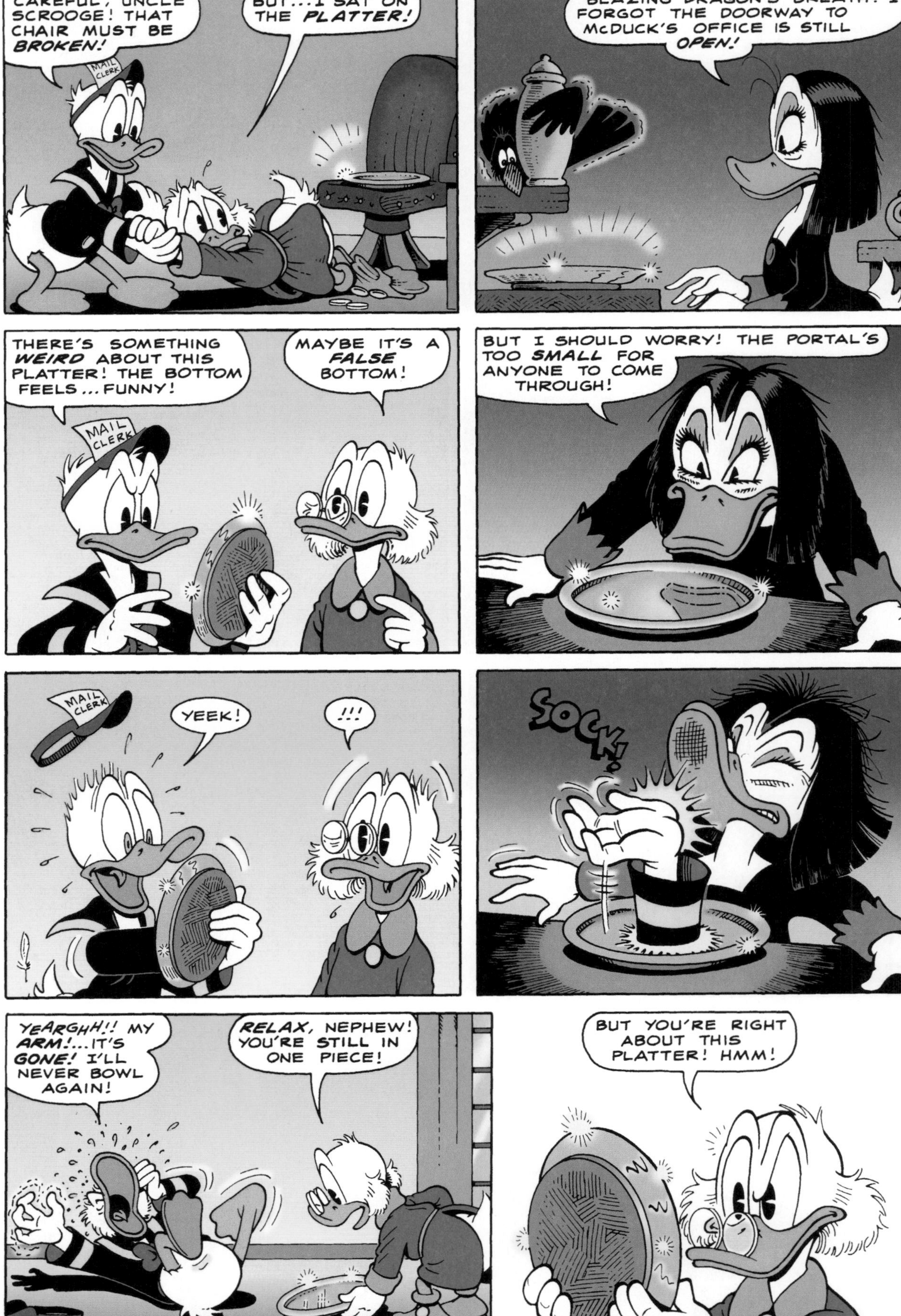
CAREFUL, UNCLE SCROOGE! THAT CHAIR MUST BE BROKEN!
MAIL CLERK
BUT...I SAT ON THE PLATTER!
BLAZING DRAGON'S BREATH! I FORGOT THE DOORWAY TO McDUCK'S OFFICE IS STILL OPEN!
THERE'S SOMETHING WEIRD ABOUT THIS PLATTER! THE BOTTOM FEELS...FUNNY!
MAYBE IT'S A FALSE BOTTOM!
MAIL CLERK
BUT I SHOULD WORRY! THE PORTAL'S TOO SMALL FOR ANYONE TO COME THROUGH!
MAIL CLERK
YEEK!
!!!
SOCK!
YEARGHH!! MY ARM!...IT'S GONE! I'LL NEVER BOWL AGAIN!
RELAX, NEPHEW! YOU'RE STILL IN ONE PIECE!
BUT YOU'RE RIGHT ABOUT THIS PLATTER! HMM!

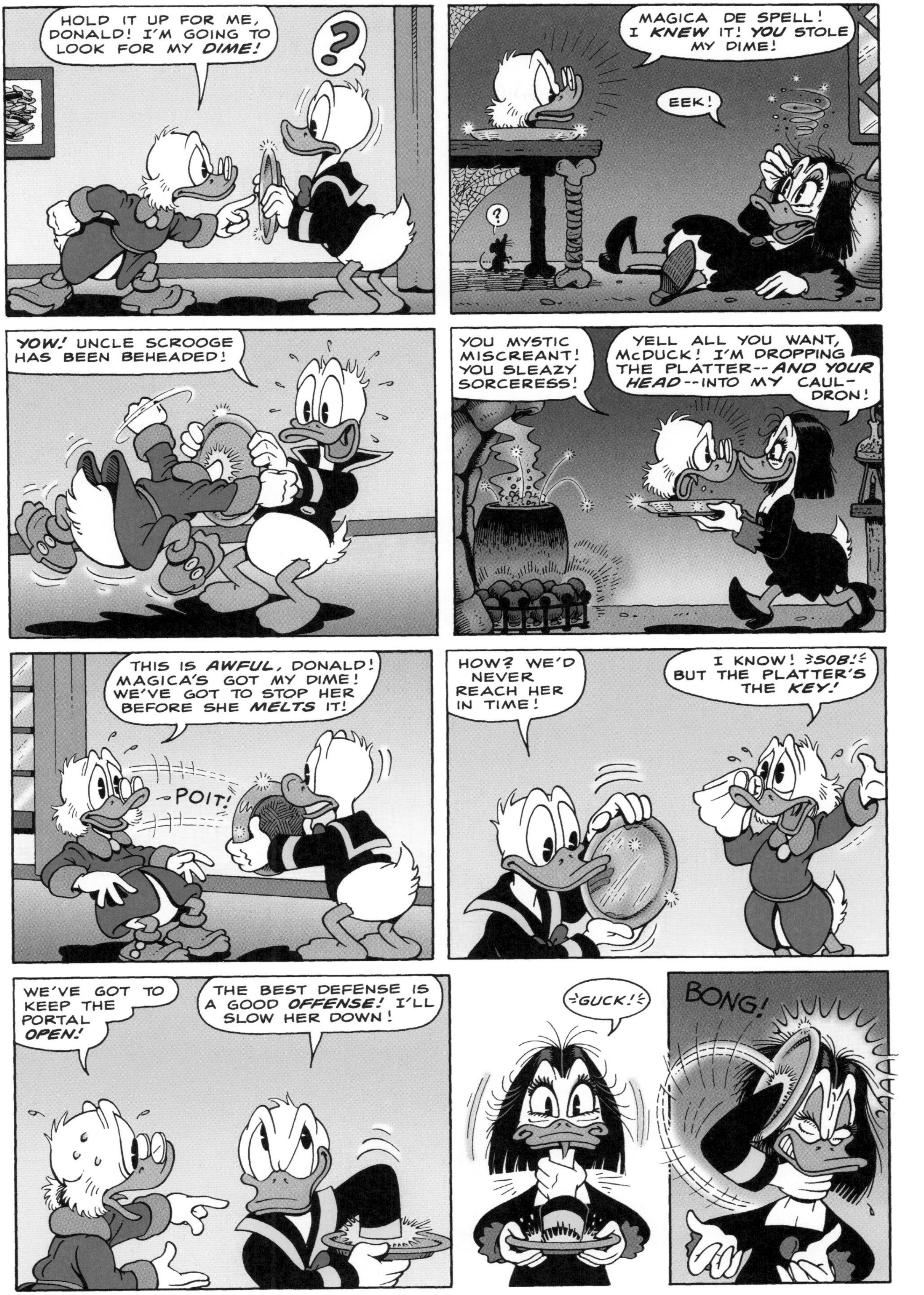
HOLD IT UP FOR ME, DONALD! I'M GOING TO LOOK FOR MY DIME!
?
MAGICA DE SPELL! I KNEW IT! YOU STOLE MY DIME!
EEK!
?
YOW! UNCLE SCROOGE HAS BEEN BEHEADED!
YOU MYSTIC MISCREANT! YOU SLEAZY SORCERESS!
YELL ALL YOU WANT, McDUCK! I'M DROPPING THE PLATTER-- AND YOUR HEAD --INTO MY CAULDRON!
THIS IS AWFUL, DONALD! MAGICA'S GOT MY DIME! WE'VE GOT TO STOP HER BEFORE SHE MELTS IT!
POIT!
HOW? WE'D NEVER REACH HER IN TIME!
I KNOW! SOB! BUT THE PLATTER'S THE KEY!
WE'VE GOT TO KEEP THE PORTAL OPEN!
THE BEST DEFENSE IS A GOOD OFFENSE! I'LL SLOW HER DOWN!
GUCK!
BONG!

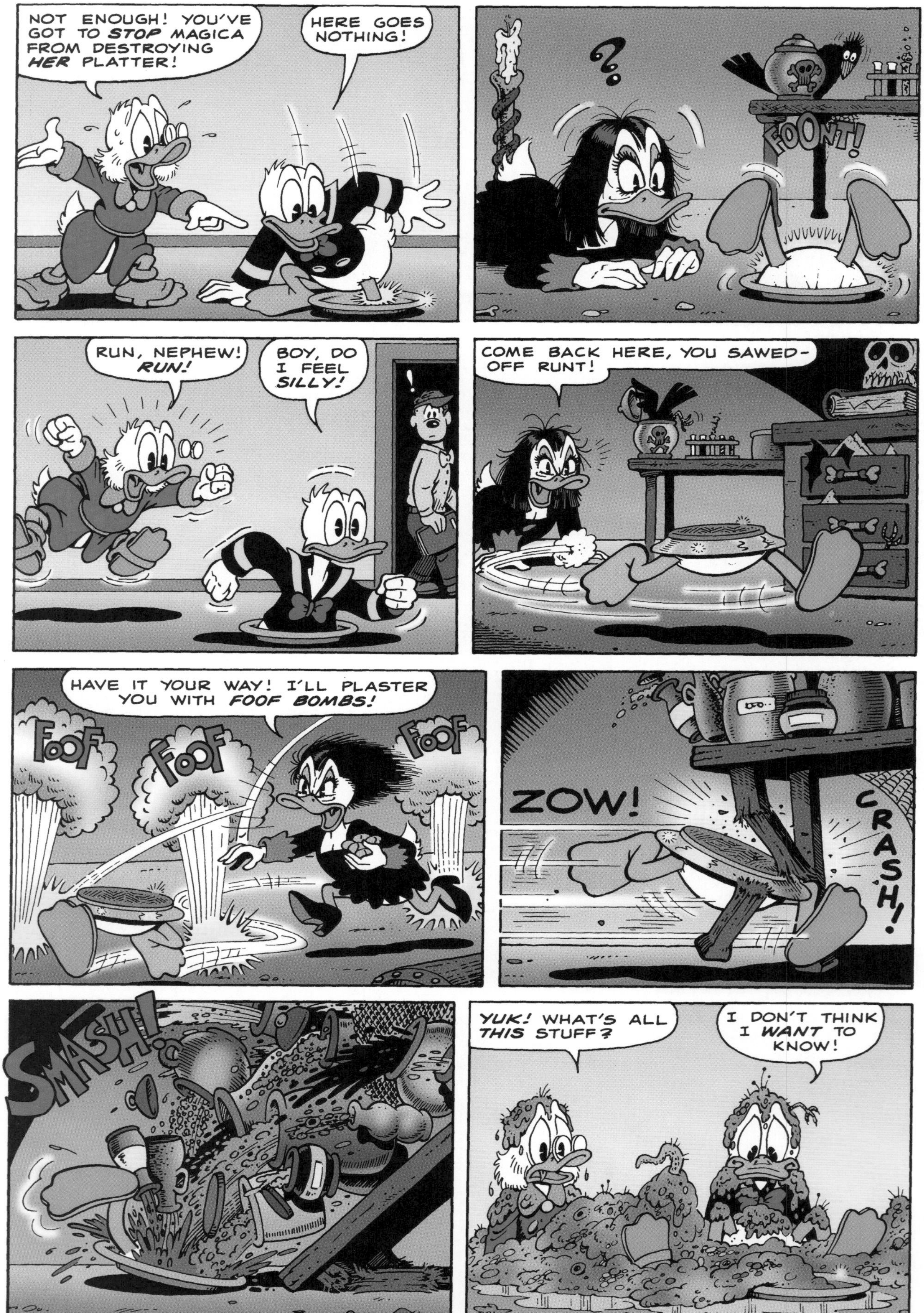
NOT ENOUGH! YOU'VE GOT TO STOP MAGICA FROM DESTROYING HER PLATTER!
HERE GOES NOTHING!
?
FOONT!
RUN, NEPHEW! RUN!
BOY, DO I FEEL SILLY!
!
COME BACK HERE, YOU SAWED-OFF RUNT!
HAVE IT YOUR WAY! I'LL PLASTER YOU WITH FOOF BOMBS!
FOOF
FOOF
FOOF
ZOW!
CRASH!
SMASH!
YUK! WHAT'S ALL THIS STUFF?
I DON'T THINK I WANT TO KNOW!

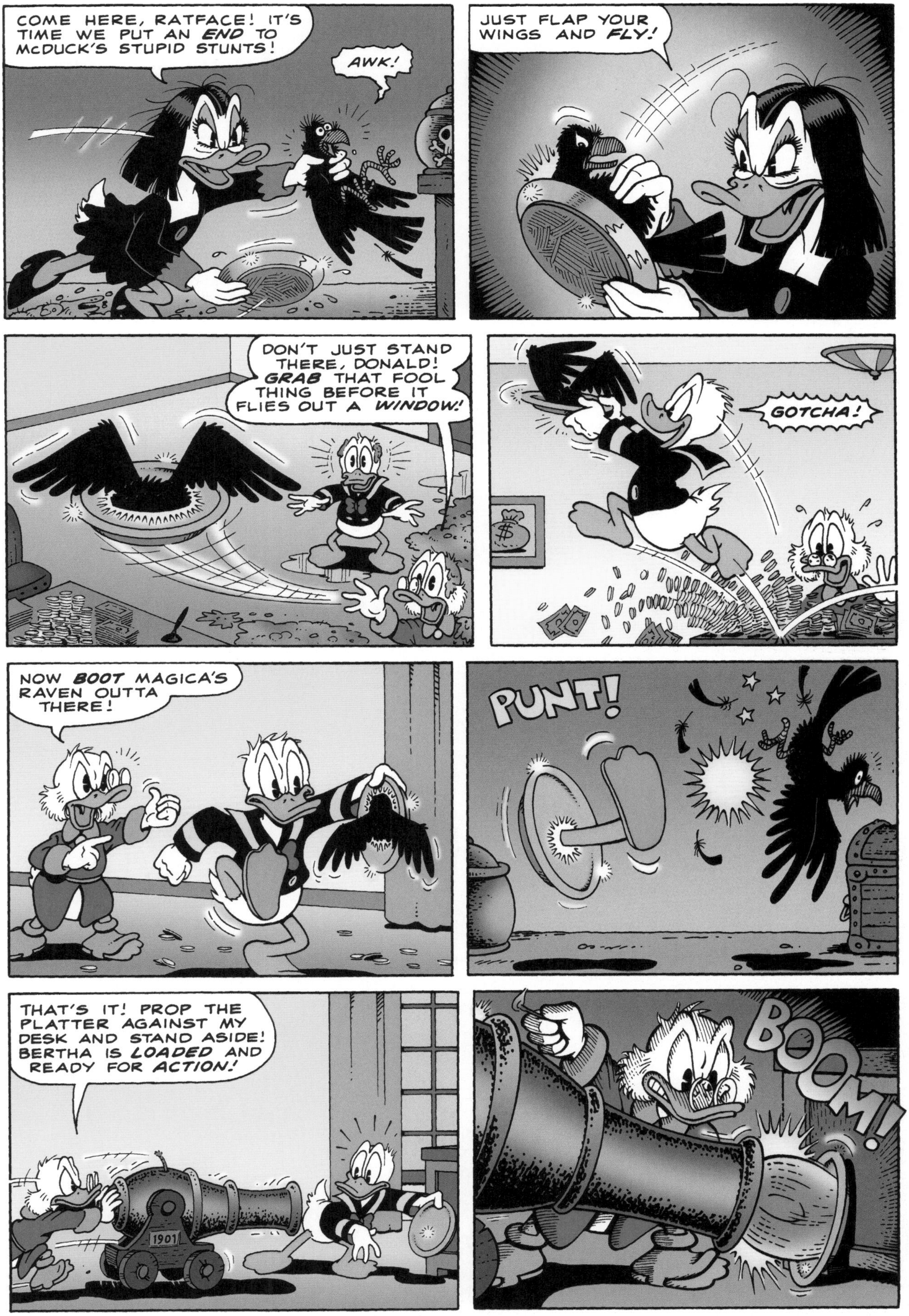
COME HERE, RATFACE! IT'S TIME WE PUT AN END TO McDUCK'S STUPID STUNTS!
AWK!
JUST FLAP YOUR WINGS AND FLY!
DON'T JUST STAND THERE, DONALD! GRAB THAT FOOL THING BEFORE IT FLIES OUT A WINDOW!
GOTCHA!
NOW BOOT MAGICA'S RAVEN OUTTA THERE!
PUNT!
THAT'S IT! PROP THE PLATTER AGAINST MY DESK AND STAND ASIDE! BERTHA IS LOADED AND READY FOR ACTION!
1901
BOOM!

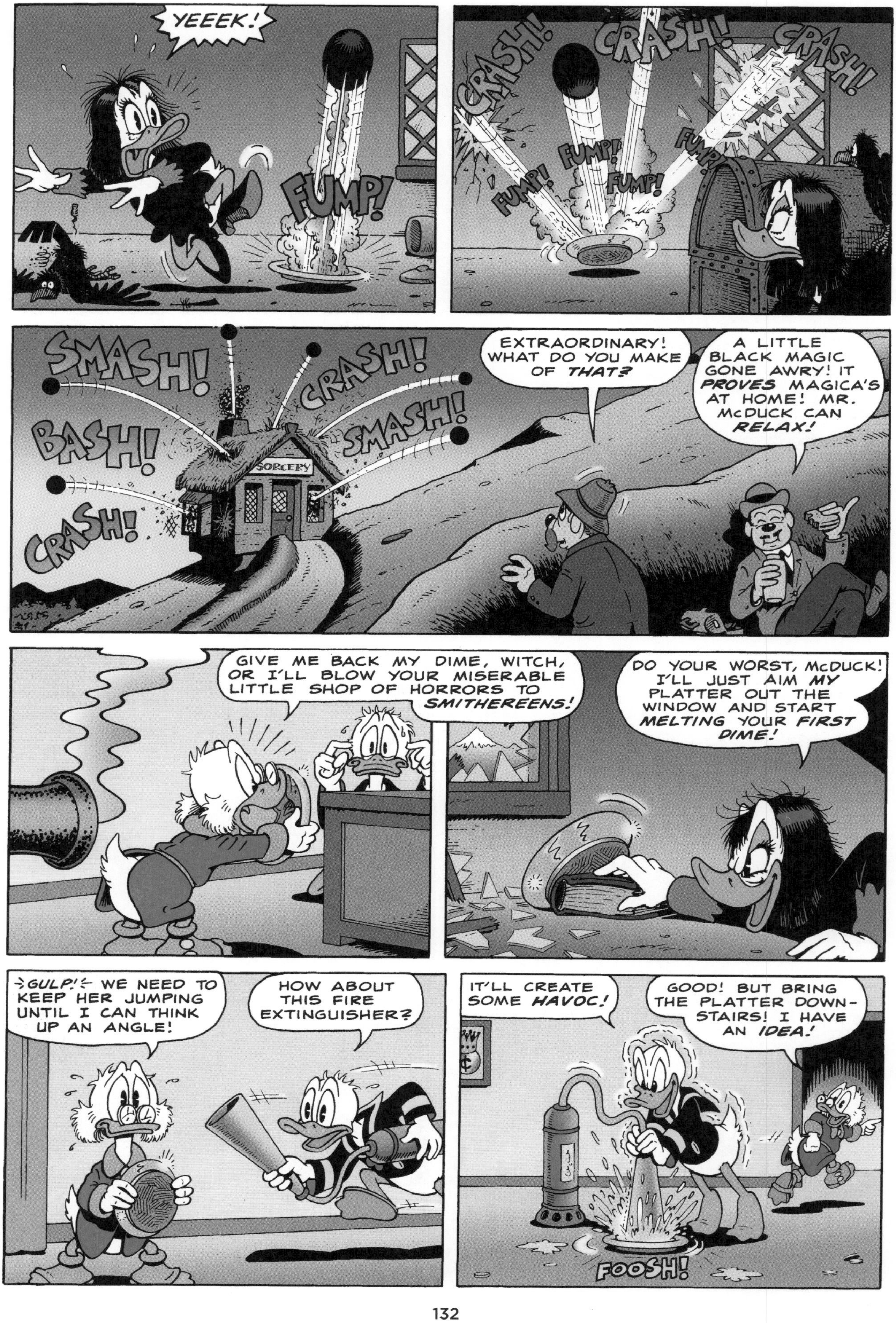
YEEEK!
FUMP!
CRASH!
CRASH!
CRASH!
FUMP!
FUMP!
FUMP!
FUMP!
SMASH!
CRASH!
BASH!
SMASH!
CRASH!
SORCERY
EXTRAORDINARY! WHAT DO YOU MAKE OF THAT?
A LITTLE BLACK MAGIC GONE AWRY! IT PROVES MAGICA'S AT HOME! MR. McDUCK CAN RELAX!
GIVE ME BACK MY DIME, WITCH, OR I'LL BLOW YOUR MISERABLE LITTLE SHOP OF HORRORS TO SMITHEREENS!
DO YOUR WORST, McDUCK! I'LL JUST AIM MY PLATTER OUT THE WINDOW AND START MELTING YOUR FIRST DIME!
GULP! WE NEED TO KEEP HER JUMPING UNTIL I CAN THINK UP AN ANGLE!
HOW ABOUT THIS FIRE EXTINGUISHER?
IT'LL CREATE SOME HAVOC!
GOOD! BUT BRING THE PLATTER DOWN-STAIRS! I HAVE AN IDEA!
FOOSH!

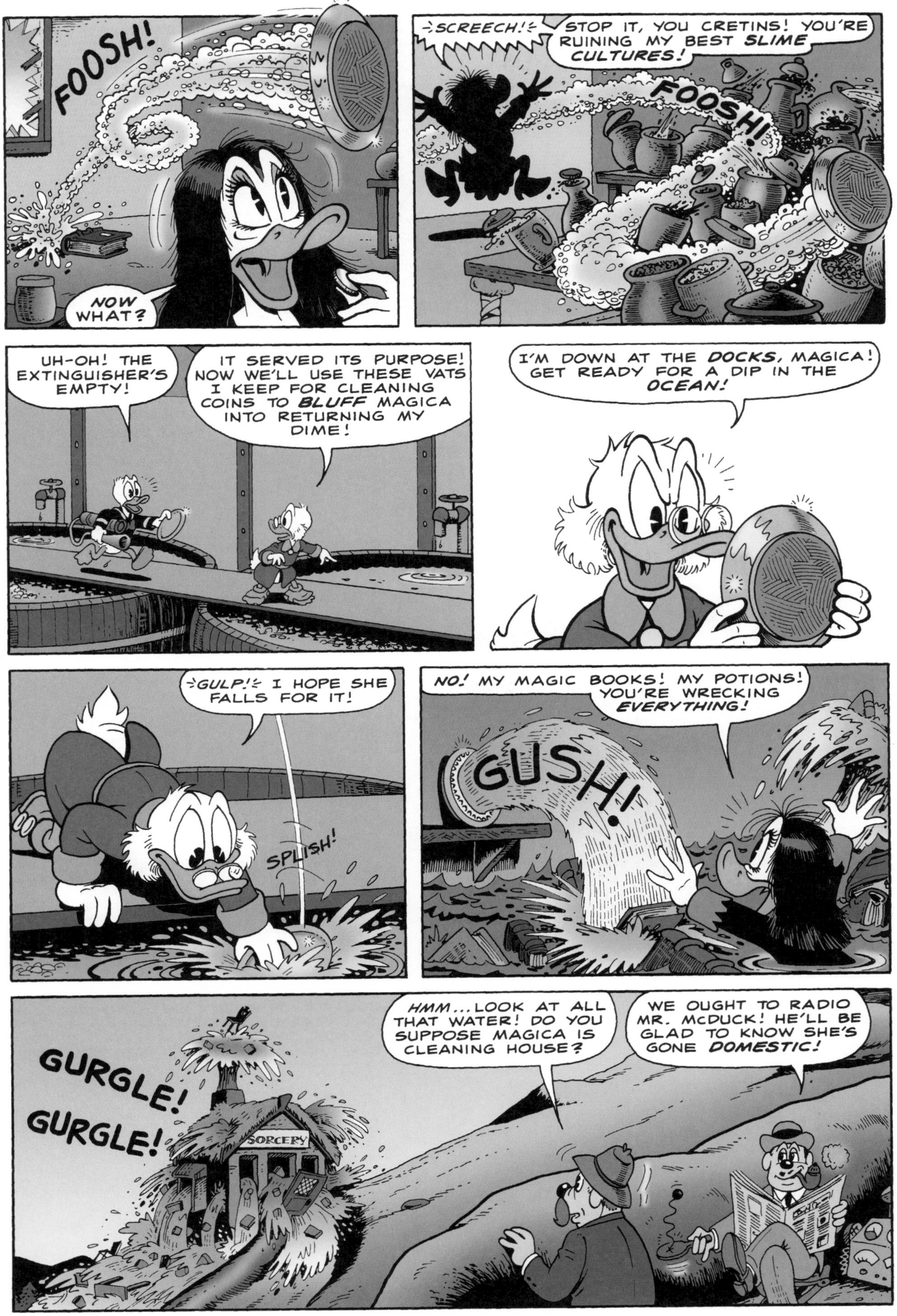
FOOSH!
NOW WHAT?
SCREECH!
STOP IT, YOU CRETINS! YOU'RE RUINING MY BEST SLIME CULTURES!
FOOSH!
UH-OH! THE EXTINGUISHER'S EMPTY!
IT SERVED ITS PURPOSE! NOW WE'LL USE THESE VATS I KEEP FOR CLEANING COINS TO BLUFF MAGICA INTO RETURNING MY DIME!
I'M DOWN AT THE DOCKS, MAGICA! GET READY FOR A DIP IN THE OCEAN!
GULP! I HOPE SHE FALLS FOR IT!
SPLISH!
NO! MY MAGIC BOOKS! MY POTIONS! YOU'RE WRECKING EVERYTHING!
GUSH!
GURGLE! GURGLE!
SORCERY
HMM... LOOK AT ALL THAT WATER! DO YOU SUPPOSE MAGICA IS CLEANING HOUSE?
WE OUGHT TO RADIO MR. McDUCK! HE'LL BE GLAD TO KNOW SHE'S GONE DOMESTIC!

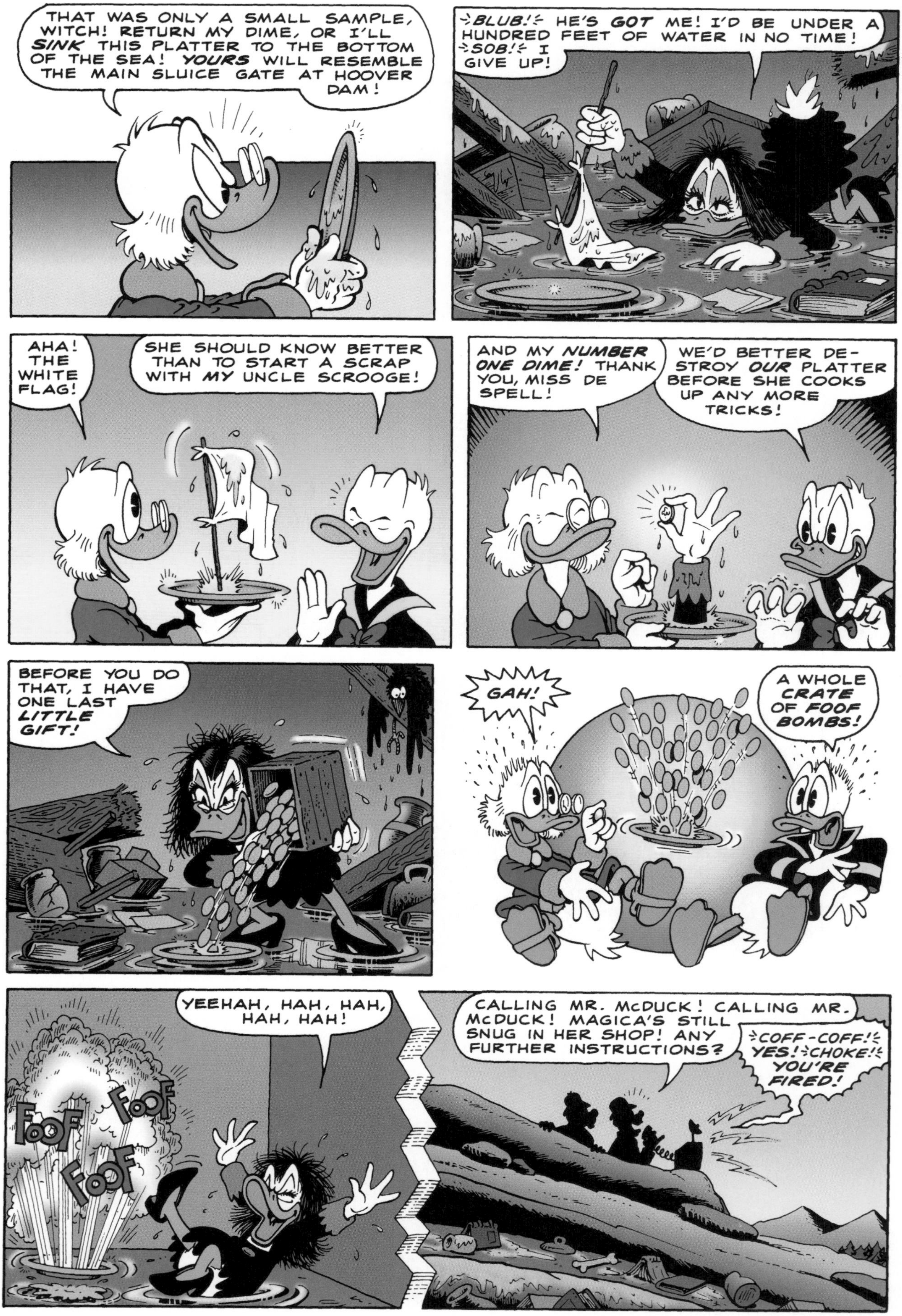
THAT WAS ONLY A SMALL SAMPLE, WITCH! RETURN MY DIME, OR I'LL SINK THIS PLATTER TO THE BOTTOM OF THE SEA! YOURS WILL RESEMBLE THE MAIN SLUICE GATE AT HOOVER DAM!
-BLUB!- HE'S GOT ME! I'D BE UNDER A HUNDRED FEET OF WATER IN NO TIME! -SOB!- I GIVE UP!
AHA! THE WHITE FLAG!
SHE SHOULD KNOW BETTER THAN TO START A SCRAP WITH MY UNCLE SCROOGE!
AND MY NUMBER ONE DIME! THANK YOU, MISS DE SPELL!
WE'D BETTER DE-STROY OUR PLATTER BEFORE SHE COOKS UP ANY MORE TRICKS!
BEFORE YOU DO THAT, I HAVE ONE LAST LITTLE GIFT!
GAH!
A WHOLE CRATE OF FOOF BOMBS!
FOOF FOOF FOOF
YEEHAH, HAH, HAH, HAH, HAH!
CALLING MR. McDUCK! CALLING MR. McDUCK! MAGICA'S STILL SNUG IN HER SHOP! ANY FURTHER INSTRUCTIONS?
-COFF-COFF!- YES! -CHOKE!- YOU'RE FIRED!

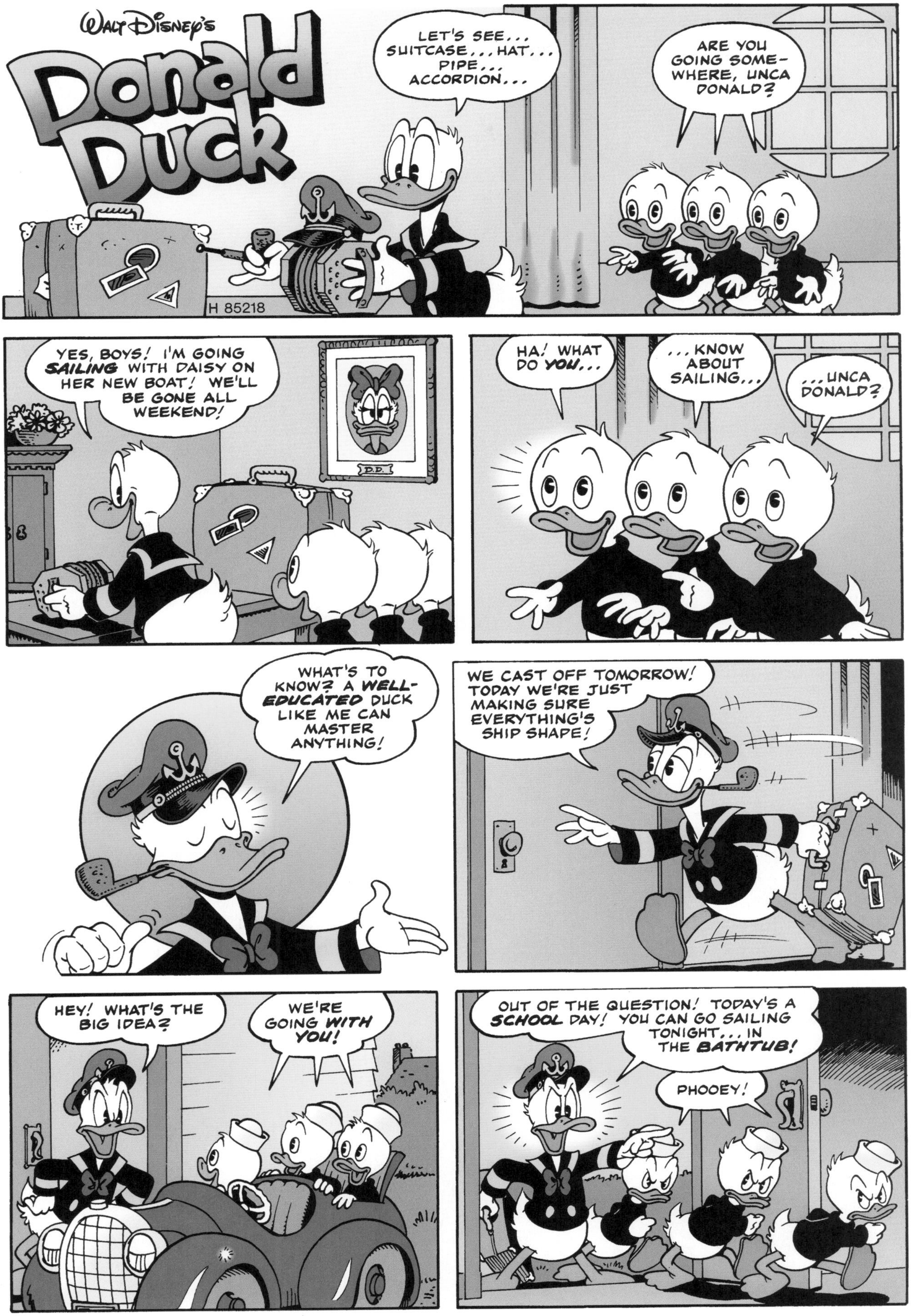
WALT DISNEY'S
Donald Duck
H 85218
LET'S SEE... SUITCASE... HAT... PIPE... ACCORDION...
ARE YOU GOING SOME-WHERE, UNCA DONALD?
YES, BOYS! I'M GOING SAILING WITH DAISY ON HER NEW BOAT! WE'LL BE GONE ALL WEEKEND!
D.D.
HA! WHAT DO YOU...
...KNOW ABOUT SAILING...
...UNCA DONALD?
WHAT'S TO KNOW? A WELL-EDUCATED DUCK LIKE ME CAN MASTER ANYTHING!
WE CAST OFF TOMORROW! TODAY WE'RE JUST MAKING SURE EVERYTHING'S SHIP SHAPE!
HEY! WHAT'S THE BIG IDEA?
WE'RE GOING WITH YOU!
OUT OF THE QUESTION! TODAY'S A SCHOOL DAY! YOU CAN GO SAILING TONIGHT... IN THE BATHTUB!
PHOOEY!

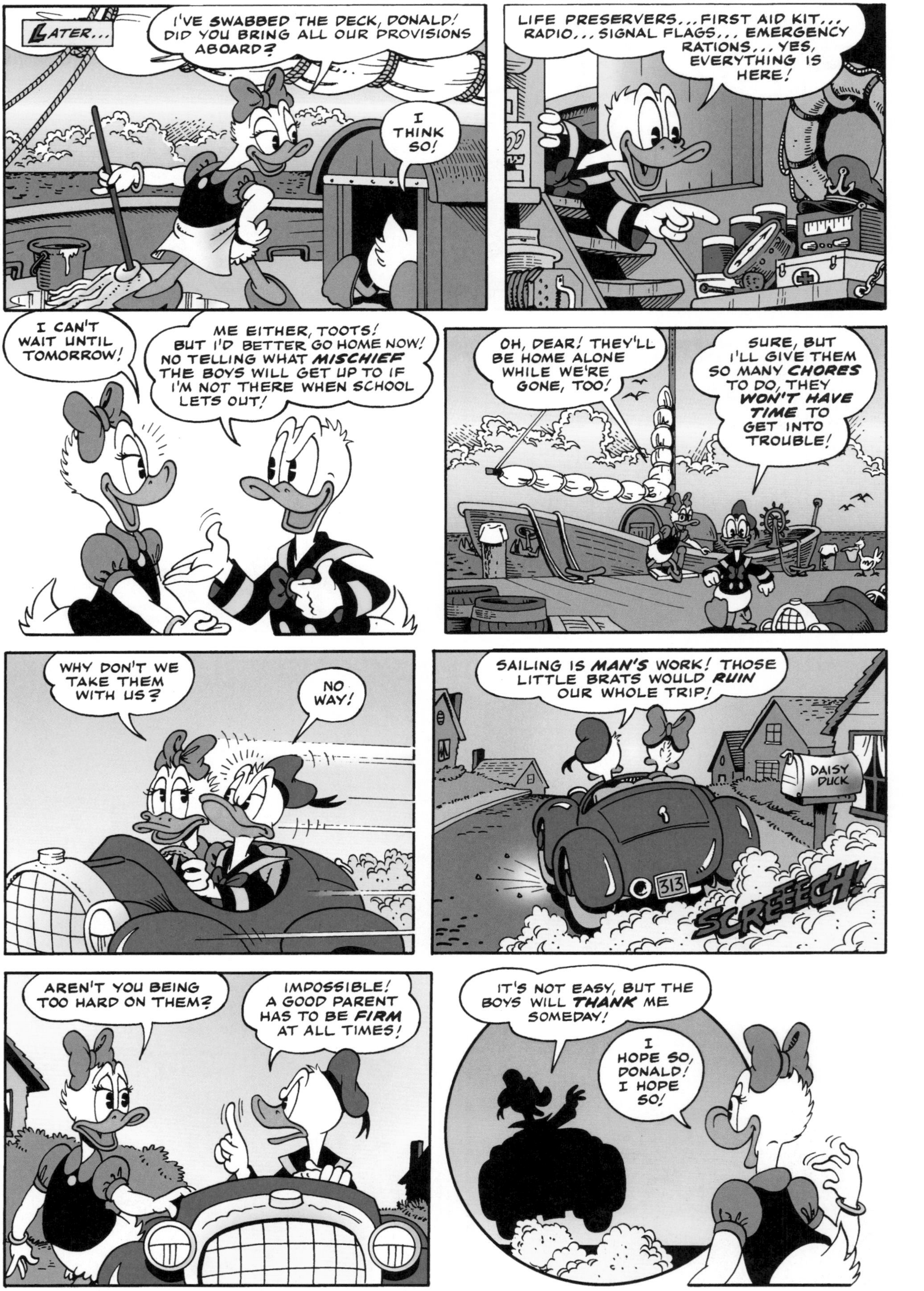

LATER...
I'VE SWABBED THE DECK, DONALD! DID YOU BRING ALL OUR PROVISIONS ABOARD?
I THINK SO!
LIFE PRESERVERS... FIRST AID KIT... RADIO... SIGNAL FLAGS... EMERGENCY RATIONS... YES, EVERYTHING IS HERE!
I CAN'T WAIT UNTIL TOMORROW!
ME EITHER, TOOTS! BUT I'D BETTER GO HOME NOW! NO TELLING WHAT MISCHIEF THE BOYS WILL GET UP TO IF I'M NOT THERE WHEN SCHOOL LETS OUT!
OH, DEAR! THEY'LL BE HOME ALONE WHILE WE'RE GONE, TOO!
SURE, BUT I'LL GIVE THEM SO MANY CHORES TO DO, THEY WON'T HAVE TIME TO GET INTO TROUBLE!
WHY DON'T WE TAKE THEM WITH US?
NO WAY!
SAILING IS MAN'S WORK! THOSE LITTLE BRATS WOULD RUIN OUR WHOLE TRIP!
DAISY DUCK
313
SCREEECH!
AREN'T YOU BEING TOO HARD ON THEM?
IMPOSSIBLE! A GOOD PARENT HAS TO BE FIRM AT ALL TIMES!
IT'S NOT EASY, BUT THE BOYS WILL THANK ME SOMEDAY!
I HOPE SO, DONALD! I HOPE SO!

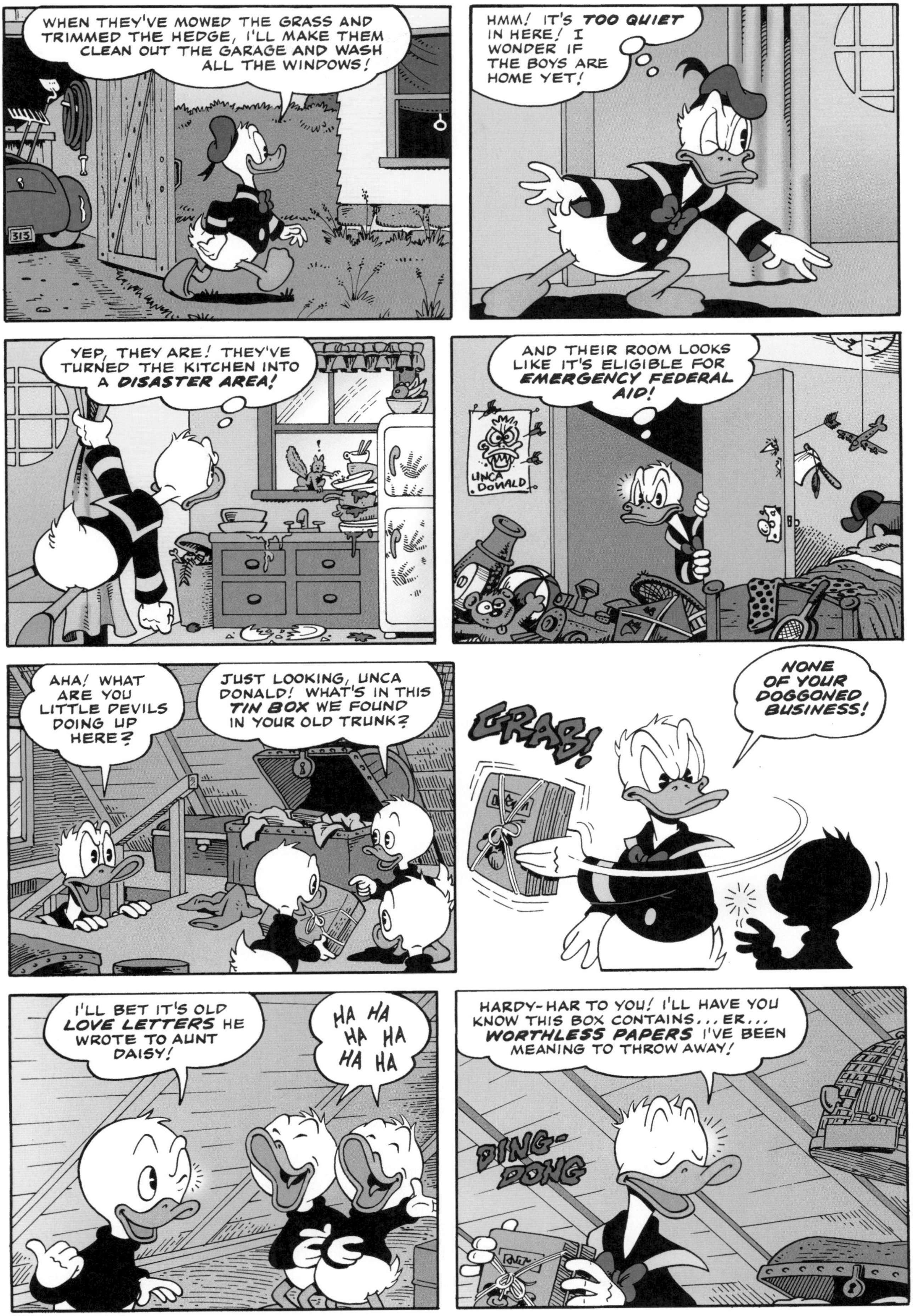
WHEN THEY'VE MOWED THE GRASS AND TRIMMED THE HEDGE, I'LL MAKE THEM CLEAN OUT THE GARAGE AND WASH ALL THE WINDOWS!
313
HMM! IT'S TOO QUIET IN HERE! I WONDER IF THE BOYS ARE HOME YET!
YEP, THEY ARE! THEY'VE TURNED THE KITCHEN INTO A DISASTER AREA!
AND THEIR ROOM LOOKS LIKE IT'S ELIGIBLE FOR EMERGENCY FEDERAL AID!
UNCA DONALD
AHA! WHAT ARE YOU LITTLE DEVILS DOING UP HERE?
JUST LOOKING, UNCA DONALD! WHAT'S IN THIS TIN BOX WE FOUND IN YOUR OLD TRUNK?
GRAB!
NONE OF YOUR DOGGONED BUSINESS!
I'LL BET IT'S OLD LOVE LETTERS HE WROTE TO AUNT DAISY!
HA HA HA HA HA HA
HARDY-HAR TO YOU! I'LL HAVE YOU KNOW THIS BOX CONTAINS... ER... WORTHLESS PAPERS I'VE BEEN MEANING TO THROW AWAY!
DING-DONG

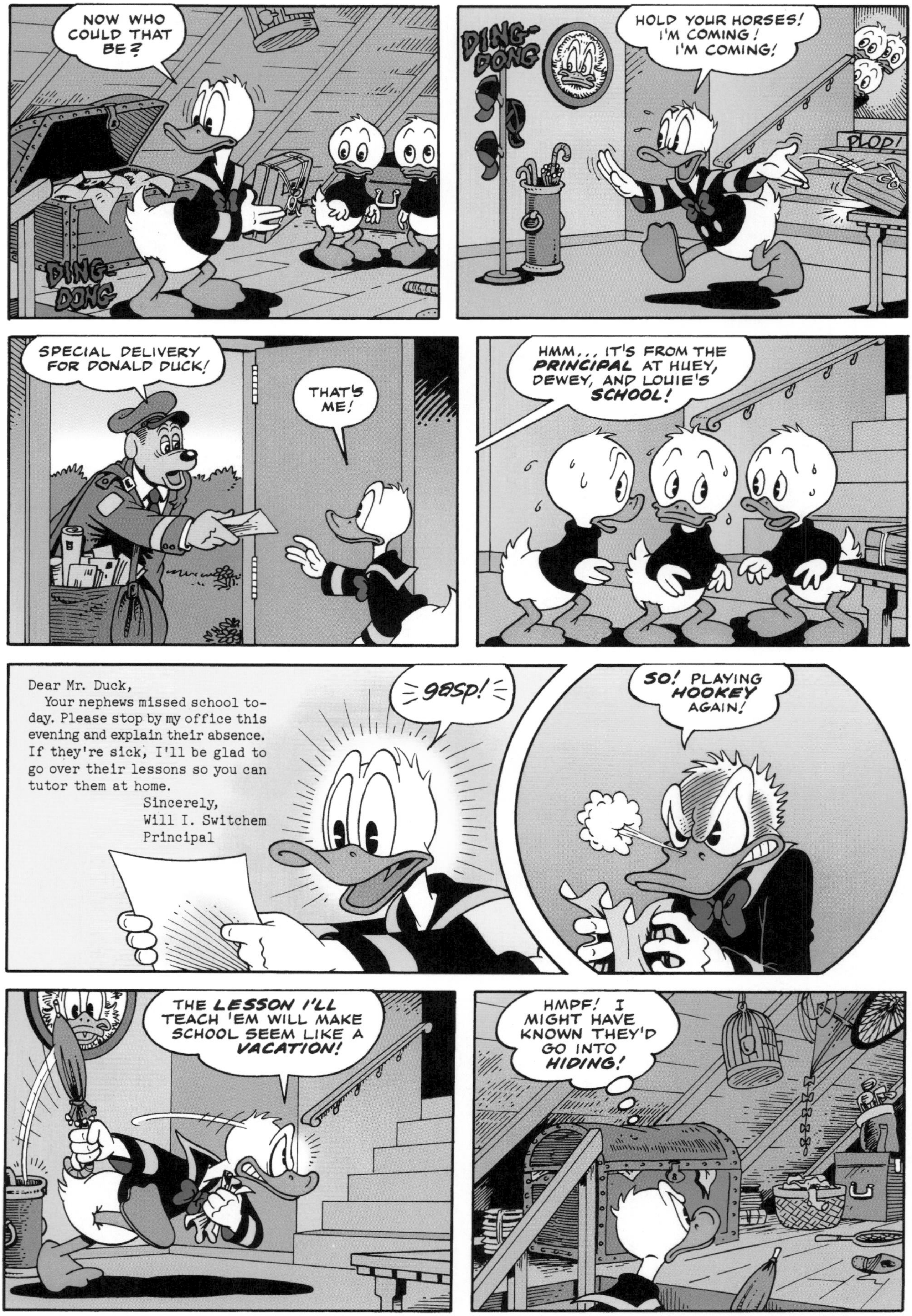
NOW WHO COULD THAT BE?
DING-DONG
DING-DONG
HOLD YOUR HORSES! I'M COMING! I'M COMING!
PLOP!
SPECIAL DELIVERY FOR DONALD DUCK!
THAT'S ME!
HMM,,, IT'S FROM THE PRINCIPAL AT HUEY, DEWEY, AND LOUIE'S SCHOOL!
Dear Mr. Duck,
Your nephews missed school today. Please stop by my office this evening and explain their absence. If they're sick, I'll be glad to go over their lessons so you can tutor them at home.
Sincerely,
Will I. Switchem
Principal
gasp!
SO! PLAYING HOOKEY AGAIN!
THE LESSON I'LL TEACH 'EM WILL MAKE SCHOOL SEEM LIKE A VACATION!
HMPF! I MIGHT HAVE KNOWN THEY'D GO INTO HIDING!

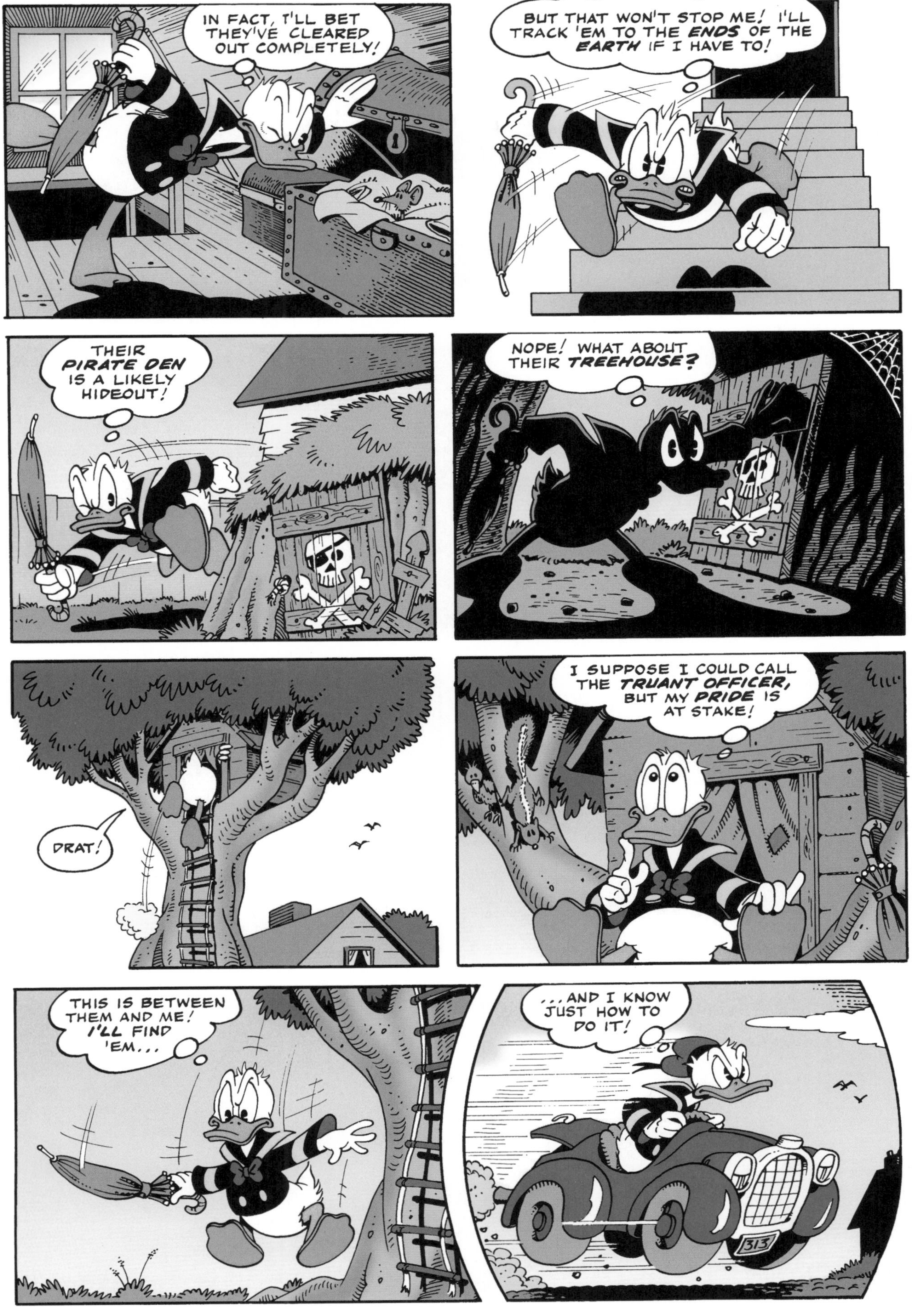
IN FACT, I'LL BET THEY'VE CLEARED OUT COMPLETELY!
BUT THAT WON'T STOP ME! I'LL TRACK 'EM TO THE ENDS OF THE EARTH IF I HAVE TO!
THEIR PIRATE DEN IS A LIKELY HIDEOUT!
NOPE! WHAT ABOUT THEIR TREEHOUSE?
DRAT!
I SUPPOSE I COULD CALL THE TRUANT OFFICER, BUT MY PRIDE IS AT STAKE!
THIS IS BETWEEN THEM AND ME! I'LL FIND 'EM...
...AND I KNOW JUST HOW TO DO IT!
313

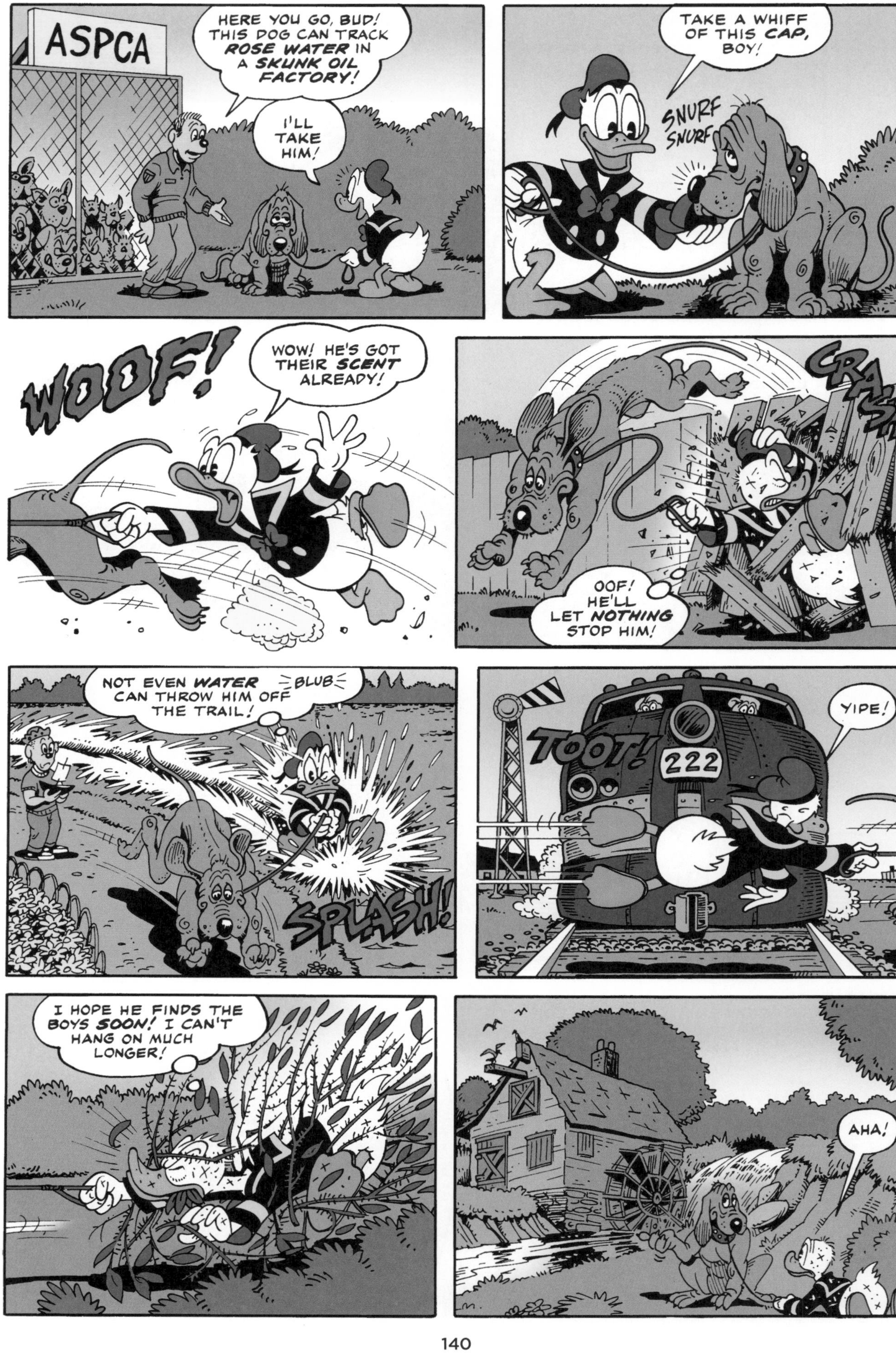
ASPCA
HERE YOU GO, BUD! THIS DOG CAN TRACK ROSE WATER IN A SKUNK OIL FACTORY!
I'LL TAKE HIM!
TAKE A WHIFF OF THIS CAP, BOY!
SNURF SNURF
WOOF!
WOW! HE'S GOT THEIR SCENT ALREADY!
CRASH
OOF! HE'LL LET NOTHING STOP HIM!
NOT EVEN WATER CAN THROW HIM OFF THE TRAIL!
BLUB
SPLASH!
TOOT!
222
YIPE!
I HOPE HE FINDS THE BOYS SOON! I CAN'T HANG ON MUCH LONGER!
AHA!

INSIDE THE MILL...

HA! UNCA DONALD WILL NEVER FIND US HERE!

PREPARE TO BE SWATTED, INSECTS!

UNCA DONALD!

PSST! DON'T PANIC, MEN! WE'VE STILL GOT OUR ACE IN THE HOLE!

WE'RE NOT COMING OUT UNTIL YOU PROMISE NOT TO PUNISH US! AND TAKE US SAILING WITH YOU!

WHAT! HOW DARE YOU MAKE DEMANDS?

OR MAYBE YOU'D LIKE US TO MAIL THIS PACKAGE TO AUNT DAISY? SHE SHOULD KNOW WHAT A DUNCE YOU REALLY ARE!

WHAT'S IN IT?

THAT TIN BOX FULL OF YOUR "WORTHLESS" PAPERS!

YES! YOUR OLD REPORT CARDS!

MIGHTY WORTHLESS, INDEED!

DAISY DUCK 1313 WEB DUCKBURG Cal.

DON'T BE RIDICULOUS! BRING ME THAT BOX THIS INSTANT!

NOT UNTIL YOU AGREE TO OUR TERMS!

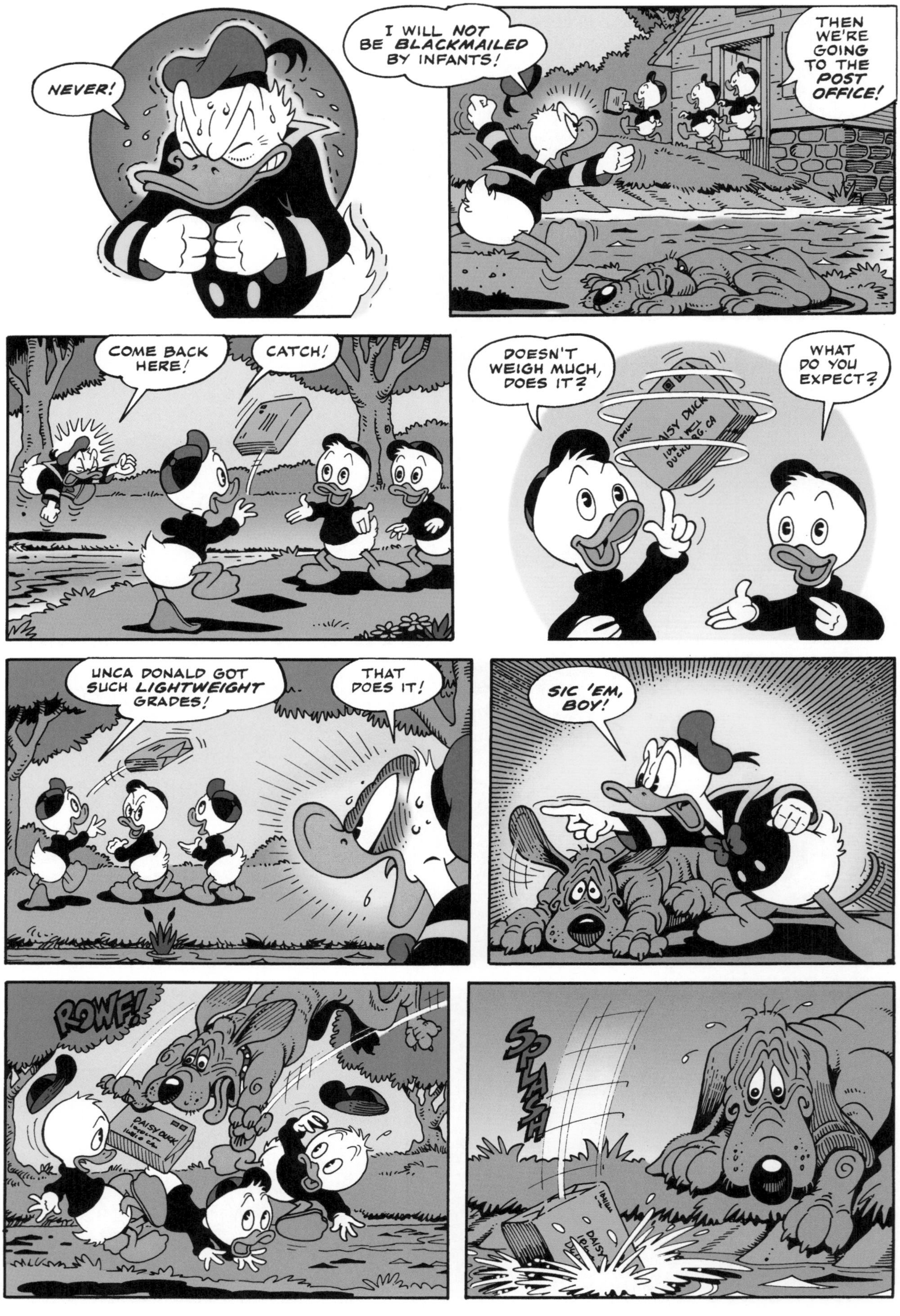
NEVER!
I WILL NOT BE BLACKMAILED BY INFANTS!
THEN WE'RE GOING TO THE POST OFFICE!
COME BACK HERE!
CATCH!
DOESN'T WEIGH MUCH, DOES IT?
WHAT DO YOU EXPECT?
UNCA DONALD GOT SUCH LIGHTWEIGHT GRADES!
THAT DOES IT!
SIC 'EM, BOY!
ROWF!
DAISY DUCK
SPLASH

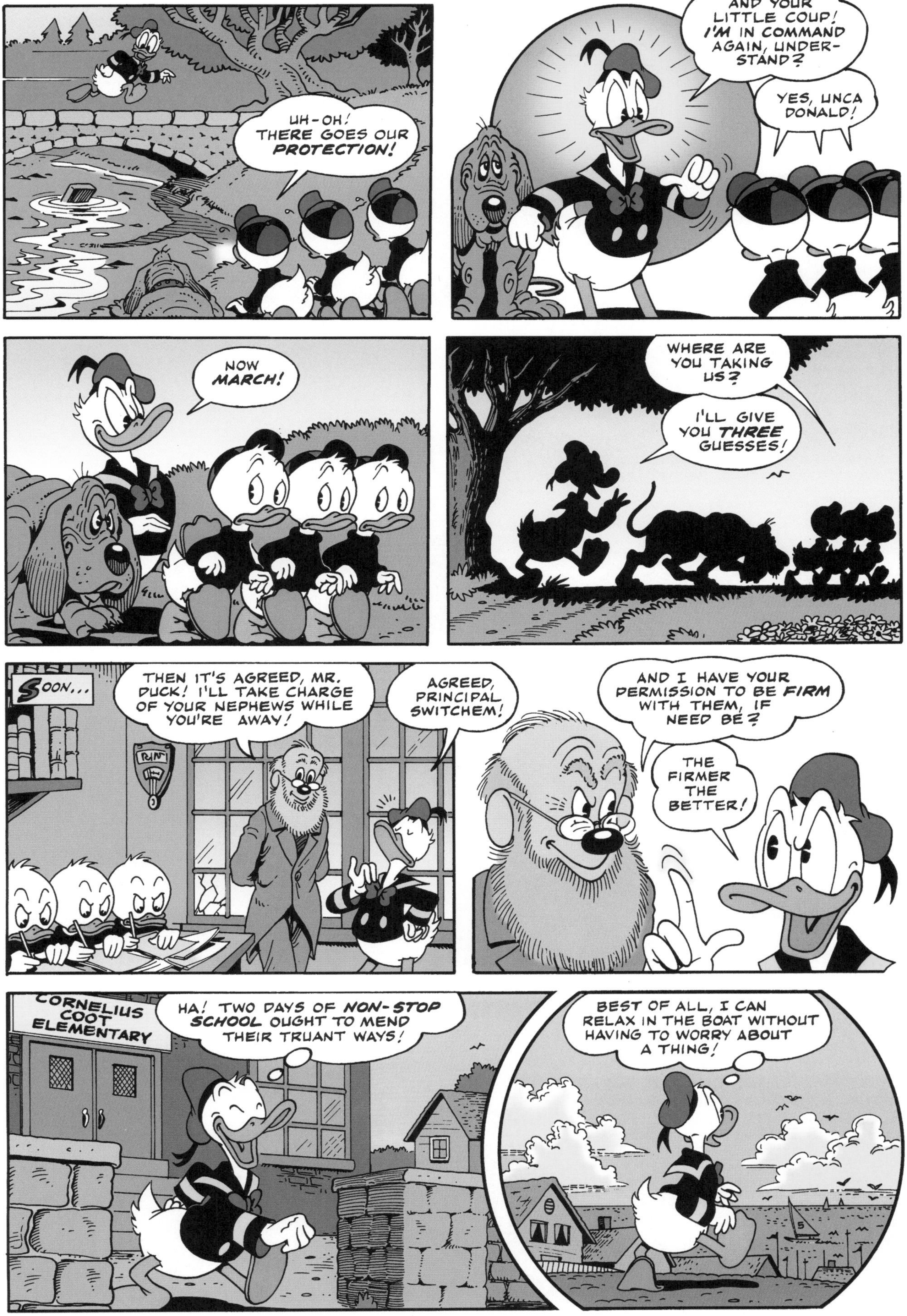
UH-OH! THERE GOES OUR PROTECTION!
AND YOUR LITTLE COUP! I'M IN COMMAND AGAIN, UNDER-STAND?
YES, UNCA DONALD!
NOW MARCH!
WHERE ARE YOU TAKING US?
I'LL GIVE YOU THREE GUESSES!
SOON...
THEN IT'S AGREED, MR. DUCK! I'LL TAKE CHARGE OF YOUR NEPHEWS WHILE YOU'RE AWAY!
AGREED, PRINCIPAL SWITCHEM!
AND I HAVE YOUR PERMISSION TO BE FIRM WITH THEM, IF NEED BE?
THE FIRMER THE BETTER!
CORNELIUS COOT ELEMENTARY
HA! TWO DAYS OF NON-STOP SCHOOL OUGHT TO MEND THEIR TRUANT WAYS!
BEST OF ALL, I CAN RELAX IN THE BOAT WITHOUT HAVING TO WORRY ABOUT A THING!

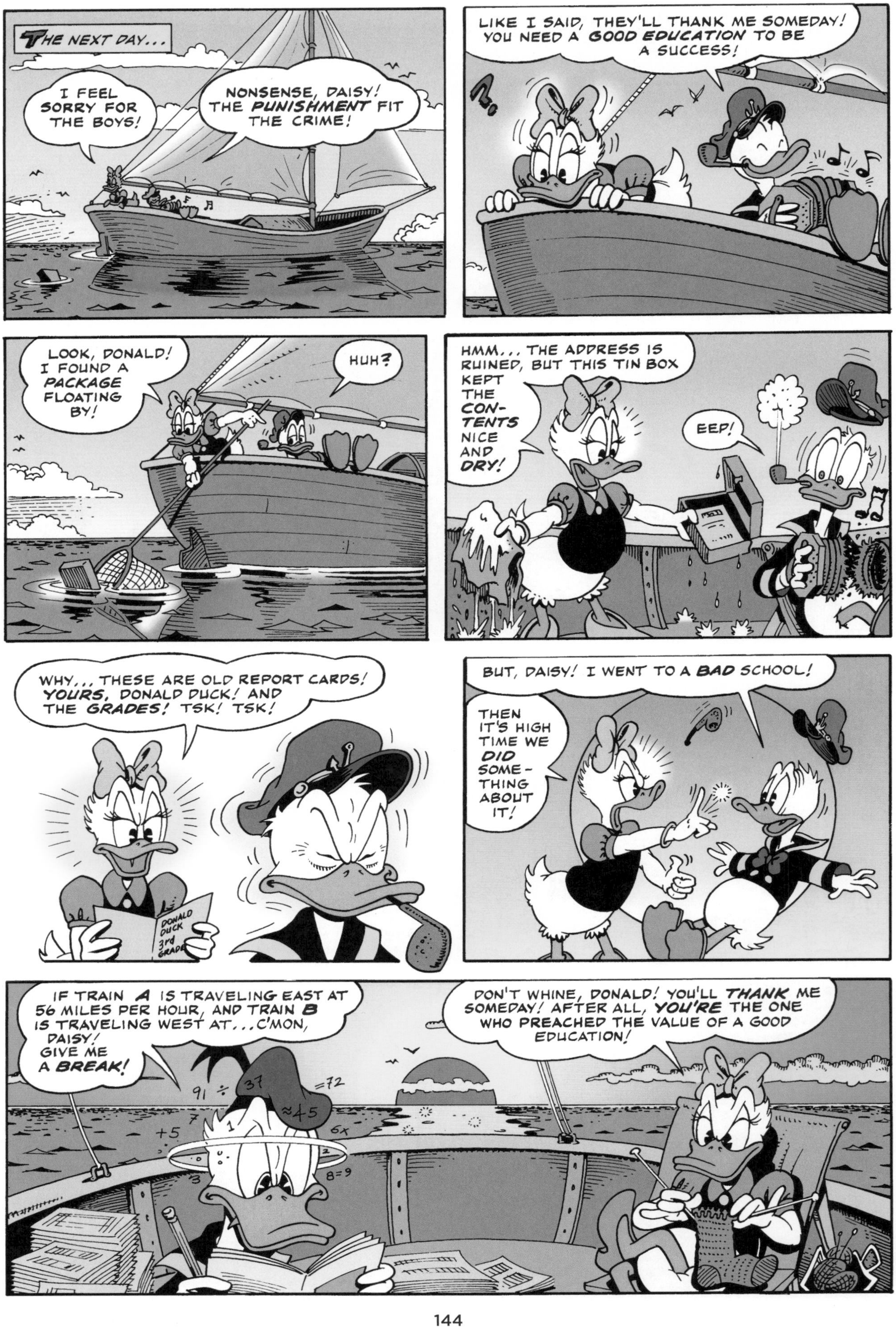
THE NEXT DAY...
I FEEL SORRY FOR THE BOYS!
NONSENSE, DAISY! THE PUNISHMENT FIT THE CRIME!
LIKE I SAID, THEY'LL THANK ME SOMEDAY! YOU NEED A GOOD EDUCATION TO BE A SUCCESS!
LOOK, DONALD! I FOUND A PACKAGE FLOATING BY!
HUH?
HMM... THE ADDRESS IS RUINED, BUT THIS TIN BOX KEPT THE CONTENTS NICE AND DRY!
EEP!
WHY... THESE ARE OLD REPORT CARDS! YOURS, DONALD DUCK! AND THE GRADES! TSK! TSK!
DONALD DUCK 3rd GRADE
BUT, DAISY! I WENT TO A BAD SCHOOL!
THEN IT'S HIGH TIME WE DID SOMETHING ABOUT IT!
IF TRAIN A IS TRAVELING EAST AT 56 MILES PER HOUR, AND TRAIN B IS TRAVELING WEST AT...C'MON, DAISY! GIVE ME A BREAK!
DON'T WHINE, DONALD! YOU'LL THANK ME SOMEDAY! AFTER ALL, YOU'RE THE ONE WHO PREACHED THE VALUE OF A GOOD EDUCATION!
91 ÷ 37 =72
≈45
7
+5
6x
8=9

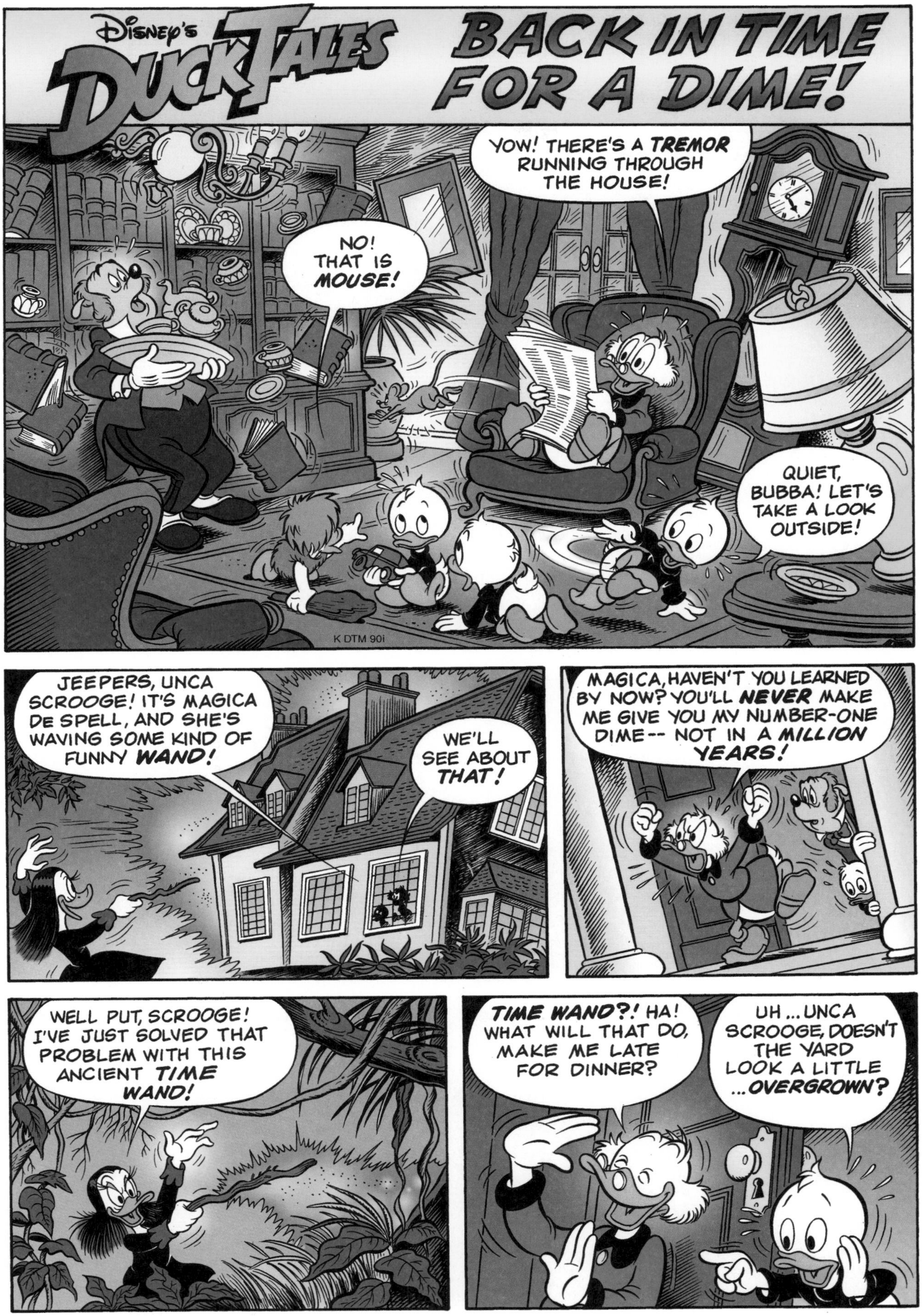

DISNEY'S DUCKTALES
BACK IN TIME FOR A DIME!
YOW! THERE'S A TREMOR RUNNING THROUGH THE HOUSE!
NO! THAT IS MOUSE!
QUIET, BUBBA! LET'S TAKE A LOOK OUTSIDE!
K DTM 90i
JEEPERS, UNCA SCROOGE! IT'S MAGICA DE SPELL, AND SHE'S WAVING SOME KIND OF FUNNY WAND!
WE'LL SEE ABOUT THAT!
MAGICA, HAVEN'T YOU LEARNED BY NOW? YOU'LL NEVER MAKE ME GIVE YOU MY NUMBER-ONE DIME-- NOT IN A MILLION YEARS!
WELL PUT, SCROOGE! I'VE JUST SOLVED THAT PROBLEM WITH THIS ANCIENT TIME WAND!
TIME WAND?! HA! WHAT WILL THAT DO, MAKE ME LATE FOR DINNER?
UH ... UNCA SCROOGE, DOESN'T THE YARD LOOK A LITTLE ...OVERGROWN?

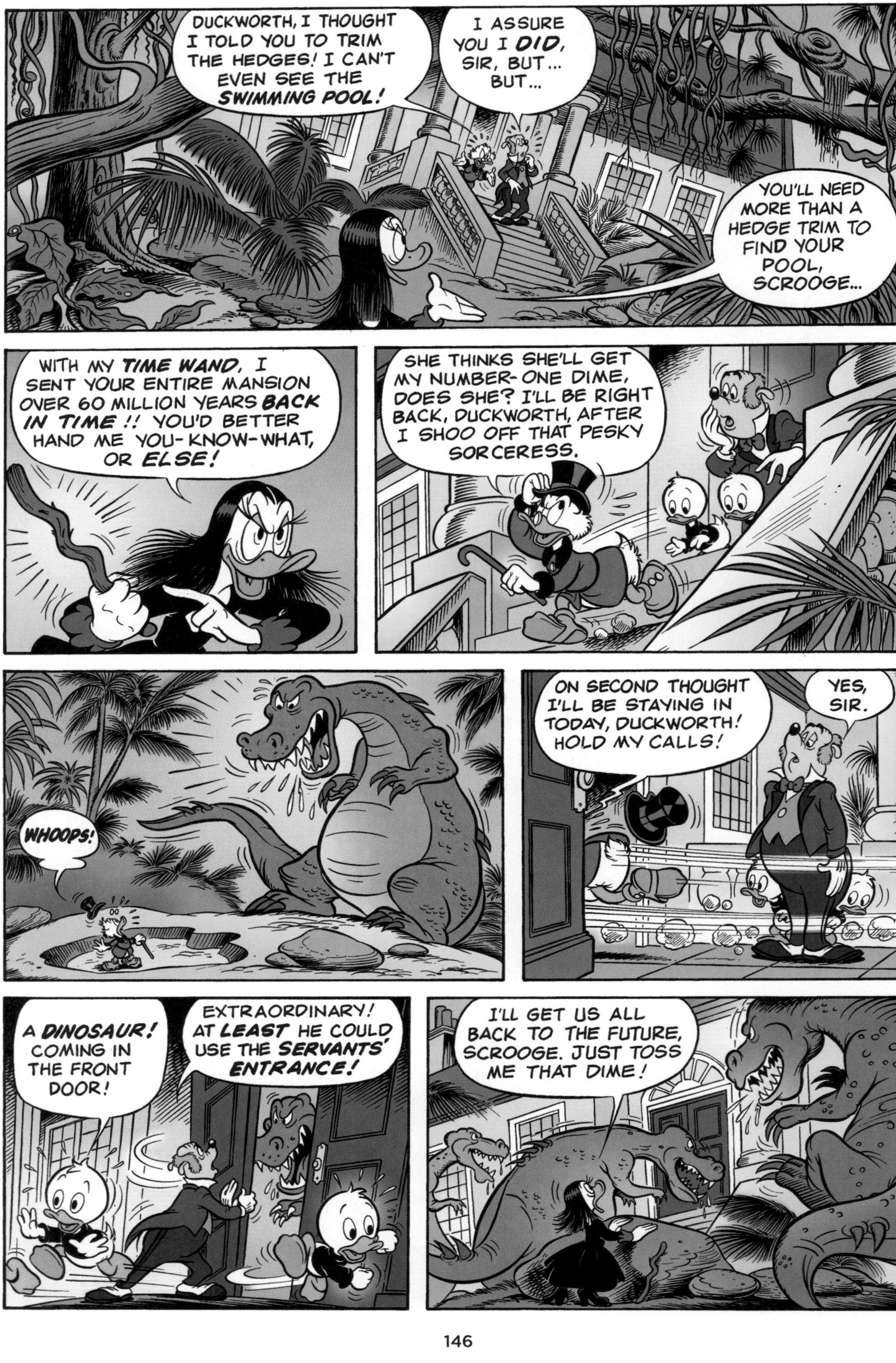
DUCKWORTH, I THOUGHT I TOLD YOU TO TRIM THE HEDGES! I CAN'T EVEN SEE THE SWIMMING POOL!
I ASSURE YOU I DID, SIR, BUT... BUT...
YOU'LL NEED MORE THAN A HEDGE TRIM TO FIND YOUR POOL, SCROOGE...
WITH MY TIME WAND, I SENT YOUR ENTIRE MANSION OVER 60 MILLION YEARS BACK IN TIME!! YOU'D BETTER HAND ME YOU-KNOW-WHAT, OR ELSE!
SHE THINKS SHE'LL GET MY NUMBER-ONE DIME, DOES SHE? I'LL BE RIGHT BACK, DUCKWORTH, AFTER I SHOO OFF THAT PESKY SORCERESS.
WHOOPS!
ON SECOND THOUGHT I'LL BE STAYING IN TODAY, DUCKWORTH! HOLD MY CALLS!
YES, SIR.
A DINOSAUR! COMING IN THE FRONT DOOR!
EXTRAORDINARY! AT LEAST HE COULD USE THE SERVANTS' ENTRANCE!
I'LL GET US ALL BACK TO THE FUTURE, SCROOGE. JUST TOSS ME THAT DIME!

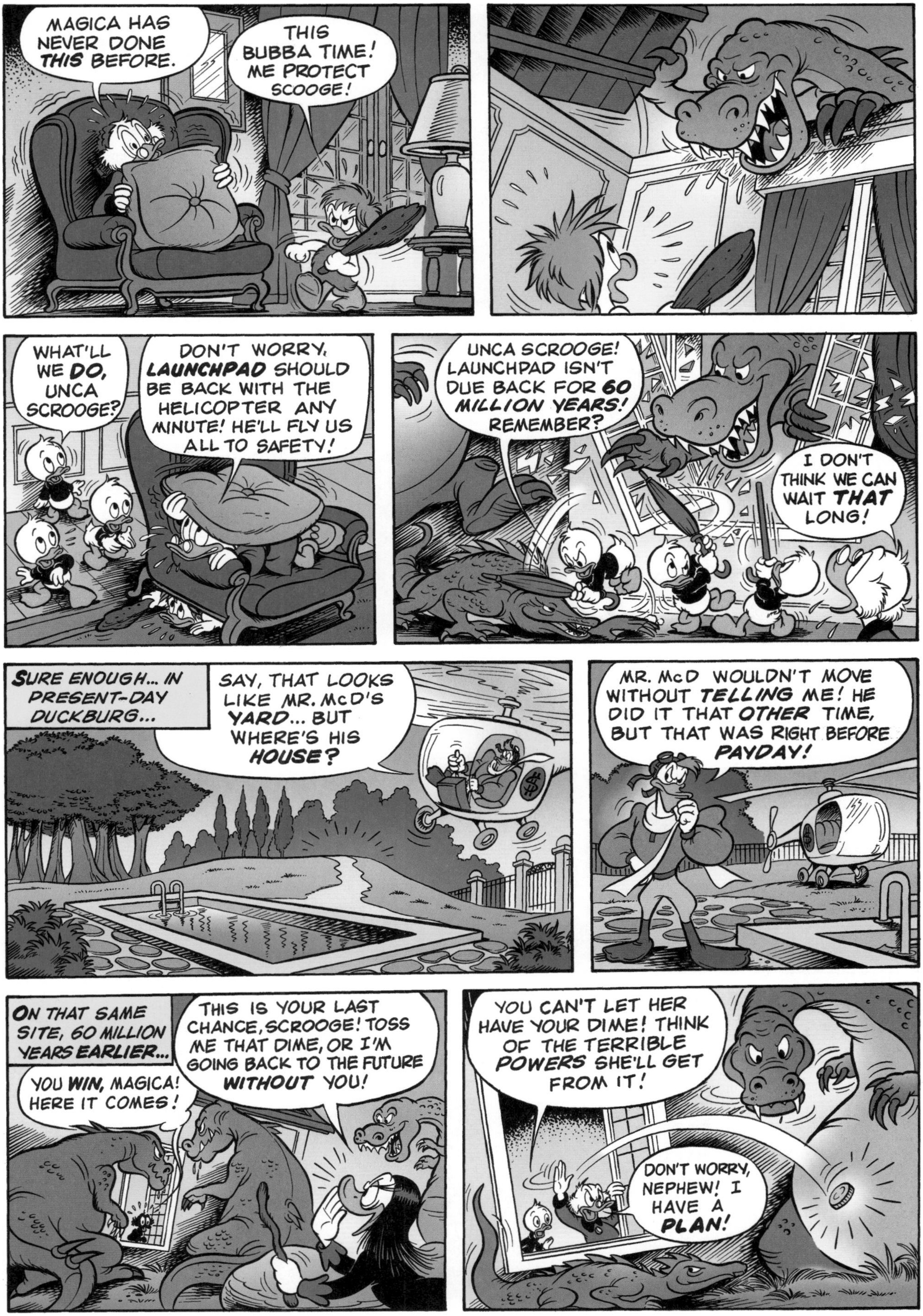
MAGICA HAS NEVER DONE THIS BEFORE.
THIS BUBBA TIME! ME PROTECT SCOOGE!
WHAT'LL WE DO, UNCA SCROOGE?
DON'T WORRY, LAUNCHPAD SHOULD BE BACK WITH THE HELICOPTER ANY MINUTE! HE'LL FLY US ALL TO SAFETY!
UNCA SCROOGE! LAUNCHPAD ISN'T DUE BACK FOR 60 MILLION YEARS! REMEMBER?
I DON'T THINK WE CAN WAIT THAT LONG!
SURE ENOUGH... IN PRESENT-DAY DUCKBURG...
SAY, THAT LOOKS LIKE MR. McD'S YARD... BUT WHERE'S HIS HOUSE?
MR. McD WOULDN'T MOVE WITHOUT TELLING ME! HE DID IT THAT OTHER TIME, BUT THAT WAS RIGHT BEFORE PAYDAY!
ON THAT SAME SITE, 60 MILLION YEARS EARLIER...
THIS IS YOUR LAST CHANCE, SCROOGE! TOSS ME THAT DIME, OR I'M GOING BACK TO THE FUTURE WITHOUT YOU!
YOU WIN, MAGICA! HERE IT COMES!
YOU CAN'T LET HER HAVE YOUR DIME! THINK OF THE TERRIBLE POWERS SHE'LL GET FROM IT!
DON'T WORRY, NEPHEW! I HAVE A PLAN!

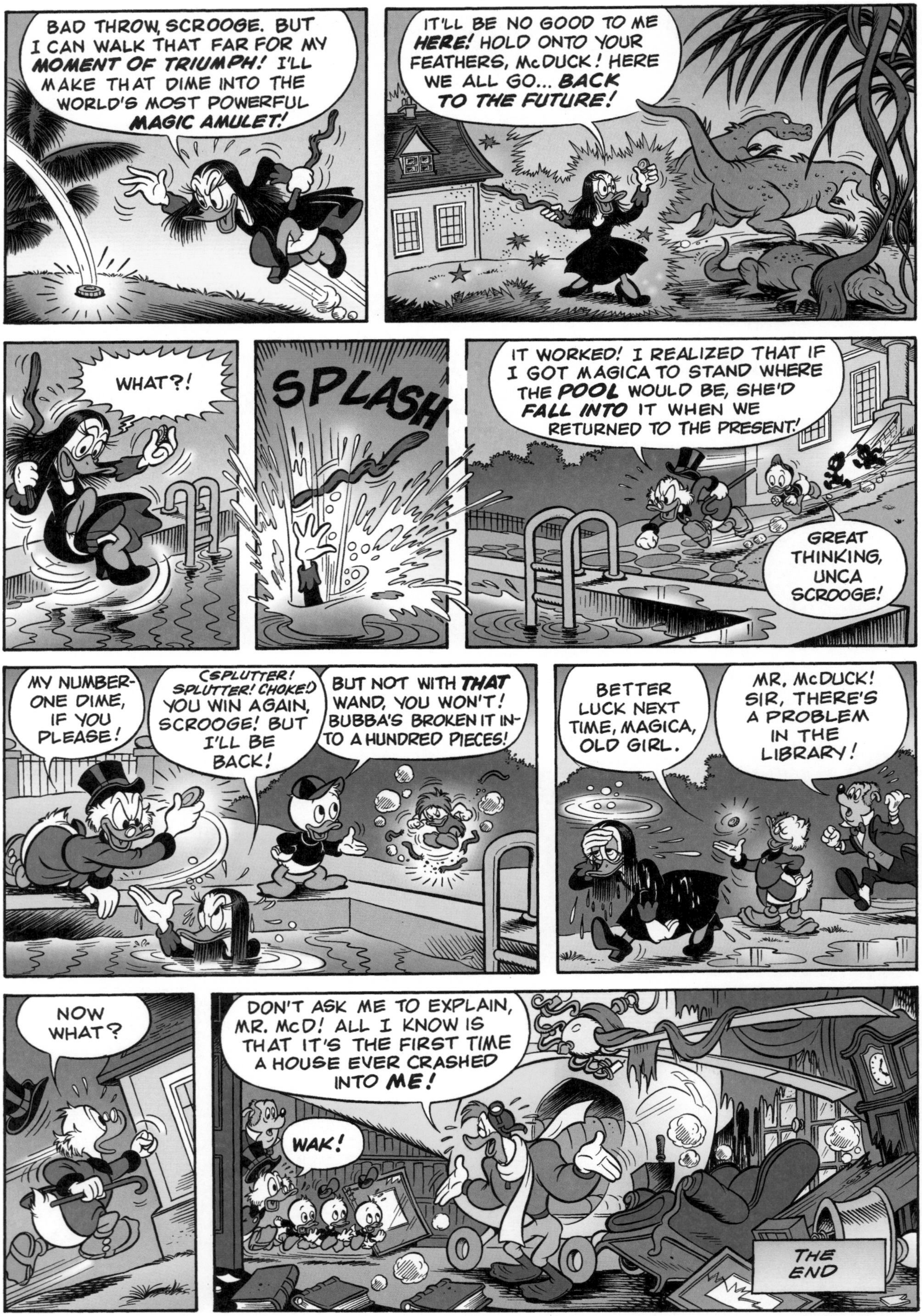

BAD THROW, SCROOGE. BUT I CAN WALK THAT FAR FOR MY MOMENT OF TRIUMPH! I'LL MAKE THAT DIME INTO THE WORLD'S MOST POWERFUL MAGIC AMULET!
IT'LL BE NO GOOD TO ME HERE! HOLD ONTO YOUR FEATHERS, McDUCK! HERE WE ALL GO... BACK TO THE FUTURE!
WHAT?!
SPLASH
IT WORKED! I REALIZED THAT IF I GOT MAGICA TO STAND WHERE THE POOL WOULD BE, SHE'D FALL INTO IT WHEN WE RETURNED TO THE PRESENT!
GREAT THINKING, UNCA SCROOGE!
MY NUMBER-ONE DIME, IF YOU PLEASE!
(SPLUTTER! SPLUTTER! CHOKE!) YOU WIN AGAIN, SCROOGE! BUT I'LL BE BACK!
BUT NOT WITH THAT WAND, YOU WON'T! BUBBA'S BROKEN IT INTO A HUNDRED PIECES!
BETTER LUCK NEXT TIME, MAGICA, OLD GIRL.
MR. McDUCK! SIR, THERE'S A PROBLEM IN THE LIBRARY!
NOW WHAT?
DON'T ASK ME TO EXPLAIN, MR. McD! ALL I KNOW IS THAT IT'S THE FIRST TIME A HOUSE EVER CRASHED INTO ME!
WAK!
THE END

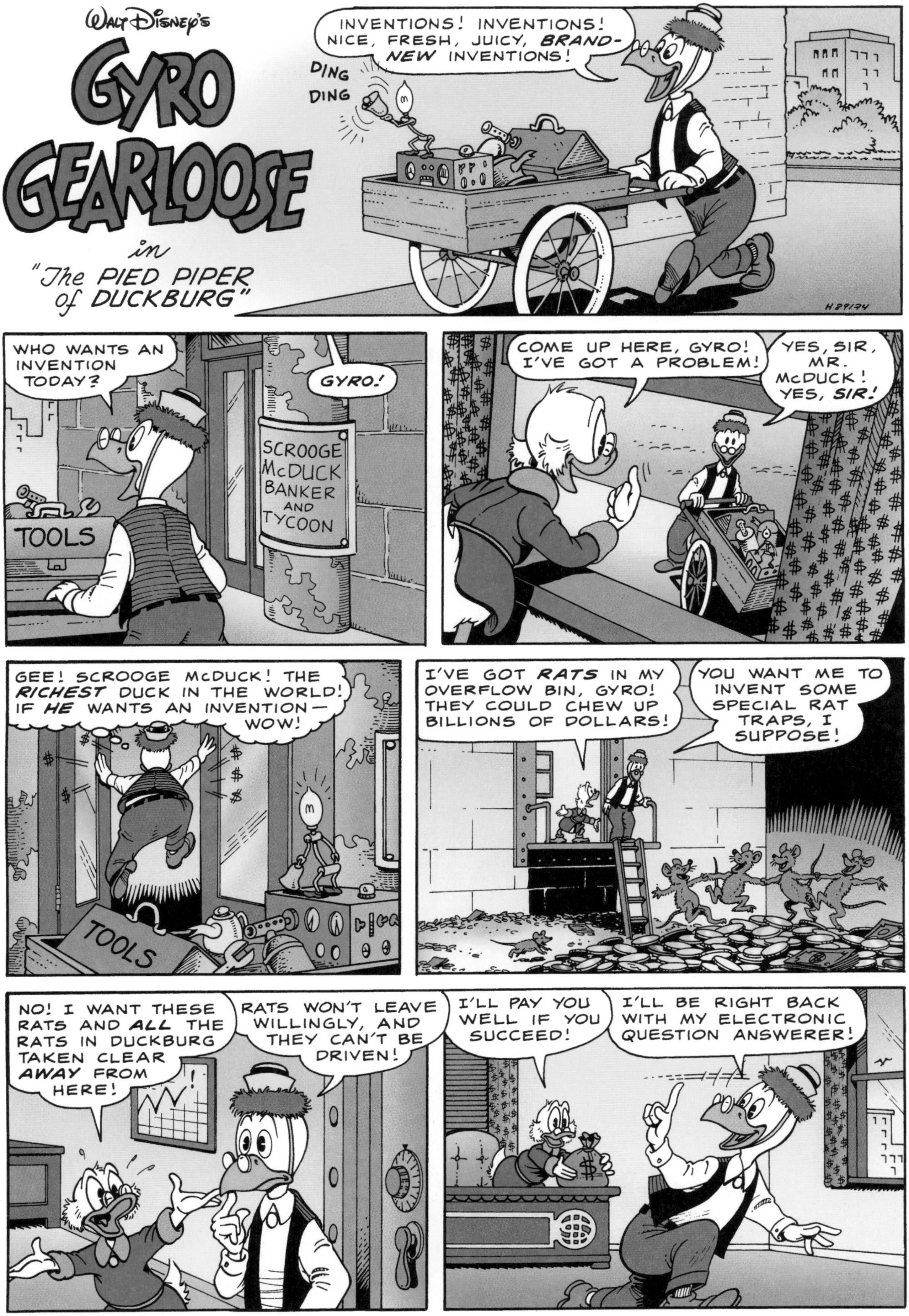

WALT DISNEY'S
GYRO GEARLOOSE
in
"The PIED PIPER of DUCKBURG"
INVENTIONS! INVENTIONS! NICE, FRESH, JUICY, BRAND-NEW INVENTIONS!
DING DING
H 89174
WHO WANTS AN INVENTION TODAY?
GYRO!
SCROOGE McDUCK BANKER AND TYCOON
TOOLS
COME UP HERE, GYRO! I'VE GOT A PROBLEM!
YES, SIR, MR. McDUCK! YES, SIR!
GEE! SCROOGE McDUCK! THE RICHEST DUCK IN THE WORLD! IF HE WANTS AN INVENTION — WOW!
TOOLS
I'VE GOT RATS IN MY OVERFLOW BIN, GYRO! THEY COULD CHEW UP BILLIONS OF DOLLARS!
YOU WANT ME TO INVENT SOME SPECIAL RAT TRAPS, I SUPPOSE!
NO! I WANT THESE RATS AND ALL THE RATS IN DUCKBURG TAKEN CLEAR AWAY FROM HERE!
RATS WON'T LEAVE WILLINGLY, AND THEY CAN'T BE DRIVEN!
I'LL PAY YOU WELL IF YOU SUCCEED!
I'LL BE RIGHT BACK WITH MY ELECTRONIC QUESTION ANSWERER!

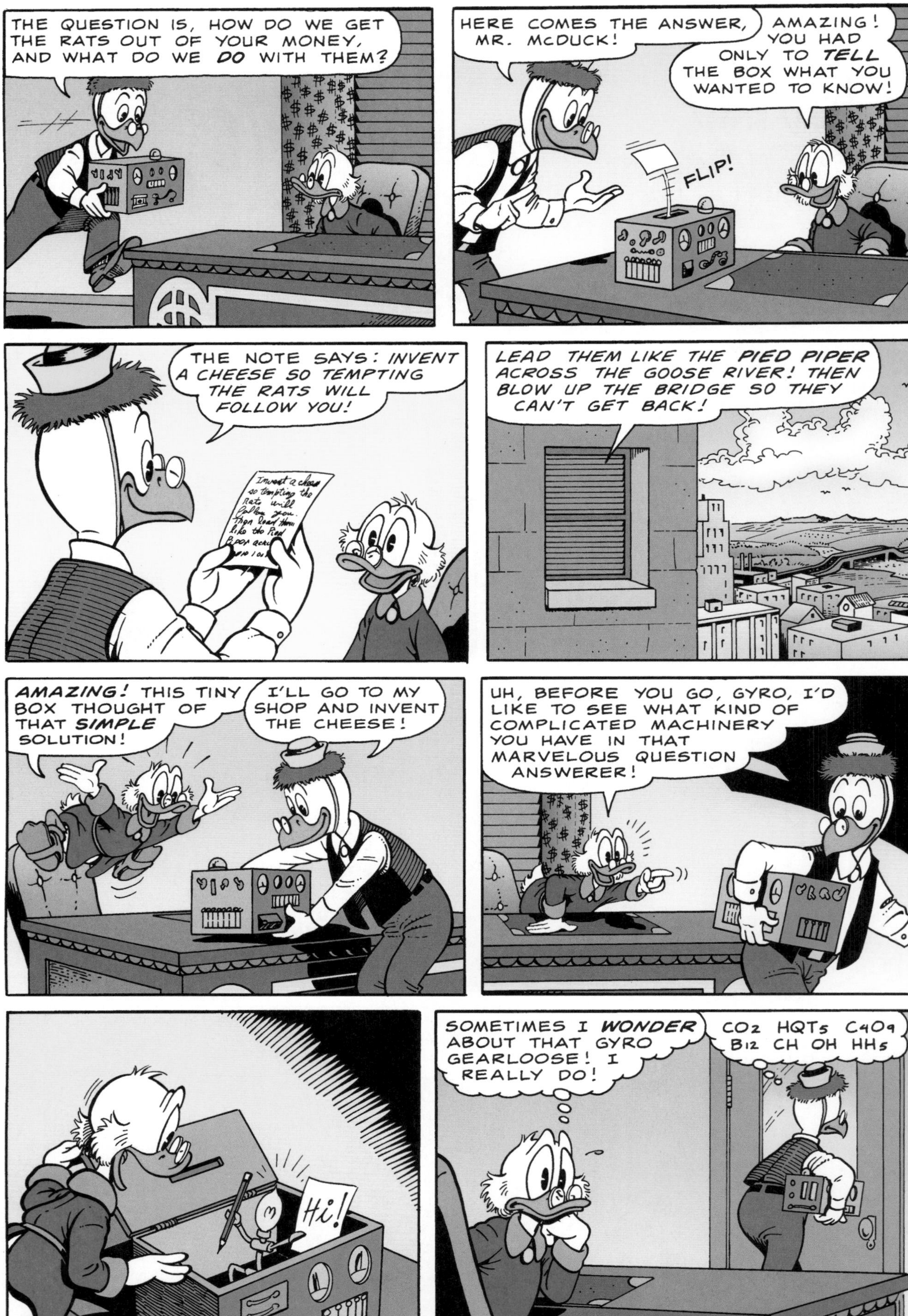
THE QUESTION IS, HOW DO WE GET THE RATS OUT OF YOUR MONEY, AND WHAT DO WE DO WITH THEM?
HERE COMES THE ANSWER, MR. McDUCK!
AMAZING! YOU HAD ONLY TO TELL THE BOX WHAT YOU WANTED TO KNOW!
FLIP!
THE NOTE SAYS: INVENT A CHEESE SO TEMPTING THE RATS WILL FOLLOW YOU!
LEAD THEM LIKE THE PIED PIPER ACROSS THE GOOSE RIVER! THEN BLOW UP THE BRIDGE SO THEY CAN'T GET BACK!
AMAZING! THIS TINY BOX THOUGHT OF THAT SIMPLE SOLUTION!
I'LL GO TO MY SHOP AND INVENT THE CHEESE!
UH, BEFORE YOU GO, GYRO, I'D LIKE TO SEE WHAT KIND OF COMPLICATED MACHINERY YOU HAVE IN THAT MARVELOUS QUESTION ANSWERER!
Hi!
SOMETIMES I WONDER ABOUT THAT GYRO GEARLOOSE! I REALLY DO!
CO2 HQT5 C4O9 B12 CH OH HH5

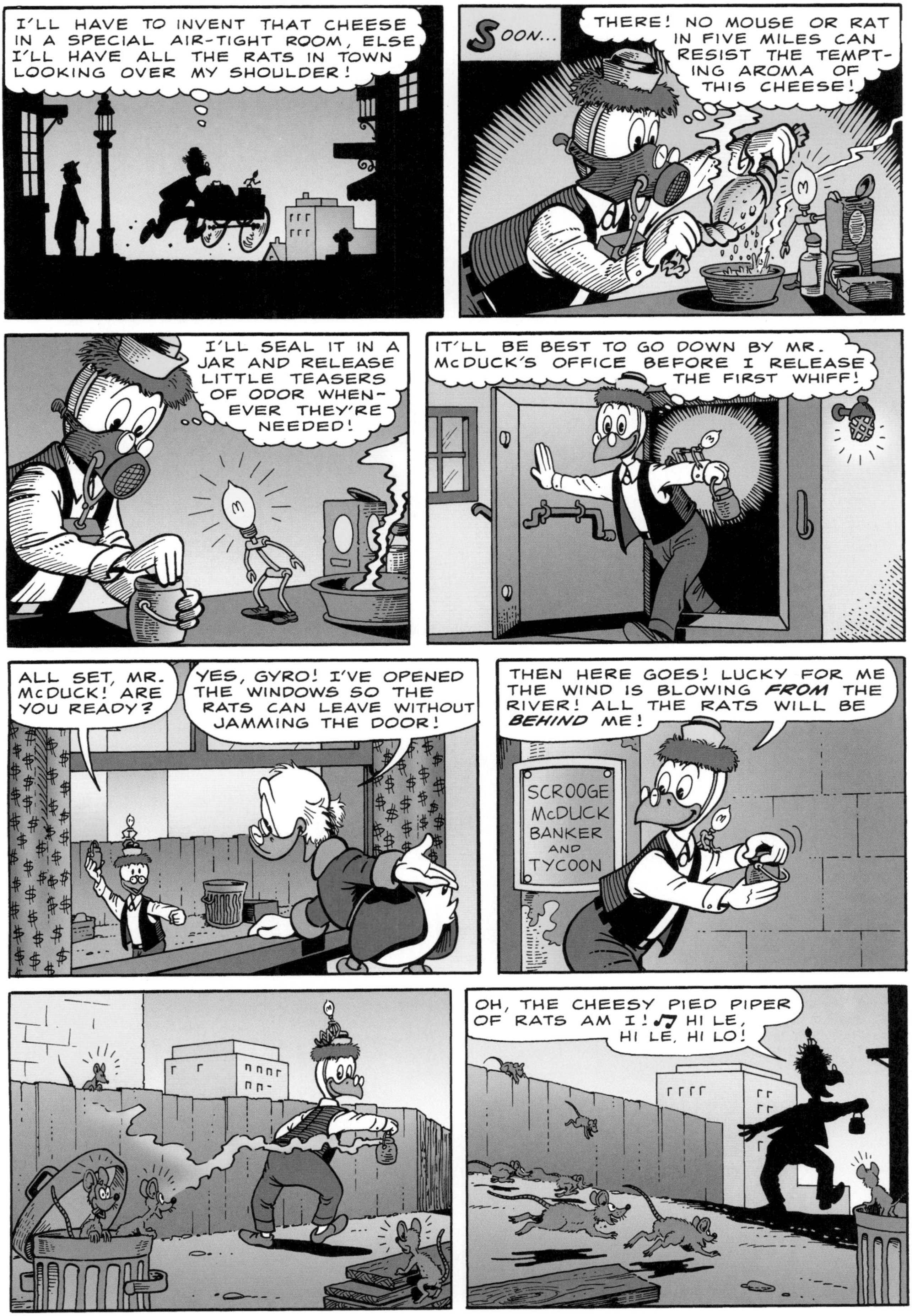
I'LL HAVE TO INVENT THAT CHEESE IN A SPECIAL AIR-TIGHT ROOM, ELSE I'LL HAVE ALL THE RATS IN TOWN LOOKING OVER MY SHOULDER!
SOON...
THERE! NO MOUSE OR RAT IN FIVE MILES CAN RESIST THE TEMPTING AROMA OF THIS CHEESE!
I'LL SEAL IT IN A JAR AND RELEASE LITTLE TEASERS OF ODOR WHENEVER THEY'RE NEEDED!
IT'LL BE BEST TO GO DOWN BY MR. McDUCK'S OFFICE BEFORE I RELEASE THE FIRST WHIFF!
ALL SET, MR. McDUCK! ARE YOU READY?
YES, GYRO! I'VE OPENED THE WINDOWS SO THE RATS CAN LEAVE WITHOUT JAMMING THE DOOR!
THEN HERE GOES! LUCKY FOR ME THE WIND IS BLOWING FROM THE RIVER! ALL THE RATS WILL BE BEHIND ME!
SCROOGE McDUCK BANKER AND TYCOON
OH, THE CHEESY PIED PIPER OF RATS AM I! HI LE, HI LE, HI LO!

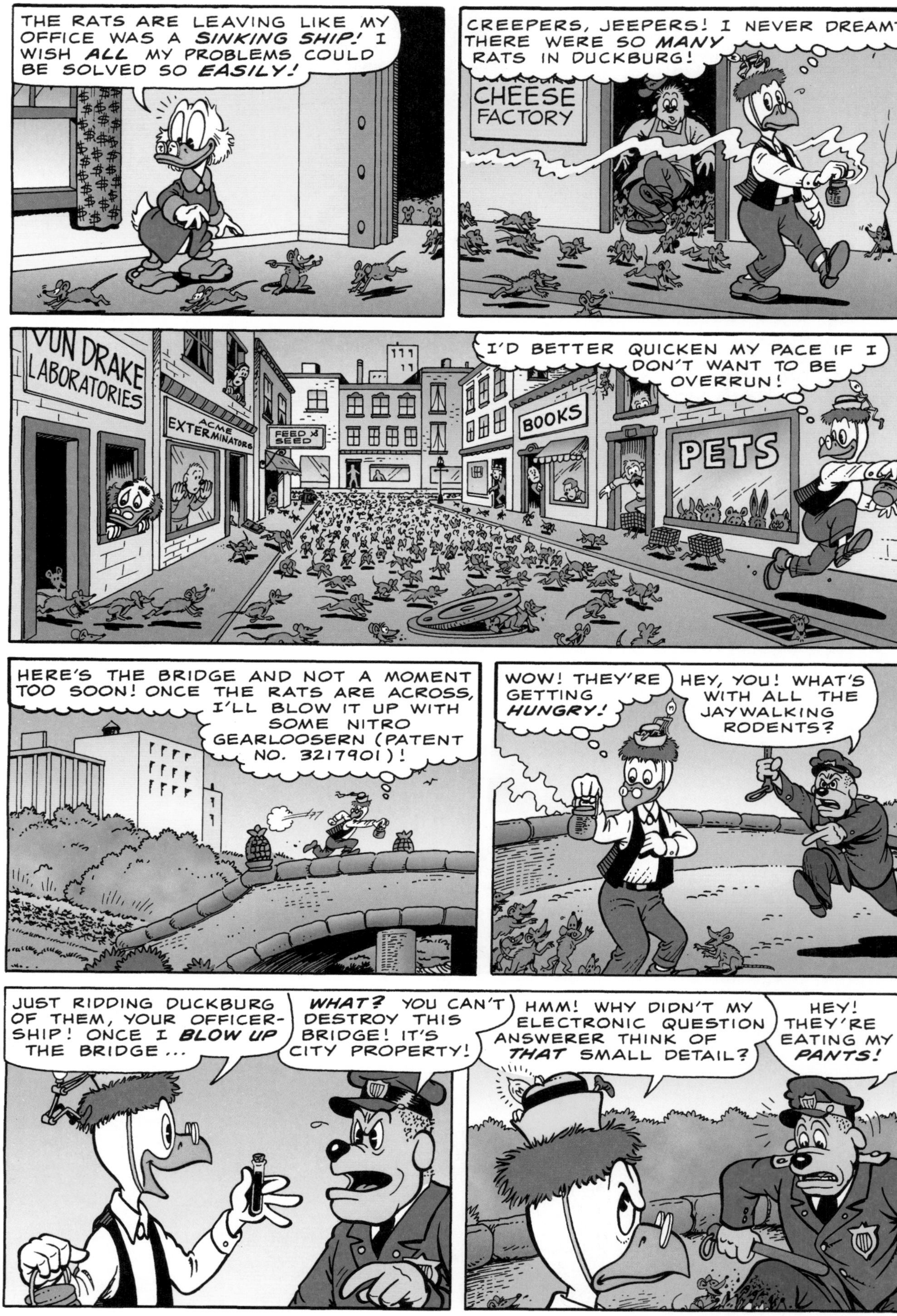
THE RATS ARE LEAVING LIKE MY OFFICE WAS A SINKING SHIP! I WISH ALL MY PROBLEMS COULD BE SOLVED SO EASILY!
CREEPERS, JEEPERS! I NEVER DREAMT THERE WERE SO MANY RATS IN DUCKBURG!
CHEESE FACTORY
VON DRAKE LABORATORIES
ACME EXTERMINATORS
FEED & SEED
BOOKS
PETS
I'D BETTER QUICKEN MY PACE IF I DON'T WANT TO BE OVERRUN!
HERE'S THE BRIDGE AND NOT A MOMENT TOO SOON! ONCE THE RATS ARE ACROSS, I'LL BLOW IT UP WITH SOME NITRO GEARLOOSERN (PATENT NO. 3217901)!
WOW! THEY'RE GETTING HUNGRY!
HEY, YOU! WHAT'S WITH ALL THE JAYWALKING RODENTS?
JUST RIDDING DUCKBURG OF THEM, YOUR OFFICER-SHIP! ONCE I BLOW UP THE BRIDGE ...
WHAT? YOU CAN'T DESTROY THIS BRIDGE! IT'S CITY PROPERTY!
HMM! WHY DIDN'T MY ELECTRONIC QUESTION ANSWERER THINK OF THAT SMALL DETAIL?
HEY! THEY'RE EATING MY PANTS!

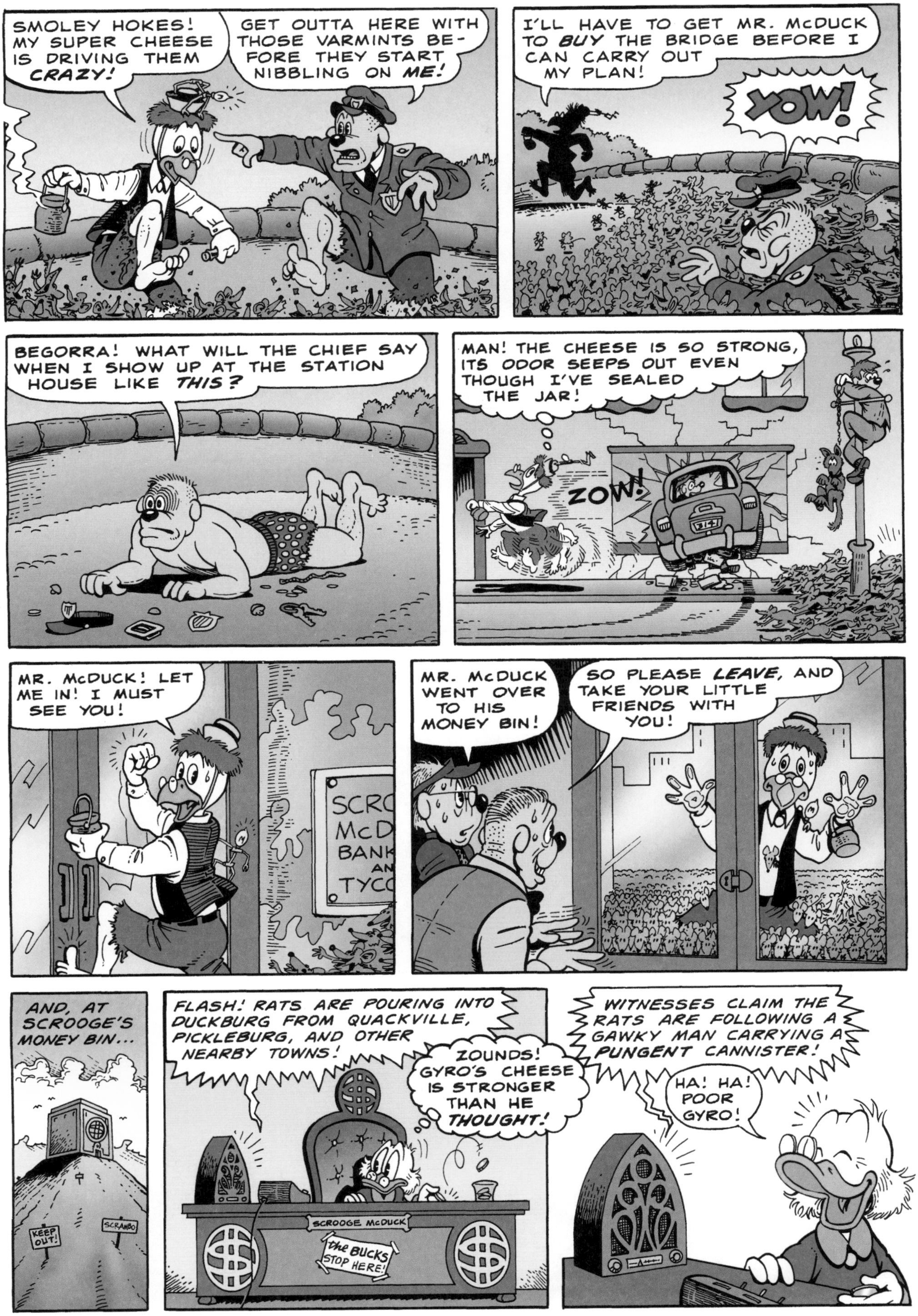
SMOLEY HOKES! MY SUPER CHEESE IS DRIVING THEM CRAZY!
GET OUTTA HERE WITH THOSE VARMINTS BE-FORE THEY START NIBBLING ON ME!
I'LL HAVE TO GET MR. McDUCK TO BUY THE BRIDGE BEFORE I CAN CARRY OUT MY PLAN!
YOW!
BEGORRA! WHAT WILL THE CHIEF SAY WHEN I SHOW UP AT THE STATION HOUSE LIKE THIS?
MAN! THE CHEESE IS SO STRONG, ITS ODOR SEEPS OUT EVEN THOUGH I'VE SEALED THE JAR!
ZOW!
MR. McDUCK! LET ME IN! I MUST SEE YOU!
MR. McDUCK WENT OVER TO HIS MONEY BIN!
SO PLEASE LEAVE, AND TAKE YOUR LITTLE FRIENDS WITH YOU!
AND, AT SCROOGE'S MONEY BIN...
KEEP OUT!
SCRAMBO
FLASH! RATS ARE POURING INTO DUCKBURG FROM QUACKVILLE, PICKLEBURG, AND OTHER NEARBY TOWNS!
ZOUNDS! GYRO'S CHEESE IS STRONGER THAN HE THOUGHT!
SCROOGE McDUCK
the BUCKS STOP HERE!
WITNESSES CLAIM THE RATS ARE FOLLOWING A GAWKY MAN CARRYING A PUNGENT CANNISTER!
HA! HA! POOR GYRO!

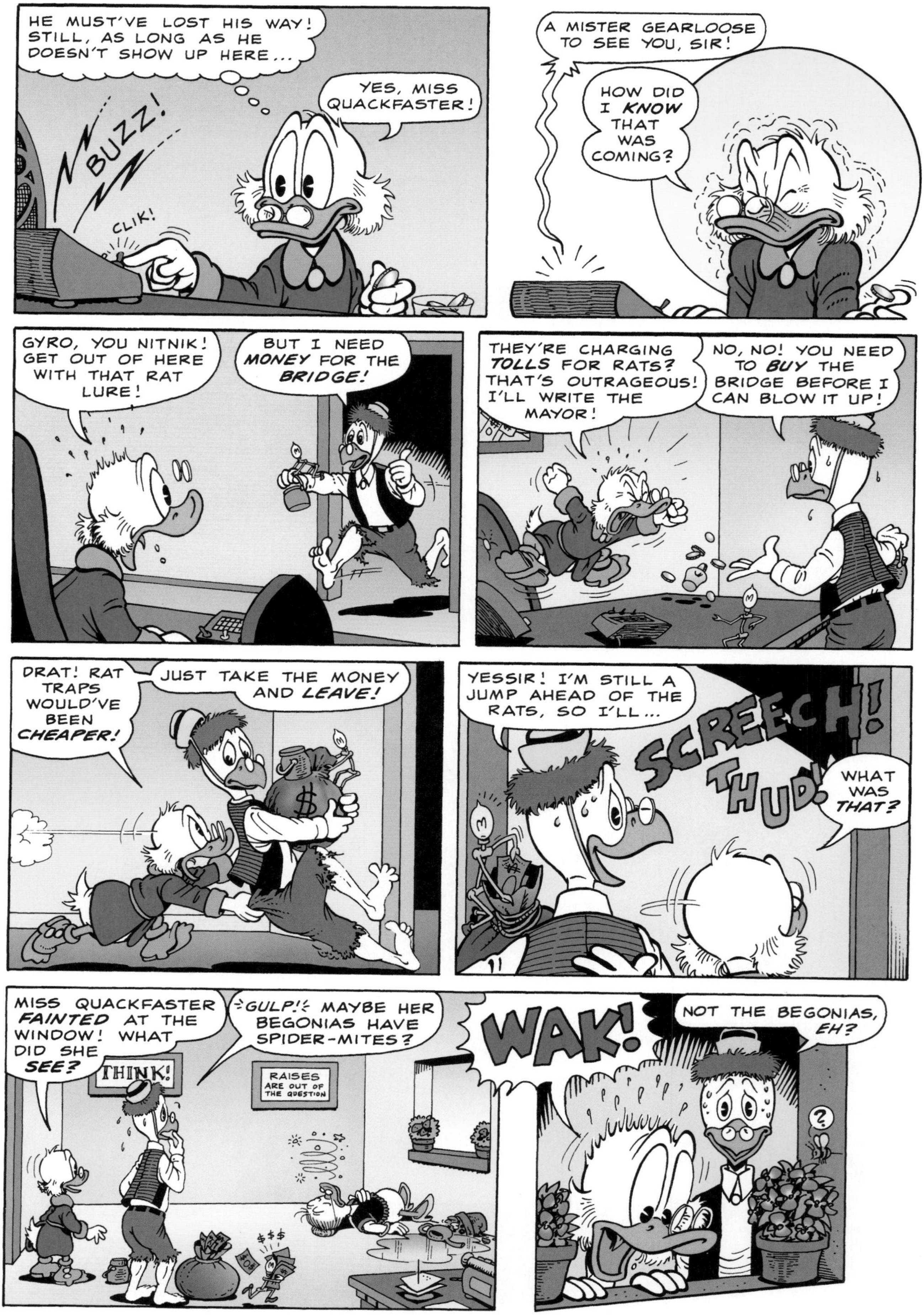
HE MUST'VE LOST HIS WAY! STILL, AS LONG AS HE DOESN'T SHOW UP HERE...
BUZZ!
CLIK!
YES, MISS QUACKFASTER!
A MISTER GEARLOOSE TO SEE YOU, SIR!
HOW DID I KNOW THAT WAS COMING?
GYRO, YOU NITNIK! GET OUT OF HERE WITH THAT RAT LURE!
BUT I NEED MONEY FOR THE BRIDGE!
THEY'RE CHARGING TOLLS FOR RATS? THAT'S OUTRAGEOUS! I'LL WRITE THE MAYOR!
NO, NO! YOU NEED TO BUY THE BRIDGE BEFORE I CAN BLOW IT UP!
DRAT! RAT TRAPS WOULD'VE BEEN CHEAPER!
JUST TAKE THE MONEY AND LEAVE!
YESSIR! I'M STILL A JUMP AHEAD OF THE RATS, SO I'LL...
SCREECH!
THUD!
WHAT WAS THAT?
MISS QUACKFASTER FAINTED AT THE WINDOW! WHAT DID SHE SEE?
GULP! MAYBE HER BEGONIAS HAVE SPIDER-MITES?
THINK!
RAISES ARE OUT OF THE QUESTION
WAK!
NOT THE BEGONIAS, EH?

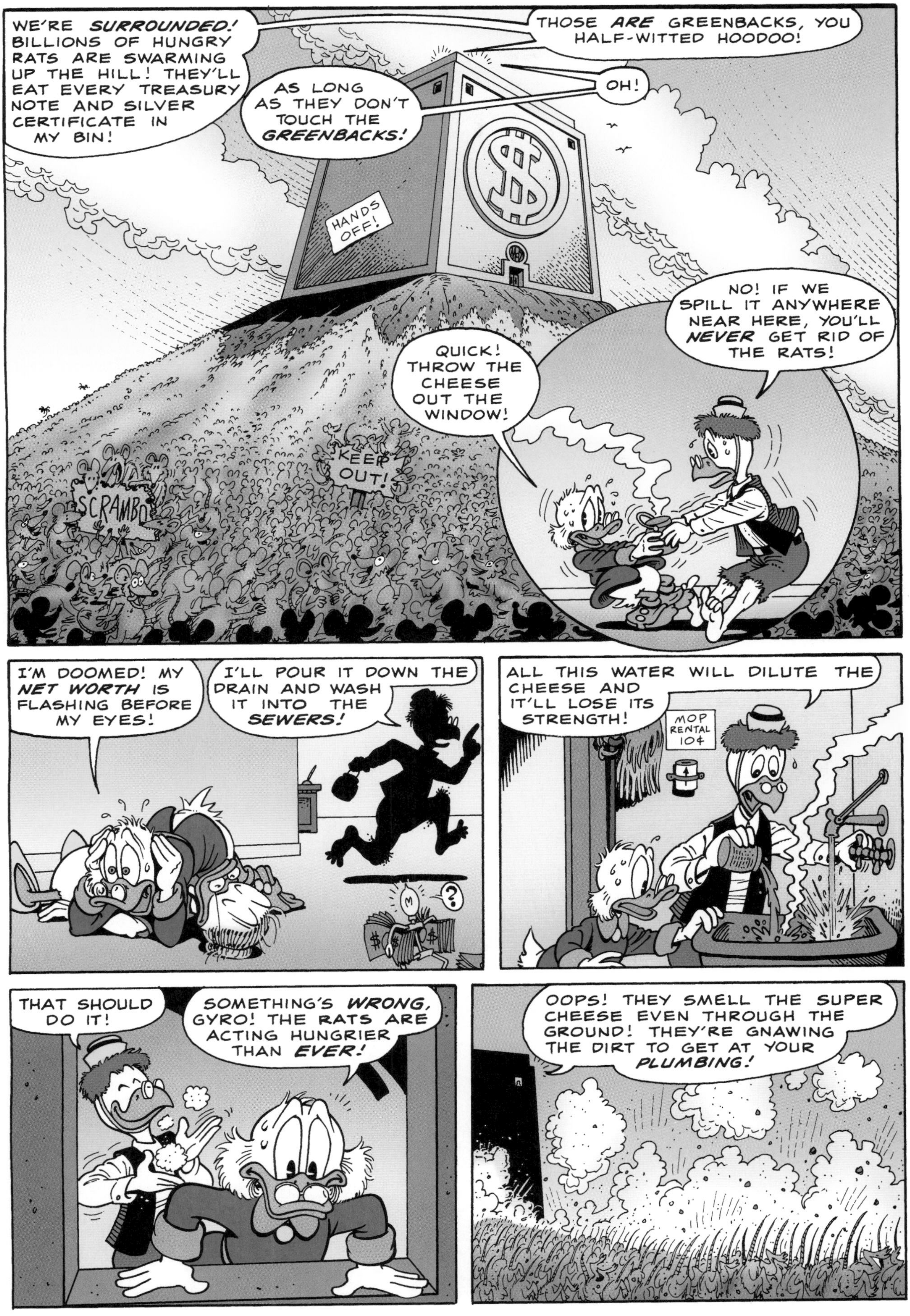
WE'RE SURROUNDED! BILLIONS OF HUNGRY RATS ARE SWARMING UP THE HILL! THEY'LL EAT EVERY TREASURY NOTE AND SILVER CERTIFICATE IN MY BIN!
THOSE ARE GREENBACKS, YOU HALF-WITTED HOODOO!
AS LONG AS THEY DON'T TOUCH THE GREENBACKS!
OH!
HANDS OFF!
KEEP OUT!
SCRAMBO
QUICK! THROW THE CHEESE OUT THE WINDOW!
NO! IF WE SPILL IT ANYWHERE NEAR HERE, YOU'LL NEVER GET RID OF THE RATS!
I'M DOOMED! MY NET WORTH IS FLASHING BEFORE MY EYES!
I'LL POUR IT DOWN THE DRAIN AND WASH IT INTO THE SEWERS!
ALL THIS WATER WILL DILUTE THE CHEESE AND IT'LL LOSE ITS STRENGTH!
MOP RENTAL 10¢
THAT SHOULD DO IT!
SOMETHING'S WRONG, GYRO! THE RATS ARE ACTING HUNGRIER THAN EVER!
OOPS! THEY SMELL THE SUPER CHEESE EVEN THROUGH THE GROUND! THEY'RE GNAWING THE DIRT TO GET AT YOUR PLUMBING!

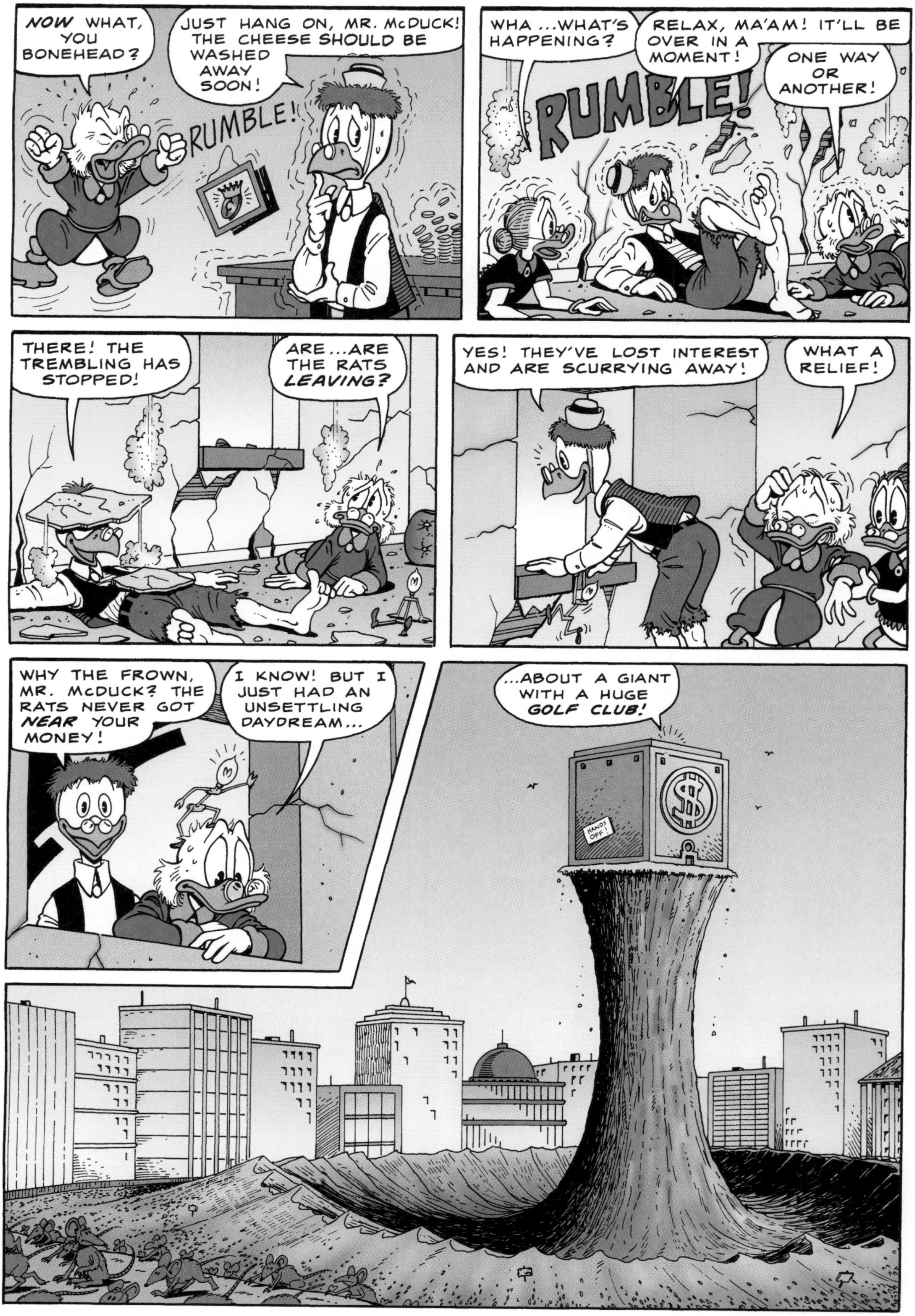
NOW WHAT, YOU BONEHEAD?
JUST HANG ON, MR. McDUCK! THE CHEESE SHOULD BE WASHED AWAY SOON!
RUMBLE!
WHA...WHAT'S HAPPENING?
RELAX, MA'AM! IT'LL BE OVER IN A MOMENT!
ONE WAY OR ANOTHER!
RUMBLE!
THERE! THE TREMBLING HAS STOPPED!
ARE...ARE THE RATS LEAVING?
YES! THEY'VE LOST INTEREST AND ARE SCURRYING AWAY!
WHAT A RELIEF!
WHY THE FROWN, MR. McDUCK? THE RATS NEVER GOT NEAR YOUR MONEY!
I KNOW! BUT I JUST HAD AN UNSETTLING DAYDREAM...
...ABOUT A GIANT WITH A HUGE GOLF CLUB!
HANDS OFF!

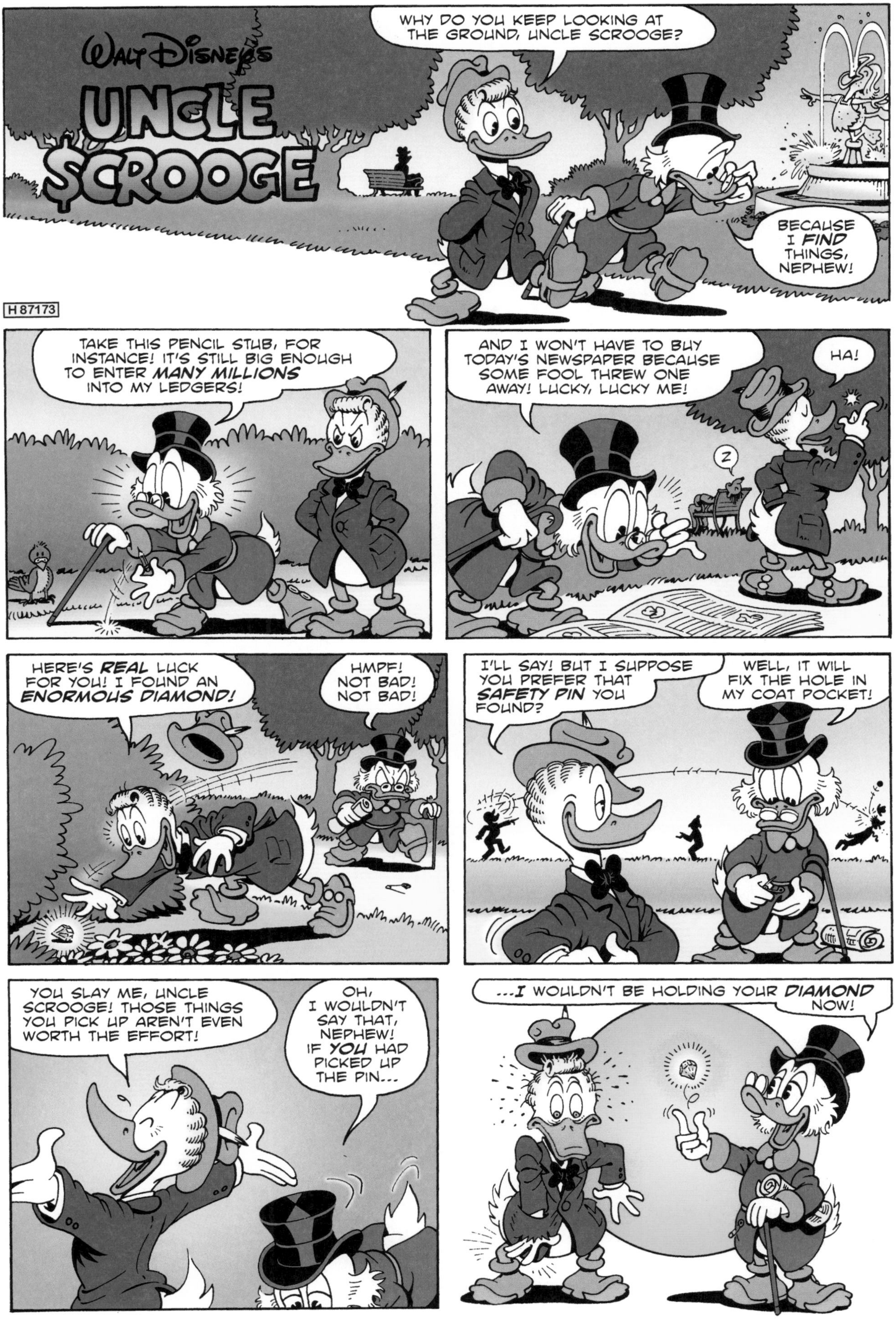
WALT DISNEY'S
UNCLE $CROOGE
WHY DO YOU KEEP LOOKING AT THE GROUND, UNCLE SCROOGE?
BECAUSE I FIND THINGS, NEPHEW!
H 87173
TAKE THIS PENCIL STUB, FOR INSTANCE! IT'S STILL BIG ENOUGH TO ENTER MANY MILLIONS INTO MY LEDGERS!
AND I WON'T HAVE TO BUY TODAY'S NEWSPAPER BECAUSE SOME FOOL THREW ONE AWAY! LUCKY, LUCKY ME!
HA!
HERE'S REAL LUCK FOR YOU! I FOUND AN ENORMOUS DIAMOND!
HMPF! NOT BAD! NOT BAD!
I'LL SAY! BUT I SUPPOSE YOU PREFER THAT SAFETY PIN YOU FOUND?
WELL, IT WILL FIX THE HOLE IN MY COAT POCKET!
YOU SLAY ME, UNCLE SCROOGE! THOSE THINGS YOU PICK UP AREN'T EVEN WORTH THE EFFORT!
OH, I WOULDN'T SAY THAT, NEPHEW! IF YOU HAD PICKED UP THE PIN...
...I WOULDN'T BE HOLDING YOUR DIAMOND NOW!

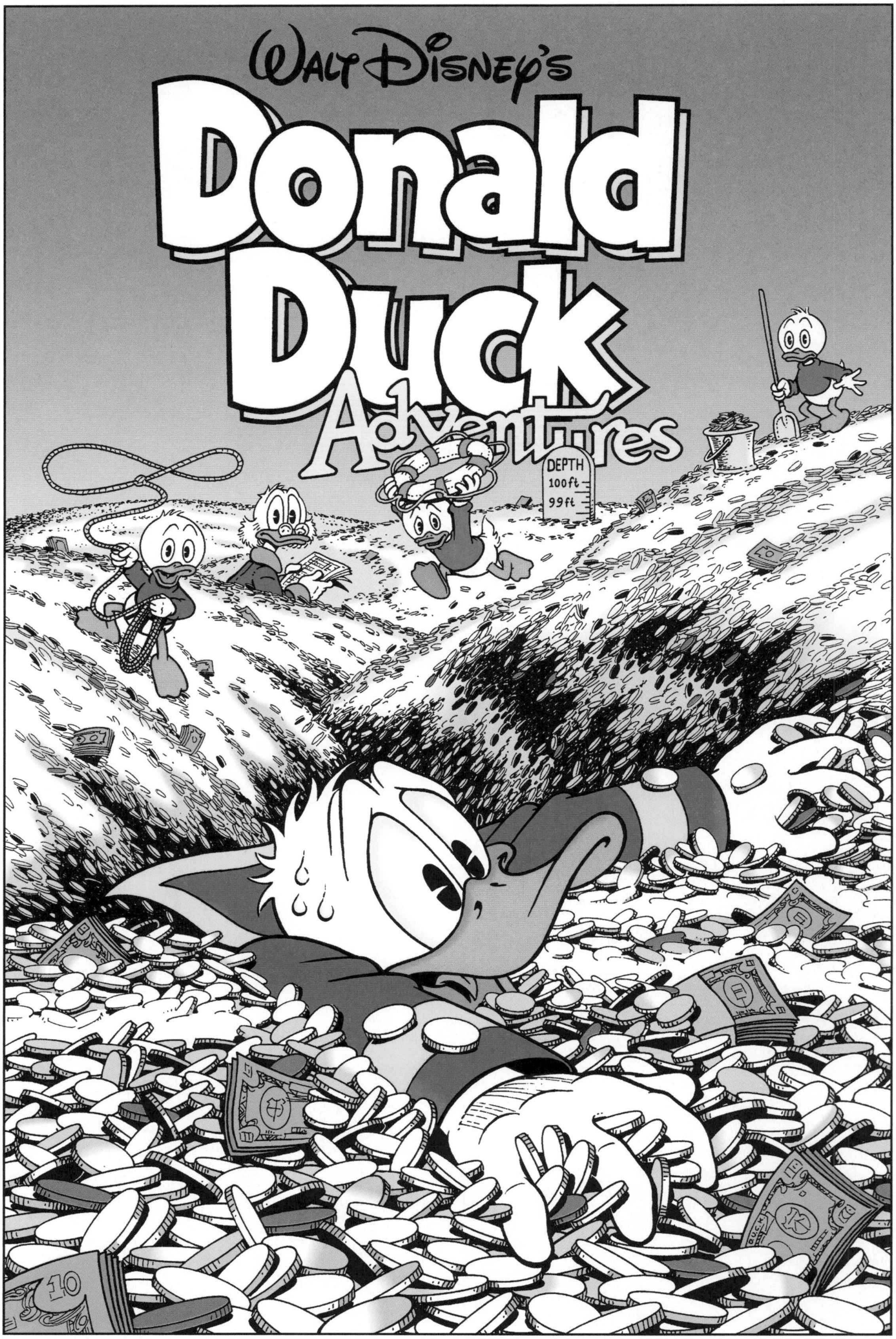
Walt Disney's
Donald Duck
Adventures
DEPTH
100ft
99ft

THE MONEY PIT
Donald Duck Adventures [series II] 1, June 1990; color by Jo Meugniot with David Gerstein

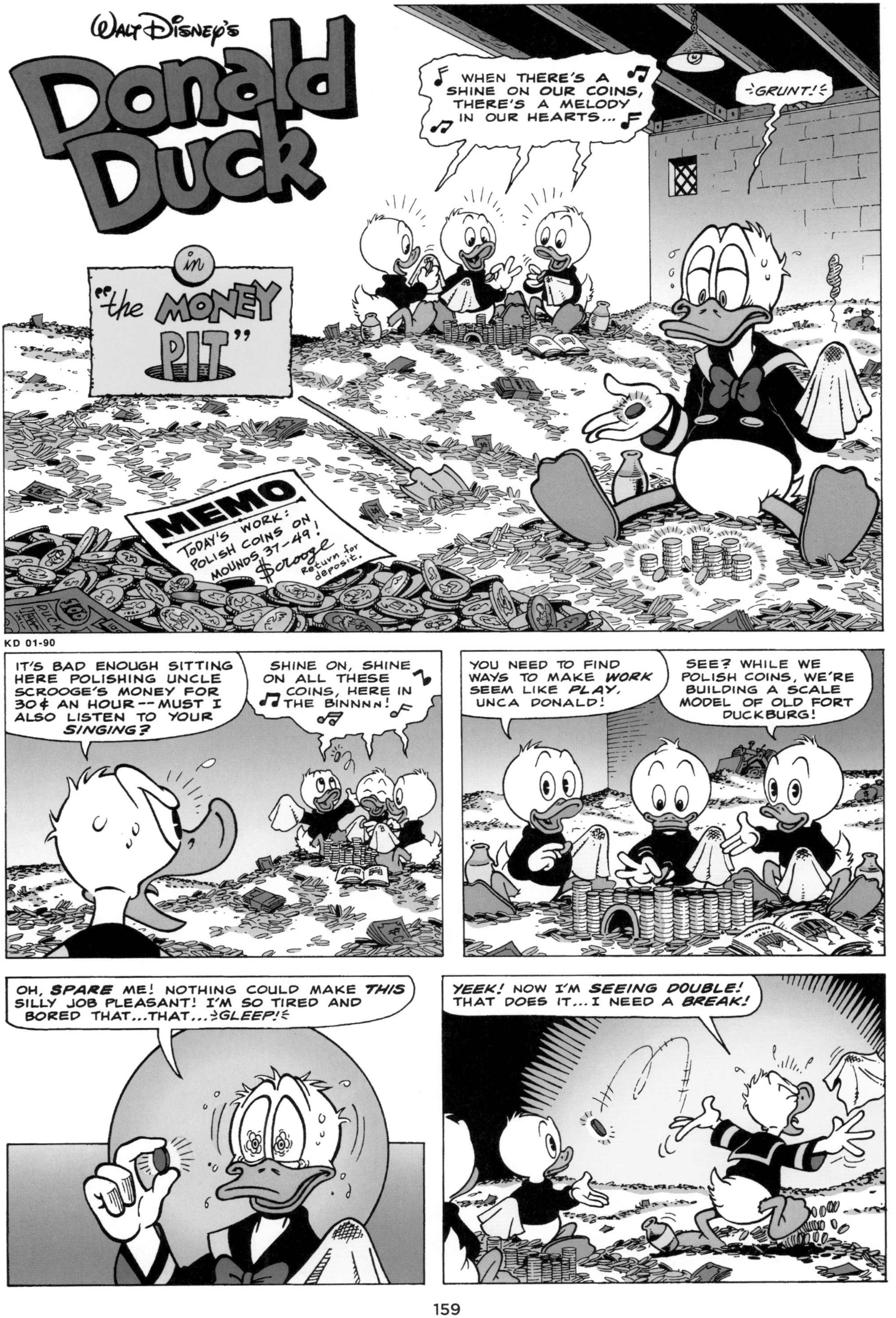

WALT DISNEY'S
Donald Duck
in "the MONEY PIT"
WHEN THERE'S A SHINE ON OUR COINS, THERE'S A MELODY IN OUR HEARTS...
GRUNT!
MEMO
TODAY'S WORK: POLISH COINS ON MOUNDS 37-49! $crooge
Return for deposit.
KD 01-90
IT'S BAD ENOUGH SITTING HERE POLISHING UNCLE SCROOGE'S MONEY FOR 30¢ AN HOUR -- MUST I ALSO LISTEN TO YOUR SINGING?
SHINE ON, SHINE ON ALL THESE COINS, HERE IN THE BINNNN!
YOU NEED TO FIND WAYS TO MAKE WORK SEEM LIKE PLAY, UNCA DONALD!
SEE? WHILE WE POLISH COINS, WE'RE BUILDING A SCALE MODEL OF OLD FORT DUCKBURG!
OH, SPARE ME! NOTHING COULD MAKE THIS SILLY JOB PLEASANT! I'M SO TIRED AND BORED THAT...THAT... GLEEP!
YEEK! NOW I'M SEEING DOUBLE! THAT DOES IT... I NEED A BREAK!

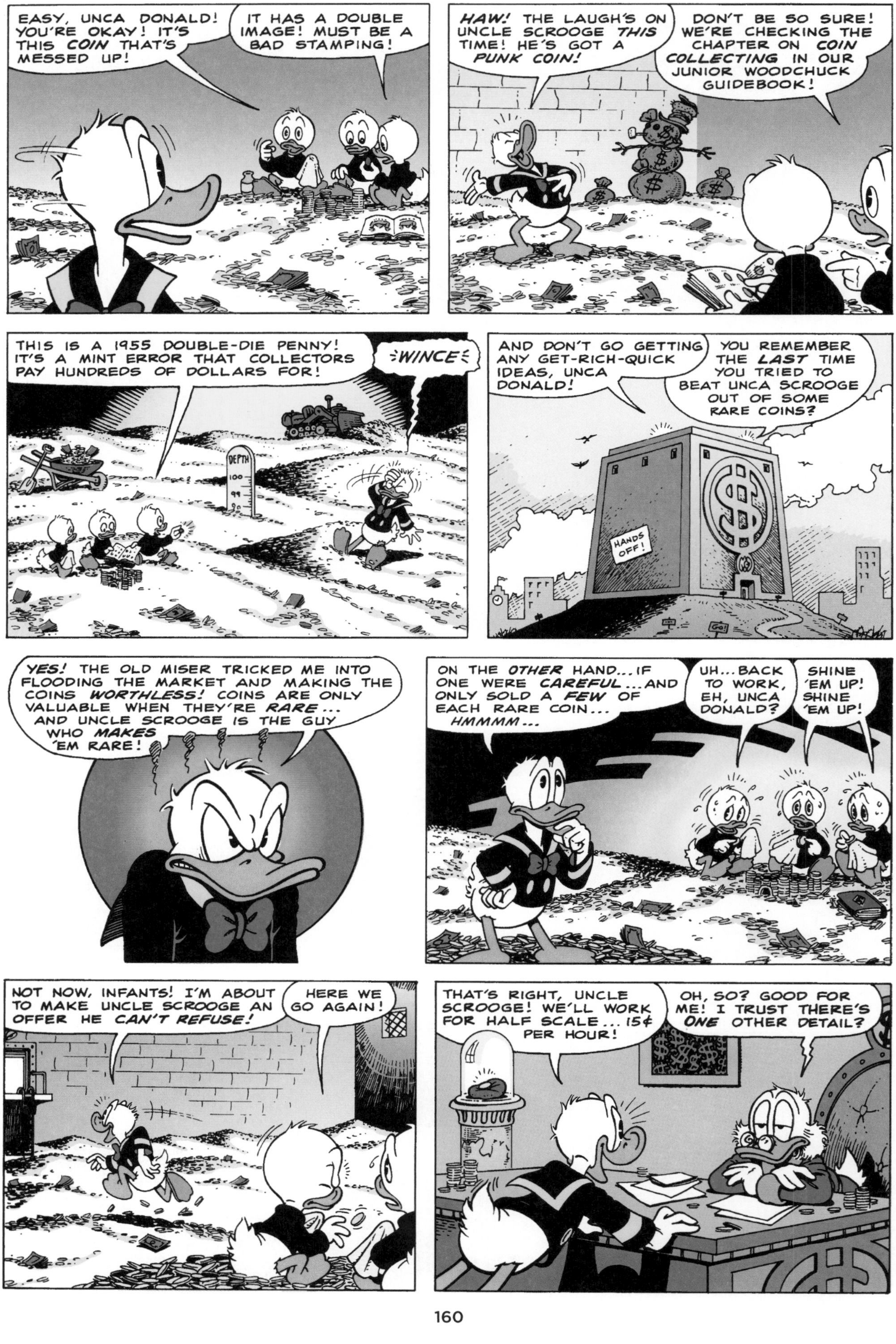
EASY, UNCA DONALD! YOU'RE OKAY! IT'S THIS COIN THAT'S MESSED UP!
IT HAS A DOUBLE IMAGE! MUST BE A BAD STAMPING!
HAW! THE LAUGH'S ON UNCLE SCROOGE THIS TIME! HE'S GOT A PUNK COIN!
DON'T BE SO SURE! WE'RE CHECKING THE CHAPTER ON COIN COLLECTING IN OUR JUNIOR WOODCHUCK GUIDEBOOK!
THIS IS A 1955 DOUBLE-DIE PENNY! IT'S A MINT ERROR THAT COLLECTORS PAY HUNDREDS OF DOLLARS FOR!
WINCE
DEPTH 100 99
AND DON'T GO GETTING ANY GET-RICH-QUICK IDEAS, UNCA DONALD!
YOU REMEMBER THE LAST TIME YOU TRIED TO BEAT UNCA SCROOGE OUT OF SOME RARE COINS?
HANDS OFF!
YES! THE OLD MISER TRICKED ME INTO FLOODING THE MARKET AND MAKING THE COINS WORTHLESS! COINS ARE ONLY VALUABLE WHEN THEY'RE RARE... AND UNCLE SCROOGE IS THE GUY WHO MAKES 'EM RARE!
ON THE OTHER HAND... IF ONE WERE CAREFUL... AND ONLY SOLD A FEW OF EACH RARE COIN... HMMMM...
UH... BACK TO WORK, EH, UNCA DONALD?
SHINE 'EM UP! SHINE 'EM UP!
NOT NOW, INFANTS! I'M ABOUT TO MAKE UNCLE SCROOGE AN OFFER HE CAN'T REFUSE!
HERE WE GO AGAIN!
THAT'S RIGHT, UNCLE SCROOGE! WE'LL WORK FOR HALF SCALE... 15¢ PER HOUR!
OH, SO? GOOD FOR ME! I TRUST THERE'S ONE OTHER DETAIL?

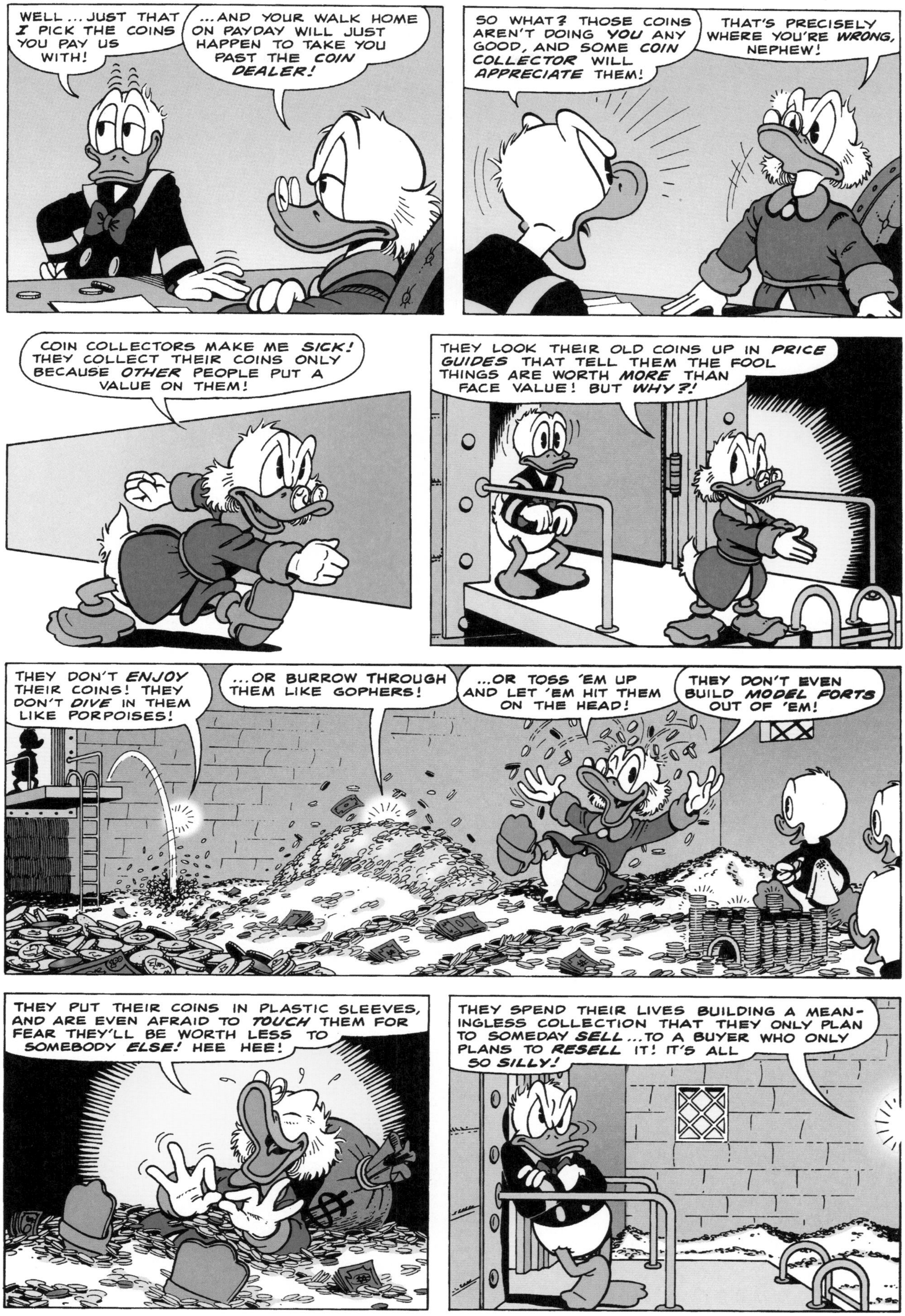
WELL ... JUST THAT I PICK THE COINS YOU PAY US WITH!
...AND YOUR WALK HOME ON PAYDAY WILL JUST HAPPEN TO TAKE YOU PAST THE COIN DEALER!
SO WHAT? THOSE COINS AREN'T DOING YOU ANY GOOD, AND SOME COIN COLLECTOR WILL APPRECIATE THEM!
THAT'S PRECISELY WHERE YOU'RE WRONG, NEPHEW!
COIN COLLECTORS MAKE ME SICK! THEY COLLECT THEIR COINS ONLY BECAUSE OTHER PEOPLE PUT A VALUE ON THEM!
THEY LOOK THEIR OLD COINS UP IN PRICE GUIDES THAT TELL THEM THE FOOL THINGS ARE WORTH MORE THAN FACE VALUE! BUT WHY?!
THEY DON'T ENJOY THEIR COINS! THEY DON'T DIVE IN THEM LIKE PORPOISES!
...OR BURROW THROUGH THEM LIKE GOPHERS!
...OR TOSS 'EM UP AND LET 'EM HIT THEM ON THE HEAD!
THEY DON'T EVEN BUILD MODEL FORTS OUT OF 'EM!
THEY PUT THEIR COINS IN PLASTIC SLEEVES, AND ARE EVEN AFRAID TO TOUCH THEM FOR FEAR THEY'LL BE WORTH LESS TO SOMEBODY ELSE! HEE HEE!
THEY SPEND THEIR LIVES BUILDING A MEANINGLESS COLLECTION THAT THEY ONLY PLAN TO SOMEDAY SELL ...TO A BUYER WHO ONLY PLANS TO RESELL IT! IT'S ALL SO SILLY!

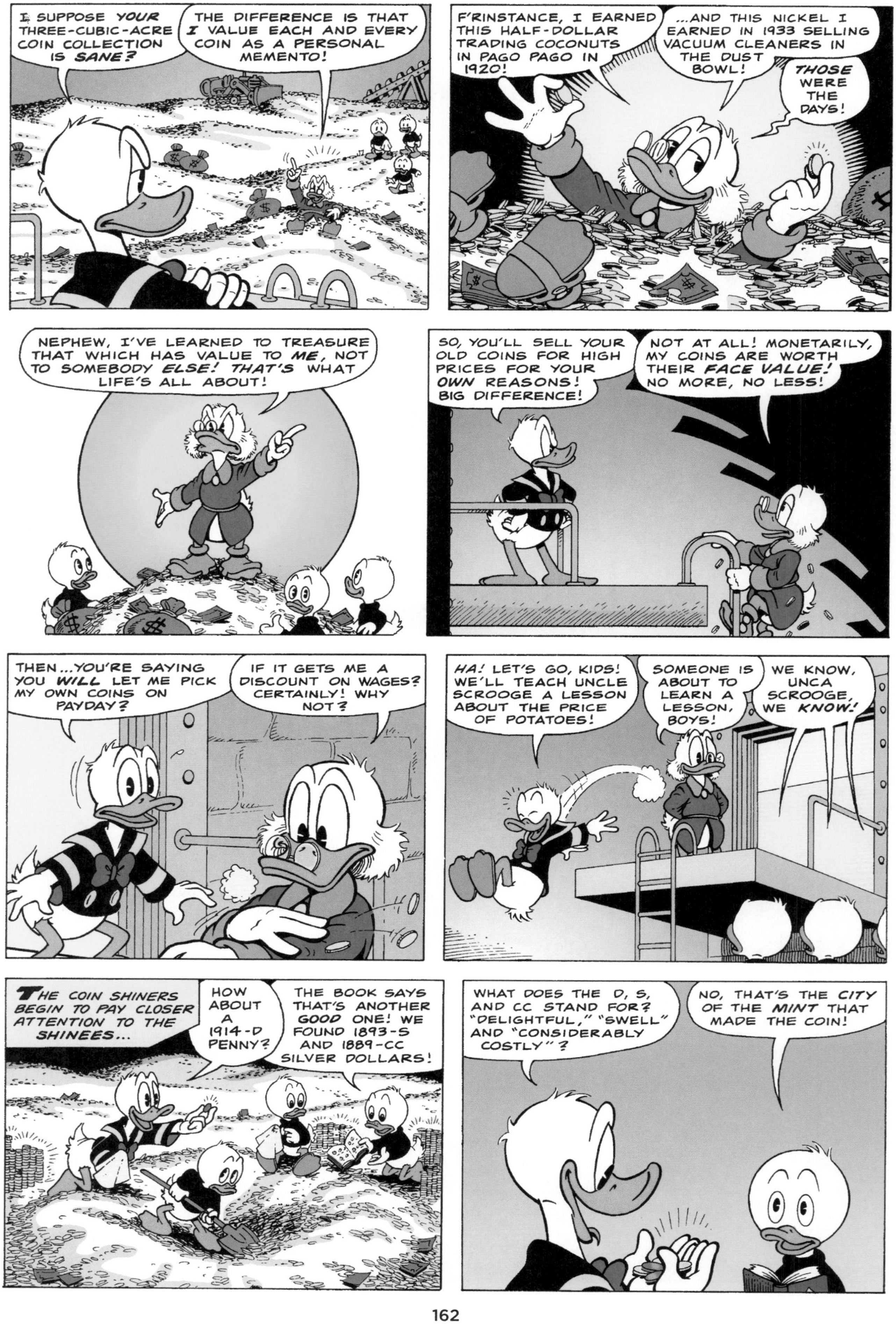
I SUPPOSE YOUR THREE-CUBIC-ACRE COIN COLLECTION IS SANE?
THE DIFFERENCE IS THAT I VALUE EACH AND EVERY COIN AS A PERSONAL MEMENTO!
F'RINSTANCE, I EARNED THIS HALF-DOLLAR TRADING COCONUTS IN PAGO PAGO IN 1920!
...AND THIS NICKEL I EARNED IN 1933 SELLING VACUUM CLEANERS IN THE DUST BOWL!
THOSE WERE THE DAYS!
NEPHEW, I'VE LEARNED TO TREASURE THAT WHICH HAS VALUE TO ME, NOT TO SOMEBODY ELSE! THAT'S WHAT LIFE'S ALL ABOUT!
SO, YOU'LL SELL YOUR OLD COINS FOR HIGH PRICES FOR YOUR OWN REASONS! BIG DIFFERENCE!
NOT AT ALL! MONETARILY, MY COINS ARE WORTH THEIR FACE VALUE! NO MORE, NO LESS!
THEN...YOU'RE SAYING YOU WILL LET ME PICK MY OWN COINS ON PAYDAY?
IF IT GETS ME A DISCOUNT ON WAGES? CERTAINLY! WHY NOT?
HA! LET'S GO, KIDS! WE'LL TEACH UNCLE SCROOGE A LESSON ABOUT THE PRICE OF POTATOES!
SOMEONE IS ABOUT TO LEARN A LESSON, BOYS!
WE KNOW, UNCA SCROOGE, WE KNOW!
THE COIN SHINERS BEGIN TO PAY CLOSER ATTENTION TO THE SHINEES...
HOW ABOUT A 1914-D PENNY?
THE BOOK SAYS THAT'S ANOTHER GOOD ONE! WE FOUND 1893-S AND 1889-CC SILVER DOLLARS!
WHAT DOES THE D, S, AND CC STAND FOR? "DELIGHTFUL," "SWELL" AND "CONSIDERABLY COSTLY"?
NO, THAT'S THE CITY OF THE MINT THAT MADE THE COIN!

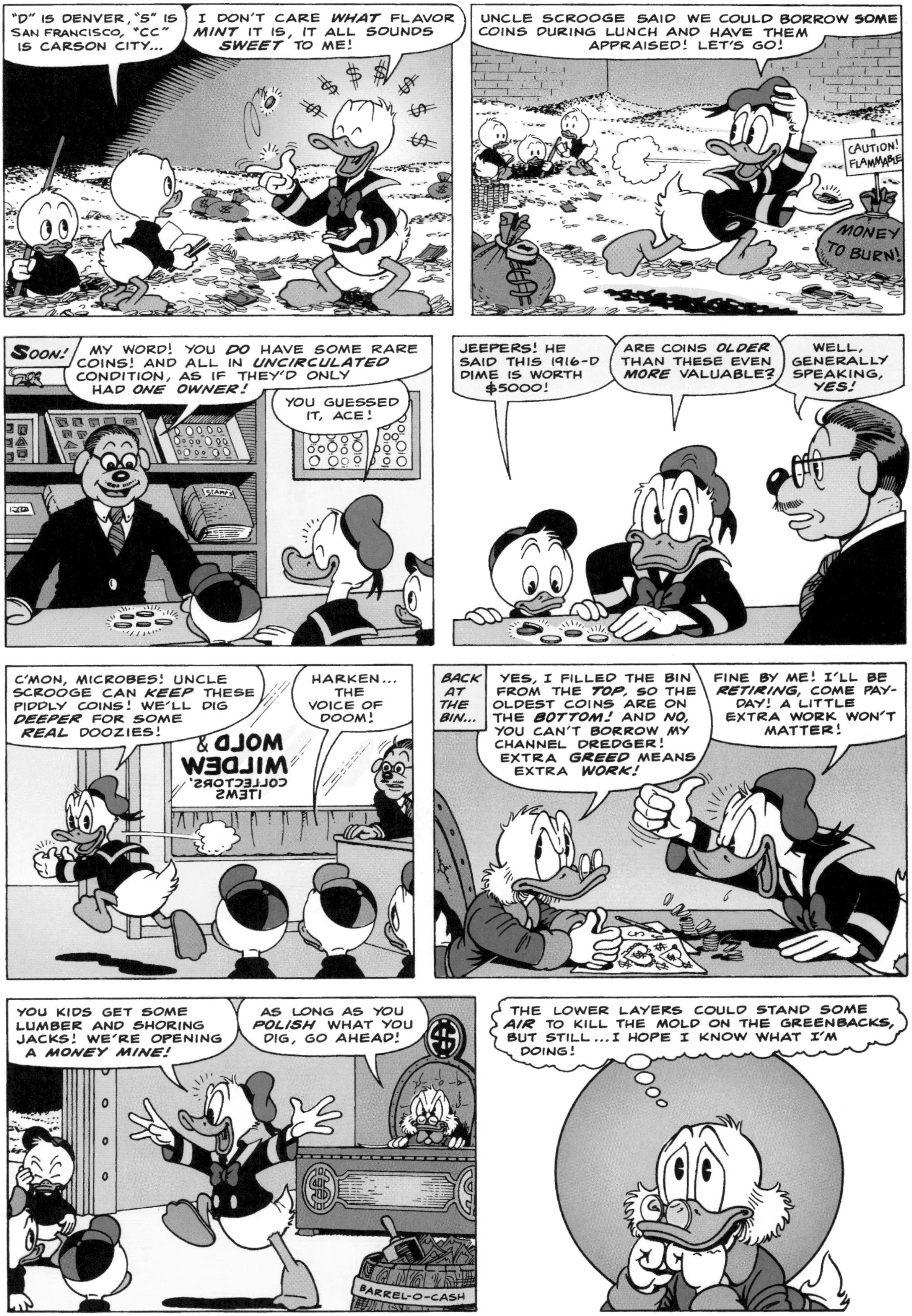
"D" IS DENVER, "S" IS SAN FRANCISCO, "CC" IS CARSON CITY...
I DON'T CARE WHAT FLAVOR MINT IT IS, IT ALL SOUNDS SWEET TO ME!
UNCLE SCROOGE SAID WE COULD BORROW SOME COINS DURING LUNCH AND HAVE THEM APPRAISED! LET'S GO!
CAUTION! FLAMMABLE
MONEY TO BURN!
SOON!
MY WORD! YOU DO HAVE SOME RARE COINS! AND ALL IN UNCIRCULATED CONDITION, AS IF THEY'D ONLY HAD ONE OWNER!
YOU GUESSED IT, ACE!
STAMPS
JEEPERS! HE SAID THIS 1916-D DIME IS WORTH $5000!
ARE COINS OLDER THAN THESE EVEN MORE VALUABLE?
WELL, GENERALLY SPEAKING, YES!
C'MON, MICROBES! UNCLE SCROOGE CAN KEEP THESE PIDDLY COINS! WE'LL DIG DEEPER FOR SOME REAL DOOZIES!
HARKEN... THE VOICE OF DOOM!
MOLD & MILDEW COLLECTORS' ITEMS
BACK AT THE BIN...
YES, I FILLED THE BIN FROM THE TOP, SO THE OLDEST COINS ARE ON THE BOTTOM! AND NO, YOU CAN'T BORROW MY CHANNEL DREDGER! EXTRA GREED MEANS EXTRA WORK!
FINE BY ME! I'LL BE RETIRING, COME PAY-DAY! A LITTLE EXTRA WORK WON'T MATTER!
YOU KIDS GET SOME LUMBER AND SHORING JACKS! WE'RE OPENING A MONEY MINE!
AS LONG AS YOU POLISH WHAT YOU DIG, GO AHEAD!
BARREL-O-CASH
THE LOWER LAYERS COULD STAND SOME AIR TO KILL THE MOLD ON THE GREENBACKS, BUT STILL... I HOPE I KNOW WHAT I'M DOING!

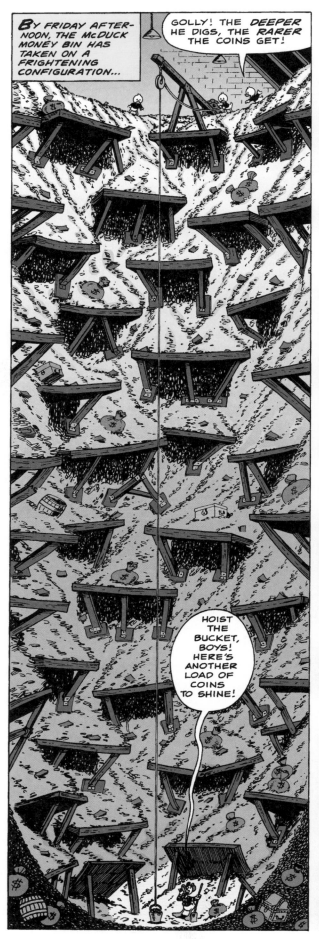

BY FRIDAY AFTERNOON, THE McDUCK MONEY BIN HAS TAKEN ON A FRIGHTENING CONFIGURATION...

GOLLY! THE *DEEPER* HE DIGS, THE *RARER* THE COINS GET!

HOIST THE BUCKET, BOYS! HERE'S ANOTHER LOAD OF COINS TO SHINE!

THIS 1894-S DIME LISTS AT A *HUNDRED THOUSAND DOLLARS!*

YOW! THIS 1913 V-NICKEL IS WORTH A QUARTER OF A MILLION BUCKS! ONLY *FIVE* ARE KNOWN TO EXIST!

YEAH? WELL, I FOUND A WHOLE *FLOUR SACK* FULL OF 'EM! KEEP THAT *ONE* AND I'LL *REBURY* THE REST!

I'M SENDING UP MORE *GREENBACKS* WITH THE VACUUM HOSE! STAND BY!

HEY! WHAT'S THAT?

SU-U-UCK!

GOLD!!! I'VE STRUCK A VEIN OF *GOLD* PIECES! OH, BE STILL, MY HEART!

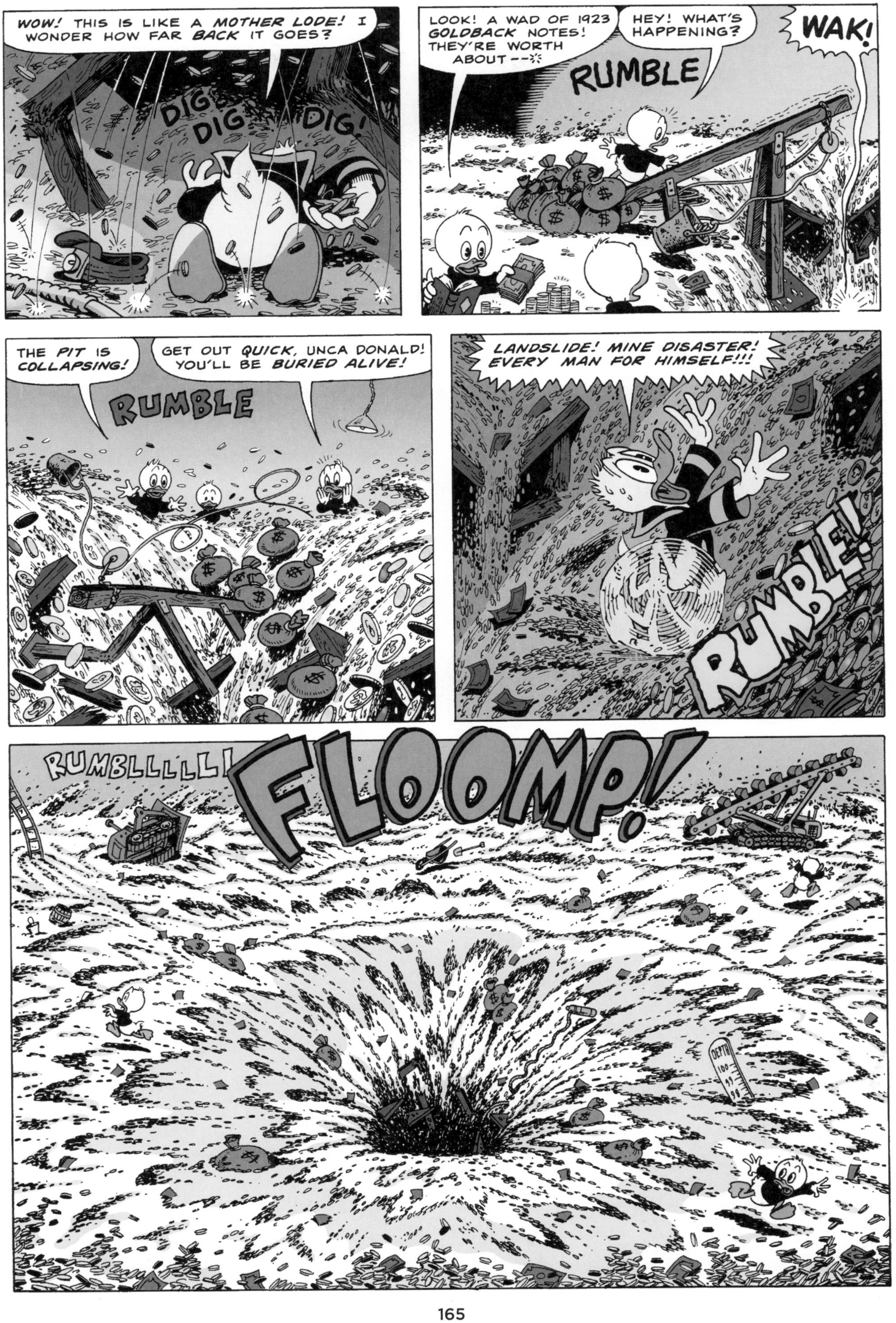

WOW! THIS IS LIKE A MOTHER LODE! I WONDER HOW FAR BACK IT GOES?
DIG DIG DIG!
LOOK! A WAD OF 1923 GOLDBACK NOTES! THEY'RE WORTH ABOUT --
HEY! WHAT'S HAPPENING?
RUMBLE
WAK!
THE PIT IS COLLAPSING!
GET OUT QUICK, UNCA DONALD! YOU'LL BE BURIED ALIVE!
RUMBLE
LANDSLIDE! MINE DISASTER! EVERY MAN FOR HIMSELF!!!
RUMBLE!
RUMBLLLLLL
FLOOMP!

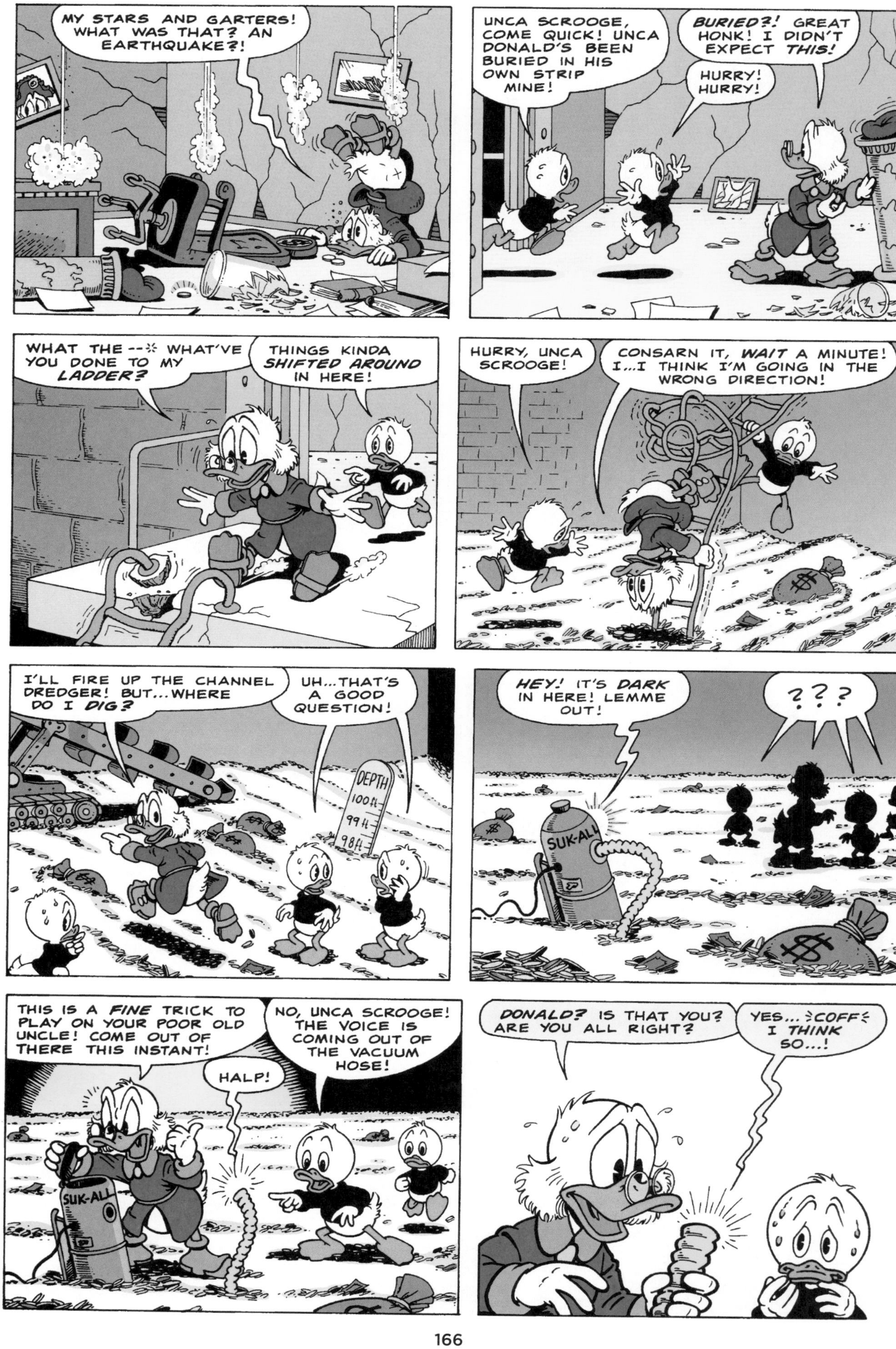
MY STARS AND GARTERS! WHAT WAS THAT? AN EARTHQUAKE?!
UNCA SCROOGE, COME QUICK! UNCA DONALD'S BEEN BURIED IN HIS OWN STRIP MINE!
HURRY! HURRY!
BURIED?! GREAT HONK! I DIDN'T EXPECT THIS!
WHAT THE --※ WHAT'VE YOU DONE TO MY LADDER?
THINGS KINDA SHIFTED AROUND IN HERE!
HURRY, UNCA SCROOGE!
CONSARN IT, WAIT A MINUTE! I...I THINK I'M GOING IN THE WRONG DIRECTION!
I'LL FIRE UP THE CHANNEL DREDGER! BUT...WHERE DO I DIG?
UH...THAT'S A GOOD QUESTION!
DEPTH
100 ft
99 ft
98 ft
HEY! IT'S DARK IN HERE! LEMME OUT!
SUK-ALL
???
THIS IS A FINE TRICK TO PLAY ON YOUR POOR OLD UNCLE! COME OUT OF THERE THIS INSTANT!
NO, UNCA SCROOGE! THE VOICE IS COMING OUT OF THE VACUUM HOSE!
HALP!
SUK-ALL
DONALD? IS THAT YOU? ARE YOU ALL RIGHT?
YES... COFF I THINK SO...!

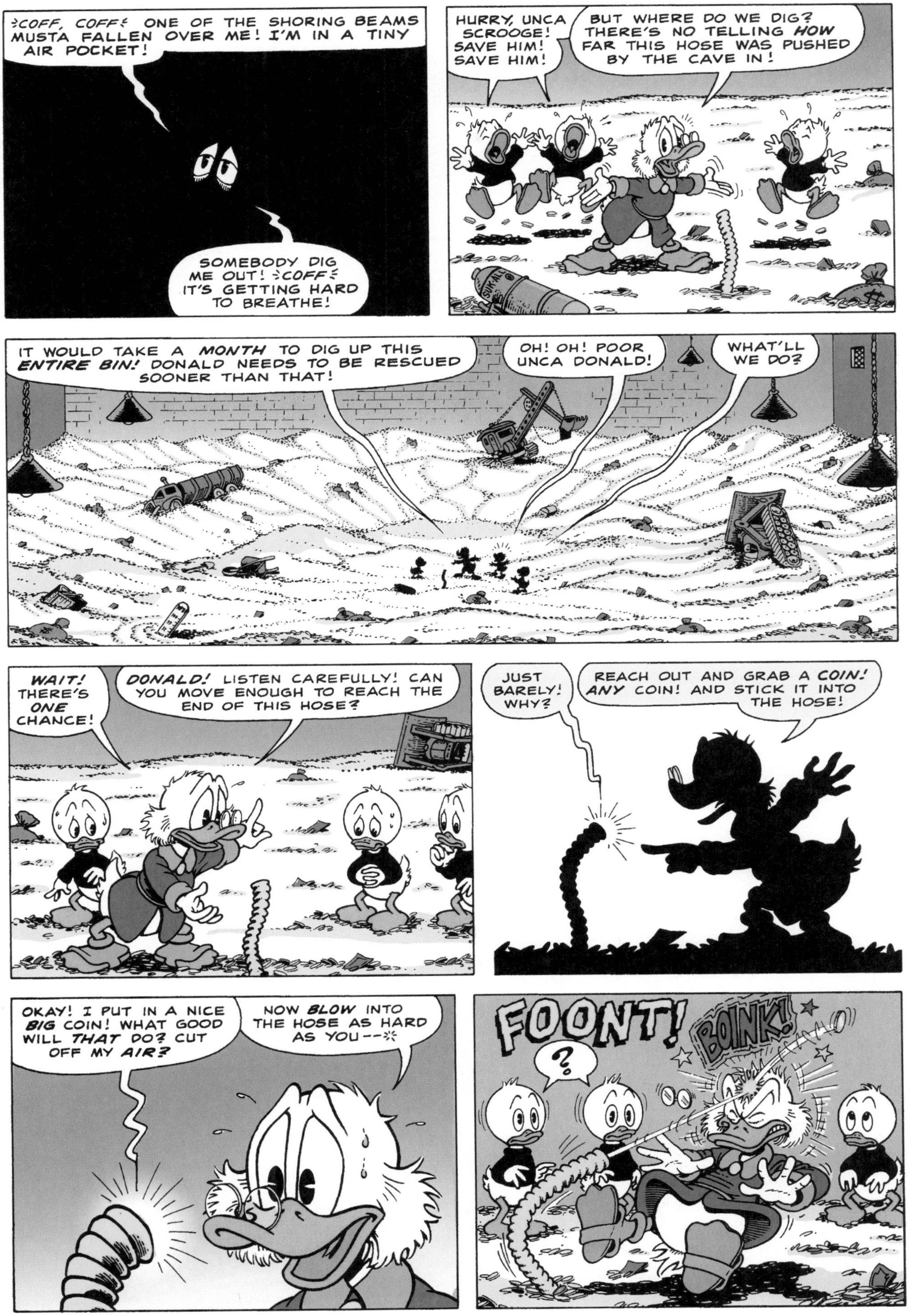
COFF, COFF! ONE OF THE SHORING BEAMS MUSTA FALLEN OVER ME! I'M IN A TINY AIR POCKET!
SOMEBODY DIG ME OUT! COFF! IT'S GETTING HARD TO BREATHE!
HURRY, UNCA SCROOGE! SAVE HIM! SAVE HIM!
BUT WHERE DO WE DIG? THERE'S NO TELLING HOW FAR THIS HOSE WAS PUSHED BY THE CAVE IN!
IT WOULD TAKE A MONTH TO DIG UP THIS ENTIRE BIN! DONALD NEEDS TO BE RESCUED SOONER THAN THAT!
OH! OH! POOR UNCA DONALD!
WHAT'LL WE DO?
WAIT! THERE'S ONE CHANCE!
DONALD! LISTEN CAREFULLY! CAN YOU MOVE ENOUGH TO REACH THE END OF THIS HOSE?
JUST BARELY! WHY?
REACH OUT AND GRAB A COIN! ANY COIN! AND STICK IT INTO THE HOSE!
OKAY! I PUT IN A NICE BIG COIN! WHAT GOOD WILL THAT DO? CUT OFF MY AIR?
NOW BLOW INTO THE HOSE AS HARD AS YOU--
FOONT!
BOINK!
?

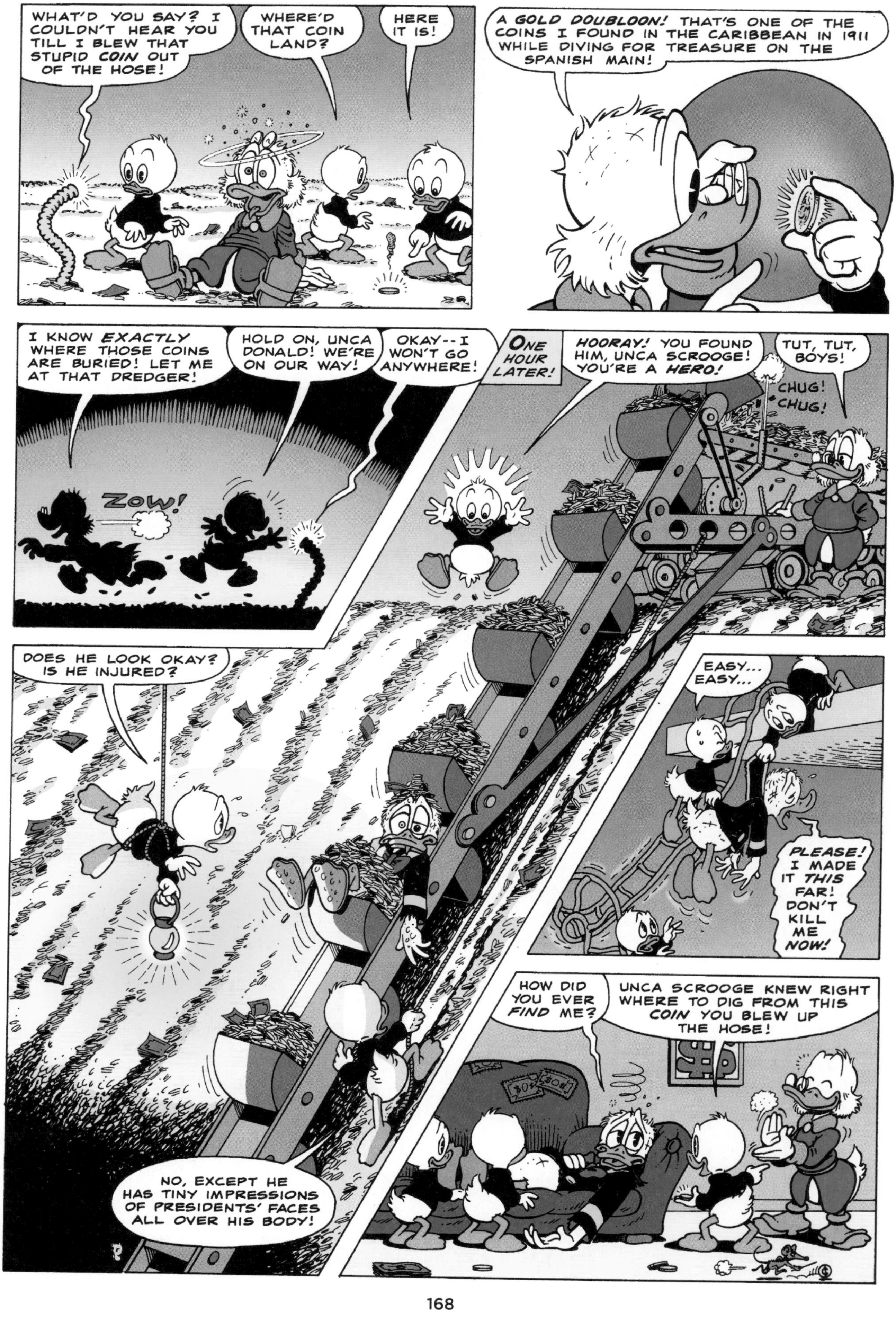
WHAT'D YOU SAY? I COULDN'T HEAR YOU TILL I BLEW THAT STUPID COIN OUT OF THE HOSE!
WHERE'D THAT COIN LAND?
HERE IT IS!
A GOLD DOUBLOON! THAT'S ONE OF THE COINS I FOUND IN THE CARIBBEAN IN 1911 WHILE DIVING FOR TREASURE ON THE SPANISH MAIN!
I KNOW EXACTLY WHERE THOSE COINS ARE BURIED! LET ME AT THAT DREDGER!
HOLD ON, UNCA DONALD! WE'RE ON OUR WAY!
OKAY-- I WON'T GO ANYWHERE!
ZOW!
ONE HOUR LATER!
HOORAY! YOU FOUND HIM, UNCA SCROOGE! YOU'RE A HERO!
TUT, TUT, BOYS!
CHUG! CHUG!
DOES HE LOOK OKAY? IS HE INJURED?
NO, EXCEPT HE HAS TINY IMPRESSIONS OF PRESIDENTS' FACES ALL OVER HIS BODY!
EASY... EASY...
PLEASE! I MADE IT THIS FAR! DON'T KILL ME NOW!
HOW DID YOU EVER FIND ME?
UNCA SCROOGE KNEW RIGHT WHERE TO DIG FROM THIS COIN YOU BLEW UP THE HOSE!

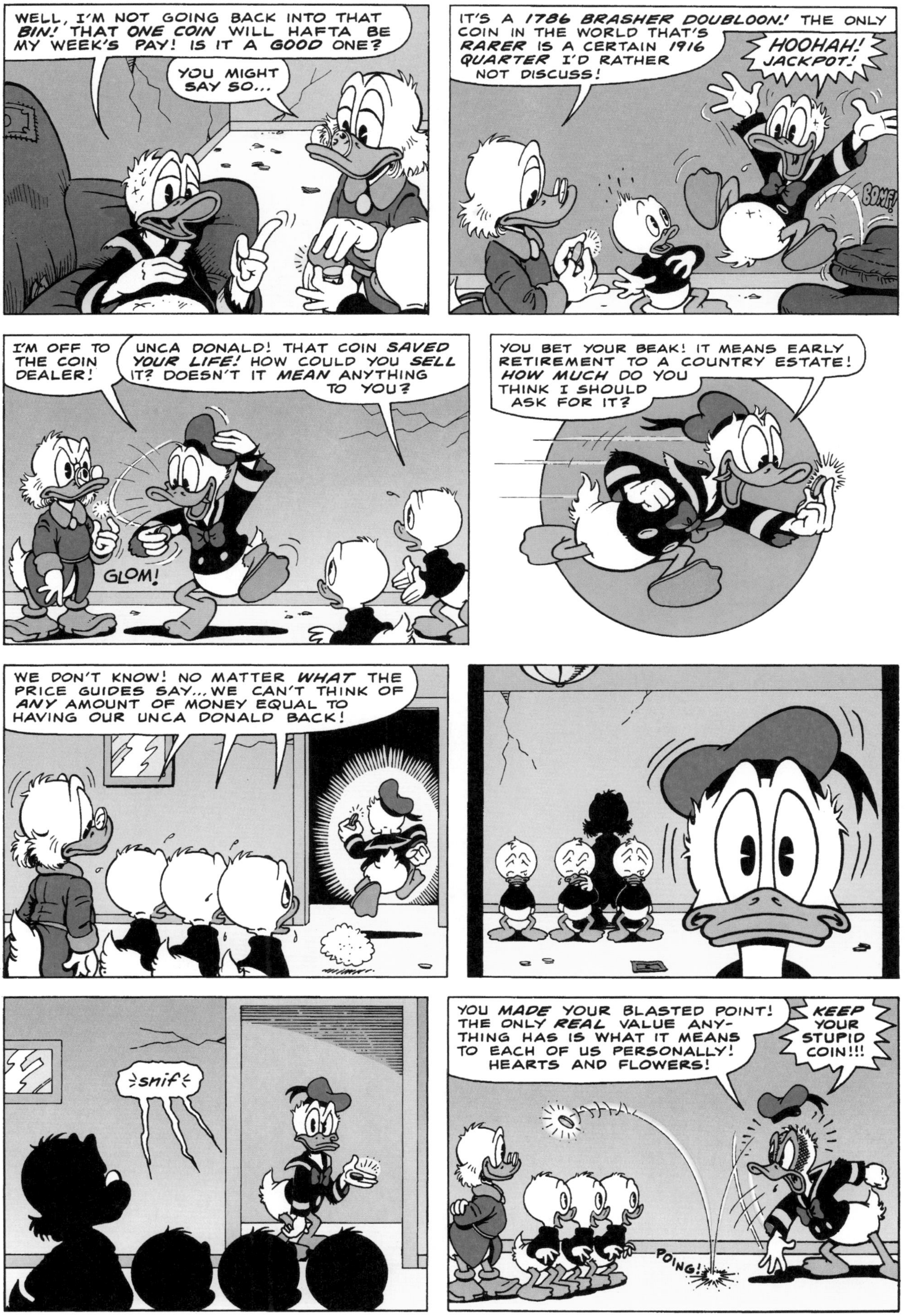
WELL, I'M NOT GOING BACK INTO THAT BIN! THAT ONE COIN WILL HAFTA BE MY WEEK'S PAY! IS IT A GOOD ONE?
YOU MIGHT SAY SO...
IT'S A 1786 BRASHER DOUBLOON! THE ONLY COIN IN THE WORLD THAT'S RARER IS A CERTAIN 1916 QUARTER I'D RATHER NOT DISCUSS!
HOOHAH! JACKPOT!
BOMF!
I'M OFF TO THE COIN DEALER!
UNCA DONALD! THAT COIN SAVED YOUR LIFE! HOW COULD YOU SELL IT? DOESN'T IT MEAN ANYTHING TO YOU?
GLOM!
YOU BET YOUR BEAK! IT MEANS EARLY RETIREMENT TO A COUNTRY ESTATE! HOW MUCH DO YOU THINK I SHOULD ASK FOR IT?
WE DON'T KNOW! NO MATTER WHAT THE PRICE GUIDES SAY... WE CAN'T THINK OF ANY AMOUNT OF MONEY EQUAL TO HAVING OUR UNCA DONALD BACK!
snif
YOU MADE YOUR BLASTED POINT! THE ONLY REAL VALUE ANYTHING HAS IS WHAT IT MEANS TO EACH OF US PERSONALLY! HEARTS AND FLOWERS!
KEEP YOUR STUPID COIN!!!
POING!

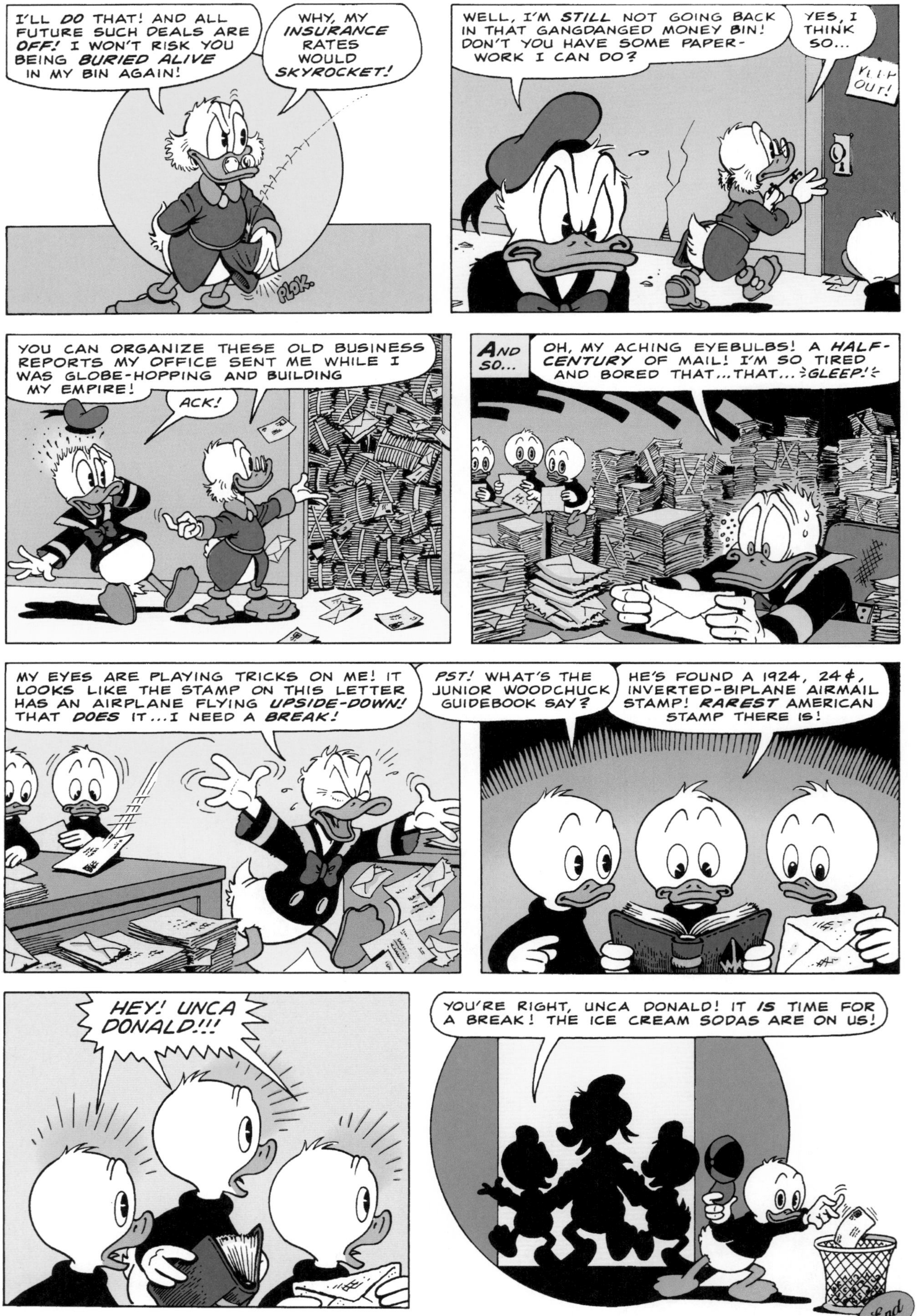
I'LL DO THAT! AND ALL FUTURE SUCH DEALS ARE OFF! I WON'T RISK YOU BEING BURIED ALIVE IN MY BIN AGAIN!
WHY, MY INSURANCE RATES WOULD SKYROCKET!
PLOK.
WELL, I'M STILL NOT GOING BACK IN THAT GANGDANGED MONEY BIN! DON'T YOU HAVE SOME PAPER-WORK I CAN DO?
YES, I THINK SO...
KEEP OUT!
YOU CAN ORGANIZE THESE OLD BUSINESS REPORTS MY OFFICE SENT ME WHILE I WAS GLOBE-HOPPING AND BUILDING MY EMPIRE!
ACK!
AND SO...
OH, MY ACHING EYEBULBS! A HALF-CENTURY OF MAIL! I'M SO TIRED AND BORED THAT...THAT... GLEEP!
MY EYES ARE PLAYING TRICKS ON ME! IT LOOKS LIKE THE STAMP ON THIS LETTER HAS AN AIRPLANE FLYING UPSIDE-DOWN! THAT DOES IT...I NEED A BREAK!
PST! WHAT'S THE JUNIOR WOODCHUCK GUIDEBOOK SAY?
HE'S FOUND A 1924, 24¢, INVERTED-BIPLANE AIRMAIL STAMP! RAREST AMERICAN STAMP THERE IS!
HEY! UNCA DONALD!!!
YOU'RE RIGHT, UNCA DONALD! IT IS TIME FOR A BREAK! THE ICE CREAM SODAS ARE ON US!
End

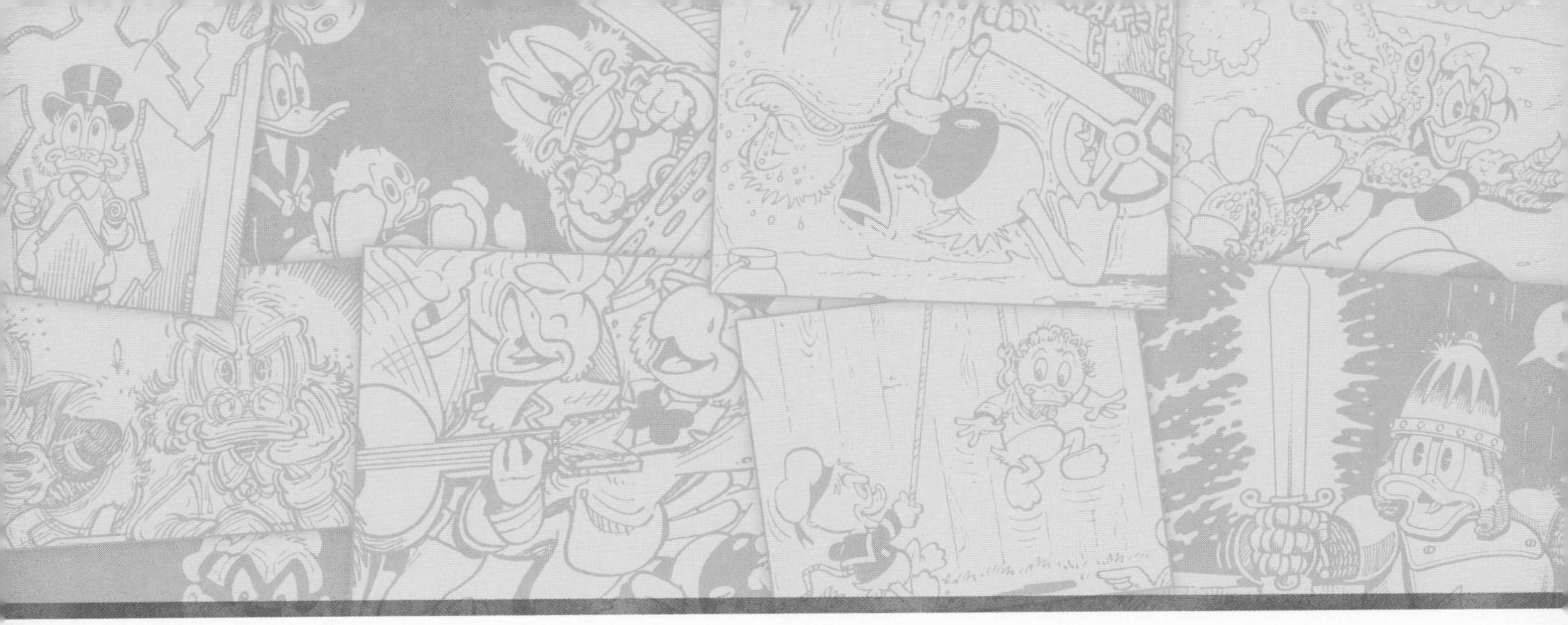

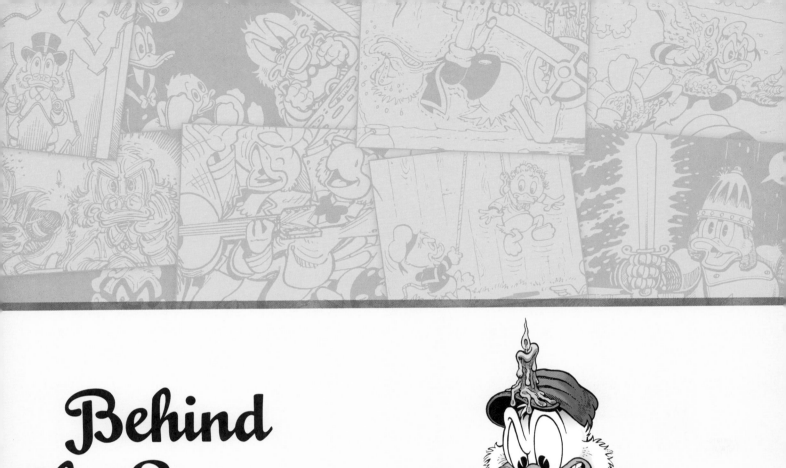

Behind the Scenes

BY

Don Rosa

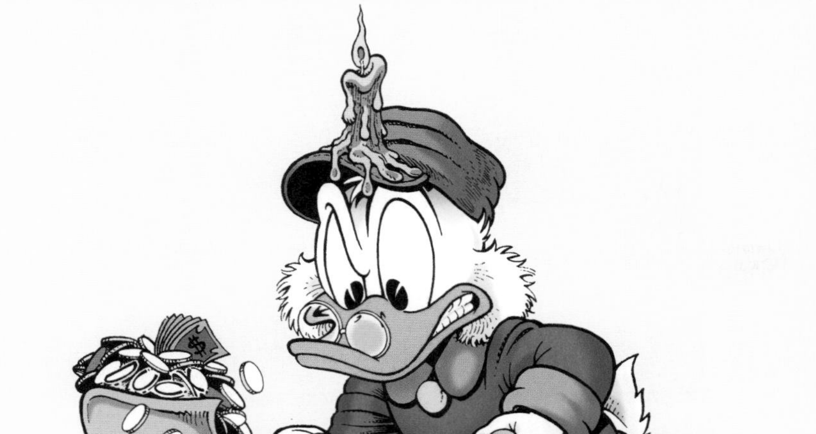

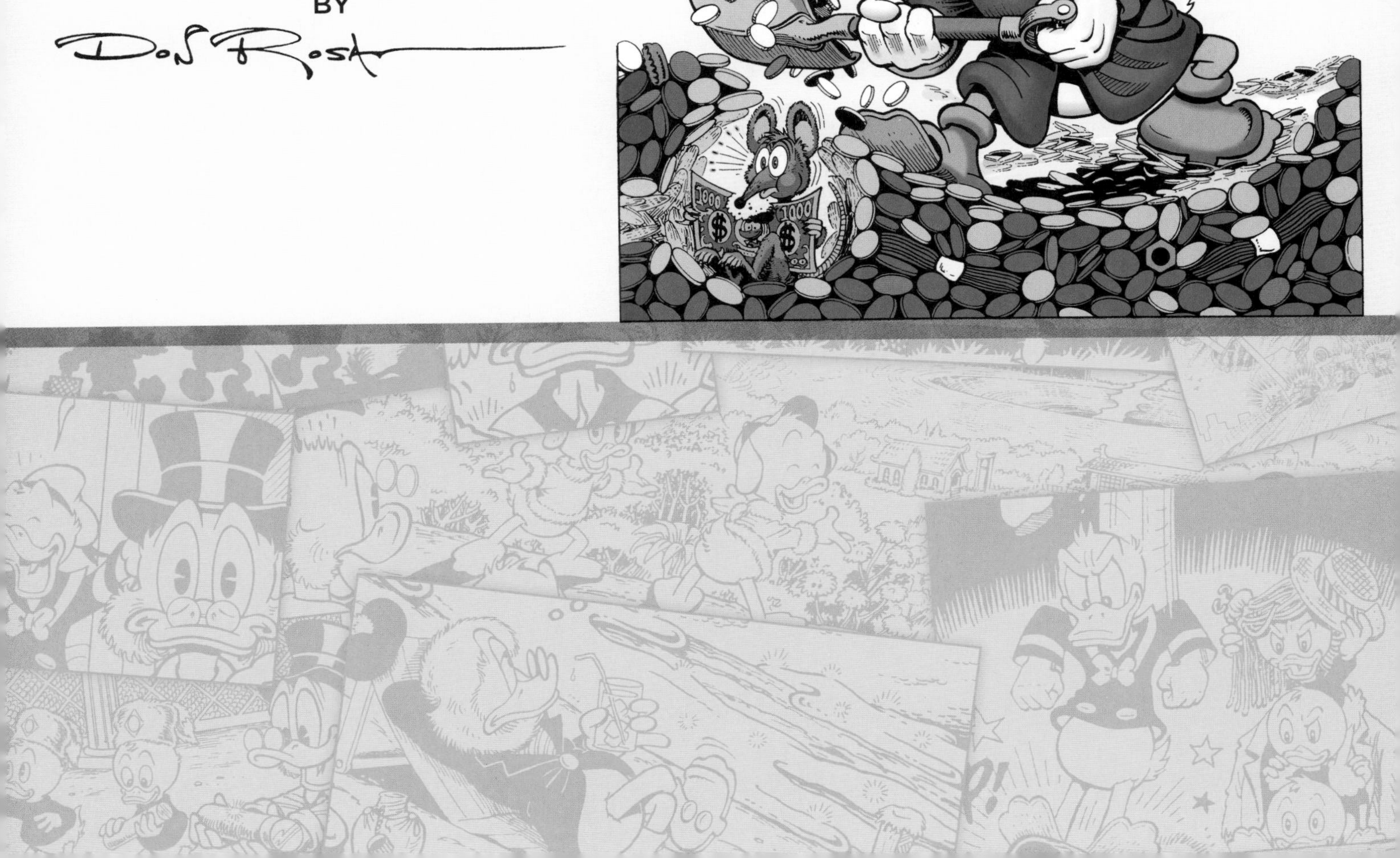

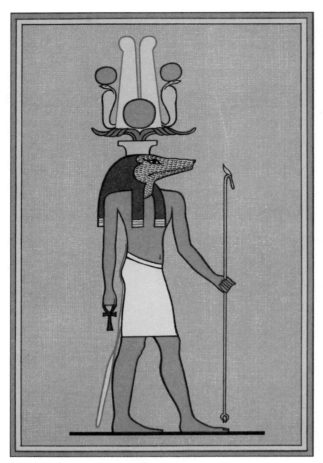

The crocodile deity Sebek as illustrated in *The Gods of the Egyptians* (1904), a research work by pioneering Egyptologist E. A. Wallace Budge.

THE CROCODILE COLLECTOR *p. 9*

I have fond memories of this story! It was the first Duck adventure I wrote/drew that was based on extensive, historically accurate facts and research, and I still recall how much fun it was to hunt down obscure facts in obscure books in university libraries and manage to create a story using that research.

First off, I must tell the story behind the story. While working for Gladstone Publishing in 1988, I was asked by the editor to do a story based on a Barks cover from *Four Color* 348, Donald Duck in "The Crocodile Collector," so that they could reprint the cover for the fans to admire. Barks had only contributed the cover to that old issue, not the interior story it referred to.

If I did a story to match his cover, it seemed to me there would then simply be *two* non-Barks stories to match the Barks cover. But I said I'd give it a try.

The first thing I noticed was that the cover obviously depicted Donald hunting for a crocodile to kill and skin to make a crocodile-hide purse. Horrors! As an animal lover I could never tell such a tale! What had I gotten myself into?! What could I do? But look at the cover—why is Donald

using a magnifying glass and holding a purse up? It's as if he were trying to find a detail on the croc to match something he sees on the purse! Yeah! And though I naturally could not (and *would* not!) suggest the publisher make a change to the Barks cover art, it would be okay if they added something to the art with color only... a color marking on the purse which Donald seeks to find on the live croc's back? Yes! (And you can see the original Barks cover, with its color modified that same way, on page 8 of this volume.)

So now what? The usual—I start doing research. The most interesting thing I soon learned about crocodiles is that they were regarded as gods in ancient Egypt. There was actually a Temple of Sebek, the crocodile god of the Nile, and therein lay the mummified remains of many a royal crocodile, all adorned with golden rings. The location of this temple has never been discovered—perfect! I recall that I had to spend a day in the University of Louisville Historical Library to do research into the matter, and I even located a hieroglyph dictionary which showed me the "Mark of Sebek" to use as the emblem that could be added to Barks' cover art in color form. So—that is not something I made up, that mark on the croc's back! That's the actual ancient Mark of Sebek, and if an ancient Egyptian bought a copy of this book, he'd open to this page and immediately say "Yo! Sebek! Dude!"... or something similar.

Aside from all of the absolutely authentic history and geography in this adventure, it is just plain filthy with in-jokes! Let me point some of them out for my amusement if not yours, in the section I like to call...

INSANE DETAILS TO LOOK FOR: My Duck stories take place in the 1950s, as many of you folks know. On page 1, I have Donald berating his nephews for paying half-cover-price for some used comic books. Here I'm laughing at myself, as a collector of old used comic books from the 1940s-60s—since I would sure like to get them for only half-cover-price, rather than the 500 or 1000 times cover price that I must pay to fill in the holes in my collection! But I always knew that Donald's nephews are smarter than I am!

On page 2 we see Scrooge's private zoo: an unusual luxury for the old skinflint, perhaps revealing a love for animals he won't admit to, but something that Barks once wrote of in his "Trail of the Unicorn" story. In fact, there's the unicorn that Donald captured for him in that adventure.

When Donald rents a riverboat to navigate the backwaters of Lake Victoria on page 11, some scenes parody *The African Queen* (1951), a classic movie in which Humphrey Bogart and Katherine Hepburn traverse those same waters.

And when the gang reaches the lost temple, on a column near the altar you'll see a caricature of Mr. Barks in the same form he once drew, himself, onto a "Wanted" poster in the background of one of his own stories.

D.U.C.K. SPOTTER'S GUIDE: "D.U.C.K." ("Dedicated to Unca Carl from Keno," Keno being my actual first name) is the special dedication to Carl Barks that I hide somewhere on the first page of most of my stories.

In "The Crocodile Collector," you'll find "D.U.C.K." hidden in a flower in the foreground of the first panel.

MOUSE SPOTTER'S GUIDE: I stick Mickey into the background of many stories, just for fun, to give readers one more detail to hunt for. There are three different "hidden Mickeys" in this tale. In the last panel on page 5, look at the shape formed by the broken pot on Donald's head. In the first panel of page 9, check the walls of the skinner's hut for a Mickeylike animal pelt. And on page 14, panel 2, you'll find Mickey in an obelisk engraving.

HIS FORTUNE ON THE ROCKS *p. 27*

Of all the stories I've ever done, this story was surely the most difficult—to *translate*! No, I didn't translate it to or from another language. But unbeknownst to me, *others* would soon be translating it, and oh! The problems I gave them!!!

During this period from 1986-1988, when I was still making comics for Gladstone Publishing in the United States, I had no idea that foreign Disney publishers would ever reprint the stories I was creating. I thought I was working strictly for the American market. As a result, often the stories would involve plays-on-words and puns which would only make sense in English—and "His Fortune On the Rocks" was created specifically to make puns based on geological terms I had learned in engineering college!

In pursuing a Civil Engineering degree, I took courses in geology and hydraulics, since civil engineers often build dams and bridges and other structures involving earth and water. Sitting in geology class, I would make jokes in my head about some of the terms I was studying, and I wanted to make good use of those little gags in a Duck story. So this entire story was built around a series of geological puns!

From "That's *your* fault!" to "Unca Scrooge will give you the *chert* off his *pack*," I leapt from one word-joke to the next, never imagining the headaches they would cause overseas. Later, I would avoid too much complicated wordplay for that reason. But that's just a peek into what we Duck story creators must get used to over time.

INSANE DETAILS TO LOOK FOR: Donald references the "Little Booneheads," his old boy scout troop from Carl Barks' "Ten-Star Generals" (*Walt Disney's Comics* 132, 1951).

D.U.C.K. SPOTTER'S GUIDE: In the first panel, look closely at the pointy-leafed plant to the left of Scrooge's jeep.

Uncle Scrooge's ornery unicorn recovers his strength—and his temper!—in Carl Barks' "Trail of the Unicorn" (*Four Color* 263, 1950).

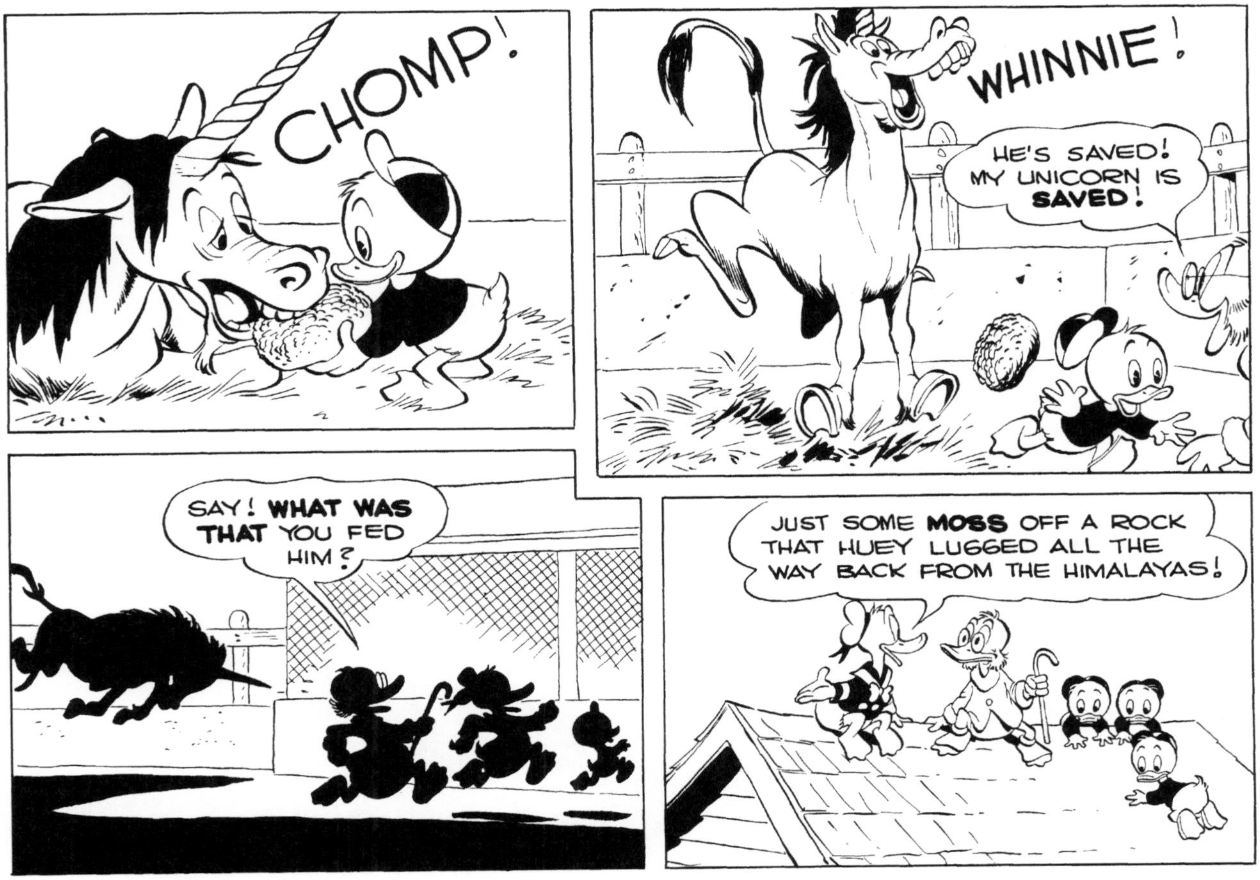
CHOMP!
WHINNIE!
HE'S SAVED! MY UNICORN IS SAVED!
SAY! WHAT WAS THAT YOU FED HIM?
JUST SOME MOSS OFF A ROCK THAT HUEY LUGGED ALL THE WAY BACK FROM THE HIMALAYAS!

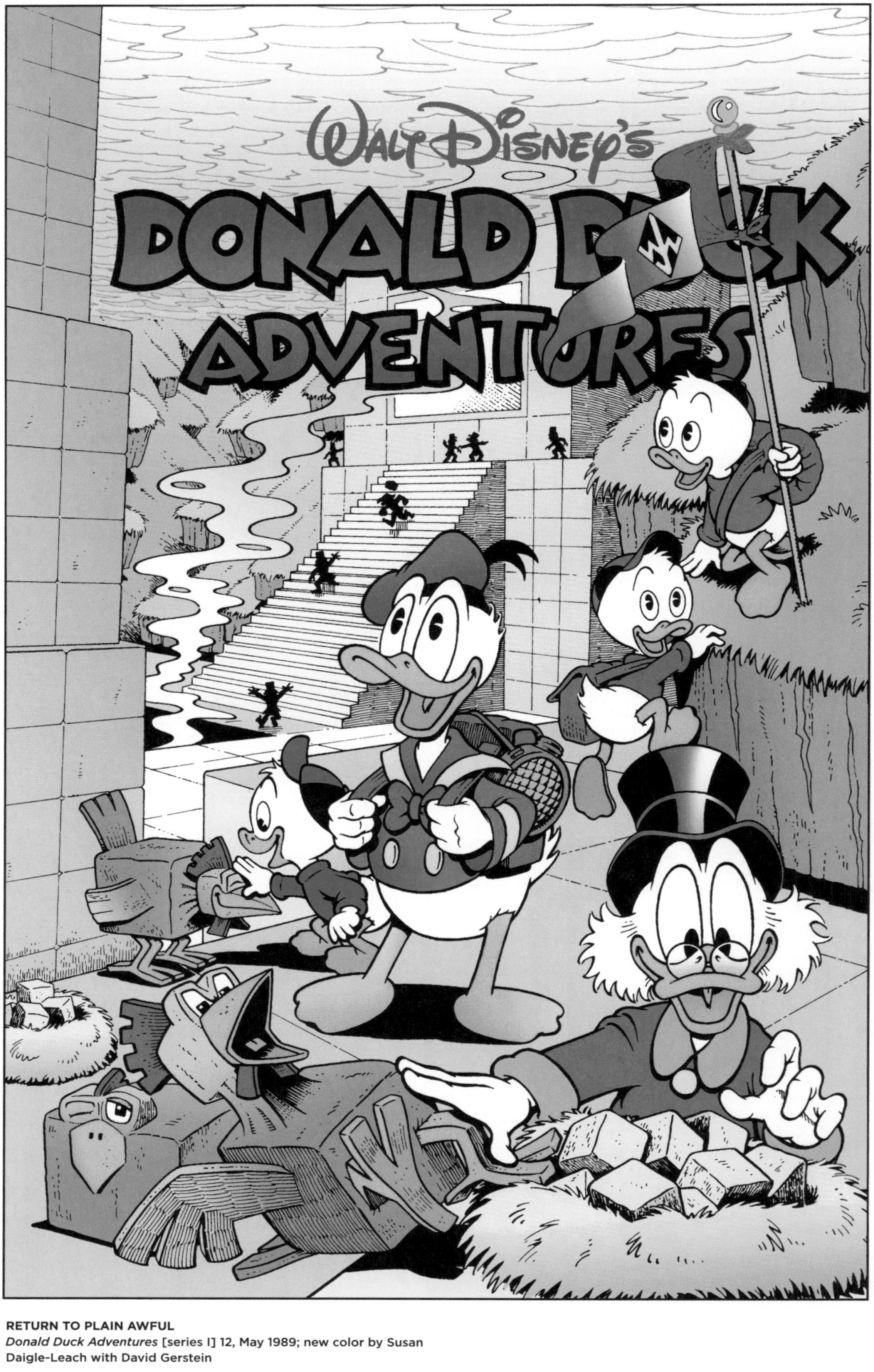
Walt Disney's
Donald Duck Adventures

RETURN TO PLAIN AWFUL
Donald Duck Adventures [series I] 12, May 1989; new color by Susan Daigle-Leach with David Gerstein

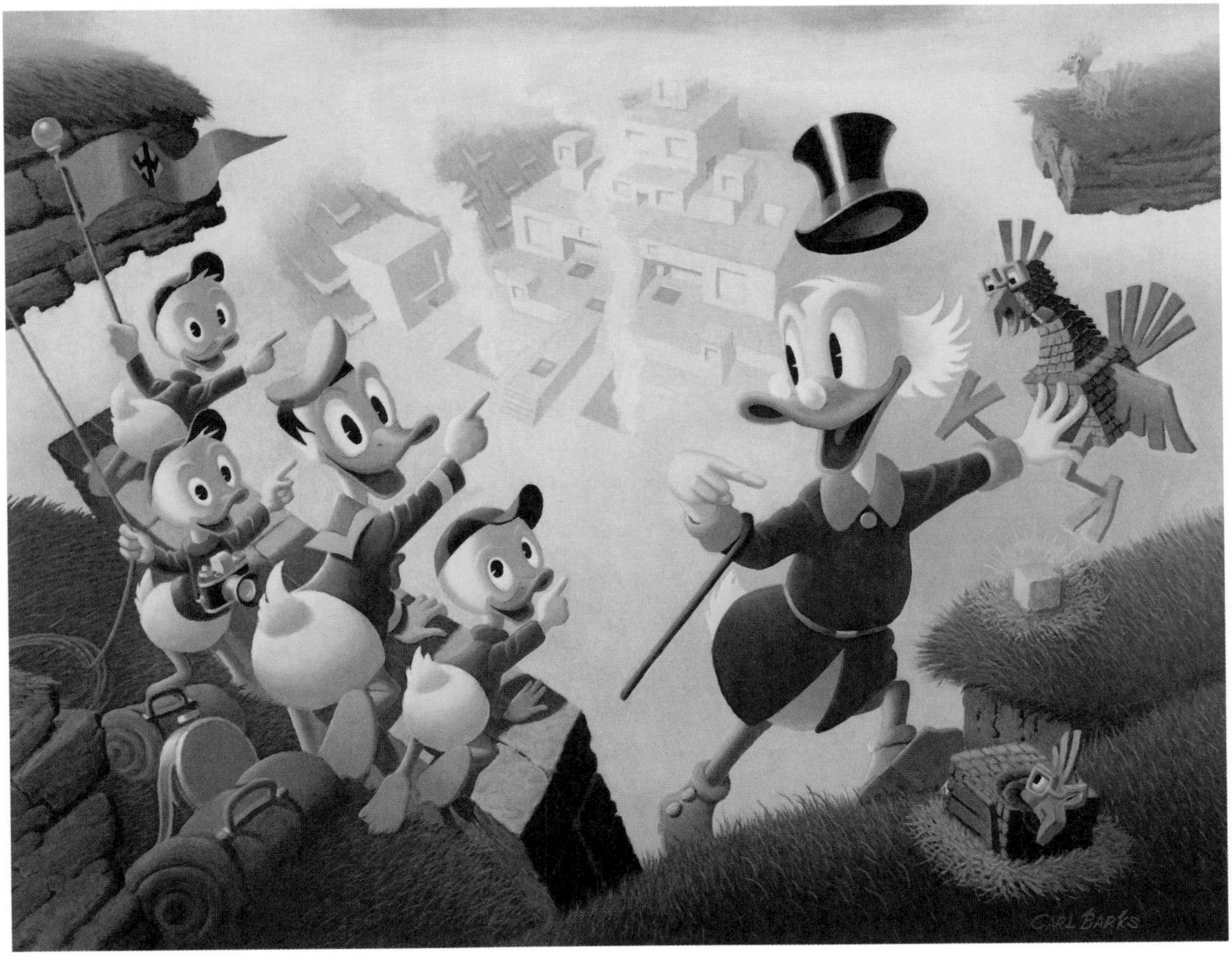
CARL BARKS

Carl Barks' painting "Return to Plain Awful" (1988)—the image that started it all.

RETURN TO PLAIN AWFUL *p. 39*

This was the first full-fledged sequel to a Carl Barks story that I was ever asked to do. Before this, I had done stories that *referenced* events or characters from the Barks stories I'd grown up with; but such references were done only for my own amusement. I used the "cabbage professor" from Barks' "Mysterious Stone Ray" in my "Cash Flow," since my plot involved a ray gun and that wacky scientist had invented a petrifying ray in the old Barks story. I'd used my favorite one-appearance Barks character Glittering Goldie in "Last Sled to Dawson"—which was *slightly* closer to being a sequel, since my story also took place in the same Canadian province as Barks' Goldie story, "Back to the Klondike."

But I'd never had a reason to consider doing a *direct* sequel to an old Barks classic.

However, in 1988 Bruce Hamilton, CEO of Gladstone Publishing, called me and said he needed a sequel to Barks' top classic story "Lost in the Andes"—the legendary tale of Plain Awful, the land of square eggs! Gladstone's sister company, Another Rainbow, produced the lithographs of the oil paintings that Barks was then creating for sale to fans and collectors. Barks called his next subject "Return to Plain Awful": essentially, a scene from "Lost in the Andes," but with Scrooge McDuck added to it. Scrooge did not appear in the original "Andes" story, but Bruce figured he could sell more lithographs if the ever-popular Scrooge was included in the scene. And he wanted me to write and draw a sequel to the Barks classic, which would become a Gladstone comic book and be included in the sale of the lithographs. It certainly sounded like fun!

Right away I could easily see the reason for a return to Plain Awful. This wasn't difficult—the Junior Woodchucks would want to return those poor displaced square roosters to their home, and Scrooge would certainly want to get his hands on those square eggs that Barks' original story claimed were so valuable. But what might have happened since Donald last visited the lost valley? If the Awfultonians were so easily influenced by a single visit from their first outer-world guest—the "Professor from Birmingham"—they would have been ripe for a new influence to shape their isolated culture. So, instead of a valley of Southern

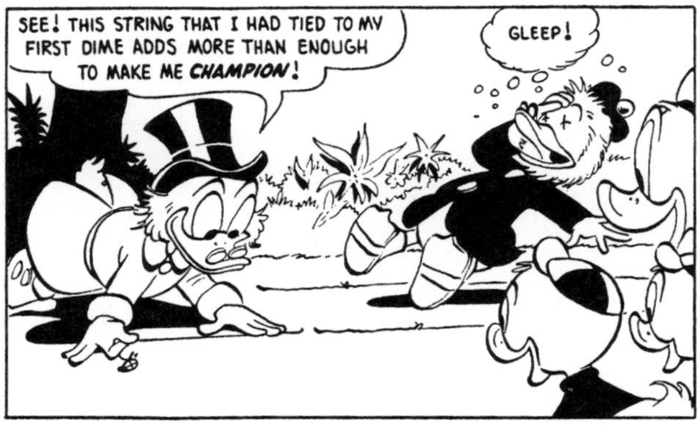
SEE! THIS STRING THAT I HAD TIED TO MY FIRST DIME ADDS MORE THAN ENOUGH TO MAKE ME *CHAMPION*!
GLEEP!

Scrooge outsaves Flintheart Glomgold by a thread! From Barks' "The Second-Richest Duck" (*Uncle Scrooge* 15, 1956).

gentlemen, the Ducks now find that Plain Awful has been reshaped to the mold of Donald... i. e. the average American suburbanite. They are later reshaped by even newer influences, and if you check the last page, you'll see a suggestion that they might be about to become a Utopia of Junior Woodchucks... not a bad fate for them.

A few years later I learned that "Return to Plain Awful" was one of the reasons Egmont, the big Danish-based Disney comics publisher, was glad to have me start doing stories for them directly. Their European readers were very familiar with all the old Barks Duck adventures, and apparently had been requesting sequels to their favorite old Barks classics for many years.

But a few years beyond that, I learned more about doing sequels. A minority of Barks fans really resented it, for some reason. I'll always find that odd. They don't mind if I do stories about Barks' Scrooge, draw him with the same top hat and cane, use all the same background aspects like the Money Bin or the Number One Dime, or use the Beagle Boys or Magica De Spell, etc., etc.—that's all okay. But if I use an element of an old story as a springboard for a new adventure, or make any reference to something Scrooge mentioned doing in his youth, some longtime fans get incensed. It's as if they feel that my sequel somehow damages the original. But no matter how lame my sequels might be, when I look again in my old comics, I still see the Barks originals exactly as they were, as wonderful as ever, in spite of my mucked-up sequel. Oh, well. I can't worry about it.

I am never fazed by a critic who might say that my writing is bad, or my artwork is amateurish and ugly (I particularly agree with that latter criticism!). But I can't help but be disappointed by the few critics who have claimed that when I am doing a sequel to a Barks story, I am taking a "shortcut" and simply "reusing" an old plot. Doing these sequels is more difficult a project than simply creating a whole new set of circumstances. Not only does it require extra attention and reference to the original tale, but I think it's also important to develop *only* the ideas and situations that already existed in the original stories—and *not* to inject whole new ideas of my own into those classic situations. This further limits my own options for the potential plots for sequels and makes creating them that much more difficult, but it's how I think it should be done.

Also due to the myriad different details I need to keep in mind in order to be accurate to an old Barks story, I still make goofs! The old vicuna hunter who makes a return appearance here, to lead the Ducks back to Plain Awful, had said—in the original "Lost in the Andes"—that he was nearly blind without his glasses. So, Barks fans have asked me, how can the old boy *see* well enough to be a mountain guide? Um... new contact lenses?

There's one other element in Barks' original that I did not exactly *change*, but—well, sorta *twisted* to my own ends. "Lost in the Andes" had the leader of Plain Awful say that it was a crime to make anything "round" in their land of squareness. But if you read that great old story (and if you haven't, drop this book and go do so immediately—I'll wait!), you see that what the nephews were condemned for doing was making something *spherical* (the bubble-gum bubbles they blew). The actual crime in Plain Awful was to make something *spherical* in the land of *cubism*! After all, the Awfultonians proudly displayed the Professor from Birmingham's *round* compass in their public museum.

But the problem is that the words "spherical" and "cubic" would not be understood by many readers, whereas the words "round" and "square" are concepts every child understands. So the word Barks originally used was "round," even though he meant "spherical." But seizing on the literal meaning of that word, it seemed like such a fun idea (and still does) to use the introduction of Scrooge's famous *round* Number One Dime as the turning point in my plot. Even without Magica De Spell around, that Dime seems to attract big trouble!!!

D.U.C.K. SPOTTER'S GUIDE: This is another early story where I simply wrote the dedication in plain sight, this time on one of the signs on Scrooge's hill in panel 1.

INSANE DETAILS TO LOOK FOR: All details of Plain Awful's looks, inhabitants, rules and regulations: "Lost in the Andes" (Donald Duck *Four Color* 224, 1949).

The Ducks' spying rivals at the bottom of page 3 are all classic Barks foes. From left to right, we see the Maharajah of Howduyustan (*Walt Disney's Comics* 138, 1951), Azure Blue ("The Golden Helmet," Donald Duck *Four Color* 408, 1952), the Brutopian Consul ("A Cold Bargain," *Uncle Scrooge* 17, 1957), Chisel McSue (Uncle Scrooge *FC* 495, 1953), and Longhorn Tallgrass, the Fabulous Cattle King (*US* 21 and 24).

Flintheart Glomgold's African money bin, and "*that* string" to which Scrooge's Dime is tied: "The Second-Richest Duck" (*Uncle Scrooge* 15, 1956). When Glomgold and Scrooge compared their fortunes, Scrooge was richer only by virtue of having saved more string—with the thread tied to the Dime making the difference!

THE CURSE OF NOSTRILDAMUS *p. 67*

DELL
NO. 1
25¢
Walt Disney's
UNCLE SCROOGE GOES TO
Disneyland
GIANT

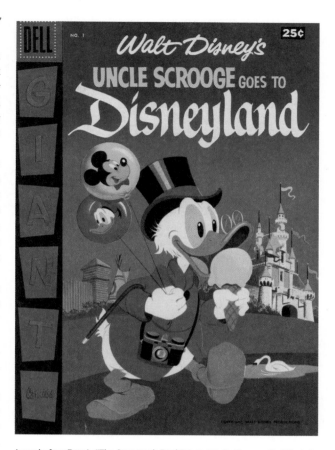

Long before Rosa's "The Starstruck Duck" (see overleaf) came Carl Barks' "Fantastic River Race," a much more typical Disney theme park tie-in story. Published in this 1957 giant-size comic, "Race" features very little of Scrooge at Disneyland—focusing instead on a flashback to Scrooge's younger days on the Mississippi.

When making comics, I always tried to alternate between long stories and short stories. I preferred long, complex adventures, but they were *really* an exhausting use of energy and time. And doing them exclusively would have spaced my paychecks out to maybe four months apart! So after completing a long adventure, I liked to then do a short story to get some more cash in the till.

But there's not much to say about the creation of these short stories. Maybe I can use this one as an example of where ideas for my stories came from. That's the most frequent question asked of any writer—"where do your ideas come from?" And there's really no answer to that. For people with active imaginations, I suppose coming up with story ideas is really very easy. They sometimes come too fast and thick (they might not be good ideas, but they keep comin').

I recall that the idea for this story hit me when I was watching a TV documentary about Michel de Nostredame (Nostradamus), the famous 16th century French astrologer who supposedly predicted many events of the past 400 years. The documentary told of the legend that Nostradamus had threatened a death curse on anyone who someday disturbed his grave. And then we were told there was another legend: that anyone who drank using Nostradamus' empty skull as a goblet would gain his gift of foretelling the future. (One might wonder how such an idea as that could ever have come about; but when you consider all the screwball urban legends that people still believe today, it seems rather mild by comparison.)

The documentary continued with the alleged incident of a grave robber who used the confusion of the French Revolution to dig up Nostradamus' skeleton; and as he stood over the grave, drinking wine from the old boy's skull, a wild musket-shot from a riot outside the cemetery hit the grave robber and killed him instantly, thereby fulfilling the curse. The thought that immediately struck me was: if the guy had just gained the power to see into the future by drinking from that skull, *why didn't he duck down?!*

And right then I, too, gained the power to foretell the future—in the sense that I could see the entire plot of the next Uncle Scrooge story I would write. Of course, I thought it prudent to have my story deal with the wearing of an amulet rather than drinking from somebody's skull.

So, that will give you an idea of just one way we writers get these ideas. Maybe they hit us while we watch a movie, as did "His Majesty McDuck" in this very volume. Maybe while we're reading a history book, which is also exemplified by part of that same story. Maybe when we stare at a nice sunset.

The one thing I've learned is that when I get an idea, I must immediately make a *note* of it. There have been times when a story idea has struck me and I've thought, "That's a brilliant plot idea! And it's so obvious! It's staring me in the face! Oh, heck, I don't need to write that down! I'll *definitely* remember *that* when I get back to writing!" And you can see where this is going, eh? When I later tried to remember that absolutely unforgettable idea... it was long gone.

As for individual gags, those sometimes also come from personal experience. A friend once told me how when he was young, he had a maiden aunt who (like maiden aunts do) was always sending him small inexpensive gifts... just odd things she would buy, perhaps at a flea market with her limited income. And my friend's mother would always have him be polite and dutifully send back a thank-you note, regardless of how trifling the well-intentioned gift was. One time the aunt sent a pack of tiny plastic monkeys, probably like those you see in the *Toy Story* movies. My friend said he felt so foolish writing to tell his aunt "thank you for the plastic monkeys." So, in "The Curse of Nostrildamus," when I needed Donald to do a bad job of translating the deadly curse written on the tomb, the most absurd phrase I could think for him to come up with *had* to be what my friend had told his aunt in his thank-you note.

D.U.C.K. SPOTTER'S GUIDE: Page 1, panel 1, on the telegraph tape.

THE STARSTRUCK DUCK *p. 77*

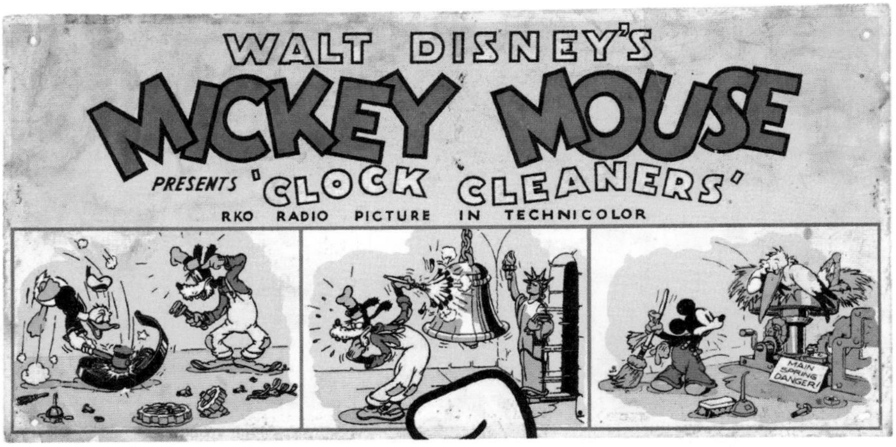
WALT DISNEY'S
MICKEY MOUSE
PRESENTS 'CLOCK CLEANERS'
RKO RADIO PICTURE IN TECHNICOLOR
MAIN SPRING DANGER!
An advertising card for the cartoon *Clock Cleaners* (1937) shows the giant bell that Donald encounters in Rosa's "The Starstruck Duck." The large thumb-shape at the base of the card marks where it was to be inserted into the hand of a Mickey display figure. Image courtesy Heritage Auctions.

Hey, why is this tale presented not as finished art, but only as a storyboard-script? Because that's the only way it exists!

Late in 1988 I was asked by Gladstone to create a very special story. The Disney-MGM Studios theme park was nearing completion, and Disney had asked Gladstone Publishing to create a Donald Duck story to promote the new park—an assignment the editors passed to me. This was especially interesting because I was then invited to have a special VIP tour of the unfinished park! I stopped by Walt Disney World for that purpose while returning from a Christmas vacation in Key West, and I was given a private tour of the entire place. I made various notes and sketches that I would use in writing a Donald Duck story set in the park.

When I was growing up in the mid-1950s, Dell's Disney comics featured similar promo stories, where Donald was shown visiting the brand-new Disneyland theme park in California; promo stories surely requested by Disney then, just as they had requested a Disney-MGM Studios promo story from Gladstone now.

The way in which those old Dell stories worked was that we would see Donald taking his nephews to Disneyland; then after about a page, he would say "y' know, this reminds me of the time that..." and the story would switch from involving Disneyland to a flashback tale of something else altogether. Well, I wanted to do something *better* than that! I would actually have my *entire* story take place in the new Disney-MGM Studios park. I would have Donald interact with every attraction in the new park, even with geographic accuracy as he moved around. I would have lots of funny references to old Disney films and history. And I would even use Mickey Mouse in the story!

Now, a few of you may know that in *my* personal view of the Donald Duck "universe," Mickey Mouse does not really exist... at least not as a chum with whom Donald might sometimes interact. But I thought it would be an amusing situation if I treated Mickey as a famous "movie star" in Donald's world, and if I had the action involve a Keystone Kops-like chase through the Park that results when Donald tries to get the famous Mouse's autograph. And I thought I did a really magnificent job accomplishing all that! I spent most of January creating a masterpiece of promotion, spotlighting every square meter of that new theme park.

But the story was never produced. While Disney much later approved it for publication in the form you see here, back in 1989, a Disney supervisor rejected my script when Gladstone showed it to her.

The reason I was given for the story's rejection was that it was considered "too commercial." My tactic of having the *entire* story take place in the park apparently backfired: I showed *too much park* for somebody!!! But wasn't promoting the park the whole idea?

Anyway, this is the only Duck story I ever wrote that I never completed with finished art. But I naturally saved my storyboard-script, and in 2004, Egmont asked to use it in its chronological place in the first complete anthologies of my work. And so it has appeared in such collections ever since—and I finally got paid for that lost month of work I did way back in January 1989! Hoo-hah!

D.U.C.K. SPOTTER'S GUIDE: Sorry... there's no D.U.C.K. when there's no completed art to hide it in.

MOUSE SPOTTER'S GUIDE: Uh—he's everywhere!!! But besides the "real" Mickey and a Mickeylike water tower, you'll find a hidden Mickey in the map at page 2... and a not-so-hidden Mickey in Donald's disguise on page 5.

INSANE DETAILS TO LOOK FOR: Page 2, panel 1: the map is an insanely accurate depiction of Disney-MGM Studios at its opening! The four locations with shortened names are Production Center, Min and Bill's Dockside Diner, Dinosaur Gertie's Ice Cream of Extinction (named for the pre-Disney animated short *Gertie the Dinosaur*), and the Epic Stunt Theater.

Page 3, panel 4: *Clock Cleaners* (1937) is, of course, an actual Mickey Mouse cartoon—co-starring Donald Duck, though "my" Donald insists he "never saw that one."

HIS MAJESTY, McDUCK *p. 87*

Many Duck fans say that this story, done in 1989 for Gladstone Publishing, is my best duck adventure ever. The simplest ideas are often the best, and this tale is such an example. But I never liked the idea that I did my best story just two years into my career! I always wanted to think my *best* story was still in the future!

This tale has one simple premise and not too much plot, so I was able to keep piling on short gags as if it were an overextended ten-pager. It deals with the founding of Duckburg and refers to many old Barksian tales in the process (as I always love to do). In fact, in my original script, the villain who hired the Beagle Boys was Azure Blue from my very favorite Donald Duck story, Barks' "The Golden Helmet" (*Four Color* 408, 1952). But my editor Byron Erickson had me change Blue into a new villain, probably because he did not want me to make too many blatant references to old Barks stories. You see, in 1989, American Disney comics were still recovering from many years of low circulation—and a few years of being out of print entirely. So readers at that time were not as familiar with those old tales, and would not have recognized Blue or his partner, Lawyer Sharky. But Byron generously offered the suggestion that I create a new villain with the smarmy personality of Uriah Heep from Charles Dickens' novel *David Copperfield*. And so this new villain, Akers MacCovet, was born.

Years later, my original script for "The Lost Charts of Columbus" (see upcoming Vol. 6 of this series) had MacCovet meeting Blue and Sharky about another ancient land ownership deal. But whereas MacCovet was added to "His Majesty, McDuck," he was eliminated from "Columbus." The poor guy!

There are many cinematic aspects to "His Majesty, McDuck": movie spoofery is another of my favorite ingredients. The basic story idea loosely parodies an old British movie titled *Passport to Pimlico* (1949), which involved a small neighborhood in London discovering it was technically a separate country from England. This presented both benefits and problems, as does a similar situation for Scrooge in my story. The poor guy!

Certain other scenes pay tribute to other old movies; in fact, some of my top all-time favorites! The Cornelius Coot Memorial Library parodies the memorial library from *Citizen Kane* (1941). And the sword-duel climax of this story recalls *The Adventures of Robin Hood* (1938: Errol Flynn versus Basil Rathbone), or maybe *The Mark of Zorro* (1940: Tyrone Power versus Basil Rathbone). Movie heroes were always picking on Basil Rathbone. The poor guy!

The history that I use as a basis for this tale is authentic (as is all the history I use in my stories, as you know by now). Sir Francis Drake actually did land somewhere on the California coast in 1579 and claim the land for England. The history of North America—and perhaps the

Long before *not* appearing in Rosa's "His Majesty, McDuck," Azure Blue and Lawyer Sharky sailed to villainous glory in Carl Barks' "The Golden Helmet" (Donald Duck *Four Color* 408).

RECKLESSLY, AZURE BLUE DRIVES HIS SHIP BETWEEN THE BERGS!
WE CAN'T GO ON, SIR! IT'S TOO RISKY!
IT'LL BE MORE RISKY TO TURN BACK! KEEP GOING, I SAY!
I'LL BE OWNER OF NORTH AMERICA ONLY IF I'M FIRST TO FIND THE GOLDEN HELMET! AND I'M GOING TO BE FIRST!
YOKUS, CROKUS, SPOKUS! WHICH MEANS, "THE BOSS SPEAKETH A JAWFUL!"

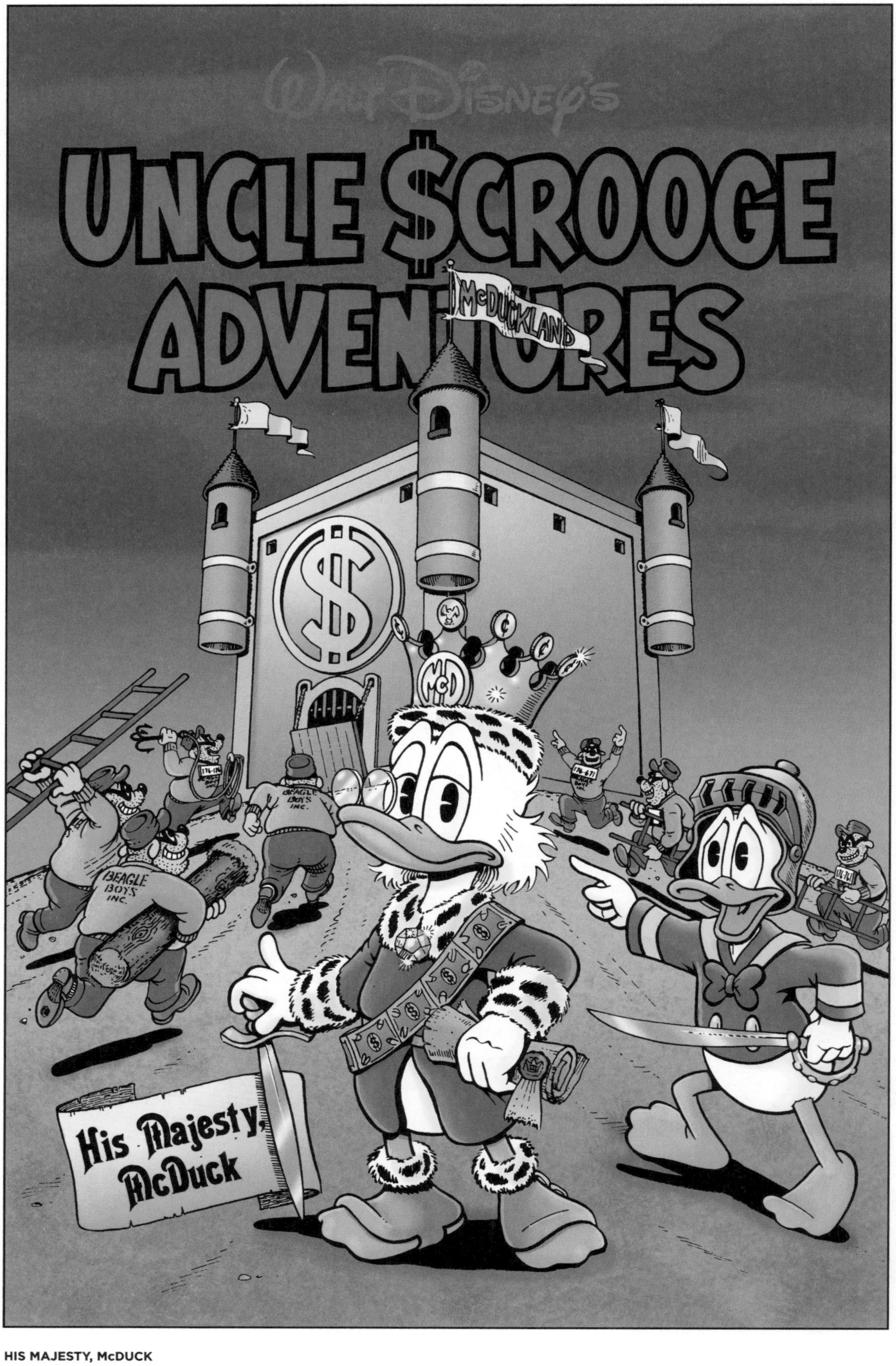

Walt Disney's
UNCLE $CROOGE ADVENTURES
McDUCKLAND
BEAGLE BOYS INC.
His Majesty, McDuck

HIS MAJESTY, McDUCK
Uncle Scrooge Adventures 14, August 1989; new color by Kneon Transitt.
The title scroll at Scrooge's feet, seen here approximately as originally drawn, was moved upward to overlap the Money Bin in all previous printings. Restoration by David Gerstein.

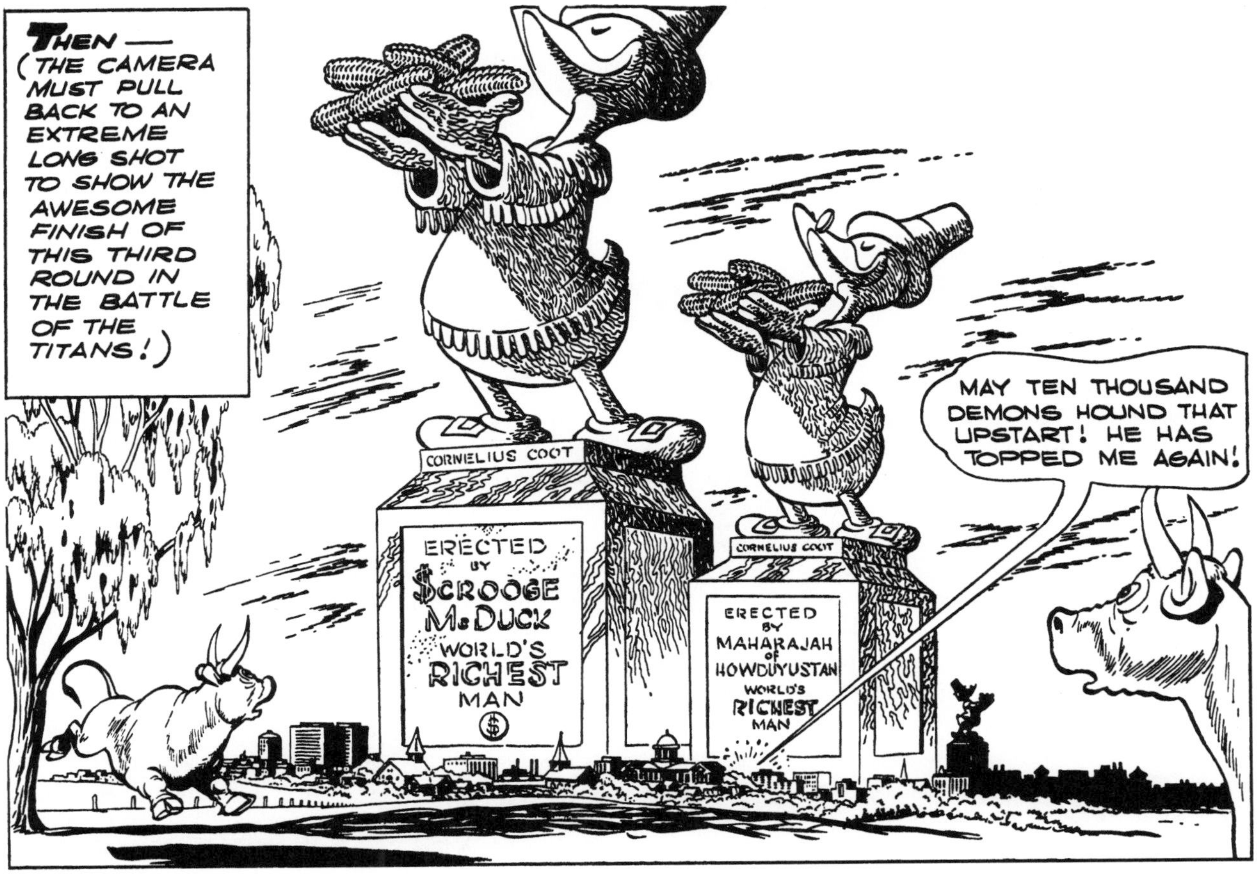
THEN — (THE CAMERA MUST PULL BACK TO AN EXTREME LONG SHOT TO SHOW THE AWESOME FINISH OF THIS THIRD ROUND IN THE BATTLE OF THE TITANS!)
CORNELIUS COOT
ERECTED BY $CROOGE McDUCK WORLD'S RICHEST MAN
CORNELIUS COOT
ERECTED BY MAHARAJAH OF HOWDUYUSTAN WORLD'S RICHEST MAN
MAY TEN THOUSAND DEMONS HOUND THAT UPSTART! HE HAS TOPPED ME AGAIN!

Carl Barks' "Statuesque Spendthrifts" (*Walt Disney's Comics* 138, 1952) first showed these mighty statues of Cornelius Coot—and their corny load of king-size cobs.

world—might be quite different today if not for the fact no one could ever locate the bronze plaque that Drake left behind to prove England's ownership of the western United States. In my tale, I decide that the site of this landing was the future site of Duckburg, and that Cornelius Coot came into possession of the land grant in such a way to explain why the statues of him that stand in Duckburg often show him holding ears of corn aloft. Fans know that Cornelius, as well as Fort Duckburg, can be seen in several Barks stories of the 1950s. (And of course, you'll recognize the Coot statue in "His Majesty McDuck" as being one of those that were built in "Statuesque Spendthrifts" [*Walt Disney's Comics* 138, 1952], that legendary Barks ten-pager about Scrooge's rivalry with the Maharajah of Howduyustan.)

D.U.C.K. SPOTTER'S GUIDE: Look in the bristles of Scrooge's pushbroom in panel 1.

MOUSE SPOTTER'S GUIDE: In the last panel of page 7, if you look closely, you'll see an interesting member of the Spanish force invading the fort.

INSANE DETAILS TO LOOK FOR: On page 10 you'll see Scrooge's trunk of memorabilia that I used years later throughout the "Life and Times of Scrooge McDuck" series... and you'll also see Scrooge open an old safe-deposit box which he would later look into in Chapter 9 of that series. In "His Majesty McDuck," he finds that the box is where, many years earlier, he had stashed the Goose Egg Nugget (the item that was the basis for all his wealth!), and in later stories I showed the Nugget as an exhibit in his Trophy Room.

Fort Duckburg as depicted by Carl Barks in "The Money Well" (*Uncle Scrooge* 21, 1958).

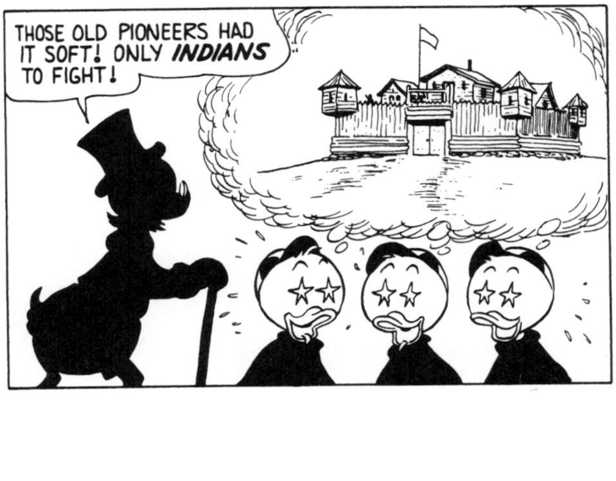
THOSE OLD PIONEERS HAD IT SOFT! ONLY INDIANS TO FIGHT!

I have Scrooge use the suits of armor from Castle McDuck, first seen in Barks "The Old Castle's Secret" (Donald Duck *Four Color* 189, 1948). And if you check Sir Swamphole's armor on page 17, you'll see that his skeleton is still inside (as so indicated in "Old Castle's Secret").

GIVE UNTO OTHERS *p. 115*
FORGET ME NOT *p. 122*
MAKING THE GRADE *p. 135*
LEAKY LUCK p. 157

These four stories... well, three stories and a one-page gag... are Duck stories that I illustrated but *did not write*; therefore, I am limited in what I have to say about them. They are scattered through the book in publication order, but are grouped together here in my commentary because they're most easily dealt with as a whole. So—how *did* I come to draw them?

Gladstone Publishing was a tiny company. Disney comics were and are the world's most popular comics, but they had not been easily available in America for so many years that they had lost the public's recognition. Gladstone's sales were fairly good, but after licensing fees, their profit margin was small. So they could not keep me busy 100% of the time. In fact, they say they *lost* money when they hired me to do a new story for them; but hired me anyway, because they didn't want to be known as a strictly-reprint publisher.

I had liquidated my construction company and I needed steadier pay than part-time freelance work. But... reading the information appearing in those same Gladstone comics, I was beginning to learn that there were Disney comics publishers in *other* countries! Who would have thought?! The Dutch Disney comics publisher was then called Oberon, and I found that they could use a few extra stories in their inventory. Great! But... I was thinking that if I wrote stories for Oberon, I would try to write the *best* stories I could... and if I really liked a new script, I would want to save it to draw it myself for Gladstone. So I surmised that I would really prefer to only illustrate *other* writers' scripts for Oberon, and save my own script ideas for the next job Gladstone wanted.

The results were these four jobs. I wasn't told at the time who the actual writers were, and even to this day the Dutch publisher is the *only* Disney publisher left on earth who leaves the names of the writers and artists out of most of their printed magazines. Only online, and in certain special albums, do credits appear.

But let's get back to the stories. Starting with "Give Unto Others"... uh... I don't like my *own* scripts too often, but I don't even understand the ending of this one. Donald knows his nephews love fishing; somebody gave him a free fishing pole; he desperately needs to find a gift for his nephews to please Daisy... so why doesn't it occur to him to give them the fishing pole he has in his hands? Boing!

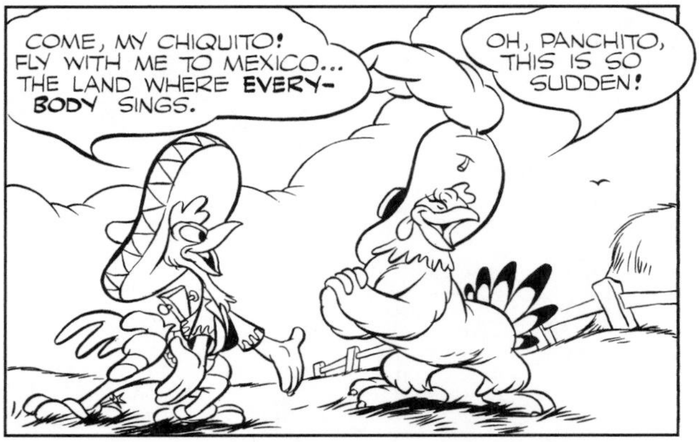
COME, MY CHIQUITO! FLY WITH ME TO MEXICO... THE LAND WHERE EVERY-BODY SINGS.
OH, PANCHITO, THIS IS SO SUDDEN!

The operatic chicken Clara Cluck, included in Rosa's art-only "Forget Me Not," was rarely used by Carl Barks. She more frequently featured in other creators' Disney comics—like this *Panchito* story by Ken Hultgren (*Walt Disney's Comics* 38, 1943).

"Forget Me Not": once again, the ending doesn't make sense to me—somebody plans their own birthday party, invites the guests, then forgets it? I don't have much admiration for Daisy Duck as a character, but I at least give her credit for more brains than that. You'll also notice that the script compelled me to include Clara Cluck, who is not a character that I personally recognize as existing in my "Barks universe." However, one distinction this story has is that it is the first of only two times when I used Daisy's nieces. And also notice that strangely *short* Gyro Gearloose, if he's not kneeling down behind Gladstone Gander! Oh, well... I guess I sure can't ever criticize a *writer* if I can't *draw* better than this!

"Making the Grade" is written in the style of the Barks ten-pagers of the '40s, when Donald was often battling with his nephews—who were not yet the sterling Junior Woodchuck-type characters that I would later grow up with in the Barks stories of about ten years later. The nephews in "Making the Grade" are not simply hooky-players; they even attempt to *blackmail* their Unca Donald into letting them drop out of school! These are *not* the nephews I grew up admiring!

Of this group of four Dutch stories, the only one I like is the cute one-pager "Leaky Luck." I also see I added some funny background bits in my usual effort at "needless and irritating details." Well, the Dutch editors knew I wasn't a real "professional" and they really didn't like my art so much, so I can't blame them for not giving me their very best scripts to illustrate. Anyway, this collection is including these Dutch stories for purposes of completeness.

D.U.C.K. SPOTTER'S GUIDE: Don't try to find any hidden dedications in these stories. On the few stories I drew for Gladstone and the Dutch that were based on scripts by someone else, I decided it would be improper to include my dedication. Each story was a joint effort, and it would be wrong for me to dedicate someone else's script to Carl Barks.

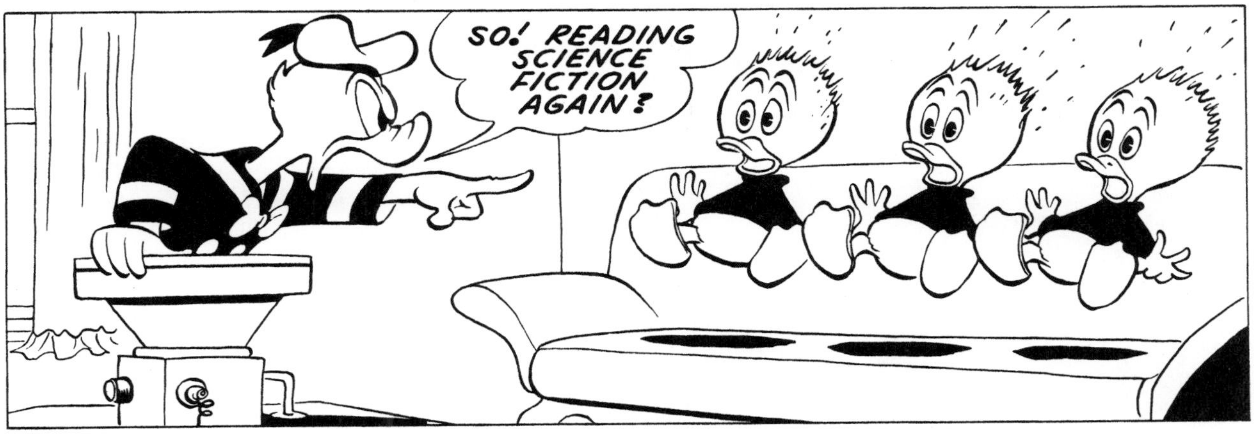
SO! READING SCIENCE FICTION AGAIN?

Donald emerges from Gyro's teleportation device in Barks' "Stranger Than Fiction" (*Walt Disney's Comics* 249), a spiritual precursor to Rosa's "On a Silver Platter."

ON A SILVER PLATTER *p. 125*

I wrote "On a Silver Platter" for Gladstone Publishing in 1988. But when circumstances intervened (see the autobiographical feature in the back of this book), I decided to offer the finished job to the Dutch Disney publisher, who already had me on tap from the four art-only stories. Thus "On a Silver Platter" was produced for the Dutch, and if several of the close-up Duck faces look un-Rosa-like—particularly in the first two pages—it's because the Dutch art director sent me some corrections to my pencil-pages for me to copy into ink. No art directors have tried to help me draw since this story, though... because I have been unanimously declared to be a "stylist" in my approach to Disney art—I take this label to mean "not very good, filled with needless and irritating details, but funny, so don't mess with it."

I personally find ten-page gag stories more difficult to write than my usual adventure stories, since my mind (unfortunately) seems to thrive on complexities. It's a hard job to come up with one simple idea good enough to carry a short gag story for ten pages, and I envy writers who can accomplish that! But "On a Silver Platter" was one instance where the basic idea struck me and the story seemed to write itself before my eyes in a matter of minutes.

Whenever I need to wrestle with a story idea to get it to make sense and be funny, that's a sure sign that the idea was flawed in the first place. So, because "On a Silver Platter" was such a breeze to write, I've always thought it must be one of my very best short stories! This is also a clue that if I want my job to be easy, all I need to do is a superbly good job all the time and it will be a cinch. What a simple solution!

I especially like the idea in this tale that Scrooge has an all-out fight with Magica De Spell, yet Scrooge never leaves his Money Bin in Duckburg and Magica never crosses the threshold of her sorcery shoppe on the slopes of Mt. Vesuvius, thousands of miles away. I was later reminded that Barks had done a short story in 1961 involving a similar transporting device ("Stranger Than Fiction," Walt Disney's Comics 249): a story that I must have read when I was nine years old. I wasn't thinking of that tale when I wrote mine, but I'll bet it was in my subconscious mind waving at me.

D.U.C.K. SPOTTER'S GUIDE: Well, as I said, I did this story for Holland, and it looks like those editors removed the dedication. Sorry!

BACK IN TIME FOR A DIME! *p. 145*

I've always viewed Disney's *DuckTales* TV series as a sort of "counterfeit" version of Barks' Duckburg characters. But I was momentarily involved with it... sort of!!! In 1990, there was also a *DuckTales Magazine*, featuring games and puzzles aimed at very young kiddies. Though I forget the circumstances, I was offered a job of writing a four-page comic strip that would be featured in each issue of the magazine. But they didn't want my drawings—the Jaime Diaz Studio, based in Argentina, would supply the art.

I sent in a four-page script which wasn't too bad... and I even tried to make good use of the *DuckTales* TV characters, such as Launchpad McQuack and (choke!) Bubba Duck. Launchpad, the inept pilot, is not a bad character; and if he had existed in the comics I grew up with, I wouldn't have minded using him in my normal comic stories. On the other hand, I was compelled to use this character named Bubba Duck—this was a caveman Duck from prehistoric times... what he was doing living with Scrooge McDuck I didn't know and I really didn't care. Heck, in my view of things, Scrooge would never even let Huey, Dewey and Louie live with him! But the comic book Scrooge is not the "kindly old grandpa" figure as portrayed on TV.

Anyway, I supplied the script and the Diaz Studio illustrated it in a very "cute" Disney manner. It's much better art than I am capable of with my limited abilities, but I still don't care for that "cute" style. Still, I know plenty of readers don't like *my* "weird" style, and I'm usually in *agreement* with them: "one man's meat is another man's poison," right?

SPRING 1990
Disney's
DuckTales
Magazine
A TREETOP TREASURE HUNT!
A TRIP THROUGH TIME (FOR A DIME!)
THE SCOOP ON BUBBA DUCK!
$1.95
Canada $2.50

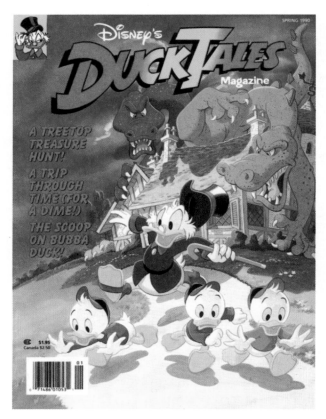

The Jaime Diaz Studio's original cover to "Back in Time For a Dime!" (*DuckTales Magazine*, Spring 1990).

Desperate as I was for work at the time, I might have submitted more scripts, even if I had a hard time getting paid for this one. But they never asked. And as it turns out, "Back in Time" is—and will likely remain—the only comic story that I will ever write but not illustrate myself.

THE PIED PIPER OF DUCKBURG *p. 149*

As with "On a Silver Platter," I wrote this story in 1988 for Gladstone, but offered it to the Dutch publisher a year later when I was otherwise out of work. I had written one long adventure, too (next volume's "Treasure Under Glass"), but the Dutch did not want long stories in their Disney comics—nor did they want more work from me after this story, since they weren't too keen on Rosa Duck work.

Now... this story has a *very special* history! It can be looked upon as the only time Carl Barks and I worked on a story together. No, it can't be regarded as a collaboration—you see, his work on the story took place in 1959 while my work took place in 1989, fully 30 years later!

Here's how that happened...

Western Publishing put out a wide variety of Disney one-shots in its famous *Four Color* line. Five issues of *Gyro Gearloose* were part of this group. Each contained a mix of seven- and eight-page stories, mostly by Barks.

"The Pied Piper of Duckburg" was to have been an eight-page story. But Barks shelved the story three pages in. He later told Michael Barrier that "I felt I was getting into something too involved for such a short story. Also I would have to draw whole swarms of kids and rats and people, and the page rates weren't worth it."

Until the 1980s, that is. Bruce Hamilton, who had been loaned the three-page pencil script by Mr. Barks, thought it would be an interesting idea if I tried to think up an ending for the story and complete the job! With Barks' approval, he sent me copies of the three pages of pencil art (you don't suppose he'd let me ink directly onto the priceless original art!).

I noticed that the story started out with Gyro pushing an "invention cart" along the street, looking for work—the only one of those old Gyro comics that featured such a pushcart was the first issue in 1959, so it seemed that I was going to try to complete a story started exactly 30 years earlier! Okay—I set to work. I am just the sort of nut who—unlike Mr. Barks—would *relish* the idea of drawing thousands of rats swarming around Duckburg, no matter how low the page rate was!

The only problem that I saw was that the story clearly showed the McDuck Money Bin being on a downtown street corner rather than looming majestically over Duckburg from atop Killmotor Hill, which is where I always depict it to be. Barks was not so concerned about such details; he always showed the Money Bin on its proper hill in the pages of *Uncle Scrooge* comics, but when he featured Scrooge as a secondary character in a Gyro or Grandma Duck or Daisy Duck story, he would place the Bin wherever it was most convenient for the plot.

This lack of continuity shouldn't necessarily bother readers, but I was one of the readers that it did bother when I was growing up; and I also knew a secret that Mr. Barks never did—that there are *untold millions* of fervent and loyal Duck fans (created by his work!) who are reading every story and never miss a detail! I could not place the Money Bin anywhere but atop Killmotor Hill in one of my own stories. So I proposed one tiny change to the dialogue on page 1, panel 5—instead of Scrooge referring to the cache of money as his main Money Bin, I begged Hamilton to allow the tiny change of having Scrooge refer to the room as an "overflow bin" at a downtown bank. I would have the action transfer up to the main Money Bin later in the story.

Granted that favor, I made a stab at completing the script. I'm sure my story is nothing like what Mr. Barks had planned; at the time, I didn't know that his letter to Barrier mentioned *kids*, another type of critter attracted by the Pied Piper. But I did my best. (Personally, I think my ending is kinda lame.) However, I had to leave Gladstone before I could draw the story, and completed the project for the Dutch a year later. (*Continued on Page 188*)

Facing page and overleaf: Carl Barks' original, unfinished three-page scribble for "The Pied Piper of Duckburg." Barks supplied these pages to Gladstone in the 1980s, leading to Rosa's completion of the story.

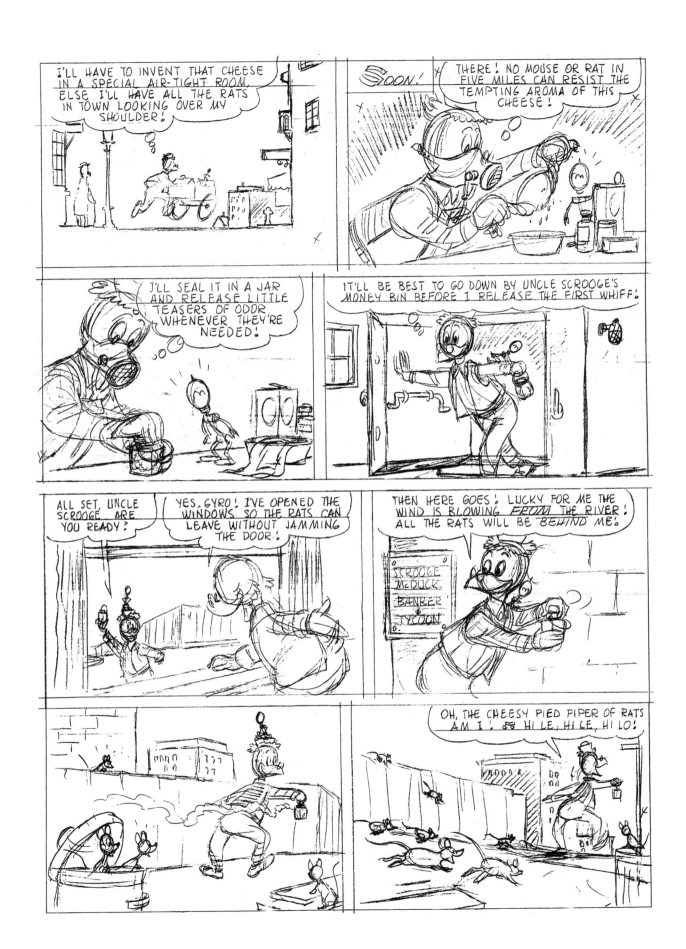

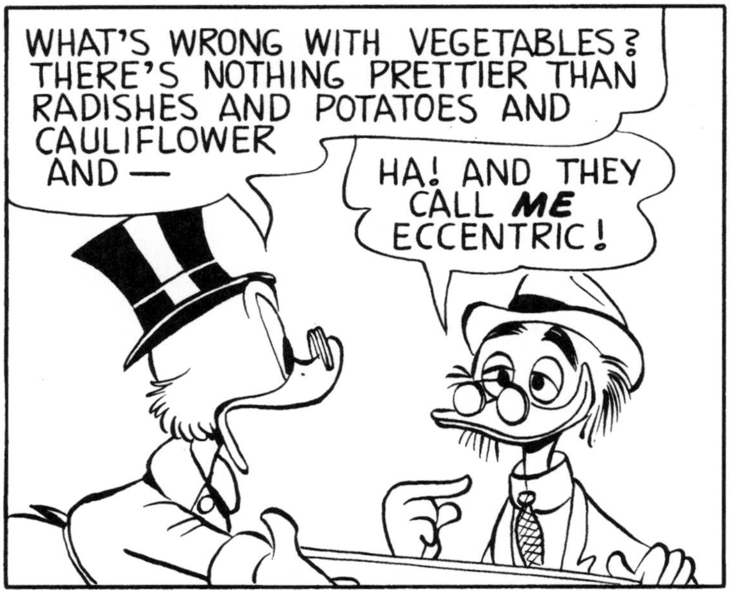
WHAT'S WRONG WITH VEGETABLES? THERE'S NOTHING PRETTIER THAN RADISHES AND POTATOES AND CAULIFLOWER AND —
HA! AND THEY CALL ME ECCENTRIC!

Carl Barks' single use of Ludwig Von Drake came in the one-page gag "Flowers Are Flowers" (*Uncle Scrooge* 54, 1964).

D.U.C.K. SPOTTER'S GUIDE: The Dutch editors took it out this time, too. Look really closely and... you *still* won't see it!!!

MOUSE SPOTTER'S GUIDE: Page 7, panel 1: Look for Mickey in the lower right corner.

INSANE DETAILS TO LOOK FOR: On page 4 you'll see one of the only two times I've used Ludwig Von Drake! The other was when I secretly showed him from the back sitting on the stage in my 50th anniversary Scrooge McDuck story, "A Little Something Special" (see upcoming Vol. 7 of this series).

I was not allowed to use Ludwig later, after I went to work for Egmont, because the editors in the 1990s regarded him as a "no longer existing" character. Maybe they thought he was too much like Gyro Gearloose? But that can't be—Gyro is a busy screwball inventor and Ludwig is an effete, pompous know-it-all. But I like Ludwig, and I snuck him into the background on those two occasions.

THE MONEY PIT *p. 159*

For various reasons, I am usually not very happy with my own stories. But this tale, written in 1988 and drawn several years later in 1990, is one of my personal favorites due to the philosophies of life that it expounds. The plot seems to be about coin collectors, but it really pertains to *all* collectors who are interested only in the monetary value of their collection rather than in their own personal interest in the items they collect—the latter, after all, being the only sane reason for spending all of one's free time in pursuing a particular hobby.

And you can take a hint—from Scrooge's remark about collectors who put their items into "plastic sleeves"—that my main focus is specifically *comic book collectors*: specifically, the type who are more interested in preserving their comics for future resale than in enjoying the darn things themselves. This also extends to the increasingly idiotic *toy* collectors who never take toys out of the cartons in which they are sold!

We Americans have a shallow preoccupation with greed rather than intellect when it comes to our hobbies. As many of you have no doubt seen, we have actually had "collectible" comic books sold *already sealed* into plastic bags, with the buyers told that if they should be so crass as to open the bag to try to read the comic, the comic would lose all of its "collector's value"... as with that toy-collector mentality!

Therefore these kids will buy the comics and never unwrap them and look at them! And *then* there are the comic collectors who are willing to buy the same issue up to *five times* simply because each one has a variant cover!

And the collectors who buy "gold editions," identical to the regular editions except for a bit of gold ink! And collectors who... well, never mind. Don't get me started!

Anyway, as a lifelong collector of many "interesting" things myself, I differentiate between *true* collectors and the "collectibles louts": those who don't understand the point that Scrooge makes on pages 3 and 4 of this story—particularly when he says, "I've learned to treasure that which has value to me, not to somebody else! That's what life's all about!" I am responding to that philosophy in the persona of the middle Duck nephew in that panel.

As I'll further explain in the autobiographical feature at the back of this book, I drew this "Money Pit" story for Disney's short-lived in-house comic book publisher. The ironic thing is that Disney published the story in the first issue of one of their new series; then took groups of all their number-one issues, *sealed* them into a plastic-wrapped box, and sold them as a costly "collectibles" set... with buyers, presumably, getting the idea that they could never open the box without destroying its "collectible" value! So these people would never read the story sealed therein that gave my opinion on that very concept! That's kinda funny and sad all at the same time, eh? Only in America...

D.U.C.K. SPOTTER'S GUIDE: The dedication is written on a dollar bill in the first panel.

INSANE DETAILS TO LOOK FOR: The tale itself is a follow-up to a classic Barks ten-pager (*Walt Disney's Comics* 130, 1951) in which Donald also tried to profit from Scrooge's rare coins—and as Donald recalls in my story, "the old miser tricked me into flooding the market." •

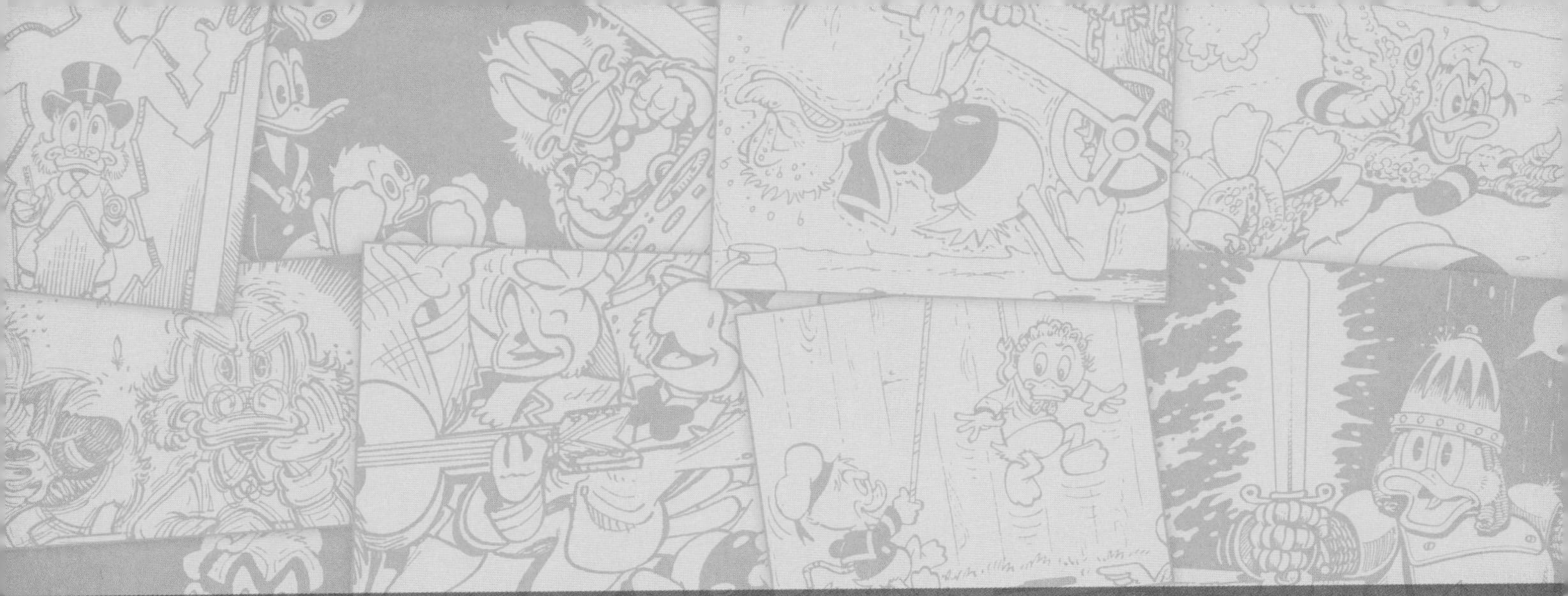

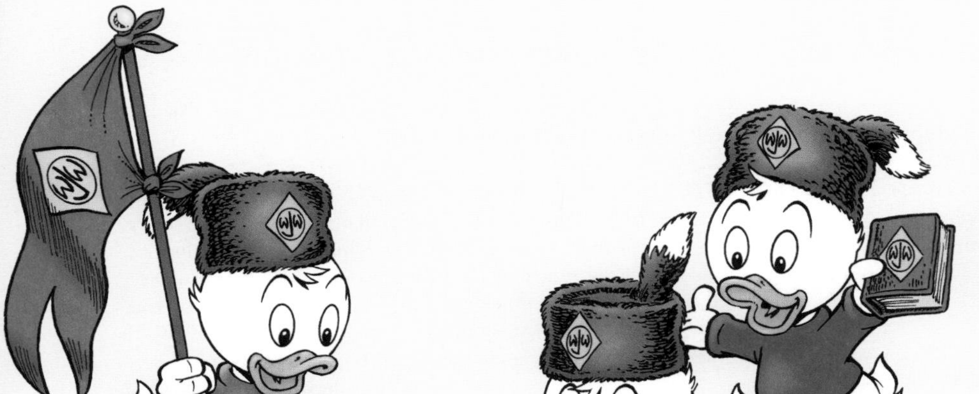

The Rosa Archives

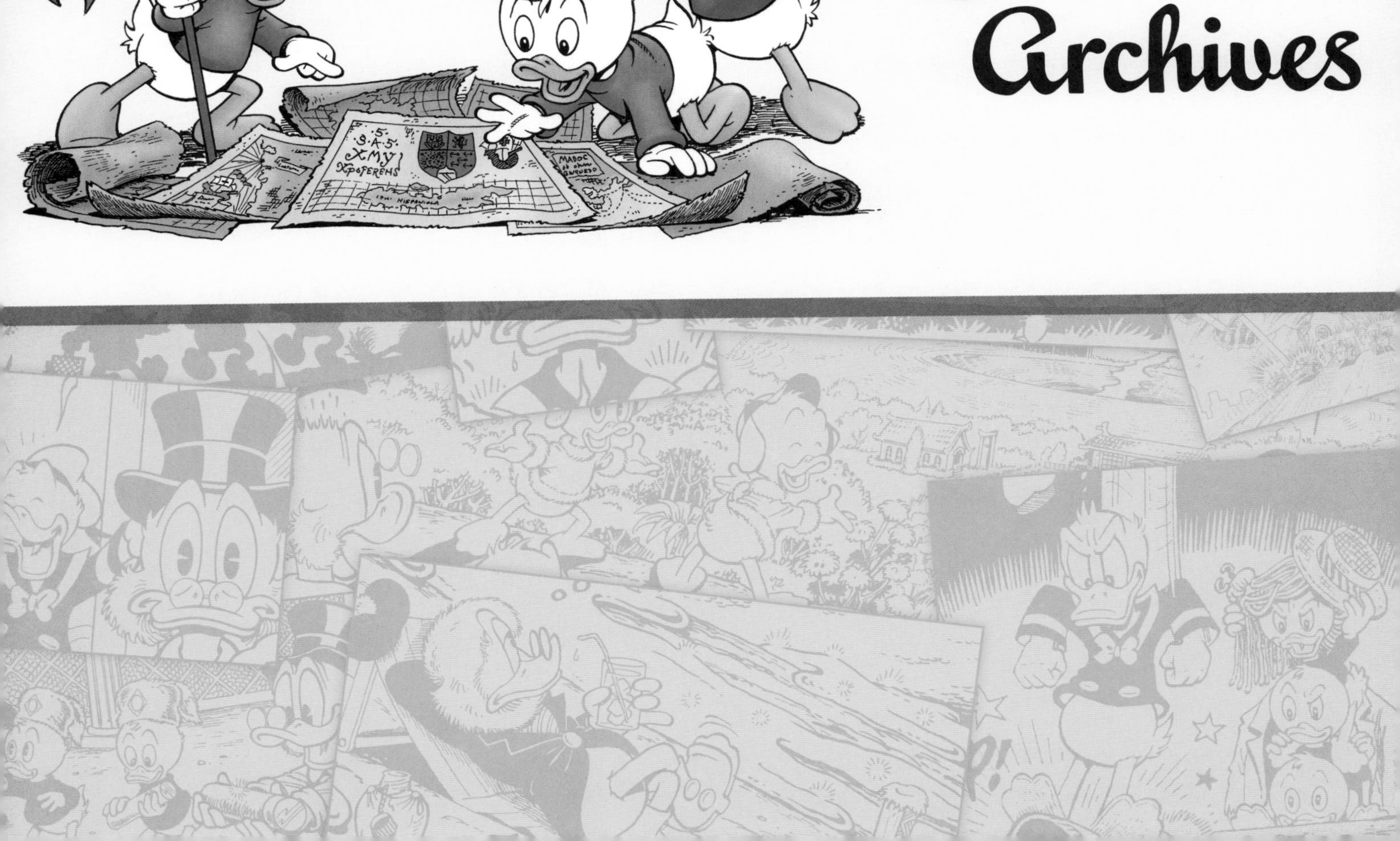

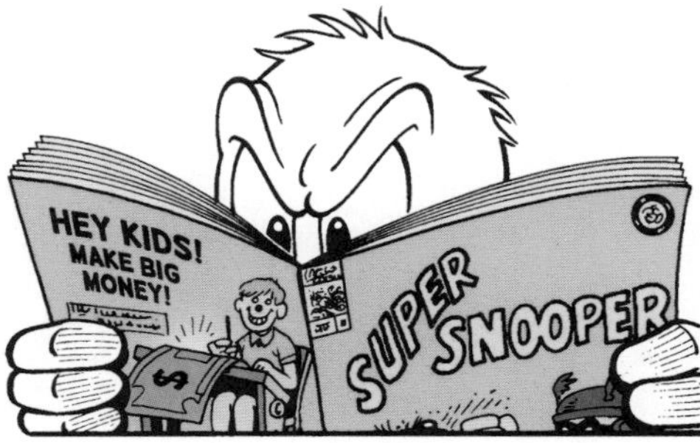
HEY KIDS!
MAKE BIG
MONEY!
SUPER
SNOOPER

This Should Cover It All!

(Additional Covers, 1990)

By Don Rosa

Earlier on in this volume you've seen the "Don-Rosa-story-specific" covers that I did in 1989 and 1990. To be precise: if I did a cover for one of my Duck stories near the time of its first printing, then Fantagraphics has run that cover either alongside the story itself, or alongside my "Behind the Scenes" annotative text.

But what about all the covers done not for my *own* stories, but for Barks classics and other projects? That's what *this* gallery is for.

Turn the next few pages for a spin through these "non-Don-Rosa-story-specific" covers. Or look below for my comments on many of them:

A STITCH IN TIME *p. 191* • This is one of only two covers I ever did which was a scene from a story by someone other than Barks or myself. Gladstone needed a cover to go with a time-machine story drawn by Daniel Branca. Looking at this cover, I can see that I borrowed the horse's pose from a book of reprints of Hal Foster's *Prince Valiant*!

THE SUNKEN CITY *p. 192* • I drew this cover to accompany a Barks story: the untitled 1954 tale about the sunken city of Atlantis and Scrooge's ten-skyrillion-dollar 1916 quarter. In the first printing, the editors redrew all of the bubbles that I had so painstakingly drawn around the Ducks. Naturally, as the engineer-cartoonist I am, I had rendered many of the bubbles as perfect circles, drawing each one with a different size circle template.

A COLD BARGAIN *p. 195* • Don't compare this cover with my cover to "The Golden Fleecing" in our previous volume! It looks like the same layout, only flipped: Scrooge carrying something round and valuable, running and looking back at a flying pursuer who's trying to wrest the precious item from his grasp; the other Ducks also fleeing. I wonder if I did that on purpose?

MAHARAJAH DONALD *p. 196* • While I still wasn't drawing especially good Ducks in 1990, I certainly *couldn't* draw decent tigers! Those look like werewolves or something.

DON ROSA SPECIAL *p. 197* • Now *here's* a special moment in my life!!! This was an album reprinting my own "Cash Flow" and "Last Sled to Dawson." But more than that, its full title was *Uncle Scrooge and Donald Duck Don Rosa Special*! Can you imagine what that felt like for me? This scene combines elements from the two featured Scrooge adventures. And you might recognize it as the back cover of Fantagraphics' *Don Rosa Library* Vol. 1.

INTENDED *WALT DISNEY'S COMICS IN COLOR* COVERS *pp. 198-201* • This series of giant-size albums took unsold copies of earlier *Gladstone Comic Albums* and rebound four issues under a new cover. Now, sometimes an edition would contain a mixture of Donald Duck and Uncle Scrooge *and Mickey Mouse* albums. So I had to draw Mickey for the only times in my professional career! (Well, other than how I hide him in the corners of panels in my stories.)

For my first attempt, I completed these four cover ideas, involving all three characters in gag scenes. I sent them to Gladstone, but they were rejected for use on this album series. It was felt that scenes showing the Ducks interacting with the Mouse would lead buyers to think that the stories inside *also* featured the Ducks interacting with the Mouse. Instead, Gladstone's Disney liason asked that I create covers featuring the three characters *together*—but *not interacting* in the same scene. Huh?!?!? What the...? So these first four cover drawings were only published on other comics years later, and this book marks their first appearance with the logos and aspect ratios I intended.

***WALT DISNEY'S COMICS IN COLOR* COVERS** *pp. 202-209* • Okay, time to produce the *final* covers. For starters, there were a few *Comics in Color* albums with only Duck stories, so "covering" those was easy. That left the Duck/Mouse covers. Well, I figured nobody could object to some of Disney's own ideas, right? So I based one cover on the idea of the characters drawing each other, as Disney had featured on some toy store posters. For another cover I recreated a "Spirit of '76" scene that Disney had used during the 1976 bicentennial; I just replaced Goofy with Uncle Scrooge. For another, I simply did a pose of Donald and Mickey ignoring each other, smiling at the reader (which I enjoyed, since I drew Donald bigger than Mickey to prove he was a "bigger star" in my view). Then I ran out of ideas on how to draw the characters *together* yet not *interacting*... and that resulted in my desperate idea for the cover used on page 204, which is probably the weirdest cover I have ever drawn—and ever hope to draw! •

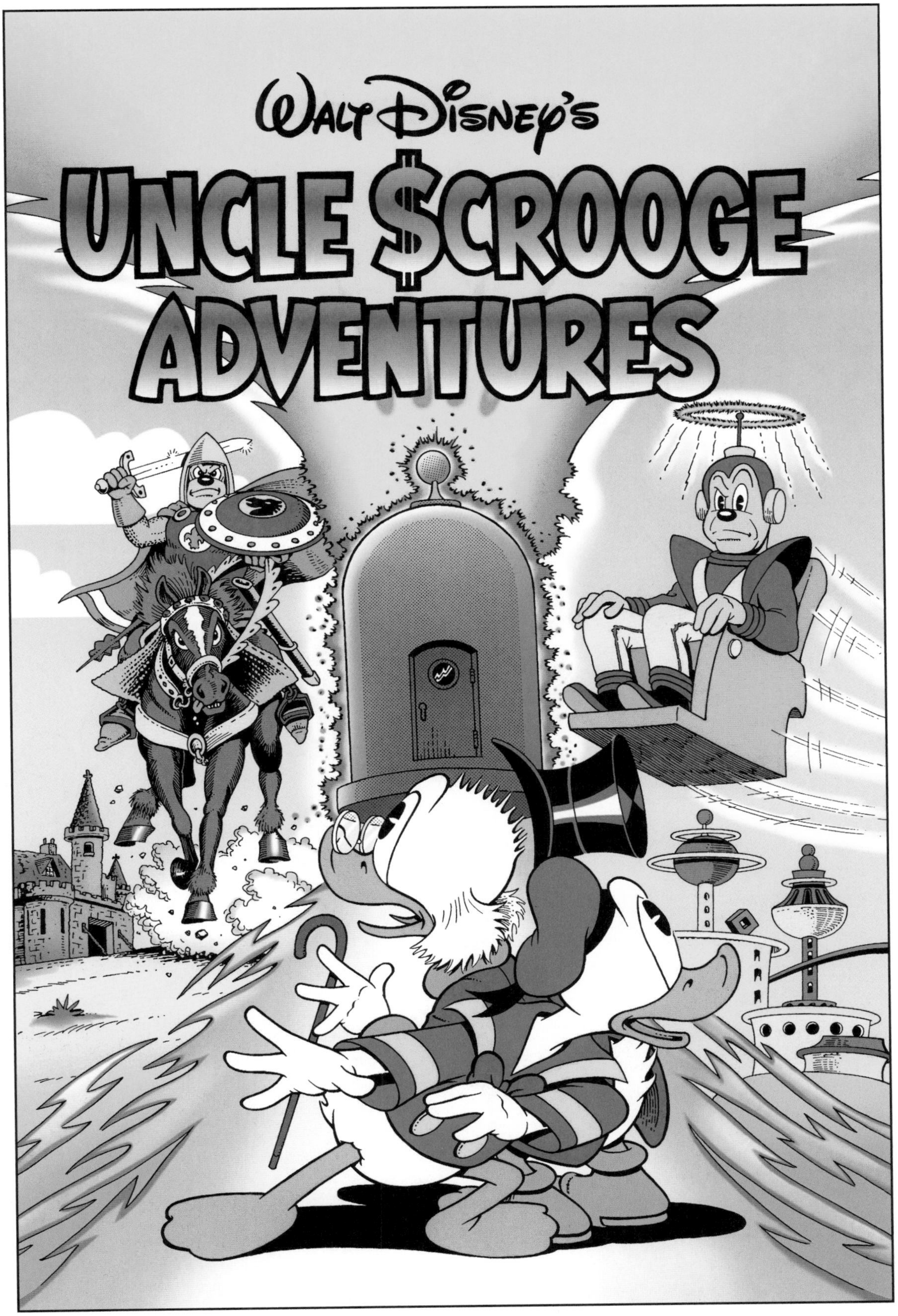
WALT DISNEY'S
UNCLE $CROOGE ADVENTURES

A STITCH IN TIME • *Uncle Scrooge Adventures* 19, January 1990; new color by Digikore Studios. Illustrating a new story written by Patsy Trench and Bob Bartholomew and drawn by Daniel Branca.

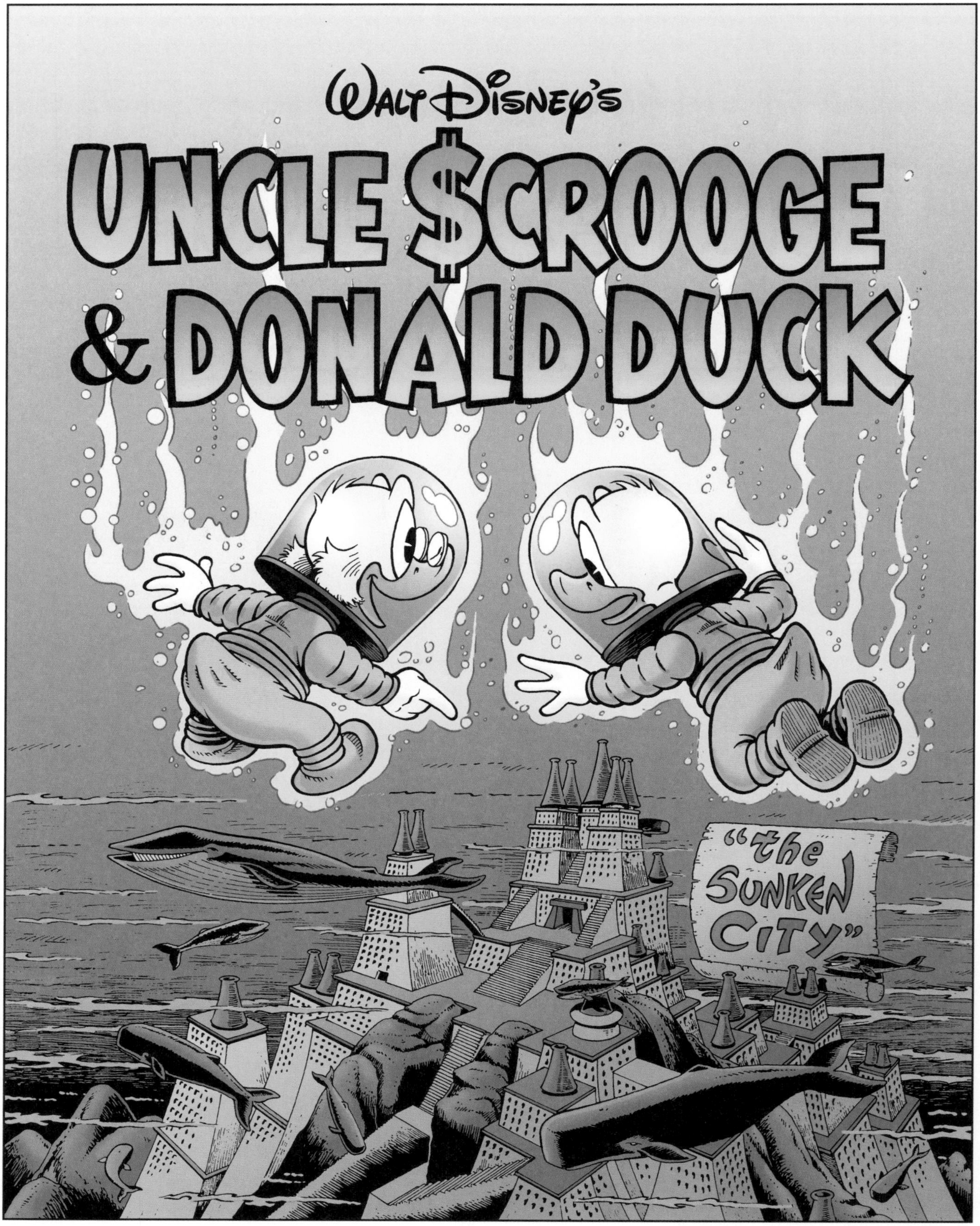
Walt Disney's
Uncle $crooge
& Donald Duck
"the Sunken City"

THE SUNKEN CITY • *Gladstone Giant Comic Album Special* 2, February 1990; restoration and new color by Kneon Transitt. Illustrating a story written and drawn by Carl Barks (*Uncle Scrooge* 5, March 1954). The streams of bubbles around Donald and Scrooge, seen here approximately as originally drawn, were replaced with non-Rosa artwork in all previous printings.

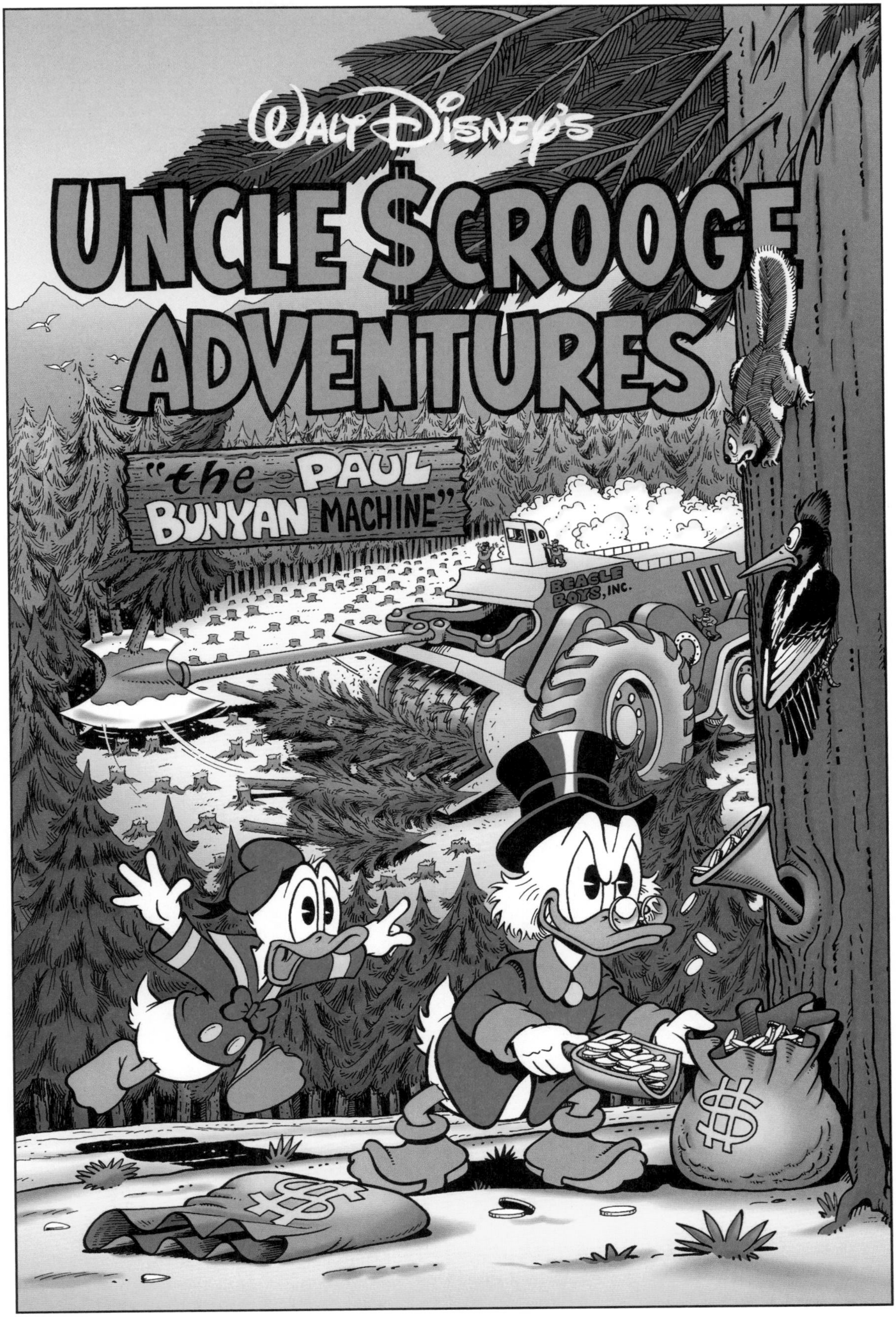
Walt Disney's
UNCLE $CROOGE ADVENTURES
"the PAUL BUNYAN MACHINE"
BEAGLE BOYS, INC.

THE PAUL BUNYAN MACHINE • *Uncle Scrooge Adventures* 20, March 1990; new color by Digikore Studios. Illustrating a story written and drawn by Carl Barks (*Uncle Scrooge* 28, December 1959).

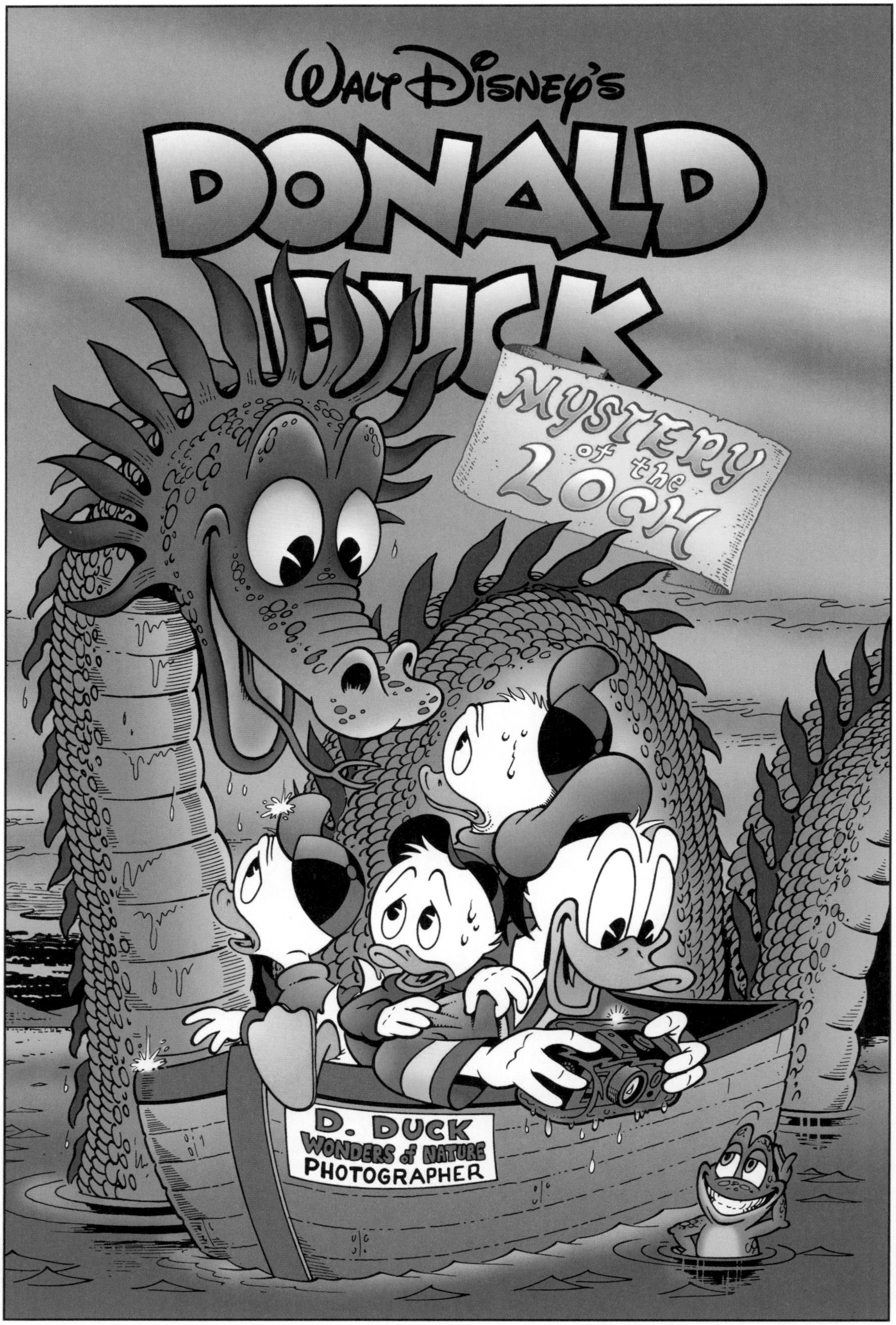
WALT DISNEY'S
DONALD DUCK
MYSTERY of the LOCH
D. DUCK
WONDERS of NATURE
PHOTOGRAPHER

MYSTERY OF THE LOCH • *Donald Duck* 278, March 1990 (interior cover); new color by Susan Daigle-Leach. Illustrating a story written and drawn by Carl Barks (*Walt Disney's Comics and Stories* 237, June 1960).

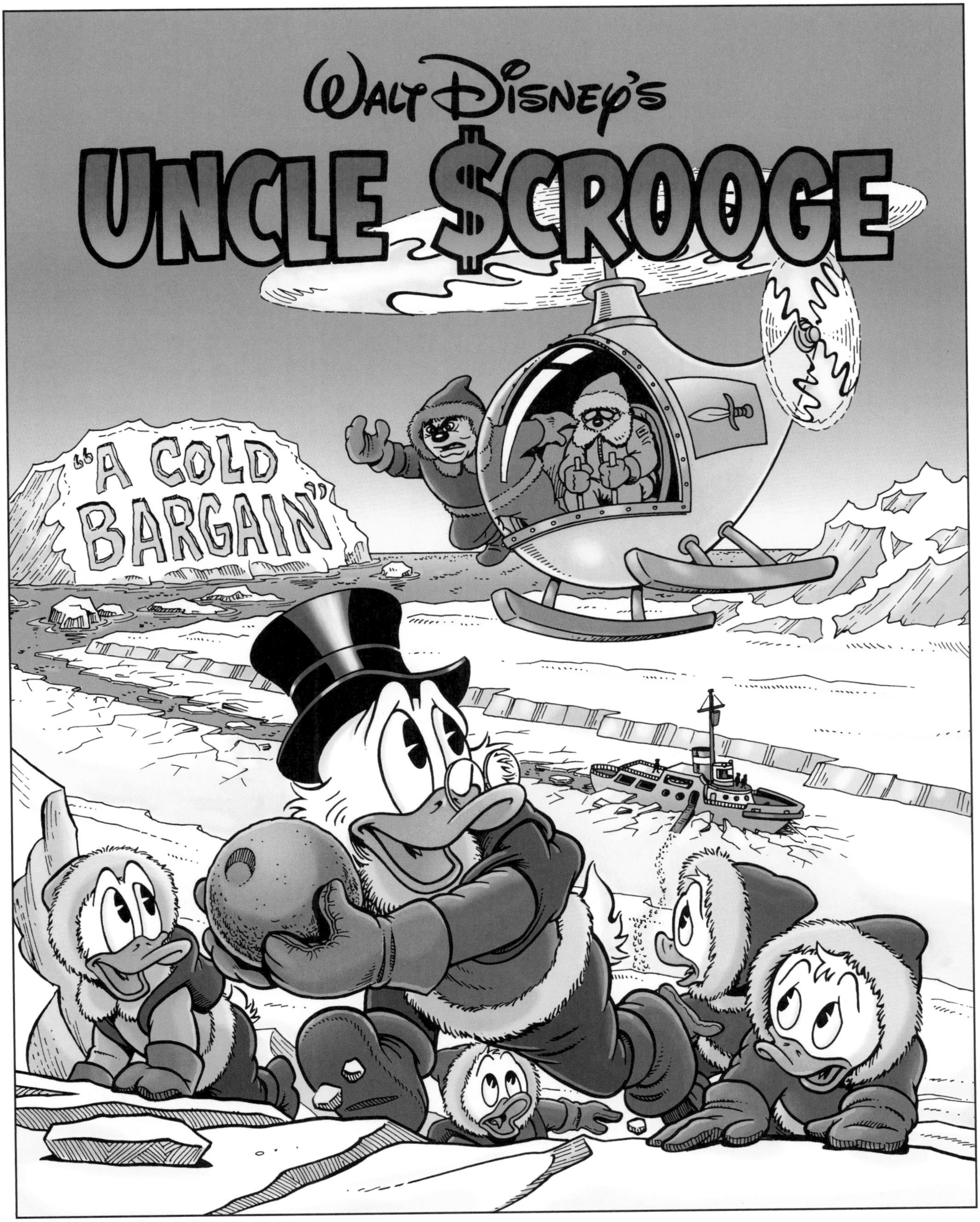
WALT DISNEY'S
UNCLE $CROOGE
"A COLD BARGAIN"

A COLD BARGAIN • *Gladstone Comic Album* 24, March 1990; new color by Kneon Transitt.
Illustrating a story written and drawn by Carl Barks (*Uncle Scrooge* 17, March 1957).

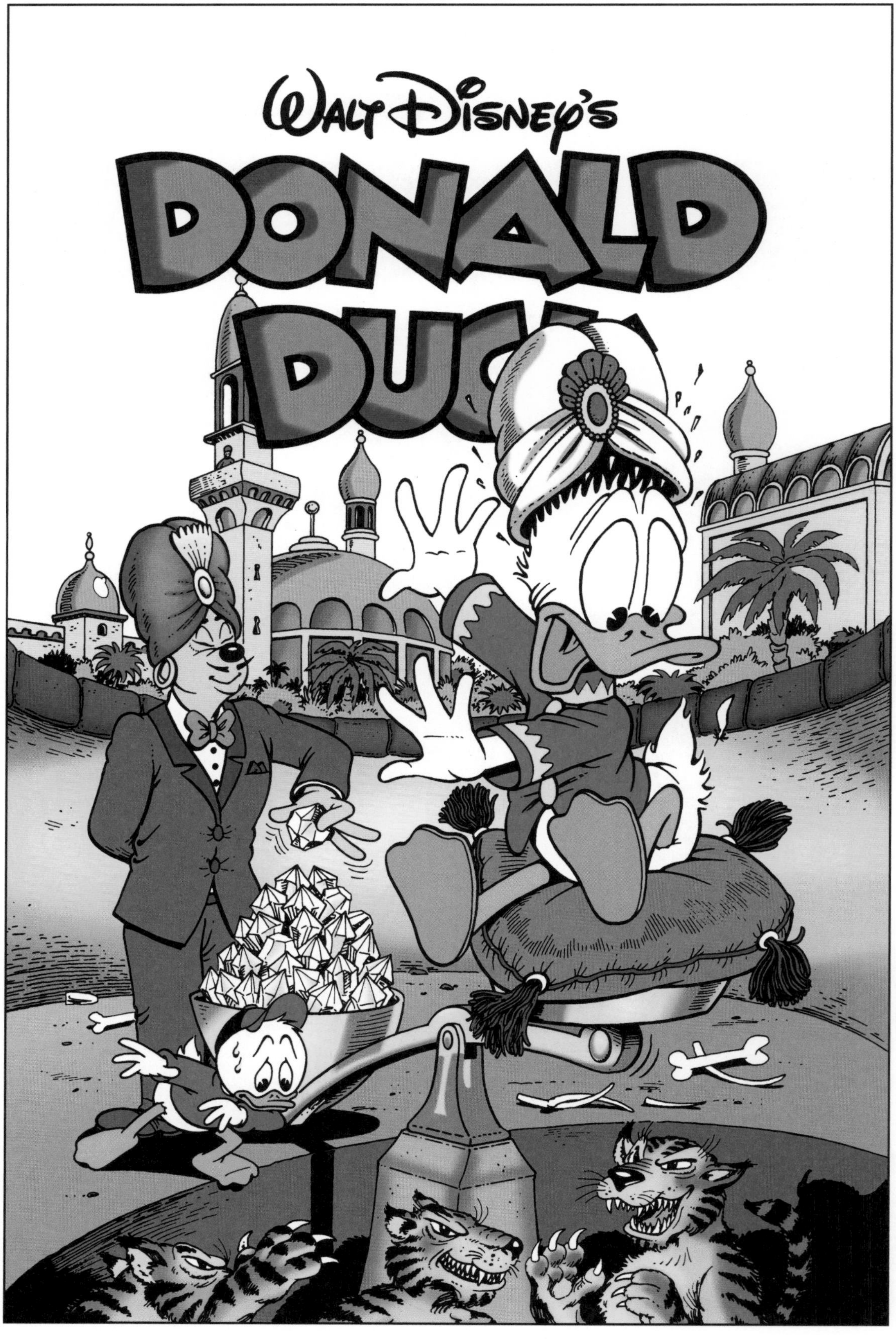
WALT DISNEY'S
DONALD
DUCK

MAHARAJAH DONALD • *Donald Duck* 279, May 1990; new color by Digikore Studios.
Illustrating a story written and drawn by Carl Barks (*March of Comics* 4, 1947).

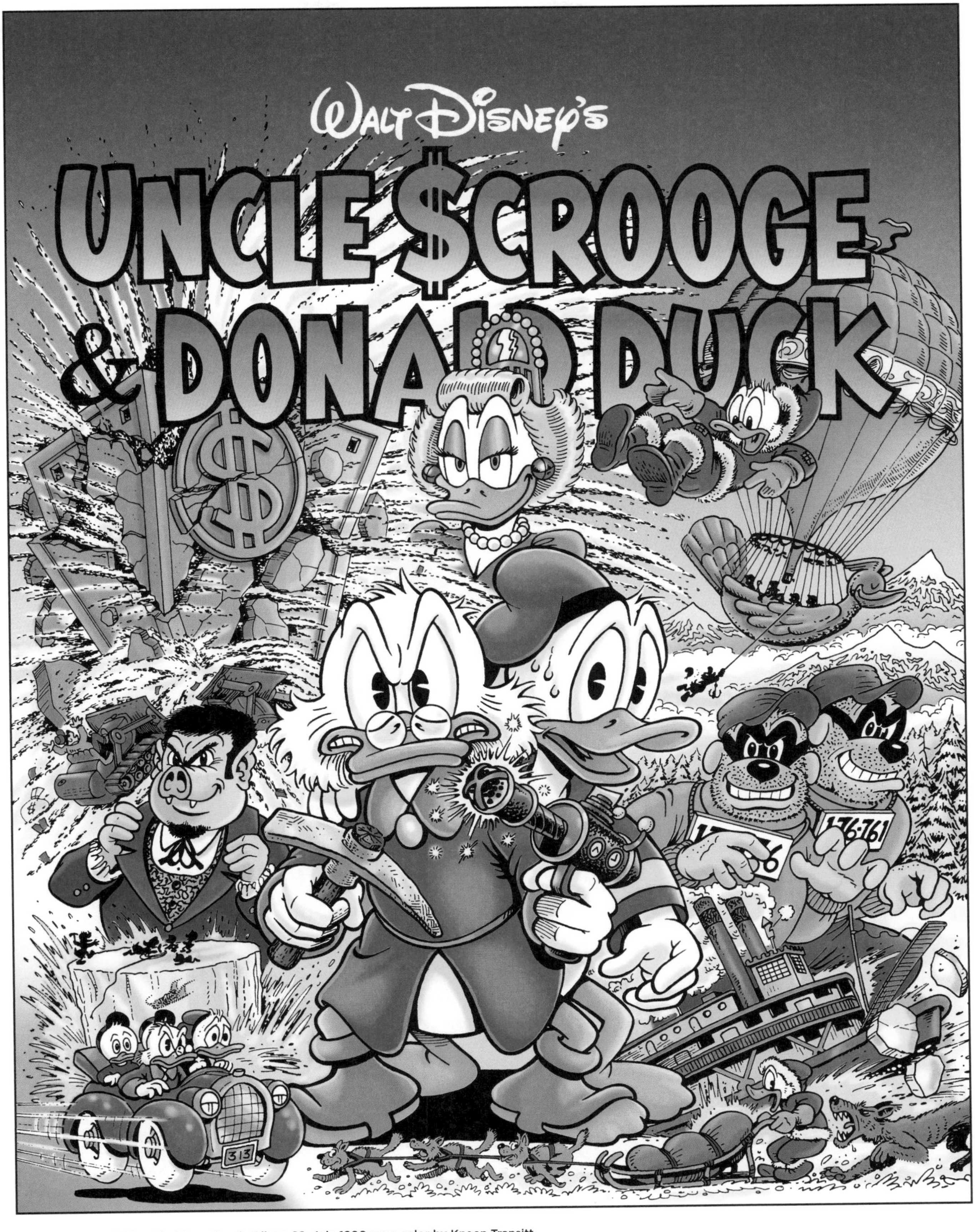
Walt Disney's
Uncle $crooge
& Donald Duck
176-761
313

DON ROSA SPECIAL • *Gladstone Comic Album* 28, July 1990; new color by Kneon Transitt.
Illustrating Rosa's "Cash Flow" (*Uncle Scrooge* 224, December 1987) and "Last Sled to Dawson" (*Uncle Scrooge Adventures* 5, June 1988).

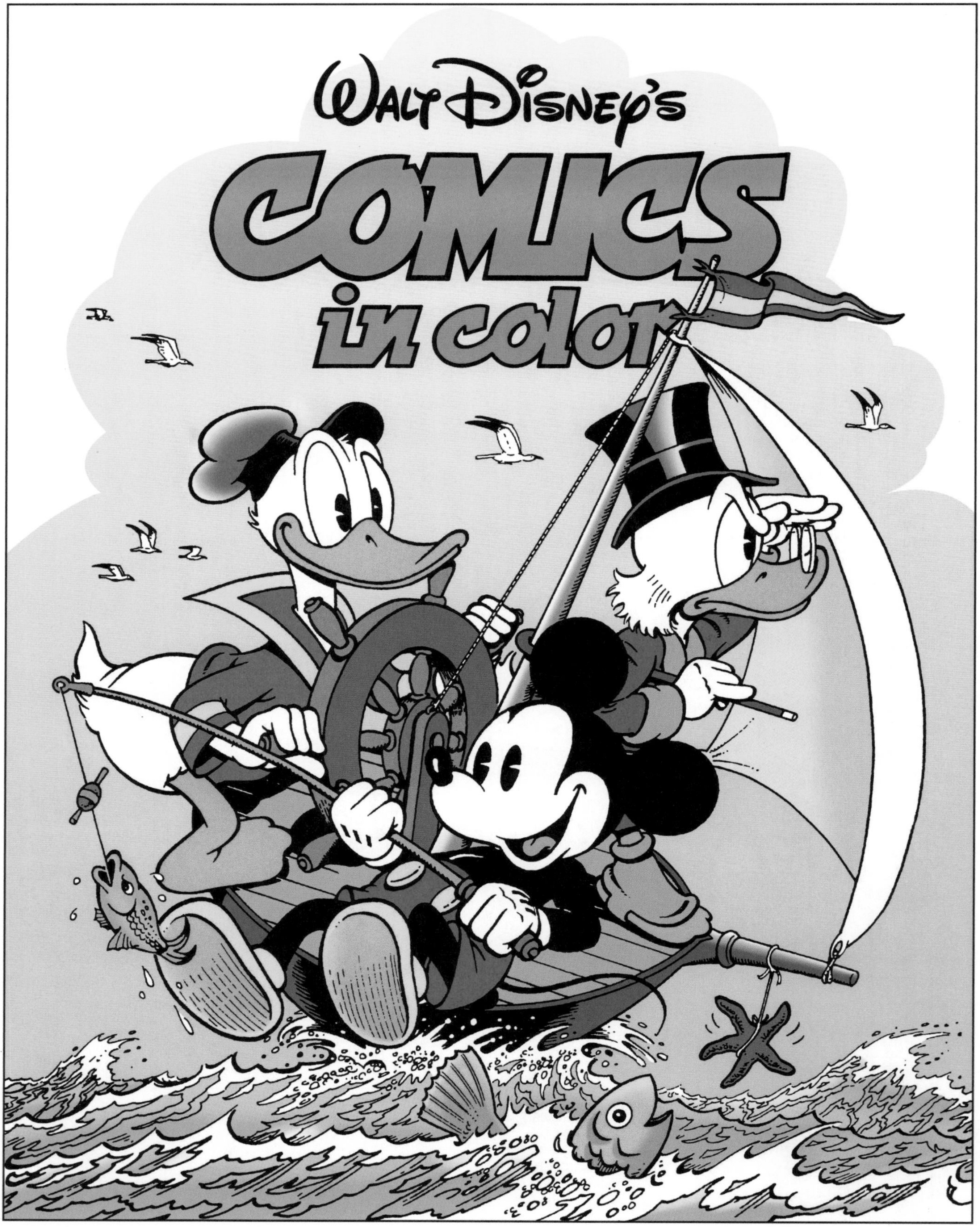
Walt Disney's
COMICS
in color

SAILING THE SPANISH MAIN • Intended for an issue of *Walt Disney's Comics in Color* [series I], 1990; actual first printing on *Walt Disney's Comics in Color* [series II] 1, 1997. New color by Digikore Studios

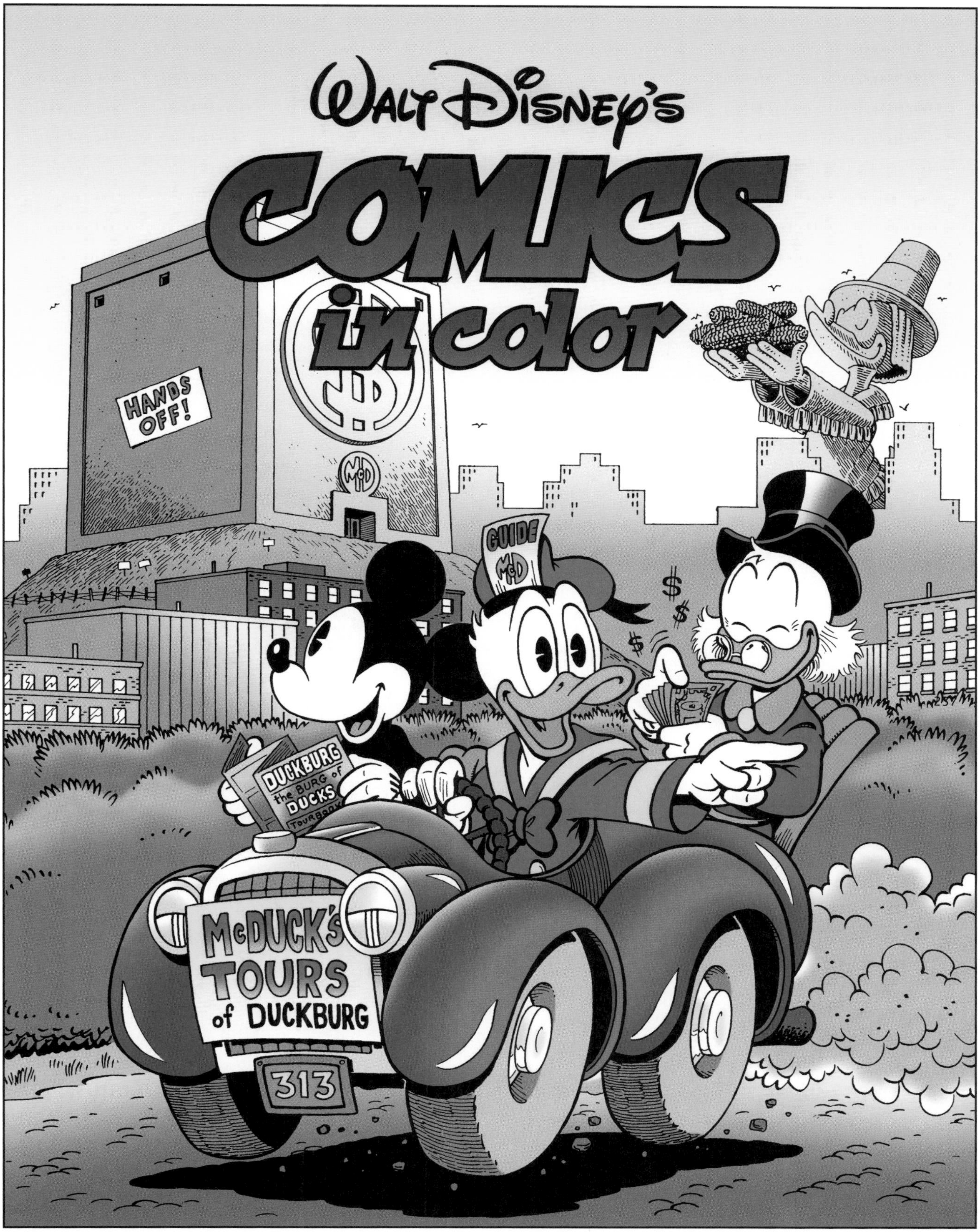
Walt Disney's
COMICS
in color
HANDS OFF!
GUIDE
McD
DUCKBURG the BURG of DUCKS TOURBOOK
McDUCK'S TOURS of DUCKBURG
313

McDUCK'S TOURS OF DUCKBURG • Intended for an issue of *Walt Disney's Comics in Color* [series I], 1990; actual first printing on *Donald and Mickey* 29, May 1995. Color by Susan Daigle-Leach, David Gerstein and Digikore Studios

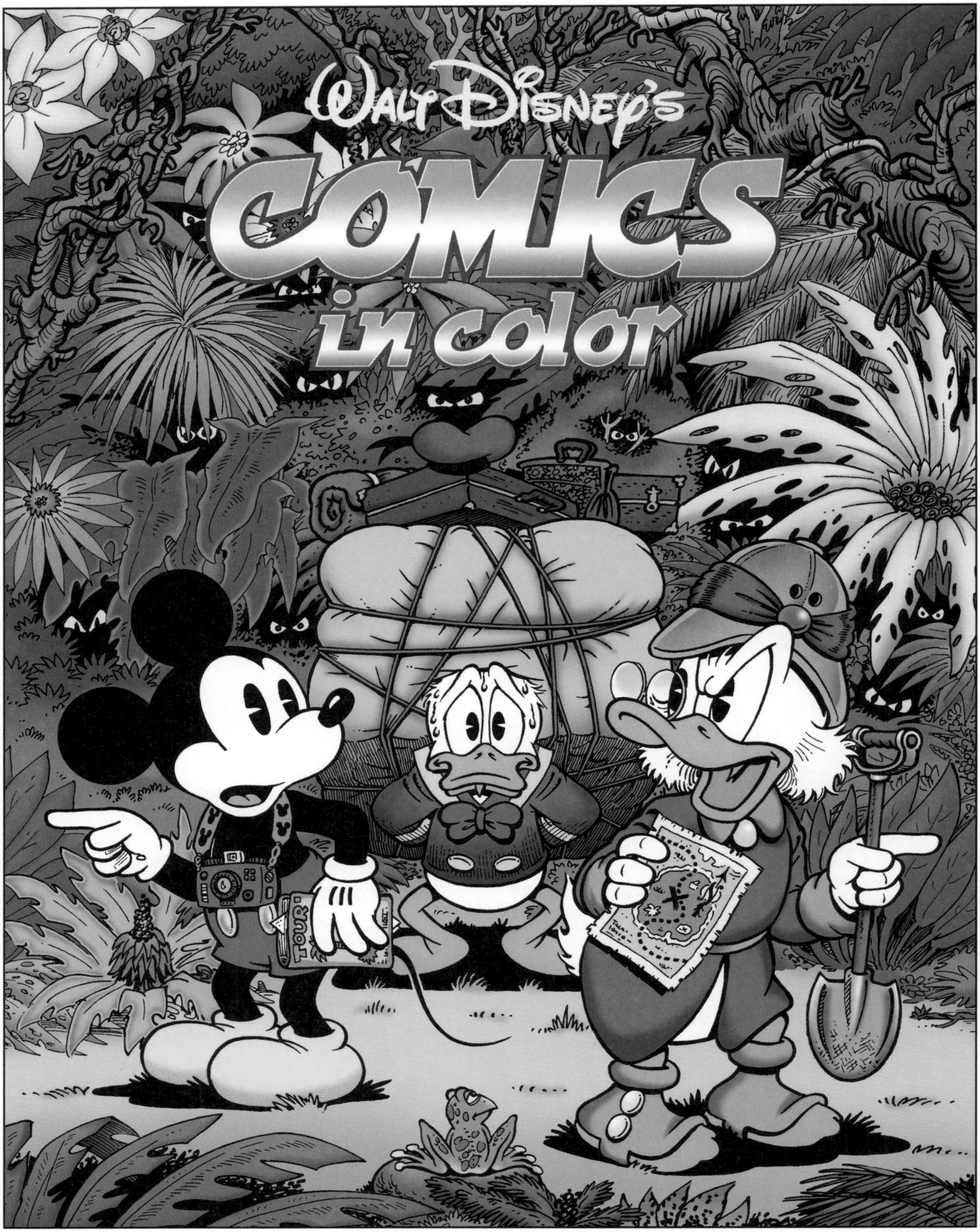
WALT DISNEY'S
COMICS
in color

Untitled cover intended for an issue of *Walt Disney's Comics in Color* [series I], 1990; actual first printing on *Uncle Scrooge* 317, January 1999. Color by Gary Leach and Digikore Studios

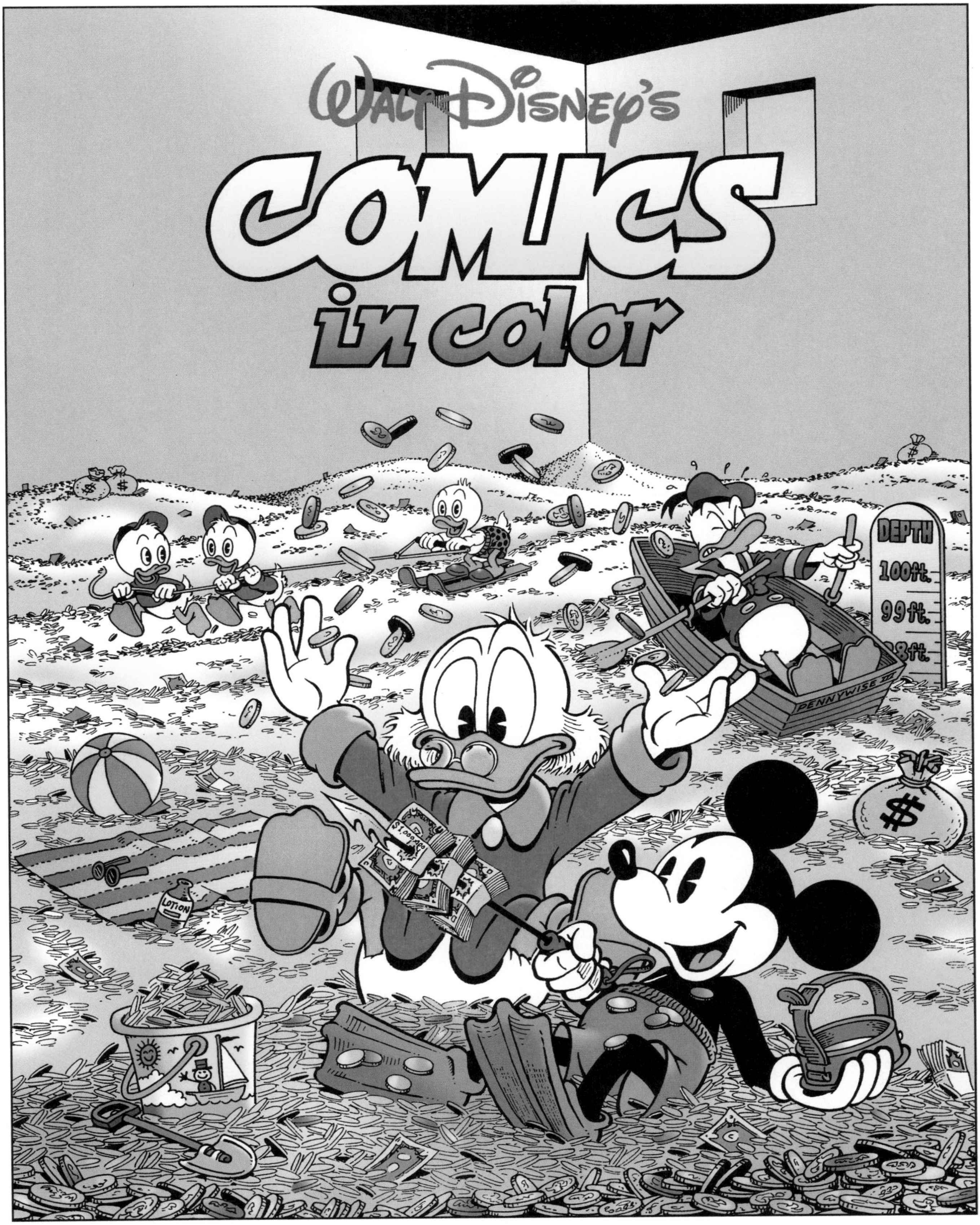
WALT DISNEY'S
COMICS
in color
DEPTH
100ft.
99ft.
PENNYWISE
LOTION

WATER SPORTS IN THE MONEY BIN • Intended for an issue of *Walt Disney's Comics in Color* [series I], 1990; actual first printing on *Walt Disney Treasures* 1, 2006. Color by Travis Seitler with Kneon Transitt

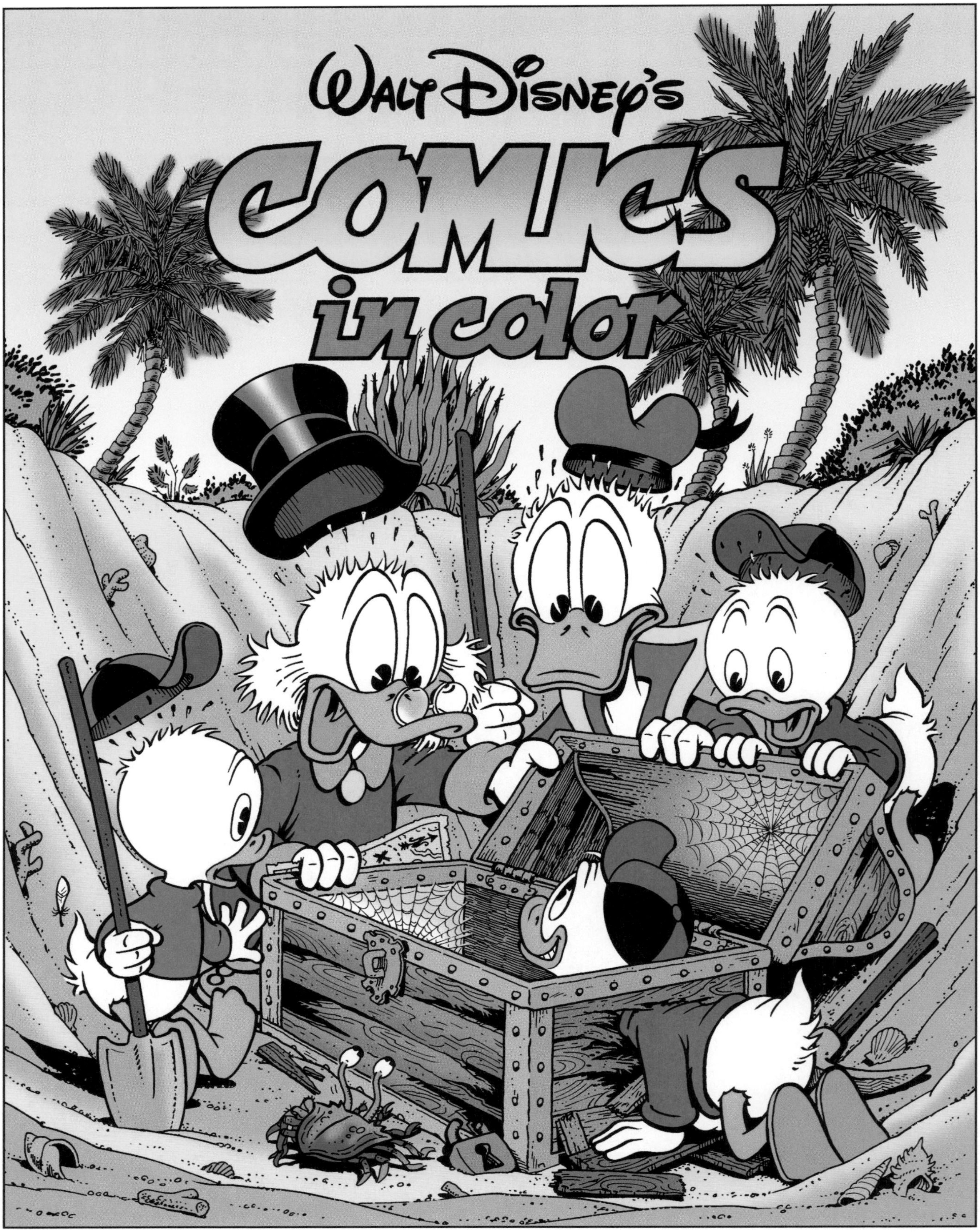
Walt Disney's
Comics
in color

Walt Disney's Comics in Color [series I] 1, 1990. Color by Susan Daigle-Leach with David Gerstein

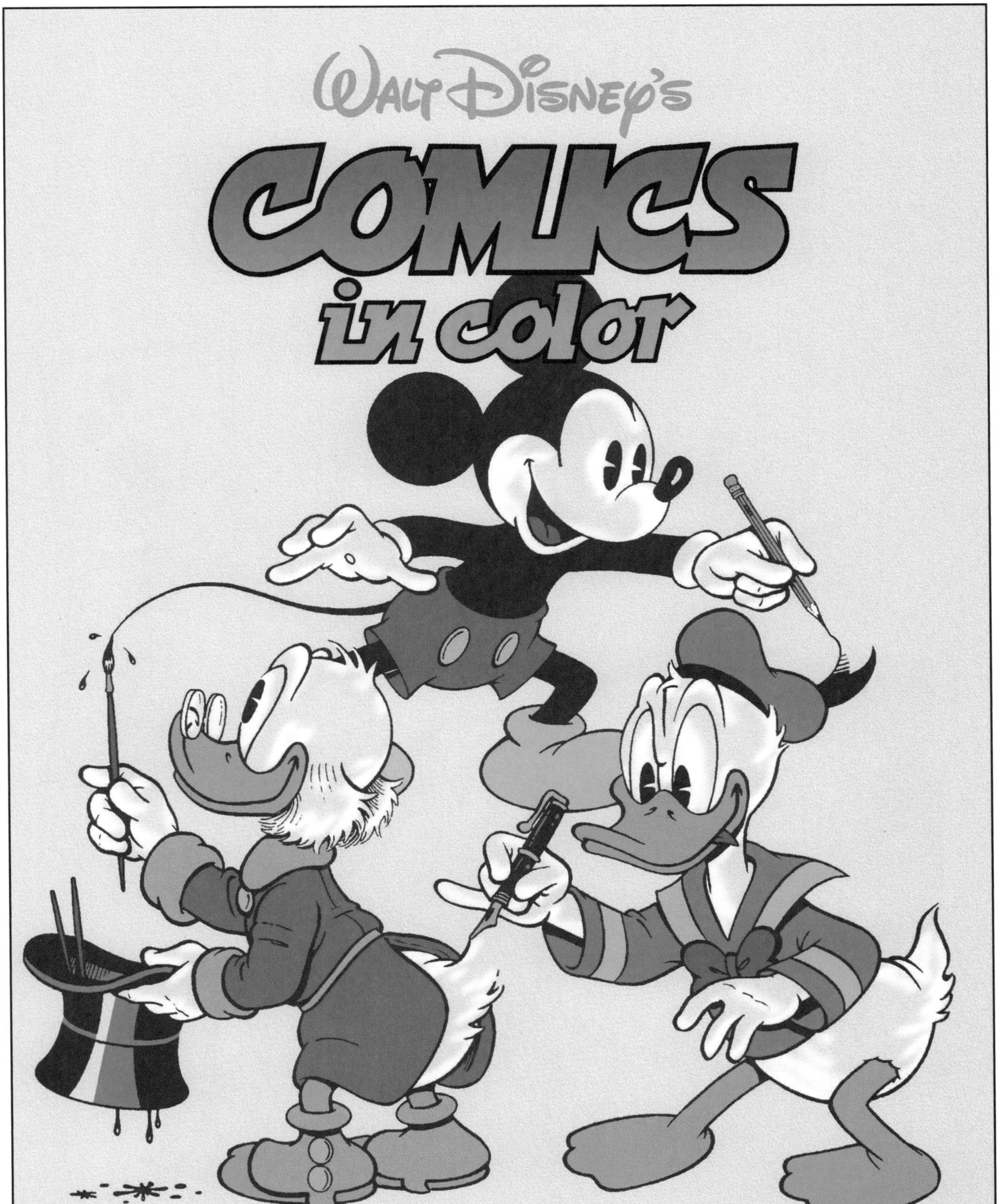
WALT DISNEY'S
COMICS
in color

Walt Disney's Comics in Color [series I] 2, 1990. Color by Gary Leach

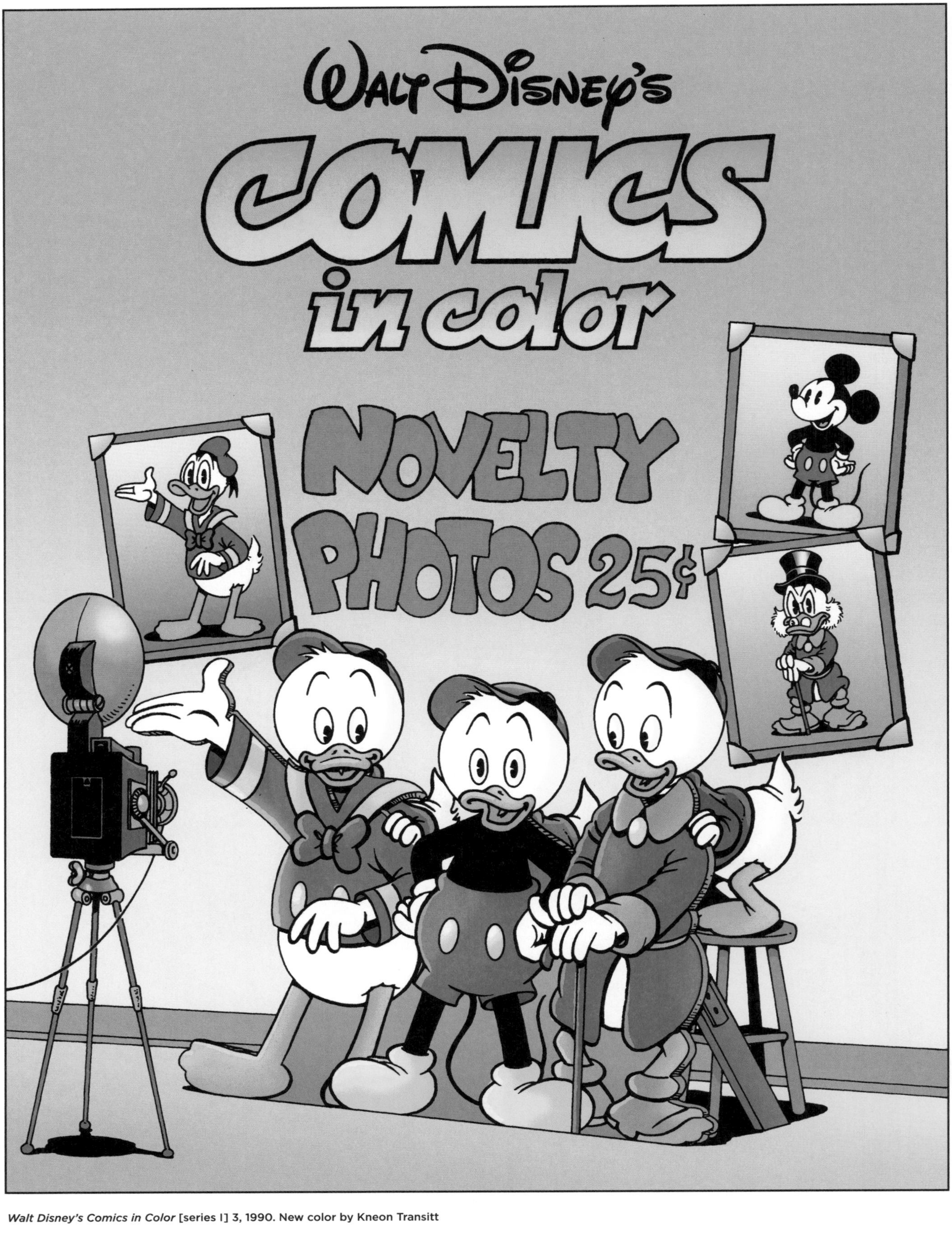
WALT DISNEY'S
COMICS
in color
NOVELTY
PHOTOS 25¢

Walt Disney's Comics in Color [series I] 3, 1990. New color by Kneon Transitt

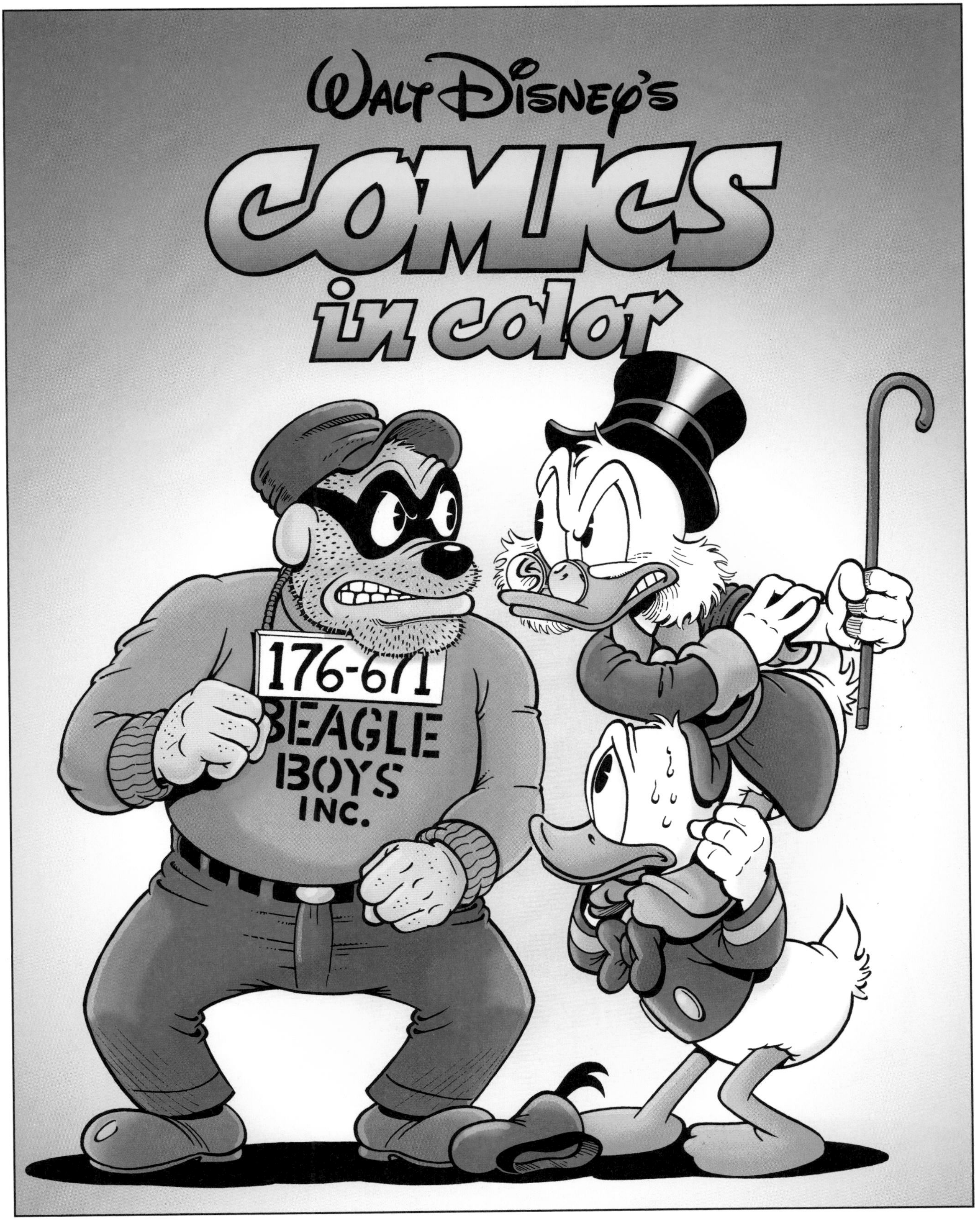
Walt Disney's
Comics
in color
176-671
BEAGLE
BOYS
INC.

Walt Disney's Comics in Color [series I] 4, 1990. New color by Kneon Transitt

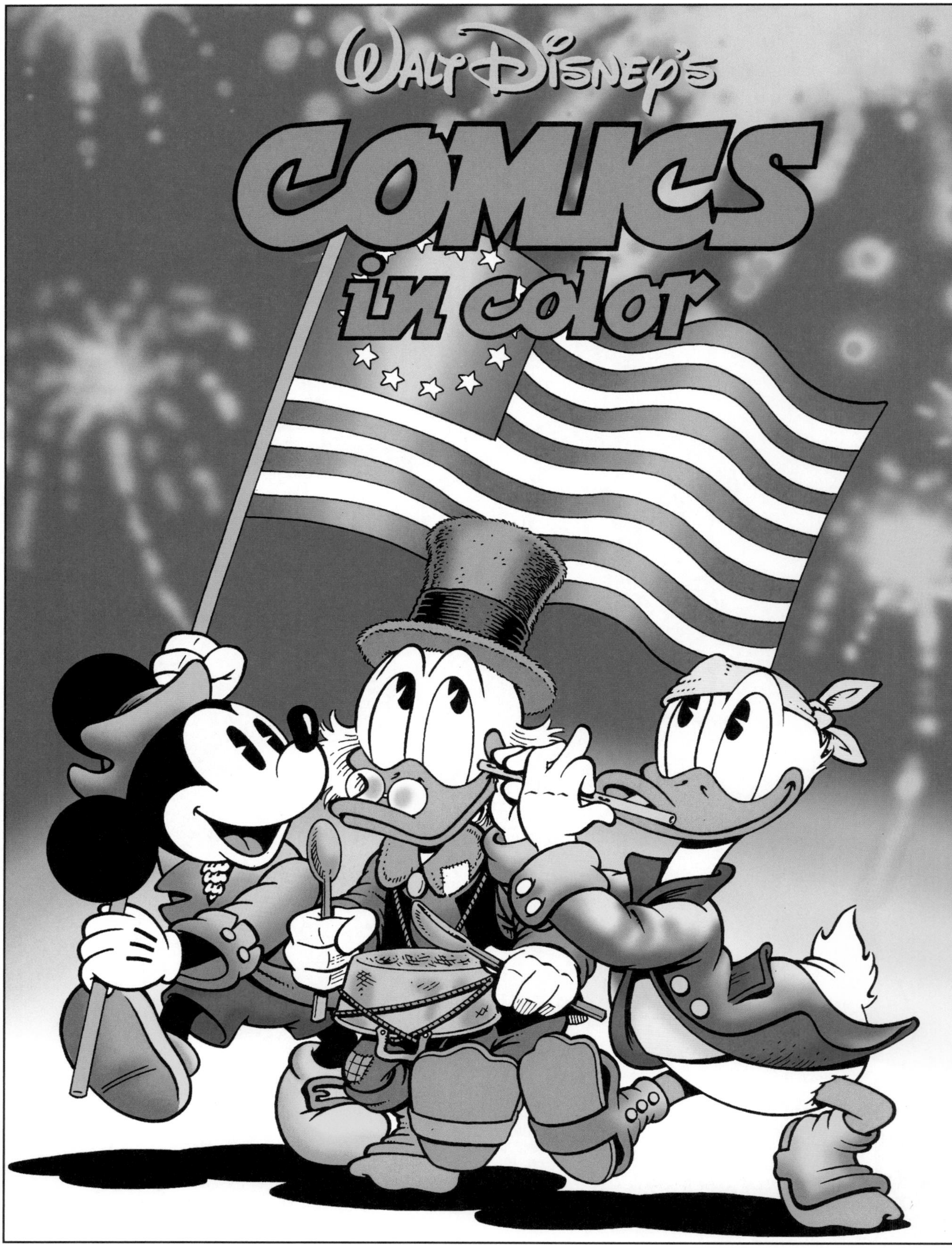
WALT DISNEY'S
COMICS
in color

Walt Disney's Comics in Color [series I] 5, 1990. Color by Gary Leach with Kneon Transitt

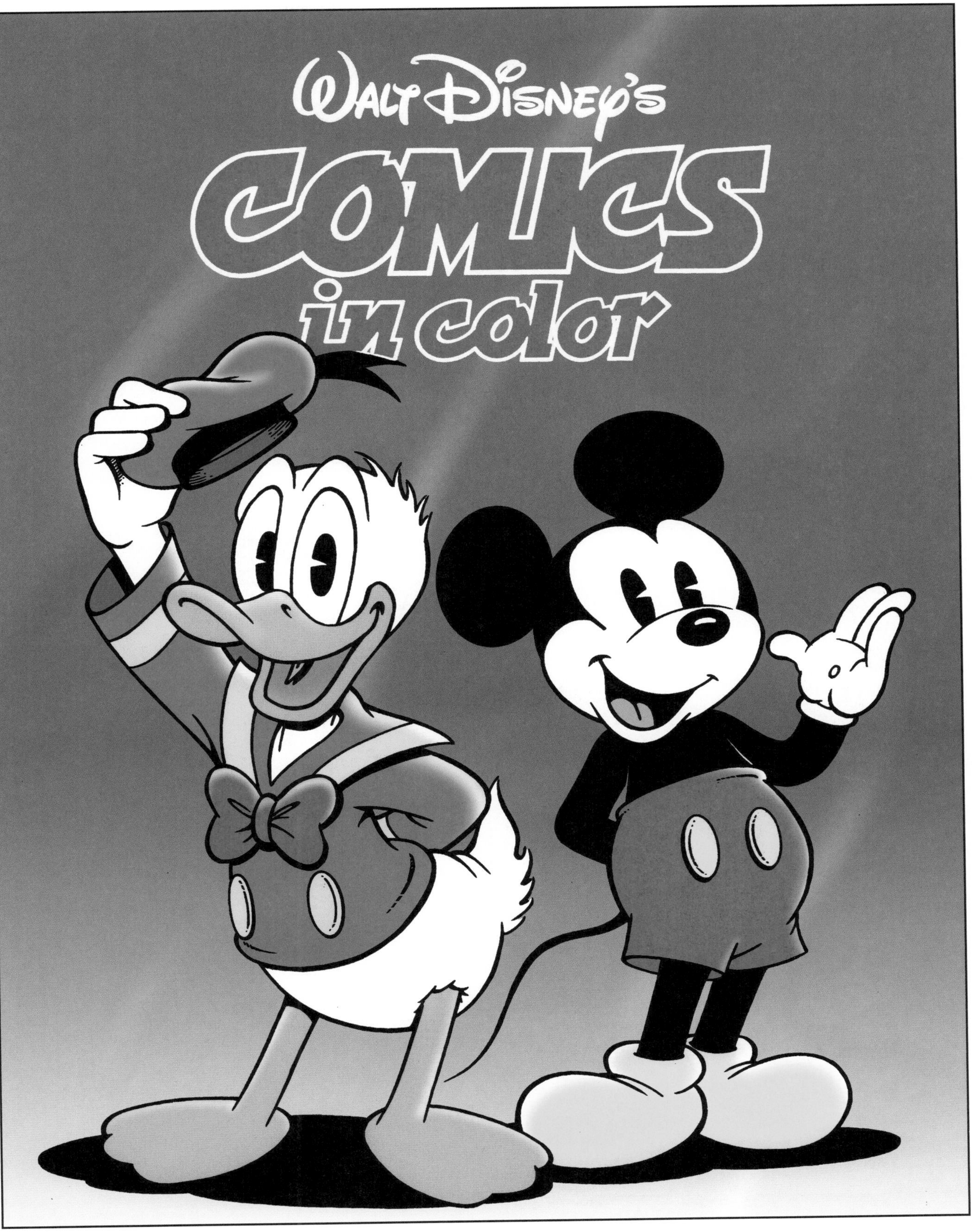
Walt Disney's
Comics
in color

Walt Disney's Comics in Color [series I] 6, 1990. Color by Gary Leach with Kneon Transitt

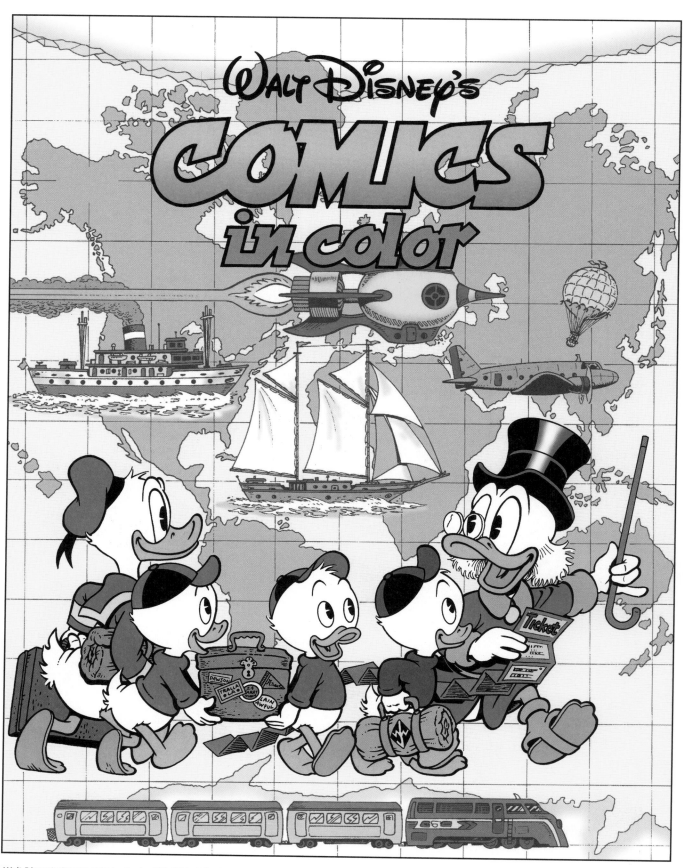

Walt Disney's
Comics
in color
Ticket
DAWSON
TRALLA LA
PLAIN AWFUL

Walt Disney's Comics in Color [series I] 7, 1990. Color by Gary Leach with David Gerstein

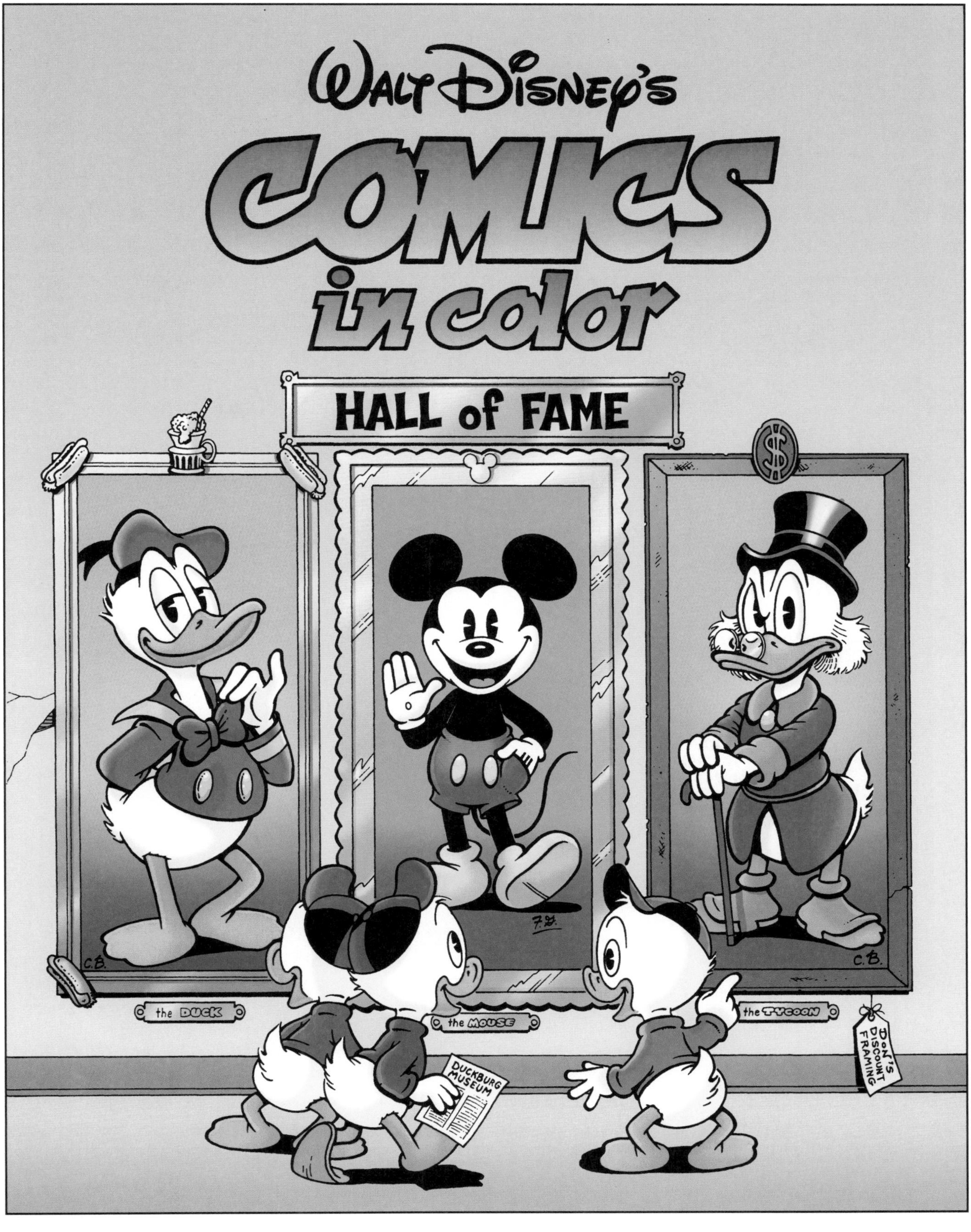
WALT DISNEY'S
COMICS
in color
HALL of FAME
C.B.
F.G.
C.B.
the DUCK
the MOUSE
the TYCOON
DON'S DISCOUNT FRAMING
DUCKBURG MUSEUM

HALL OF FAME • Intended for unpublished *Walt Disney's Comics in Color* [series I] 8, 1990; first printing on *Walt Disney Giant* 5, 1996. New color by Kneon Transitt

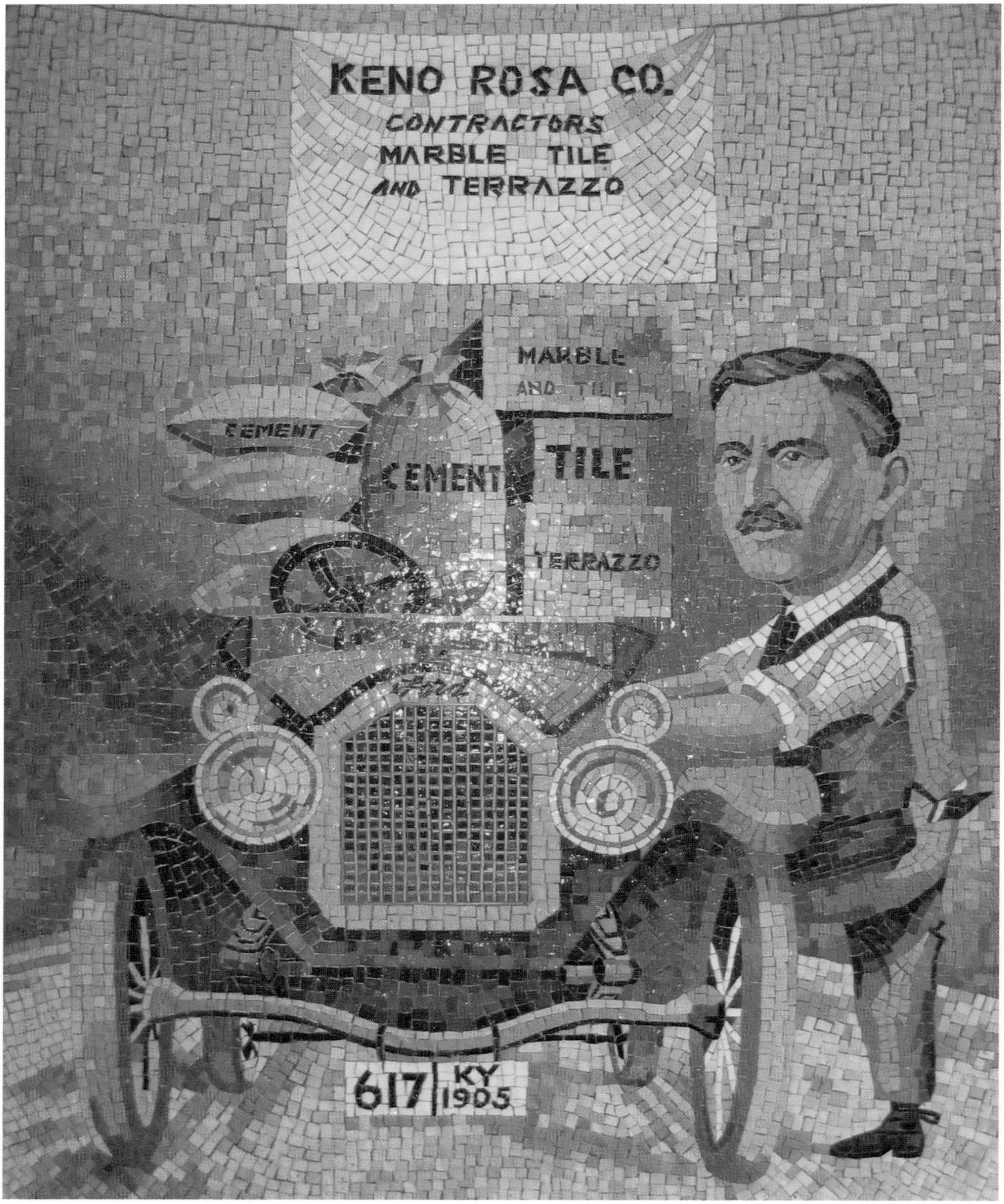
KENO ROSA CO.
CONTRACTORS
MARBLE TILE
AND TERRAZZO
MARBLE
AND TILE
CEMENT
CEMENT
TILE
TERRAZZO
Ford
617 KY 1905

This large mosaic—made by the Keno Rosa Company—depicts Don Rosa's grandfather, the founder of the firm. Portraying him as an illustrious entrepreneur, it is based on a cartoon (facing page) drawn by Alexander J. Van Leshout for his 1926 caricature book, *Louisvillians and Their Hobbies*. The Rosa family's copy of the book carries an enigmatic note: on the page with his caricature, Keno wrote the event and date of Don Rosa's birth—almost as a foretelling of his cartooning career! All photos with this article © and courtesy Don Rosa.

The Life and Times of DON ROSA

PART 2: “The New Laird of Cape Suzette”

This volume’s mini-autobiography will cover my cartooning career from about mid-1988 to mid-1990. These were probably the most challenging two years of my life, but they had a very positive and happy outcome. I could write volumes about these two years; whereas the subsequent years discussed in future volumes were much more pleasant, but actually uneventful compared to 1988-90.

I’ll try to be brief, but the very first major event in this period that concerned my drawing career was a freak accident—one that will take more time to explain than the other aspects of this period, even though those other aspects changed the course of my life a lot more.

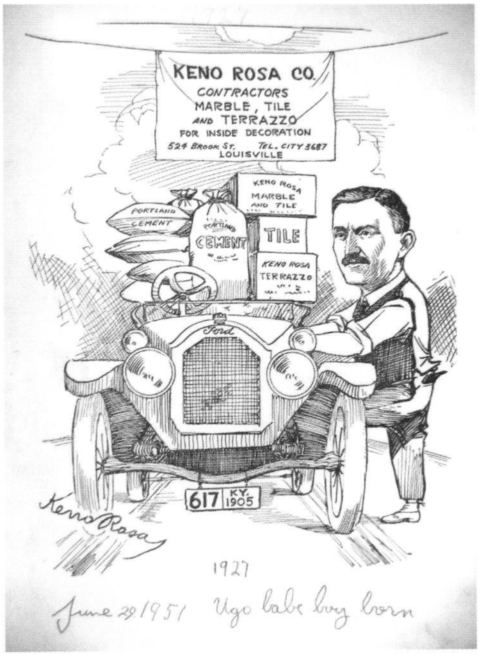
KENO ROSA CO.
CONTRACTORS
MARBLE, TILE
AND TERRAZZO
FOR INSIDE DECORATION
524 BROOK ST.
TEL. CITY 3687
LOUISVILLE
KENO ROSA
MARBLE
AND TILE
PORTLAND
CEMENT
CEMENT
TILE
KENO ROSA
TERRAZZO
Ford
617
KY.
1905
Keno Rosa
1927
June 29 1951
Ugo babe boy born

I had recently moved to a home out in the country, and my nearest neighbor had a horse ranch with various pieces of handy equipment. With a high-lift bucket bulldozer he was helping me clear some old fencing debris off my land. We loaded a pile of the debris into the ’dozer’s bucket. There was a thick three-meter fencepost that would not fit into the bucket, but was waterlogged and too heavy to move otherwise; so we laid it across the bucket arms for transport to his dumpster. Once there, my neighbor raised the bucket to dump the debris; and while he was watching the bucket, I looked up and saw the huge round fencepost rolling down the bucket arms—and on the verge of dropping onto his head from about a three-meter height!

In a split-second decision, my very brave (but actually rather stupid) impulse was to reach out and try to break the fall of the wooden post with the only defense I had: my two hands. I yelled, too, causing my neighbor to jump out of the way; but the beam fell full force on my right hand, slamming it hard against the metal top of his tractor.

For comparison, imagine putting your hand on an anvil and letting the blacksmith smash it with his sledgehammer. It hurt!

Later, x-rays showed that the post had crushed the bones inside my right hand in the knuckle region of the last two fingers. I was panic-stricken that I’d ruined my drawing hand forever; but I recall that within hours I forced myself to try to draw, to see what damage was done. Fortunately, the fingers used for drawing are the other three of those five, so all seemed well. And that was good, since no insurance would have covered my injury or the loss of my career—I was later told that I had “voluntarily placed myself in jeopardy through no fault of the other party,” even though I thought I was trying to save his life.

Though I could still draw, I later noticed that I could not bend my last two fingers to properly grasp a tool or such. So I eventually had hand surgery to restore part of the mobility of those fingers. Thankfully, this accident did not end my drawing career.

Aside from getting my drawing hand almost squished, 1988 had been a great year! I wasn’t making much money—maybe half of what I had earned at my now-liquidated family construction company. But who cared?! Not only had I realized the dream of my lifetime—writing and drawing adventures of Carl Barks’ characters—but now Gladstone Publishing was also asking me for sequels to Barks stories I grew up with! And they also needed cover art for classic Barks adventures for which there were originally no matching Barks covers.

So doing Disney comics was going along just fine! But then, in late 1988, things started getting in the way. The first thing that happened was minor: Gladstone’s

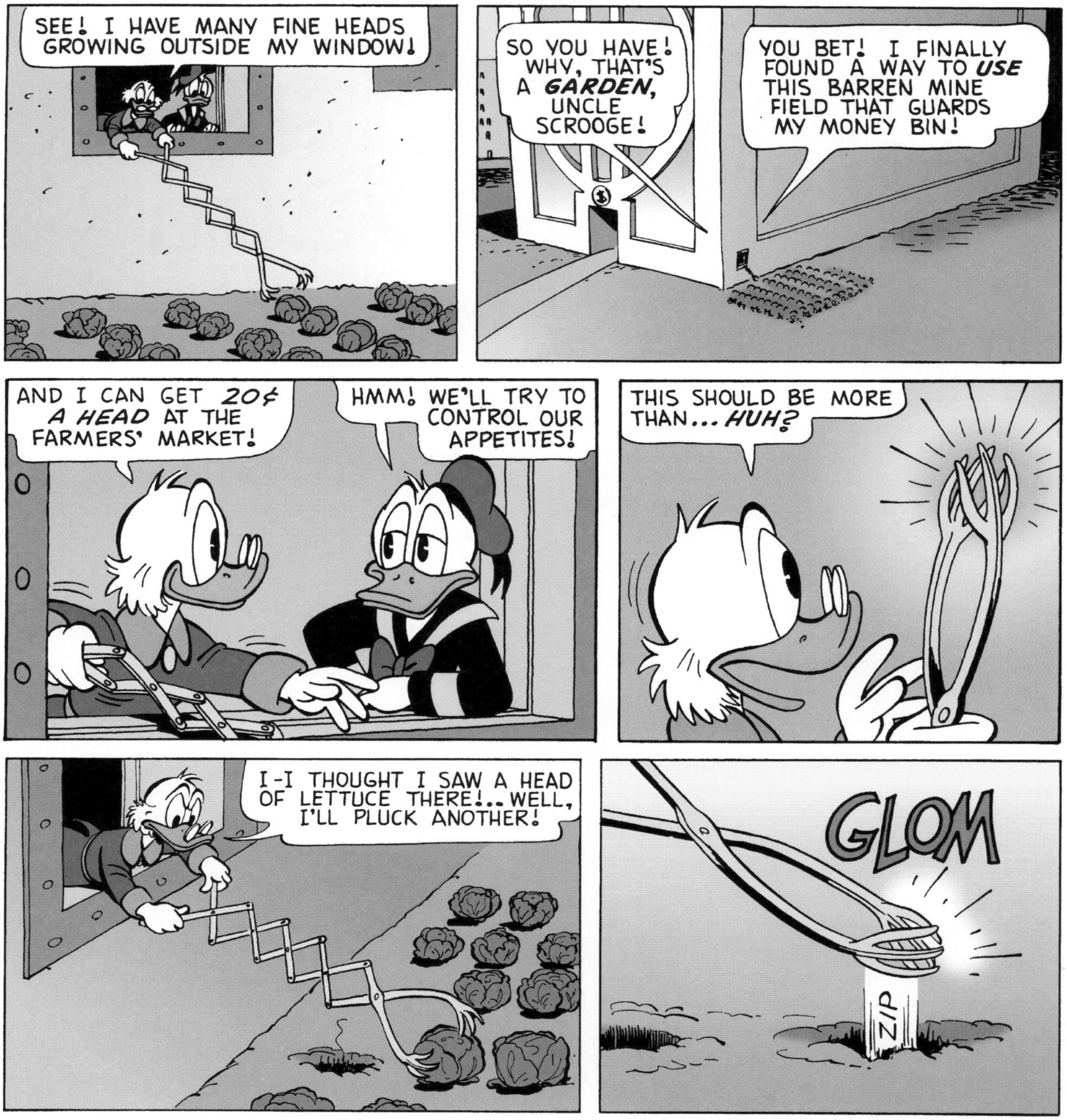
SEE! I HAVE MANY FINE HEADS GROWING OUTSIDE MY WINDOW!
SO YOU HAVE! WHY, THAT'S A GARDEN, UNCLE SCROOGE!
YOU BET! I FINALLY FOUND A WAY TO USE THIS BARREN MINE FIELD THAT GUARDS MY MONEY BIN!
AND I CAN GET 20¢ A HEAD AT THE FARMERS' MARKET!
HMM! WE'LL TRY TO CONTROL OUR APPETITES!
THIS SHOULD BE MORE THAN... HUH?
I-I THOUGHT I SAW A HEAD OF LETTUCE THERE!.. WELL, I'LL PLUCK ANOTHER!
GLOM
ZIP

One more Gladstone-era Disney comic *partly* by Rosa. Barks' "How Green Was My Lettuce" (*Uncle Scrooge* 51) had several panels excised from its first printing in 1964 to make way for a subscription ad. For *Uncle Scrooge* 241 (1990), Rosa drew two new panels to fill the gap. Can you spot them?

brand manager at Disney began asking to approve my scripts before they were drawn. When my Gladstone editor told me that I had to wait for Disney approval on "His Majesty, McDuck," no problem; I'd just write another script and then I'd be one ahead.

So I wrote "The Pied Piper of Duckburg." Then I wrote "On a Silver Platter." That was two short stories, so next I wrote a longer story, "Treasure Under Glass," which took me another two or three weeks. But aha! Disney's approval had finally come on "His Majesty, McDuck," so I finally started in on drawing it. Since I was only paid for stories after I drew them, I had by now done nearly two months of "free" writing, but I figured I'd get paid for that work later when the art was done.

I was perhaps halfway through the art on "His Majesty, McDuck" when I received a call from Gladstone publisher Bruce Hamilton about one thing or another. And I still recall how, at the end of the conversation, he casually mentioned a new licensing policy: Disney now expected Gladstone to keep possession of my art after publishing it.

Boing! I don't think either Bruce or his Disney liaison realized that this was a serious issue—and yet it was. I was not a Disney employee or even a Gladstone employee; I was a freelance self-employed writer-artist who sold my labor to Gladstone. A freelance artist's artwork is his property; he only sells the publication rights to a publisher and/or licensing company. The physical pages of artwork should remain the personal property of the freelance artist. But the new policy of 1988 contradicted this.

Happily, just a few years later, this all would change: Disney would again allow publishers to return freelancers' art. But back in 1988, the policy as it stood created a problem for me. At the time I had been squeaking by, making about half of the income I had made at my construction company; but that was only because I was selling my original Duck artwork to collectors. If I didn't have that art to sell, my income would now become only one quarter of what it had been before.

Still, I knew Gladstone had already scheduled "His Majesty, McDuck" for an upcoming comic, so I managed to complete the job and send it in to them. But all those weeks I had spent writing additional scripts, expecting to draw them when I completed "His Majesty"—well, I couldn't financially justify drawing them now.

I can't put into words how this felt. I had been a Disney fan all my life, particularly a Disney comics fan. And I had been a Disney booster at every chance I had, writing indexes in fanzines of all their comics and movies for other Disney fans. And yet now I couldn't afford to work with their characters. I had liquidated my near-century-old family company, so I couldn't go back to that. Yet I had a mortgage to pay. What could I do?

I was reduced to estimating construction jobs, at minimum wage, for my former employees at the Keno Rosa Co., who had formed their own small construction company after they lost their jobs with me. My whole life was suddenly topsy-turvy. If I didn't find a solution to this catastrophe, I would soon go bankrupt.

But there was one chance. I could, of all things, take a job being offered to me by... Disney! Walt Disney TV Animation had noticed my Scrooge comics, and about a year earlier had been asking me to work on their version of Barks' Ducks, which they titled *DuckTales*. I wasn't at all interested in being a screenwriter, so I'd declined their kind offer. But now... I was desperate. I called them to see if that job was still open... but it wasn't. *DuckTales* was already out of production. However, they were planning a new show

A big cast, but not big enough to stop the artist from drawing: Don Rosa at the drawing board in 1988, after an injury that threatened to stall his newborn comics career.

titled *TaleSpin* (apparently someone really liked this "Tale" word). They invited me out to Hollywood at their expense to get in on the beginning of the new show.

I had never intended to be a professional cartoonist, but I had stumbled into it when I wanted to create one Scrooge story for Gladstone. I had also never had any intention to be a screenwriter, and suddenly—bang, I'm a screenwriter. Some people work hard for years to get into either of these fields, but I had stumbled into them both effortlessly. And yet it clearly wasn't due to my meager abilities... I was an amateurish cartoonist, and I'd never written a screenplay in my life; I saw it all as what we call "serendipity"... the art of happy accidents (not that I felt very happy at this point in my life). I didn't want to be a screenwriter, but now I'd give it a try.

TaleSpin was an interesting show—set in the fictional city of "Cape Suzette," it was based on old adventure movies of the 1930s, which were certainly one of my interests! I soon was getting enthusiastic about giving it my best shot. I even did storyboards for my own scripts for free, just to see if I could make myself seem valuable. A screenwriter who can also do his own storyboards was just as rare as a comic writer who can draw his own scripts. It turned out that I wrote the first two episodes of the show that were completed, even though they were not the first episodes broadcast.

The two episodes were "It Came from Beneath the Sea Duck" (a parody of 1950s giant monster movies), and "I Only Have Ice for You" (they liked puns as story titles). I recall that the first script was animated almost exactly the way I wrote it, while the second one was altered totally. But even so, the producers were very gracious; I had written that second script based on the story synopsis they had given me, and they later said that they needed to see that synopsis in script form to realize that it would not work—so I still received full pay and a good review.

But I could see this was not the job for me. I had always been in complete control of my work. Good or bad, when I completed a comic story, it had been 100% my work and no one else's. Sure, the results would have looked prettier if someone else drew it, but I still was very proud that my comics were all my own work. Screenwriting was too small a portion of the entire package. When I did a comic book, I was the screenwriter, but also the director, photographer, art director, choreographer, make-up artist, special effects manager, sound designer, costume designer, and filled every other of the hundreds of jobs that creating a motion picture required. I needed to get back to that.

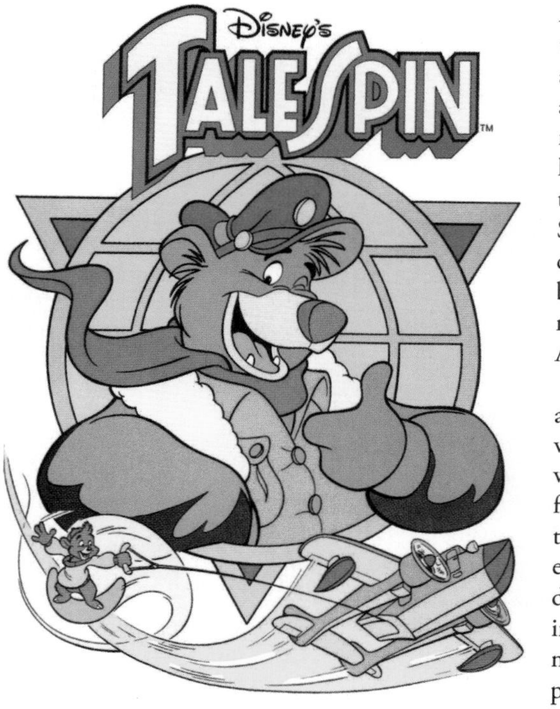
Disney's
TaleSpin

The two *TaleSpin* screenplays gave me enough cushion in the bank account to see if I could return to creating comics. I had those three completed comic scripts left over from when I had to quit Gladstone, and I offered them to the Dutch Disney publisher with the stipulation that I be the stories' artist as well. They accepted! So I happily completed "The Pied Piper of Duckburg" and "On a Silver Platter" for Oberon (today Sanoma), a Dutch company that properly returned all artwork to its freelance artists. Things were looking up a bit.

But back in the United States, times were changing. In late 1989, Disney took the comics license away from Gladstone. And surprisingly, Disney decided—for the first time in domestic licensing history—to publish their own comic books in-house! One of the associate editors, Bob Foster (a great friend of mine), called me up to ask me to work for this new Disney Comics company. I told him that I would not sign a contract stating that others could keep my physical artwork without buying it separately. But to show Bob—since he was a good egg!—that I would be willing to work for Disney Comics, Inc. if that policy were changed, I would write and draw one story for him before going back to working for the Dutch. And for that story, I now recalled that I had a fourth unused script left from the Gladstone days... one that Gladstone Editor-in-Chief Byron Erickson had rejected with no interest in a rewrite: "The Money Pit." That story involved lots of authentic references to rare American coins and would not have worked well for a European publisher. So I proceeded to draw "The Money Pit" for Disney Comics, Inc.

But now the story gets interesting! It's late 1989 and I'm working on that "Money Pit" story. The Dutch art directors had not been very pleased with my amateurish drawing style, and I could sense that they were not interested in me as a steady worker. And by this time I had learned that the biggest Disney publisher and producer of Disney comics, actually perhaps the biggest magazine and newspaper publisher on the planet Earth, was this "Gutenberghus Publishing Service" (today Egmont): a company based in Copenhagen, but with publishing branches in numerous other European and Asian countries.

I had been certain that such a huge company with all the best writers and artists would never want an inexperienced fan-artist from Kentucky working for them. But I was desperate. My entire future was now looking dim. I wanted to contact them in a way that would be noticed, more than simply by sending a postal letter.

Naturally, I couldn't afford a telephone call to Europe (ha-ha—me calling Europe! What a crazy idea!) and nobody had invented e-mail yet, so I tried an old-fashioned trans-Atlantic telegram. I asked "whom it may concern" if they could use one more Duck comics writer and artist...

Little did I know what would happen next. But in Volume 3 of Fantagraphics' *Don Rosa Library*, you'll find out. (You'll even see what became of my final wayward Gladstone script, "Treasure Under Glass!" Be here.) •

Above: Disney's Baloo evolved into a cargo pilot for TV's *TaleSpin*.

Opposite: Rosa's *TaleSpin* episode "It Came From Beneath the Sea Duck" pays homage to a scene from Carl Barks' "Ghost of the Grotto" (Donald Duck *Four Color* 159, 1947). An attacking giant octopus is fended off with a dose of hot pepper disguised as a tasty treat: a prime rib in Barks, a tub of ice cream in *TaleSpin*.

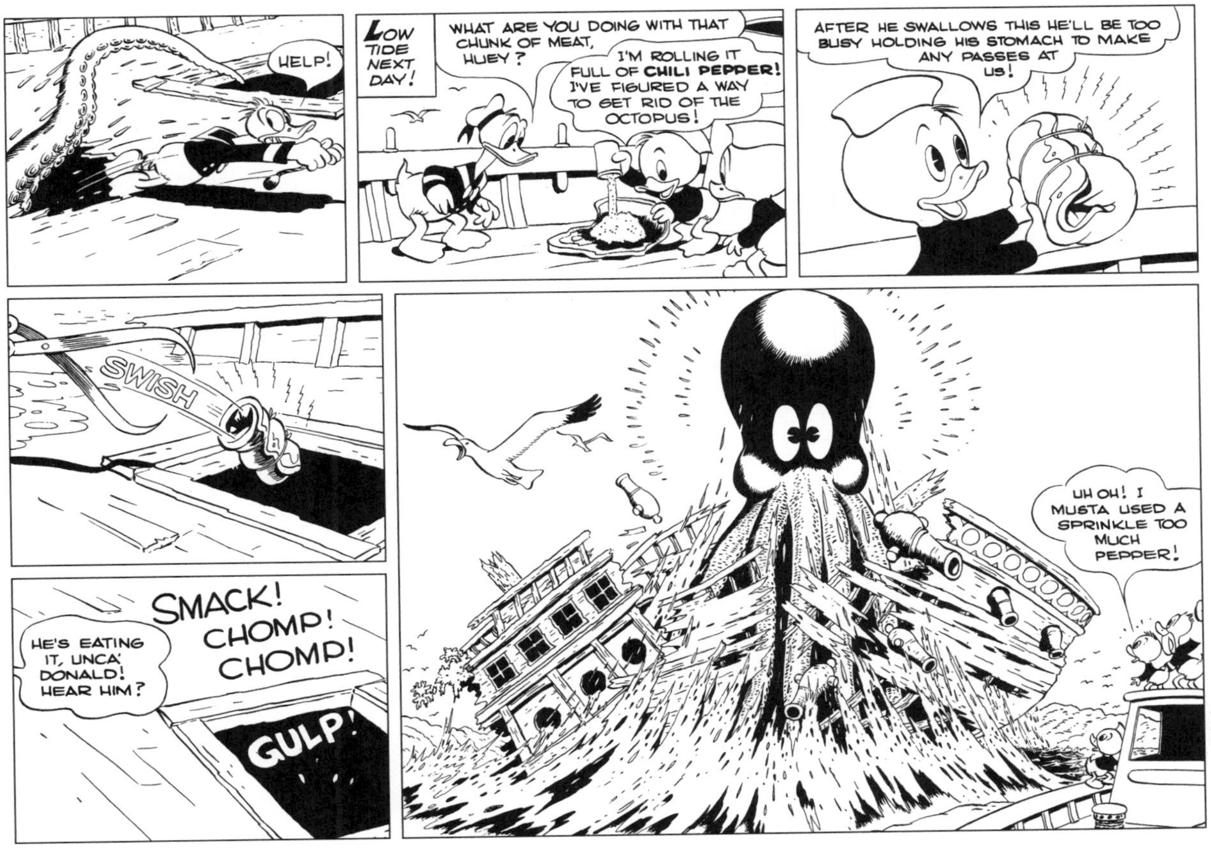
HELP!
LOW TIDE NEXT DAY!
WHAT ARE YOU DOING WITH THAT CHUNK OF MEAT, HUEY?
I'M ROLLING IT FULL OF CHILI PEPPER! I'VE FIGURED A WAY TO GET RID OF THE OCTOPUS!
AFTER HE SWALLOWS THIS HE'LL BE TOO BUSY HOLDING HIS STOMACH TO MAKE ANY PASSES AT US!
SWISH
HE'S EATING IT, UNCA' DONALD! HEAR HIM?
SMACK! CHOMP! CHOMP!
GULP!
UH OH! I MUSTA USED A SPRINKLE TOO MUCH PEPPER!

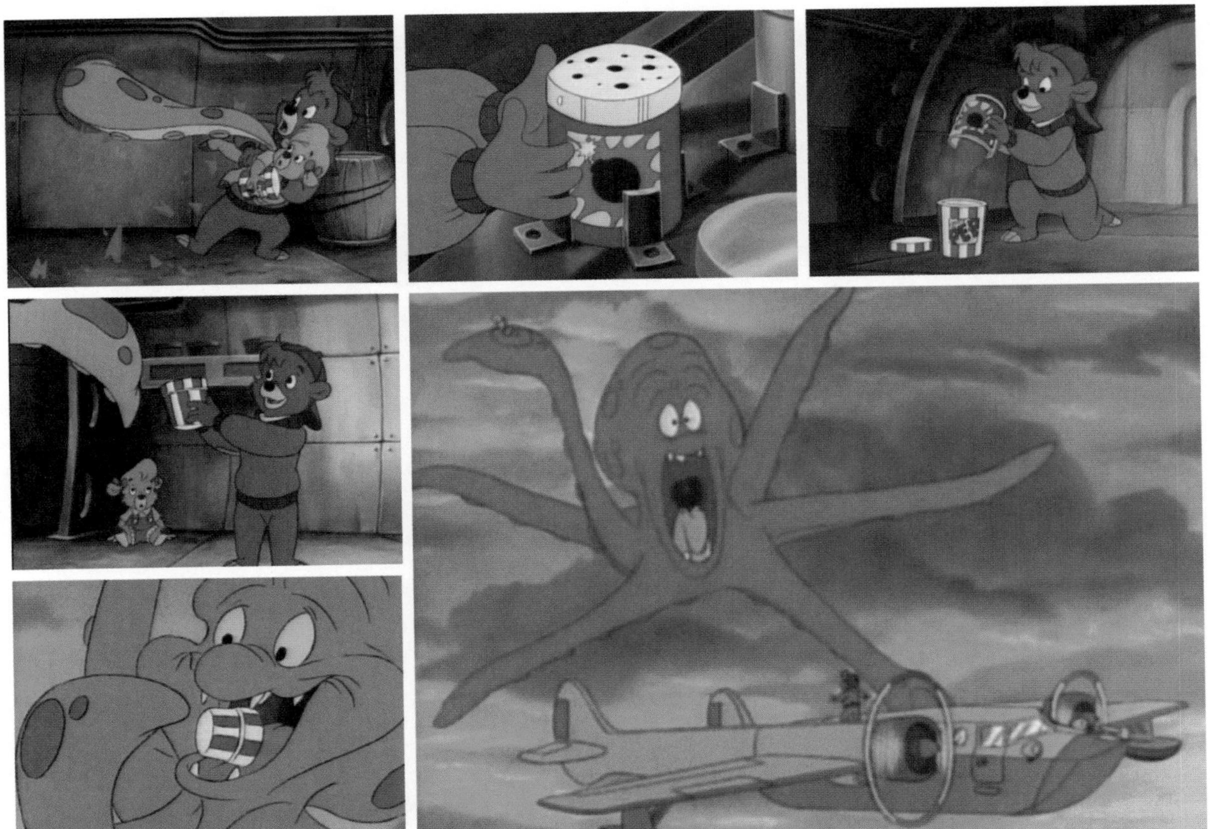

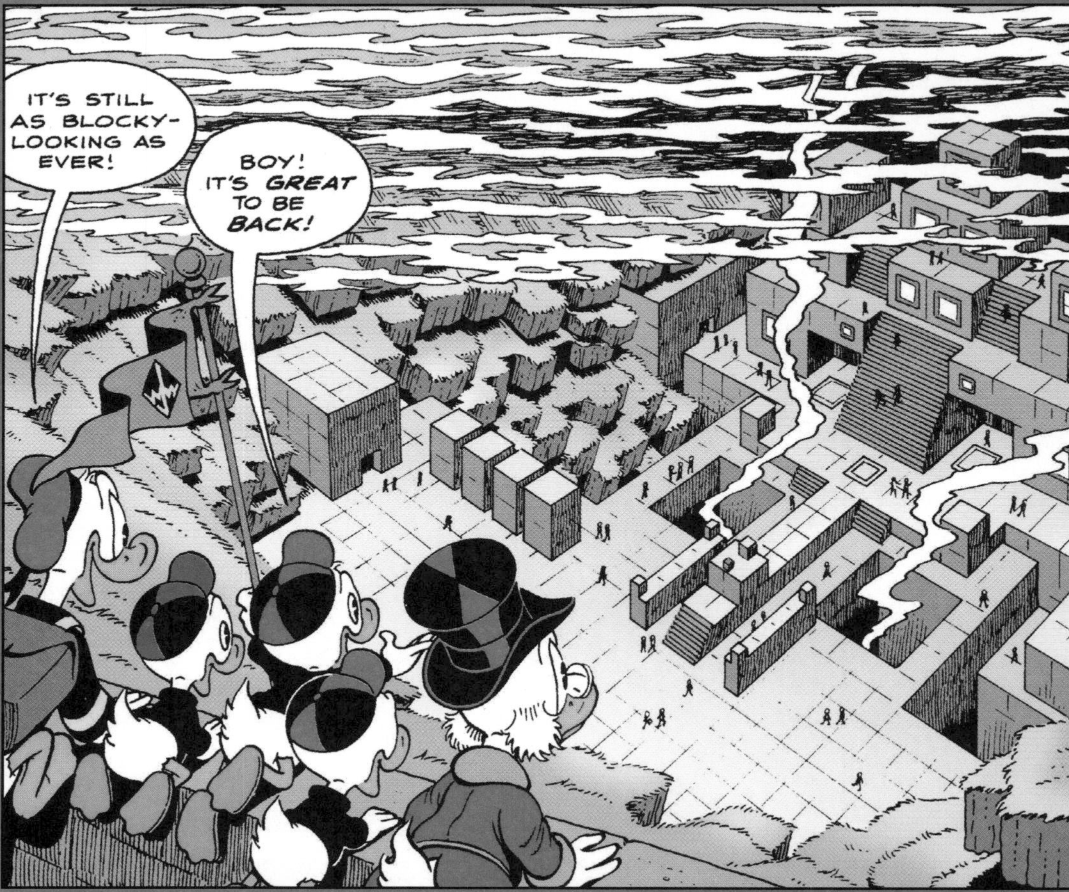
IT'S STILL AS BLOCKY-LOOKING AS EVER!
BOY! IT'S GREAT TO BE BACK!

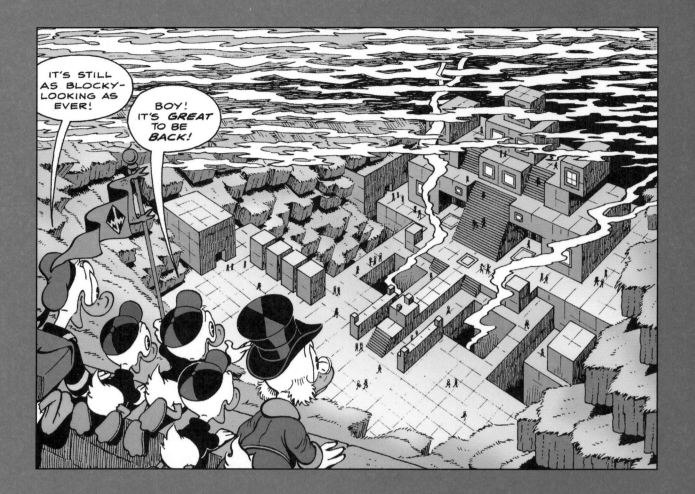

About the Editors

DAVID GERSTEIN is an animation and comics researcher, writer, and editor working extensively with the Walt Disney Company and its licensees. His published work includes *Mickey and the Gang: Classic Stories in Verse* (Gemstone 2005); *Walt Disney Treasures – Disney Comics: 75 Years of Innovation* (Gemstone 2006); and *The Floyd Gottfredson Library of Walt Disney's Mickey Mouse* (Fantagraphics, 2011-present). David has also worked with Disney in efforts to locate lost Oswald the Lucky Rabbit cartoons and to preserve the *Mickey Mouse* newspaper strip.

GARY GROTH has been publishing Don Rosa since 1970. Oh, and he also co-founded Fantagraphics Books in 1976. Fantagraphics is still going strong and he's still publishing Don Rosa. Life can't get any better than that.